TO Buffalo
July 29, '11
From: Berta
Happy Birthday !!

D1011012

COUNSEL
FOR THE
SITUATION

COUNSEL
FOR THE
SITUATION

SHAPING THE LAW TO
REALIZE AMERICA'S PROMISE

William T. Coleman Jr.
with Donald T. Bliss

BROOKINGS INSTITUTION PRESS
Washington, D.C.

ABOUT BROOKINGS

The Brookings Institution is a private nonprofit organization devoted to research, education, and publication on important issues of domestic and foreign policy. Its principal purpose is to bring the highest quality independent research and analysis to bear on current and emerging policy problems. Interpretations or conclusions in Brookings publications should be understood to be solely those of the authors.

Copyright © 2010
THE BROOKINGS INSTITUTION
1775 Massachusetts Avenue, N.W., Washington, D.C. 20036
www.brookings.edu

All rights reserved. No part of this publication may be reproduced or transmitted in any form or by any means without permission in writing from the Brookings Institution Press.

Library of Congress Cataloging-in-Publication data

Coleman, William T. (William Thaddeus), 1920–
    Counsel for the situation : shaping the law to realize America's promise / William T. Coleman, Jr. ; with Donald T. Bliss.
        p. cm.
    Includes bibliographical references and index.
    ISBN 978-0-8157-0488-1 (hardback : alk. paper)
    1. Lawyers—United States—Biography. 2. United States—Officials and employees—Biography. I. Bliss, Donald T. II. Title.
    KF373.C625A3 2010   2010033339
    340.092—dc22

9 8 7 6 5 4 3

Printed on acid-free paper

Typeset in Adobe Caslon

Composition by Cynthia Stock
Silver Spring, Maryland

Printed by R. R. Donnelley
Harrisonburg, Virginia

CONTENTS

FOREWORD

Stephen Breyer

WHEN BILL COLEMAN TRIED OUT for the swim team at his Philadelphia high school, the school eliminated the team rather than risk racial integration. That is the world in which Bill grew up. And that is the world that Bill Coleman helped to change. He did so directly when called upon for help by Thurgood Marshall. And he did so indirectly through the power of example—the example of a man of unusual ability who became successful as a skilled attorney, a wise counselor, and a dedicated public servant.

Bill Coleman's story is one that younger generations should mark and inwardly digest, lest they forget the pioneers who helped to make a better America possible. That story also shows us something important about the legal profession, helping us understand how in the mid-twentieth century an individual could become, at one and the same time, a great lawyer, a wise statesman, and a leader in the fight for equal rights.

Coleman started life with enormous natural abilities, including intelligence, perseverance, and the capacity for hard work. After graduating summa cum laude from the University of Pennsylvania, he entered Harvard Law School, where he became a member of the *Harvard Law Review*. His law school education was interrupted by World War II when he volunteered for service in the Army Air Corps. After the war, he graduated from the law school first in his class, earning the Fay Diploma. He had just begun to serve as a law clerk for Judge Herbert Goodrich of the Third Circuit Court of Appeals when he received a call offering him a clerkship with Supreme Court Justice Felix Frankfurter. Bill accepted. He spent the next year at the Court, learning from Justice Frankfurter about the law, discussing law and literature (including Shakespeare and Pushkin) with his fellow clerk (and later attorney general) Elliot Richardson, and even arguing fine points of constitutional theory with Justice Hugo Black, whose views differed considerably from those of Justice Frankfurter.

Bill then entered private practice, where he thrived. He enjoyed a variety of assignments. An early one involved addressing an entertainment star's fear that someone else had received higher billing. Ever practical, Bill simply took a ladder to a Broadway theater at three o'clock on a rainy morning, put it up against the marquee, and measured the height of the letters in Cole Porter's name. Bill is pragmatic. He once solved a complex legal problem by insisting that his clients, worried about which country's laws would govern a particular contract, sign the contract over the Pacific in midflight. Bill is highly skilled. He argued nineteen cases in the Supreme Court. Bill is wise. That fact is known to the many young lawyers who have seen him as a mentor as well as to the many clients who have sought advice from him on more than purely legal issues.

At the same time, Coleman's career extends well beyond that of private practitioner. He is one of that breed of (now sadly vanishing) statesmen-lawyers whose careers combine private practice with public service. They include William "Wild Bill" Donovan, Henry L. Stimson, Dean Acheson, Lloyd Cutler, and many others who took to heart Roscoe Pound's admonition that law is a profession "imbued with a spirit of public service." That public service, in Bill Coleman's case, included work with the Warren Commission, an appointment as our nation's secretary of transportation, and membership on numerous local, state, and national public and private advisory boards, commissions, foundations, and similar entities. To each he has devoted his intelligence, energy, and imagination, always looking for workable solutions.

I saw him at work firsthand when the government was considering whether to grant landing rights for the Concorde, the British-French airplane that both flew and boomed supersonically. Bill, then transportation secretary, resolved the controversy by presiding personally over lengthy public hearings about landing rights in Washington, D.C., and New York. By opening up the process, by giving everyone a chance to be heard, he helped ensure acceptance of a compromise solution that might otherwise have satisfied no one.

Yet to describe Coleman simply as a private lawyer and public servant would be highly misleading. Bill is a man of color who grew up at a time when that fact meant hardship, humiliation, and prejudice at the hands of a society that embraced not simply invidious discrimination but legalized segregation as well. Those horrors, of course, touched Bill's life directly: An army that segregated units by race and refused officer club membership to those of the "wrong" race; a national capital where a law clerk at the Supreme Court found it difficult to find a restaurant where he and his fellow clerks could have lunch together; a legal profession that initially denied him a job, despite his stellar Harvard Law School record and his Supreme Court clerkship; and more, much more, and worse besides.

What was Bill's reaction? Don't agonize, just get down to work, let's end this evil, and let's cure society of that malignant disease. His method: To use what was best about America, the law's commitment to equal justice, to end what was worst about America, its blatant racial discrimination. That is why Bill helped write the brief in *Brown* v. *Board of Education.* That is why he agreed to fight for integration by representing minority clients in the *Girard College* case, which he won. That is why he became chairman of the NAACP Legal Defense and Educational Fund. That is why he became a leader and an integral part of the civil rights struggle, which has transformed the culture of our nation. At the same time, Bill enabled others to point to him, to his talents, to his achievements, to his having crossed what had previously seemed all-white thresholds—the *Harvard Law Review,* the Supreme Court clerkship, the president's cabinet—to illustrate that racial discrimination and prejudice were not only morally and legally wrong but simply absurd in depriving the nation of a tremendous pool of talent and character.

Perhaps now it is easy to understand why I hope many will read this book. Bill Coleman's story is that of a man who became successful in his career while making an enormous contribution to American life—all in the face of formidable obstacles. He never gave up on America. He never considered working outside its legal system. And he led by example. Anyone interested in the history of the civil rights movement will consequently find in Bill Coleman's story an explanation of how brilliant and tenacious lawyers brought about a quiet revolution in the law and an inspiration for future generations upon whose shoulders fall the many challenges confronting our society today.

Salvador de Madriaga, a great Spanish patriot, once argued for breadth of vision, breadth of learning, breadth of spirit, and breadth of experience by cryptically warning that "he who is 'nothing but', is 'not even.'" Bill Coleman must have taken that advice to heart. It is no wonder this nation awarded him its Medal of Freedom. Elliot Richardson, discussing how Bill Coleman's friends feel about Bill, described him as "an individual of strong loyalties, deep commitment to human values, and solid practical judgment. Harnessed to a clear and analytical mind and unflagging energy, these qualities make him an effective force in all of the many arenas in which he engages. Add a quick sense of humor and a gift for friendship, and you have in every sense a man for all seasons."

I would add the following: After Bill Coleman completed his clerkship at the Supreme Court, Justice Frankfurter sent him a letter, which said, "What I can say of you with great confidence is what was Justice Holmes' ultimate praise of a man: 'I bet on him.' I bet on you, whatever choice you may make and whatever the Fates have in store for you." This book makes crystal clear the accuracy of Justice Frankfurter's judgment.

PROLOGUE

Achieving the American Dream as Counsel for the Situation

Dream no small dreams for they have no power to move the hearts of men.

—GOETHE

AT SOME POINT EACH OF US enters the stream of history. We have no control over the time or place, or the sandbars, boulders, or floating obstructions we may confront along the way. I entered the stream on July 7, 1920. I began to chart a course through most of a transitional century, a time unique in the annals of American and world history. This was the century in which a youthful pluralistic nation began to fulfill the promise of its declaratory charters, recognizing the rights of all its citizens to reach their full potential and resolve their differences within a framework of law. Fortunately for me, it was the time when persons of extraordinary vision and great charisma actually changed the course of history's stream—Eleanor Roosevelt, Dwight Eisenhower, Earl Warren, Lyndon Johnson, Charles Houston, William H. Hastie, and Thurgood Marshall, to name but a few.

As the doors of opportunity slowly began to open, I chose a career in the law. I have sought to uphold the highest traditions of my profession—as "counsel for the situation" in the private practice of law, through public and community service, as an innovative advocate helping to shape the law, by bringing my lawyer's skills to the corporate boardroom, and, perhaps most challenging of all, by attempting to balance (not always successfully) family with work. Among the high priests in a secular society, lawyers often are the means by which we resolve conflict peacefully. We are the grease that lubricates the engine of a dynamic, growing economy. The leading members of the bar are "experts in relevance" who can tackle complex problems with analytical skill and commonsense judgment. In this age of increased specialization, volatile global economic cycles, and intensely competitive legal practices, I hope we never lose the vision of the special role lawyers perform in a regulated private economy and diverse free society. That role often calls on us to undertake voluntary legal services and serve the public in advisory and full-time capacities.

It has been my privilege and luck to know and advise in varying ways presidents of the United States of both political parties, to serve in President Ford's cabinet as secretary of transportation, to argue nineteen cases in the Supreme Court of the United States on issues as diverse as antitrust, energy, banking, and constitutional law, to represent leading corporations in major mergers and "bet-the-company" litigation, and to serve as a director of some of America's great corporations, among them IBM, Chase Manhattan Bank, Pan Am, CIGNA, and PepsiCo.

I was also privileged to play a part in the peaceful legal revolution in which the Supreme Court finally faced up to the U.S. Constitution's unfulfilled promise of equality of opportunity, resurrecting its somnolent post–Civil War amendments and eradicating American-style apartheid. Like my mother and father and their parents and grandparents before me, I firmly believed that it is incumbent on each generation not only to challenge the establishment but, more important, to become a creative force within it.

The path that I have taken, therefore, is somewhat different—although hardly unique—from that of most civil rights leaders and politicians of color with whom I have worked, whom I greatly admire, and to whom all Americans are much indebted. Through their struggles, opportunities have opened up for Americans of color and for many others as well. As the barriers came down, I found myself well prepared to seize the unprecedented opportunities presented at that extraordinary time in history. My greatest ambition was to be a practicing lawyer in all the many dimensions of that profession, in the courtroom, in the boardroom, and in the corridors of government. I wanted to be an integral part of an interconnected global economy, reaping the just fruits of my labor.

Nurtured by a strong and loving family, including my wife and children, I had had ingrained in me the values of insatiable curiosity, hard work, and the best possible education obtainable through talent and effort. My parents were proud to be Americans and proud of the particular, significant heritage they each brought to the American experience. They contributed greatly to their community, instilled in me a strong sense of justice, and taught me to value the diverse contributions of many cultures and races in the long march of history and in our great nation.

As Philadelphians, the ringing words of the Declaration of Independence—that all men are created equal—resonated for my parents as an unfulfilled and incomplete promise, a buoy toward which the ship of state would sail in search of a more perfect union. The compromised U.S. Constitution—strangely silent on the singular sin of slavery—was also drafted in Philadelphia. It established a structure of government that could lurch forward with stops and starts and occasional reversals toward a more just and fair society, tempering legislative and executive power with an independent judiciary that was intended to apply wisdom and experience to the resolution of conflicts and the interpretation of the Constitution. The first ten amendments (the Bill of Rights) fleshed out the lofty promise of the Declaration of Independence, initially mostly for the benefit of propertied white males.[1]

Still reeling from the festering wounds of the great Civil War, the states ratified the Thirteenth, Fourteenth, and Fifteenth Amendments, expanding that promise to men of all races and eventually to women. Yet the federal government—all three branches—fell into a deep slumber, anesthetizing the post–Civil War amendments through neglect and subservience to anachronistic theories and traditions like racial inferiority and segregation, nurtured— one recalls with regret—by some of our great writers, philosophers, scientists, political and religious leaders, and academicians.[2] It took almost two centuries and a new generation of leadership to translate the vision of equal opportunity imbedded in the Declaration of Independence and the amended Constitution into a legal framework in which all American citizens, regardless of race, place of birth, religion, ethnicity, or gender, could and most often do participate fully in a working democracy and free market economy.

As I entered the stream of history, racial discrimination permeated both public policy and private decisionmaking throughout the nation. My own experience was usually with the more subtle brand of Yankee racism. Having graduated first in my class at the Harvard Law School, served my country as a U.S. Army Air Corps officer in World War II, and clerked for two distinguished jurists, Judge Herbert F. Goodrich of the U.S. Third Circuit Court of Appeals and Justice Felix Frankfurter of the United States Supreme Court, I nevertheless pounded the pavement in my hometown of Philadelphia, in Boston, in Washington, and on Wall Street in search of a law firm job. I had no offers and was rarely granted an interview. But the times they were a-changin'.

During my young adulthood, giant visionaries again emerged to lead us toward that more perfect union. I was blessed with the opportunity to get to know and work with many of these great leaders, some of whom are icons of American history and others whose behind-the-scenes work has never been fully appreciated or even completely disclosed. They became mentors, advisers, competitors, and colleagues as I pursued my legal career. They were Democrats and Republicans, politicians and professors, counselors and corporate executives, conservatives and liberals, and women and men of all colors and creeds. Despite their differences, they shared a strong commitment to a healthy democracy dependent on participatory decisionmaking by all Americans. They shared the strong conviction that individual talent, brilliance, and effort can and will change the course of history.

I empathize with the view of Chief Justice John Marshall: "The events of my life are too unimportant and have too little interest for any person not of my immediate family, to render them worth communicating or preserving."[3] Yet many friends and colleagues have suggested that I owe it to the nation and future generations to record both the opportunities presented to me and the hurdles along the way, as well as the extraordinary contribution of those in past and present generations who made those opportunities possible.[4]

It is my earnest hope that future lawyers will learn from my successes and failures, that historians will find fresh insights on the period when America's promise of equality of opportunity was largely embraced in the law and accepted by just about all Americans, and that the essential truth will again be reaffirmed that presumptions about character and ability should never be based on shades of skin color.

As I look back over my ninety years, I am grateful to have entered the stream of history at the time I did. During this short period of time we have learned that the nation and its citizenry gain when Americans of all races, genders, and ethnicities enter the current of America's flowing, ever-expanding stream. I am grateful for my parents and for so many transformative leaders who taught me this lesson and took a personal interest in my career.

And I am grateful for the American people, who, sometimes begrudgingly and not always peacefully, have nevertheless generally come to accept that the promise of America's dream will be realized only when all of its citizens are able to participate fully in democratic self-government and a competitive, dynamic, free economy.

ONE

Mr. Coleman Goes to Washington

Government is a trust, and the officers of government are trustees; and both the trust and trustees are created for the benefit of the people.

—HENRY CLAY, 1829

ONE THURSDAY AFTERNOON IN LATE 1974, I was sitting in my law offices at the Dilworth firm in Philadelphia, preparing for a court hearing. My assistant buzzed me on the intercom: "It's Mr. Donald Rumsfeld on the line."

"I'll take it," I said. I knew and admired Don Rumsfeld from my days on President Nixon's productivity and price commissions. When Gerald Ford assumed the presidency after Nixon's resignation, Rumsfeld became his chief of staff. That afternoon, in his usual brisk but courteous manner, Rummy told me that President Ford wanted to see me in the Oval Office the next afternoon.

I was in the middle of seeking an injunction against the local transit unions on behalf of the Southeastern Pennsylvania Transportation Authority, the regional transit authority. But one does not lightly turn down an invitation from any president of the United States. I had great respect for Gerald Ford, with whom I had worked closely when he was a member of the Warren Commission, formed to investigate the assassination of President Kennedy, and I was one of its six senior legal counsel. Ford was a decent, bright, down-to-earth, practical politician, and I thought he had made a great start as president under most difficult circumstances. While Rumsfeld did not say why the president wanted to see me, I knew that Ford was in the process of assembling his own team, consisting of some veterans from the Nixon administration, like Secretary of State Henry Kissinger, who would provide continuity in our delicate international relationships, and some new faces who would enable Ford to put his own stamp on the presidency and differentiate his tenure, in style and content, from that of his predecessor.

On the train down to Washington, the next morning, I rehearsed in my mind what the president might say to me and how I should respond. I was content with my responsibilities at the Dilworth firm as the head of its thriving litigation department, with the challenging corporate, securities, labor, regulatory, and appellate work that I was doing there, and with the private corporate boards on which I was sitting. I felt that I was reaching the pinnacle of my lifelong ambition to become a successful lawyer in my hometown, Philadelphia. As chairman of the NAACP Legal Defense and Educational Fund, I was fully engaged as a volunteer in the continuing legal assault on racial discrimination, following in the footsteps of my mentor Thurgood Marshall, then a justice of the U.S. Supreme Court. From a more practical standpoint, I was paying hefty tuition bills for my two older children, who were at Yale Law School, and my younger son, who was attending Williams College. I shored up my resolve not to accept a full-time position in the Ford administration if one were offered and hoped that what the president had in mind was an advisory role, perhaps on a commission to address the challenges of stagflation, the high inflation and jobless rates that haunted the economy.

When I arrived at the Oval Office at 2:00 p.m. Friday afternoon, President Ford greeted me warmly. We chatted briefly about the findings of the Warren Commission. In 1963 Ford had raised some of the toughest questions about whether there had been a foreign conspiracy involving the Cubans or the Soviet Union in the Kennedy assassination, which was my primary area of investigation. The president then abruptly changed the subject. He came right to the point: "Bill, I would very much like you to join my cabinet as secretary of housing and urban development."

I was flattered. But in some ways the president's offer of this particular job made it easier for me to stick by my resolve and turn down full-time government service. President Johnson had appointed the extraordinarily well-qualified Robert Weaver as secretary of housing and urban development, the first American of color ever to be appointed to a cabinet position. (That is, unless we are able to verify what some historians recently have reported, that Alexander Hamilton, born on the Island of Nevis in the Caribbean, had some Negro blood. If so, then—by the peculiar U.S. tradition in defining race—George Washington appointed the first American of color to the cabinet when he selected Hamilton, who became an outstanding secretary of the treasury. I would be proud to claim him.)

In some respects, the offer of the HUD post was unsettling. Was the department considered to be the "black" cabinet chair at the table? Candidly, I was then no fan of HUD—or of federal housing policy, for that matter. America's inner cities were cluttered with federally subsidized high-rise housing projects that spawned vertical black ghettos—the result of well-intended but ill-conceived policies dating back to Franklin Roosevelt's administration that had created almost insurmountable obstacles for those of us who fought to desegregate schools and communities. It was easy for me to decline the offer, politely pleading my financial obligations to three university-aged children.

President Ford seemed disappointed but then asked me tentatively if I would feel the same about being the ambassador to the United Nations. He noted my service as an alternate delegate to the twenty-fourth U.N. General Assembly and my work with Henry Kissinger in freeing Namibia from South Africa. It wasn't so much a firm offer as an exploration of my resolve. Again, I said that I simply wasn't in a position to take a full-time post in government at that time.

With a discouraged look on his face, the president rose from the couch, walked toward the Wilson desk (which dates back to President Grant's administration), turned abruptly, and said, "Bill, you were a pilot. You represent public transit companies. You are on the Pan Am board. How would you feel about secretary of transportation?"

I was caught off guard and feeling a little guilty about my lack of responsiveness to the president's persistent interest in recruiting me for his administration. Moreover, I was not about to admit that I didn't even know that there was such a thing as the U.S. Department of Transportation. My resolve began to crumble, and I said, with some hesitation in my voice, "Well, Mr. President, I'll have to think about it. Can you give me a couple of days to think it over and discuss it with my wife, Lovida?" He agreed, and the meeting ended on a positive note.

When I discussed the offer with my family over the weekend, it was fortunate that my daughter, Lovida Jr., was home from Yale Law School. She was, as she always is, direct and to the point: "Look, Dad, there probably have been only about two hundred Americans in the history of this nation who have served in the cabinet—and only one other black person that we know of. I really don't see how you're qualified to be secretary of transportation, but it's a great privilege to be offered the job. It's a chance for you to do something important for your country—especially now, when the nation is going through this post-Watergate trauma."

"President Ford is a decent and honest man," she continued. "He graduated from my law school, and he's trying to restore trust in government. You know, Dad, several of my professors at Yale have said that Ford got the highest grade in the course on legal ethics. He needs to assemble his own team, and he obviously thinks you can help him bring back integrity and quality to the federal government. How can you turn him down?"

First thing Monday morning I called Rumsfeld. "If the President still wants me," I said, "I will serve as secretary of transportation."

Rummy sealed the deal. As it turned out, President Ford appointed Carla Hills as secretary of housing and urban development. She did a superb job, much better than I would have done. I hope that my obstinacy did not deprive her of the opportunity of being secretary of transportation. The HUD building was across the street from the Department of Transportation, and Carla and I worked on many projects together during the Ford administration; in subsequent years she and her husband, Rod, became close personal friends of my family. Rod is a client, and their son-in-law, Steve Bunnell, is one of my outstanding law partners.

A creature of Congress, President Ford knew the importance of keeping the congressional delegations informed about prospective appointments. He immediately called Senator Hugh D. Scott, a close friend of my father's, who, I suspect, leaked the news to one of Philadelphia's newspapers. That was a bit unsettling because I was in active negotiations with the transit unions on behalf of the regional transit authority at that time. On the other hand, the newspapers put a more positive spin on the prospective appointment than the FBI, whose investigators traipsed around my Mount Airy neighborhood questioning curious neighbors about my character and integrity. With the FBI clearance completed, the president sent up my nomination, and, after some courtesy visits to key senators, I testified before the Senate Commerce Committee, which reported favorably on my nomination, without objection, and the Senate confirmed my appointment by acclamation. (My daughter remarked that nobody objected because I hadn't done anything worth objecting to.)

Shortly thereafter my beloved wife, Lovida, and I packed our bags and eagerly headed down to Washington.

PART I

The Formative Years

When I was younger, I could remember anything, whether it happened or not.

—MARK TWAIN

TWO

Roots

Children have never been very good at listening to their elders, but they have never failed to imitate them.

—JAMES BALDWIN, 1961

"SOMEDAY, WILLIAM, YOU WILL MAKE a wonderful chauffeur." My English teacher, Miss Egge, had intended to compliment the poised oral presentation that I, one of the four tenth-graders of color at Germantown High, then one of Philadelphia's finest public high schools, had just given.

Yet somehow I didn't take it quite that way. So I answered, foolishly and from the gut, "You'll probably end up as my driver, you [blank] white woman," using epithets that I'd heard on the football field after an illegal block, which I am too embarrassed to repeat even to this day.

I was promptly kicked out of school. The next morning my parents arrived at the principal's office, promising to wash out my mouth with soap and teach me not to use such language—at least not in the classroom. Taken aback by their proper manner, dress, and presence, Miss Egge quickly realized the folly of her comment. We hugged. She became a great friend, supporter, and inspiring teacher.

Although I grew up in the sheltered comfort of a middle-class family, I had attended segregated elementary schools, and therefore Germantown High presented me with some new challenges. The academic grounding was superb, but on occasion I also confronted Yankee-style racism.

Soon after I arrived, I decided to go out for the high school swimming team. I had been a swimmer at the Wissahickon Boys' Club and Emlen summer camp, both of which my father directed, since the age of six and a swimming teacher since I was fourteen, and I had raced competitively. My unofficial times in the 50- and 100-yard freestyle were comparable to times reported in the newspapers for swimmers on teams from the best public and private high schools. I introduced myself to Coach Schwartz, who informed me, "Unfortunately, Bill, Negroes cannot be members of the swimming team."

My parents protested. Schwartz responded: "Now, let's not be the dog in the manger."

"Human dignity is more important than avoiding controversy," my father replied. "No one is going to crush the spirit of any of our three children." Germantown High, which was not about to condone racial discrimination, acted expeditiously. It eliminated its swimming team. On January 29, 1938, the day I graduated from high school, with letters in track and cross country and a coveted letter of admission to the University of Pennsylvania, a notice was posted prominently on the school bulletin board: "Tryouts for the high school swimming team begin on February 1."

While the scars of this lost opportunity remained for years, I bore Coach Schwartz no ill will. In fact, I remember him as a superb teacher of history and political science, who gave me exceptionally high grades and my best letter of recommendation to Penn. Years later, when I returned to campus to speak as a lawyer to the morning assembly, Schwartz pulled me aside and confessed the real reason for denying me a place on the swimming team. Practice and competitive meets were held at the Germantown YMCA, which did not allow colored folks to swim in its pool.* He told me he had not wanted to risk the school's relationship with the Y by raising the issue at that time, devilishly emphasizing the "C" in YMCA.

A more amusing example of racial stereotyping involved my music class—and it happened more than once. When I first entered class as a new student, the music teacher would greet me warmly, assuming (no doubt based solely on the color of my skin) that here was someone who could lead the singing. But I was pitifully tone deaf. My laughable efforts at song were unfortunately viewed as defiance, and I would be sent home from school. My father or mother or both would have to bring me back, explaining that all the Colemans (at least until my children's generation) were genetically incapable of carrying a tune.

I grew up in Philadelphia, our nation's cradle of liberty, and my experiences with racial discrimination and stereotyping pale in comparison with the violent versions encountered in parts of the old South—the lynchings, the Jim Crow laws and Black codes, and the denial of access to restaurants, accommodations, and basic services. In certain times and places, such experiences were to be found in the North as well—the lynchings and race riots in Springfield, Illinois, in 1908 come to mind. Yet my vivid youthful impressions linger to this

---

*Racial appellations are always tricky, especially for those of us who have lived through so many renditions of political correctness. I hope the younger generations will forgive my penchant for a time-tested, period-appropriate approach, which I explain in chapter 40.

day, serving as a constant reminder that our nation's progress in race relations remains uneven.

Having been nurtured in an educated and disciplined but loving family of modest means, I was better prepared than most to respond to the slings and arrows of Yankee racism. I understood the ignorance from which they sprang. Because I was confident in my own deeply rooted family values, such incidents motivated me to work a little harder to demonstrate my worth, to prove the precipitators wrong and foolish. Such slights also strengthened my resolve to hold my ground—to fight back with a tenacity and combativeness that served me well during the civil rights movement. On occasion my feistiness may have offended some of my white colleagues and friends in later years as they adjusted to the forces that were integrating formerly closed sectors of our society. My formative years provided me, unlike some young men of all races today, with a deep reservoir of strength.

Life began for me shortly after 12:15 a.m., the morning of July 7, 1920, in a small temporary apartment in North Philadelphia. My parents had moved to be near Dr. Stephen Hamil, who was married to one of my mother's close relatives. My mother would not risk a hospital birth, where one newborn could—mistakenly or intentionally—be substituted for another. Dr. Hamil delivered me at home, as was the case with all the Coleman children. My family returned to their actual home in adjacent Germantown two days after my birth.[1] A few days later, the doctor needed to lance a boil on my neck, and this bit of minor surgery was witnessed by my beloved sister, Emma Louise Coleman, then four years old. We were joined seven years later by our brother, Robert Van Tyle Coleman.

My parents, William Thaddeus Coleman Sr. and Laura Beatrice Mason, were born and raised in Baltimore, where they were wed on June 29, 1915. My mother, the fifth of six children, was born on Druid Hill Avenue, next door to the home in which Thurgood Marshall was later born in 1908. Grandfather Mason, a Republican, received a patronage appointment as a postman during President William Howard Taft's administration. Upon the election of Democrat Woodrow Wilson, my grandmother Mason went down to the Baltimore post office headquarters and staged a sit-in (decades before Rosa Parks), waiting patiently until she was able to plead—successfully—for the retention of her husband despite the change in political parties. Her compelling brief: my grandfather was the sole support of six children. Grandfather Mason was one of the few Republicans who kept his job during the Wilson administration—and for many years the only postal worker of color in Baltimore.

Like her sisters, Mother finished high school early, with high grades. She later graduated from the Baltimore Coplin Normal School, a black teacher's college, with high honors. She taught German—language and history—in the segregated Baltimore public high schools until she married my father. My parents then moved to Philadelphia in 1915 when my father decided to pursue a career in social work. Mother would object vigorously whenever anyone said that she had stopped working after marriage. She insisted that raising three children, providing a welcoming home, and sustaining a loving marriage were rewarding pleasures—but awfully damn hard work. She quoted Ben Franklin (who, frankly, did not practice what he preached): "For there is no rank in natural knowledge of equal dignity and importance with that of being a good parent, a good child, a good husband, or wife."[2]

Mother loved to speak German to the Pennsylvania Dutch in the Montgomery County farm country, where we spent eleven weeks each summer at Camp Emlen. When she walked into the Clements's country store in Morwood, the other customers occasionally would shift to German, unaware that she understood their language extremely well. At dinner she would regale the family with tales of what they were saying—good or bad—about the colored folks who summered in their neighborhood. Mother attempted to teach me German, but lamentably I had inherited my father's lack of genes for language facility, as several of my college professors of European philosophy would later attest, as they called on me to read Hegel in the original German.

According to a genealogy prepared by my mother's oldest sister, Emma, Mother's great grandfather was an African named Peck, who was educated for the ministry in England. While he was home in West Africa on vacation one summer, he went down to the wharf for a stroll and was abducted by slave traders and thrown onto a ship headed for America. As the ship arrived at the port of Baltimore, he escaped. Befriended by similarly situated colored friends, he found work, completed his education for the ministry, and married the illegitimate daughter of a slave owner. They had a large family. Peck was a successful minister, and he and his wife operated a stop along the Underground Railroad. He helped free many slaves by running them up to Canada in his hay-covered wagon. One of his daughters, Eliza, was my mother's grandmother. She married John Burgess, a Quaker painter from rural Maryland. They had twelve children, one of whom was my mother's mother, who lived in Baltimore. She married Charles Pinckney Mason, as noted above, who worked for the U.S. Post Office in Baltimore.

Richard Mason, Charles's father—and my great grandfather—was born in the West Indies. According to Emma's genealogy, he was the son of a West Indian woman who had married a noble Napoleonic refugee who migrated to the islands when Napoleon was imprisoned in France. Richard's mother brought him to Baltimore as a young boy, where he was apprenticed to a shoemaker. He made a very good living crafting custom-made shoes. He married Anne Young, and they raised my grandfather, Charles.

My mother also told me that some of our ancestors had lived in Alsace, in the Rhine Valley. That may explain her interest in the German language and her affinity for the Alsatians. Mother would recount for us the suffering of the Alsatians in 1871, when they surrendered to the newly created German Empire during the Franco-Prussian War. She rejoiced when, after fierce German resistance, the Americans seized their first major German city on October 21, 1944—Aachen, near the Belgian-Dutch border, at one time the favorite residence of Charlemagne.

Mother's great uncle, the Reverend Bishop, had been an Episcopal minister in St. Louis. He was active in the Underground Railroad. My grandmother would talk of seeing colored strangers in the attic of her uncle's St. Louis house for a day or two. They would then disappear suddenly, on their way to Canada, where they would be free. In his youth Reverend Bishop had been among the valiant Negro troops under General Grant and General Hooker, who stormed Lookout Mountain, Tennessee, in the Battle of the Clouds on November 24, 1863, driving General Bragg's Confederate forces off the mountain and eventually out of eastern Tennessee.

Mother was strikingly beautiful and well read, with a knowledge of world history and a love of literature. She was always available to help with difficult homework and to enrich her children's school experience.

We shared with our parents and other Philadelphians pride in living in the birthplace of the American experiment, with its antecedents in Great Britain, France, Rome, and Greece. We also learned a lot about the allegorical history of Ethiopia, founded three thousand years ago by Menelik, the first son of King Solomon and the Queen of Sheba, a woman of color. Menelik allegedly brought the Ark of the Covenant to Ethiopia and founded the Solomonic dynasty, of which Haile Selassie was the last reigning emperor. The young Coleman kids knew a lot more about the Queen of Sheba than about Queen Elizabeth I of England. My parents read with sadness and bitterness about the Italian invasion of Ethiopia in 1935 and the callous rejection by the League of Nations of Emperor Haile Selassie's passionate pleas for help.

In dinner conversations and family outings, our parents told stories about the many contributions made by persons of color in world and American history, filling a deep void in the history lessons presented in the Philadelphia public schools. We had an abundance of role models who, I fear, are unknown to many youngsters today, regardless of race.

The Coleman children heard stories about the achievements of Hannibal, François-Dominique Toussaint L'Ouverture, the Dumas (father and son),

Alexander Pushkin, Frederick Douglass, Ida B. Wells, Booker T. Washington, and William Edward Burghardt (W. E. B.) DuBois, a friend of Mother's older sister. Mother introduced us to the literature produced by colored Americans—Langston Hughes, Countee Cullen, James Weldon Johnson—along with the German classics of Goethe, Kant, and Schiller that she so loved. Her favorite writers were Mark Twain, Pushkin, Tolstoy, Dickens, and Plutarch.

My parents took pride in the fact that when their ancestors came to this country, mostly as free men and women, they brought their own special histories and traditions, which, along with those of the early Americans, melded into and strengthened the greater whole—in the language on the Great Seal of the United States, "E Pluribus Unum." With her knowledge of and respect for history, other cultures, and the promise of America, my mother was able to instill in her children an appreciation for our mixed heritage in the context of the multicultural society in which we were encouraged to thrive.

My parents believed that a good education, integrity, discipline, hard work, and a bit of luck were essential to success, and they consistently and persistently fought against artificial barriers based on race. In their view, the historic path toward racial equality of opportunity began with Abraham Lincoln's opposition to slavery as "a moral, social, and political wrong."[3] They loved to tell the story of the abolitionist John Brown at Harper's Ferry. My uncle Lovett Groves had gone to school at Harper's Ferry, so we felt a family connection. In their day, segregation and racial discrimination were the critical challenges. My parents challenged any impediments to their children's ability to succeed. They knew and appreciated deeply what persons of color had accomplished in fighting racial injustice and opening up opportunities, and they firmly believed that America was enriched as all races entered the flowing stream. Like Alexander Hamilton, they wanted to be known simply as Americans.

Mother could be very persistent (a trait I no doubt inherited). One day in early 1975, when I was sworn in as secretary of transportation in President Ford's cabinet, she arrived at the northwest entrance to the White House with my brother and his wife. My sister-in-law's name had been omitted from the guest list. Mother informed the White House security guard that unless her daughter-in-law was admitted, even without identification, my mother would wait at the curbside until after the ceremony. The guard relented, in a breach of security that likely could not be replicated today (except by expert White House state dinner crashers).

President Ford had asked Justice Thurgood Marshall to administer the oath of office for the swearing-in. A special chair on the podium was provided for my aging mother. In his introduction to the three hundred guests at the ceremony, President Ford said some flattering things about his soon-to-be cabinet officer. As he concluded his remarks, there was a tug at his arm: "Mr. President," whispered my mother. "I have two other children who are here today. Please say something nice about them too."

Without any briefing paper, President Ford could not have known that my sister, Emma, was a high school teacher in Atlantic City and my brother, Robert, was the key spatial architect at the Budd Company in Philadelphia. Fortunately, the ceremony proceeded onward, as I had already started my remarks, and an awkward moment for the president was avoided. My oldest child, William T. Coleman III, afterward said that he was never so happy to hear my voice.

My father, William Thaddeus Coleman, was born on Division Street in Baltimore. His middle name (and mine also) was given to him in honor of Thaddeus Stevens (1792–1868), a Republican Pennsylvania congressman. As a leader of the Radical Reconstructionists, the feisty and irascible Stevens led the fight for the civil rights acts adopted shortly after the Civil War and for the Fourteenth Amendment to the U.S. Constitution, which mandates due process and equal protection of the law for all Americans regardless of race. With his uncompromising tenacity, Thaddeus Stevens was a bit of a dark knight. In my mind he remains an unsung patriot in realizing the American dream.[4] In embracing his name, no doubt I took on a few of his less-than-elegant traits as well, but they have served me well in some tight situations, and I am comforted by the fact that, according to my mother, Thaddeus was also the name of an apostle and cousin of Jesus Christ.

My grandfather Louis Coleman was, beginning in 1890, the maitre d' of the main dining room of the Charles, at the time Baltimore's most exclusive hotel. Although my grandfather died before I was born, I knew my grandmother, Bessie Coleman, well. She would often visit us in Philadelphia. She was a wellspring of Ben Franklin–style aphorisms—"Early to bed, early to rise, makes a man healthy, wealthy, and wise," she would say, although she also advised me that being wise is more important than being wealthy. Perhaps foreshadowing my future time in government, she warned that "three may keep a secret, if two of them are dead" and reinforced that admonition with a similar one: "If you would keep a secret from your enemy, tell it not to a friend." Grandmother Coleman owned and managed a domestic cleaning and assistance service for unmarried men, white and colored, which brought her in touch with many prominent members of the community. She was very close to Carl Murphy and his family, for forty-nine years the publisher of the *Afro-American*, then the leading colored newspaper in the United States. She always brought news about the politics of racial ferment, which energized many a family dinner conversation.

My father was a handsome man both inwardly and outwardly. Articulate, straightforward, and caring, he was capable of displays of temper when they were justified. He was courtly, by today's standards a bit old fashioned in the respectful way that he valued and treated women.

In his second year in high school in Baltimore, my father and his classmates routinely passed a local Chinese laundry on the way home from the segregated public school. One day he joined the chorus of boys taunting the owner. The Chinese proprietor threw a hand iron at my father. Father threw it back, fortunately missing the gentleman but unfortunately smashing to smithereens the large storefront window of the laundry. Within minutes, almost every policeman in the precinct was on the hunt for my father. In desperation Grandmother Bessie called a childhood friend, the president of Hampton Institute, saying, "You must take my son, Bill, into the Hampton Institute."

"Of course, Bessie, just send him down immediately." And the next day Bill was on a train to Hampton, Virginia.

That traumatic experience undoubtedly contributed to my father's lifelong abhorrence of racial discrimination in any form. When he arrived at Hampton, the school authorities learned for the first time that he was only fourteen years old, hardly eligible for college admission. Fortunately, Hampton had an affiliated trade school. My father registered in the cabinetmaker program until he was of age to matriculate at the college. My father always prized the skill that he had acquired by working with his hands, and he developed a special appreciation for artisans. One of his inlaid tables still stands in our bedroom.

Father graduated from Hampton Institute in 1913 with a bachelor's degree in sociology and social work. He taught for a year at a segregated public high school in North Carolina, for a salary of $75 a month. His request for a raise the following year was denied by the white superintendent, who instead offered to call him Professor Coleman. Dad resigned and went north to Philadelphia to continue his studies. After completing a social work course of study at the University of Pennsylvania, he was hired as the executive director of the Wissahickon Boys' Club, an institution established by the Germantown Quakers.

The spark behind the club was John T. Emlen. The Emlen family was very wealthy, epitomizing what we ordinary Philadelphians often said about the Quakers: "Sent by William Penn to Philadelphia to do good, they did very well."

THREE

Making Jewels Out of Rough Diamonds

A boy is a diamond in the rough; add character and you have a jewel.

—WILLIAM T. COLEMAN SR.

MY FATHER REJECTED THE SEPARATE-BUT-EQUAL doctrine, but he would probably have to admit that the Wissahickon Boys' Club was without equal in the nation. Owing to the generosity of the Quakers and Father's leadership, the club developed a physical plant and membership numbers from the 1920s through the 1940s that rivaled those of any boys' club in the country, colored or white.

The club opened in 1903 as one of the original fifty-three boys clubs in the country and the first to serve youth of color. Its roots were in several organizations that had served the Negro community since the late 1870s. In 1906 representatives from the fifty-three clubs met in Boston to bring some organization to the movement. They formed the Federated Boys' Clubs and launched a drive to spread the concept across the country. In 1915 the Federated Boys' Clubs changed its name to Boys' Clubs Federation. When my father was hired in 1915, he was the first paid professional American of color in the federation.

At first the Wissahickon Boys' Club board of directors, composed of successful businessmen or their spouses, was all white. Later a director of color was appointed, Daniel Brooks, who had a doctorate from the University of Pennsylvania. Brooks, who was principal of the Reynolds School, a segregated public school in North Philadelphia that included kindergarten through eighth grade, was the first colored principal in the Philadelphia public school system. He lived a block from my family. Two very active and committed women on the boys' club board were Mrs. Frances Strawbridge, whose husband was an owner of the leading Philadelphia department store, Strawbridge & Clothier, and Mrs. Stephen Carey, whose husband was an owner of the Leeds and Northrop investment firm. Since the Wissahickon Boys' Club was part of the Community Fund, an organization of nonprofits in the Philadelphia area, my father got to know the Philadelphia business community well. He became fully engaged in local business, city governance, and community affairs.

The clubhouse was located in the Germantown district on the north side of Coulter Street and Pulaski Avenue, adjacent to a neighborhood on the south side of Coulter known as the colored ghetto of West Germantown. The name Wissahickon comes from the name of the Indian tribe that used to inhabit the area in and surrounding nearby Fairmont Park. The boys' club facilities included a basketball gym, poolroom, game room, boxing room, an outdoor swimming pool, lockers, and a small balcony for basketball spectators. When I was fourteen years old, Dad put me in charge of the poolroom from 4:00 to 9:00 p.m., paying me a dollar a week out of his own pocket.

The gym was cramped for playing basketball—its walls were at the court's boundaries, and the ceiling was not very high. Some of the best basketball players in the city learned to play there. Wilt Chamberlain was one of them. Some went on to play college ball, some to the Negro Basketball League, and some later on to the National Basketball Association.

A house connected to the club building was converted to classrooms where boys could be tutored in the evening or could use the library. One night a week classes in carpentry, traditional storytelling, music, reading, and cooking were offered. One day a young white lady, a Miss Fox, showed up at the club's front door and offered to teach cooking to the boys for free, which she did for twenty-five years. We never knew much about her background, but she never missed a class. She taught with grace and enthusiasm and became a good friend of my mother.

My father firmly insisted that the club should be open whenever the boys were not in school, so it was open five days a week from 2:30 to 6:00 p.m. and, after an hour for dinner, from 7:00 to 10:00 p.m. On Saturdays it would be open from 9:00 a.m. to 10:00 p.m., later when there were basketball games there. At least two days a month there would be a social, with a good band and dancing. On Saturday nights there were movies. I especially enjoyed Rin Tin Tin, Tarzan, and Tom Mix movies. Most important, from my father's perspective, was that we were spared the humiliation of sitting in the segregated section of the movie houses on Germantown Avenue.

Many club boys, as my father called them, went on to have significant careers. Bill Cosby was one of them. One of his early television skits was about playing basketball in the club's undersized gym. Herb Adderly, another club boy, played football at Michigan State and went on to become the star defensive halfback of the Green Bay Packers, winning the national championship in his first year. With his championship bonus he bought his mother a new home and a Cadillac, enabling her to move out of her apartment in a segregated federal housing project near the boy's club that was constructed during the Depression.

On Friday afternoons many of my club friends and I would walk over to the athletic fields of Penn Charter, Germantown Academy, Chestnut Hill Academy, or Germantown Friends School, four nearby private white schools. We would watch the competition between the prep schools, listening to the enthusiastic cheers from the players' parents, grandparents, maids, butlers, and chauffeurs. Many of the athletes would go on to play for Ivy League colleges. On the way home, some of us were heard to grumble, "I bet we could beat those guys if we had the chance. They didn't look all that great to me. I'd like to see how much they could score against a really tough defense."

We also trekked to baseball games at Shibe Park, the home of Connie Mack's Athletics (the American League) and Baker's Field, where the Phillies then played (the National League). We wondered why there were no men of color on the teams. When we got to see Satchel Paige, Buck Leonard, and Josh Gibson play in the Negro Baseball League, we knew that whatever the reason, it was not based on talent.

It wasn't easy being the son of the executive director. In a unique twist on affirmative action, the coaches would make sure I made the team even though many of the boys had more natural athletic talent. It could be embarrassing. For example, I was able to play starting quarterback of the football team in the days of the single wing because I could call the signals from the blocking back position and let the tailback do the passing. My one advantage was that I could remember plays and signals better than most. With the advent of the T formation, my football career ended. Swimming and track (quarter mile, half mile, and cross-country) became my sports.

In the thirty-one years of Dad's leadership, only one club boy was arrested (defining "arrested" narrowly to mean actually being booked at the police station and thereby acquiring a police record). His boys did get into trouble. Because my father had an arrangement with the Fourteenth Police District, whenever a boy was picked up by the police, day or night, he would be brought to the boys' club or to our home instead of the police station. My father would call the parents and the issue would be worked out. My father strongly believed that "there is no such thing as a bad boy, just a good boy doing something wrong"—or that, as he often put it, "a boy is a diamond in the rough; add character and you have a jewel."

In 1920, the year of my birth, the Emlen family once again demonstrated their Quaker generosity. They purchased and gave to the Wissahickon Boys' Club a thirty-acre farm about thirty miles northwest of Philadelphia, in Morwood, Montgomery County, the heart of Pennsylvania Dutch country. The farm was to be used as a summer camp for boys ages six to eighteen. The campground included a beautiful river-fed lake—wonderful for swimming, fishing, rowing, and canoeing—surrounded by a grove of trees. There was also a big barn that was used as an auditorium and for recreation on rainy days. And so that my father would not be separated from his family for eleven weeks during the summer, the Emlens built a five-room cottage at the edge of the farm for my parents.

About eight years later, a regulation swimming pool filled by artesian well water was built on the camp grounds; the swimming pool was considered safer than the lake for young city boys who would be swimming for the first time. There was one drawback. Each Sunday evening the pool had to be drained for cleaning and then refilled by nine o'clock the next morning. The ten o'clock Monday morning swim class was a sight to behold, as inner-city boys were baptized by full immersion in the ice-cold spring waters of rural Pennsylvania. By Tuesday the sun had warmed the water to a more bearable level.

Camp was open from the last Monday in June through Labor Day, and each summer about twelve hundred boys attended. The very young campers (ages six to nine) lived in the original farmhouse, boys from ten to twelve lived in a large converted chicken coop, and those thirteen to eighteen years old lived in one of eight tents on the hill, each tent holding twelve to fourteen boys. The counselors had smaller tents in front of the row of camper tents. They were mostly school teachers, principals, and older college students, and each year the staff included a medical doctor who had just completed his first year of internship.

Many of the campers were sponsored by charitable institutions. The Wirtz Foundation paid for about a hundred boys to attend, each for a two-week stay. The Country Week Association of Philadelphia sponsored about thirty poor kids from inner-city Philadelphia each week. At first the boys would arrive on Monday afternoons with an identification tag on their shirts. As charity-supported campers, they often were called "country weekers" by the other boys and sometimes even by the counselors. Dad quickly ended that practice, insisting that once boys set foot on the campgrounds, there would be no distinction among them.

There was an interesting social and economic mix among the campers, including boys from poor families and boys whose parents paid for as much as a ten-week stay, the sons of teachers, college presidents, doctors, and other professionals. They came from throughout the eastern United States and from as far away as New Orleans. There was a more exclusive camp for children of color in Massachusetts, Camp Atwater, but it took boys only during July. Some of the wealthier colored kids would then spend the rest of the summer at Camp Emlen, where many of them were exposed to inner-city kids for the first time. Sometimes a sponsored camper would return on his own dime, either because his parents were doing better or because he had worked after school to save money. My father always thought that that was the best testament to the value of the experience. In later years, there were a significant number of white campers, who often were called "whitey" until Dad put a stop to it.

The camp offered track, tennis, boxing, hiking in the rolling hills nearby, water sports, and a playground for the youngsters. Competitive athletics were important. Roy Campanella attended Camp Emlen when he was twelve. As the catcher he threw the ball so hard and accurately that even I—a lefty—could play second base that year. When he did not return the next summer, opting at the age of thirteen for the Negro Baseball League instead, I lost my second-base position and was relegated to the outfield. Campanella was one of the first Negroes to join Branch Rickey's legendary Brooklyn Dodgers, along with teammate Jackie Robinson, and he was named the National Baseball League's most valuable player three times. He is now comfortably ensconced in the Baseball Hall of Fame.

A high point each year was the baseball games played against the whites-only Germantown Boys' Club, which owned a camp about ten miles down the road. Edward Harris, who was the executive director, and my father were friendly rivals. Anxious for their campers to win, they would import some of their most athletic club boys just for the weekends on which the games were played. The other great rivalry was with the Pennsylvania Dutch boys who lived on and worked the nearby farms.

One day board member Mrs. Strawbridge appeared at the club. "Mr. Coleman," she announced, "my husband and I have just purchased a new car, and we'd like to give our three-year-old Cadillac to the club to transport the boys' baseball and basketball teams to away games." After thanking her for her generosity, my father said that the cost of gas and servicing such a car would be beyond the club's means. He then suggested that if she had no objection he could sell the car and use the proceeds to upgrade the club's sports facilities.

"That makes perfect sense, Mr. Coleman. I hope you get a good price for the car because when you do, I will match it dollar for dollar."

Believe it or not, a high point of each camper's week was Sunday chapel. The camp had built an open wooden chapel in a grove of trees next to the lake. By Sunday the boys had lived together for at least a week, learned new skills, tested one another's physical and mental stamina, and gained the confidence that comes from being away from home. The Sunday morning bath had also done wonders, as during the week cleanliness to be had was from swimming in the pool or capsizing a canoe. A few counselors were budding ministers. We were well up on the struggles of the day, from racial injustice to President Roosevelt's myriad attempts to pull the nation out of the Great Depression. We heard many speeches, and occasionally the oratory crescendoed, surging to heights comparable to Martin Luther King Jr.'s "I Have a Dream" speech. I took away some oral skills that were to serve me well in later years in the courtroom and on the political trail, regardless of the demographic mix of the audience.

In the last half of my senior year of high school my father hired me as a camp counselor. The salary was $300 for ten weeks, a not insignificant sum in June 1937, considering that room and board were free. However, I did not fare so well in my first responsible job. The last week of camp, my father was under a lot of pressure, hoping once again that the season would end without any serious mishaps. He directed all counselors to remain on the campgrounds in the evenings, even when they had no specific assignment. One evening that week some of us nevertheless decided to go to a movie in the town of Souderton, four miles away. After all, the summer was ending and it was our last time together. My father called an emergency meeting that night, and we didn't show up. On our return to camp he met us with a stern rebuke. Showing no favoritism, he fired me on the spot. Even more humiliating, I was demoted to the rank of camper, with a 9:00 p.m. bedtime. It was the last time that I ever disobeyed an order to stay on the job.

For most of his forty-three-year working career my father held three jobs: executive director of the Wissahickon Boys' Club, from 1916; director of Camp Emlen, from 1920; and field secretary for the Federated Boys' Clubs from 1926. As the first national officer of color, he would spend about ten weeks a year traveling throughout the eastern United States, establishing and raising funds for new clubs for boys of color.[1]

In 2006 the Boys and Girls Clubs of America published its official centennial report, *Changing Lives, Changing America: 100 years of Boys and Girls Clubs*. The book acknowledged that in the early years "'separate but equal' was the law of the land, particularly in the South. Clubs operated within these parameters." The book further explained that before the U.S. Supreme Court decision in "*Brown v. Board of Education* overturned segregation, there were some 40 club branches and/or organizations serving exclusively Black American youth, South and North."[2] The first and oldest club to serve the black community, the book notes, was the Wissahickon Boys' Club, which also was unique in that it was founded by an interracial group. Not surprisingly, it was among the first to attract white as well as black members.

As the national federation's only officer of color, my father was often faced with racial prejudice. Efforts were made to bar him from serving as a delegate or participating in social activities at national conventions in, among other places, Indianapolis, Birmingham, and Washington. He stood his ground, insisting on his right to serve as a delegate but occasionally forgoing social events if a compromise were necessary to ensure his participation on policy matters. My father never talked about these incidents at home. I learned about them from reading about his life. Well before the modern civil rights movement, he was opening doors for Americans of color.[3]

As I look back on the importance of the boys' club experience in my life, I wonder whether as we address the seemingly intractable problems of the inner city—Southside Chicago for example—there isn't a lot that we could learn from this period in history. Long before the Great Society, the minority community provided the support systems needed to nurture and ensure the assimilation of its youth (many of whose families had migrated north in search of greater opportunity) into the American mainstream. It was also a time when the greater community, including wealthy individuals, felt a personal and philanthropic responsibility to lend a hand to the less fortunate. For inner-city kids, the club and camp experiences provided college-educated role models, lessons in developing self-discipline and a sense of personal responsibility, and the challenge of healthy competition in accordance with established rules—all essential prerequisites to successful entry into the mainstream of American society.

My father continued to serve the Wissahickon Boys' Club until his retirement in 1955. The organization carries on to this day, making jewels out of rough diamonds.[4] As Ben Franklin once wrote, "It is prodigious that quantity of good that can be done by one man, if he will make a business of it."[5]

FOUR

Home Sweet Home

The example of good men is visible philosophy.
—ENGLISH PROVERB

THE GREAT DEPRESSION HIT THE nation in 1929 when I was nine years old. My dad's workload greatly increased, and the Colemans always had food on the table, decent clothes on our backs, and a comfortable home. Dad worked with many families on relief, encouraged boys to join the federal Civilian Conservation Corps, and undertook additional charitable work. For example, he persuaded many of the Wissahickon Boys' Club's directors, who were wealthy people with large properties, to make some of their sizable backyards available to jobless people to grow food for consumption or sale.

Through his many community activities, Dad was well known in Germantown and almost as well known in the greater Philadelphia area, yet he never had any interest in political or public life. He did meet Hugh D. Scott when Scott first ran for Congress from the Sixth Congressional District, where we lived, and they developed a close alliance, each providing valuable support to the other through the years. In 1958 Hugh was elected to the U.S. Senate, rising to minority leader and, at one time, the Republican Party chair. He provided invaluable help to me when I was secretary of transportation, guiding me through the Senate's byzantine rules and arcane customs as we worked for legislation to advance the country's transportation system.

Despite my father's many activities, he always made time for the family. He was friendly, humorous, gentle, and patient but, when necessary, a tough disciplinarian. Rarely would a few months go by without my getting a whipping, after which, of course, Mother would console me.

We went to the Episcopal church every Sunday. By the age of twelve, I became an acolyte. Sunday dinner after church was a special occasion, usually including one or two guests; either chicken or lamb, the choice of "cultured" families, was served. One Sunday my father abruptly left the table when my mother served ham. The conversation would be wide ranging, although if one of the club boys had achieved a significant success, that would be the first topic to be discussed. When we got older, our parents would take us to the theater or to hear an army or navy band.

My aunt Emma Mason Groves, my mother's oldest surviving sister, was a special delight. She and her husband, Lovett B. Groves, lived in Boston. In the 1930s Emma would take a trip south twice a year to Baltimore and Washington, visiting us on her way home. Lovett Groves held two jobs. From 9:00 a.m. to 5:00 p.m. each day, he was deputy secretary of the Massachusetts Bureau of Motor Vehicles. After an early dinner he slept from six until eleven, and from midnight until eight in the morning he was an official in the U.S. Post Office in Boston.

While Emma and Lovett cherished their weekends together, Emma's active mind and outgoing nature kept her busy during the week. W. E. B. DuBois, a good friend, would often visit and escort her to social events during the week. A graduate of Fisk College and the first man of color to receive a doctorate from Harvard, DuBois was well known among colored intellectuals for taking an aggressive stand on race relations and serving as a foil to Booker T. Washington, who held more docile views.[1] DuBois's energetic discussion of race with my parents on one occasion when he visited our home left an indelible impression on me, an impressionable young boy.

The Groveses knew many of the leaders of emerging colored organizations, such as Walter White, head of the NAACP, and Lester Granger of the National Urban League. The intellectual ferment created by such men gave rise to the civil rights movement and helped shape my attitudes and resolve growing up. When Aunt Emma visited us in Philadelphia on her return trip to Boston, she would bring us the latest news from the lawyers, professors, doctors, and other professionals who were leaders in the Negro community. She would bring us up to date on the happenings at Howard University in Washington, Morgan College in Baltimore, and Lincoln College in Oxford, Pennsylvania. She was our own special precursor to CNN, bringing us the breaking news, the gossip, the cutting-edge issues, the controversies, and the achievements pulsating among what we then called "colored people."

At a time when role models in politics, the media, and sports were predominantly white, there was a substantial group of black achievers of whom we were enormously proud. Information about their achievements spread by word of mouth. There was the handsome, articulate Charles H. Houston—a summa cum laude graduate of Amherst College and a magna cum laude graduate of Harvard Law School—who was the first editor of color of the *Harvard Law Review* and who later became dean of Howard Law School and counsel to the NAACP. Houston won a brilliant victory in the U.S. Supreme Court in 1938, when, ending a long drought on civil rights, the Court held that a person of color had the right to attend the University of Missouri Law School.[2]

There was Houston's second cousin William H. Hastie, who also attended Amherst, where he was a member of Phi Beta Kappa, and Harvard Law School, where he also was an editor of the *Harvard Law Review.* Hastie, along with Houston, taught Thurgood Marshall at Howard Law School and in 1937 became the nation's first district court judge of color, sitting in the Virgin Islands. He was also the country's first federal appellate court judge of color, appointed by President Truman to the U.S. Court of Appeals for the Third Circuit in 1949, and he later became its chief judge. According to former attorney general Nicholas Katzenbach, Bobby Kennedy recommended Hastie for appointment to the Supreme Court.[3] John F. Kennedy, however, took a less controversial route and nominated the more conservative Byron White, the former University of Colorado all-American and National Football League halfback, who was at the time Bobby's deputy. With the success of such legal luminaries as Houston and Hastie filling our evening conversations, it is no wonder I gravitated toward a career in the law.

We had great non-lawyer role models as well: Alain Leroy Locke, a Rhodes scholar, literary critic, and philosophy professor who popularized the Harlem Renaissance;[4] Dr. Charles Drew—also a graduate of Amherst, summa cum laude, and of Harvard Medical School, magna cum laude—who developed dried blood plasma; and Ralph Bunche, a Harvard Ph.D., foreign policy expert, international mediator, and Nobel Peace Prize laureate. Outside our immediate circle, we all admired George Washington Carver, who had developed and promoted the farming of peanuts and other agricultural products that helped save the South from economic disaster following the decline of cotton farming. And we revered Duke Ellington, Fats Waller, Cab Calloway, Lena Horne, Ella Fitzgerald, Billie Holiday, and Louis Armstrong as the undisputed kings of the jazz world, Marian Anderson as the queen of the classical music concert, and Josephine Baker as the toast of Paris.

In Germantown, we lived in a two-story twin house in the 200 block of West Earlham Terrace on a dead-end, transitional street with a mix of residents about evenly split between colored and white. With no through traffic, my older sister, younger brother, and I could play baseball, touch football, or volleyball or just run the block to practice for the track team. The streets to the north were occupied by whites, but to the south, the Germantown colored ghetto began.

On the north side of Earlham Terrace, the houses were large and beautiful. Within walking distance from our house were four private, exclusively white academies, including the Germantown Friends School. Mrs. Stephen Carey, a

Quaker, was on the board of both the Wissahickon Boys' Club and the Germantown Friends School. Her maid's son Charles was a club boy. Mrs. Carey was heartbroken that she could not get Charles into the Germantown Friends School, especially since she and her family had contributed a lot of money to the school. Later her athletic son, Steve Carey, became president of Haverford College and a close family friend. I once visited him in a Washington jail, where he had landed after marching with Martin Luther King Jr. By the time of the *Brown* v. *Board of Education* decision, the four private academies had accepted a few children of color, including my two sons and daughter. In 1974 Steve and his wife helped me celebrate my White House swearing in.

My best friend in the late twenties and the early thirties was Stewart Webster, one of six children of the Webster family, who lived two houses down from us. Most of the Webster family were very fair in skin color; indeed, they easily could be mistaken for white. The oldest sister Anna, who worked in sales at the downtown Wanamaker's Department Store, apparently was hired as white. We were instructed never to call her by her first name when shopping there. Her husband, of a darker shade but still relatively fair, could not accompany her downtown. We thought this odd and foolish—indeed mean, despicable, and cruel. We thought that this had to end; fortunately, I have lived to see that, for the most part, it has.[5]

FIVE

School Days

I am always ready to learn, although I do not always like being taught.

—WINSTON CHURCHILL

IN SECOND GRADE, I WAS a difficult child. Much to the class's enjoyment, I often would talk back disrespectfully to the teacher, who always was a woman. One day, while I was acting up, my classmates' laughter ceased and silence pervaded the room. When I looked to the door, my father was standing there. He chastised me in front of the class, making good use of his powerful hand and belt. He made me apologize to the teacher, Miss Walters. My days as class clown came to an abrupt end.

In 1925 the public schools in Philadelphia, though north of the Mason-Dixon Line, were strictly segregated by race through the sixth grade. All the teachers in the colored schools were colored, but the principals were white. Starting in junior high school, the schools were integrated, and both the teachers and the principals were white.

I started kindergarten at the age of five in the Meehan School, about an eight-minute walk from home, two blocks into "Pulaski town," the heart of the smaller West Germantown Negro ghetto; it was tough, but not as tough as the Sharpnack Street Negro ghetto in East Germantown. The Fitler School was much closer to home but was for white children exclusively.

Miss Adams, my kindergarten teacher, was an attractive woman who apparently saw some potential in me. When I finished grade 1B, I was skipped to 2B, which meant that thereafter, until I finished college, I always started a new grade or school in February rather than September.

It was Miss Walters in 2B who noticed that I had what appeared to be a speech defect. Since there was no speech teacher at Meehan, I was sent to the all-white school, Fitler, for speech instruction two periods a week. I discovered only much later in adulthood that I did not have a speech defect. Rather, I had no feel for phonetics and could not pronounce complicated words unless I had heard the word pronounced by someone else. The Fitler school never picked up on the real reason for my so-called speech defect.

The physical facilities at Fitler were far superior to those of the segregated school to which I was assigned. Unlike Fitler, Meehan had no gym or play-room; to keep from freezing in the winter when we went outside for recess or lunch, we crowded in a group up against the wall in a game called "Hybo Sally." Pushing and shoving, we tried to move to the positions closest to the wall. To avoid facing the cold at recess time, I often invented an extra study project, like trying to write a poem, which permitted me to remain inside.

The Meehan School included kindergarten through fourth grade. For fifth and sixth grades, we went to the Joseph E. Hill School, a racially segregated school less than two miles from home. It was a tough school, as the poorer kids from the Sharpnack Street ghetto thought that they controlled the turf. I also was the new boy on the block because most of the other kids had started at Hill in kindergarten. I learned to stand up to bullies and ruffians, but on occasion I got the hell knocked out of me, arriving at home with a bloody nose or a black eye. Fortunately, in those days the weapon of choice was just a bare fist. After the first year it got better. Some of the kids had discovered the Wissahickon Boys' Club. Some went to Camp Emlen, as beneficiaries of the Wirtz Foundation or the Country Week Association. My days at the Hill School were character building, exposing me to a different kind of discrimination, one based on poverty, class, and envy rather than race. The teachers were relentless, and they gave me a good grounding in mathematics.

In sixth grade, I took over a newspaper route, delivering the two evening Philadelphia dailies—the *Evening Bulletin* and the *Daily News*. On Thursdays I would deliver the three weekly Negro papers, the *Pittsburgh Courier,* the *Afro-American,* and the *Philadelphia Tribune,* to the colored neighborhoods. I later decided to increase my income by standing in the late afternoon on a corner at Wayne Avenue and Coulter Street, where people who worked in downtown Philadelphia and commuted to Manayunk or Schuylkill Falls (where Grace Kelly and her brother Jack, of boat-racing fame, grew up) had to change from the Route 53 trolley to the Route 52 trolley. It was a great spot to sell the late-afternoon editions of the *Bulletin* and the *Daily News*.

One Thursday, however, when the employees were on strike at both daily newspapers, I had the bright idea of selling the *Pittsburgh Courier* hot off the press. One white purchaser begrudgingly paid me the ten cents (the *Bulletin* was only two cents) and started reading the *Courier,* with its pictures of colored people. He angrily demanded, "Why are you charging me five times the price for this rag?" Taken aback, all I could think to say was, "Because it costs a lot more to color the pictures." That really set him off. He became almost threatening. I burst into tears and ran home, asking my mother why the white person hated the paper that I had attempted to sell him. My mother's reply was that the poor fellow probably had never even heard about Pushkin or the Queen of Sheba.

Seventh grade opened entirely new vistas for me. I was off to Roosevelt Junior High School, which had about twenty-five hundred students and a modern physical plant. Almost all of the students were white, and all the teachers and the principal were white. Only a handful of us were colored.

Roosevelt Junior High was more than three and a half miles away from our house. I walked to school and back each day. Enough adults recognized me as a Coleman kid that if I got into trouble along the way, someone would report it to my parents. For two years I endured the seven-mile round-trip trek each day, bundled up to brave the harsh Philadelphia winters. In later years when, in civil rights litigation and also as a member of President Ford's cabinet, I defended the busing of school children to more distant desegregated schools, I would look back on those years for reassurance that it was worth it—it was.

At Roosevelt, I competed with white students, benefiting from first-class facilities, textbooks, and equipment. I also was introduced to art, science, geography, and foreign languages (my mother's failed attempt to teach me German notwithstanding). During those days little emphasis was placed on speaking ability, and I was able to master the grammar and vocabulary of Latin and French. I learned about Roman and Greek history and philosophy and was even introduced to the work of Alexander Pushkin, Russia's greatest poet. My mother had pointed out to us that some of the ancient Greeks and Romans were colored and earned full rights of citizenship. Most interestingly, she informed me that Pushkin was a man of color through his maternal great-grandfather, General Abram Petrovich Gannibal, who came as a child slave from what was then Ethiopia. He was educated in Paris, became a military adviser to Tsar Peter the Great, and oversaw Russia's defense by building its forts. Gannibal fought courageously at Peter's side in Russia's victory in 1709 over Charles XII of Sweden in the Battle of Poltava—the first time the Russians defeated a European power—facts of which my white teachers were unaware.

After three years at Roosevelt, I started tenth grade at Germantown High School, which was only a mile and a half from home. The teachers, facilities, and curriculum were all first rate. I ran cross-country and track, lettering in both sports, and finished fourth in the Penn Relays, in which all the Philadelphia high schools competed, running the second leg of the mile relay. Germantown High thrived during the Great Depression, ironically because many of the wealthier families could not afford to send their children to private schools. The Philadelphia school board placed the best teachers there and kept the physical facilities in great condition.

Unfortunately, that is no longer the case, as a visit to Roosevelt and Germantown High today would confirm. That lesson was not lost on me in later years as we tackled the issues of "separate but equal" and school-financing reform. The brutal fact is that schools that serve the children of the well-to-do are usually significantly better financed and supported than schools in poorer neighborhoods.

My best friend in high school was Robert Tresville, whose father, a man of color and a career army officer, led the U.S. Army band at Fort Benning, Georgia. After finishing the tenth grade in Georgia, Bob was sent to Germantown to live with an uncle to escape the segregated schools of the South and to receive the academic preparation he needed to apply to West Point. We became close friends on the track team, where Bob was a pole vaulter. He also was a superb, nationally ranked tennis player and won the Sojourner Truth championship. We would visit the tony Chestnut Hill Country Club, where he easily beat the very best tennis players—but where he could not use the locker room to dress or shower.

Bob spent his first year of college at Penn State and then was accepted at West Point. After graduation he was sent to train as a fighter pilot in Tuskegee, Alabama, where I bumped into him again. Since he was a first lieutenant and I was only an aviation cadet, technically we could associate only on the tennis court, although we found surreptitious ways to breach the Army–Air Force protocols. Bob was the first person of color to graduate directly into the U.S. Army Air Corps. He went overseas with the 332nd Fighter Group, an all-black unit, and commanded a 100-fighter squadron, obtaining the rank of captain. On June 9, 1944, his group shot down five enemy planes in one day. He lost his life on the morning of June 24, when he crashed into the Tyrrhenian Sea while leading his squadron in a low-approach mission to strafe an Italian munitions supply center in extremely hazardous weather. That afternoon a cable arrived at his base, announcing his promotion to major.[1]

There are few people whom I have admired as much as I did Bob. His infectious smile, forthright and confident manner, and competitive enthusiasm were exhilarating. No man had more love for his country or courage and determination to defend its ideals and dreams. I wish God had spared him, even though I know Bob would have rejoiced, knowing that if he had to die, it would be in defense of the nation that he and his family loved so well. That so perfect a human being would have given his life in defense of so imperfect a country—a country that had relegated him to second-class citizenship—had a profound personal effect on me and on my aspirations to help make this nation worthy of my best friend's sacrifice.

SIX

Sibling Rivalries

A ministering angel shall my sister be.

—WILLIAM SHAKESPEARE, *Hamlet*

"DON'T YOU EVER FORGET IT, Bill. When you were buried in books in the school library, I was out on the front lines, fighting for civil rights in the old South."

My sister Emma, who passed away at the age of ninety-three, was right. I learned a lot from her example. The immediate Coleman family of five was close knit, but we siblings were always competitive. My sister's practical wisdom and my brother's practical jokes enlivened many dinner table conversations and family outings.

Whether in the classroom or in the family, Emma was a born teacher. She taught me the most important lesson of my life: how to live meaningfully with the opposite sex. Several of her experiences also had a substantial effect on shaping my career, increasing my awareness of the evils of racial discrimination and fortifying my resolve to see it end.

During the 1920s and 1930s, the Philadelphia school board had implemented a secret and, in my judgment, unlawful policy of giving lip service to racial integration while forcing most children of color in Germantown to attend predominantly colored and manifestly inferior schools. As a result, Emma was sent to the mostly black Gillespie Junior High and Gratz High schools, which were well outside our school district and more distant from our home. Although Emma's high school preparation was inferior, she did very well. In her junior year, she decided that she wanted to teach home economics in high school. She applied to Temple University in Philadelphia, which offered a strong home economics curriculum, but she was informed that during their junior year, home economics majors had to live in a particular dormitory. Colored students were not allowed in that dormitory or in any other dormitory on the Temple campus at that time. Trying to be helpful, the admissions folks suggested that she spend her junior year at Cheney State

Teachers College, then a Negro school at least sixty miles outside of Philadelphia that had a markedly inferior academic reputation.

Emma and our parents rejected that suggestion. Instead, she enrolled at the Hampton Institute, my father's alma mater. After graduation she was home manager in a segregated federal housing project in Virginia. Shortly thereafter she began teaching at St. Paul's, a private religious high school in Virginia, where she met and married a fellow teacher, Wilburn Dooley. They both left in 1944 to teach in the public high schools of Atlantic City, from which she retired at the age of sixty-five.

While teaching at St. Paul's, Emma and her husband engaged in a civil rights struggle that, she would often remind me with her competitive smile, preceded any efforts of my own by many years. The "redneck" mayor (as she called him) of the Virginia town in which they lived had a long history of discriminating against the large colored population, denying them city employment, access to public facilities, and even the vote. The Negro leadership decided the mayor must be replaced. However, the commonwealth of Virginia and its political subdivisions had active, willful programs to deter people of color from registering and voting. Consequently, few Negroes were registered to vote.

Emma and Wilburn registered. To do so, they had to pay three years of back poll taxes and then take a written exam. The white examiner gave each of them a blank sheet of paper, on which they had to write down—word for word, from memory—the question, which he gave them orally, and an answer that satisfied the examiner. Many years later, in 1992, Emma recalled that her answer included the statement that she had never fought in a duel.

Afterward, Emma and Wilburn worked hard to get other people of color to register. It took two years of evening meetings in schools, homes, apartments, and churches, but finally, the people of that Virginia town, including a large number of people of color, were able to vote the mayor out of office.

Not only did Emma inspire me to work against racial discrimination, she also inadvertently may have affected my choice of law as a career. In mid-November of each year, my mother and father would begin a lengthy discussion about how much they could afford to spend on family presents for Christmas. Since my parents were adamant that their children would attend college, setting aside funds for education was their first priority. I think I was the only kid in my neighborhood who did not have a bicycle by the age of twelve; the money went instead into a college savings account. After meeting their savings target, my parents would make a final decision on Christmas expenditures, usually about the tenth of December. Mother would take all of us to downtown Philadelphia after school to shop at Philadelphia's two great department stores, John Wanamaker's and Strawbridge & Clothier, which were across the street from Philadelphia City Hall, where the Supreme Court of Pennsylvania, the Orphan's Court, and the Common Pleas Court of Philadelphia County were located.

Emma would suggest to Mother that they shop first so that Emma could return home early and begin preparing dinner. In later life I often complained that Emma got the more expensive Christmas gifts because Mother would run short of money by the time she got to my brother and me. Emma's scheme had an unintended consequence. At fourteen years of age, I did not want to hang around in the women's department, and so I went outside to take a walk for an hour or so in the cold, mid-December weather. I wandered into city hall to warm up, ending up on the fourth floor, where the state supreme court was in session. Not knowing what the cases were about, I nevertheless listened to several arguments. I remember one lawyer being chewed out by a justice because he was not aware of a case that was directly on point on which the court had handed down an opinion a month before. To this day, I habitually review the recent opinions of a court on any subject before making an oral argument before the court.

When I got home I asked my parents, "Do people really get paid for just talking?" They tried to explain what lawyers did, citing the examples of Charles Houston, William H. Hastie, Raymond Pace Alexander, his wife, Sadie T. M. Alexander, Louis Brandeis, and Clarence Darrow. From that day on, I knew that lawyering was an option, even though Mother probably wanted me to follow the Mason family tradition and become an Episcopal minister, Father probably wanted me to be a social worker, and they both urged me to consider becoming a medical doctor.

My brother, Bobby, seven years younger than I, also went to the public schools in Philadelphia. In Roosevelt Junior High School, he was an underperformer. His grades were quite mediocre, to put it charitably, and he was embarrassed by comparisons with his siblings. He would even promise to do Emma's and my chores at home if we would delay showing our report cards to our parents. My parents were very constructive in addressing Robert's challenges; they were unwilling to accept a downward spiral to mediocrity from any of their children. They had learned about the success of the Palmer Institute in bringing out the latent talents of young minority boys, and soon Bob was on his way to North Carolina.

The principal of the Palmer Institute touched him with fire, recognizing Bob's mathematical skills and seeing in him the potential to be a superior spatial architect. Bob graduated with high grades and was admitted to the Hampton Institute. After finishing Hampton, he was hired by the Budd Manufacturing Company in Philadelphia, which at the time made automobile bodies for Ford, General Motors, Chrysler, and other companies. Bob had a rare talent for judging space and clearances and soon became the company's leading spatial architect, planning the manufacturing floor for each new model as he traveled throughout the world to advise the various Budd facilities.

On a business trip to London in 1979, I received the sad news that Bob had had a heart attack and died as he was being rushed to the hospital. We miss him greatly, especially his sense of humor, which had always lightened up our sometimes heavy family discussions. He left one son, Robert Van Tyle Coleman Jr., who has had a successful career at PepsiCo.

SEVEN

College Years

The man who doesn't read good books has no advantage over the man who can't read them.

—MARK TWAIN

WHEN THE LIGHTS WENT OUT and the Emlen campers were supposed to be asleep, serious talk began among the counselors. "Where do you want to go to college, Bill?" the senior counselor from Howard University asked me. "I was thinking about an Ivy League school, maybe Penn," I responded. "You're setting your sights pretty high, aren't you?" he retorted. "I don't want to sound too much like Booker T. Washington," the counselor from Morgan State chimed in, "but I do believe that a Negro college gives us the most practical grounding for success."

"A Negro college was good enough for your mom and dad and your sister, Bill," the Lincoln sophomore spoke up. "But come on, guys," the Temple junior interrupted. "You've read DuBois's *The Talented Tenth*. If you've got the grades, Bill, you've got to go for it. Ain't no whitey goin' to lead us to the Promised Land."

The contentious intergenerational debate among people of color in those days was over whether Negroes should humbly demonstrate their worth through hard work, training, thrift, and self-help, as counseled by Booker T. Washington, or rather should rise up in outrage against suppression by the dominant white majority, as espoused by W. E. B. DuBois. Armed with his Harvard doctorate, DuBois urged the most talented tenth of the Negro population to pursue excellence in higher education and to rise to leadership positions in society. That excellence could come from a Howard or a Harvard, as men like Thurgood Marshall and Charles Houston demonstrated. Although both Washington and DuBois had useful and not always contradictory ideas for racial progress, they were set up as polar opposites. DuBois was winning the hearts of the younger generation, laying the foundation for the modern civil rights movement.

The twenty-three counselors spent many hours revisiting the Washington-DuBois debate, exploring the value of religion and discussing local, state, and national politics and, of course, the facts of life. Sometimes the head counselor, Aubry Huxter, the principal of an Atlantic City high school, and Dr. John Graves, the camp physician who had just finished his first year of residency at the Mercy-Douglass Hospital in West Philadelphia, would join the discussion. From those discussions and from my experience in predominantly white schools after my first six years in segregated schools, I became increasingly committed to entering the white-dominated mainstream. I would swim hard against any current that threatened to divert me to a separate channel.

Finishing Germantown High in January 1938 with highest honors, I started at the University of Pennsylvania in early February 1938. My family paid the tuition, $400 a year. I lived at home, commuting by trolley and subway. The trolley ride (Route 53) proceeded down Wayne Avenue and Coulter Street to Erie Avenue and Broad Street. I then took the Broad Street subway to South Street and transferred to another trolley, traveling along South Street through some of the city's poorest neighborhoods to 25th Street, until I finally reached the beautiful blocks of the Penn campus. The ride home was the same in reverse, except that I traveled down Lombard Street instead of South Street. The living conditions along Lombard Street were even more horrible than those along South Street. Every day I traveled back and forth between my parents' home and this exclusive Ivy League school, where I was immersed in discussions about the grand American experiment, which began in Philadelphia. As I looked out the clouded windows of the trolley car, I could not avoid noticing the chasm between academic theory and reality, the stark contrast between the poor colored ghettos and the white middle-class neighborhoods.

When I entered Penn I was still struggling with the choice between a career in law or in medicine. Six months later, during the summer break of 1938, when I had returned to Camp Emlen as a senior counselor, Dr. Graves took me to Mercy-Douglass Hospital to observe a stomach cancer operation. My stomach fared only slightly better than the patient's. I quickly decided that medicine was not for me.

At Penn I made the freshman track team, running the quarter mile and half mile and participating again in the Penn Relays, this time as a college freshman. Like most track enthusiasts of the late 1930s, I dreamed about being in the 1940 Olympic games. My fantasies began to dissolve, however, when my track times fell far short of those of Johnnie Woodruff of the University of Pittsburgh and Ben Johnson of Columbia. Then, on September 1, 1939, World War II broke out in Europe, ending all hope for an Olympics in 1940.

In the fall of 1939 I worked at the Main Street Post Office at 30th and Market Street in Philadelphia in the evenings and on weekends. I also worked at the 30th Street railway station dining room on the day of the Army-Navy football game. The money from those two jobs enabled me to attend my new fraternity's black-tie dinner dance during the weekend of the Penn relays. In my junior year, after surviving a mild hazing during the rush process, I had been accepted in the Alpha Phi Alpha fraternity, a colored fraternity started at Cornell University. Because there were fewer than twelve colored undergraduates attending Penn at that time, the fraternity drew from all the colleges in the Philadelphia area.

My friendship with Melvin J. Chisum, who was two years behind me, was one of several enduring relationships that began at college. Chisum became a brilliant physician after graduating with distinction from Penn's medical school. We took Robert A. Brotemarkle's psychology course together. We were very competitive, and we got the two top marks in the class. I don't recall who scored higher on the examination, but the decisive answer was "Neither" to the question, "On what side of the cow's brain is its Broca area?" The Broca area of the human brain controls speech; since cows cannot speak, there is no such area in their brain. I also made some close white friends, among them Leonard Joseph and Stuart Marks, who later accompanied me to Harvard Law School in September 1941, where we were in the same student study group.

Academics at Penn were challenging and broadening. My classes in literature, philosophy, mathematics, psychology, political science, economics, history, the natural sciences, French, and Latin provided me with a true liberal arts education that not only gave me confidence as a budding Renaissance man but also served me well during my legal career by showing me the interconnections of human thought. A successful lawyer needs to address legal issues in their broader historical, cultural, and social context. That was certainly the case in our work on *Brown* v. *Board of Education* and other civil rights litigation. Analogies to art, literature, science, history, and even sports enhance the persuasiveness of a legal argument. Throughout my career I have drawn upon what I have learned from my parents and from the stimulating courses and after-class discussions at Penn to enrich my advocacy for a client's position.

Two quick examples come to mind. Fast forwarding a few decades, in 1980 I was involved in a transaction that came about because of a discussion I had with a prominent Algerian and two Saudi Arabians about the important contribution of the Arabs to mathematics, especially the invention of algebra and the concept of zero. My Arab friends appreciated the fact that a Westerner knew of and respected the historic contribution made by their ancestors. The conversation segued into the financial potential of the acquisition of an oil services company in the Middle East—a new business opportunity.

The second example involved a visit that PepsiCo chairman Don Kendall and I made to Moscow before the 1980 Olympics, when Coke was threatening to replace Pepsi as the soft drink of choice in the Soviet Union. As we were waiting for a meeting to begin, I mentioned to the Soviet chairman, Leonid Brezhnev, through his interpreter how much I admired Pushkin and even quoted a few lines that my mother had taught me. As we talked about how Pushkin's Ethiopian great-grandfather, General Gannibal, had fought in Russia's victory over Sweden, Brezhnev's face lit up. We became fully engaged in a lively conversation about Russia's literary icon, until the chairman was called away on an urgent matter. He soon returned to our meeting, but before he did, an aide mentioned to Don Kendall and me that we had not yet said what we really wanted. We explained that we wanted to continue Pepsi's present business activities in the Soviet Union and, indeed, expand them. The aide replied, "That shouldn't be a problem. The chairman told me how much he enjoyed talking to both of you. He said he would work out a fair decision when you get around to making your request."

For my classmates at Penn and me, the Great Depression and President Franklin Roosevelt's New Deal were the subject of much debate. We anxiously monitored Hitler's rise to power in Europe. We admired the valiant, gutsy stand of Great Britain and, more grudgingly, the Russians, once the Nazis turned on them. We suspected that eventually the United States would be drawn into the war, but with two great oceans protecting our borders, we felt secure. We paid little attention to the gathering storm in the Pacific. Given the Eurocentric nature of education in those days, we knew little about Asia and had only slight knowledge of Japan's ambitions.

In studying American history and political science, I shared the pride of my classmates in the role that Philadelphia played in drafting our Declaration of Independence, Constitution, and Bill of Rights. I especially appreciated the perceptive insights of the young Frenchman Alexis de Tocqueville, who, as he demonstrated in *Democracy in America*, understood the potential of the American ideal better than most American writers of that time or, for that matter, of any other time.[1] Not surprisingly, I brought to the discussions a perspective different from that of many of my classmates. We all embraced the declaration that "all men are created equal" and the concepts of freedom and democratic government. But I could not understand why so many white Americans could eagerly embrace those concepts for themselves and their families and friends but reject them with equal vigor for some of their fellow citizens, merely because of skin color or other physical characteristics.

The Thirteenth, Fourteenth, and Fifteenth Amendments (the so-called Civil War amendments) notwithstanding, more than a few of my classmates and even some professors still didn't get it. They were willing to apply due process and equal protection of the law to economic issues as whites competed with one another, but they failed to see how those amendments pushed the boundaries of inclusiveness beyond the historical status quo. Increasingly, I recognized that it was the responsibility of my generation to expand the reach of the worthy precepts of the Philadelphia framers to all the citizens of our great nation.

In history class, we touched on a great stain on America's conscience—slavery. We read about the abolitionists, the Civil War battles won by great generals, the Emancipation Proclamation, and the Radical Reconstructionists—white men who rescued the republic from the scourge of slavery. There was little discussion of the long period of post–Civil War regression, with the rise of Jim Crow and discriminatory policies in housing, education, and commerce. Nor were we introduced to the substantial contribution of free men and women of color from colonial days to the present. No one mentioned that 20 percent of the troops fighting for the Union, which won the Civil War, were men of color.

Near the end of my second year at Penn, a partner in one of Philadelphia's great law firms who sat next to my father at a United Fund luncheon mentioned to him how important it is for any good lawyer to understand business, economics, and finance. Justice Holmes's prediction in 1897, that the lawyer of the future would be "the man of statistics and the master of economics," had come to pass.[2] After my father conveyed that useful insight to me, I began to take a third of my courses at the Wharton School of Finance and Commerce, the renowned business school at the University of Pennsylvania. I took courses in accounting, economics, public and private finance, insurance, and corporate law. We studied John Maynard Keynes, who in 1936 had published his important treatise *The General Theory of Employment, Money, and Interest*.[3] In 1939 Alvin H. Hansen of Harvard had perceived the breakthrough value of Keynes's work, and it became the undisputed coin of the realm in economics during my junior year at Penn. In recent years, Keynes has had a revival, although I am concerned that some politicians appear to have grossly oversimplified his theories to fit them into media sound bites.

In my newfound fascination with economics I discovered that I could take extra courses at the college and Wharton School without paying additional tuition. I increased my course load from the required seventeen credits to twenty-two credits and graduated in June 1941 after three and a half years, finally overcoming the disadvantage of having skipped from first grade to the second semester of second grade in grammar school.

I graduated summa cum laude with distinction in government, economics, and political science. I was accepted in the Pi Gamma Mu honor society for political science and government majors. A colored student, Leroy Brown, had received a Phi Beta Kappa key at Penn two years earlier, in 1939, but when I was examined for the society, I was rejected. Apparently there was some controversy within Phi Beta Kappa, which did not want to replicate that groundbreaking event too quickly. Brown went on to Penn medical school and became an outstanding Philadelphia physician, as did his brother a few years later.

Many years later, when I was secretary of transportation, Martin Meyerson, then the president of Penn, reviewed my 1938–41 academic record and awarded me a Phi Beta Kappa key in 1976, earned as of April 1941, the date that I was originally considered. Perhaps I set a useful precedent: we should wait at least three decades to see what an honor student accomplishes before awarding the individual a Phi Beta Kappa key. I later discovered that Mrs. Sadie T. M. Alexander, who was the wife of Raymond Pace Alexander and with him constituted an incredible husband-and-wife legal team in what was then Philadelphia's preeminent colored law firm, had a comparable experience when she was considered for Phi Beta Kappa membership.[4]

PART II

Learning to Be a Good Lawyer

None of us got where we are solely by pulling ourselves up by our bootstraps. We got here because somebody—a parent, a teacher, an Ivy league crony, or a few nuns—bent down and helped us pick up our boots.

—THURGOOD MARSHALL

EIGHT

Harvard Law School

Fragile as reason is and limited as law is as the institutional-
ized medium of reason, that's all we have standing between
us and the tyranny of mere will and the cruelty of unbridled,
undisciplined feeling.

—JUSTICE FELIX FRANKFURTER

"ARE YOU ON YOUR WAY to the law school?" he asked, noticing the bewildered look on my face.

"Yes," I replied.

"I'll show you the way. I know the territory pretty well. I just finished Harvard College. Where did you go to college?"

"University of Pennsylvania," I answered. "No surprise, I was raised in Philadelphia. Are you from Boston?"

"Born and bred in Brookline, just outside Boston."

I climbed the few remaining steps from the Harvard Square subway and accompanied this chisel-faced young man with his swept-back hair and his crisp Boston Brahmin accent. We walked across the famous Harvard Yard, a place I had only seen in the movies or read about in books and magazines. His friendly manner and wry smile seemed in stark contrast to the austere Romanesque style of H. H. Richardson's Austin Hall or the massive Langdell Hall, named after the law school's first dean and father of the case law method of teaching. The campus was, for many of us, a surreal dream, inhabited by the ghosts of Justice Holmes and Justice Brandeis and imbued with the living presence of Justice Frankfurter, the Hands—Learned and Augustus—Roscoe Pound, Paul Freund, and Joseph H. Beale (*Treatise on the Conflict of Laws*), and, especially meaningful for me, Charles H. Houston, William H. Hastie, and Raymond Pace Alexander.

My fellow student turned to me and shook my hand vigorously. "My name is Elliot Richardson," he said, pronouncing each syllable with his typically deliberate style.

"Why are you going to law school?" I asked.

"Well," said Elliot, "my father was a doctor and both my brothers are going to medical school, so I had to differentiate myself from the rest of the family

43

somehow. Actually, I think, law is the best route to public service. I am interested in exploring a career in politics. How about you?"

"Well, it was either law or medicine, and my stomach really couldn't take the operating room. More seriously, though, I think that lawyers are in the best position to bring about peaceful change and progress in our society. And I wouldn't mind making some real money, if you know what I mean."

The law school took about 20 percent of its new students from Harvard College, and as we entered the registration hall, it was apparent that Elliot knew a lot of people there. He introduced me with the enthusiasm of someone who is introducing a new friend to an old friend.

Two days later, on a balmy fall Tuesday in September 1941, I settled anxiously into my assigned seat in Property Law 1. Warren Barton Leach Jr. opened the class with the Harvard Law School mantra: "Look to the right of you and to the left of you. One of you won't be here next year."

My entering class of almost four hundred fifty students included only three persons of color. In fact, there were only eight of us in the law school, including the master's and the doctoral programs. There were no women. They were not eligible for admission, and they were not even allowed in the classrooms. Each class had about one hundred and ten students.

In the law school tradition, Professor Leach launched immediately into the Socratic case method of instruction. Mischievously eyeing his seating chart, he called on an unsuspecting student to recite the facts from a judicial opinion that we had been assigned to read from our case book. In a series of rapid-fire questions, he sought to elicit from the student an understanding of the legal principles that were applied to the facts of the case. Was the judge's decision correct? Assuming hypothetical variations of the basic facts, how should the opinion be altered? As soon as he had sufficiently demolished one student's attempt at analysis, he would move on to another, gleefully savoring the intellectual carnage left behind.

I still remember dreaming night after night about a wild fox running across an open field after Leach destroyed my cocky analysis of *Pierson* v. *Post*.[1] Through this painful process we learned the law of personal property and the importance of a clear and comprehensive grasp of the facts. We also learned how to apply legal principles to real-life situations and to support our conclusions with skilled analysis and sound reasoning. Some of the cases are as clear in my mind today as they were then, more than sixty-five years ago. This method of teaching was in stark contrast to the way Chief Justice John Marshall or Abraham Lincoln learned the law, by reading treatises, like Blackstone's *Commentaries*, or serving as an apprentice in a law firm. However, it taught us lesser mortals analytical and advocacy skills that could be applied to almost any situation.

As the school year began, more than two-thirds of my classmates wore Phi Beta Kappa keys, but as the weeks progressed and as these best and brightest of the Ivy League colleges were humiliated and embarrassed by their feeble responses to the sharp questioning of the professors, the keys gradually began to disappear. It didn't help, of course, that Roscoe Pound, former dean and Carter Professor of Law, strutted the hallways wearing a substantially larger Phi Beta Kappa key, causing some classmates to start the false rumor that those with regular-size keys were the not-really-smart ones.

My professors presided over their classes like Greek gods. I learned contracts from Lon Fuller, who brought his extraordinary wisdom and grasp of legal philosophy, ethics, and morality to bear on a simple agreement between two human beings. I learned judicial procedures and trusts from Austin Wakeman Scott, who was a major force in developing the law in those fields. And I learned conflict of laws and federal jurisdiction from Paul A. Freund, who was a mentor for so many lawyers, law clerks, judges, and constitutional scholars of subsequent generations. Freund's precise and pristine interpretations of the Constitution were so precious that I audited all his courses in constitutional law even though I had not been assigned to them.

My experience in Paul Freund's classes demonstrates the extraordinary impact that a brilliant and caring teacher can have on an impressionable student. Many law students consider the study of conflict of laws dreary and dry. It is a complex subject that specifies which state's or nation's law should be applied by a court to resolve a certain legal issue when all or some of the events that gave rise to the issue happened in different jurisdictions. Paul Freund made the course come alive. I could not wait until 10:00 a.m. on Thursdays, when I settled into my seat in Austin Hall, awaiting the arrival of Professor Freund, who entered into the lecture room like Laurence Olivier stepping onto the stage in *Henry V.*

In 1941–42 conflict-of-laws principles were in ferment. For many years most courts had accepted fairly simple and somewhat inflexible rules. For example, in a contract dispute, the laws of the place where the contract was signed would govern. That was the position of Joseph H. Beale, a leading conflict-of-laws specialist and scholar at Harvard. Other scholars, led by Arthur Linton Corbin of Yale Law School, argued for a more flexible approach, taking into account the law of the state where the alleged breach had occurred, if different from the law of the state where the contract was executed. The more flexible approach, which might apply the laws of several states in addressing the formation of the contract, the wrongful breach, or the intent of the parties, introduced significant complexities and potential inconsistencies among state and federal court precedents. The complexities were compounded when the courts were required to interpret and apply the constitutional obligation to grant full faith and credit to the acts and judicial decisions of other states. Frankly, the state of the law was a mess. As Justice Robert H. Jackson aptly observed, "It [is] difficult to point to any field in which the Court has more completely demonstrated a more candidly confessed lack of guiding standards of a legal character than in trying to determine what choice of law is required by the Constitution."[2]

The American Law Institute was working on a restatement of the law on conflicts, and therefore the nation's academic community was out in full force. Professor Freund taught the class with great skill, bringing us onto the battlefield of ideas. He had been a brilliant U.S. deputy solicitor general during the New Deal phase of the Roosevelt administration. Justice Frankfurter often said that Freund was the best student he had ever had, and Frankfurter's colleagues on the court thought Freund about the best lawyer ever in the office of the solicitor general. He was the best teacher I ever had, and he became a dear, admired friend. He quietly supported me in a lot of ways, some of which I learned about long after his death. In reading Todd C. Peppers' book on Supreme Court law clerks in 2007, I learned that in 1947 Freund had recommended me to Justice Frankfurter as one of his two law clerks for the October 1948 term.[3]

The examination at the end of the course on conflict of laws was very difficult. The extra time and effort that I put into the class to prove myself worthy of such an inspiring teacher paid off. I received the top grade, and as a result I won the Joseph H. Beale Prize for performance in the conflict of laws course, which included a check for $400, a lot of money in 1946.

Freund's course on federal jurisdiction was equally exciting and contemporaneous. Here too, there were surges of change and conflict. Freund led us through the thicket of federal diversity of citizenship jurisdiction dissecting the evolving and not always consistent line of cases that determined whether state or federal law applied to various procedural and substantive issues.

We explored issues arising out of the Great Depression. With bankruptcies, foreclosures, and unemployment reaching frightening heights, many states had enacted statutes restricting the rights of private property owners, who would immediately obtain injunctions in the federal courts, alleging that the statutes were an unconstitutional denial of due process and tying up the states' emergency antipoverty programs for years. Congress amended the Urgency Deficiencies Act of 1913 to require that a federal constitutional challenge to a state statute be heard by three federal judges, rather than one, sitting as a district court and that one of the three be from the federal circuit court.[4] There was also a direct right of appeal to the U.S. Supreme Court, bypassing the federal appeals court. Similarly, if a state court declared a federal statute unconstitutional, the losing party had a direct right of appeal to the

U.S. Supreme Court. The expedited process of judicial review would enable timely implementation of emergency relief. Given the direct right of appeal, the Supreme Court could not easily avoid deciding a delicate issue, as it could when the usual route of petition for a writ of certiorari from a federal appellate court was followed.

The Supreme Court is highly selective in taking appeals from the federal circuit courts. Today, the Court takes only about eighty cases a year, usually those involving an issue of national importance that has led to conflict in the federal appellate courts. Of the almost 10 million cases filed in federal and state courts each year, about eight thousand certiorari petitions are filed seeking review by the Supreme Court. Of those, only 1 percent are granted. Excluding petitions *in forma pauperis* (by indigent petitioners), the percentage is a bit higher, perhaps 2 to 4 percent, and petitions filed by the U.S. solicitor general fare much better—25 percent or so may be granted.

In this area in particular, the law, techniques, and analysis that I learned in Paul Freund's federal jurisdiction class were of significant help to me in later years in the civil rights litigation strategy we pursued under the leadership of Thurgood Marshall. That strategy led in 1954 to the Supreme Court's *Brown v. Board of Education* decisions, declaring state-sanctioned racial segregation in the public schools a violation of the Constitution. Given the odds against a successful certiorari petition, it is highly possible that without the right of direct appeal from a three-judge panel, *Brown v. Board of Education* would never have reached the Supreme Court at the time it did.

While I audited Freund's courses in constitutional law, I was assigned to the class taught by Thomas Reed Powell. His constitutional law course was divided into two parts. The first semester dealt with the commerce clause of the Constitution and the second semester focused on the provisions in the Bill of Rights and the Thirteenth, Fourteenth, and Fifteenth Amendments (the so-called Civil War amendments) that protect persons against the wrongful actions of federal and state governments.

In Powell's class, supplemented by Freund's special insights, I was introduced to constitutional issues that were very much in flux and continued to evolve in varying ways during my legal career. Indeed, I was later involved in a number of cases in both civil rights and business litigation in which we were able to help shape the legal interpretation of issues such as the applicability of the Bill of Rights to states, the meaning of state action under the Fourteenth Amendment, and the applicability of the Thirteenth Amendment to private action deemed to result in a "badge of slavery."

Similarly, a sophisticated understanding of the commerce clause and the cases applying it proved invaluable to me in both business and civil rights litigation. Powell had been counsel in a Supreme Court case in which he had challenged the constitutionality of a Texas statute requiring certain safety devices on interstate trains traveling through Texas. Because the Texas requirements were completely different from those in adjacent states, the interstate trains had to stop at the border and change their equipment. The Supreme Court held the Texas statute unconstitutional, as an undue burden on interstate commerce.

The railroad safety case had nothing to do with race, but Professor Powell mentioned in passing that perhaps the same principle could be applied to statutes that required segregation on trains passing through a state. That observation opened up a vista for me. It became a cornerstone of the civil rights litigation strategy—relying on cases in which race played no part to establish a principle within the common law tradition that logically could be applied to prohibit racial discrimination. Ironically, in *Hall* v. *DeCuir* (1878) the Supreme Court had declared unconstitutional a Louisiana law passed during the Radical Reconstruction period that prohibited segregation on interstate carriers, on the ground that it interfered with congressional oversight of interstate commerce. Applying the principle Powell employed in winning his case, William Hastie and Thurgood Marshall persuaded the Supreme Court in *Morgan* v. *Virginia* (1946) to void a Virginia statute that required racial segregation on interstate buses passing through Virginia. Later, in *Boynton* v. *Virginia* (1960), the Supreme Court held that the Interstate Commerce Act prohibited whites-only lunch counters serving interstate bus passengers. The core lesson from Powell's precept is that civil rights lawyers must master all fields of law because one never knows where the winning nuggets—the applicable legal principles—may be found. Many victories in civil rights cases were achieved by relying on precedents that had nothing whatsoever to do with race.

While a law student I occasionally met with Charles Houston and William H. Hastie when they visited the law school to meet with Freund, Powell, Professor Henry L. Hart, and Dean Erwin Griswold to seek their advice on the civil rights litigation strategy that they were spearheading from their base at Howard Law School. Sometimes their former star student, Thurgood Marshall, would accompany them. Houston and Hastie had been students of Felix Frankfurter's. They shared with me stories about his quick mind and his great decency. When Frankfurter heard cases argued by Houston or Hastie, the air in the courtroom was magical. Despite his tough critical questioning—no favoritism displayed there—the justice's pride in his former students shone through.

Whatever the subject at the Harvard Law School—contracts, criminal or civil law, federal securities law or creditors rights, constitutional law, trusts or estates, corporate, labor or administrative law—the emphasis was on analytical thinking and mastery of the common law, with its roots in early English law, and the founding documents of the nation, as interpreted by the Supreme Court. I hope this is still true. In recent years there has been a proliferation of specialty courses, indulging the appetites of students for the esoteric. I also am concerned that law schools place too much emphasis on preparing students for the actual practice of law, offering clinics on how-to techniques to teach them how to argue appeals, take depositions, or cross-examine witnesses. In my view that is not what the leading law schools should be doing. It is not their grist. As leading scholars in their disciplines, few law school professors have the practical experience to teach the nuts and bolts of daily practice. Instead, they should be stressing analytical skill and reasoning, scholarship, clarity of written and oral expression, the theoretical and ethical implications of legal precedents, and the historical roots of the law. A graduate of a premier U.S. law school should be prepared to act as a wise counsel for any situation.

As a practicing lawyer, I have found it remarkable how useful a knowledge of the common law can be in finding the correct answer to difficult and novel constitutional, statutory, or business issues. In interpreting the words of a statute of Congress or a state legislature, it is crucial to understand the historical context from which the words derive. The framers who shaped the institutions and contours of the Constitution and the federal court system were profoundly influenced by their training in common law. So were the members of the First Congress, who passed the Judiciary Act of 1789 and the several Process Acts of the 1790s, which define the working rules for the federal government and its courts. Most of all, Chief Justice John Marshall established the practice of interpreting a written constitution as the supreme law of the land through an adversarial process that originated in the common law of England. Throughout my career, in many different types of cases, I have drawn on the rigorous analytical foundation in the common law that Harvard Law School provided me.

Although the University of Pennsylvania Law School had offered me a full scholarship, my parents fully supported my decision to go to Harvard Law School and agreed to pay my tuition and train fare. I lived with Aunt Emma and Uncle Lovett in Dorchester during my first year and commuted on the MTA to Harvard Square.

In those days the examinations that determined course grades were given at the end of the school year, except the exam in criminal law, which was given at the end of the first semester. While I had never had much interest in criminal law, I was intrigued by some of the constitutional guarantees contained in the Bill of Rights. I scored a 77 on my exam. While that may not sound like much, Harvard Law School had a peculiar grading system. A score of 75 and above was an A. With a 75 average, a student would graduate magna cum laude; an

80 or above would qualify for summa cum laude, a distinction that was granted only once or so every decade. (There were none in my graduating class.)

Apparently my 77 caused quite a stir at the law school, drawing some early attention from many of my classmates and a few professors. The dean wrote me a letter saying that the law school was granting me a full scholarship and enclosing a check refunding the $300 that my parents had already paid of the $400 tuition for my first year. I pocketed the $300 and told my parents that they didn't have to pay the additional $100. For many years that deception haunted me. I rationalized that I had used much of the $300 to court my future wife, the lovely Lovida Hardin of New Orleans, then a freshman at Boston University who was also being pursued by several other determined suitors. In any event, my conscience was relieved about nine years later when Lovida and I purchased a car for my parents, at a cost of about $9,000.

In addition to the analytical training, a great benefit of the Harvard Law School experience was the lifelong friends that I made. As one of only three Americans of color in my class, I had a special bond with Bill Dennis Edwards, a graduate of Columbia University. He was my roommate during my second year, when I moved into a law school dormitory.

When traveling between Boston and Philadelphia on the way to or from the law school I would stay in New York City overnight, sometimes at the home of Bill's family in Harlem. By 1941 there were a lot of colored singers, musicians, bands, and other artists who performed in the midtown and downtown dining rooms and night clubs. They also performed in Broadway musicals. The dining rooms and night clubs did not admit Negroes as customers, nor did most of the midtown or downtown restaurants, which closed at about one in the morning. The father-in-law of Clifford Alexander, secretary of the army in the Carter administration, was a prominent surgeon at Harlem Hospital. He and his wife, who had been in the theater, would often host parties starting after the clubs and restaurants had closed. Performers such as Lena Horne, Hazel Scott, Cab Calloway, Lionel Hampton, and Duke Ellington would show up, and the jamming would really begin. For the first time I experienced the rare ability of talented artists to improvise. The parties often continued until five in the morning. All kinds of people would show up. On one occasion I met Nelson Rockefeller. On another I met Fidel Castro. Bill Edwards and I still could catch the 6:00 a.m. train to Boston and make a class if it started after 11:00 a.m. These informal jam sessions were some of the best entertainment I have ever experienced.

My other classmate of color was Wade Hampton McCree, who had graduated summa cum laude from Fisk University. He was witty, sharp, and quick, a great storyteller and an exceedingly persuasive writer. Wade's time at law school was interrupted by the war, as was mine. He served with great courage and leadership as an officer in the 92nd Infantry, fighting from Anzio to Rome. Wade went on to have an exceptional career. For a short time he practiced law in Detroit, where his wife, Dores, was a librarian. When Soapy Williams was elected governor of Michigan, he appointed Wade as a state trial court judge, and in 1961 President Kennedy appointed him to the federal district court. President Johnson then appointed him to the U.S. Court of Appeals for the Sixth Circuit. President Carter persuaded Wade to leave the bench to become solicitor general of the United States, where he won a number of Supreme Court arguments. I am quite confident he would have become a Supreme Court justice if there had been a vacancy during President Carter's term of office. After the Carter administration, he became a professor at the University of Michigan Law School, where he was a superb teacher.

From our first encounter at the top of the subway exit in Harvard Square until his death a few years ago, Elliot Lee Richardson was my closest friend and confidant. Elliot may be best remembered for his resignation as attorney general, after he refused to follow President Nixon's order to fire Archibald Cox, the special prosecutor in the Watergate scandal, in what became known as the Saturday Night Massacre. Elliot should be remembered even more as the paragon of a public servant, applying the analytical tools he learned at Harvard Law School to the development of sound public policy. A skilled politician, Elliot saw public service as a means of achieving good results for the American people rather than as a stepping stone for public recognition or private gain. Elliot came from what I pray is not a vanishing breed—Americans who view public service as a responsibility of good citizenship, not as a path to a career. Some in Congress today seem to have forgotten that responsibility, focusing instead on raising money for their reelection in order to sustain a lifetime career in public office. Elliot gave the so-called revolving door a good name as he spun around from the private sector to public service.

Elliot's father had been a renowned Boston surgeon. He had suffered a stroke at a young age and was confined to a wheelchair; after that he became a practitioner of internal medicine, a new field that he helped pioneer. Elliot's mother died when Elliot was very young, leaving three children, Elliot and his two brothers, who later became medical doctors. They lived in Brookline, Massachusetts, and a Miss Brown was charged with managing the house.

On several occasions, Elliot invited Lovida and me to dinner with other guests, such as Ted Beale and his wife, a cousin of Elliot's, and Bill Bundy, who usually attended without his wife, Mary, the daughter of Dean Acheson, who was recovering from tuberculosis. Bundy was from an old Boston family with deep roots in the Democratic Party, in contrast to Elliot's moderate Republican roots. Ernest Sergeant, who would become the managing partner of the Boston firm of Ropes and Gray, also was a frequent guest. Miss Brown sat at the dinner table with the rest of us but never participated in the conversation except to make sure we were all well taken care of. We delighted in her savory New England cooking.

We talked about law, politics, and the economic life of the nation. Elliot, Ernie, Bill, and Ted enjoyed vigorous conversation. Elliot thought and talked in paragraphs, with long pauses in between, carefully formulating his thoughts in a way that allowed transcripts of his remarks in later life to be published without editing. He did not have the crisp staccato delivery of a John Kennedy or a politician's knack for sound bites. His friends often thought he would be a wonderful president if only his wife, Anne, could make the campaign speeches. Bill Bundy expressed himself in more pungent terms. The three of us had great disagreements, but there were never any hard feelings. My dinner companions, products of private prep schools and Harvard or Yale, were better versed in Shakespeare and Wordsworth, but once in a while I could slip in an insight from Langston Hughes, Alexander Pushkin, or a recent arrival on the literary scene, Richard Wright, with his now classic *Native Son* and *Black Boy*.

Over the years my appreciation of Elliot grew as a fellow lawyer, cabinet officer, scholar, and close, caring friend, a true Renaissance man whose breadth of interests never ceased to amaze me. That he apparently thought a lot of me as well was a great boost to my self-confidence. Years later I was deeply touched when I came across a quotation in which he described me as "an individual of strong loyalties, deep commitment to humane values, and solid practical judgment. Harnessed to a clear and analytical mind and unflagging energy, these qualities make him an effective force in all of the many arenas in which he engages. Add a quick sense of humor and a gift for friendship and you have in every sense a man for all seasons."

Another classmate for whom I had great admiration was Harold D. Osterweil, a graduate of the University of Michigan. As students, he and I concluded that the mastery of what had been discussed in previous classes was probably more important than preparing for the next class. In fear of being called on and made a fool of by the professor, too many classmates would focus entirely on the next assignment, neglecting to absorb the valuable information that the professor had imparted in previous classes, which would become the grist for examination. Harold and I would sit together in the Langdell Hall library and review our notes for about an hour and then walk around outside for fifteen minutes, exchanging ideas. At the end of the first year we were tied for first place in the class. Tragically, Harold was killed on D-Day on the beach of Normandy.[5]

We law students, like the rest of the nation, were in a state of shock when the Japanese attacked Pearl Harbor on December 7, 1941. The next day we gathered in Memorial Hall to hear President Roosevelt speak over the radio.

The following day Germany declared war on the United States. We would soon be at war in Europe. Some of my classmates who had been in ROTC left immediately. Professor Leach's admonition—"Look to the right and left of you"—was quickly fulfilled, but for unforeseen reasons. Elliot Richardson and Bill Bundy were among those who immediately volunteered. Because Elliot failed the vision test, he was assigned stretcher duty as a medic in the infantry, racing across Europe with General Patton's army; he won a battlefield promotion to lieutenant. Bill Bundy joined the American cryptologists at the highly secret decoding facility at Bletchley Park, Britain. The unit was able to break the German code daily.[6] After the U.S. Army's success at Normandy, Bundy asked to be transferred to the Pacific for active combat duty. Given his proven talent, he was assigned to work on the Japanese code.

I volunteered as a cadet in the U.S. Army Air Corps to be trained as a fighter pilot. My call to active duty was delayed, however, because only a few recruits of color were being taken at a time, and therefore I was able to continue at the law school. By May 1942 at least 20 percent of the class had left for the war—some for assignments in various government departments in Washington. I stayed through the final examinations at the end of the school year and took additional courses during the summer of 1942, essentially starting my second year.

Much to my pleasant surprise, I received an invitation by special delivery letter in early June 1942 from the president of the *Harvard Law Review*. The top fifteen students in each class, with a grade average of at least 75, were invited each year to join the *Law Review*. With the exception of my grade in criminal law, I had not yet received any of my first-year grades. The invitation meant that I had done better than I expected. When I finally received my report card, my grade average was 77. The invitation to work on the review greatly changed my law school experience because the review staff were expected to work seven to eight hours a day on writing and editing the *Law Review*, which published eight issues a year.

Because I was required to spend so much time at Gannet House, home of the *Law Review*, I decided in June 1942 to move into the law school dormitories. I was assigned to Walter Hastings Hall, suite 53, with my classmate Bill Edwards. We often would have visitors in uniform because many students leaving for war received their initial military training at Harvard. That provided for some interesting contacts. On one occasion, a young lieutenant junior grade in a full-dress Navy uniform, a strikingly handsome dude, arrived—Lieutenant John F. Kennedy, to whom I was introduced by Tudor Gardner, whose father had been governor of Maine. We had a long talk, and near the end of our conversation, Kennedy said he had heard that there were a lot of attractive girls at Radcliffe, Smith, and Mt. Holyoke, who no doubt were friends of mine. He thought it would be a good idea if we went out on a double date, perhaps to hear some great music. He also said that he had a lot of friends in Boston and could arrange a date for me with some of his female friends at a later time.

About a week later, Lieutenant Kennedy called.

"Hi, Bill, this is Jack Kennedy, do you remember me?"

"Of course, Lieutenant, nice to hear from you," I replied.

"You remember our chat, Bill? Well, I'm free tomorrow night, and I thought maybe you could arrange for a couple of dates with some of your friends and take in a concert. What do you think?"

"Well, Lieutenant," I replied, pausing because I was most unsure of what to say. I didn't have a whole lot of friends at these women's colleges, as Kennedy had assumed. So I blurted out, "Since I'm in your town, Jack, don't you think you should be the first one to arrange a double date with me and your friends?"

I heard the click of the receiver; the conversation was over. I didn't hear from Jack Kennedy for another fourteen years, when, as I was going through the receiving line at the White House, President John F. Kennedy greeted me with a mischievous smile: "I know you—you're Bill Coleman. You lived at 53 Hastings Hall." A year later his brother, Robert, called to tell me that the president wanted to appoint me as a judge on the U.S. District Court for the District of Columbia. For the second time, I turned down an offer from Kennedy, pleading my financial obligations in providing for the education of my growing family.

In December 1942, my draft number (11093886) hit the top. I was to follow so many of my classmates, part of the great generation that fought in World War II. Because the Army Air Corps called up only about twenty-five Negro air cadets a month, I continued studying through the summer of 1942, which moved me a class ahead of many of my friends. When I finally got the call to report to Biloxi, Mississippi, for basic training, the law school campus seemed eerily quiet.

As I reflected on the extraordinary events that had unfolded during my months in New England—and the unforeseen dangers that lay ahead—of one thing I was certain. The most important person whom I had met while living in Boston was Lovida Hardin. I met her at a get-acquainted party after I had been at law school for about a month. A friend, Lorena Cousins, had sponsored a mixer for the colored students at the various universities, a segregated affair. As a graduate student I was reluctant to go and initially sat along the sidelines reading a law book. Then this pretty young lady from New Orleans caught my eye, and I mustered the courage to ask her to dance.

Lovida had attended Boston Latin School for Girls for her last year in high school so that she would be able to apply to Boston University, where she was then enrolled as an education major. No matter where the U.S. Army took me, I would continue my pursuit of Lovida, as she was—and is—a beautiful and thoughtful person, willing to put up with my relentless drive and ambition. She was to become and has remained my wife for more than sixty-six years. It is impossible for me to find appropriate words to express the invaluable contributions, the love, and the understanding that she has brought to my life and how she has adjusted to and handled the many new difficulties and challenges that we faced as a growing family.

NINE

War

Once let the black man get upon his person the brass letters, U.S.; let him get an eagle on his button, and a musket on his shoulder and bullets in his pocket, and there is no power on earth which can deny that he has earned the right to citizenship.

—FREDERICK DOUGLASS

"HEY, NIGGER, WHERE'RE YOU GOING?"

I kept on walking.

"Hey, boy, where're you going?"

No response. He moved closer, his six-foot, muscular frame towering over me.

"Hey, boy, did you hear me? Get over here."

In cowardly fashion, I settled for the lesser but still obviously insulting question for a man of twenty-three. I told him where I was going. It was my first experience of southern racial intimidation, a valuable lesson for later years when we would be fighting racial discrimination in southern courts.

The white, rosy-cheeked Army sergeant with the choleric disposition had been waiting at the train station in Biloxi, Mississippi. "Get in that truck," he said. "I've been instructed to take you to Biloxi Air Base." He waited for a while to see if other colored recruits would be arriving but found none. A couple of white enlisted soldiers who had been in town on twenty-four-hour passes were looking for a ride back to the base. Having space in the truck, he offered them a ride back. Their boisterous banter, no doubt, was maliciously intended for my ears.

"How come there're so many spiffy, highfalutin' niggers in town?" one said.

"Seems like Eleanor Roosevelt has convinced her crazy husband that these niggers can fly," the sergeant answered.

The sergeant dropped me off at the induction center and sped off, leaving me covered in a cloud of dust. Such was my welcome to the U.S. Army Air Corps and the war effort.

While I admired the patriotic spirit of my law school friends who immediately volunteered after Pearl Harbor, I had had my own doubts about volunteering for the segregated military. And it wasn't just the segregation. Soldiers of color were mostly restricted to menial, noncombat tasks such as kitchen and cleanup duty. They were undertrained and ill equipped. We had regressed since the Revolutionary War and the Civil War, in which black soldiers had fought valiantly, but the military command in 1941 appeared to have little grasp of that history. In early January 1942 I had dropped in to see Charles Houston in his Washington office. He was then dean of Howard Law School, the "West Point of the Civil Rights Movement."[1] A handsome, lean six-footer with the face of a matinee idol, perpetually sad eyes, and a deep baritone voice, Houston welcomed me warmly.

"Dean Houston," I asked, "how in good conscience can a person of color go into the U.S. Army these days, when it segregates American citizens by race?"

"Well, Bill, I faced the same dilemma in the First World War. Like you, I was deeply troubled. But I made the judgment that with all its faults, we still live in the best country in the world. Someday well-trained, knowledgeable, and dedicated lawyers will rid the United States of the racial caste system. In the meantime, if I wanted to claim full citizenship in this great nation, I had to be willing to serve it during times of crisis. I entered officers' training school and served as a second lieutenant in the segregated U.S. Army field artillery unit in France. The French government awarded some twenty-five soldiers in my battalion the Croix de Guerre for their heroism in combat."

"Was it worth it?" I asked.

"Almost 400,000 Negro troops were recruited for World War I, and when it was over, all we got was a parade in Harlem. That's about it. President Wilson would not allow any soldiers of color in the massive 1919 victory parade in Washington. I came back convinced that it would take the same kind of courage and determination to continue the war against racism—but in the courts, not the blood-soaked trenches."[2]

After talking to Dean Houston, I decided to volunteer for training as a fighter pilot. Up until that time, the U.S. Army Air Corps had flatly refused to accept persons of color for flight training or for any other officer school on an integrated basis. At the persistent urging of Eleanor Roosevelt, the Air Corps reluctantly began to open up opportunities for Negroes to train to be pilots of single-engine fighter aircraft, but only at the segregated Tuskegee Air Base in Alabama. It still refused to take them as bomber pilots, navigators, or bombardiers.

I did not get called up for training as an aviation cadet until March 1943, and my call to active duty came mainly because Bill Hastie had made a fuss. He had resigned a federal judgeship in the Virgin Islands to serve as a civilian aide to the secretary of war, Henry L. Stimson. Hastie had argued forcefully against the foolish segregation policies of the U.S. military, which were depriving the nation of valuable manpower during a time of war. Hastie denounced these "reactionary policies and discriminatory practices" and resigned in protest.[3]

Gradually, the War Department began to call up the more qualified colored men for pilot training. Because Tuskegee could only handle twenty-five new entrants each month, I was called up for pre–flight school basic training in Biloxi, Mississippi.

And so I made arrangements for my first trip to the Deep South. I was at first denied a ticket on the Pullman car because, I was told, there was no separate sleeping car for blacks. That was unacceptable. In law school I had read a Supreme Court decision holding that if a railroad company did not offer a separate Pullman car for blacks, it must accommodate them in a nonsegregated Pullman car.[4] Charles Houston had argued creatively that the Interstate Commerce Act of 1887, as amended, required all passengers to be treated equally. (The law was not enacted with race in mind.) It was one of eight cases that Houston argued in the Supreme Court—seven of which he won.

Armed with Houston's victory, I confronted the Army Air Corps office in Boston. I said that if I were forced into a segregated car on the way to Mississippi, I would leave the train; they would have to search for a lost soldier roaming around someplace south of the Mason-Dixon Line. The sympathetic sergeant booked me on a first-class sleeper all the way from Boston to Biloxi.

My father accompanied me on the train from Boston to Philadelphia, tears streaming down his cheeks. I had never seen the stoic man in such a state. "Good-bye," he said. "Do your duty for our nation, son, but please, please stay alive for your mother's and my sake." Here was a man who had dedicated his life to helping young colored boys cope with the challenges of a yet immature country, and his first-born son, who had amazed him by rising to the top of his class at Harvard Law School, was off to war and an uncertain fate. My heart swelled with enormous gratitude for the loving support and confidence of my parents.

I remained in Biloxi for three weeks and then transferred to the Tuskegee Institute to attend extended pre-flight school. At Biloxi and then at Tuskegee I went through basic training, learning how to march in formation and shoot an M-1 rifle. In July 1943, while at Tuskegee, I was called up as an aviation cadet in Class 44C. During my third month I began training on a Stetson (P-17) bi-wing plane. My fellow cadets were high achievers from colleges around the country. They were talented, articulate, and fun to be around. After six flights with a civilian flight instructor, the most skilled were able to fly solo. Not me. Fortunately, a Mr. Anderson, who knew me from Wissahickon Boys' Club days, was the chief civilian aviation instructor. He gave me three additional hours of unrecorded flight training. Years earlier, my father had hired Anderson to fly a bi-wing with a trailer advertising Camp Emlen. With his special help I learned to take off, land, get out of a spin, and pass all the other tests as a solo pilot in a double-wing plane. Having passed the first phase of training, I was a qualified pilot and eligible for fighter pilot training.

After I'd completed twelve hours of basic fighter pilot training, the flight instructor informed me that I did not have the special athleticism required of a fighter pilot, whose survival depends on his reflexive skills in aerial combat. He consoled me by saying that I might make a good bomber pilot or navigator if such opportunities were open to people of color. The military could not countenance the possibility of integrated crews in those days. In one of the great disappointments of my life, I "washed out" of basic fighter pilot training. My future in the Air Corps would depend more on skills of the mind than of the body.

I was sent to the Air Corps Officer Training School in San Antonio, Texas, where I was the only minority member of my class. About thirty days later, thanks to the strong recommendation of Senator Hugh Scott, I was transferred to the Harvard Business School to be trained as a statistical control officer.[5]

The one very positive consequence of my washing out in the third stage of training to be a fighter pilot was that on my return to Boston I again saw a lot of Lovida Hardin as she was completing her B.S. degree in education at Boston University. It was in the nick of time. A beautiful, charming conversationalist with practical, commonsense judgment, she was very popular and had lots of friends. One friend we both grew to admire was Eddie Brooke, a handsome, debonair rising star on the legal scene. Eddie would later become attorney general of Massachusetts and the first U.S. senator of color—a Republican—since Reconstruction.

My time in Boston made me feel all the more deeply that Lovida was the partner with whom I wanted to spend the rest of my life. I pursued her persistently. She may have found me at times a bit bookish and cocky, but I guess she figured that she could handle my eccentricities. After gaining her father's consent, which was not easily obtained, I proposed to Lovida, and we became engaged to be married. Her father, a respected physician in the New Orleans Creole community, interviewed me and checked out my references.

After Lovida graduated, she left for New Orleans to live with her parents as she started her job teaching first grade. Although she had specialized in junior high school education at Boston University, there were no openings at that level in the segregated New Orleans school system.

After two months in Boston, I completed my training as a statistical control officer and was commissioned a second lieutenant. I was assigned to the

477th Composite Fighter-Bomber Group stationed at Godman Field, Kentucky, adjacent to Fort Knox. The 477th opened up new opportunities for people of color as multiengine pilots, navigators, bombardiers, gunners, and radio operators. It was the only unit in the entire U.S. Army Air Corps that combined fighters and bombers in a single group, although complete segregation of personnel was maintained. The commanding officer was Colonel Robert J. Selway, a white West Point graduate.

The 477th had a short but troubled history. Many of the old-line military commanders, including Colonel Selway, resisted the pressure to open up opportunities for soldiers of color. On the other hand, as the Allied Forces were becoming increasingly successful in North Africa and Europe, the Army chief of staff, General George C. Marshall, began to focus on what was needed to end the war in the Far East, where the Army Air Forces had had a relatively small role. To bring more air power to the Pacific, the U.S. government started to train Negroes as pilots on both the B-25J bomber and the P-51 fighter plane. The cramped facilities at Godman Field proved to be woefully inadequate, and on March 1, 1945, the 477th moved to Freeman Field in Indiana. Some of the new fighter planes had innovative technologies that required additional training, although jets were not yet part of the Air Corps fleet.

The Germans had a few fighter jets. One of my aviation cadet classmates, Roscoe Brown, was among the first Americans to shoot one down, an Me-262 fighter, and he figured out how to do it without any instruction. Instinctively Roscoe decided to let the German aircraft get on his tail but then immediately pulled back on the throttle. Given its great speed, it passed him, and when it did, Roscoe shot it down. After the war, Roscoe received a Ph.D. from New York University and became a university president and radio and television host.

The extraordinary accomplishments and the reputation of the Tuskegee airmen in North America and Europe have been well documented. The unit shot down 111 enemy planes and destroyed or damaged 272 on the ground. They lost more than seventy brave pilots, killed in action or missing.[6] They escorted the American bombers, mostly piloted by white Southerners, on missions as far as Berlin. They never lost one bomber to enemy fire. The Tuskegee pilots were brought back from Europe en masse and stationed at Freeman Field in Indiana to prepare for reassignment in the Pacific.

The happiest event of my life occurred in February 1945, when I took military leave to visit Lovida, boarding the train at Nashville for New Orleans. At the railroad station I bumped into a white classmate from Harvard Law School who also was going to New Orleans. He suggested that we sit together, but regretfully, I told him, I could not sit with him in the whites-only car. I reluctantly decided to board the segregated car, as required by law, even though I wore a military uniform just like him. I could not risk being thrown off the train because I was on the way to my wedding.

My classmate joined me. When the conductor saw my white classmate, he ordered him to move to another coach, but my classmate told the conductor that he was one-eighth Negro. We had a great trip together, talking about Harvard Law School all the way to New Orleans. When I got to New Orleans, I took a bus to the Hardin residence. When I rose to give my seat to a pregnant white woman, she scowled, preferring to stand rather than sit in the "colored section."

On February 10, 1945, Lovida and I were married by a Catholic priest in a large family wedding. I had taken instruction in the Catholic faith to please Lovida's parents. It did not stick, however, and I soon reverted to my Episcopalian upbringing, which I thought demanded less devotion and extracted less guilt. Of the Coleman family, only my mother and father were able to attend the wedding. My brother was fighting in Europe, and my sister and her husband were teaching school in Atlantic City. One of the flower girls at the wedding was Sybil Hydel, who later married Ernest Nathan Morial, who became the first New Orleans mayor of color, serving from 1976 to 1986. Their son, Marc, also became mayor of New Orleans, serving from 1994 to 2002; he then became the president of the National Urban League.

Lovida's parents were prominent citizens of New Orleans. Dr. Joseph Hardin had a thriving general practice. Dr. Hardin and John Minor Wisdom (who became a great Fifth Circuit Court judge) led the Louisiana delegation to the Republican National Convention in 1952, switching their support from Senator Robert Taft of Ohio to Dwight David Eisenhower. As a reward, President Eisenhower appointed Dr. Hardin commissioner of the Port of New Orleans. His principal part-time duty was to inspect each incoming ship to make sure the sailors lived in healthy conditions and were treated properly on the voyage. Before Lovida's father's death, the city of New Orleans named a public school and a park after him.

Shortly after the wedding, Lovida and I found an apartment in Atterberry, Indiana. I continued to work at Freeman Field. We were happy newlyweds, except that Lovida had a hard time keeping the fire going in the wood stove (our sole source for cooking and heating), a common problem in the segregated housing project in which we lived.

My work as a statistical control officer was not especially interesting. Word got around that I had some legal training, and a few officers and enlisted men who had been charged in general courts martial asked me for some legal assistance. In about five months I handled at least twenty cases and obtained nineteen acquittals.

I was assigned to one defendant who was charged with writing fourteen bad checks on a gambling binge. I got him acquitted of thirteen of the fourteen charges by arguing that at the time that he wrote each check, there were sufficient funds in his bank account. Recalling the teachings of my Harvard professor Lon Fuller, I found some cases that held that the mere writing of a check does not assign funds in the bank to the payee; that assignment occurs only when the check is actually cashed by the bank. Except for the fourteenth check, there had been sufficient funds in the bank to cover each of the previous checks individually.

About this time some of the Tuskegee-trained pilots who had been assigned to Freeman Field came to see me. They had been denied admission to the only officers' club on the airbase. A separate facility, previously a club for noncommissioned officers, had been made available to them, but it was much inferior. Unlike the elite officers' club, it had no game room, billiard table, card tables, ping pong tables, fireplace, mess hall, or guest rooms. We called it "Uncle Tom's Cabin."

Colonel Selway claimed that the elite officers club was limited to base instructors. The separate facility was for everyone else on the base, including officers who had flown combat missions in North Africa and Europe because—incredibly—they were now only trainees for reassignment to the Pacific. Those officers all happened to be men of color. The new instructors, on the other hand, were all young white officers, fresh out of flight school, who had never been overseas or experienced enemy fire. Some of the Tuskegee pilots had flown fifty or more combat missions and held a rank as high as colonel. Some had been shot down by German and Italian pilots. But they were considered only trainees! Sadly Selway's up-the-chain command was fully supportive of this ruse. Die-hard segregationists employed every artifice to resist integration in any form.

In April 1945, 101 officers of color on the base had a meeting. One of the leaders was Second Lieutenant Coleman A. Young, who later was to become mayor of Detroit. They decided to test the truth of Colonel Selway's claim that access was determined on the basis of status—instructor or trainee—rather than race. They sent three officers up to the club, one of whom was very light-skinned. The light-skinned officer was ushered into the club while the other two were kept out. The only relevant factor was race; rank and insignias of combat were irrelevant.

The 101 officers of color reconvened their meeting. Since I was the only person present who had attended law school, they pressed me for the legal arguments that I would make to defend them for violating a direct order of their commanding officer. I thought of many arguments. In the end I assured them that as long as Franklin Roosevelt was president, Eleanor would never allow 101 Tuskegee airmen who had so valiantly served their country in Europe, the Middle East, and North Africa to go to jail. The officers went to the white officers club in small groups over a couple of days. As they entered the club, their names were recorded and they were placed under arrest. By the end of the second day, sixty-one officers had been placed under house arrest and confined to the bachelor officers' quarters and mess hall. The protest continued.

On the morning of April 15, 1945, the radio blasted the news—President Roosevelt had died the previous evening. President Harry Truman, a Missouri twang in his voice, announced the sad event. Unaware of Truman's commitment to civil rights, the airmen grew anxious. When I went to see my clients, now under confinement, they blurted out, "For Christ's sake, Coleman, that was some advice you gave us. We couldn't even count on the white guy living long enough to keep us out of jail."

Emotions were running high, and some of the most radical of the young men (they averaged less than twenty-three years of age) suggested some desperate, even violent, tactics. At one point I stood up and, according to one participant, said:

"I have been sitting here listening to a bunch of damn dummies planning how to get all of you hanged or sent to prison for life. Now if you don't know what you are doing, you'd better ask someone. You're not just challenging a colonel or a general, you're challenging the War Department and the United States Government. Believe me, they are just waiting for you to make one big mistake—one mistake, and they will be on you like a bunch of tigers."

The room calmed down a bit. One of the radicals sarcastically piped up: "Well, if this gentleman is so smart, smarter than all of us dummies, I am sure he will tell us what we should do to save our necks."[7] I told them that I would draft a letter for them requesting the right to consult with and be represented by counsel. Since there was no typewriter available, they each copied my letter by hand.[8]

Meanwhile, Colonel Selway and his staff had belatedly drafted a regulation that attempted to clarify the distinction between the two clubs. He called in each of the Tuskegee airmen and asked them to sign a certificate that they had read the regulation. He then read to them Article 64 of the Articles of War (willful disobedience of a direct order) and suggested they could be charged with mutiny. Most would not sign. Some signed but added compelling statements such as the following: "There is no officer in the army who is willing to fight harder, or more honorably, for his country and the command than the undersigned, nor is there an officer with a deeper respect for the lawful orders of superior authority. The undersigned does not expect or request any preferential treatment for the render of this service, but asks only [for] the same identical opportunities for service and advancement offered all other military personnel, and the extension of the identical courtesies extended to all other officers of the Army."[9]

It was time for reinforcements. The next day I called Thurgood Marshall. He recommended that I get in touch with Theodore Berry, a Cincinnati lawyer who was also a member of the city council. Berry was an excellent trial lawyer. His son-in-law Togo West would become secretary of the army and later secretary of veterans affairs in the Clinton administration.

The arrest of the Tuskegee pilots generated a lot of publicity in the national media, and members of Congress were inundated with letters from irate constituents. The War Department was flooded with letters from senators, congressmen, and the public protesting the discriminatory practices of the armed forces. Concerned about rising tensions and the lack of sufficient security at Freeman Field, Colonel Selway decided to transfer the 477th Composite Fighter-Bomber Group back to Godman Field, Kentucky. The airmen were loaded onto an air transport but not told their destination. A rumor was spreading that they were headed to Fort Leavenworth Prison. As a young Negro photographer attempted to take pictures, a white soldier grabbed his camera and confiscated the film, which he threw to the ground and mashed under his boots.

On arrival at Godman Field, the Tuskegee airmen were greeted by white military police brandishing machine guns.[10] I painfully observed the heroic officers being marched under guard to the segregated mess hall for lunch while about a hundred German prisoners of war, who were being held at Fort Knox under better conditions, watched with befuddled curiosity as they ate with the white American soldiers. On April 23, 1945, General George C. Marshall, probably on direct orders from President Truman, ordered the release of the 101 airmen, pending trial.[11] A few of us headed down to Dave's Bar in Louisville for a celebratory drink.

The War Department also wisely decided to replace Colonel Selway with Colonel Benjamin O. Davis, the Tuskegee-trained commander of the 332nd Fighter Group and a graduate of West Point, who was just back from Europe; however, Selway remained at Godman Field as commander.

Three officers who had allegedly jostled a guard upon entering the club were set for trial. Ted Berry and I went to work as defense counsel. I subpoenaed Colonel Selway because we wanted his testimony on why he had issued the order denying the Tuskegee airmen admission to the officers' club. The colonel directed me to report to his office for a meeting as an officer still under his command, not as a lawyer defending a group of clients. He then informed me that he was not going to appear at the court martial and defiantly waved my officer rating sheet in my face. I told Colonel Selway that he ought to consult his lawyer because his failure to obey the subpoena would constitute a serious crime.

Colonel Davis presided over the all-colored court martial board. Ted Berry and I exercised a preemptory challenge, excusing Colonel Davis from the board, relieving the new commanding officer from the untenable position of judging his new command. Colonel Selway did appear at the trial. Rejecting long-standing tradition, he refused to salute the court, only the flag behind the court. Under cross-examination, despite his hostility and probable prevarication, Selway's explanation for excluding "trainees" from the officers club completely collapsed. The only way that the club managers had distinguished "trainees" from "instructors" was by the color of their skin.

In presenting our case we relied in significant part on a 1919 army regulation, 210-19, requiring that a base officers club be open to all officers assigned to that base. The regulation had nothing to do with race. The reason for the 1919 regulation was that after World War I, the West Point officers had wanted to have exclusive officers clubs that would not be open to officers in the National Guard, the ROTC, or those who had won battlefield commissions. When the non–West Point officers (all of whom were white) complained, Congress forced the War Department to adopt the regulation. Through our exhaustive research we had found a document that we could rely on to support a defense against racial segregation even though that was not the intent of the regulation and at that time there was no specific prohibition against racial segregation or even discrimination in the armed forces. This was another opportunity to use Charles Houston's strategy of applying precedents in other areas of the law to race cases. All the officers were acquitted except one, Ralph C. Terry, who received a fine of $150 for "jostling" a guard to get into the club.

The acquittal of the Tuskegee airmen was a great victory. It made the front page of most newspapers in the United States. Soon thereafter President Harry Truman issued an order that no recreational facility on any army base could deny the admission of commissioned officers, noncommissioned officers, or enlisted men on the basis of race, and in July 1948 he issued an executive order racially integrating the armed forces. It was President Eisenhower, however, who fully implemented the order.[12] Today the U.S. armed services are the least racially segregated institution in American life. Soldiers, sailors, and airmen and airwomen of all races serve with valor in the nation's defense. It was not until 1995, however, that the Air Force finally expunged the letters of reprimand in the files of many of the Tuskegee airmen who participated in the Freeman Field incident and set aside the court martial conviction of Ralph C. Terry.

Immediately after the trial a lieutenant colonel came from Washington to interview me. He suggested that I was foolish to get involved in an incident like this because it would risk my admission to the bar. He seemed sympathetic and implied that he would try to prevent it from adversely affecting my military record.

A few days later, I received a letter from the Department of War, informing me that I had been given the lowest possible rating as an officer, inviting me to respond, and warning me that I could be asked to resign my commission. After doing some research, I responded to the letter, pointing out that less than a month earlier I had received the highest positive rating possible and that army regulations expressly prohibited my receiving a second rating within thirty days of the previous rating unless it was superior to the first rating. I also described my performance as a statistical control officer.

I never received a response to my letter. I did, however, receive an honorable discharge when I resigned my officer's commission to return to Harvard Law School in December 1945. Although I have been subjected since to numerous security clearances, background checks, and confirmation hearings, the issue has never come up again.

The public outrage generated by the media coverage of the treatment of the Tuskegee airmen at Freeman Field—despite their extraordinary service in Europe and North Africa—likely was the catalyst that compelled Presidents Truman and Eisenhower to desegregate the armed services completely. And the successful integration of the military undoubtedly prepared the American people for actions later taken by the Supreme Court and Congress to eliminate state-sanctioned racial segregation in other sectors of American life. For if Americans of color had fought and died to secure the blessings of liberty, surely they had an equal right to partake of them.

Throughout the nation's history, despite the strange silence of history teachers and history textbooks, soldiers of color have valiantly fought for the right to defend the freedoms that they hoped one day would be extended to them, fulfilling the nation's promise of equal opportunity for all its citizens. Soldiers of color fought with the American colonists in the French and Indian War and nearly every major battle in the Revolutionary War, from Bunker Hill, Massachusetts, and Trenton, New Jersey, to Yorktown, Pennsylvania, where Cornwallis finally surrendered to George Washington. General Washington was constantly accompanied on foot and horseback by his mulatto aide, Billy Lee.[13] When Washington could not fill his ranks with white recruits, he established a racially integrated Continental Army, in which coloreds and whites fought side by side, a condition that was not replicated (with few exceptions) until the Korean War.[14] Few school children of any race learn about the contribution of soldiers of color during the War of 1812. Andrew Jackson won the Battle of New Orleans with the help of two battalions, one of free men of color and the other of Haitian immigrants whose courage more than compensated for Jackson's retreating militia.[15]

Before the popular film *Glory* appeared, little was generally known about the contribution of soldiers of color to the victory of the North in the Civil War through their service at Lookout Mountain and Fort Wagner, among other battles. Some two hundred thousand free men of color fought for the Union.[16] Twice that number were recruited by the Army after April 1917, when the country entered World War I, mostly serving in supply, although two infantry divisions saw active combat in France.[17] Nor is there a widespread awareness that colored troops joined white troops at the Battle of the Bulge in World War II, holding back the Germans until the skies cleared and the Allied bombers and fighter planes could do their job and General Patton could advance with the Third Army.[18]

In recent years there have been several films—and belated honors—for the extraordinary accomplishments of the Tuskegee airmen in World War II, but there remain many other untold stories. In Korea, Vietnam, Iraq, and Afghanistan, soldiers of color have served—sometimes disproportionately—with courage and distinction as part of our fully integrated armed forces. Why do I raise this subject, however briefly? Because an essential part of the American story—the part that conjures up the strongest feelings of patriotism—is the sacrifice of fallen soldiers in defense of freedom. As a nation we celebrate two national holidays—Memorial Day and Veterans Day—to honor the soldiers who made the ultimate sacrifice to preserve our liberty. Yet few Americans are aware of how many soldiers of color throughout our history have made the ultimate sacrifice.

After the new commanding officer, Colonel Davis, assumed control, life on the base returned to normal. Colonel Davis had known my parents in civilian life and was familiar with my court martial defense work. He decided it was time for me to render service to the other side and put me in charge of prosecutions under the military code.

A word about Benjamin O. Davis Jr., a genuine American hero.[19] Our paths were to cross on several occasions, including in later years when we served together in the Ford administration. President Clinton awarded each of us the Presidential Medal of Freedom. Davis's father was the Army's first Negro general. He sent his son, who had been sponsored by Oscar De Priest of Chicago, then the only Negro member of Congress, to West Point. In his four years at West Point, Davis roomed alone and mostly ate alone, shunned by his classmates. Initially rejected by the Army Air Corps, which did not accept persons of color, he was (due to Eleanor Roosevelt's persistence) assigned to the first training class at Tuskegee Army Air Field and rose to lead the fabled

Tuskegee airmen, the 332nd Fighter Group, personally flying more than sixty missions. Davis was the first general of color in the U.S. Air Force. He served as chief of staff for the United Nations Command and U.S. Forces in Korea and as commander of the Thirteenth Air Force at Clark Air Force Base in the Philippines. At the time of his retirement from the Air Force, he was deputy commander of the U.S. Strike Command. He continued to serve the public as a civilian, and in 1998 President Clinton awarded him a fourth star.

When the war with Japan ended on August 25, 1945, Colonel Davis made up a list of officers who could leave the service. I was near the top of the list. As I moved through the discharge line at an Air Force base in New York, I was offered the opportunity to join the Army Air Corps Reserve, which would have provided some additional income and a promotion in rank to major. As tempting as the offer was, I turned it down; my sights were focused entirely on returning to law school and becoming a practicing lawyer. The man behind me in line accepted the offer. He was called up during the Korean War, where he earned accolades as one of America's greatest fighter pilots. He was also a top fly fisherman and hitter for the Boston Red Sox. His name was Ted Williams.

TEN

After the War

Make your friends your teachers and mingle the pleasures of conversation with the advantages of instruction.
—BALTASAR GRACIANI, *The Art of Worldly Wisdom*

LOVIDA AND I HAD PLANNED to return to Boston at the conclusion of my military service in November 1945 so I could complete my studies at Harvard Law School. The next semester did not begin until the end of January 1946. In the interim we returned to Philadelphia to live with my parents. I got a job working for Raymond Pace Alexander, undoubtedly the most prominent lawyer of color in Philadelphia and a graduate of the University of Pennsylvania and the Harvard Law School. His wife, Sadie T. M. Alexander, was also a lawyer and a partner in his firm, having served on the *University of Pennsylvania Law Review*. I worked on both civil and criminal cases. The civil cases were mostly personal injury cases, such as a slip and fall on the icy Philadelphia sidewalks.

One series of criminal cases involved charges against several South Philadelphia Italian American women who allegedly had poisoned their husbands to collect life insurance. The first two cases were defended by prominent white criminal defense attorneys. The newspaper coverage was substantial. Each case resulted in a conviction for murder or manslaughter. The third defendant came to Raymond Pace Alexander for representation. Alexander tried the case before a packed courtroom and convinced the jury to bring back a verdict of not guilty on the murder charges. His client was convicted only for practicing medicine without a license. Shortly thereafter his office was flooded with other accused women begging Alexander to defend them. He worked out satisfactory solutions in each of the cases.

Another series of cases involved suits by plaintiffs for injuries sustained after slipping on the icy pavement after a heavy snowstorm in Philadelphia. Pennsylvania case law was fairly clear: a plaintiff must prove that the snow had turned to ice or was more than six inches deep and that the storm had ended more than forty-eight hours before the snow was removed. The key issue was how to prove that the snow was more than six inches. Alexander would have plaintiffs testify that they had fallen with outstretched arms and that the snow reached up to their elbows. He would then ask the court's permission to measure the distance of the person's arm from the fingertip to the elbow; of course, it always measured more than six inches.

As much as I enjoyed my work with the Alexander law firm, I realized that I did not want to restrict my legal career to these types of cases. My studies at the Wharton School had aroused my curiosity about the world of business and economics, and my experiences in the Army Air Corps strengthened my resolve to work to end racial discrimination in all its many forms. I vividly remember reading a story in *Time* magazine about the Marines who stormed the beaches at Iwo Jima. The noncombat Quartermaster Corps and the Coast Guard who manned the boats delivering the soldiers to the hostile beaches were often men of color. The *Time* story was about a soldier of color who pleaded with a white Marine to teach him how to fire a rifle so he could join the invasion as the Marines were under heavy enemy gunfire from the bunkered Japanese, who greatly outnumbered them.

The *Time* writer probably intended to show that all Americans—black and white—were committed to defeating the enemy. For me, however, the story raised a disturbing question: How could a person of color be sent to war without being fully trained and equipped and without the opportunity to demonstrate his patriotism and courage in defense of his country? I wanted to change this shortsighted practice.

The Alexander firm offered me a job when I graduated. They warned me that no white firm would hire a lawyer of color, and even if it did, the lawyer would spend his time in the library or in a warehouse searching for records and reviewing stale documents. While the Alexanders' advice was probably accurate at the time, it only fortified my stubborn resolve to force a change. I fully intended to swim in the legal mainstream.

Lovida and I returned to Cambridge in late January 1946 to a reunion with old friends. Bill Bundy, Elliot Richardson, and Ted Beale were back from the war, as were my southern compatriots Jimmy Wilson, Cuz Hardee, and Mallory Smith and my dear friend Wade McCree. Sadly, we had lost our close friend, the brilliant Harold Osterweil. Because of my late induction into the military, I was a full year ahead of Elliot and many of my former classmates.

Lovida and I rented a house in Boston from a medical doctor, and Lovida got a job working at the Harvard Graduate School of Education. One day when the law school was in recess and I was hoping to get some extra sleep, Lovida started out the door to go to her job but suddenly spun around and said, "Get up, Bill, no man of mine is going to be in bed when I have to leave for work." So I sheepishly arose. After all, she was the income producer in the family. She had purchased my first civilian suit after military service. Lovida had noticed that I always let others—male and female—ascend the stairway before me. While others thought this was simply an act of courtesy instilled by my mother, Lovida knew that the real reason was that all of my clothes had holes or slits in the seat of the trousers.

Working on the *Harvard Law Review* required great discipline. One habit I acquired was reading all the new cases of the U.S. Supreme Court as they were handed down each Monday morning during the session, a habit that I have continued until this day. The close working relationships and social interaction with the brightest second- and third-year students was both challenging and stimulating. On one occasion I was assigned the task of editing a note by a student who later was elected president of the *Review* and went on to be a Supreme Court law clerk, law professor, and law school dean. He wrote extremely well, but I convinced him that his analysis and logic were inconsistent with various precedents he professed to be relying on. After some initial resistance, he came around to my point of view and substantially improved his published product as well as my own self-confidence in my ability to hold my own with the best and the brightest.[1]

Some of my colleagues put up my name for president of the *Review*. An election was held, which I lost to James H. Wilson Jr., a brilliant student from Georgia who had served with great distinction in the U.S. Navy. The following year there was a spirited contest for *Review* president between Elliot Richardson and Bill Bundy. News of an election between the scions of two Boston Brahmin families for an office thought to be the most important prize of the realm spilled over into the parlor rooms and the offices of the white-shoe Boston law firms, social clubs, and faculty lounges.[2] The two contenders conducted themselves as the perfect gentlemen they were, neither overstating their qualifications nor understating their opponents. Elliot prevailed.

Harvard Law Review alumni like Felix Frankfurter, Paul Freund, and Erwin Griswold instilled in us the elitist conceit that being an editor of the *Review* prepared one uniquely to serve as counsel for any situation. As evidence, they cited the abundance of successful judges, government officials, leading members of the bar, and corporate executives. Charles Houston and Bill Hastie had served on the *Review* before me, but I was privileged to be the first American of color to graduate at the top of my class in 1946 and belatedly to receive the Fay Prize for the highest grade average. For reasons reminiscent of my Phi Beta Kappa days, Harvard seemed to take its time in awarding me the prize. I finally received the elegant Fay diploma, marking my class ranking entirely in Latin in—would you believe?—June 2009. If

Harold Osterweil had not died in the war and if Elliot and Jimmy Wilson, whose grades were better than mine, had not left the law school early to serve in the war, any of them might have led the class ranking and won the coveted prize. Nevertheless, it was viewed as something of an achievement for a man of color. It would be another forty-plus years (until 1990) before a man of color would be elected president of the *Harvard Law Review*. It was a special thrill when I read that Barack Obama had been elected president of the law review on February 5, 1990.

ELEVEN

Clerking for the Good Judge

Hold fast to dreams,
For if dreams go,
Life is a barren field,
Frozen with Snow.

—LANGSTON HUGHES

"HAVE YOU LINED UP A job yet, Bill?" Elliot inquired. He had just been elected president of the *Harvard Law Review,* and we were chatting at its sixtieth anniversary dinner as Justice Felix Frankfurter walked by.

"Not yet," I replied, sheepishly. Although I had graduated magna cum laude at the top of my class, my job search had so far been unsuccessful. I was one of the few graduates of the law school who had not yet received an offer.

Perhaps I had set my sights too high. In June 1946 I had boldly written to Justice Hugo Black about a possible clerkship.[1] After setting forth my law school record, I wrote, "Despite my training, owing to the fact that I am a Negro I have encountered considerable difficulty in getting a suitable position. Your efforts and expressions in your judicial utterances led me to inquire whether you would consider me for the position as your legal clerk." Justice Black replied: "My clerk was selected some months ago, and I have no prospect of a vacancy until he finishes his job. You have made an excellent record, and I congratulate you on it." Other graduating law review members had been snatched up for judicial clerkships or by major law firms in Boston, New York, Philadelphia, Washington, and Chicago and on the West Coast.

Elliot, with his ingrained spirit of fairness, could not understand why I could not find a job. Unlike others, he did something about it. The next morning he called his uncle, Henry L. Shattuck, a distinguished Boston lawyer who had been the only Republican on the Boston city council. From April through October Shattuck slept on his yacht every night, instructing the crew to cast off when he arrived at the dock about half past six in the evening and to make sure that he was back in Boston Harbor by eight o'clock the next morning. He was at work by a quarter to nine. When Elliot's father died, Shattuck became the Richardson brothers' surrogate father.

The morning after Elliot's call Shattuck's chauffeur arrived at the rented house in Cambridge, Massachusetts, where Lovida and I were living, bringing five books on the law and instructions to drive me to Shattuck's law office in downtown Boston. After a short interview Shattuck devilishly called Charles B. Curtis, a leading lawyer in one of Boston's top law firms, a Democrat, and a member of the state legislature. Curtis had gotten a lot of newspaper coverage lately because of the strong stance he was taking on the floor of the state legislature on the moral imperative to eliminate segregation and discrimination against people of color. As I sat in the office, Shattuck placed the call.

"Good morning, Charlie," Shattuck said, a wry smile on his face as Curtis answered the phone. "Have I got a great opportunity for you. I have sitting in my office a young lawyer who just graduated from Harvard Law School and is looking for a job. His name is Bill Coleman and he was the best student in his class."

"That sounds real interesting, Henry," said Curtis, sounding suspicious, "By the way, Henry, you should tell your nephew Elliot to come talk to me when he finishes law school."

"I'll do that, Charlie, but Bill Coleman is available right now. Having listened to your statement on the floor of the General Assembly yesterday, I know that the fact that Bill is colored would not be a problem for you. Indeed, it's an opportunity to put into practice what you've been preaching lately," Henry said, with a quiet chuckle and a wink in my direction. There was a long pause.

"Henry, I just couldn't do that. My law firm and clients would not accept a Negro lawyer. You know that, Henry." The conversation was over. Henry Shattuck had tried, and he would try again, more successfully, a few years later.

Many months before, however, I had applied for a clerkship with the Honorable Herbert F. Goodrich, a judge on the U.S. Court of Appeals for the Third Circuit sitting in Philadelphia. An unsuccessful Democratic candidate for governor of Pennsylvania, Judge Goodrich, a Harvard Law School graduate, had been dean of the University of Pennsylvania Law School. He was a leading scholar in the field of conflict of laws so I hoped he would note that I had received the Beale Award for my grade in Paul Freund's conflicts course.[2] Indeed, he did, and he invited me to be his law clerk, starting in May 1947 when the term of his present law clerk ended. I quickly accepted.

Fortunately, Dean Griswold arranged for me to become a Langdell teaching fellow at the law school until my clerkship began. This was a relief since I was about to have a child to support. I supplemented my income by tutoring five second-year law students who were having trouble with their courses. In addition, I helped a second-year law student to negotiate a deal for the movie production of parts of John Dos Passos's classic, the U.S.A. trilogy. We worked on "The Forty-Second Parallel" (1930), "Nineteen Nineteen" (1932), and "The Big Money" (1936).

Over a two-month period, I saw a lot of John Dos Passos. Considered in the 1930s to be one of America's greatest writers, Dos Passos wrote fervently about the corruption of industrial society and the growing disparity between the wealthy and the poor, reinforced by a political system that betrayed the vision of the founding fathers. By this time, his pendulum was swinging from the fiery radical to the reactionary conservative. He had lost his wife and one eye in an automobile accident; and he was growing disillusioned with the radical left. The trilogy was perhaps the most innovative, passionately written commentary on America for its time, but the thin, bespectacled author with a strange accent was no longer fully vested in the project. While I could empathize with his view of two unequal nations, I never bought into his radicalism, and, in the end, neither did he. A contract was signed and I received my compensation, but to my knowledge the film was never produced.

During this period I also studied for the Pennsylvania bar exam, which I took in early December 1946. I had instructed my parents to open any mail addressed to me from the Pennsylvania Board of Law Examiners and to call me immediately. For the next two months each tension-filled morning was spent waiting for the results—an apprehension most law school graduates can appreciate. Finally, one evening at 7:02 p.m. my father called with the news I'd been hoping for: "I have some good news, Bill. You passed the bar."

"That's a relief," I said, "But why are you calling me so late? You must have gotten the mail by ten o'clock this morning."

"I was waiting for the reduced evening telephone rate, Bill. Money doesn't grow on trees you know."

Our first child, William Thaddeus Coleman III, was born in Boston on April 20, 1947. Shortly thereafter, Lovida, our young son, Billy, and I took the train to Philadelphia to live with my parents. After searching for a few months, we were able to purchase a comfortable home in West Mount Airy. It was a modest twin house with a nice front and back yard and a comfortable space for entertaining. I could afford the down payment because the chief judge of the Orphans Court of Philadelphia County, Lewis Van Deusen Sr., had appointed me the guardian for the children of a deceased father in a substantial estate matter. The fees awarded to me by the court covered the down payment. Lovida's father also provided some financial support.

The day I started work with Judge Goodrich, both Philadelphia daily newspapers, the *Bulletin* and the *Inquirer*, carried pictures of Judge Goodrich and me, noting in the caption that I was the first nonwhite law clerk in the entire federal court system in the United States.

Each relationship between a judge and his or her law clerk is unique. Judge Goodrich engaged his clerks in a discussion of the law and facts and then assigned them legal research. A respected legal scholar, he would often write the first draft of an opinion, leaving blanks for his clerks to complete. The judge and I also wrote an article together, "Pennsylvania Marital Communities and Common Law Neighbors," which was published in the *University of Pennsylvania Law Review*.[3] On a few occasions when the judge had other duties, I taught his class on conflict of laws at Penn Law School. The judge shared with me his views about the great lawyers of the Philadelphia Bar, what made them effective and what constituted persuasive advocacy before his court.

While Negro lawyers had their own bar association, the National Bar Association, I did not apply for membership, even though Raymond Pace Alexander had served as its president from 1929 to 1931. Consistent with my personal commitment to enter the mainstream, I applied to the American Bar Association in 1947. Judge Goodrich and his good friend William Mason of Morgan, Lewis, and Bockius sponsored my application, and I became a member—one of its first members of color. The American Bar Association had opened its membership to Negroes four years earlier, but there had been few takers. I strongly felt it was important for lawyers of color to be fully integrated in professional associations, but it was not until the 1960s that the association became fully engaged in issues of importance to many attorneys of color.

Even more important, Judge Goodrich inculcated in me a strong appreciation for the work of the American Law Institute.[4] At the time, the judge served as its executive director. Based in Philadelphia, the institute, through a careful and deliberative process, drafts and republishes restatements of the law, model codes, and other proposals for legal reform to promote the clarification, modernization, and improvement of the law. I became a member of the institute in June 1955 and was elected to its council on June 10, 1970.[5] I remain an active member to this day.

On February 15, 1948, I was checking the citations in an opinion for Judge Goodrich when the telephone rang. It was a call from Henry L. Hart, one of my professors at the Harvard Law School.

"Is this Bill Coleman?" he asked.

"Yes, Professor Hart, it is good to hear from you," I responded to the totally unexpected phone call.

"I have a question for you, Bill. Starting September 1948, would you accept appointment as law clerk to Justice Felix Frankfurter for the 1948 term beginning in October? You would have to move to Washington. You should know, Bill, that I also have recommended Elliot Richardson, who is now clerking for

Learned Hand, chief judge for the Second Circuit Court of Appeals, as the other law clerk." As the good news sunk in I responded immediately, "Yes, sir. I would be honored." I knew that no American of color had ever served as a law clerk to a Supreme Court justice, and my heart leaped to the skies.

Two months went by and I heard nothing further from Professor Hart. Justice Frankfurter did not call me for an interview either, so I muscled up my courage and called Professor Freund. Freund knew that Henry Hart had spoken to me, apparently because Freund was the one who had recommended me to Justice Frankfurter. Freund later told me of Hart's response to my query. "Coleman must not be as bright as you said, Paul. How could he imagine I'd ask him that question if I did not have the authority to close the deal if he said yes?" The next day I got a call from Elliot Richardson. He said how happy he was that we were going to be clerks together. Although the Court term did not begin until the first Monday of October, he was going to start on June 30. He knew that I would not start until September 1 because Frankfurter wanted one of his clerks to remain over the following summer to organize, index, and compile the files and appendix of the work completed during the 1948 term and to brief the two incoming law clerks.

At last it was clear and real. I really was going to clerk for one of the great justices in the history of the Supreme Court, and clerking with me would be my first and closest friend from Harvard Law School. For a guy who couldn't get a job in a law firm, fortune seemed to be shining brightly on me.

TWELVE

Justice Frankfurter

*All our work, our whole life is a matter of semantics, because
words are the tools with which we work, the materials out
of which laws are made, out of which the Constitution was
written. Everything depends on our understanding of them.*

—JUSTICE FELIX FRANKFURTER

MY YEAR WITH JUSTICE FRANKFURTER (from September 1, 1948, to August
31, 1949) remains among the most meaningful and enjoyable of my life. Having greatly admired a legend from afar, I discovered, working with him daily
for most of the year, that he was even more brilliant, caring, widely read,
informed, witty, and, yes, demanding than I could ever have imagined. Each
day was a thrill, walking up the steps into the grand Supreme Court building.
My associations with the sixteen other law clerks, who arrived from various
parts of the country, bringing different philosophies and perspectives, was
both stimulating and collegial. They were the select few from my law school
generation who had scaled these steeples of excellence. I also quickly learned
to appreciate the professionalism and helpfulness of the Office of the Clerk
and the Supreme Court marshals.

Working in this oasis of intellectual ferment and civilized tranquility, I was
able to ignore for the most part the brutal fact that our nation's capital at that
time was almost completely racially segregated, including the hotels, theatres,
schools, department stores, and restaurants, except for the Supreme Court
cafeteria, the railway station, and a few other isolated eating places. Lovida
and I rented an apartment in a segregated neighborhood because the 1948
Washington Real Estate Board Code of Ethics expressly declared that no
property in a white section of the city should ever be sold, rented, advertised,
or offered to colored people. Even the employment practices of the city and
federal government were highly discriminatory.

Starting on September 1, Elliot and I were in Frankfurter's chambers every
day. Although the justice did not return to Washington until September 15,
he was on the phone with us three or four times a day discussing various issues
and giving us assignments. While on summer vacation he had read and reread

all the printed petitions for writs of certiorari and jurisdictional statements, which were delivered to him by pouch wherever he was in the world.

When Elliot and I were preparing for our clerkships, we read all the articles and briefs of Felix Frankfurter before he was appointed to the bench. Frankfurter strongly advocated positions advanced by the American Civil Liberties Union, the NAACP, and New Deal proponents. Our reading was useful only because it confirmed Frankfurter's independence as a justice. He completely put aside his personal views and addressed only the facts of a particular controversy, adhering to the specific meaning of the words of the governing statute, whether or not he personally agreed with the legislative policy underlying it.

On September 17, Justice Frankfurter made his grand entrance as he dashed through our offices on the way to the bathroom. In the presence of my new employer I felt like Manasseh Cutler, a Massachusetts minister, when he first met Benjamin Franklin: "My knees smote together."[1] Yet, I thought to myself, he is human like the rest of us, having to answer the call of nature.

When we met at ten in the morning I was immediately put at ease by the justice's unassuming style. Again the words of Manasseh Cutler describing Ben Franklin captured perfectly my impressions of that first meeting:

> I was highly delighted with the extensive knowledge he appeared to have of every subject, the brightness of his memory, and clearness and the vivacity of all his mental faculties. . . . His manners [were] perfectly easy, and everything about him seem[ed] to diffuse an unrestrained freedom and happiness. He [had] an incessant vein of humor, accompanied with an uncommon vivacity, which seem[ed] as natural and voluntary as his breathing.[2]

It is true that as I got to know the justice better that year and over subsequent years, I learned that he did not suffer fools gladly and sometimes chafed at the obstinacy of slower men and women, regretting the waste of time it took to explain and persuade even his acknowledged peers, including law professors and justices.

The justice was a fairly short man, even shorter than my five feet seven inches. But no one ever thought of him as little or ordinary. An impeccable dresser, he had boundless energy, walked fast, and spoke with a commanding presence. He was a true scholar whose knowledge of the history and precedents of the Supreme Court was unmatched. With his insatiable curiosity he had amassed an understanding of American, European, and ancient history that gave context to his analysis of current issues. With his roaring laugh and affable personality, Frankfurter was a friend and adviser of the leaders of the executive branch and foreign governments. For this reason, some historians have questioned his judicial independence. I am not sure we would be better off by adopting as a model a Supreme Court justice who lives in isolation, aloof in an ivory tower, unconnected to the world around him.

Much has been written about Frankfurter's informal advice to President Roosevelt on issues like the lend-lease program and his opposition to punitive measures against Germany after World War II, which were being urged by Henry Morgenthau Jr., the secretary of the treasury. Frankfurter's contribution to these world events was extremely valuable. I cannot imagine that such communications compromised his judicial independence. If we appoint individuals of high ethical standards to key positions, then intricate regulatory restrictions may not be as necessary. We might find that there is great benefit in having great minds interact on great issues. It seems each time our government is embarrassed by the ethical lapse of an unethical official, it further tightens and complicates the regulatory regime, which deters good people from government service. Have we lost sight of the critical objective—appointing persons of proven quality and integrity in the first place?

In my experience each justice had a different relationship with, and set of expectations of, his law clerks. The relationships in a particular chamber would also vary depending on the personality and strength and weaknesses of the law clerk. Among his clerks, past and present, Justice Frankfurter had been family. He took us into his confidence completely, treated us as intellectual sparring partners, shared his sometimes acerbic opinions of prominent people, including his colleagues on the Court, and showed a genuine interest and affection for our families—spouses, parents, and children. He enjoyed talking to my parents when they visited the chambers, eliciting from my mother her substantial knowledge and well-spoken opinions about history and world affairs. When my first child, Billy, was three years old, he visited the chambers, and before long the justice was rolling on the floor pushing Billy's red toy car around the carpet.

Much has been written about Justice Frankfurter by legal historians and Court observers, but some of his former law clerks, who went on to substantial careers in their own right, have described the special relationships he developed within his chambers. Frankfurter himself described the relationship as a partnership:

> They are, as it were, my junior partners—junior only in years. In the realm of the mind there is no hierarchy. I take them fully into my confidence, so that the relation is free and easy. However, I am, they will tell you, a very exacting task-master; no nonsense, intellectually speaking, is tolerated, no short-cuts, no deference to position is permitted, no yes-sing, however much some of them in the beginning be awed.[3]

Former law clerk Andrew Kaufman described the relationship from the clerk's perspective:

> [Frankfurter] was loyal to his friends. Once he admitted you to that circle—and the circle was very large—you were his friend for life. There was one group that was admitted en masse: his law clerks. Frankfurter treated us like colleagues; he was interested in our lives; he included our families in his interest; and he kept his clerks as his friends and as his colleagues forever. It is hard not to reciprocate the affection of someone who cares passionately for you.[4]

We worked six days a week at the Court. On weekdays, the justice would leave at about seven in the evening for dinner with Mrs. Frankfurter. Elliot and I would spend an hour preparing for the next day. Still a bachelor, Elliot would go out for the evening. I would join Lovida with our young son Bill III at our apartment in Northwest Washington. Our second child, Lovida Hardin Coleman Jr., was born on May 21, 1949. Elliot Richardson is her godfather.

On Saturdays the Court met in conference until three o'clock. Frankfurter would rush back to his chambers after the conference and until about six o'clock would recount in vivid detail what had transpired. He also left with us his black book, in which he had written many notes and comments. Frankfurter gave Elliot and me a sophisticated feel for how the secretive conference actually worked. Only the nine justices were present. They greeted one another with a handshake. When someone knocked on the door, usually to bring documents requested by a justice, the most junior justice would open the door, receive the papers, and deliver them to the appropriate justice. I had also heard, although I cannot verify it, that the junior justice on some occasions would serve coffee to the other justices at the conference table.

The Court would turn its attention to the cases argued since the last conference. When Frankfurter joined the Court in 1939, Charles Evan Hughes Jr. was the chief justice. Frankfurter marveled at Hughes's great talent in stating the facts and issues of each case without signaling how he was planning to vote on the merits. Thereafter, each justice, in the order of seniority, would comment on the case. Then the voting would begin. The most junior justice voted first, and the chief justice voted last. If the chief was in the majority, he would assign the case to himself or one of the other justices in the majority to write an opinion for the Court. If the chief was in the minority, the most senior justice in the majority would make the assignment.

Frankfurter indicated that when Harlan F. Stone became chief justice in 1941, he followed the same practice of presenting the case at the conference but tended inadvertently to signal how he was going to vote. Apparently when Fred M. Vinson became the chief justice in 1946, he was even less subtle in indicating the way he was going to vote. I have been told that Justice Earl Warren simply told his colleagues in the conference how he was going to vote when he presented the case.

Another key purpose of the Saturday conference was to determine which cases the Court was going to hear. Petitions *in forma pauperis* were initially reviewed by the Office of the Chief Justice, and those not thought worthy of discussion at the conference would be placed on the so-called dead list. Occasionally Justice Frankfurter or another justice requested that a case be removed from the dead list and considered in conference. All other petitions were discussed in conference, and if four justices voted in favor, an order was issued setting the case down for oral argument. For jurisdictional statements, five votes were required. On a few occasions, the merits of a case were discussed, and the case dismissed for lack of jurisdiction.

With the formal beginning of the 1948 term on the first Monday in October, the work pace of the law clerks quickened. Unlike the other clerks, Elliot and I were not tasked with writing memorandums on petitions for writs of certiorari or jurisdictional statements. Justice Frankfurter had carefully read them all. He considered this an essential part of his job. This was also his way of keeping informed on the issues that were percolating in the federal and state courts. Nor did his clerks write pre- or post-bench memorandums for each argument. After the oral argument, the justice would begin to discuss the issues with his clerks. If the opinion was assigned to Justice Frankfurter or if Frankfurter decided to write a dissent or concurring opinion, the work would begin in earnest.

In most cases the justice wrote the first draft of an opinion. He would ask for detailed legal research on critical issues. For example, when the Court decided to hear *Wolf* v. *Colorado* (1949), the question presented was whether the admission in a state court of illegally seized evidence by a state official violates the due process clause of the Fourteenth Amendment. The issue had been resolved for federal courts: evidence seized in violation of the Fourth Amendment cannot be introduced in federal criminal trials. Elliot had spent most of July researching how state courts had handled this issue. His research revealed that thirty of forty-seven states had expressly rejected the federal rule that such evidence could not be used. After reviewing charts derived from the research, the justice incorporated them in his opinion in *Wolf* v. *Colorado*.[5]

Frankfurter organized his chambers differently from the other justices, reflecting his collegial style. The justice, Elliot, and I worked together with his secretary in the center office room. Frankfurter forfeited the usual justice's office in a large end room, with its fireplace and bathroom, because he wanted to work between his clerks and his secretary. Constant drafts and revisions were exchanged. We soon appreciated one another's strengths and tacitly recognized

Senior partner and senior counselor William T. Coleman Jr. of O'Melveny & Myers LLP, Washington, D.C.

Reverend and Mrs. Peck and family, William Coleman's maternal great-great-grandparents. Trained for the ministry in the United Kingdom, Peck was abducted by slave traders on his return to West Africa. He avoided slavery, however, by escaping at the port of Baltimore and joined the community of free men and women of color in the early 1800s.

Coleman's parents, Laura Beatrice Mason Coleman and William T. Coleman Sr.

William T. Coleman Jr.,
age 16, in 1936

The U.S. Army sent Coleman to Harvard Business School in 1944 for training as a statistical control officer. Lieutenant Coleman was assigned to the 477th Army Airforce base unit. Bored with his duties, he began defending soldiers in court martial proceedings at Godman Field in Kentucky and Freeman Field in Indiana.

Bill Coleman and Lovida Hardin on their wedding day in the Hardins' home in New Orleans, February 10, 1945.

Above: The Coleman children, William T. Coleman III, Lovida Jr., and Hardin, in front of their home on Easter Sunday.
Left: Lovida Hardin Coleman in 1945

The *Harvard Law Review* staff of 1945–46. Bill and his lifelong friend Elliot Richardson were members. Coleman is the fourth from the left in the fourth row. Richardson is the last person in that row. Also pictured are James H. Wilson Jr., William P. Bundy, and Jerry Hyman, who worked closely with Coleman on Pan Am matters, and Mickey Rudin, who retained him to represent Frank Sinatra.

Coleman lands a job as law clerk to Third Circuit judge Herbert F. Goodrich in 1947.

Justice Felix Frankfurter at the end of Coleman's clerkship during the 1948 term of the Supreme Court of the United States.

Charles Hamilton Houston, architect of the civil rights litigation strategy, was the first man of color to serve as an editor of the *Harvard Law Review*. Houston went on to become dean of Howard University Law School and litigation director for the NAACP.

Coleman's lifelong friend Judge Louis Pollak, who was also a Supreme Court clerk in 1948, fellow associate at Paul, Weiss, and former dean of the Yale and University of Pennsylvania law schools

Secretary of Transportation William T. Coleman Jr. and wife Lovida visiting the Smithsonian's new Air and Space Museum in 1976.

The Coleman family in 1975, Hardin, Lovida, Lovida Jr., Bill, and William III.

In 1995 Coleman received the Presidential Medal of Freedom from President Clinton. Pictured from left are Hardin Coleman, William T. Coleman III, Jesse Coleman, President Clinton, Aaron Coleman, Hillary Rodham Clinton, Bill Coleman, Lovida H. Coleman Jr., Lovida H. Coleman, and Gail Coleman

The Coleman family in 2006. On the far left are William III and his wife, Allegra, with their children Amadeus and William IV. Bill Coleman and Lovida stand in the middle with Lovida Jr. and Aaron to Lovida's left. On the stairway are Hardin, Gail, and Jesse.

Photo by Carl Cox Photography

one another's weaknesses. The justice and Richardson wrote better than I did, but they acknowledged on more than one occasion that I had a superior knack for picking up inconsistencies or logical flaws in their arguments.

The justice had a tendency to complete one thought in a sentence and start a new thought in the same sentence. We were constantly rewriting sentences to smooth them out. Like Justice Brandeis, Frankfurter often tried to incorporate material that friends and scholars, domestic or foreign, had sent him. Elliot and I would often rearrange paragraphs and entire sections of the opinion into a more cohesive form.

When the three of us worked together on an opinion, we would sometimes run into one another delivering papers to the printer, which was then in the Supreme Court building. The justice would make constant, continuing corrections, strikeouts, revisions, or additions to the printed galleys. He thought it essential, especially in state criminal cases, to cite state court precedents to assure the state judges that the Court understood and respected their rulings.

Justice Frankfurter served on the Court for twenty-three years. He wrote 247 opinions, 132 concurring opinions, and 251 dissents. He is viewed as an advocate of judicial restraint, which often caused him to dissent from decisions that he viewed as judicial activism.[6] He consistently called for narrow rulings, especially on issues that sharply divided the nation. He said the Court should "avoid putting fetters upon the future by needless pronouncements today."[7] Chief Justice John Roberts recently referred with unmistakable enthusiasm to Frankfurter's suggestion "that courts should focus on the concrete issues and not embarrass the future too much."[8]

Not surprisingly, in later years Justice Frankfurter's well-known propensity to avoid reaching a constitutional question if there were any other possible grounds on which a case could be disposed of was of great concern to the litigation team in preparing for *Brown* v. *Board of Education*. My experience told me that Frankfurter's fundamental decency and abhorrence to discrimination in any form would override his process-oriented instincts. I assured my colleagues that Frankfurter would vote to overrule the separate-but-equal doctrine of *Plessy* v. *Ferguson*.

There was another reason why I was hopeful about Frankfurter's support. In June 1949, near the end of the term, Thurgood Marshall filed a petition for a writ of certiorari challenging South Carolina's segregation of the public schools under the *Plessy* v. *Ferguson* doctrine on the grounds that the colored schools were grossly inferior to the white schools. Governor Byrnes, formerly an associate justice of the Supreme Court, then filed a petition requesting that the case be sent back for trial to hear evidence about a new South Carolina statute imposing a tax on soda pop, the proceeds of which would be used exclusively to make the separate schools equal. Thurgood Marshall opposed

South Carolina's remand petition on the grounds that even if the schools were physically equal, segregation would still violate the Fourteenth Amendment. Elliot and I urged the justice to reject Governor Byrnes's petition and vote to hear the case. At the justice's request, we drafted a memorandum that would support a decision that even physically equal racially segregated schools would violate the Fourteenth Amendment without having to overrule *Plessy* v. *Ferguson* expressly. The Court nevertheless sent the case back to permit Governor Byrnes to put into evidence how the expenditures under the new state tax would equalize the schools.

I do not know how Frankfurter voted on that particular petition, but I was surprised to receive a telephone call in early 1953 from Alexander Bickel, who was then clerking for Justice Frankfurter, requesting a copy of the memorandum that Elliot and I had drafted on how to hold public school desegregation unconstitutional without overruling *Plessy* v. *Ferguson*. I retrieved a copy from my files and sent it on immediately.

I was confident that Frankfurter would find a way to right the moral wrongs of school segregation without violating his own principles of judicial restraint and, more important, would work to persuade his more conservative colleagues.

From my clerkship experience I knew that Frankfurter had a lot of influence with other justices, such as Robert H. Jackson, Thomas C. Clark, Harold H. Burton, Charles E. Whittaker, and Sherman Minton and that he worked very hard at persuading them to support his positions. He especially sought to indoctrinate new justices coming on to the Court. Some of his more activist colleagues, such as Justice Hugo Black and Justice William O. Douglas and in later years Chief Justice Warren and Justice William Brennan, were not often persuaded by Frankfurter's tireless and talkative advocacy, which they sometimes viewed as pedantic.

Elliot and I took great care to ensure consistency with previous Frankfurter opinions and especially with Holmes and Brandeis opinions, to which we gave great deference. On a few occasions we would painstakingly distinguish a Holmes opinion. Frankfurter respected Holmes's views on the limits of judicial review and his steadfast deference to the policy decisions of the elected branches of government, whether he agreed with them or not. Holmes's later opinions on free speech were also highly respected, as his views evolved—probably in consultation with Zechariah Chaffee of the Harvard Law School, who had published in 1919 a classic article on freedom of speech during wartime.[9]

If I had focused more on some of Justice Holmes's opinions on race, I most likely would have enlivened the discussions in the justice's chambers about how much weight to give Holmes's opinions.[10] Much to my chagrin, Justice

Holmes wore a shocking blinder when it came to racial discrimination. Most of his opinions completely ignored the Thirteenth, Fourteenth, and Fifteenth Amendments. He gave zero weight to the civil rights acts passed after the Civil War. In *Giles* v. *Harris* (1903), despite the clear language in the Fourteenth and Fifteenth Amendments, Holmes wrote an opinion upholding state laws that concocted a variety of ruses to prevent nearly all black voters from casting ballots. The first Justice John Marshall Harlan dissented.[11] And in *Bailey* v. *Alabama* (1911), Holmes dissented from the majority opinion, which held that the Alabama peonage statute, criminalizing an employee's failure to work out a debt to his employer, violated the Thirteenth Amendment. Justice Holmes also joined the majority in *Kentucky* v. *Berea College,* which upheld a Kentucky law that banned a corporation from operating a school with both white and black pupils. Incredibly, he dissented in *Buchanan* v. *Warley* (1917), outlawing residential segregation laws.

Although I do not recall ever discussing with Justice Frankfurter the Holmes opinions on race, I do recall with some amusement Frankfurter's efforts to persuade me that former chief justice Roger B. Taney had some redeeming qualities. Chief Justice Taney had written the infamous *Dred Scott* decision in 1857 in which he had used language that I still find horrendous: "[Negroes are] beings of an inferior order, and altogether unfit to associate with the white race, either in social or political relations; and so far inferior that they [have] no rights which the white man [is] bound to respect." Frankfurter once described the *Dred Scott* decision as "one of the Court's great self-inflicted wounds." Without any effort to justify such odious rhetoric, Frankfurter would point out to me that Taney, one of the longest-serving chief justices in history, had done some good things in other areas, such as civil liberties and the commerce clause. When President Abraham Lincoln suspended habeas corpus in 1861, Chief Justice Taney had the courage personally to serve the commanding officer of a military fort with a writ of habeas corpus even though the president had threatened him with imprisonment. The chief justice also had written many leading cases on the commerce clause with which Frankfurter agreed, and he had helped to clarify the constitutional relationships between the federal and state governments. Taney recognized the dual authority of the federal and state governments to regulate commerce so long as there was no conflict between them, but where there was a conflict, he held that congressional legislation was controlling and supreme. Frankfurter would occasionally send me an article or opinion about Taney that would shed a more favorable light on his work than the dreadful *Dred Scott* case.[12]

Despite Frankfurter's efforts, Chief Justice Taney will never be rehabilitated in my eyes. The nation would have been far better off if he had never served on the Court. Many years later I heard an interesting anecdote about how Taney was appointed, illustrating the randomness of history. Chief Justice Warren had appointed me to the federal Civil Rules Advisory Committee under the chairmanship of Dean Acheson. At our meeting, federal district judge Charles Wyzanski explained why some lawyers had refused appointment to the Supreme Court. Just as Wyzanski finished his point, Chief Justice Warren interjected and, to the best of my recollection, said, "Charlie, you missed the best case of all, the case of John R. Carroll." Charlie started to blush. He did not like being told he did not know everything. The chief justice then recounted the story that when the great chief justice John Marshall died, President Andrew Jackson decided that the next appointee should come from Maryland. He initially selected John R. Carroll, a prominent lawyer of a leading Catholic family in Maryland. He summoned Carroll to the White House and, according to Warren's anecdote, said, "I have decided to appoint you Chief Justice of the United States."

Carroll's startling response was, "No, Mr. President, I cannot accept it." Jackson tried to persuade him, "It's the fourth most important position in the United States. There are only four positions specifically mentioned in the Constitution. The Court sits only four months a year and you live only forty miles away, so you can spend most of your time at your grand estate in Maryland."

Mr. Carroll sheepishly responded, "Mr. President, I have always felt that if this country was willing to bestow such a high honor on one of its citizens, he should be willing to give up his mistress or to marry her. I am not willing to do either." Given the public opprobrium that President Jackson faced about his own marital situation—rumors circulated that the first lady was not divorced from her first husband when she married Jackson—the president readily understood the reason for Carroll's rejection. He decided to find another Catholic from Maryland. He appointed Roger B. Taney.[13]

On the way back from Acheson's lovely farm where the advisory committee had been meeting, I mulled over the chief justice's tale. Instead of the perceived private immorality of John Carroll, the nation got the public immorality of the *Dred Scott* decision, with its devastating consequences in the decades that followed. I began to think that maybe the French have a point—that our somewhat puritanical sense of private morality does not always lead to the best results for the country.

THIRTEEN

Life at the Supreme Court and in the Nation's Capital

Wisdom too often never comes, and so one ought not to reject it merely because it comes late.

—JUSTICE FELIX FRANKFURTER

Verily, it is vastly better to yield to wisdom at last, than not at all.

—MARK TWAIN

MOST MORNINGS, JUSTICE FRANKFURTER WALKED to work with Secretary of State Acheson from their homes in Georgetown to the old Executive Office Building, next to the White House, which then housed the Department of State.[1] They would talk about the issues of the day. Often the justice, according to Acheson, would not stop talking even when they reached the office building. Finally, the secretary had to make the rule that when they reached a certain line on the pavement outside the building the conversation would stop. The justice would avoid ending the conversation by stopping just ten steps before the agreed-on mark. When the justice arrived at the Court, he was bubbling over with tidbits to share with Elliot and me about what was going on in Europe, Japan, the Marshall Plan, and NATO.

While the justice was walking to work, Elliot and I would spend a half hour each morning reading Shakespeare or the English romantic poets to each other. Apparently Elliot had made this a condition of his acceptance of the clerkship—a condition that the justice wholeheartedly embraced. We also played badminton on the roof of the court to clear the mind and work off excess energy.

Working in Frankfurter's chambers gave us the opportunity to meet many fascinating figures of the day. Each year when the American Law Institute met in Washington, Learned Hand, chief judge of the Second Circuit Court, would drop by for a chat. Elliot kept a picture of Learned Hand hanging on the wall, with a learned inscription, hand-written and addressed to Elliot, which looked like Greek to me—in fact, it was in Greek. Frankfurter would generously bring Elliot and me into conversations with British Labour Party leader Harold Laski, the famed Nuremberg prosecutor Lord Hartley Shawcross, the law chancellor of Great Britain, and the prime minister of Australia. McGeorge Bundy, by then dean of Harvard, was a frequent visitor. On one occasion, Bundy saw the *Memoirs of Hecate County*, by Edmund Wilson, on the shelves of the justice's chambers, a humorously erotic story of multiple affairs and sexual fantasies that had been banned in New York state. Although Frankfurter was widely read, his personal library was not noted for its salacious content. The book was there because it was in the record of a case before the Court on whether its contents violated New York's obscenity law. Bundy said he would demonstrate how to read a dirty book, grabbing it off the shelf and letting it fall open naturally to the pages in which the most licentious material appeared, obviously the well-worn pages of the book. As it turned out, Frankfurter recused himself from this obscenity case for reasons he never disclosed; perhaps it was his friendship with the author. The Court affirmed the lower court's holding that the book was obscene, in a divided opinion, 4-4.[2]

Each year Justice and Mrs. Frankfurter would host a black-tie dinner for all current and past Frankfurter law clerks. I was the twelfth. Among the group were Phil Graham, the publisher of the *Washington Post;* Edward F. Pritchard Jr., a member of the Roosevelt brain trust who had gone to jail for voter fraud and stuffing the ballot box but then redeemed himself as an education reformer; Tommy "the Cork" Corcoran, the epitome of the Washington lawyer; Adrian "Butch" Fisher, legal adviser to the State Department; Phil Elman, whose support from the solicitor general's office in *Brown* v. *Board of Education* was extraordinary; and Joseph L. Rauh Jr., of the Americans for Democratic Action. As the author of President Roosevelt's Executive Order 8,802, establishing the Fair Employment Practices Committee, Joe Rauh coined the phrase "No discrimination on grounds of race, color, creed, or national origin"—words that elevated the pithy promise of the Declaration of Independence to a higher, more specific, and more inclusive level.

After dinner Mrs. Frankfurter made humorous remarks, classifying each law clerk from barbarian to milquetoast. Dean Acheson was usually the only outside guest. He also would speak, followed by the justice, who would talk about the Court or the state of the world or how to conduct oneself in public life (which occasionally bordered on the pedantic, like Polonius's advice to Laertes in *Hamlet*). Justice and Mrs. Frankfurter always thought of his law clerks as the sons they never had.

The law clerks of that term got along quite well—truth to tell, a lot better than some of the justices, who became more fractious as their tenure lengthened. We clerks used to exchange gossip and information about the justices.[3] Frankfurter thought that Justice Robert Jackson was the best writer on the

Court. We all agreed. As the year went on our respect for Justice Douglas declined, and this view was shared by Frankfurter. We all greatly admired Justice Black, as did Frankfurter, although as the years went on their views increasingly diverged and their friendship became strained. A former senator from Alabama who had been a member of the Ku Klux Klan, Justice Black had changed his views radically on the Court. At that time he was a consistent, dedicated defender of the Bill of Rights, civil rights, and civil liberties. The standing joke about Justice Black was that he traded in the white robe he had used to scare blacks for a black robe to scare whites.[4] In later years Black appeared to slip from his pedestal on civil rights, defending some of the traditions of the Old South.

On one occasion, witnessing Justice Black's handling of a case left a lasting impression, affecting some of my practices later as secretary of transportation. The case involved a suit by a union against a state, alleging that the union's actions were protected by the First Amendment and therefore could not be in violation of the state's antitrust laws. In the conference after the argument, the Court voted 7-2 in favor of the union's position, the dissenters being Frankfurter and Jackson. The chief justice assigned the opinion to Justice Black. Three months later Justice Black circulated an opinion to which was attached a memorandum stating that he had tried for more than two months to write the opinion to support the way he had voted. It just did not mature. Instead, the attached opinion reflected the opinion of the dissenters, an opinion that Justice Black now realized was the correct one. All but one of the justices were persuaded by Black's memo and revised draft opinion. The Court issued its decision, 8-1.

Many years later as a cabinet officer I confronted a number of complex and controversial issues. The discipline of explaining the reasons for my decision in writing before making a final decision and releasing it to the public helped me achieve a more responsible result. There were some occasions when I actually wrote, or had written on my behalf by one of the young lawyers who worked with me, two decisions, one affirming and the other denying the recommendation before me. Through this process I was able to support my decisions with transparent, persuasive reasoning. While inevitably the secretary of transportation was sued by the losing party, we never lost a lawsuit in which I had issued a written decision after going through this process. For this string of victories, I am indebted to Justice Black.

Elliot and I made lasting friendships with the other law clerks during the 1948 term. It was the beginning of my long association with Louis H. Pollak, who clerked for Justice Wiley Rutledge. Through the decades, our paths would frequently cross. We were to become fellow associates at Paul, Weiss, Rifkind, Wharton, and Garrison. His future father-in-law, Louis S. Weiss, offered me my first law firm job. Pollak and his future wife, Kathy, dated on several occasions in our Philadelphia home. In the 1950s Pollak and I were part of Thurgood Marshall's brain trust. We worked together on the *Brown* v. *Board of Education* briefs. Pollak later became a distinguished professor and dean of the Yale Law School, where he taught two of my children. Later he moved to Philadelphia, where he became a professor and then dean of the law school of the University of Pennsylvania and thereafter a federal judge on the U. S. District Court for the Eastern District of Pennsylvania. Through the years we worked on more projects than I can count. He has never hesitated to lend a sympathetic ear and helpful hand to many of the concerns—public and private—that have challenged our interwoven careers.

Another friend, Truman Hobbs, a graduate of Yale Law School, clerked for Justice Black. Truman would often drive me home after work. His other passenger was his father, Sam Hobbs, a member of Congress of the Alabama old school. After the first week of awkwardness with the sullen man sitting in the back seat, we became lively friends, arguing and sharing a joke or two. His son returned to Alabama and eventually became a judge on the U.S. District Court for the Middle District of Alabama.

The law clerks worked hard, but we were not nerdy bookworms. We had a lot of fun together. There was the House of Truth in Georgetown. This group house had been founded by Felix Frankfurter in 1911 with a number of other ambitious young men, many of whom pursued notable public careers. Justice Holmes gave it the name House of Truth, sarcastically referring to the brainy fast talkers who occupied it. Elliot, along with eight other bachelors, rented the house, equipped with cooks, servants, and butlers. They hosted many dinner parties and lunches, but the high point was the Sunday brunch starting at eleven in the morning and lasting until at least midafternoon.

To move quickly into the swing of conversation, it was important to have read both the Sunday *New York Times* and *Washington Post* before arriving. Elliot made sure that Lovida and I were invited most Sundays, even if he was to be out of town. Many of the other law clerks showed up, including some former Frankfurter law clerks. Frequent visitors also included columnists Joe Alsop, Scotty Reston, and Tony Lewis. Senators, cabinet officers, justices, and members of the House of Representatives attended from time to time. There were vigorous discussions about the current issues of the day. Whatever was said at the House of Truth was left at the House of Truth. Imagine the excitement for young professionals like me when General George Marshall, Dean Acheson, or one of the Supreme Court justices showed up for Sunday brunch, sharing their insights from living history.

Although the House of Truth continued for many years, it is no more. One of my regrets is that with the Washington Redskins' Sunday football games and with most members of Congress flying home to their districts each weekend to raise money and run for reelection, these informal intergenerational get-togethers have disappeared. We now have to rely on CNN, Fox News, and the Sunday morning talk shows to spoon feed us through the media prism. We seem to have lost the art of passing along wisdom and information from one generation to the next through informal social networks and discourse. It is not a coincidence, in my judgment, that we also seem to have lost some of the respect and civility that characterized communications between generations and among those of very different political and philosophical orientations.

All good things come to an end, as did the 1948 October term of the Supreme Court on the last Monday in June 1949. The justice and Elliot left, but by earlier arrangement I stayed on until August 31 to organize the papers of the term and brief the two incoming Frankfurter law clerks, one of whom, Al Sachs, went on to become dean of Harvard Law School and the other, Fred Fishman, a successful partner in the Kaye Scholer firm in New York.

It bears repeating: the year I spent with Justice Frankfurter was the most rewarding of my life thus far. The opportunity to work closely with Elliot and the beginning of a lasting friendship with Louis Pollak made the year all the more memorable. After the end of the 1948 term, the justice wrote me the following letter (handwritten) from his summer home in Charlemont, Massachusetts:

Dear Bill: Nothing has given me more satisfaction since coming on the Court than the association with you and Elliot—and hardly anything as much. And the root reason, apart from the personal congeniality of both of you, lies in the hold that Law has for you—so comprehensively put by you when you say that "without strict adherence *to reason* and refraining from permitting personal biases to enter adjudication, judges become covert little Hitlers."

You have the judicial temperament and you are constantly disciplining yourself to practice it. The actual form that one's life takes—whether one becomes a judge or not—is to a very large extent a function of contingency. I have never known anyone more equipped, better suited for judging than you. And I ardently hope our country may have that service of those faculties in you. But, it is not in mortals to command success—if success means a particular post. And no truly wise man focuses his ambition on a specific place rather than on a direction for his effort. Too many so-called liberals and high-winded lads at that are seduced by what Justice Brandeis rightly called the "odious doctrine that the end justifies the means."

You, I know, never will pursue false gods—let alone false man. It was a joy to have worked with you for the year, and I shall watch your future with confident, great hopes. My wife joins me in the best of good wishes and may they attend your whole family.

Yours very sincerely, Felix Frankfurter[5]

Another letter from the justice followed early the next year:

Let me say a final word. Chance is a most influential—I think almost a decisive factor in the career of men. What is important is that one should have a direction of purpose as you have and not aim for a particular realization of it, through a particular job. That is almost fatal, for the contingencies of life are too many. What I can say of you with great confidence is what was Justice Holmes's ultimate praise of a man: "I bet on him." I bet on you, whatever choice you may make and whatever the Fates may have in store for you.[6]

And in my volume of the opinions, which we worked on in the October 1948 term, the justice inscribed, "Dear Bill: Here is the 'end-product' of our happy collaboration during the 1948 Term. Everything in it that's wrong is mine exclusively. Sincerely yours, Felix Frankfurter."[7]

The clerkship with Justice Frankfurter, though a one-year job, became a relationship that lasted through the justice's life. Neither was it an employer-employee relationship: we were equals—except in brains, age, pay, and charm. We exchanged differing views, sometimes cathartically; we opened up depths of understanding and new vistas. Through the years we talked often. I visited the justice whenever I was in Washington. Occasionally he would call me in Philadelphia and say, "Why don't you come down tomorrow, Bill. We will take our shoes off and just talk about life, law, and the nation for an hour." He often commented on the sheer brilliance and passionate dedication of his former students Charles Houston and William H. Hastie.

While I was the first American of color to clerk for a justice of the Supreme Court—every justice throughout the history of the United States (until the appointment of Justice Marshall in 1967) was a white male—I was received in the sanctity of the Court with dignity, grace, and respect for the achievements that had brought me there. As I interacted in the justices' chambers and in private social events with the leaders of the nation and the world, I felt for the most part accepted and respected for the views and perspectives that I brought to often lively discussions. And I should not underestimate the value of my presence in giving these white male leaders the opportunity to engage in social interaction with a person of color. Nothing breaks down artificial barriers of discrimination more than human interaction—people of different backgrounds simply getting to know one another as individuals. There was all too little opportunity for such social interaction in those days (and probably not enough even today, according to Attorney General Holder).[8]

The thrill of the ride in those hallowed halls made it easy to forget the Jim Crow conditions in Washington, but there was an occasional reminder of this abhorrent reality. One sunny holiday when the justices were working but the Court's cafeteria was closed, I was in the chambers researching an antitrust case. At noon, Elliot stuck his head into the room and said that all the clerks were going downtown to eat at the Mayflower Hotel, inviting me to join them. I said I would meet them in about ten minutes. Elliot said he would wait for me. When I joined Elliot later, the others had already left for the restaurant, and Elliot said, "It's getting late, Bill, and I've got an awful lot to do. Why don't we take a short walk over to Union Station and have lunch there?" Later that day I walked in on the justice and Elliot, who looked very upset. Elliot confessed that he had called the Mayflower and had been told that it would not serve colored people in its dining room.

There is an interesting coda. In 1946 a student at Howard University was refused admission to a restaurant in downtown Washington. When he returned home, his grandmother said that when she was a young girl all of the restaurants in the city were open to colored people. She recalled that there was an ordinance to that effect. The students could not find it in the 1919 District of Columbia Municipal Code, so one of their professors challenged his class to search for the missing ordinance. They found evidence that when the 1919 code was sent up to Congress, the person who compiled the existing ordinances had purposefully omitted an 1873 prohibition against denying service to colored people because the compiler didn't like it. He argued that the doctrine of desuetude (that is, that the law had fallen in disuse) justified the omission.

The Howard professor and his students brought a lawsuit to enforce the 1873 ordinance. In 1953 the Supreme Court, in *District of Columbia* v. *John R. Thompson Company*, unanimously held that under the 1873 ordinance Washington restaurants cannot refuse service to Negroes. Although the ordinance was not included in the municipal code compiled in 1919 and voted on by Congress, the Court reasoned that it was still valid law because the codification statute explicitly stated that the code should include all the existing, still effective ordinances of the District of Columbia. In a memorandum prepared at the time, Justice Douglas apparently cited Frankfurter's chagrin at my being unable to join my co-clerks at the Mayflower. Even Justice Reed, an austere and very proper southern gentleman, went along with this decision, though, according to several law clerks who served in that term, he was greatly disturbed by the social implications. After all, Justice Reed and his wife lived at the Mayflower Hotel. According to Richard Kluger, in his wonderful book *Simple Justice,* "the Justice was reported to have exclaimed, upon returning from the conference at which the *Thompson* vote was taken: 'Why—why, this means that a nigra can walk into the restaurant at the Mayflower Hotel and sit down to eat at the table right next to Mrs. Reed!'"[9] Thanks to Elliot's thoughtful phone call, Mrs. Reed was at least spared that possible embarrassment in 1949.

PART III

New York, New York

Now is the accepted time, not tomorrow, not some more convenient season. It is today that our best work can be done and not some future day or future year. It is today that we fit ourselves for the greater usefulness of tomorrow. Today is the seed time, now are the hours of work, and tomorrow comes the harvest and the playtime.

—W. E. B. DuBois

FOURTEEN

From the Ivory Tower
to the Working World

*A little less complaint and whining, and a little more dogged
work and manly striving, would do us more credit than a
thousand civil rights bills.*

—W. E. B. DuBois

SUCH IS THE NATURE OF the human condition that life—like a roller coaster ride—can descend from high to low and back to high with rapid acceleration. As my clerkship was coming to an end, I returned on several occasions to my home town of Philadelphia in search of a job. It was time to descend from the ivory tower of the Supreme Court to the working world. I thought I was reasonably well prepared—a graduate summa cum laude of the University of Pennsylvania; an editor of the *Harvard Law Review* graduating first in my class; a commissioned officer during World War II; a law clerk for a highly regarded U.S. Third Circuit judge sitting in Philadelphia; and a clerk for one of the great justices of the U.S. Supreme Court. It wasn't a bad resume for a twenty-nine-year-old kid born and raised in Germantown and nurtured by parents who had contributed greatly to the Philadelphia community.

Was it too much to expect that the City of Brotherly Love would embrace my return? Was I expecting too much from my classmates at Penn and Harvard when I asked them for help in arranging an interview with the established Philadelphia law firms where they were working? Judge Goodrich and Justice Frankfurter wrote many letters and made phone calls. I prepared thoroughly for interviews. Few were offered.

On one occasion I showed up for a scheduled interview. The receptionist looked frustrated as I announced, "Good morning, I am Bill Coleman, and I have an appointment for an interview with Mr. White at 10:00 a.m."

"Yes, Mr. Coleman, I will see if he is available," she replied as she cupped the telephone receiver with her hand and explained the predicament to Mr. White's secretary.

A few minutes later an ashen secretary appeared and with a forced smile said, "I am sorry, Mr. Coleman, but Mr. White had to leave for an urgent meeting with a client and will not be able to keep his ten o'clock appointment."

"I would be happy to wait until he returns," I replied.

"That will not be necessary, Mr. Coleman. He is not likely to return to the office today."

"Well, can you reschedule the appointment?"

"I am afraid not. Mr. White's calendar is completely jammed for the rest of the month."

I did only a little bit better at the next law firm, a few floors up. A young partner came out and chatted with me for about five minutes in the reception area.

"You have a great record, Bill. I would think that you would be a great catch at one of the local law firms. I would suggest you talk to Austin Norris or Sadie and Raymond Pace Alexander. I would be happy to give them a call and arrange an interview for you."

"That won't be necessary," I replied. "They are good friends of my family and I worked at the Alexander firm for three months after I returned from the Army Air Corps. As you know, they specialize in criminal and tort law, but my interests are in business and constitutional law."

"Well, I am sorry we can't help you then, Bill. We're just not hiring right now. Good luck on your job search." He quickly terminated the conversation, stretched out his hand for a quick shake, and turned his back to return to his office and resume his billable hours.

My job search often took me to Boston, Washington, and Wall Street. The result was always the same. "Our clients simply would not understand," remarked one partner with unusual candor. My entry into the mainstream current had hit an eddy. In those days many Wall Street firms did not accept any minorities, including women, Latinos, and Jews and in some cases even Catholics. Law firms tended to cluster around specific ethnicities, but the white Anglo-Saxon Protestants defended their stranglehold on the best business. The major corporations were not any better in reaching out to women and minorities.

With September 1st fast approaching, I recalled a rule of property law from Professor Leach's class. "There should be no gap in the seisin."* I had a wife and two children to support. I picked up the telephone, called Louis Weiss of Paul, Weiss, Wharton, and Garrison in New York City, and got another interview. Elliot's uncle Henry Shattuck had also put in a good word for me with Lloyd K. Garrison. I was hired on the spot with a starting salary of $6,700, slightly more than I had made as a law clerk. This was before the days when Supreme Court law clerks got huge signing bonuses as they do now, often

---

* Possession of a freehold estate. A gap in the chain of ownership could jeopardize free and clear title.

starting off with two to three times the income of the justices for whom they have clerked.

Having beat the streets in Philadelphia, Boston, Washington, and New York for several weeks looking for a job, I was surprised by the gracious offer I received from Weiss. I have often wondered what the backroom conversations might have been among the partners. After all, this may well have been the first time ever a major law firm in any U.S. city had hired a person of color as an associate.

Lovida and I searched for housing in New York. We ruled out Harlem north of 110th Street because we did not want to live in a strictly black neighborhood. We explored the suburbs of New York City as far out as Seacliff, Long Island, and Plainfield, New Jersey, but could not find affordable housing. I had been admitted to the Pennsylvania bar, but to become a member of the New York bar I would have to live in New York state or in a state sharing a border with New York. Fortunately, Pennsylvania touches New York. Lovida and I decided to stay in our house in the Mount Airy neighborhood of Philadelphia, which we had rented out when we moved to Washington for my clerkship.

On September 1, 1949, my alarm went off at 5:50 a.m. in our comfortable house in Mount Airy. I quickly showered, shaved, and dressed and caught the Chestnut Hill local train to the North Philadelphia station. After a change in Newark I transferred to the Hudson Tube to Wall Street. From there I walked at a fast pace (recall that I'd been a quarter miler) to 61 Broadway in the Wall Street financial district where Paul, Weiss was then located, shooting for a 9:35 a.m. arrival. This was my routine six days a week for two years. If all went well—no crisis or emergency or overtime demand—I could leave the office in time to get the 6:45 p.m. train out of Newark and arrive at home by 8:30 p.m. for dinner. On Saturday the Paul, Weiss lawyers usually knocked off around three o'clock, and I could get home by six.

While my commute was a little longer than it would have been from New Jersey or Long Island, there were some advantages. A first-class unlimited ticket for a Pullman car seven days a week then cost only $37 a month, and Pennsylvania Railroad employees did not strike nearly so often as Long Island Railroad employees did. The long commute also enabled me to do a lot of legal work on the train.

Moreover, as a commuter of color in the early 1950s I was easily recognizable. A number of Philadelphia businessmen and stockbrokers acknowledged me as a fellow traveler. Everyone soon got to know my name. Over time several became clients, and one even asked me to join his board of directors when he became the chief executive of a public company in Philadelphia. Through the years it is amazing how many professional opportunities have come to me from chance encounters on trains and planes. It says something for first-class travel—a diminishing commodity in these days of cost cutting.

At that time Paul, Weiss had only about fifty lawyers. Each day one of the firm's practice groups would have a lunch, and on Friday all the attorneys had lunch together. To defray the cost of my daily commute I took advantage of the free lunch by joining the various practice groups. This gave me exposure to interesting work and a broad understanding of the many facets of private practice in a large law firm. It was excellent grounding, for my aspiration was to be a counsel for the situation with an interdisciplinary mastery of the law. I joined both the entertainment group, where I had exposure to such clients as the Playwright Group, Cole Porter, Cinerama, Robert Sherwood, and Arthur Miller, and the litigation or trial group, where I worked with former judge Simon Rifkind, who joined the firm soon after my arrival after a great career as a federal judge for the U.S. District Court for the Southern District of New York. I also got to know Sam Silverman and Mike Mermin, experienced litigators, and the corporate transactional and tax group, which included Randolph Paul, Carol Agger (the wife of Supreme Court justice Abe Fortas and the first woman to become a partner in a major U.S. law firm), Adrian DeWind, and a young lawyer named Mortimer Caplan, who later became U.S. commissioner of internal revenue.

One of my first assignments in the entertainment group was working on the production of Cole Porter's *Kiss Me Kate*, a musical based on Shakespeare's *Taming of the Shrew*. One evening when I was working late at the office my phone rang about eleven o'clock. It was senior partner John Wharton, telling me that Betty Comden, of the preeminent musical comedy duo Comden and Green, had complained that the marquee in Times Square displayed Cole Porter's name in larger letters than the marquee displaying her name and that of Adolph Green on a rival theatre, even though the contract my firm had drafted required that they be exactly the same size. It was my job to measure them, which I did—at three in the morning in driving rain. The letters, as it turned out, were exactly the same size. More than once I've cited this example to young associates who complain about the tedious work involved in reviewing documents or doing research. "If you want to climb the ladder of success, you have to start at the bottom rung," as I did in those predawn hours on Broadway in a rainstorm. At least it's a lot drier in the library.[1]

Another memorable theatrical production for which I did the legal work was *Lost in the Stars*, a musical with book and lyrics by Maxwell Anderson and music by Kurt Weill. It starred Robert Todd Duncan, the first American of color to sing with a major American opera company. Selected by George Gershwin for *Porgy and Bess*, Duncan had played Porgy more than eighteen hundred times, except once in 1936, when Duncan led the cast in a protest against the National Theatre in Washington, vowing that he would never play in a theatre which barred him from purchasing tickets to certain seats because of his race. The theatre relented and allowed its first integrated performance. His son joined the staff of the NAACP Legal Defense Fund.

I also worked with the tax lawyers at the firm who negotiated contracts for the seven authors who made up Playwright, Inc. The writers' income would fluctuate widely from year to year, spiking when a play was produced on Broadway or rights were sold to Hollywood or to the fascinating new medium called television. In those years the federal income tax would hit 90 percent in the top bracket. We negotiated contracts to spread out their income and reduce their tax liability.

Another well-known name partner of the firm, Lloyd K. Garrison, had been appointed special master by the Supreme Court in *State of Georgia* v. *Pennsylvania Railroad, et al.,* an antitrust case in which Georgia had alleged that the Pennsylvania Railroad and other northern interstate railroads had conspired to charge higher freight rates in the South. Garrison, a direct descendant of the abolitionist William Lloyd K. Garrison, asked me to help him prepare his final report to the Supreme Court. There was an enormous amount of work to complete the report before the end of the term, but a side benefit was that Lovida and I would spend the weekends at Garrison's grand summer home on the New England coast, working during the mornings but sailing and swimming in the late afternoon and attending sumptuous dinner parties with their seashore friends. Garrison thanked me for my concentrated effort by arranging a bonus of $2,500—a lot of money in 1950.

Another interesting case involved two leading New York families that had invested in the tobacco business. Thirty years before they had formed a corporation in which each owned 50 percent of the common stock. One family, our client, wanted to dissolve the corporation but the other did not. Under New York law a corporation could be dissolved only if a majority of shareholders voted for liquidation. With each party owning 50 percent of the stock, our client did not have the majority required to dissolve the corporation. Each year a novice associate would be given the file and told to develop legal arguments to resolve the problem. In 1951 the baton was passed to me.

One day as I was riding the train from Philadelphia to New York I decided to read in its entirety the charter of the corporation. I had learned in corporate law that the boilerplate fourth paragraph of a charter of incorporation usually states: "This Corporation shall have perpetual existence." Much to my shock, I read in paragraph four of the charter: "This Corporation shall be in existence for 25 years." I quickened my pace from the Tube station to the law firm and burst into the senior partner's office, the charter in hand, pointing out what I had just read. There were a lot of sheepish and embarrassed looks around the office that day. We quickly moved to dissolve the corporation. A few of the doubters, if there were any, may have thought that the gamble of hiring Bill Coleman might well have been worth the risk.

This practical experience was the first test of the admonition I had learned from Erwin Griswold, the eminent tax lawyer, former dean of Harvard Law School, and former solicitor general, who would interrupt a babbling student and say, "Don't think great thoughts; read the statute."

One of the pleasures of practicing law with an outstanding law firm is being involved in cutting-edge issues in the arts, politics, and international affairs. As a lowly associate I was involved in several transactions that opened up new vistas and stretched my understanding of unfolding current events. One was setting up the initial finances for the Cinerama Corporation, a new technology in the film industry. The second was working on the first Securities and Exchange Commission's registration statement for the Bonds of Israel transaction. Each day I worked on the project I had to rewrite the description of the boundary lines of the State of Israel as the military struggle ebbed and flowed. I learned that no matter how small a part a lawyer may have in an overall client matter, it is important to understand the overall context to which his or her work contributes. While my role might have been small and menial, I would imagine myself as the senior partner in charge of the entire matter and assume that in fulfilling my responsibilities I was responsible for advancing the client's objectives.

The arrival of retiring judge Rifkind was a great event for the law firm. He circulated a memorandum to all lawyers working with him, instructing them to keep him informed of client matters they were working on because he would occasionally bump into clients at social events or when walking in Central Park and he wanted to be able to respond to any questions that might arise. This advice was invaluable, and I've tried to make it a point to keep my law firm partners, associates, and clients informed of the status of matters on which I am working. This is not only a simple courtesy but a matter of good client relationships in the development of continuing business. Yet it always amazes me how rarely attorneys take the trouble to keep their colleagues and clients informed.

Of the three other tips I learned from Simon Rifkind only the first remains valid: always bring to court the written order you wish to have the judge sign; always bring plenty of dimes to call back to the office if you need urgent help on a particular issue; and make sure you get your boss a cab in front of 10 Foley Square in New York City at 4:55 p.m. on Friday, which is twenty-five minutes after the courts adjourn for the week.

Rifkind asked me to work with him in preparing for an oral argument before the Supreme Court. He represented Emerson Radio Phonograph in a challenge to the standards for color television transmission adopted by the Federal Communications Commission. Unfortunately the Court affirmed the commission's action approving the standards proposed by CBS.

One day, Rifkind noticed my chagrin when an important firm client called late one Friday afternoon in the middle of the summer requesting that I prepare certain documents for delivery to him by 10:00 a.m. Monday morning. This was a complex deal, and it was the third time I had received such a request from the client late on a Friday afternoon. Rifkind shared with me one of the many techniques he had learned over a long career: "Stay calm, Bill, think of some papers that the client would have to deliver to you before the end of the day on Friday so you can meet his Monday morning deadline. Then call the client and tell him you plan to work all weekend but will need certain documents that you can pick up at his office or home. I assure you, Bill, your client will say he can't get you the information until Tuesday morning. He will be on his way out the door headed for his summer place in the Hamptons or Martha's Vineyard."

I followed Rifkind's advice and my weekend was saved. This technique has worked well over the years, except when dealing with Thurgood Marshall, as he had no summer home and for him work on a summer weekend was like work on any other weekend or a normal working day. Marshall used to say that the only way to get an advantage over the brilliant Wall Street lawyers, like the acclaimed John W. Davis, was to outwork them on the weekends—a work ethic that would consume my weekends and evenings for several years to come.

As extraordinary as my legal training at Harvard Law School and through my clerkships was, the experience at Paul, Weiss added an entirely new dimension. My opportunity to work with some of the nation's great trial lawyers and corporate, entertainment, and tax lawyers in a law firm that contributed so much to the city and the state of New York—and remains today one of the nation's outstanding law firms—prepared me well for a life practicing law and in public service. Elliot Richardson, after finishing his clerkship with Justice Frankfurter in July 1949, returned to Boston to become an associate at Ropes and Gray. Elliot recommended that Ropes and Gray send me a significant insurance matter, which earned the firm an impressive legal fee, perhaps demonstrating that the gamble on Bill Coleman also paid off in hard currency.

While I was supporting my growing family, Elliot was still the attractive, eligible bachelor—a great catch in the Boston community. Then he met Anne Hazard, a Radcliffe College graduate, who was teaching school in Cambridge. Bright, beautiful, and charming, she was a perfect match for Elliot. Lovida and I attended their wedding in August 1952 at the Hazards' summer home in Rhode Island. We stayed for the weekend with one of Anne's close relatives.

Among the wedding guests were Justice Frankfurter and Judge Learned Hand. Adlai Stevenson had just made his historic acceptance speech at the Democratic National Convention as he prepared to run for president in 1952. At the reception, everyone was quoting Stevenson's ringing words. The only Democrat in the room who did not join in the praise of Stevenson was Frankfurter. Hand kept trying to find out why Frankfurter remained silent. Finally about three o'clock in the morning, after constant badgering and after the bride and groom were long gone, the justice finally confessed, "Do you really want to know why I don't think he would be a good president?" All parties held their breath, thinking there was some skeleton lurking in Adlai Stevenson's closet. Frankfurter continued, "Adlai Stevenson flunked out of Harvard Law School."[2]

In late December 1949, while I was sitting in the library at Paul, Weiss in Manhattan, the telephone rang. "Mr. Coleman, good morning. My name is Thurgood Marshall. I am chief counsel of the NAACP Legal Defense and Educational Fund."

"Yes, sir, Mr. Marshall. I know who you are. I am a great admirer of your work. We met at the Harvard Law School a few years ago when you were visiting with Mr. Houston and Mr. Hastie. I learned a lot from watching you argue before the Supreme Court when I was clerking for Justice Frankfurter."

"Let me get right to the point, Mr. Coleman. Bill Hastie has had some very fine things to say about you. I would like to invite you to a meeting early next month of about twenty-five lawyers to talk strategy. Some of us believe this is the time to bring lawsuits attacking racial segregation head-on in the public schools in the South—kindergarten through twelfth grade. We have a good group coming in January: Robert Carter, Constance Baker Motley, Jack Greenberg, Spottswood Robinson, James Nabrit Jr., George Hayes, and others. John Davis, from Lincoln University [Marshall's alma mater] will also be coming to describe some recent studies on the psychological damage of racial segregation on colored children."

"Let me know the time and place, Mr. Marshall. I'll be there."

FIFTEEN

American History
in Black and White

*We make movies about Malcolm X, we get a holiday to honor
Dr. Martin Luther King, but every day we live with the
legacy of Justice Thurgood Marshall.*

—JUAN WILLIAMS

AFTER I HUNG UP THE phone that December day, a surge of elation quickly
yielded to trepidation. I had just been invited by Thurgood Marshall to a
three-day summit of preeminent civil rights lawyers and legal scholars. We
were going to plot a strategy to take our great nation to the next milestone in
the struggle for equal rights for all Americans regardless of color.

I had a challenging full-time practice at Paul, Weiss, where I was determined to prove the wisdom of Louis Weiss's groundbreaking decision to hire
me. Yet from law school and my clerkships, I recognized the obligation of
lawyers to volunteer their time to serve the public interest. Fortunately, in
the three law firms where I have practiced, there has been a deep tradition of
public service and strong support for voluntary representations in the public
interest, also known as pro bono work.

When I spoke to the partners at Paul, Weiss about my phone call with
Thurgood Marshall, they were enthusiastically supportive. In the ensuing
years I would work full-time at Paul, Weiss and later at the Richardson Dilworth firm, using my spare evenings and weekends to research the law on
segregation and traveling to the Legal Defense and Educational Fund's offices
in New York or Washington to work with Marshall and his brilliant team of
lawyers. The extra workload deprived my family of the fatherly attention they
deserved and increased the burden on Lovida. But I had aspired to be a counsel for any situation, and eliminating the racial caste situation then existing in
the United States clearly needed wise counsel.

Marshall's invitation to join his team was indeed an honor. With Charles
Houston as dean and William Hastie, a young professor, Howard Law School
had become the laboratory in which the civil rights litigation strategy was
incubated. Thurgood Marshall was their prize pupil, having graduated first in
his class in 1933. Harvard Law School dean Roscoe Pound offered him a full

scholarship to study for a doctorate of law degree, as had both Houston and Hastie before him, but Marshall had caught the litigation bug and preferred to pursue his postgraduate education in court with his mentor, Charles Houston. Starting out as a practicing lawyer in his home town of Baltimore, he took on a number of civil rights cases and became affiliated with the local chapter of the NAACP. For a time he shared an office with Baltimore's most prominent attorney of color, Warner T. McGuinn, who had attended Yale Law School on a full scholarship anonymously provided by Mark Twain. By mid-1938, Marshall had succeeded Charlie Houston as the chief counsel to the NAACP in New York, which gave him a platform and the resources to pursue civil rights litigation aggressively throughout the United States.[1]

Marshall's success became legendary. He attracted a team of the best and brightest advocates. Houston and Marshall had teamed up to win a case in the Maryland state courts, *Pearson* v. *Murray,* resulting in the admission of a person of color, Donald Murray, to the University of Maryland Law School. The victory had special meaning for Marshall, who years before had been denied admission to Maryland's law school. Over his career Thurgood Marshall argued more than thirty cases in the Supreme Court and countless more in the lower courts.[2]

Walter White, president of the NAACP, had established the Legal Defense Fund (LDF) in 1939 as a separate nonprofit arm.[3] By the time of Thurgood's phone call to me in December 1949, the baton had passed from Houston and Hastie to Marshall as the leading lawyer of the civil rights movement. A good listener and tireless worker, Marshall had an uncanny ability to ask the right questions and pick the right strategy. Some perhaps thought he was not the best writer or the most articulate member of the team, but his judgment was impeccable. He had an instinct for the arguments and facts that would work, but more important, he was quick to reject advice that fell flat. He worked like an accomplished artist who was able to select the small brush strokes and colors from his palette that would create a pleasing (and persuasive) painting.[4]

Marshall could provoke passion and brutal candor from his many compatriots, but just when emotions were about to explode, he'd diffuse the situation with a joke or folksy story that brought laughter and a reminder that we were all on the same team. Incredibly, he made the twenty-hour days and work-filled weekends fun.

We respected him not only for his charisma and sagacity but also because of his courage. In his lonely vigils through the South fighting the worst forms of racism and building the case for school integration, his life was threatened on several occasions. Yet he always treated his opponents with deference and respect. He could pull up a chair and sit across from a redneck sheriff, engage in small talk, and find enough common ground to get his way.

As I prepared for the meeting with the Marshall team in January 1950, I began to think about the historical context in which we would face the challenges ahead. These memoirs are not the place to tell the complete story of the struggle from slavery to legal equality of opportunity for persons of color; these stories have been told well by many others, beginning with the late John Hope Franklin, in his *From Slavery to Freedom*.[5] I do want to explain, however, the perspectives we brought to the January strategy meeting.

My view of American history differed substantially from what most Americans learned in history books and political science courses. History books are mostly silent about the participation of people of color in the early exploration and settlement of North America. Did you know that the navigator on Columbus's third voyage was a Negro named Pedro Alonso Niño?[6] That among the settlers of Jamestown, Virginia, in 1619 were about twenty indentured servants of color?[7] Or that the prominent Boston preacher Cotton Mather reported in 1721 that a slave named Onesimus had told him how to treat patients for small pox, a precursor to inoculations?[8] That Crispus Attucks, a runaway slave, was the first of the five people killed by the British in the Boston Massacre of 1770?[9] That before the Constitutional Convention, free blacks were eligible to vote in "at least five States"?[10]

Although this kind of information may be conveyed during Black History month or in the popular African American studies programs at some universities, the students who take black studies are not necessarily the ones who need to have a full accounting of American history—black and white. As interesting as the phenomenon of black studies may be, it is far more important, in my judgment, to integrate the role and participation of people of color into regular courses in American history and political science, starting in elementary school.

We all learn in American history about that extraordinary document, the U.S. Constitution, creating the separation of powers and the system of checks and balances, that has worked so well to protect and preserve democratic government—and an exceptional document it is. Soon after the Constitution was adopted, eager to preserve the concepts of liberty embraced by the founders, the states ratified the first ten amendments, the Bill of Rights, securing fundamental freedoms for the citizens of the new country.

Four provisions in the Constitution that are of little interest to most Americans were a major focus for those of us working to end racial discrimination through the legal system. When the Constitution was drafted in 1787 and adopted in 1788, the framers studiously avoided the words *slave* and *slavery*. The words do not appear in the Constitution. That slavery, at least in the South, was implicitly condoned is beyond question. Without using the word *slavery*, Article I, section 2 counts "the Whole number of free Persons . . . and three-fifths of all other Persons" when determining congressional representation and the apportionment of taxes. Article I, section 9 denies Congress the power to prohibit the "importation of . . . Persons" until 1808. Article IV provides that persons cannot escape their duty to render service or labor by traveling to another state, and if they do, the receiving state must return them. Finally, Article V provides that the Constitution itself cannot be amended before 1808 to ban the importation of "certain Persons."[11]

Even the most fervent opponents of slavery among the founders were willing to compromise on this issue in order to create the United States of America with thirteen states and the western territories. Adoption of the Constitution required ratification by at least nine of the thirteen states, and without the support of the slave states the nine votes could not have been secured in 1788. Was the implicit recognition of slavery a pact with the devil? People of color may answer this question differently from the vast majority of whites, for whom unprecedented liberties were enshrined in the founding documents of the nation. For people of color, those often overlooked and untaught constitutional provisions were a great stain on the nation's conscience. The legacy of this immoral compromise reverberated throughout the decades, and eventually we all paid the price in a tragic Civil War and the legacy of racial discrimination in its wake.

It is disturbing that the three-fifths compromise was the resolution of a power struggle between large and small states and between slave and free states. It apparently did not occur to the founding fathers to question the morality of calling any human being three-fifths of a person.[12] The sad fact is that but for a small enlightened minority, the conventional wisdom of the time was that the Negro was biologically and intellectually inferior—neither capable of nor prepared for the rights of citizenship. These misperceptions lingered on for decades, permeating our most venerable academic institutions and even influencing the thought of our most revered leaders.[13]

In retrospect, the three-fifths compromise appears all the more abhorrent because most of the founders were opposed to slavery. They understood the inconsistency between the declarations of liberty and the institution of slavery. The Northwest Ordinance of 1787, adopted by the Congress of the Confederation of the United States, prohibited slavery north of the Ohio River.[14] Yet no such explicit prohibition was incorporated in the later-drafted Constitution. Instead, because the views of the North and South continued to diverge during the period of western expansion, the echoes of the original compromise were replicated in the Missouri Compromise of 1820 and the Compromise of 1850. Some new states would be admitted to the union as free states, and some as slave states.

The nation continued on this regressive path. To implement Article IV of the Constitution, the Fugitive Slave Law was enacted by a southern-dominated

Congress in 1850. An unintended consequence of this contemptible legislation was that it radicalized the North. While some Northerners were willing to overlook the evils of slavery in the South, they deeply resented a law that encouraged bounty hunters to come north to capture escaped slaves and the requirement that Northern federal marshals and magistrates support efforts to hunt down fugitive slaves and return them to their southern masters.[15]

For the legal scholars who were to assemble in January 1950, the nadir of the nation's immoral compromise was the infamous Supreme Court decision in *Dred Scott* v. *Sanford* in 1857. In that case, the Supreme Court held that no person of color—slave or free—was a citizen entitled to sue in federal court. Having denied Dred Scott access to the courts, the Supreme Court nonetheless gratuitously added that the former slave did not become free by living and marrying in a free state or territory. He remained the property of his owner, who could not be deprived of his property without due process of law. The Fifth Amendment that anchored individual rights against tyrannical government was turned on its head. The Constitution protected the property rights of the slave owner but accorded no rights to the person of color. The Court struck down an act of Congress (the Missouri Compromise, which forbade slavery in parts of the western territories) for only the second time (the first being *Marbury* v. *Madison*), ruling that under the Constitution, even Congress could not outlaw slavery in the territories.

In language that completely shattered any aspirations of people of color that the promise of the nation's founding documents was intended to embrace them, Chief Justice Taney wrote the following erroneous interpretation of the founders' intent:

It is too clear for dispute, that the enslaved African race were not intended to be included and formed no part of the people who framed and adopted this declaration; for if the language, as understood in that day, would embrace them, the conduct of the distinguished men who framed the Declaration of Independence would have been utterly and flagrantly inconsistent with the principles they asserted. . . .

They perfectly understood the meaning of the language they used, and how it would be understood by others; and they knew that it would not in any part of the civilized world be supposed to embrace the Negro race, which, by common consent, had been excluded from civilized Governments and the family of nations, and doomed to slavery. . . . The unhappy black race were separated from the white by indelible marks and laws long before established, and were never thought of or spoken of except as property, and when the claims of the owner or the profit of the trader were supposed to need protection."[16]

The highest court in the land had ruled wrongfully that blacks were "so far inferior that they had no rights which the white man was bound to respect."[17]

Taney wrote a supplement to his original fifty-five-page official decision, which was not made public until his biography was published in 1872. Even more vitriolic on race, its purpose was to address any questions that might arise about the scope of his decision. In the supplement Taney referred to the colonialists' view that imported slaves were "ignorant, degraded, savage[s] . . . packed like bales of merchandise and sold in markets like bales of woolen goods or puncheons of rum."[18] Such was the wisdom of the chief justice of the United States in the middle of the nineteenth century. If those of us on the Marshall team ever became weary of the long hours and longer odds of the struggle in which we were engaged, we had only to reread the *Dred Scott* decision to stimulate a burst of adrenaline and rededication.

In his 1858 senatorial campaign Abraham Lincoln denounced the *Dred Scott* decision.[19] After Lincoln's election as president, he appointed Dred Scott's lawyer, Montgomery Blair of Maryland, as postmaster general. Lincoln's attorney general, Edward Bates, issued a legal opinion that even today is not given sufficient attention by legal scholars. Bates, who had never rejected slavery before his cabinet career, was asked whether a black captain of a commercial schooner plying the coastal trade met the requirement of naval law that only a U.S. citizen may command a ship flying the American flag. Bates carefully researched the definition of citizenship dating back to Greek and Roman times and concluded that the *Dred Scott* decision was wrong in declaring that blacks were not citizens. Citizenship, according to Bates, is determined on the basis of place of birth, not color of skin.[20]

On December 20, 1860, sixty-one days before Lincoln assumed office, South Carolina withdrew from the union. As every school child knows, the Civil War began on April 12, 1861, when Confederate general P. G. T. Beauregard's troops fired on the federal Fort Sumter in South Carolina. In 1862 President Lincoln signed the Emancipation Proclamation, effective on January 1, 1863. The proclamation, an exercise of presidential war powers under Article II of the Constitution, applied only to Negro slaves in the states in active rebellion. Lincoln, the careful lawyer, thought that abolishing slavery and conferring U.S. citizenship on all persons of color would have required at least an act of Congress and, more probably, an amendment of the Constitution.

The Civil War essentially ended on April 9, 1865, in Appomattox, Virginia, when General Lee surrendered to General Grant. President Lincoln was assassinated five days later. Once the war was over, the nation addressed the unfinished business of 1787. For Americans of color, the great American democratic experiment really only began in 1865 when the nation adopted the Thirteenth

Amendment (making slavery illegal everywhere in the United States); in 1867 with the adoption of the Fourteenth Amendment (providing that all persons born or naturalized in the United States are citizens thereof and of the state in which they reside and that no state shall deprive any person of due process or equal protection under the law); and in 1870 with the adoption of the Fifteenth Amendment (providing that no citizen can be denied the right to vote by states or the federal government because of his or her race, color, or previous condition of servitude). Believe it or not, it would be many more decades before the Supreme Court would breathe life into these pillars of equality.

Over the veto of President Andrew Johnson, Congress also passed the Civil Rights Act of 1866, providing citizenship and federal court protection for the civil rights and immunities of the freed slaves. Among the rights conferred by the act were the right to enter into and enforce contracts, to buy, sell, and own property, to sue, and most important, the right to "full and equal benefit of all laws and proceedings for the security of person and property."[21] To secure passage, John Bingham, the Radical Republican leader in the House of Representatives, struck language from the bill that expressly prohibited racial discrimination. Then, arguably to achieve the same purpose, Bingham introduced the Fourteenth Amendment, which prohibited state action that denied persons equal protection under law. The amendment was ratified on July 9, 1868. The significance of these actions would be the subject of much debate and research by the Marshall team.[22]

In 1870 and 1875 Congress passed additional civil rights legislation, implementing the enforcement provisions of the Fourteenth Amendment. The Civil Rights Act of 1875 declared that all people regardless of race or color were guaranteed "the full and equal enjoyment of the accommodations . . . of inns, public conveyances on land or water, theaters, and other places of public amusement" and that no one was to be disqualified for jury service "because of race, color or previous condition of servitude." Despite the broad reach of his legislation, Senator Sumner failed in his effort to include desegregated schools among the guaranteed rights.[23]

In March 1867, under the leadership of Thaddeus Stevens and Charles Sumner, Congress passed the first of four reconstruction acts to facilitate the integration of former slaves into the political and economic life of the South. Under Radical Reconstruction, voters elected one U.S. senator and ten representatives of color to Congress as well as hundreds of local and state officials.

These giant steps forward were short lived. The ascendancy of Andrew Johnson to the presidency undermined support for the Republican majority in Congress.[24] In eleven short years much of the progress unraveled. The razor-close 1876 election was thrown into the House, which appointed a commission to resolve disputed electoral votes. The ultimate winner would depend on how the Electoral College counted the votes of three southern states, Florida, Georgia, and Alabama. The Hayes-Tilden Compromise of 1876 settled the political matter. To win the election (by one electoral vote), Republican candidate Rutherford B. Hayes compromised away many of the Republican Reconstruction principles. More troubling, he agreed to withdraw immediately all federal troops from the South who were there to protect the rights of Negroes and enforce the Reconstruction laws. Once the federal presence was withdrawn, the South returned with a vengeance to a path toward state-mandated segregation.

The Jim Crow era began in the South and spread to much of the North. Having regained political power, the white-dominated southern states began to pass laws segregating the races, creating obstacles to voters of color, and enacting the Black Codes, which imposed tightly restrictive regulations on the movement and behavior of former slaves.[25] Instead of facilitating the Negro's transition from the total dependence of slavery, these laws suppressed any prospect of education, mobility, or economic progress, approximating the conditions of slavery. Exacerbating the legal suppression, groups like the Ku Klux Klan, the Knights of the Golden Circle, the Sons of Washington, the White Leagues, and the Red Shirts fanned the flames of hatred. Racial discrimination took a violent turn. Blacks were humiliated and abused. Lynchings were commonplace.[26]

There was nary a word in my schoolboy history texts about this sordid chapter in American history, but it has been well documented by many authors. Again, I turn to *Simple Justice* for the context in which these regressive laws and practices set the stage for the *Brown* v. *Board of Education* team. Richard Kluger presents a compelling example: "A black charged with murdering a white man was seized and hauled to the local theater, where an audience was invited to witness his hanging. Receipts were to go to the murdered white man's family. To add interest to the benefit performance, seat holders in the orchestra were invited to empty their revolvers into the swaying black body while those in the gallery were restricted to a single shot."[27] That same year, Congress and President Taft declined to advance an antilynching bill or enforce the Fourteenth Amendment because "it was a matter for States to handle."[28]

A succession of presidents turned a deaf ear. Even presidents of great achievement in other areas sat by silently while Jim Crow laws proliferated. During Woodrow Wilson's administration, the previously integrated District of Columbia became highly segregated. Franklin Roosevelt perpetuated a racial caste system in the military and in federal housing policy—the sins of which are visited on inner-city children to this day.

Perhaps more troubling—shocking, in fact—for those of us on Thurgood Marshall's legal team is that almost all Supreme Court decisions from the end of the Civil War until *Missouri ex rel. Gaines* v. *Canada* (1938) were decided adversely to persons of color. One exception was the 1879 opinion in *Strauder* v. *West Virginia* overturning a West Virginia statute that limited jury service to white males, on grounds that the Fourteenth Amendment was "primarily designed" to eliminate discrimination against the colored race. Frequently cited by the LDF, the decision was mostly ignored by the courts until *Brown* v. *Board of Education*. Instead, six years after the adoption of the Fifteenth Amendment, Chief Justice Morrison Waite wrote in *United States* v. *Reese* that the Fifteenth Amendment did not confer on Americans of color a right to vote. Only a state could grant such a right. According to Waite, the Fifteenth Amendment merely provides that a person may not be denied a right to vote solely because of his race. Poll taxes, grandfather provisions, and biased literacy tests were not a problem as long as they did not expressly exclude Negroes on the basis of race. In *United States* v. *Cruikshank,* Chief Justice Waite again held that the right of suffrage is not a necessary attribute of natural citizenship and that the actions of a riotous mob that broke up a meeting of Negro voters was not state action under the Fourteenth Amendment. In *United States* v. *Harris,* the Court found no violation of the Fourteenth Amendment when an armed mob took a group of Negroes from the custody of the sheriff, killing one of them and beating the others. The lynch mob was not judged to be state action.

In the *Civil Rights Cases* of 1883 the federal government attempted to enforce the Civil Rights Act of 1875 barring discrimination in public accommodations. Writing for the Supreme Court, Justice Joseph Bradley declared that Congress had exceeded its authority under the Fourteenth Amendment, which, in his reading, outlawed discriminatory action only when taken by the states themselves and not private persons. Associate Justice John Marshall Harlan dissented. Addressing various state ruses designed to set up insurmountable obstacles to voters of color, the Supreme Court in *Williams* v. *Mississippi* refused to find such restrictive codes unconstitutional on the ground that they did not expressly discriminate against Negroes.

For Thurgood Marshall's team the huge boulder blocking the path was the 1896 Supreme Court decision in *Plessy* v. *Ferguson.* On June 7, 1882, a light-skinned colored man named Homer Adolph Plessy boarded an East Louisiana interstate railway train in New Orleans and sat down in a first-class car reserved for whites.* The conductor asked him to move to the car

*Plessy was "seven-eighths Caucasian and one-eighth African blood; the mixture of colored blood was not discernible in him." *Plessy* v. *Ferguson* 163 U.S. 537, 538 (1896). In bringing the suit to challenge the Louisiana Jim Crow law, apparently a group of people of color and the railroad company (which found the restriction burdensome) thought that the light-skinned Plessy would show the absurdity of the segregation law.

for colored passengers. When Plessy refused to move he was arrested and brought before Judge John Ferguson of the New Orleans criminal court. The court rejected Plessy's argument that the rail car segregation law violated the Fourteenth Amendment. The ruling was appealed to the Louisiana Supreme Court, which granted Plessy's petition to appeal to the Supreme Court of the United States.

Writing for the Court, Associate Justice Henry Billings Brown stated that while the objective of the Fourteenth Amendment was to enforce equality of the two races before the law, it was not intended to abolish distinctions based on color or to enforce social equality or a comingling of the two races on terms unsatisfactory to either. Justice Brown proclaimed that laws requiring separation of the races do not necessarily imply the inferiority of either race and are generally recognized as within the competency of state legislatures in the exercise of their police power. In support of this assertion, Brown referred to the widespread practice of school segregation, citing the *Roberts* v. *City of Boston* opinion of the Massachusetts Supreme Judicial Court in 1849, which upheld a decision by the Boston school committee to segregate children of color into separate schools. (Brown's opinion failed to mention that the Massachusetts legislature voted to prohibit school segregation just six years after the state court's decision in *Roberts*.) Justice Brown concluded that state statutes requiring segregation of public facilities by race were a reasonable exercise of state police powers, provided the facilities were equal, because segregation reflected "established usages, customs, and traditions of the people" and were intended to promote "their comfort, and the preservation of the public peace and good order."[29]

Again, the first Justice Harlan dissented, as he did in 316 other Supreme Court cases during his thirty-three years on the Court. Harlan's eloquent dissent went to the heart of the matter: segregation of public facilities, under the guise of giving equal accommodations for whites and blacks, was intended to protect the dominant status of the white race and prevent the freed slaves from the full enjoyment of the blessings of liberty as the Fourteenth Amendment required. Harlan's solitary voice for more than a third of the century offered those of us on the Marshall team hope that ultimately reason would prevail, despite the Supreme Court precedents to the contrary.[30]

When the triumvirate of Charles Houston, Bill Hastie, and Thurgood Marshall began their courageous march to end state-sanctioned racial discrimination, there had been at least five Supreme Court decisions that held unequivocally that state-mandated segregation in the public schools, transportation, and other governmental facilities was lawful and did not violate any federal constitutional or statutory provision. In 1914 the Supreme Court, in *McCabe* v. *Atchison, Topeka and Santa Fe Railway*, upheld an Oklahoma law requiring separate but equal accommodations for whites and blacks but also held that the railroad did not have to provide sleeping and dining cars for blacks if there was insufficient demand to fill the separate car. Sadly, among the majority in that decision was Justice Holmes.

In *Gong Lum* v. *Rice*, Chief Justice William Howard Taft upheld a decision by a Mississippi school superintendent to deny admission to a nine-year-old Chinese girl to attend an all-white public school. In dismissing her petition, the chief justice wrote in 1927 that a full argument was unnecessary because the same question had been many times decided to be within the constitutional power of the state legislature without interference by the federal courts. Taft cited an earlier unanimous opinion by Justice Harlan in 1899 in the case of *Cumming* v. *Richmond County Board of Education* in which the Court rejected a demand by Negro parents that the school board close the county's white school until the black high school was reopened. While the opinion was something of an aberration for Harlan, it demonstrated the risk of over-reaching by the plaintiffs. Closing the white school would not have helped the children of color and would have denied white youngsters an education.

The Marshall strategy team noted that in both the *Gong Lum* and *Cumming* cases the issues presented and the remedies requested—overruling a school superintendent's decision of what constitutes "colored" and taking punitive action against white students by closing their school—created a high hurdle for a successful outcome. It was unlikely at that time that a direct attack on school segregation, or even an attack on the inequality of facilities provided under the separate-but-equal doctrine, would have prevailed, but the additional Supreme Court precedent implicitly accepting the *Plessy* doctrine now made a challenge all the more difficult. Defining the right issue, presenting the best factual case, seeking the appropriate remedy, and selecting the best forum would be critical tactical decisions if additional adverse precedents were to be avoided.

The above digression has not been a pleasant accounting of American history, and it is not the story most school children learn even today. But it is the historical experience of Americans of color. It explains, I believe, the passion and commitment of Thurgood Marshall and his team and the odds they faced as they prepared for their greatest courtroom battle. Yet the storm clouds rising had their silver lining. A string of modest successes had chipped away at the unconscionable precedents that besmirched the promise of the post–Civil War amendments. Those successes were the fruits of the Houston-Hastie-Marshall triumvirate, on which our strategy sessions would build.

SIXTEEN

Chipping Away at *Plessy*

*It is the measure of the Negro's circumstance that, in America,
the smallest things usually take him so very long, and that,
by the time he wins them, they are no longer little things but
miracles.*

—Murray Kempton

Charles Houston was the anchor and architect of the strategy—and his strategy yielded some significant successes in laying the foundation for a frontal attack on public school segregation. Houston was not only a brilliant strategist and mesmerizing advocate, he was above all a mentor and teacher who would ensure that progress would not depend on the fortunes of a single leader. When he died of a massive heart attack at the age of fifty-four, our shock and sadness quickly turned to resolve and renewed dedication to see his mission fulfilled.[1]

Houston, Hastie, and Marshall, with their strong support team, searched for the point of greatest vulnerability in the southern wall of resistance. They surmised that at least the more open-minded white southern judges would understand why it was important that lawyers of color have the opportunity to attend the same law school as other members of the local bar, their colleagues on the bench, and elected officials. As successful lawyers, these judges would understand the benefits of professional networking in their own legal careers.

For this reason, the first Supreme Court case successfully brought in 1938 by Houston and Marshall, *Missouri ex rel. Gaines* v. *Canada,* involved law school admissions. The state of Missouri cleverly sought to satisfy *Plessy's* separate-but-equal test without investing in a separate law school for persons of color. Instead, the state offered to pay the law school tuition of any colored person in Missouri who was accepted in any law school in the country, including Harvard, Yale, or Columbia. Houston and Marshall convinced the Supreme Court that the alternative educational opportunity, even at an elite law school, would not be equal to what Lloyd Gaines would get at the University of Missouri, where he would rub elbows with the lawyers who more likely would become fellow members of the bar, judges, and government officials.

Although the Court upheld the separate-but-equal doctrine of *Plessy*, it made clear that it would begin to examine carefully the facts underlying the state's assertion of equal treatment. More important, the Court recognized the right of a Negro citizen to assert a claim of unequal treatment and obtain a remedy.

Marshall's next Supreme Court victory was in *Sipuel* v. *Oklahoma State Board of Regents* (1948). The Court held that the plaintiff, Ada Sipuel, could not be denied admission to the University of Oklahoma Law School unless Oklahoma established a law school for persons of color. When Oklahoma quickly assembled a law school, admittedly far inferior to the established university, Sipuel wisely turned down the offer of admission. Marshall came back to the Supreme Court, arguing that the university had defied the Court's mandate. But the Court was unwilling to go further, holding in a 7-2 decision that the *Sipuel* case did not squarely present the issue of whether the mere establishment of a separate law school for Negroes was sufficient to satisfy the equal protection clause.

In *Gaines* and *Sipuel*, the NAACP Legal Defense Fund challenged the practical implications of the doctrine of separate but equal. Houston and Marshall argued that true equality in a law school education involved far more than the physical facilities. It required the free exchange of ideas and opinions among the students and faculty. Marshall argued that excluding one group on the basis of race automatically imputes a badge of inferiority to the excluded group. Having suffered a setback in the Court's refusal to follow through on its *Sipuel* opinion, Marshall again took the issue head on in *Sweatt* v. *Painter* in 1950, involving the University of Texas Law School. Although Texas had established a law school for persons of color several years earlier, Marshall was able to persuade the Court that it was not equal to the prestigious state university law school. The Court ordered that Hemon Marion Sweatt be admitted to the University of Texas Law School.

In his brief before the Supreme Court, Marshall argued for the first time that *Plessy* v. *Ferguson* should be overruled. The main focus of his argument was that segregation was illegal because true equality could never be achieved with provision of separate facilities for persons of color. Chief Justice Fred Vinson wrote the opinion for the Court in *Sweatt* on the more narrow ground that the new law school for Negroes simply did not provide an equal educational opportunity. The chief justice noted that the University of Texas Law School possessed qualities of greatness, which included the reputation of its faculty, the influence of the alumni, and its standing in the community. The chief adroitly avoided the issue of whether a state could meet its constitutional obligation by establishing a separate but equal law school for Negroes. Nevertheless, this was the first time the Supreme Court had ordered that a student of color be admitted to a school previously open only to white students, on the ground that the colored school established by the state failed to offer an equal educational opportunity.

One of the ironies of Supreme Court practice is that by the time the lofty abstract principles reach the Court, the reality on the ground has often shifted. While *Gaines* and *Sweatt* seemed great victories for Marshall and *Sipuel* a disappointment, the reality was quite different. By the time Gaines was admitted to Missouri's law school, he had simply disappeared without a trace.[2] Sweatt actually attended law school at the University of Texas, but he was met with burning crosses and racial slurs. He became ill, divorced his wife, and flunked out during his second year.[3] Ada Sipuel fared much better. Fearing further litigation, the Oklahoma attorney general had a change of heart. On the recommendation of the sympathetic university president, Sipuel was admitted to the university law school, where she was welcomed by the white students, who helped her catch up after her late start in the school year. Although during her first semester she was required to sit in a separate section in the back of the classroom, marked "colored," the signs came down in the second semester and she moved to the front row.[4]

On the same day the *Sweatt* decision was announced, June 5, 1950, Chief Justice Vinson issued an opinion in *McLaurin* v. *Oklahoma State Regents for Higher Education*. The sixty-eight-year-old George McLaurin had been admitted to the doctoral program at the University of Oklahoma but had been subject to humiliating restrictions. He was forced to sit alone in separate sections of the classroom, the library, and the cafeteria. The Court found these restrictions impermissibly handicapped his graduate instruction, impairing his ability to study and exchange views with other students. Artfully avoiding the broader issues raised by school segregation, the Court recognized the importance of the "intellectual comingling of students" and acknowledged the harmful effects of the practice of segregation. Thurgood Marshall once told me that the studious, elderly McLaurin was the perfect plaintiff: his case was free of the sexual undercurrents often at play in desegregation cases, where white parents feared their perception of the social intermingling of their young daughters with testosterone-charged adolescent boys of color.

The Court issued a third civil rights decision on that same day involving *Henderson* v. *United States*, one of the few cases that was not brought by the Thurgood Marshall team. Elmer Henderson complained that the Southern Railway had forced him to sit separately in the dining car behind a curtain. In a unanimous opinion by Justice Harold Burton, the Court again sidestepped the larger issue of separate but equal but held that the discriminatory and humiliating treatment of Henderson was not permissible.

My first strategy meeting with the Marshall team in January 1950 preceded the favorable Supreme Court decisions in Sweatt, McLaurin, and Henderson issued in June of that year. But as the Marshall team later assessed the three decisions issued on June 5, 1950, the LDF reluctantly had to concede that in each case the Court simply had figured out a clever way to affirm the *Plessy* doctrine of separate but equal by finding the treatment unequal. Arguably the LDF had not chipped away at the underlying doctrine but simply forced the Court to apply it in cases of egregious inequality. Unless the Court confronted directly the legality of segregation itself, we might have to spend the rest of our lives arguing the inequality of education and transportation facilities on a case-by-case basis. Clearly, and most important, if Americans of color were to be fully integrated into the mainstream of American culture, the system of legal apartheid would have to be abolished once and for all.

Increasingly, Marshall had raised the argument in his briefing that it was time to outlaw state-mandated segregation and overrule *Plessy v. Ferguson,* but tactically he did not want to risk a loss on the issue that would further strengthen the Court's commitment to that despicable doctrine. Realizing the Court's propensity to seek the narrowest possible basis for a ruling, he always gave the Court the opportunity to apply the *Plessy* doctrine and find that the facilities offered to persons of color were unequal. Had he been too timid? As he consulted a broader group of advisers, the fundamental question he asked was whether now was the time to mount a frontal attack on school segregation per se in public elementary and high schools. If so, how should that objective be achieved tactically? The Court had begun to acknowledge in *Sweatt* and *McLaurin* that in certain circumstances segregation by race could adversely affect a student. But these cases involved individual adults voluntarily pursuing a graduate professional degree. How would the Court react to a broad-based challenge to all segregated public schools, K–12, and all the raw emotion, political volatility, and cultural tradition implicated by such a challenge?

I have presented here a summary of my views on the historical context as I began to work with the Marshall team. The comprehensive story is told with extraordinary clarity, passion, and insight in Richard Kluger's seminal book, *Simple Justice,* which should be read and reread by all Americans who are interested in a full and fair accounting of American history.

SEVENTEEN

The *Brown* Team

Never doubt that a small group of thoughtful, committed citizens can change the world. Indeed, it is the only thing that ever has.

—MARGARET MEAD

IN JANUARY 1950 I WALKED into the conference room of the NAACP's Legal Defense and Educational Fund, Inc., on West 40th Street in Manhattan. We sometimes called it the "Inc" Fund. Some faces were familiar and some were not, but over the next five years I came to know the most dedicated, energetic, and innovative group of people whom I've ever had the privilege of working with. Many went on to extraordinary careers as judges, law school deans, and practicing lawyers, where they continue to improve the nation's laws.

Like Marshall, Robert Lee Carter had graduated from Lincoln University and had been a star pupil at Howard Law School under the tutelage of Hastie and Houston before receiving a master of law degree at Columbia. Carter came to the LDF in 1944, at the age of twenty-seven, after a career in the Army Air Corps, where he'd been a troublemaker, fighting racial discrimination and segregation at every turn. He became Marshall's deputy and ran the staff with an iron fist, making sure that court deadlines were met and freeing up Marshall to travel the country. He was more radical than most of his colleagues and was more interested in results than theoretical strategizing. Carter was the lead attorney in the Topeka school desegregation case, one of the five cases that were consolidated for argument in *Brown* v. *Board of Education*. He later served as general counsel of the NAACP under Roy Wilkins and, even though a Democrat, was appointed by President Nixon as a U.S. district judge for the Southern District of New York. In 2007 New Jersey named its state education building after Judge Carter. In the 1950s Carter and Marshall were an effective duo, complementing each other in skill and temperament, although they later went their separate ways.

Spottswood W. Robinson III was also a Howard Law School graduate and a student of Houston's and Hastie's. He and his law partner, Oliver W. Hill

Jr., were in charge of the Virginia school desegregation cases. Robinson later became the dean of Howard Law School and was appointed to the U.S. Court of Appeals for the District of Columbia Circuit, where he became its chief judge. Robinson was Marshall's cerebral soul mate, a pragmatic strategist, a graceful writer, and a smooth oral advocate. He was respected for his mastery of the record and responsiveness to judicial interrogation, even by unsympathetic southern judges. The tall, balding Oliver Hill had been a classmate of Thurgood Marshall, with whom he had competed for first place. Fiercely competitive and focused, he was a skillful trial lawyer and was the first person of color to serve on the Richmond, Virginia, city council.[1] He lived to the age of 100 and received the Presidential Medal of Freedom. Virginia named its Court of Appeals building after him.

Constance Baker Motley, a graduate of Columbia Law School, had passed the bar a couple of years earlier and joined the LDF as its expert on housing issues. Quiet but tenacious, she earned the respect of her male compatriots for her persistent advocacy. As a woman of color, Motley had her own quiet battles in the mostly male macho atmosphere of the civil rights warriors. She later became U.S. district court judge for the Southern District of New York, and was eventually appointed its chief judge.[2]

One of the few white faces around the table was that of Jack Greenberg, a twenty-five-year-old lawyer just out of Columbia Law School. After many years as director-counsel of the LDF, Greenberg became dean of the College of Columbia University.[3]

Robert R. Ming Jr. was a graduate of the University of Chicago Law School and a member of its law review. He practiced law for the government and in a private firm, was a professor of law at Howard for ten years, and later taught at the University of Chicago. An excellent writer, he drafted many of the key briefs.

James M. Nabrit Jr., who had grown up in poverty in southwestern Georgia, worked his way through Northwestern Law School, graduating at the top of his class as an editor of the school's law review. He became a successful partner in a black law firm in Houston, representing Native Americans in oil well disputes and blacks in voting rights cases. He later served as dean of the Howard Law School, president of Howard University, and an ambassador to the United Nations. His son James Nabrit III, whom I had taught to swim at my father's Camp Emlen in Pennsylvania, also attended. A graduate of Bates College and Yale Law School, he joined the LDF right out of law school. His father and George Hayes were the lead counsel in the Washington school desegregation case. George Edward Chalmers Hayes graduated from Brown University and Howard Law School; he later taught law at Howard and served as its general counsel. Although he had served a term on the District of Columbia school board, he was not reappointed because of his spirited advocacy for desegregation.

Another young attorney who joined us was Charles T. Duncan, the son of the burnished baritone, Robert Todd Duncan. A graduate of Dartmouth and captain of its ski team, Charles graduated from Harvard Law School. He later became a professor and dean of Howard Law School and corporate counsel to the District of Columbia.

There were several white faces on the team: Louis H. Pollak, my friend and fellow associate at Paul, Weiss; Charles Black, a quirky Texan and professor at Yale Law School; and Jack Weinstein, a professor at Columbia Law School and evidence expert. Weinstein later became a federal district judge for the Eastern District of New York.

In our several strategy sessions at the offices of the Legal Defense Fund over many months, Thurgood Marshall invited us to think outside the box. Should we launch a frontal assault on public school segregation, K–12, asking the Court to overrule *Plessy*? Were a majority of the Supreme Court justices prepared to take on such a socially explosive issue? Would President Truman support our position? How would the moderate Republican and Democratic elected leaders respond? Would we get a fair shake from the national press? Would most Americans of color, especially Southerners, support our position? What about Negro principals and school teachers who might fear losing their jobs? Would Chief Justice Vinson be willing to overrule *Plessy*, a decision he had worked so hard to distinguish in *Sweatt* and *McLaurin*? Should we build a strong case based on sociological and psychological evidence on the debilitating effects on colored children of school segregation, or should we focus on a purely legal analysis of the constitutional amendments and judicial precedent?

Few arguments were off limits. Robert Ming suggested we argue that being a Negro was in fact belonging to a religion. Applying the Supreme Court precedents holding that the First Amendment was incorporated into the Fourteenth Amendment, we could argue that any state action discriminating against Negroes was a violation of the free exercise of religion. He also invoked several provisions of the United Nations Charter. According to *Missouri* v. *Holland*, interpreting Article VI of the Constitution, the U.N. Charter treaty provisions on human rights would override even an interpretation of the Fourteenth Amendment such as that in *Plessy* v. *Ferguson*.[4]

As a younger, newer member of the team, I listened in awe to the debates, forming my own views from the heated arguments among the battle-scarred veterans. I supported Robinson and Carter's passionate plea for a strong frontal no-holds-barred attack on segregation per se. But I was wary of Jimmy

Nabrit's view that we should not even allege the inferiority of the unequal colored schools lest we give the Vinson court yet another opportunity to sidestep the issue of *Plessy*'s continuing constitutional validity. Like Marshall, I favored the hedge strategy—the "two-string bow." We would argue that at the very least the facilities were inferior and therefore unconstitutional but also that separate facilities were inherently unequal. We would never concede equality without desegregation, but we would not risk a total loss if the Court proved unwilling to overrule *Plessy*.

I was skeptical of Carter's proposal to use the research of psychologist Kenneth B. Clark (a City College of New York professor) on the adverse effect of segregation on black children. Clark and his wife, Mamie, had conducted tests on Negro children using black and white dolls. The Negro children liked the white dolls better—they thought white dolls were smarter and prettier. I agreed with Robinson that we should make a purely legal case.[5] From my clerkship days I imagined with horror how the skeptical justices might derisively view evidence based on children's dolls. James Patterson has quoted me as saying, "Jesus Christ, those damn dolls! I thought it was a joke."[6] But Marshall was persuaded by Carter to use whatever sociological or psychological evidence supported our position.[7] And some say it worked.[8]

Each lawyer in those meetings knew to the very last footnote every opinion of the Supreme Court and every decision of a state or federal court having to do with race. They knew all the civil rights statutes from the first one enacted in 1866 and every opinion interpreting them. Although the knowledge and experience of my colleagues was intimidating, the one thing I brought to the table was an innovative look at how we might apply precedents in other areas of the law. During my military service, which interrupted my law school education, I had methodically reviewed my case books and class notes at least once a month. I had a good retention of the case law in a wide area of legal disciplines.

When Judge Hastie visited the group he reinforced my interest in exploring analogous case law, pointing out that it was easier to induce a federal judge, especially one born and educated in the South, to extend established legal principles to the issue of race than to tackle the issue of racial discrimination head-on. This is how Hastie and Marshall had approached the Democratic Party primary voting cases. Overruling its own precedent, the Supreme Court found that the exclusion of black voters in the Democratic Party primaries in the South did not violate the Fifteenth Amendment because party primaries were private organizations and "state action" did not apply. Hastie and Marshall invoked the Supreme Court decision in a criminal case, *United States* v. *Classic,* holding that federal law prohibited fraud in both party primaries and federal general elections. Based on this precedent, they argued that the

Fifteenth Amendment must also apply to primary elections. The Supreme Court agreed in *Smith* v. *Allwright* (1941) and *Terry* v. *Adams* (1953), also known as the Jaybird Democratic Primary case.

The Legal Defense Fund's successful strategy in the voting rights cases was critical to our litigation planning. We invoked Charles Houston's argument that persons of color could not be denied accommodation in a Pullman car as that would violate provisions in the Interstate Commerce Act requiring railroads not to discriminate among its customers, even though Congress was addressing price discrimination in the statute.[9] As the group sought to broaden our scope of inquiry we invited leading legal scholars like Paul Freund, Benjamin Kaplan, and Dean Griswold to meet with us and share their insights, which they willingly and eagerly did.

We decided to declare war on public school segregation. Total victory meant getting the Supreme Court to overrule the doctrine of separate but equal in *Plessy* v. *Ferguson*. We worked days and nights, weekends, and sometimes twenty-two-hour days to develop and implement a strategy that would create a record optimizing our chance for success in the Supreme Court. The strategy required that we file five cases, four in the federal district courts in South Carolina, Virginia, Kansas, and the District of Columbia and one in the state court in Wilmington, Delaware. Jack Greenberg suggested that the chief judge of the Court of Chancery, Collin Seitz, might be more favorable to our position than the judges in the federal district court in Delaware.

After a fairly tense debate we concluded that in Kansas, South Carolina, and Virginia, each claim in the complaint and other pleadings should allege the unconstitutionality of a state statute or constitution. This would establish jurisdiction in a federal three-judge district court proceeding and a direct right of appeal from an adverse decision to the Supreme Court. Thurgood Marshall was concerned that a three-judge court in the South would ensure a loss at the lower court level, whereas our prospects would be better if we were to draw a sympathetic single judge and jury.[10] Marshall knew some judges who were sympathetic to our cause, but there was no guarantee they would be assigned the case.

I argued that the trial court provided the opportunity to make a strong record, but the ultimate objective was to persuade the Supreme Court to overrule *Plessy*. The direct right of appeal would substantially increase the likelihood of Supreme Court review. If we followed the usual path of a trial before a single judge, the normal appeal would be to a federal circuit court consisting mostly of southern judges, who in any event would not be in a position to overrule Supreme Court precedent. And if we lost in the circuit court, which was likely, the Supreme Court would have complete discretion in deciding whether to grant certiorari to review the appellate court's decision. Based on my clerkship experience, I worried that a number of the justices would probably prefer to avoid the controversy. I thought it likely that certiorari would be denied.

Marshall raised the concern that since school segregation was often the policy of a local school district, an allegation of the unconstitutionality of a state statute might be a stretch in some jurisdictions. After a full airing of the pros and cons we reached a consensus that we were far more likely to ensure review by the Supreme Court through a three-judge panel. Our tactical consensus worked.

Bob Carter led the team in Kansas. The team presented evidence that showed the inherent harm to the Negro child of a segregated classroom. Their expert witness, Kenneth B. Clark, testified that the differential treatment of children based solely on their race had an adverse effect on their ability to learn. The court in Kansas made findings that accepted Clark's testimony but held as a matter of law that racial segregation did not violate the Fourteenth Amendment. Walter Huxman wrote for the three-judge panel:

> If segregation within a school as in the *McLaurin* case is a denial of due process, it is difficult to see why segregation in separate schools would not result in the same denial. Or if the denial of the right to comingle with the majority group in higher institutions of learning as in the *Sweatt* case and gain educational advantages resulting there from is lack of due process, it is difficult to see why such denial would not result in the same lack of due process if practiced in the lower grades.

Judge Huxman acknowledged that these decisions involved only higher education and that the Supreme Court had not overruled *Plessy*.[11] The court's findings of fact were even more helpful. The eighth finding of fact stated that

> segregation of white and colored children in public schools has a detrimental effect upon the colored children. The impact is greater when it has the sanction of law; for the policy of separating the races is usually interpreted as denoting the inferiority of the Negro group. A sense of inferiority affects the motivation of the child to learn. Segregation with the sanction of law, therefore, [deprives Negro children of] benefits they would receive in a racially integrated school.

The record proved immensely helpful.

In the Virginia case similar evidence was introduced. Unfortunately for Spottswood Robinson and Oliver Hill, the commonwealth mounted a substantial defense, investing significant resources to counter the plaintiffs' evidence. The court made a finding of fact that racial segregation did not have an adverse effect on the Negro child and was not unconstitutional.

In South Carolina, the court upheld the constitutionality of the segregated schools, noting that the contradictory evidence on the effect of segregation on colored children raised a matter of legislative inquiry and did not implicate a constitutional right. Judge Waites Waring filed a courageous, fiery twenty-page dissent, concluding that "segregation is *per se* inequality."[12]

In Delaware, Collins Seitz, the state chancellor, ruled that the colored schools were vastly inferior and a denial of equal protection, ordering the white schools to admit the children of color. He further suggested that separate schools might be inherently unequal and invited the Supreme Court to consider this further. Seitz's spirited decision was affirmed by the Delaware Supreme Court.[13]

The case in the District of Columbia presented difficult legal and factual issues. The constitutional challenge was based not on the Fourteenth Amendment, which applies only to state action, but on the due process clause of the Fifth Amendment. At the time the Fifth Amendment was adopted in 1791, slavery was an accepted practice in the South and arguably Congress had implicitly approved the District of Columbia's segregated school system. Because the Fourteenth Amendment's equal protection clause was not in play, the LDF lawyers did not contend that the Negro schools were inferior. For the trial leader, the adequacy of the colored schools was irrelevant. James Nabrit saw segregation as a fundamental per se denial of liberty and was the strongest proponent of a broadside attack on public school segregation. Unlike the more cautious Marshall, the tenacious Nabrit was willing to risk all and not give the Supreme Court a pathway to avoid overruling *Plessy*. As expected, the district court ruled against him. The adverse decision was pending appeal to the District of Columbia Circuit Court when Chief Justice Vinson called Nabrit and asked him to petition the Supreme Court for review so that the District of Columbia case could be heard along with the other four cases.[14] Because the legal theories and factual record differed from the state cases, the District of Columbia case was docketed separately as *Bolling* v. *Sharpe*.

In each case, except for the state case filed in Delaware, the federal district court upheld racial segregation in public schools. The five cases were then scheduled for argument in the Supreme Court.

As I made the daily commute between the Manhattan offices of Paul, Weiss and the LDF and my home in Philadelphia, juggling a lively private legal practice, a growing family, and the demands of the Marshall team, my life was about to take another turn.

PART IV

A Philadelphia Lawyer

He who would be great anywhere must first be great in his own Philadelphia.

—Russell H. Conwell

EIGHTEEN

The City of Brotherly Love

In Boston, they ask, how much does he know? In New York, how much is he worth? In Philadelphia, who were his parents?

—MARK TWAIN

As I WAS DRAFTING A contract for an Arthur Miller production at Paul, Weiss in 1952, the phone rang. "Bill, this is Richardson Dilworth."

After a few pleasantries, he went on, "Bill, I know you have had an interest in practicing law in Philadelphia. I have just been elected Philadelphia district attorney and am looking for some bright young lawyers to assist me. Would you be willing to drop by my office at my law firm in the Fidelity building sometime next week to discuss employment in the district attorney's office?"

"Well, I am honored, Mr. Dilworth, that you would consider me for such a position. You're right. I've always wanted to practice law in my home town. Lovida would really appreciate not having to rouse me before six every morning to catch the train to New York. Could I come by first thing Monday morning?"

"That sounds fine, Bill. Let's say 9:30 a.m."

"I'll be there."

Richardson Dilworth was one of the great trial lawyers in Philadelphia's history. A marine officer in both world wars, he had been a cowboy and oil well driller in the Southwest during his summer college breaks. He learned in the foxhole to respect toughness, commitment, and loyalty. He didn't care whether a person was rich or poor, a recent immigrant or a fifth-generation Philadelphia Main Liner. A great trial lawyer, in Dilworth's mind, was like a wrestler who could get his knee on the neck of an opponent and yield only when he pleads "enough." He flooded his opponents with discovery, gleefully exposed their most closely guarded secrets, and was a vicious cross-examiner.

A converted Democrat, Dilworth was a reformer. Unlike most other major northern cities in the United States, especially those with large Negro populations, Philadelphia had been run for decades by a Republican machine. The city council, the mayor, and the so-called row offices (lesser city offices such as controller and treasurer) were staunchly Republican. Even FDR did not carry Philadelphia until 1936.

When Dilworth and another young Republican lawyer named Joseph E. Clarke Jr. returned from World War II, they were disturbed by what they saw. The city named by the Quaker William Penn after the Greek *philos* (love) and *adelphos* (brother), once the second-largest city in the British Empire, the birthplace of the nation's founding charters, their beloved hometown of Philadelphia, had become a grimy, poverty-ridden, and corrupt postindustrial city in decline. Garbage dumps burning along the Delaware River dissuaded ships from using the once-thriving Philadelphia port. Public officials ignored the large slums of the burgeoning colored population that had migrated north in search of jobs, joining the indigenous population of former slaves from colonial days. The politicians made peace with organized crime. Several city officials had committed suicide rather than account for their use of public funds. The hundred-year-old Republican machine had brought to a halt Philadelphia's progress as a modern American city.

Wealthy, articulate, and socially prominent, Dilworth and Clarke joined the Democratic Party. Dilworth started his own law firm, Dilworth, Paxson, Kalish, and Green. Clarke joined the white-shoe law firm of Dechert, Price, and Rhodes. The Democratic Party was under the leadership of Representative William Green, who, though a more traditional politician, welcomed the energetic young reformers into the political mix. The three crusaders launched a drive for a new city charter. They also invigorated the Americans for Democratic Action.

In 1951 Joe Clarke ran for mayor and Dilworth ran for district attorney of Philadelphia County. Each won decisively, ending a sixty-seven-year era of Republican control. This caused an extraordinary upheaval in city politics. Dilworth became a celebrity. He was elected mayor in 1955 and served two terms.

The Dilworth-Clarke reform era demonstrated what courageous, public-spirited political leadership can accomplish. Between 1952 and 1964, they reformed city government, aggressively pursued corrupt politicians and organized crime, planned the outlines of a modern city, including Society Hill and Independence Mall, created a network of parks and recreation facilities, cleaned up pollution and established trash collection, and launched one of the nation's premier regional transit authorities, the Southeastern Pennsylvania Transportation Authority, to replace the crumbling city bus system. Regrettably, the reformers were eventually succeeded by a Democratic political machine, and years later Philadelphia reverted to its old ways. Today it struggles, like other large eastern cities, with a host of old and new challenges.

As a third-generation Republican whose political roots were firmly anchored in the party of Lincoln, I learned from Dilworth what Mark Twain often professed: that character trumps party politics every time. Throughout my career I have worked with outstanding public servants of both political parties.

When Richardson Dilworth called me in 1952, he was still with his law firm but preparing to move to his new position as district attorney. As we agreed, I visited him in his office at the Dilworth firm. He told me his plans to reorganize the district attorney's office, which had been dominated by Republicans for many years. At the end of our meeting he intrigued me with an offer of deputy district attorney of Philadelphia for appellate matters. He told me that I had been highly recommended by Judge Goodrich. Another friend, Henry L. Sawyer Jr. of Drinker, Biddle, and Reath, who'd just been elected to the city council as a Democrat, had also put in a good word for me.[1] I was stunned by the offer. I very much wanted to work in Philadelphia, but until that moment the door to a mainstream legal career in my hometown had been slammed shut in my face. I was torn. The district attorney's office simply was not the career path I had in mind. I told Dilworth I would mull it over, talk to Lovida, and get back to him. I kept putting off a decision.

A couple of days later when I was back working at Paul, Weiss, I received another phone call from Dilworth. He asked me to come over to his office again at three o'clock the following afternoon. When I got there I noticed four people sitting in the waiting room. They all were friends of my father: Austin Norris, a lawyer; Luther Cunningham, a minister; William Gray, also a minister; and Charles Baker, a businessman. These four men of color had worked hard to elect the Clarke-Dilworth team, generating votes in the colored community, which had made the difference in the 1951 elections. As I met with Dilworth alone, he said to me, "Bill, we have a bit of a problem. Some of the Negro Democrats who worked very hard for my election have pointed out to me that you, your mother, and your father are registered Republicans. They told me, however, that they knew and respected you and your parents. They told me that if you would ask them to recommend you to me, they would do so and I could then announce your appointment to the press."

"With all due respect, sir, if I do that, I would be beholden to them. If there is one thing I learned in Washington," I replied pontifically, recalling a statement I overheard Secretary Stimson once make to Justice Frankfurter, "it's that when you accept a public job, you should not have obligations to anyone except the general public."

Dilworth was more than a little annoyed. "Grow up, Bill," he said as he paused, recovered his composure, and regained the modulated tone of a trial lawyer talking to a jury. "I can assure you that if any of these four ever ask you for something that in your judgment you should not deliver, you have the authority to turn them down and ask them to leave your office. I'll support you fully."

I thought about ending that long commute to New York City six days a week and struggled internally for about five minutes. In the end I said, "I'm deeply honored by your offer. I'd very much like to work in Philadelphia, but I simply don't think that being a prosecutor is right for me at this time. I've enjoyed my work at Paul, Weiss, both the business transactions and corporate litigation. This is the kind of legal work I'd like to continue doing in Philadelphia, if I ever get the opportunity. To be honest, there is another reason. I've begun to get involved in the school desegregation cases, working with Thurgood Marshall on a voluntary basis. I want to continue my work on these cases. I know I couldn't do so if I were a public employee."

"Well, I'm disappointed, Bill. But I understand your point. I fully support the work you're doing on the school desegregation cases. You may be doing a greater public service by pursuing that litigation than you could do as my deputy."

A few days later I got another call from Dilworth. I answered the phone with some trepidation because I thought he might be trying to persuade me to reconsider my decision. Much to my surprise Dilworth was on a different tack. He said, "My partners and I would like you to become an associate in my law firm, Dilworth, Paxson, Kalish, and Green."

I accepted immediately.

On March 31, 1952, Paul, Weiss, Rifkind, Wharton, and Garrison gave me a going-away party. Just about every one at the firm attended. Senior partners called me aside, showered me with flattery, promised to send me legal business, told me I was welcome back any time, and said I'd been on the fast track to becoming partner. While I appreciated all the flattery, the most useful if unwelcome advice came from a contemporary associate who pulled me aside and said, "Bill, let me be blunt. Sometimes you act like an arrogant bastard. Maybe you think you're the smartest person in the room. I suspect you're simply trying to prove you're up to the job. You ought to be more aware of the impression you make on the people you are working with."

That night, on my last train commute home, I had many recollections and reflections about my experience at Paul, Weiss. I was gratified that at last, six years after finishing Harvard Law School, a Philadelphia law firm of some note would finally give me the opportunity to practice law in a productive environment, as so many of my classmates had been doing in their hometowns. I thought about how happy my father and mother would be that I would become a part of the Philadelphia community. Finally, reflecting on both the diversity of my practice at Paul, Weiss and the challenging opportunities ahead, I looked forward to continuing a multidimensional legal practice. While specialization has become the trend in today's complex legal world, a good lawyer must be familiar with developments in the major legal disciplines and able to move at ease among them or at least to identify the key issues that must be resolved by a specialist who is brought onto the team. I remembered Justice Frankfurter telling me about his response in 1944 to Jean Monnet, when the great French economist and founder of the International Monetary Fund asked him why so many outstanding public officials in the United States are lawyers. Frankfurter told him that the highest talent of any lawyer is to become quickly an expert in what is relevant. That is the primary precept of a counsel for the situation.

NINETEEN

Expert in Relevance

*The highest talent of any lawyer is to become quickly an
expert in what is relevant.*

—Justice Felix Frankfurter

At last I was in fact and reality a Philadelphia lawyer.

The term *Philadelphia lawyer* has had several meanings through the years.
In 1952 it meant a very competent counsel who is knowledgeable in the most
minute aspects of the law and uses that knowledge in a shrewd and creative
manner to benefit his or her client.

The term originated with Andrew Hamilton, who had obtained the acquittal of a German printer, John Peter Zenger. In 1735 Zenger was charged with
publishing "seditious libels and treasonable defamation" about the New York
Royalist governor William Cosby. Zenger had been unable to find a New York
lawyer brave enough to defend him. Andrew Hamilton from Philadelphia took
on the case. He made a spellbinding argument to the jury. He conceded that
Zenger had printed scurrilous information about the governor but argued that
the libel law was immoral and should be nullified by the jury. The issue, he told
the jury, was not whether Zenger was guilty of violating the law but whether he
should be free to expose and oppose the government's abuse of power by speaking and writing the truth. Hamilton's "free speech" argument preceded the First
Amendment by more than a half century. When Zenger was acquitted, a cry
arose from the galleries: "Only a Philadelphia lawyer could have done it!"

During the Great Depression the term *Philadelphia lawyer* was invoked
to describe the innovative work of lawyers in creating railroad bailment-lease
transactions. Through such a device, bankruptcy was avoided and much-
needed funding was generated for the Pennsylvania railroads.

In 1952 Philadelphia was the third-largest city in the nation. The legal
community was well established and highly respected. The Dilworth firm was
an upstart at that time and probably not yet considered among the leading
firms.[1] Philadelphia lawyers were highly competitive, conscious of university degrees and social status, and inclined to keep tabs on their victories and

defeats in lawyerly jousts in the courtroom and beyond. On the whole, cama-
raderie prevailed, rooted in shared social values and long-standing traditions.

As Dilworth the reformer had penetrated the Republican fortress of city
governance, so Dilworth the law firm was slowly breaking into the exclusive legal club by matching and outperforming the more venerable leading
law firms. The firm's primary clients then included Triangle Publications,
owned by Walter L. Annenberg, which published the *Philadelphia Inquirer,*
the *Philadelphia Daily News, TV Guide, Seventeen,* the *Armstrong Daily Race
Sheet,* and the *Official Detective Magazine.* Triangle owned five television and
radio stations. Other clients included the owner of the major motion picture
theaters and Levitt and Sons, which had just finished building Levittown,
New York, and was about to embark on Levittown projects in Pennsylvania and New Jersey. The Dilworth firm was clearly the most diverse in the
city, including Protestants, Catholics, Jews, Republicans and Democrats,
persons from socially prominent Main Line Philadelphia families and persons from working-class neighborhoods, and now even a person of color. We
were a scrappy, determined group of talented lawyers, eager to demonstrate
our superior skills to the more established Philadelphia firms. Dilworth and
Harold E. Kohn, then thirty-five, were recognized as among the top litigators
along the eastern seaboard.[2]

My arrival was not without its challenges. My confidence was slightly shaken
when I learned that a group of secretaries had gone to see Harold Kohn, the
managing partner, to tell him they were quitting because the firm had hired a
Negro lawyer. Kohn immediately reached out to Dilworth, who rushed over to
the office and met with the secretaries. As I was later told, he said,

> Each of you is a damn good secretary, but we can find someone almost
> as good to replace you. We are lucky to have found Bill Coleman. His
> record is superb. Judge Goodrich, Henry Sawyer, and the Paul, Weiss
> firm have recommended him highly. I don't think we could replace him.
> If you get to know him, you'll find he's a decent human being. So I
> ask you to stay around and give him a chance. Oh, by the way, Walter
> Annenberg, who, as you may know, is our most important client, called
> to congratulate me on being the first law firm in Philadelphia to break
> the color barrier. Walter told me that as long as Bill Coleman is with this
> firm he'll continue to send us his business.

Dilworth had diffused the situation, and the secretaries decided to stay.
Many of them became good friends and were willing to work all night and
on weekends on cases in which I was involved, even volunteering for work on
the school desegregation cases and my other public service commitments. In
those days we used the term *secretaries;* today the more politically correct term

is *assistant*. It seems that *secretary* is now reserved for positions like secretary of state or secretary of transportation.[3]

Although I had not met Walter Annenberg at the time, we later worked together on several legal matters for Triangle Publications. I did legal work for the *Philadelphia Inquirer* and kept the *TV Guide* trademarks effective, preserving their value for an eventual sale. Annenberg was always gracious and appreciative, and I carry a heavy debt of gratitude to him. Many years later, in June 1998, while he was serving as the U.S. ambassador to the Court of St. James during the Reagan administration, he and I sat together on the platform as we each received honorary degrees from Harvard University.

My first big break came when Paul, Weiss referred a new client to me, American Houses Company, which built prefabricated houses to meet the great demand of returning veterans. Its principal factory was on leased land that it had acquired by assignment from the U.S. government, which in turn had leased the land from the property owner at the onset of World War II. The express term of the lease was "the length of World War II plus six months." Because all of American Houses' building operations were in this factory, loss of the lease would almost certainly have ended its thriving business. Imagine the shock when a letter arrived from the landlord stating that the term of the lease was over. President Harry Truman had issued an order declaring World War II over, which, surprisingly, received practically no newspaper coverage. The *Federal Register* was not daily reading for most business people.

Caught by surprise, American Homes came to the Dilworth law firm hoping to obtain equitable relief on the ground that it was unfair to oust a tenant who was unaware of the triggering event terminating the lease. Unfortunately we knew that the Pennsylvania courts would deny such relief because the state case law was crystal clear that equitable relief could not override explicit written provisions on the term of the lease. While we could seek relief in federal court claiming diversity of citizenship as a basis for federal jurisdiction, we knew that under the *Erie R.R.* v. *Tompkins* decision, a federal court would apply state law in federal diversity cases, and thus the unfavorable Pennsylvania precedent would prevail. We were able to obtain a temporary restraining order *ex parte* to hold the status quo for ten days as we undertook comprehensive day and night research. We could find no case under Pennsylvania law that would support an equitable right to continue occupation.

As I lay awake in bed at three o'clock on the morning of our scheduled court appearance, totally exhausted and about to admit defeat, I faintly heard the voice of Professor Freund from my federal jurisdiction class: where the federal government was involved, federal law rather than state law applies. This was known as the Clearfield doctrine.[4] I quickly rose and headed to the office in the predawn hours. We amended the complaint to allege jurisdiction based on a federal question. We argued that because the original lease was between the landlord and the federal government, American Houses, as the assignee, was entitled to all the rights of its assigner, the United States government, and thus should have the same right to apply the Clearfield doctrine that the United States government would have. The federal court accepted our argument. The lease was saved. It was a great victory. American Houses paid the Dilworth firm a $150,000 legal fee. Since my associate salary for the year was under $12,000, I thought I had earned my keep.

Bigger opportunities were soon to come. In their political campaigns in 1951, Dilworth and Clarke had promised action to address the rapidly deteriorating Philadelphia public transit services. The Philadelphia Transit Company (PTC), a private company, operated transit services under a 1907 agreement with the city, which provided that after fifty years the city could purchase all the assets of the PTC at book value on six months' written notice. Book value was essentially the purchase price minus depreciation. The Dilworth-Clarke reformers had proposed to create a new regional transportation system, the Southeastern Pennsylvania Transportation Authority (SEPTA), which would include Philadelphia and the four surrounding counties. Under the proposal the city would acquire the PTC assets under its 1907 agreement and transfer them to SEPTA.

In anticipation of the creation of SEPTA and the sale of the PTC to the regional authority, the city wanted to keep fares down and ridership up. It also wanted to ensure a fair accounting of the privately held transit company, in response to swirling charges that the PTC had engaged in imaginative accounting techniques, greatly inflating the book value. The city retained Harold Kohn and me to represent it. There were several issues that required our immediate attention.

First, the PTC's labor contracts were coming to an end. We were charged with keeping labor costs down to avoid fare increases. Harold and I became labor negotiators on behalf of the City, and the labor contract was settled with only modest increases for transit employees.

Second, the PTC filed for a substantial rate increase with the Pennsylvania Public Utility Commission. The City opposed the increase. Harold and I participated in the commission hearings and later court proceedings. Since we were new at the game of utility commission accounting, we really dug in and attacked many of the cost entries that had been accepted in previous PTC rate cases. We were able to get significant items knocked out of the rate base and to increase accrued depreciation, thus reducing the net book value of the PTC assets in anticipation of their sale to the City and transfer to SEPTA.

The third urgent issue was to preserve the validity of the 1907 agreement between the City and the PTC providing for a sale based on book value. If the City had to condemn the PTC transit facilities, it would cost at least five times the book value because the City would be required to pay the current fair market value or replacement value of the PTC's properties. Not surprisingly, the PTC sought to force the City to condemn its assets by invalidating the 1907 agreement. They argued that the agreement violated the common-law rule against perpetuities. Under that arcane rule, any future interest in real estate had to vest in the new owner within the lives of the people named in the written instrument plus twenty-one years. Its purpose was to prevent the dead hand of a deceased from controlling the disposition of his estate in perpetuity. The PTC argued that there were no lives actually set forth in the agreement and therefore twenty-one years was the maximum period allowed. The fifty-plus years for the City to exercise its purchase option was obviously much longer than the twenty-one years allowed under the rule against perpetuities.

Recalling my class with Warren Barton Leach, the world's leading authority on the rule against perpetuities, I rushed over to the public library and researched early English common law. I learned that the rule did not apply against the king because its purpose was to ensure that the king knew which noblemen owned land and were obliged to fight for him. Here, the City was king, and we argued in the trial court and on appeal that the rule should not be applied to void a contract with the City.

This was but one of many instances where my Harvard Law School training in common law proved to be invaluable and decisive in a successful outcome. The Supreme Court of Pennsylvania upheld our legal position by a 4-3 vote. Our opponent, Hamilton Connors, a senior partner of Ballard, Spahr, and Ingersoll, Pennsylvania Transit Company's longtime outside counsel, filed a petition for a writ of certiorari with the U.S. Supreme Court, which was denied.

The case went back to the lower court for a trial on the merits to fix the purchase price. Morgan, Lewis, and Bockius, then Philadelphia's leading law firm, joined the Ballard firm as co-counsel for the PTC. During the course of the trial the parties engaged in intensive settlement negotiations, which eventually resulted in an oral settlement during a morning court break. When all the senior lawyers left for lunch, I went back to the office to prepare a written agreement that would be ready for a three o'clock meeting at the Dilworth firm. Although it had not been specifically discussed, I included a provision that the PTC would pay all of the local, state, and federal taxes resulting from the transaction. I thought there might be some city and commonwealth real estate transfer taxes, and since the issue had not been raised, I considered the inclusion of this provision simply appropriate tidying up of the agreement in accordance with good real estate practice. When the opposing partners returned from their celebratory lunch, they signed the agreement with congratulations all around.

A few days later, when our tax and corporate lawyers got deeply involved in drafting the final agreement based on the settlement, they discovered that because the agreement involved the purchase of assets rather than stock, the PTC would have a substantial federal income tax liability resulting from IRS Code provisions dealing with accelerated depreciation. This was quite a shock to the PTC's new controlling shareholder, John McShain, then a leader in the Democratic Party and one of the most successful building contractors in the nation. Over the years McShain's construction company was the prime contractor for more than a hundred buildings in Washington, including the Pentagon, the Kennedy Center for the Performing Arts, and National Airport. At that time, he had just completed the renovation of the White House. Upon hearing the bad news from his lawyer, McShain immediately fired his law firm and hired Philadelphia's second largest law firm, Dechert, Price, and Rhodes.[5] My partner Richard Levy, a superb tax lawyer, was able to configure the transaction in a way that reduced the adverse effect of accelerated depreciation on the PTC's taxable income. By applying more sophisticated accounting for pension liabilities, Levy reduced the PTC's federal tax liability so much that the federal government had to pay a refund. This was not because of Levy's otherwise generous nature. In drafting the SEPTA-PTC purchase agreement, we had also included a provision that SEPTA would be entitled to 50 percent of all tax refunds.

Although I was assigned to the litigation department at Dilworth, my work on the transit system reinforced what I had learned at Paul, Weiss. An effective lawyer must have a grasp of all the principal areas of legal practice. My exposure to transactions, tax, real estate, and labor law were critical in providing the best representation for our client in administrative and judicial proceedings.

One evening in 1956 Harold Kohn walked into my office. He told me that I had just been elected a partner of the Dilworth firm. The next morning a congratulatory letter arrived from Richardson Dilworth, then the newly elected mayor. There was little fanfare or celebration even though by this time the Dilworth firm was recognized as one of Philadelphia's best law firms, and the admission of a partner of color was a threshold event, among the first of its kind in the nation. Partners in the elite firms were beginning to understand that law firm diversity was an advantage, not a detriment, as we expanded our representation of SEPTA, the city of Philadelphia, and several major corporations headquartered there.

Our work for SEPTA continued. We soon confronted a major scandal. The Pennsylvania Transit Company had misused $4 million in funds loaned by the city to repair the Frankford El. The city attorney, David Berger, retained Kohn and me to sue the PTC. We won the case, to much acclaim in the local newspapers. There was even a complimentary editorial in the *Philadelphia Bulletin* humorously heralding the success of Philadelphia's outstanding new law firm: Berger, Kohn, and Coleman.

The publicity surrounding our victories was a great boost for the reputation of the Dilworth firm and for my own legal career. In my work with Harold on the transit cases, we had confronted and prevailed over many of the top lawyers in the major Philadelphia firms, most of whom had rejected my request for an interview in the years between 1946 and 1952. I acknowledge that this gave me some sense of satisfaction.

We also did a lot of labor work. I got to know Matthew Guinan, the president of the National Transport Workers Union, quite well as he carried on skillfully in the shoes of the legendary union leader Mike Quill. Every two or three years there would be a new labor agreement to negotiate. The days and nights were long, the issues intense, and failure would mean a disruptive citywide transit strike. Settlements were seldom made before two o'clock in the morning after the contract ended at midnight. I learned from informal conversations with Matt how to tell whether there would be a strike or a settlement. If at half past ten at night the buses were still picking up passengers, there was not going to be a strike. If the buses were passing up passengers, then I knew that the drivers had to get their vehicles back to the garage before midnight.

Once SEPTA became the owner and operator of the transit system, Pennsylvania state law prohibited the union employees from striking. On one occasion Matt Guinan and I reached a settlement on a labor agreement for the local TWU 234, but the president of the local union rejected it and called for a strike. I immediately went to court seeking an injunction, which was granted; but the union refused to honor it. The city was completely gridlocked. The next morning we initiated a court hearing to hold the local president Dominick deClerico and the officers of the union in contempt of court. Much to everyone's surprise, especially the press, Matt Guinan sat at the counsel table next to me. He supported SEPTA's position. When the press asked him why, he stated publicly that he had made an agreement with Mr. Coleman and SEPTA that was fair and equitable. He was not going to let the local union reject it.

The contempt hearing went on before a packed courtroom full of union members until almost midnight. The judge announced adjournment until ten o'clock the next morning. He then instructed the sheriff to take the local union president to Holmesburg Prison for the night before returning the next morning. I stood up and said something along these lines: "Your Honor, Dominick deClerico is a human being only doing what he mistakenly believes is in the best interest of his workers. Please parole him to me. I will make sure he returns by ten o'clock tomorrow morning."

The judge said, "If he does not, Mr. Coleman, you both will be in contempt. There is no reason why you can't wear your Brooks Brothers suit to jail."

Matt and I sat up all night with deClerico. At 10:00 the next morning he returned to the courthouse with his local officers. He stood up and announced to the court that he was ordering his men back to work. The strike was over.

As I have learned on so many occasions during my career practicing law, the best business development for a law firm is success for your existing clients. Sometimes this means more work from that client, which was thoroughly demonstrated in the many new matters we undertook for SEPTA. Sometimes it means new clients who have observed your success in addressing similar issues. Occasionally it even means representing a new client who gained respect for you by suffering a significant defeat at your hands. From our SEPTA work we generated a lot of new business of all three types.

Our successes with SEPTA brought us new clients, which in turn brought us other new clients. The city of Cincinnati retained the Dilworth firm to acquire a local private transit company. That relationship led to our being retained to negotiate a revised contract between the city and the Cincinnati Reds for the construction of a new baseball stadium. The mayor of Cincinnati at that time was Ted Berry, whom I had met in 1945 when we acted as co-counsel defending the officers of color who were excluded from the white officers club at Freeman Field in Indiana.[6]

Because business development is such a central focus today in the competitive law firm environment, it may be instructive to draw three lessons from our representation of Cincinnati. First, that the mayor and I had worked together many years earlier in volunteering our services on a civil rights matter led to a lucrative private engagement. Pro bono work pays. Second, it is important to stay in touch with people with whom you have had a successful professional and personal relationship, as you never know when they may surface again with a new business opportunity. Networking pays. Third, the diversity of the Dilworth firm was a plus in obtaining business from a city government whose elected officials represented a diverse population. Diversity pays. While this idea may have been novel in 1954, today it is a truism. The major law firms compete for talented law students of color because they recognize that diversity is critical to obtaining and retaining business from government and private entities that serve a diverse population.

Like my legal practice, the Coleman family was growing in Philadelphia. In 1952 our son Billy and daughter Lovida Jr. had a new baby brother, Hardin L. Coleman. With a little, or should I say with very little, help from me, Lovida worked hard at raising all three of our wonderful children. When they were of school age, they entered the venerable Quaker Germantown Friends School, where they were among the first students of color.

Although raised a Catholic, Lovida decided to become a Quaker as she undoubtedly took refuge from the hubris of the Coleman household in that still small voice of calm. Her charm, thoughtfulness, and spirit made her a welcome part of the school community, which soon expanded into the greater Philadelphia community. She made friends easily, breaking down social barriers. We began receiving invitations to the homes of longtime Philadelphians, completely discrediting the stereotype of Philadelphia Main Liners as aloof and unwelcoming to newcomers. Invitations were extended to summer homes in Vermont, New Hampshire, and Maine. We visited the Horace Mann family in Deer Isle, Maine, where we sailed in Penobscot Bay off the coast south of Bar Harbor. The water seemed awfully cold, even by comparison to the Camp Emlen swimming pool.

Our lives in Philadelphia were busy and fulfilling as the color barrier disintegrated both professionally and socially.

TWENTY

The Tipping Point

Out of public schools grows the greatness of a nation.

—MARK TWAIN

THE SUPREME COURT SCHEDULED THE five school desegregation cases for argument on December 9, 1952. I spent many evenings and weekends and much of my vacation time in New York and Washington, working on the briefs and preparing Marshall, Carter, Robinson, Nabrit, Hayes, and Greenberg for oral argument. Neither my name nor that of Louis H. Pollak could be on the briefs filed in 1952. Former Supreme Court law clerks were prohibited from appearing before the Court for three years after their clerkships ended.

When December 9 arrived, I entered the courtroom and sat nervously in the lawyers' section. Chief Justice Vinson presided. Marshall made a passionate and effective argument, also displaying his wry sense of humor. When Justice Robert Jackson offered a backhanded compliment, suggesting that Marshall might want to bring some lawsuits on behalf of Native Americans who also lived under segregation, Marshall's reply drew a tension-easing laugh: "I have a full load now, Mr. Justice." The questions from the bench revealed both skepticism and divisiveness indicative of deteriorating relationships among the justices in the Vinson Court. John W. Davis, counsel for South Carolina, interpreted the questions as suggesting a win for the segregated school districts. As he walked out of the Supreme Court building, he was overheard saying to a colleague that based on the comments and questions of the justices, he was likely to win by 5-4 or perhaps 6-3.[1]

We waited restlessly, interminably for a decision. No decision came down. On June 8, 1953, as the term came to a close, the Court issued an order scheduling all five cases for reargument on October 12, 1953. According to his clerk Alex Bickel, Justice Frankfurter had urged the Court to hold over the *Brown* cases for reargument, preventing a defeat.[2] Justice Douglas later wrote that if the Vinson Court had decided the cases, *Plessy* v. *Ferguson* would have been upheld, 5-4.[3]

143

The court order directed the parties "to discuss the following questions insofar as they are relevant to their respective cases":

1. What evidence is there that the Congress which submitted and the state legislatures and conventions which ratified the Fourteenth Amendment contemplated or did not contemplate, understood or did not understand, that it would abolish segregation in public schools?

2. If neither the Congress in submitting nor the states in ratifying the Fourteenth Amendment understood that compliance with it would require the immediate abolition of segregation in public schools, was it nevertheless the understanding of the framers of the amendment (a) that future Congresses might in the exercise of their power under Sec. 5 of the amendment, abolish segregation, or (b) that it would be within the judicial power, in light of future conditions, to construe the amendment as abolishing such segregation of its own force?

3. On the assumption that the answers to questions 2(a) and (b) do not dispose of the issue, is it within the judicial power, in construing the amendment, to abolish segregation in public schools?

4. Assuming it is decided that segregation in public schools violates the Fourteenth Amendment, (a) would a decree necessarily follow providing that, within the limits set by normal geographic school districting, Negro children should forthwith be admitted to schools of their choice, or (b) may this Court, in exercise of its equity powers, permit an effective gradual adjustment to be brought about from existing segregated systems to a system not based on color distinctions?

5. On the assumption on which questions 4(a) and (b) are based, and assuming further that this Court will exercise its equity powers to the end described in question 4(b), (a) should this Court formulate detailed decrees in these cases; (b) if so, what specific issues should the decrees reach; (c) should this Court appoint a special master to hear evidence with a view to recommending specific terms for such decrees; (d) should this Court remand to the courts of first instance with directions to frame decrees in these cases, and if so, what general directions should the decrees of this Court include and what procedures should the courts of first instance follow in arriving at the specific terms of the more detailed decrees?[4]

I saw the hand of Felix Frankfurter, crafting a balanced set of questions (like a law school exam) that would tilt to neither side nor reveal the Court's inner conflicts. The reaction of the Marshall team was mixed. Greenberg was upbeat and thought the Court was marshalling support to overrule *Plessy*. I initially agreed with Jack. Carter was more skeptical. His skepticism increased, as did mine, as the results of the research we had assigned various historians began to flow in from around the country.

Then, quite unexpectedly, in September 1953 Chief Justice Vinson died from a heart attack. As the Congress was not in session, President Eisenhower made a recess appointment of California governor Earl Warren to be the chief justice of the U.S. Supreme Court. Because Warren's Senate confirmation was delayed, reargument was postponed from October 12 until December 7, 1953. Warren was confirmed by the Senate on March 1, 1954.

During the summer months the Marshall team worked day and night, sacrificing their family vacations. With Marshall's approval, I asked a Harvard Law School classmate or former co-clerk in every southern state to research the state's legislative history on the adoption of the Fourteenth Amendment. Each of my contacts was white. Most of the relevant material was available only at the library of the state capitol. Each of my classmates and co-clerks provided a clear and thoughtful memorandum on what the state legislators thought the amendment meant when they voted to ratify it.[5] My co-clerk in the 1948 term, Truman Hobbs, no fan of school integration, gave me a careful, comprehensive analysis of the Alabama legislative history. My law review president, James Wilson, then practicing law in Atlanta, wrote a brilliant memo. The research by Hobbs, Wilson, and my other colleagues from the southern states were acts of courage, as their careers could have been severely damaged if their cavorting with the Legal Defense Fund radicals had become widely known.[6]

On the basis of this research I came up with an argument that I thought quite persuasive. Each southern state that had seceded from the Union, except Tennessee, was required to vote for ratification of the Fourteenth Amendment in order to be readmitted to the Union.[7] Pursuant to the Reconstruction Act, Congress examined the amended constitutions and statutes of the rebel states to determine whether they were in conformity with the Constitution of the United States as amended in all respects. At the time each state seceded from the Union, it had in place laws either prohibiting the education of Negroes or requiring that Negroes be educated only on a segregated basis. Some southern states actually made it a criminal offense to teach a black person to read and write. These laws were repealed for the most part by the southern states before they voted to ratify the Fourteenth Amendment. After they were readmitted, and after Reconstruction in the South began to unravel as the Radical Republicans lost power, many states either reenacted or reinstated the laws requiring segregation. In my view, shared by Lou Pollak, this was strong evidence that the southern states recognized that at the time it was ratified, the Fourteenth Amendment prohibited state laws requiring segregation. We presented this innovative argument to Marshall. I could see his brow furrow and his eyes narrow. "Didn't some of the northern states have statutes mandating or permitting segregated schools at the time they ratified the Fourteenth Amendment?" he asked rhetorically. Marshall rejected my argument. Most of my colleagues agreed that the argument was too risky, and we did not include it in the brief.[8]

We did subtly incorporate in the brief another argument I had advocated. While the extensive research conducted over the summer by the historians and legal contractors we had hired had turned up a few nuggets, any objective analysis of the evidence would have had to concede that there was little support for the proposition that Congress or the states affirmatively intended to outlaw public school segregation under the equal protection clause of the Fourteenth Amendment. I argued that this did not really matter. The framers of the basic documents—the Declaration of Independence, the Constitution, and the post–Civil War amendments—had avoided explicit confrontational language such as *slavery* and *racial discrimination* and instead resorted to broad concepts in order to obtain ratification by the states while ensuring the nation's capacity to grow into "a more perfect union." The Supreme Court, as ultimate interpreter of the Constitution, would give life and meaning to these concepts in the context of specific cases and current circumstances. In my view the founders had three fundamental objectives: to create a national government (replacing the Confederation); to create a government that was directly responsive to the people and not simply to the colonies or states; and to preserve freedom and liberty for all its citizens.

Mindful of the need to secure ratification from the southern states, the framers, most of whom opposed slavery, avoided the term in the Constitution. Even the drafters of the Thirteenth, Fourteenth, and Fifteenth Amendments were aware of the need for state ratification. They therefore chose resilient language capable of adapting to changing circumstances. Despite several reckless wrong turns in the *Dred Scott* and *Plessy* v. *Ferguson* decisions, the Supreme Court ultimately would recognize, as the drafters no doubt intended, that all Americans were citizens of one nation, based on their place of birth or naturalization and not on the color of their skin—a concept of citizenship firmly rooted in Greek and Roman societies and endorsed by the Americans, black and white, who voted to ratify the Constitution and the post–Civil War amendments.

The language adopted in the Fourteenth Amendment, like that of many products of the legislative process, was a compromise. It was sufficiently vague so as not to threaten moderates but sufficiently elastic to embrace and encourage the advance of civilization. It was a living Constitution that was being amended, adaptable to accommodate changes beyond the imagination of the founding fathers, as the Court's expansive interpretation of the commerce clause had attested. The framers could not have imagined that the commerce clause would be invoked by Congress to regulate airlines, pension programs, or worker safety. In the post–Civil War amendments, the nation adopted certain fundamental values of citizenship and equality of treatment, regardless of race or prior condition of servitude. Those amendments repaired the imperfections of the original Constitution. They anticipated that these values would be applied in future decades to unforeseen and changing circumstances, such as the rise of public schools in the South. They could not predict the extraordinary changes in the demographic, economic, social, and cultural fabric of the nation over the next century, but they could express the basic values that would protect the rights of all citizens and strengthen democratic self-government.

One morning in early 1954, while I was working in the LDF offices in New York, Marshall asked me to develop arguments to answer the question why the equal protection clause of the Fourteenth Amendment required more than simply providing equal physical facilities and equal state and local expenditures per school or child. I had to return by train to Philadelphia for a court hearing on SEPTA at 2:00 p.m. After the hearing, on the train back to New York, I scribbled out nine arguments on the back of a large manila envelope. At seven that evening, I went to Marshall's office and briefed him on the points. Marshall took the envelope with him, and although I can't remember all the points, I do recall that he worked some of these thoughts into his eloquent presentation on the fallacy of the underlying premise of *Plessy* v. *Ferguson*.

Since more than three years had lapsed since my Supreme Court clerkship, I was named on the 235-page NAACP brief filed on the 1953 reargument. The Inc Fund respected the insights Louis Pollak and I brought to the table on the inner workings of the Court and the views of individual justices. There was a lot of interest in my views on Frankfurter. Some of my colleagues thought I had a pipeline to the justice's inner thoughts. I did not. We all recognized that Frankfurter had a pivotal vote in the divided Court, that he influenced some of the other justices, and that he was prodigiously preoccupied with the *Brown* cases. His brilliant clerk in the 1952 term, Alexander Bickel, had spent a year analyzing the legislative history of the Fourteenth Amendment, which he later turned into a seminal *Harvard Law Review* article.[9]

Another former Frankfurter clerk, Philip Elman, was an important link in the solicitor general's office between the Truman and Eisenhower administrations. He was critical to the vigorous stance taken by Eisenhower's new attorney general, Herbert Brownell, on the unconstitutionality of state-sanctioned school segregation. Elman had written the brief for Truman's last attorney general, James P. McGranery; Marshall thought it too tepid and gradualist in its approach. I, on the contrary, thought Elman caught the beat of the nervous justices who fretted about the unrest and civil disobedience that could arise from a precipitous pronouncement that school segregation was unconstitutional. Without any enforcement power, the justices also had to worry about whether the other branches of government and the public would accept and follow its decisions. Elman sought to assure them that peaceful transitional change was possible. Elman has been criticized by Harvard Law School professor Randall Kennedy and others for his discussions with Justice Frankfurter during the pendency of the *Brown* case, *ex parte* communications to which other parties had no opportunity to reply. Elman's curious defense of these conversations was that the solicitor general's office had an obligation to work with the justices to help fashion a solution to the toughest problem facing the Court in that century. Elman's special relationship with Frankfurter accorded him this responsibility. I do not believe this view was shared by his superiors at the Department of Justice.

Elman perhaps takes too much credit for the unanimous decision of the Supreme Court, neglecting the role of the Marshall team, which he said made the wrong argument at the wrong time. Elman claims that Justice Jackson and Justice Frankfurter toyed with the idea of stating that public school segregation violated the Fourteenth Amendment but felt it was up to Congress to enforce it under section 5 of the amendment. The gradualist approach, embodied by the phrase "all deliberate speed," Elman claims, enabled the Court to reach a unanimous decision. At one time, Elman implied that Frankfurter and I also had had *ex parte* contacts on the *Brown* case. This is not true. We scrupulously avoided any discussions of the *Brown* cases during their pendency.

Other former Frankfurter clerks played less visible but supportive roles: Phil Graham (publisher of the *Washington Post*), Joe Rauh (founder of Americans for Democratic Action and a strong civil rights advocate), and Butch Fisher (legal adviser to the State Department). Thus Frankfurter and his clerks—present and former—were involved in the *Brown* cases. We all had different roles to play. In all my dealings with Justice Frankfurter, I know he and I respected the boundaries of appropriate discussion.

Three weeks before the argument, Marshall and I had moved into a suite at the Wardman Park Hotel in Washington. We had separate bedrooms connecting to a comfortable living area, which quickly became cluttered with briefs, records, federal reporters, and a bottle or two of Jack Daniels. We worked day and night and weekends preparing for the argument. Marshall was our Henry V on the eve of Agincourt in 1415, inspiring his merry band of brothers, who were preparing the battlefield for the three most important days of his life.

About a week before the argument there was a moot court at the Howard Law School in which the lawyers scheduled to argue the five cases participated, except Marshall, who observed every moot court but did not participate.[10]

Among the Howard Law students in attendance were Douglas Wilder, a second-year law student, later governor of Virginia and mayor of Richmond, and Vernon R. Jordan, also a second-year law student, who became president of the National Urban League and later a successful attorney, investment banker, and close friend and adviser to President Clinton, now President Barack Obama, and Lovida and me.

Four days before the reargument, Marshall asked me to join him at the counsel table. Only thirty-three years old, I was to be a firsthand witness to history in the making.

TWENTY-ONE

Reargument, December 7, 1953

In the field of public education, the doctrine of separate but equal has no place. Separate educational facilities are inherently unequal.

—CHIEF JUSTICE EARL WARREN

"MR. MARSHALL," I SAID TO BREAK the palpable tension, "you're going to have to be as good as Toussaint L'Ouverture. If a colored slave could defeat Napoleon's generals in Haiti, there is hope for us today."

Sighing heavily as he shifted his lanky frame in the back seat of the taxi, Marshall looked at me quizzically and then spoke, perhaps anticipating the argument he was about to make to the Supreme Court—an argument that would validate a twenty-year struggle against all odds.

"You still don't get it, Coleman," he admonished me. (He always called me Coleman.) "It's not about them versus us. If we win, the white Americans will benefit as much, even more, than we do. History shows that when one group dominates another, the dominant group suffers more than the dominated, who at least have the spirit of their struggle for freedom."

On that brisk morning of December 7, 1953, twelve years to the day from the Japanese attack on Pearl Harbor, we called for a cab at the Wardman Park Hotel in Northwest Washington. I carted our heavy litigation bags to the trunk of the taxi in preparation for our twenty-five-minute ride to the Supreme Court.

Trying to measure up to the historic proportions of the unfolding day, I feebly quoted Thomas Paine before the battle of Trenton in 1774: "These are the times that try men's souls." Marshall agreed. Our souls had been tried and sometimes fried.

The taxi driver, a man of color, listened quietly to the uneasy banter coming from the back seat. When we arrived at the Supreme Court building, he shyly spoke up: "Neither of you gentlemen ever told me where you wanted to go. But I knew, Mr. Marshall, where you had to be at 12:00 noon. God bless you, sir."

After that few words passed between Marshall and me as we trekked up the front steps of the U.S. Supreme Court on that December day. We entered the marbled chambers, already full with observers, some of whom had waited in line outside for most of the night, hoping to gain a coveted seat. Thurgood's mother, Norma, and his terminally ill first wife, Buster, sat in reserved seats. For each, it would be one of the last of his arguments they would attend. The always lovely Lovida sat nearby.

The new chief justice Earl Warren entered the Court. I looked up at the tall, stately figure with prematurely white hair capping his black judicial robes. His presence permeated the chambers with calm and confidence; in this hallowed place, reason would prevail. We all rose. In a quiet voice, Warren called for the school desegregation cases, which had been set for three days of reargument to address the fundamental constitutional issues at stake—issues that would challenge the very fabric of the nation's social, economic, and political life.

The South Carolina and Virginia cases led the docket. Spottswood Robinson rose to speak for the appellants. He argued brilliantly and forcefully that the broad purpose of the Fourteenth Amendment to the U.S. Constitution was to achieve complete legal equality. This can be accomplished only by prohibiting all state caste laws, including school segregation statutes. Always well prepared, Robinson had mastered the thousands of pages of record and responded to the justices' few questions with confidence.

A little past three that afternoon, Thurgood Marshall rose to approach the podium in the well of the Supreme Court. My stomach knotted up. The atmosphere was tense as the six-foot Marshall leaned slightly forward and began his prepared argument. Robinson had thoroughly warmed up the justices as he laid the foundation on the purpose and history of the Fourteenth Amendment. Marshall intended to show the Court how its more recent cases on racial classification had, step by step, demonstrated the irrationality of the separate-but-equal doctrine of *Plessy* v. *Ferguson*. No one in that courtroom was better prepared to address these issues. Marshall had personally argued several of the cases, most recently *Sweatt* v. *Painter*. There the Court had catalogued the inherent inferiority of the separate law school for Negroes and ordered Sweatt's admission to the University of Texas Law School. I thought to myself that every justice sitting behind that bench had benefited from a lifelong network of professional colleagues and surely would empathize with the inherent inequality and discriminatory nature of a state law that excluded persons of color from participating in a shared law school experience.

Was not the same principle applicable to primary and secondary public school education, where lifelong relationships are also forged? The challenge that December afternoon was to persuade the Court to take the next logical step. If people of all races were to be a contributing part of the American stream of history, should not this process begin when they are young children? Even if student and teacher per capita expenditures could be equalized and comparable but separate physical facilities could be funded and constructed (which was almost never the case), the value of education is not found in concrete and mortar but in the development of social skills, the nurturance of self-respect and confidence, and engagement in the healthy exchange of ideas with classmates of different backgrounds, experiences, and beliefs. If a purpose of education in a democratic society is to create an informed citizenry, then in a segregated environment white as well as Negro children were being deprived of a full appreciation of the multicultural society in which they each lived. Most important, wasn't the constitutional right of all citizens to equality of treatment and self-respect an essential element of effective education? As Marshall analyzed the social conditions and rationale that gave rise to the *Plessy* decision in 1897, it became clear that the separate-but-equal doctrine did not make any sense in 1953, even though the Supreme Court in recent decisions had struggled stubbornly to avoid overruling it.

That afternoon, the justices were not interested in Marshall's prepared argument. More fundamental questions came with Gatling-gun rapidity. Justice Jackson quickly interrupted: he knew well the judicial precedents, but he was troubled about the propriety of the Court's exercising judicial power to overturn the acts of state legislatures. Wasn't this the prerogative of the legislature? Shouldn't the Court wait until Congress acted to outlaw school segregation?

The other justices probed the extent of the Court's power to enforce the Fourteenth Amendment. At first Marshall was taken aback. He had never thought the power of the Court to be a serious question, only its willingness to overrule opprobrious precedent.[1] Gradually he regained his footing. He argued that the Court clearly had the power and responsibility to enforce the Fourteenth Amendment. Indeed, it had done so in the *McLaurin* decision, where the Court had endorsed Bob Carter's argument that the segregated treatment of a Negro student in the classroom of a white graduate school violated the Fourteenth Amendment's equal protection clause. Justice Frankfurter was skeptical: the Court in *McLaurin* had not ruled on segregation itself, only the cruel treatment of the student in the classroom. Marshall reserved his remaining fifteen minutes for rebuttal. With a beleaguered expression, he returned to his seat next to me.

John W. Davis, the eighty-year-old patrician from West Virginia, was certainly the most esteemed lawyer in America at that time. He had been the unsuccessful Democratic candidate for president in 1924, losing to the taciturn Calvin Coolidge. Davis rose to make his 140th and final argument before the Supreme Court in defense of the South Carolina school district. He had accepted without a fee South Carolina's invitation to defend segregation in the public schools. Although there was no doubt in my mind that Davis's position was morally and legally wrong, I grudgingly have to admit that his argument was effective. He danced between eloquence and wit, articulating the best case possible for the traditions and social mores of the antebellum South from which he came. As the argument progressed he became increasingly emotional, unusually so for such an experienced advocate but befitting the high stakes drama in play. Tears welling in his eyes, Davis stressed that the southern states had determined that racial segregation was best for both races, implying a mutual pact between blacks and whites. Congress and the federal courts, including the Supreme Court, had allowed and even encouraged this practice. In his sincere view it would be a disaster for the Court to force whites and blacks to sit together in public schools.

Citing at length the historical record, Davis cogently argued that neither Congress nor the states that ratified the Fourteenth Amendment intended that it would be used to force the integration of schools. South Carolina had taken steps to provide equal schools for Negroes and whites. He invoked Aesop's fable: A dog with a piece of meat in his mouth crossed a bridge. Seeing the meat's reflection in the water, he plunged for it and "lost both substance and shadow." Here is equal education," he said, "not promised, not prophesied, but present. Shall it be thrown away on some fancied question of racial prestige?" Davis challenged the NAACP's claim that integration would enable Negroes to learn more quickly and lead a more serene life. He admonished the Court: "Your honors do not sit and cannot sit as a glorified board of education for the State of South Carolina or any other state." After Davis and the other lawyers finished their arguments for the day, the Court adjourned.[2]

Marshall and I returned to our suite at the Wardman Park Hotel, exhausted but invigorated. Lou Pollak joined us. We critiqued each of the arguments and suggested points that Marshall should emphasize in his rebuttal the following afternoon. For four hours we had a vigorous debate, facilitated by Marshall's old friend, Jack Daniels. The smoke from Marshall's ever-present Winstons stung my eyes. I urged him to focus on the Supreme Court's obligation to enforce the Fourteenth Amendment by eliminating state laws creating a caste system. Now was the time for bold action. Through the Inc Fund's effective advocacy, led by Marshall over the past decades, the Court had chiseled away at the *Plessy* precedent, demonstrating not only that the separate-but-equal doctrine did not work in practice but that it was based on the false premise of racial inferiority. Now was the time to discard this unworkable and immoral doctrine. Segregation adversely affected the self-esteem of children of color. There was no justifiable reason to doubt their ability to learn alongside their white peers in an integrated classroom, and that was their right as citizens. Marshall thrived on these no-holds-barred exchanges. As was his practice, he kept his own counsel.

The next day Marshall rose to make his rebuttal. Returning to basics, he regained the high ground. His earthy, conversational tone was in marked contrast to Davis's elegance and erudition. In simple, informal language he brought the lofty courtroom into the real world of the rural South he knew so well from his extensive travels and interviews. It was a part of the South that even Justice Black and Justice Reed had never experienced. Colored kids (he favored the term colored or Negro) and white kids, he said, would live near each other, work the farms together, separate for school and then after school meet at the ball fields to play together. State-sponsored segregation imposed by white legislators was not a mutually agreed-on pact. It reflected the misguided sentiment that "Negroes are inferior to other human beings." It was an attempt to keep the people who were formerly owned as slaves in "as near that status as possible." This was the only explanation for why "Negroes are taken out of the main stream of American life in these states." State segregation laws may reflect the popular view of the majority of whites in the South, but the Supreme Court should not make decisions on public opinion polls. His voice rising, Marshall concluded, "Now is the time, we submit, that this Court should make it clear that that is not what the Constitution stands for."[3]

Justice Jackson had asked some of the most difficult, probing questions during the oral argument, expressing great concern about whether the Court should fill the vacuum left by congressional inaction. Although he died before Justice Marshall joined the Court, Jackson and Marshall knew and admired each other. It has been reported that after the oral arguments in December of 1953, Justice Jackson burst into Justice Frankfurter's chambers and blurted out, "Wasn't that colored fellow magnificent! He simply creamed John W. Davis."[4]

U.S. solicitor general Lee Rankin followed Marshall to the lectern that afternoon. Acting on orders from Attorney General Brownell and with the active support of President Eisenhower, he told the Supreme Court, without reservation, that public school racial segregation was unconstitutional.[5] Phil Elman was a major force behind the U.S. government's brief and the preparation of Rankin's oral argument.[6]

Given the skepticism inherent in some of the justices' questions, there was no reason to be particularly optimistic at the conclusion of the arguments. While the Marshall team thought the new Republican chief justice was a welcome replacement for his predecessor, Chief Justice Vinson, we were uncertain of Warren's ability to lead the fractured Court into this new frontier. The chief justice had been mostly quiet during the marathon three-day argument. The agonizing wait began. We waited with forced patience and perfected our prayers.

We gave the Court three months, but then impatiently awaited word. Finally, the Court made its decision. On Monday, May 17, 1954, the chief justice began reading the decision of the Supreme Court to a packed, spellbound courtroom. He recited the history of the Fourteenth Amendment and the evolution of the *Plessy* doctrine in a dry matter-of-fact tone as the spectators inched forward on their seats. Finally signaling where the Court was going, the chief asked rhetorically whether segregation deprives Negro children of equal opportunity. After a pause he answered his own question: "We believe that it does." A sigh of relief arose from the Marshall team. And then, as the chief proudly stressed the word *unanimous*, which he had added to the written text of the decision, a barely perceptible smile broke out on Marshall's face. Chief Justice Warren announced, "We [unanimously] conclude that in the field of public education the doctrine of separate but equal has no place. Separate educational facilities are inherently unequal."[7]

Marshall scanned the nine justices, briefly making eye contact with Justice Reed, who nodded slightly as he wiped a tear from his eye.[8] At long last the U.S. Supreme Court had held that state-mandated racial segregation in the public schools in the United States violated the Fourteenth Amendment.

TWENTY-TWO

With All Deliberate Speed

There has been entirely too much deliberation and not enough speed.

—JUSTICE HUGO BLACK

ACCORDING TO PUBLISHED REPORTS, CHIEF Justice Warren was convinced that a decision of the magnitude of the *Brown* cases required unanimity. He had worked hard to persuade his colleagues on the bench. The last holdout most probably was southern justice Stanley Reed, who intended to write a dissenting opinion. After several lunches during which Warren urged Reed to join the opinion, Warren asked his colleague whether he really wanted to file a lone dissent that would only encourage resistance in the South and undermine the authority of the Court.

I have learned from others that Justice Frankfurter was also quite instrumental in getting Reed to join the Court's opinion. Frankfurter pointed out that historically a justice would write a dissent mainly in the hope that a future Court would embrace the dissenter's views, which would become the law of the land. With eight associate justices joining the chief justice's opinion, there was no chance here that a future Court would change its position. (Reed apparently did not invoke the first Justice Harlan's many solitary dissents to rebut Frankfurter's argument.) Reed reluctantly agreed to join Warren's unanimous opinion.[1]

While we were both elated and exhausted by the astounding victory in the Supreme Court, our work was far from over. The Court set the five cases down for further reargument precisely on what type of decree should be entered. Having taken the bold action to end state-mandated school segregation, what were we to do now? The Court had requested the parties' position on this issue in paragraphs 4 and 5 of its June 8, 1953, order but apparently was not pleased with the parties' responses. The Court no doubt thought the parties were taking extreme positions, marking the boundaries within which a reasonable remedy could be found.

Marshall's position was straightforward. The Court should order the states to stop illegal, unconstitutional action immediately, no later than the start of the next school term. His position on remedy was based on the 1953 Supreme Court decision in *Morton Salt Company*, a case that did not involve race. As a practical matter, the elimination of laws requiring school segregation would not result in the immediate integration of public schools throughout the South. Other restrictive laws, practices, customs, and traditions had played a part in the segregation of neighborhoods and school districts.

Nor were state-sponsored practices of racial segregation by any means limited to the South. Federal and northern state actions were fully implicated in the segregation of neighborhoods and societal institutions. Racially restrictive covenants, discriminatory practices of federal housing authorities, the administration of the G.I. Bill of Rights, segregated housing projects developed during the Roosevelt and Truman administrations, and racially discriminatory banking and insurance practices all contributed to the creation of shameful segregated ghettos in northern cities. To give but one example, of the 67,000 mortgages issued under the post–World War II G.I. Bill in New York and northern New Jersey, 66,900 went to white veterans who built their homes in predominately white neighborhoods.[2] Achieving the benefits of desegregated public school education throughout the country would call for some extraordinary remedies, including the busing of children.

On the other hand, the Supreme Court was well aware of the civil disturbance that could result if it ordered all the schools in the South to desegregate within the next ninety days or even within the next year. The U.S. government expressed this concern in its brief on the decree. President Eisenhower personally read and revised the government's brief to acknowledge that although segregation was wrong, it had been fervently supported by a great number of people and sanctioned by the Court for many years. Compliance with the Court's decision would therefore require understanding and goodwill. Eisenhower also changed the wording of the Department of Justice's bottom-line recommendation that "racial segregation in public schools is unconstitutional and will have to be terminated as quickly as possible," substituting the word *feasible* for possible.[3]

There was much debate among the Marshall team about what position we should now take on remedy. Having dedicated more than twenty years of his life fighting for the result in *Brown*, Marshall's instincts were to take a hard-line position, demanding immediate desegregation across the board. Spottswood Robinson and our principal expert, psychologist Kenneth Clark, supported this approach. Marshall also recognized, however, that the Court was expecting the NAACP to take a more "practical" view. In September

Marshall sent a memo to the team requesting recommendations on the position we should take in response to the court order.

In support of a hard-line approach, Kenneth Clark had developed certain data based on a sample survey of southern attitudes and progress on desegregation. Drawing on these data, I drafted a fairly tough section for the brief on implementation and sent it to Marshall. I did not sleep well that night. I thought my draft was unpersuasive and was afraid it would irritate the Court more than advance our objective.

I got up early in the morning and wrote a longer, more personal letter to Marshall. I told him that I had reached the conclusion that we would be better off under a decree that would provide for a gradual but effective transition. I proposed that the Supreme Court require the states to submit a desegregation plan to the federal district courts for approval. I argued that although this might appear to be something of a retreat, the Court would view it as statesmanship, and we would be luring the southern states into submitting plans and a timetable that they then would be obligated to implement. I did not relish the prospect of making these arguments to my colleagues, most of whom had devoted decades of their lives to a battle they had just won. Nevertheless, I thought the Supreme Court had approached this issue with great care and courage, scheduling three separate oral arguments and forging a unanimous decision in support of bold action, overruling its own precedent. By scheduling a third argument the Court clearly wanted help in fashioning a remedy that would bring about the greatest social change ever ordered by a Supreme Court.

Under my proposal the Supreme Court would issue a decree along the following lines:

1. The public school life of most children is twelve years, first through twelfth grade (thirteen if kindergarten is counted, but some people consider thirteen an unlucky number, so I avoided using it).

2. Each state would have an option. It could start at the first grade and desegregate one higher grade each year, or it could start at the twelfth grade and desegregate downward. Of course, states could start at both ends, first and twelfth grades, and complete the process in six years. If a state opted to burn the candle at both ends, it could request a one-year delay in the start-up date.

3. Whichever option the state chose, the state attorney general would submit its plan to the federal district court for approval.

4. By the end of twelve years, or perhaps earlier, all public schools would be racially desegregated.

5. Because this would be a statewide remedy, it would not be necessary to bring enforcement suits in each local school system.

Among the benefits of this approach, I argued, would be that the Supreme Court would provide detailed instructions, the states would be forced to take responsibility for developing a statewide plan that the state attorney general would be obligated to enforce under a federal district court decree, and a fixed timetable would be established.

I was not surprised and could well understand why just about everyone in the Legal Defense Fund conference room strongly disagreed with me, the young upstart who had only recently joined the team. As one participant bluntly put it, "Let me see if I understand you, Bill. You would have Mr. Marshall stand before the Court and say, 'May it please the Court. Even though you have unanimously and courageously held that public school desegregation is unconstitutional, and even though state and local officials have intentionally and willfully violated my clients' constitutional rights for decades and caused them great harm, we are willing to concede, Your Honor, that defendants do not have to stop harming our children now. We are happy to give them another decade or more to comply with the U.S. Constitution.'"

There wasn't much sentiment to pursue my proposal further. The LDF brief took a more aggressive position. It asked the Court to declare desegregation unconstitutional immediately, to require periodic progress reports, and to order that the integration of public schools be completed not later than September 1956. The U.S. government was only slightly more flexible. In a brief filed by Attorney General Brownell, it recommended that the Court require the school districts to submit desegregation plans to the district courts, that the district courts monitor the plans closely and report periodically to the Supreme Court, and that the school districts make a good start on integration after a one-year transition period. Having found desegregation "a fundamental human right supported by considerations of morality as well as law," the Eisenhower administration concluded that it was essential "to make an immediate and substantial start toward desegregation, in a good faith effort to end the segregation as soon as possible."[4]

On May 31, 1955, the Court rejected our proposal and most of the attorney general's. It handed down a decree that delegated enforcement authority to the federal district courts and directed the school districts to "make a prompt and reasonable start toward full compliance." The Court granted the lower courts additional flexibility on the timing to take into account administrative issues such as the "physical condition of school plant, the school transportation system, personnel, revision of school district and attendance areas . . . and revision of local laws and regulations." It instructed the district courts to proceed "with all deliberate speed."[5]

It has now been more than fifty years since the Supreme Court's decision, and many of the schools in the South and the North are still mostly segregated. Whether my twelve-year gradual transition plan, or some other more detailed instructions on remedy, would have accelerated the process is hard to say.

It is generally assumed that Frankfurter was responsible for the term "all deliberate speed," which he adopted from Holmes's decision in *Virginia* v. *West Virginia*. Holmes attributed it to the English Chancery, where the commonly used term was "all convenient speed," a phrase that can also be found in Shakespeare's *The Merchant of Venice*. It was not Frankfurter's (or his former clerk Elman's, for that matter) finest turn of phrase. I tend to agree with Justice Black's retrospective remark in 1964, wondering why the Court ever agreed to it. "There has been entirely too much deliberation and not enough speed."[6]

The Eisenhower administration continued its strong support for school desegregation. Without waiting for the Supreme Court's order on remedy, President Eisenhower ordered the immediate end of racial segregation in the District of Columbia schools, bringing to a quick conclusion one of the five cases that the LDF had initiated in its comprehensive strategy.

Resolution of the remaining cases and desegregation of the public schools throughout the South proved far more challenging; once again, President Eisenhower proved to be up to the task.[7]

TWENTY-THREE

Enforcing the Court's Order

The Federal Constitution will be upheld by me by every legal means at my command

—PRESIDENT DWIGHT D. EISENHOWER

A TELEPHONE CALL FROM THURGOOD Marshall during the summer of 1958 ended any hope I had of an August vacation with my family in South Pomfret, Vermont. The federal district court in Arkansas had ordered that nine Negro plaintiffs be admitted to Central High School in Little Rock beginning the day after Labor Day in 1957.

During a visit with President Eisenhower at his summer vacation spot in Newport, Rhode Island, Arkansas governor Orval Faubus had pledged yet again to cooperate with the courts and the federal government. But when the nine school children of color attempted to enter the high school on September 4, 1957, the governor ordered the Arkansas National Guard forcibly to prevent the students from entering the school. As the school week began on September 23, the brave black students returned. A mob of fifteen hundred angry white parents threatened to block their entrance to the school, spitting on them and hurling epithets. "Lynch her, lynch her," cried one foolish woman. Ostensibly to protect their safety, the governor ordered the children kept out of school. The federal district judge again ordered the Negro plaintiffs admitted. The obstinate governor then decided to close Central High School for a year.

President Eisenhower was asked whether he agreed with the *Brown* decision. He said it didn't matter what he believed, it was the law of the land. Critics have suggested that Eisenhower's comment reflected a lack of commitment to school desegregation. The facts belie such a contention. Eisenhower made clear that it was his sworn constitutional duty as president to enforce the district court order. He stated emphatically, "The only assurance I can give you is that the Federal Constitution will be upheld by me by every legal means at my command."[1] And he meant what he said.

Eisenhower federalized the Arkansas National Guard, removing it from the governor's control. He also sent the elite 101st Airborne Division to Little

Rock to keep order.[2] In the face of the military presence the protestors backed down quickly, and the Negro students attended the integrated school for the rest of the year until the summer break in June 1958. On February 20, however, the school board petitioned the district court to postpone the desegregation program because of extreme public hostility. After a hearing the seventy-four-year-old federal district court judge Harry J. Lemley granted the relief requested by the school board, barring the Negro students from attending Central High School in September 1958. The judge approved a two-and-a-half-year moratorium on the desegregation of the Little Rock school system. The court of appeals reversed but stayed the effective date of its judgment of reversal for thirty days to allow an appeal to the Supreme Court.

Marshall and I discussed how we could induce the Supreme Court, then in summer recess, to come back in a special term in early September to hear the case before school opened. We moved into action.

We were most fortunate to have as local counsel Wiley A. Branton, who later became dean of Howard Law School, a commissioner of the Federal Communications Commission, and a partner in the leading national law firm of Sidley, Austin, Brown, and Wood. Branton understood that the Supreme Court could do nothing until it had a record of the case before it. Branton moved mountains to get the record from the district court to the Eighth Circuit Court of Appeals and then on to the Supreme Court. Like many of us who practiced civil rights law during those days, Branton was adept at dealing with the tactics used by southern judges and their clerks to delay moving the record up the chain when race issues were involved.

Our next challenge was to locate the Supreme Court justice assigned to the Eighth Circuit Court, Charles Evans Whittaker. I could not track him down.

"Gosh, Coleman," Marshall exclaimed, "every justice has a Negro valet. If we can find his valet, he will know where the justice is."

"With the chambers closed for the summer, how am I going to find the valet?" I asked.

Marshall patiently replied, "Ask around and find out what church the valet goes to. Then we can find the minister, find the valet, and ask him where the justice is."

We located the valet, who told us that Justice Whittaker had taken the train at Union Station that morning to attend the annual meeting of the American Bar Association on the West Coast. Marshall got on a plane, met the train in Omaha, Nebraska, showed a picture of Justice Whittaker to the Negro porter, and located the justice in a sleeping berth on the way to California. Justice Whittaker took the appeal papers, signed them, and referred the matter to the Supreme Court for further action.

The Court was called back for a special term to hear the case *Cooper* v. *Aaron* on August 28, 1958. William Cooper was the chairman of the Little Rock school board, and John Aaron was a Negro student denied admission to Central High. We wrote a compelling brief in record time, to which Bill Taylor made an enormous contribution, as he so often did. There was a lot at stake. Was *Brown* v. *Board of Education* truly transformational or merely an empty victory from a toothless judiciary? As I sat next to him again at the counsel table, Marshall made a tremendous argument. "Education is the teaching of overall citizenship," he argued, "to learn to live together with fellow citizens and to learn to obey the law." Marshall was "not worried about the Negro children at this stage." He worried about the white children, he said, who were told "that the way to get your rights is to violate the law and defy lawful authorities." He didn't "worry about the Negro kids' future. They've been struggling with democracy long enough."[3]

School was scheduled to open on September 15, 1958. The Supreme Court issued its judgment on September 11, ordering that the Negro students again be admitted. On September 29, the Court filed a compelling and dramatic unanimous opinion. In an unprecedented show of resolve, the opinion was personally signed by each of the nine justices, three of whom were recent appointees by President Eisenhower. To my knowledge the signatures of nine justices have never—before or since—graced a decision of the Court. Broadly affirming the decision in *Brown* and expressing no tolerance for a delay in its implementation, the opinion stated:

> As this case reaches us it raises questions of the highest importance to the maintenance of our federal system of government. It necessarily involves a claim by the Governor and Legislature of a State that there is no duty on state officials to obey federal court orders resting on this Court's considered interpretation of the United States Constitution. *Specifically it involves actions by the Governor and Legislature of Arkansas upon the premise that they are not bound by our holding in* Brown v. Board of Education, 347 U.S. 483. *That holding was that the Fourteenth Amendment forbids States to use their governmental powers to bar children on racial grounds from attending schools where there is state participation through any arrangement, management, funds or property.* We are urged to uphold a suspension of the Little Rock School Board's plan to do away with segregated public schools in Little Rock until state laws and efforts to upset and nullify our holding in *Brown v. Board of Education* have been further challenged and tested in the courts. We reject these contentions [emphasis added].[4]

The significance of *Cooper* v. *Aaron* cannot be overstated. Resistance to the *Brown* decision throughout the South brought the nation back to the precipice of civil war as fossilized traditions adamantly refused to yield to a revolutionary change in the law. A large number of southern members of Congress had signed a manifesto declaring *Brown* wrongly decided and an abuse of judicial power and calling for massive resistance against integration. White citizens councils began to arise in the South to fight integration. Racial violence and lynchings increased, including the brutal murder of Emmett Till, whose killers were acquitted by an all-white jury. Congress was not helpful. It rejected an Eisenhower proposal to authorize the attorney general to intervene to protect the constitutional rights of any citizen. It rejected financial assistance to desegregating schools. The muddled resolution of the remedy phase, resulting in the vague language of "all deliberate speed," had offered the southern resisters an opportunity to test the federal resolve.

Eisenhower and the chief justice he appointed were men whose career accomplishments were anchored in relentless courage. Their response in the Little Rock case greatly narrowed the gap between the idea and the reality. Turbulent times lay ahead, but there could be no doubt of the federal government's determination—it would not back down. *Brown* and *Cooper* together had transformed the chimerical vision of equality of opportunity embedded in the Declaration of Independence into a legal foundation on which presidents, Congress, and the courts would build a legal structure of equal opportunity for all Americans. Inspired by the Supreme Court's unyielding resolve, the modern civil rights movement was launched. A year after the *Brown* decision was reached, Rosa Parks refused to sit in the back of a bus in Montgomery, Alabama, and a grassroots boycott began.

Cooper v. *Aaron* was also a major victory for the newly independent Legal Defense Fund and for its first director-counsel. Shortly thereafter, Marshall asked me to join its board of directors and to serve as its chairman.

Thurgood Marshall and the Inc Fund team dedicated decades to the fight against state-sanctioned school segregation because we believed that if children of color and whites spent time together in school they would get to know each other as individuals, not stereotyped races. They would learn from each other. All races would be enriched by the sharing of ideas and talents derived from different backgrounds and cultural experiences. False values of prejudice and racial superiority would yield to common values shared by all members of the human family as children grew into adults, made lifelong friendships, and became part of racially integrated communities and businesses. The benefits of integration would spread from the public schools like concentric ripples expanding from a stone cast in a pond, permeating the greater society as a whole. Instead of veering off into separate cultures, people of all races would enhance the cultural values of the American mainstream. Where integration has been achieved, this has often proved true. It was certainly true in my case as I moved from segregated primary schools to integrated junior and senior high schools and then on to Penn and Harvard.

We underestimated the complexity of achieving sustained integration in the face of myriad governmental policies and private sector practices that created and perpetuated racial segregation in neighborhoods and in social, religious, and business institutions. More than a half a century after *Brown*, public school de facto segregation is still common in most metropolitan areas. In this respect, the promise of *Brown* has been largely unfulfilled.

To gain a unanimous decision in *Brown*, the chief justice purposefully narrowed the specific holding to the desegregation of public schools and set no specific timetable for its accomplishment. It could be argued that *Brown*, read literally, did not achieve its objective. Yet the importance of *Brown* cannot be overestimated for two reasons that may not have been foremost in our minds at the time.

First, in the *Brown* case the Supreme Court emphatically reaffirmed that in a racially pluralistic society the rights of minorities are protected by a judicial system that upholds the Constitution where the more democratic institutions fail to act, paralyzed as captives to the whims and biases of the political majority. This truth has been demonstrated as the Fourteenth Amendment has been applied to other protected classes of disadvantaged persons who have endured discrimination on the basis of gender, physical or mental handicap, immigrant or homeless status, imprisonment, or sexual orientation. The two great Marshalls—Chief Justice John Marshall and advocate Thurgood Marshall—realized the subtle potential in the U.S. Constitution, as amended, to prod the nation toward a more perfect union. They showed that the imperfections of pure democracy as a reflection of popular will and the status quo can be countered by the talents of wise though fallible human beings through a time-tested adversarial process that translates rhetorical aspirations into justice in the living experience of all American citizens.

Second, despite limiting its holding to public schools, the *Brown* decision established the broader constitutional principle that state-sanctioned racial discrimination would not be tolerated. *Cooper* v. *Aaron*, backed by the commander-in-chief's mobilization of the 101st Airborne, made emphatically clear that there would be no retreat from that principle.

Eisenhower's response to the *Brown* decision was the diametrical opposite of Andrew Jackson's response to the Court's decision in upholding the land rights of the Cherokee Indians: "[Chief Justice] Marshall has made his decision, now let him enforce it." Ignoring our treaty obligations, President Jackson ordered that the Cherokees be forcibly removed from their lands in Georgia, precipitating the Trail of Tears and beginning one of the saddest and most reprehensible chapters in the nation's history. We had come a long way since 1830 in recognizing the integral role of the Supreme Court in our constitutional system. As the Court has carefully interpreted the law, applying time-tested transparent adversarial procedures and explaining its decisions with reasoned analysis, the Court has commanded the respect of the other, more powerful, elected branches of government. In applying the principle of equal protection under the law to abolish the racial caste system, the Court took the first dramatic step. The other branches followed. One question is worthy of reflection: what would have been the effect on the authority and legitimacy of the Supreme Court, indeed on our constitutional structure of government, if Eisenhower had taken the Jacksonian approach to the *Brown* decision?

Congress took longer to come on board. Eventually it got the message. As the civil rights movement gained momentum, Congress enacted a series of civil rights laws to reverse decades of racial discrimination in voting, housing, employment, and even the judicial enforcement of private contracts. The doors of the legislatures, government, and business opened up for all American citizens.

As new opportunities for the exercise of power emerged for Americans of color, the civil rights movement splintered into different factions. There was the Martin Luther King nonviolent, peaceful protest that raised the national consciousness. There were the Malcolm X separatists, and the Young Turks of the black power movement, proclaiming that black is beautiful. There were the victims of discrimination seeking reparations and special treatment.

In a free society, all nonviolent approaches and ideas should be welcome. For me, as for Thurgood Marshall, the battlefield was the courts and the legislatures. By eradicating state-sanctioned racial discrimination we were working toward a fully integrated society that was color blind. We weren't there yet, but that was the goal. We did not fight for school integration and equal rights to encourage black separatism. We believed that with civil rights comes the responsibility of citizenship in a lawful and democratic society. We envisioned a nation in which all Americans, regardless of gender, ethnicity, and race, could apply their God-given talents to reach their potential. America would be a stronger nation because of the contributions of its diverse populations to a greater cultural whole. We entered the stream of American history at different points, but we all became part of one giant flowing river.

Like Moses, it was Thurgood Marshall's destiny to lead his people to the promised land—a land in which the promise of the Thirteenth, Fourteenth, and Fifteenth Amendments would finally be embraced by the Supreme Court, a land in which all American citizens, regardless of race, would have an equal opportunity to succeed. While all Americans celebrate the 1776 Declaration of Independence, for many Americans of color, the idea of equal opportunity under the law did not become a reality until the Supreme Court ended state-sanctioned apartheid in 1954. Unlike Moses, who never reached his promised land, Marshall was to reach the pinnacle of his profession. In 1961 President Kennedy appointed him as the first American judge of color on the U.S. Court of Appeals for the Second Circuit. In 1965 President Johnson appointed him as the first nonwhite solicitor general of the United States. In 1967 he was nominated by President Johnson and confirmed by the Senate as the first nonwhite justice of the Supreme Court of the United States.

TWENTY-FOUR

A Lawyer's Public Service Obligation

Some people buy diamonds and rare works of art; others delight in automobiles and yachts. My luxury is to invest my surplus effort, beyond that required for the proper support of my family, to the pleasure of taking up a problem and solving, or helping to solve, it for the people without receiving any compensation.

—Louis D. Brandeis

ONE OF THE GREAT BENEFITS of practicing law in an enlightened law firm is the recognition by just about all of your partners of a lawyer's continuing and compelling obligation to serve the public. As the nation increasingly recognized the value of diverse participation in addressing the challenges we faced at the local, state, and federal levels, I was offered many opportunities for public service. Because I had a full-time job practicing law and had undertaken a substantial commitment to the Legal Defense Fund, I had to be selective in accepting these opportunities.

THE BRANCH RICKEY COMMITTEE

One I could not refuse was an appointment by President Eisenhower in 1959 to the President's Committee on Government Employment Policy, which became known as the Branch Rickey Committee.[1] Branch Rickey was part owner and general manager of the Brooklyn Dodgers when he recruited Jackie Robinson and broke the color barrier in major league baseball. The seven-member committee met in Washington about once every three weeks for two days. Its mission was to open up meaningful federal job opportunities for people of color.[2]

In those days persons of color in the federal government served mostly as drivers, messengers, and in comparable positions. There were very few professionals. The Rickey Committee called in various federal agency heads and developed a plan to recruit, hire, and retain persons of color for civil service positions. We made some progress, although it would have been hard to fail since we started with a baseline near zero.

We met with President Eisenhower on several occasions, showing him the dismal statistical record of the federal government and recommending an action plan, which the president fully supported.[3] With Eisenhower's committed leadership, the federal government began to make rapid strides in recruiting minorities to professional civil service positions. Over the years as middle-level management in the federal government became more diversified, the private sector began to catch on as well, recognizing that a diversified workforce would bring many benefits, including the ability to work more effectively with government and to serve a diversified customer base. The Rickey Committee represented an important turning point. The days of Woodrow Wilson's segregated capital city were coming to an end. A strong middle class of color was emerging.

JFK

I did not get involved in the 1960 presidential election between Jack Kennedy and Richard Nixon. Neither candidate demonstrated a strong commitment to civil rights. As I saw it, Kennedy and his advisers (especially Bobby) were concerned that a strong civil rights stance would alienate the Democratic South. His selection of Lyndon Johnson as his running mate, for whom he had little admiration, was, I then thought, a cynical ploy to win Texas and possibly a few adjacent states. Nixon's advisers, on the other hand, had cooked up the so-called Southern Strategy, seeking to peel off southern votes for the Republican Party. Nixon deserved credit, however, for accepting Nelson Rockefeller's recommendation to endorse the civil rights legislation in the Republican Party platform, antagonizing the Goldwater conservatives.

By a fluke, however, I found myself on the fringe of an event that occurred in October 1960 that may have thrown the election to Kennedy. On October 19 in Atlanta, Georgia, local police arrested Martin Luther King Jr. for refusing to leave the all-white lunch counter of Rich's department store. King had reluctantly been persuaded to join the student-led sit-in protest movement that had been arising spontaneously throughout the South. The other protestors were quickly released, but the trial judge, Oscar Mitchell, intending to teach King a lesson, denied him bail. After a hearing in which the shackled King appeared, Judge Mitchell revoked the suspension of a previous traffic violation and sentenced King to four months of hard labor. King was transferred to the maximum security prison at Reidsville.

The story received worldwide news coverage. Like the tale of the Rashomon rape, there were many (mostly self-serving) versions of what happened next.

According to one report, Jack Kennedy was relaxing in his hotel room, preparing for his fourth and final debate with Nixon, when his civil rights adviser Harris Wofford suggested he might want to intervene directly on behalf of Martin Luther King. Bobby and the other staff members prepping Kennedy advised him not to do so. His position in the South was already precarious. Instead, Kennedy called Coretta Scott King and extended his sympathies, offering to help in any way he could. The frightened Mrs. King asked him to help secure her husband's release. When Judge Mitchell relented and Martin Luther King was released from the Atlanta jail, the King family assumed that Jack Kennedy had intervened. They gave him public credit for King's release. King's grateful father, a Baptist minister and lifelong Republican, told the press that he planned to switch his vote, even though Kennedy was a Roman Catholic.[4]

My involvement in this incident suggests that Kennedy may not have lifted a finger to help King. The day after King was arrested, Phil Elman, who was still working in the solicitor general's office, called me and said that the Justice Department believed that under the Georgia statute under which he was arrested, King's sentence was probably illegal. In any event, King clearly was entitled to bail. I did some additional research and called Thurgood Marshall, who enlisted Donald Hollowell and Horace Ward, LDF civil rights lawyers in Atlanta, to represent King in securing his release from prison. Phil Elman later told me that the Justice Department was trying to reach Richard Nixon so he could make a public announcement, but the Nixon campaign staff properly deflected the issue to the Eisenhower White House, which endlessly pondered over several draft statements. Seizing the opportunity, the politically astute Kennedy staff beat the Republicans to it, followed by the King family's press conference attributing the outcome to Kennedy. Two days later Martin Luther King came by my law office in Philadelphia to thank me for my intervention with Thurgood. A picture taken that day still hangs in my office.

Kennedy's masterful public relations ploy may have won him the very close 1960 election. Word quickly spread through the Negro community, while the mainline media gave it scant attention. Harris Wofford prepared a blue pamphlet (apparently without the knowledge of the Kennedy brothers) telling the story about how Jack had rescued King. The "blue bomb" circulated widely throughout the black electorate. While Kennedy carried Illinois by only 9,000 disputed votes, he received an estimated 250,000 black votes in that state. He garnered 250,000 black votes in Michigan, which he won by 67,000 votes. Forty thousand blacks voted for Kennedy in South Carolina, and he won the state by 10,000.[5] While neither Martin Luther King nor Thurgood Marshall publicly endorsed Jack Kennedy, they probably won the election for him.

In my work with Thurgood Marshall, I deeply appreciated the support we received from Robert Kennedy's Justice Department, especially Burke

Marshall, the assistant attorney general for the civil rights division, and Nicholas Katzenbach, the deputy attorney general. They were extraordinary in carrying out the requirements of *Brown* v. *Board of Education* in the states and school districts where there was resistance. They were initially critical of Eisenhower's employment of federal troops in Little Rock, but as they faced similar crises in Mississippi and Alabama they reluctantly concluded that federalizing the National Guard was the necessary course.

THE WARREN COMMISSION

As every American knows, the nation lost its young and charismatic president, John F. Kennedy, on November 22, 1963. He was assassinated in Dallas, Texas. Lyndon B. Johnson was sworn in on Air Force One amid rumors about the assassination, which reached a crescendo when Jack Ruby killed the alleged lone assassin Lee Harvey Oswald in front of TV cameras in the Dallas police station.

Only six days after the tragedy President Johnson established a seven-member commission to conduct an official inquiry into the assassination. With the persuasive arm-twisting of which he was a master, the new president convinced a reluctant Chief Justice Warren to chair the commission. The other members were Representatives Gerald R. Ford of Michigan and Hale Boggs of Louisiana, Senators Richard Russell of Georgia and John Sherman Cooper of Kentucky, CIA director Allen Dulles, and former World Bank president John J. McCloy.

The commission selected as general counsel J. Lee Rankin, Eisenhower's solicitor general, who had been an effective ally in the *Brown* cases. About four days after his appointment Rankin invited me to be one of six senior counsel for the Warren Commission. I agreed, with the understanding that I could continue to practice law while undertaking this assignment.

I took the train from Philadelphia to Washington to meet with Lee Rankin, along with the five other senior counsel appointees. My senior counsel colleagues were quite impressive: Albert E. Jenner Jr., who founded the Chicago firm Jenner and Block; Francis W. H. Adams, a former New York City police commissioner; Joseph A. Ball, a Los Angeles trial lawyer; Norman Redlich of New York University Law School; and David W. Belin, a successful lawyer and businessman from Des Moines who later wrote two books on the assassination. Each of us would be in charge of one of six areas of inquiry. At the first meeting Rankin assigned me the task of determining whether there had been a foreign conspiracy; what Lee Harvey Oswald had done when he visited the Soviet Union and Mexico; and whether the Cubans or Russians were involved in any way.

Each senior counsel was supported by a full-time junior counsel; I was assigned W. David Slawson, who later became a professor of law at the University of Southern California. Among the other impressive junior counsel with whom I had the opportunity to work closely were John Hart Ely, a Warren law clerk, who later became a noted constitutional scholar and my general counsel at the U.S. Department of Transportation; and Arlen Specter, who has served this country with tenacious intellect for many years on both sides of the aisle as a senator from Pennsylvania. When it was finally issued, the report listed fourteen assistant counsel and twelve staff.

The commissioners were all busy men, which meant that the bulk of the work would fall on the staff. The mostly part-time staff of about twenty-five consisted mainly of young lawyers without experience in criminal investigation or cold-war intelligence gathering. Given the tight deadlines, the staff was not in a position to conduct an independent investigation from scratch. It depended heavily on the work of the professionals in the FBI and the CIA. Nevertheless, the commission and professional staff brought judgment, experience, and analytical skill to the review of the investigatory work, and they conducted many interviews of witnesses, probing all meaningful leads.

Fresh out of law school, David Slawson worked full time on the commission staff. I spent three or four days a week at the Madison Hotel working out of the Veterans of Foreign Wars building across from the Supreme Court and making an occasional visit to the Federal Power Commission on behalf of my client, Philadelphia Gas Works. I read a lot of files on the train between Philadelphia and Washington, exchanging views with my travel companion, Arlen Specter.

Slawson and I were fully aware (and appropriately apprehensive) of the gravity of the task assigned to us. President Kennedy's assassin had a record of pro-Soviet and pro-Castro activities. Oswald had tried to defect to the Soviet Union and lived in Russia from October 1959 through May 1962. He had married the daughter of a colonel in the Soviet Ministry of Internal Affairs. He had visited the Cuban and Soviet embassies in Mexico City only eight weeks before the assassination.

The failed Bay of Pigs invasion and Cuban missile crisis had occurred under the young president's watch. If Oswald had been involved in a retaliatory foreign conspiracy to murder a U.S. president, the cold war would suddenly have become hot with potentially unimaginable consequences. But if we were to conclude that Lee Harvey Oswald was not the agent of foreign conspirators (wittingly or unwittingly), we would first have to review thousands of pages of intelligence reports and interview hundreds of witnesses to determine whether any of the allegations of a foreign conspiracy had merit or any of Oswald's activities and trips abroad suggested foreign involvement in encouraging, planning, or carrying out the assassination. Given Oswald's pro-Soviet and pro-Castro activities, it is fair to say that we initially assumed we would find some evidence of Soviet or Cuban involvement, or both. We considered but rejected involvement by either China or North Vietnam early on in our investigation, even though Madame Nhu reportedly sent Mrs. Kennedy a highly offensive telegram after the assassination, rejoicing in the assassination as justified retribution for Kennedy's alleged complicity in the murder of her husband. But there was no evidence of North Vietnamese involvement.

My first task was to investigate thoroughly the files of the CIA, the FBI, the State Department, and other federal and state governmental agencies, including all the diplomatic cables, to create a detailed study of what the U.S. government knew about Lee Harvey Oswald's activities when he was in Mexico City and the Soviet Union. David Slawson and I had top security clearances and complete access to all commission information and FBI, CIA, and White House documents. We came up against the wall between the CIA and the FBI that prevented the agencies from sharing information with each other. Its purpose was to keep the CIA out of domestic activities and protect the privacy rights of American citizens, but the barrier later became an obstruction that may have precluded the sharing of critical information before the September 11, 2001, terrorist attacks in New York City and Washington.

The CIA had learned within a few hours after the assassination that some eight weeks earlier Oswald had met with Cuban officials at the Cuban embassy in Mexico City. I discovered that the U.S. ambassador to Mexico, Thomas C. Mann, a close friend of President Johnson's, had sent frantic cables to the White House after the assassination, reporting on allegations that Lee Harvey Oswald was in a conspiracy with the Cubans, who were responsible for the assassination. Ambassador Mann believed that a U.S. retaliatory attack on Cuba was imminent.

The CIA in Washington and its Mexico City station chief produced solid information that, in my judgment, demonstrated that Cuba was not involved in the assassination. The work of the CIA was professional and critical to the commission's ability to make informed judgments about the many rumors that were swirling around at that time.

David Slawson, Howard Willens, and I spent more than a week in Mexico City in April 1964, meeting with U.S., Mexican, and Cuban officials. Oswald had visited the Cuban embassy in an unsuccessful attempt to obtain a visa to travel to Cuba in transit to the Soviet Union. U.S. intelligence sources showed us intercepted messages and photographs of Oswald's visit to and communications with officials in the Cuban and Soviet embassies in Mexico City. We discussed with CIA and U.S. embassy officials their findings based on intelligence investigations and consultations with Mexican authorities. We thoroughly reviewed the credibility of various witnesses who claimed to have seen actions or heard statements that directly or indirectly linked the assassination to the Castro government. We concluded that such accounts were not credible. While we tracked down a number of leads and recommended some follow-up testimony, we left Mexico without having found any credible evidence of Cuban government involvement in the assassination.

I was frankly glad to return to the states. The atmosphere of suspicion and terror in those weeks following the assassination was not conducive to a good night's sleep. As I lay in bed restlessly in the early hours of one morning, I heard a rattling at my window. Was someone trying to break in to silence the investigator? When I got up a few hours later, I was assured by U.S. embassy personnel that the hotel window washers worked overnight and that the CIA was keeping watch over me.

We also received detailed reports from the intelligence agencies concerning Oswald's trip to the Soviet Union. The Soviet Union had provided the commission with official documents describing Oswald's activities while traveling there, his aborted attempt to obtain Soviet citizenship, his marriage to Marina, his eight-month stay in Minsk, and his decision to return to the United States. The Soviets clearly had considered how he could be of use to them, possibly for propaganda purposes, but concluded that Oswald, who attempted suicide in Russia when his application for citizenship was rejected, was unstable and of low intelligence. A Soviet defector, Yuri Ivanovich Nosenko, essentially confirmed this view, although we treated his testimony with skepticism, given the timing of his defection shortly after the assassination and his seemingly extraordinary knowledge of Oswald's Soviet experience.

Slawson and I initially were scheduled to travel to Minsk, but the FBI and the CIA persuaded Chief Justice Warren that our trip could jeopardize the confidentiality of the foreign sources on which they had relied in making their reports. When I was informed that our proposed trip had been cancelled, I was disappointed. I thought it would have been helpful to interview directly people in Minsk who knew Oswald personally and the officials who had considered his application for citizenship.

In subsequent years some skeptics have suggested that the CIA and the FBI withheld critical information from Slawson and me. There were extremely sensitive issues during the height of the cold war concerning personnel, practices, agents, and defectors, but I do not believe that relevant information was withheld. Nor was I in a position to alleviate the skepticism without revealing sources and techniques that would have jeopardized national security. For example, Slawson and I reviewed tapes of telephone calls that Oswald made to the Soviet embassy in Mexico City, but I was not about to disclose at that time that the CIA had wiretaps and surveillance cameras on the Soviet embassy in Mexico City.

Critics have written that the CIA withheld from the commission information about Operation Mongoose—a highly clandestine activity in which Robert Kennedy's Justice Department and purported representatives of organized crime, who had contacts in Havana, had considered various ways to assassinate Fidel Castro and other Cuban high officials. Apparently no gimmicky contrivance was off the table, including exploding cigars and poisoned milk shakes. If the commission had been fully aware of this nefarious activity (and if Castro had been aware of it) we would have considered this strong motivation for retaliation. In my many meetings with the CIA, from which we developed an excellent rapport, I believe I was made generally aware that such planning had been undertaken and debated. In any event, the information would not likely have affected my investigation since we had to assume Castro's antipathy toward Kennedy so soon after the Bay of Pigs failed invasion and the missile crisis.

At the time of the assassination, Castro and officials in the Kennedy administration were also engaged in back-channel communications to improve relations. I had known Fidel Castro slightly from my law school days visiting Harlem jazz clubs, as Castro was a jazz enthusiast. He was an affable, witty, mercurial, and unpredictable personality, but I found credible his comment to Senator Specter in 1998 that he was "not a crazy man" and had had nothing to do with Oswald and the Kennedy assassination.[6]

After six months of investigation, we prepared a 107-page memorandum setting forth the facts and our conclusions on Oswald's foreign contacts and connections.[7] We explored all reasonable hypotheses and applied common-sense judgments. Slawson and I made several detailed presentations to the commission and met individually with members who had particular follow-up questions. We asked questions of staff as they reported on other areas of the investigation. On several occasions I had detailed conversations with Chief Justice Warren and with Representative Ford.

David Slawson and I recommended that the commission conclude that the evidence did not support a foreign conspiracy finding. Nor was there credible evidence that any foreign individual, government, or agent had been directly or indirectly involved in the assassination. After intensive probing by several members, the commission agreed with our conclusions.

Arlen Specter had one of the most difficult assignments. He led the investigation into whether Lee Harvey Oswald had acted alone. There was much speculation in the press that there must have been at least two marksmen because President Kennedy and Governor Connolly of Texas, who accompanied him, were both shot. Specter delivered the "one bullet" theory, demonstrating scientifically that although Oswald had fired three shots, a single bullet from Oswald's rifle had struck both President Kennedy and Governor Connolly.[8]

The commission issued its report on September 24, 1964.[9] It found no evidence of a conspiracy. Lee Harvey Oswald, a depressed and disturbed man with radical political views, had acted alone. Interviews with Marina Oswald had revealed that their marriage was deeply troubled. Oswald wanted to demonstrate dramatically his manhood, as he had attempted on prior occasions. As I recall, there was evidence that Oswald had told Marina the day before the assassination that the next day he would do something that would make her very proud of him.

The commission also found that Jack Ruby had acted alone. Although I was not involved in this part of the investigation, I was privy to the staff presentation and the commission's deliberations. Given the information revealed about Ruby's connections to persons allegedly involved in organized crime and photographs that showed him stalking Oswald after the assassination (but before he shot Oswald), I thought it was important that the commission fully probe the veracity of Ruby's testimony. He had claimed that he acted alone on impulse and affection for Jackie Kennedy. I believe the commission came to a proper conclusion, weighing all the possibilities and probabilities. Despite the flurry of rumors and speculation at the time and since, there was not any solid evidence to implicate another party.

The chief justice once again demonstrated his mastery at forging a consensus. Senator Russell and Representative Ford were not completely convinced that Lee Harvey Oswald had acted alone. Warren redrafted the findings to state that the commission "found no evidence that either Lee Harvey Oswald or Jack Ruby was part of any conspiracy, domestic or foreign to assassinate President Kennedy."[10] The language left open the possibility that additional evidence would one day emerge that could change the report's conclusion.[11] In retrospect, I would rephrase the finding as follows: "The Commission found that the evidence did not support a conspiracy. . . ." We were confronted with myriad rumors and conflicting and contradictory testimony, which we had to sift through and sort out. We had to use judgment and common sense in assessing the probative value of the evidence. We spent a lot of time authenticating documents and resolving conflicting testimony in deciding on what and whom we could rely. For example, we had to consider the possibility that Oswald was brainwashed during his stay in the Soviet Union in the fall of 1959 and determine the accuracy of reports that he attempted suicide when the Russians denied him citizenship. Weighing all the evidence, we concluded that, at most, the Soviets viewed the pathetic Oswald as a possible tool for anti-Western propaganda.

As is so often the case in Washington, most of the work of the commission was undertaken by staff lawyers. As lawyers we are trained to weigh the probative value of the evidence. We have to prove our case to a disinterested party—in this case, the American public. We concluded that the evidence did not support a conspiracy finding, and our findings are supported by a voluminous record. The commission's review of that information was uneven. The chief justice was deeply and personally involved. A former prosecutor, he asked tough questions and exercised sound judgment. Gerald Ford and Allen Dulles also were actively involved at each step of the way.

Through the years many conspiracy theories have been circulated, calling into question the Warren Commission's findings. This is completely understandable given the historical cold-war context, Oswald's bizarre foreign trips, Ruby's deranged intervention, and the tragic story of the slain leader of Camelot. Moreover, the commission's work was closed to the public, and for obvious reasons we could not disclose some of the sources of our investigation or our deliberations on possible foreign conspiracies. Finally, we needed to complete our report as quickly as possible (in a little less than a year) to bring closure to these unsettling issues for both the American public and our international allies and adversaries. Nonetheless, I remain solidly behind the commission's conclusions. In the spirit of full disclosure, however, there are two bits of evidence that have always intrigued me, although I do not find them sufficiently compelling to undermine the commission's findings.

First, one witness claimed that several days before the assassination he saw Jack Ruby sitting in front of a window in the news offices where Ruby worked. From that vantage point he would have had a clear view of the place where the car carrying President Kennedy would be when the assassin's bullet hit. We investigated this claim thoroughly and located several other witnesses who stated that at the time of the shooting Ruby was not sitting in front of that particular window. Other witnesses testified that he was elsewhere in the newspaper offices. We did not find the original witness's statement credible. Even if it were true, it is not clear what significance could be attached to where Ruby was sitting at a particular point in time unless there were other supporting evidence that he was involved in a conspiracy.

The other bit of evidence that intrigued me, and continues to puzzle me, was information that I found in one of the documents the Soviets turned over to the United States after the assassination. The document described Oswald's activities in Minsk. A long-standing tradition in the village where Oswald lived was that each winter the men would go on a hunting trip. A rule of the hunting trip was that the group could not return until each man had shot and killed at least one animal. According to this document, Oswald was such a lousy shot that even after several days on the trip, he still had not successfully bagged an animal. Finally, in desperation, another hunter standing behind Oswald shot an animal and said to Lee Harvey, "You have now killed your animal"—thereby allowing the group, now all very cold, tired, and hungry, to pack up their camping gear and head home. If true, this report would have called into question how Oswald could have made such an accurate shot on November 22, 1963, as to hit both the president and Governor Connolly. There was contrary evidence in the record, however. When in the U.S. military Oswald was awarded a marksman medal. His Marine Corps reputation was that of an accurate and skillful rifleman. There were also statements in other Russian documents that contradicted the hunting story. There was further evidence that Oswald engaged in target shooting while in Texas.

As a key sentence in the commission report, a sentence that I wrote, states, the hardest thing to prove is a negative. I must confess there is a slight queasiness in my stomach when I read that the Russians are now opening up additional KGB files. Who knows what sinister information may be lurking there?

In retrospect, I wish we had had a clearer understanding of why Oswald assassinated Kennedy and why Ruby killed Oswald. We concluded that Oswald was an "unstable and neurotic character" who did not get along with other people and was "confused, dogmatic and unused to the discipline of logical thought." He "fashioned himself a potential leader and resented the fact that circumstances compelled him to do menial work," but he never finished high school and had trouble keeping even a menial job.[12] None of this really explains why he killed the president. Jack Ruby deprived us of the best evidence on this issue.

More than a half century has passed since the Warren Commission issued its report. The report and supporting evidence are now available to the public at the National Archives. All the information, including the documents and testimony of witnesses, was made available to the attorney general, Robert Kennedy, who would have left no stone unturned in determining the accuracy of the findings concerning the death of his beloved brother. To my knowledge, no compelling evidence has come forward that would disprove the commission's findings. I hope we have brought closure to this sad chapter in American history. The findings of the Warren Commission enabled the nation to complete its grieving process and move on to address the many challenges on the domestic and foreign fronts. If Slawson and I had found compelling evidence of a Cuban or Soviet conspiracy, I can only imagine how world events might have unfolded. Instead, the precarious peace of containment was maintained as we made the orderly transition to the Johnson administration.

LBJ

With his knowledge of the levers of power and skilled leadership, President Johnson seized the momentum of goodwill and national unity as the nation mourned the death of the young president. The Johnson administration's success in enacting civil rights legislation, establishing Medicare, declaring war on poverty, and enforcing judicial mandates ensured that the *Brown* legacy would become engrained in the nation's legal fabric. Johnson, the practical politician, knew that his signature on a bill alone would not solve the intractable problems of race and poverty that festered in the nation's urban and rural communities. He knew that some of the well-intended New Deal policies in welfare and housing had been counterproductive. He looked to the affected parties for practical solutions. In 1965 he called the White House Conference on Civil Rights, which was held on June 1 and 2, 1966. The conference was titled To Fulfill These Rights. More than twenty-four hundred participants met to address four areas of discussion—housing, economic security, education, and the administration of justice. As co-chair of the planning session I brought some young potential leaders like the Reverend Jesse Jackson of Chicago and the new mayor of Gary, Indiana, Andy Hatcher, into the planning process. I thought they would engage young people from the inner city who were sitting on a tinder box about to explode in frustration and protest.

One of the younger participants told me that the most foolish thing that President Roosevelt had ever done was to create large high-rise housing projects for the poor in the northern cities. I had always thought this was one of Roosevelt's greater achievements, since it provided better living conditions for many of the poor blacks who migrated north. But it also created concentrated racially segregated neighborhoods. A wiser policy would have been to create affordable housing throughout the suburbs, with racially mixed neighborhoods in which people of different ethnicities and classes could work together, learn together in school, and get to know one another. In FDR's time, that could not have happened. The times had changed, and, in my judgment and that of the commission, it was now time to address housing discrimination and neighborhood segregation. The 100-page conference report called for legislation to ban racial discrimination in housing and in the administration of criminal justice. It recommended increased federal spending to improve the quality of housing and education. After the conference, in recognition of my contribution to the conference, President Johnson invited Lovida and me to a White House dinner in honor of Princess Margaret. To Lovida's amusement, I was seated between Princess Margaret and Happy Rockefeller, whose romances had been highlighted in the tabloids of the day.

Lyndon Johnson must have been pleased with my work because, no doubt at the urging of Thurgood Marshall, he urged me to accept an appointment as a judge on the U.S. Court of Appeals for the Third Circuit. Unwilling to give up the exciting and lucrative practice of law, I turned him down. In early 1967 I got a call from Harry McPherson, counsel to President Johnson, who said, "Bill, the president was wondering whether you were planning to be in

Washington this Sunday afternoon. If so, he hoped you'd drop by his office around three o'clock."

"Well, Harry, I was planning to take a trip to D.C. on Sunday—a chance to see those elegant Dutch landscapes at the National Gallery," I improvised. That Sunday I dropped into the Oval Office and chatted with the president for forty-five minutes, mostly about the southern resistance to school desegregation and the pending civil rights legislation, which he strongly supported. I was not quite sure of the purpose of the meeting, but on the way out McPherson waved me into his office and closed the door. He said, "The conversation we are about to have never took place. The president wanted me to tell you that he has decided to nominate Thurgood Marshall to the Supreme Court."

"That's wonderful news," I replied, truly elated.

"There is one potential glitch," McPherson continued. "Our legislative people are not sure they can muster the votes for confirmation. And the president asked me to find out discreetly whether your decision to turn down an appointment to the Third Circuit Court would apply to the Supreme Court if we can't get Marshall confirmed."[13]

Stunned, I stammered, "Well, you know, Harry, the Supreme Court, well, the Supreme Court, that's an entirely different job. But we will get Thurgood Marshall confirmed, I assure you."

Johnson nominated Marshall on June 13. We proved the White House vote counters wrong. Marshall was confirmed by the Senate on August 31, 1967, by a vote of 69-11.

PHILADELPHIA COMMUNITY WORK

During the Johnson years I was also involved with Philadelphia community work. Mayor Dilworth established and appointed me chair of the Citizens Police Review Board. The board heard citizen complaints about police abuse. To my surprise I found that police mistreatment of poor minorities was not exclusively a problem of white police officers. We instituted new training initiatives for all members of the police department regardless of race or ethnicity. Mayor James Tate, who succeeded Dilworth, appointed me to a civilian advisory committee on poverty, as a representative of the Greater Philadelphia Movement, a multiracial reform movement that brought together Main Line aristocrats and political reformers to address the deterioration of the city's inner core. Through this work, I got to know and admire Samuel Evans, a black civil rights leader who spent a lifetime representing the poor until his death at the age of one hundred and five in 2008. Evans made sure that the work of this committee reflected the legitimate concerns of the poor and would not be co-opted by the establishment, including the Greater Philadelphia Movement.

When Mayor Dilworth resigned to run for governor against Bill Scranton, I fully supported him as my mentor and friend. I was therefore surprised when the victorious Governor Scranton asked me to join his cabinet as secretary of welfare. I turned him down, but shortly thereafter he asked me, as chairman of the Philadelphia Bar Association's judiciary committee, to recommend new judges for the Common Pleas Court of Philadelphia County and the Philadelphia Municipal Court.

Through the years our paths would cross on numerous occasions, on Nixon's Price Commission, in President Ford's cabinet, and on the IBM board of directors. Indeed, I believe he recommended me to President Ford when the president was forming his own cabinet.

THE TRILATERAL COMMISSION

It was through another association, however, that Lovida and I became traveling companions of Bill and Mary Scranton. While I was at the Dilworth firm, Zbigniew Brzezinski persuaded David Rockefeller, then chief executive officer of Chase Manhattan Bank, to organize a group of business leaders with public service experience from the major industrial economies of North America, Western Europe, and Japan. The group would meet periodically to discuss and promote good public policies.

From this idea was born the Trilateral Commission. I was appointed one of its five lifetime trustees. The Trilateral Commission was formed to provide a forum for leading corporate and academic thinkers from the United States, Canada, Europe, and Japan to exchange ideas about monetary policy, disarmament, fair trade, and other public policies. Members of the Trilateral Commission have gone on to serve as secretaries of state and defense, chief executive officers of major global conglomerates, and even a U.S. president. The candid, informal interaction opened up channels of communication as members moved in and out of government. Lasting friendships were forged as global competitors sought common understanding. The Trilateral Commission is a discussion group, not a decisionmaking body. It seeks to break down artificial barriers between governments and the private sector in an increasingly globalized economy. It generates trust among senior government officials who can shortcut bureaucratic channels to find common ground. Why this would seem threatening to certain far-right organizations has always puzzled me.

It was not easy to juggle public service opportunities, my work with the business community through the Trilateral Commission and on corporate boards, my continuing involvement in Legal Defense Fund litigation, a lively law practice, and growing administrative responsibilities at the Dilworth firm. Planes and trains provided critical reading time. To younger lawyers, fearful that public service and pro bono work will detract from billable hours as the building blocks of career advancement, I can only say that there was an incredible synergy in my diversified portfolio. The transference of experience and knowledge among various endeavors enriched the quality and wisdom of the contribution I was able to make. The network of contacts generated increasingly interesting and challenging professional opportunities.

TWENTY-FIVE

Managing the Dilworth Litigation Department

America is the paradise of lawyers.

—JUSTICE DAVID J. BREWER

BACK AT THE DILWORTH FIRM, I continued to be actively engaged in litigation and corporate matters. On February 12, 1962, Mayor Dilworth had resigned to run for governor of Pennsylvania. He was solidly defeated by William Scranton by more than half a million votes. Scranton, a Republican representative from Scranton, Pennsylvania, was a worthy opponent. It hadn't hurt that his brother-in-law, the editor of *Time* magazine, had put Scranton's picture on the cover of *Time* a week before the election. Dilworth told me he was happy that the margin of his loss was so great because he did not lie awake at night wondering whether with one more speech or one more visit to a rural county, he might have won.

The good news was that Dilworth returned to our law firm in 1963. The new mayor of Philadelphia, James Tate, appointed him president of the Philadelphia school board, a nonpaying job. Mayor Tate also instructed the Philadelphia Gas Works (PGW), which was owned by the City, to retain the Dilworth firm with me as the lead outside counsel. The operator of PGW was the United Gas Improvement Company, a publicly owned company listed on the New York Stock Exchange. For many decades the outside law firm for Philadelphia Gas Works and United Gas was Morgan, Lewis, and Bockius. In a devilish mood Dilworth asked me to pay a visit to Arthur W. Littleton, the distinguished leader of Morgan, Lewis, and inform him of the City's decision to transfer legal representation of PGW to the Dilworth firm, and to arrange for the delivery of all the files in pending litigation, regulatory, and transactional matters. Since Morgan, Lewis's office was three floors below the Dilworth firm's, in the Fidelity Philadelphia Trust Building, it wasn't a long journey. But Dilworth was well aware that Littleton had refused to interview me for a job at Morgan, Lewis when I had applied there after my clerkship with Justice Frankfurter.

Dilworth obviously had called Littleton in advance. Littleton's greeting was friendly and courteous. He pledged to cooperate fully with us in the transfer of all representations to our firm, with one exception. We had no lawyers in the Dilworth firm, he said, with experience in natural gas regulatory matters nor any office in Washington, where the Federal Power Commission hearings took place. I explained to Littleton that since Philadelphia was only 140 miles from Washington and the trains ran every hour until well after midnight, it would not be inconvenient for our firm to participate in Federal Power Commission hearings. I further noted that Congress had not enacted the Natural Gas Act until 1938, and the Supreme Court had not ruled that the Federal Power Commission had jurisdiction over pricing and service contracts between natural gas producers and the interstate pipelines until the *Philips* case in 1954. We were therefore confident that our firm could complete our review of all the appellate decisions and rulings of the Federal Power Commission and be ready to undertake the work immediately. Littleton reluctantly agreed to turn over all the files in pending matters, as the City had directed.

The following Monday I plunged into the extensive PGW files. I was assisted by a young associate, Robert Maris, the son of Albert B. Maris, judge of the U.S. Court of Appeals for the Third Circuit, who had recently joined the firm. Maris was a summa cum laude graduate of Haverford College and a magna cum laude graduate of the University of Pennsylvania Law School, and he'd been a member of Penn's law review. He had just finished a clerkship with a fine judge on the Court of Common Pleas, Edmond Spaeth. Bob was articulate and hard working. Many a written brief and article bearing my name reflects his talented writing skill.

While Bob Maris and I fully immersed ourselves in the arcane world of natural gas regulation, there was a flurry of discovery, motions, briefs, and preliminary hearings in the Federal Power Commission proceedings.[1] The commission's decisions were routinely appealed to the District of Columbia Court or the Fifth Circuit Court and then up to the Supreme Court. From 1965 through 1968 I argued and won four cases in the U.S. Supreme Court dealing with natural gas issues.

My first Supreme Court oral argument thus had nothing to do with race. It was *United Gas Improvement Co.* v. *Continental Oil* (1965) involving the commission's jurisdiction over sale of gas fields.* Unfortunately, because of illness, Justice Frankfurter had retired from the Court by that time. The following day I went to see him and told him about the experience. The next day he called

---

*The other three Supreme Court cases I argued and won for Philadelphia Gas Works and United Gas Improvement were *Federal Power Commission* v. *Sunray DX Oil Co.* (1968); *Permian Basin Area Rate Cases* (1968); and *United Gas Improvement Co.* v. *Callery Properties, Inc.* (1965).

to tell me that Justice Harlan had come in to visit and remarked how well I had handled the issues.

The midsixties were the heyday of pervasive government economic regulation of many sectors of industry. Not surprisingly, it also was the time when specialized Washington law firms sprung up like wild weeds in the month of May. What was good for the lawyers—and often good for industry—was not necessarily good for the consumer or for economic growth and efficiency, as we would see in the coming decades.

One sultry summer afternoon in 1958 I received a call that made me very popular among the younger Dilworth lawyers. A Harvard Law School classmate, Mickey Rudin, asked me to represent Frank Sinatra, who was a member of a group that had applied for a casino license in Atlantic City. As a part of the due diligence phase the attorney general of New Jersey had requested an interview with Sinatra. To avoid a crowd and unwanted publicity, I arranged to have the interview conducted in a private aircraft at an isolated airfield in northern New Jersey. This was the first of several occasions when I met Frank Sinatra, who was always a gentleman and appreciative of the advice I gave him. My young partners continued to do work for Frank Sinatra, which occasionally took them on hardship duty to the Hollywood social scene.

Another important client of the Dilworth firm was Levitt and Sons. In the early 1950s Bill Levitt had purchased more than ten thousand acres of land in Bucks County, Pennsylvania. The seller owned additional property with a substantial water supply, and Levitt had assumed that it would have access to the water for its planned housing development. The seller, however, said no, and Levitt was left high and dry.

Levitt asked the Dilworth firm to represent the company. We brought a lawsuit against the seller, claiming that the water reservoirs were a public utility and that Levitt had the right to purchase the water at a fair and reasonable price. We were successful. The houses were built on the land with access to a water supply.

Levitt created mass-produced affordable, comfortable homes for G.I.s returning from the war. The prefabricated communities introduced the suburban way of life, where children played safely in cul-de-sac neighborhoods surrounded by shopping centers, churches, and manicured lawns. By 1952 Levitt was building one of every eight new houses in the United States. There was a problem, however. Levitt refused to sell houses to people of color.[2]

On behalf of the NAACP's Legal Defense Fund, Thurgood Marshall and Constance Baker Motley brought a lawsuit against Levitt in federal court alleging that its refusal to sell houses to Negroes in Levittown, Pennsylvania, violated the Fourteenth Amendment. Needless to say, this put me in an extremely awkward position. As chairman of the board I was actively engaged in representing the Legal Defense Fund on a voluntary basis in other civil rights litigation. On the other hand, I felt that a law firm had an obligation to represent its long-standing clients, and Levitt had retained the Dilworth firm on many matters over the years. I did not object to the firm's taking on the representation, but I did not participate in the case.

The federal district judge dismissed the case on the grounds that since the defendant was a private company, it did not involve state action under the Fourteenth Amendment. The Legal Defense Fund appealed to the circuit court. During the course of the appeal I had several conversations with Bill Levitt on other legal matters we were handling for his company. Occasionally he would bring up the pending civil rights matter.

Levitt would ask, "Bill, do you think your law firm will prevail in the circuit court?"

"Given the current state of the law," I replied, "I think it's likely you will prevail on appeal. My guess is that the Supreme Court would not take up the case at this time."

"That's encouraging," he responded.

I continued, "In all candor, Bill, I think you should consider the long-term consequences of your position. Your business depends on the support of the public and the government. The Housing Act and the G.I. Bill are critical to your home buyers. I personally believe that federal law and policy will change. The question is whether you want to wait until this change takes place or be ahead of the curve."

A few days later Levitt asked me to arrange a dinner with Thurgood Marshall. We met for a couple of days at the Levitt home in Bucks County, and Bill finally agreed that after the first hundred homes were sold in Levittown, Pennsylvania, he would eliminate any restrictions on the sale of houses based on race in both Levittown, Pennsylvania, and Levittown, New Jersey, which was still in the planning stage. He also agreed to change the racial policies for Levittown, Long Island. Levitt's explanation for excepting the first hundred houses was that he wanted to ensure that when Negroes purchased homes in Levittown, it would be in various sections of the development and not in one section only. He rightly wanted to avoid a racial ghetto in any of his Levittown developments.

Given the importance of federal support for his projects, I suspect that Bill Levitt was very happy he had ended racial exclusions when he learned three weeks later that President Johnson planned to appoint Robert Weaver as secretary of housing and urban development. Levitt once said to me, "Can you imagine my life today if I had not followed your advice?"

With Levitt's change in policy, a few families of color moved into Levittown. They were the true heroes. They were greeted with burning crosses on their lawns, rocks crashing through their windows, mobs waiving confederate flags, and harassing phone calls in the middle of the night. But they persevered, and the Levittowns became integrated.

Richardson Dilworth and Henry Ford II had been classmates during Ford's only year at Yale, and the Dilworth firm was asked to represent Ford Motor Company in its acquisition of Philco. The representation involved some complex antitrust issues, as both Philco and Ford competed vigorously for defense contracts. The Justice Department's Antitrust Division was raising some hurdles, and Dilworth asked me if I could help set up a meeting with Attorney General Kennedy. I requested a meeting at nine on a Monday morning, two days before the closing of the transaction. The attorney general's office never asked the subject of the meeting. Apparently Kennedy assumed that I wanted to see him about the admission of James Meredith to the University of Mississippi—the hot-button topic in the media occupying much of Robert Kennedy's time. When Dilworth, Jim Sutton, and I arrived at the Justice Department with some Ford executives in tow, Kennedy seemed surprised. Having assumed that we wanted to discuss a civil rights matter, he had asked Burke Marshall, head of the Civil Rights Division, to attend the meeting. Marshall was a leading antitrust attorney who had requested the civil rights job because of his commitment to the issue. The attorney general reportedly had a lot more respect for Burke Marshall's views on antitrust than for those of the assistant attorney general, Lee Lovinger, who ran the Antitrust Division. Our meeting was successful, and the acquisition was completed on the scheduled date.

One lesson I have learned in practicing law, a lesson that every new generation of lawyers seems to have to relearn the hard way, is that a lawyer should not discuss legal matters outside the law firm or the scope of his client representation. The Justice Department had initiated a criminal investigation into allegations of contract bid–rigging by General Electric, Westinghouse, Allis Chalmers, and eighteen other major manufacturers of electrical equipment for utilities, transit systems, and cities. One day on my train commute from Mount Airy to Philadelphia I sat next to a partner in a top Philadelphia firm that was representing one of the principal defendants. He described to me his client's concern that if they lost this criminal case, the public utilities and cities could sue them civilly, claiming antitrust violations and seeking treble damages plus counsel fees.

A week later Harold Kohn mentioned at a partner's meeting that he had been approached by a lawyer in another Philadelphia law firm about defending a junior executive in an electrical manufacturing company who was under criminal investigation. He thought this represented a breakthrough opportunity for the trial lawyers at Dilworth to represent officers at some of the nation's major electrical manufacturing companies. I said, "Harold, don't touch that case." I then described the concern that had been expressed to me by my indiscrete companion on the train ride to work.

The manufacturing companies pleaded guilty to rigging government bids on turbines, switch-gears, and other heavy electrical equipment. Our firm was retained by the City of Philadelphia, Philadelphia Electric, Philadelphia Gas Works, and other distribution companies to sue the manufacturers for treble damages. The lawsuit resulted in a substantial settlement, which swelled our firm's profits for about five years and made us even more the go-to firm for antitrust work. It paid my children's tuition bills for a number of years.

There was good news and bad news in the success of the Dilworth firm. When Harold Kohn, who was among the best trial lawyers I have ever known and a friend and mentor, decided to leave the firm to set up his own practice, he took with him several of our top litigation partners. He asked me to come, but I said no. With Kohn's departure, I became, at the age of forty-three, the head of the litigation department at the Dilworth firm. They also put my name in the firm title, which became Dilworth, Paxson, Kalish, Levy, Dilks, and Coleman.

Some of the partners suggested that I recruit experienced litigators from outside the firm to replace the departing trial lawyers. I repeatedly rejected these suggestions. Over the years we had hired lawyers with outstanding academic records who had served on the law reviews of the best law schools and had clerked for federal or state court judges. As partners, I thought we had an obligation to the younger lawyers in our firm to make sure they had the opportunity to step up to the challenges and progress as quickly as their talent and efforts would allow. Mayor Dilworth, Harry Kalish, and other key partners supported my position. Today the legal business has changed substantially. Partners come and go from law firms like customers through a revolving door on a President's Day sale. I fear we have lost something important in the process, probably never to be regained.

Mayor Dilworth would sometimes subtly intimate that in hiring prospective litigators, my requirement of an outstanding academic record and preferably a clerkship for a distinguished judge may have prevented me from considering some very capable young lawyers of color. Perhaps to make this point, he took it upon himself to interview and recruit a young Yale Law School graduate named David Pattinsky. After he described David's law school record to me I heartily agreed that he would be an excellent choice. I was surprised when David showed up at the office for his first day at work with a skin color like mine. His mother was black, his father Jewish. During my years practicing law I did not lower the bar in recruiting and supervising lawyers of color. Although I then supported affirmative action programs to ease entry into law schools of persons from disadvantaged backgrounds, I believed it was their responsibility to work extra hard thereafter to establish a reputation of excellence, as Houston, Hastie, and Marshall had done. Once minority lawyers with superior records were hired, I made sure they were given the opportunities to work for important clients on major business matters having nothing to do with race. Too often the large firms assign minority lawyers to discrimination defense work or pro bono matters. Today there are many highly qualified minority law students for whom the major firms compete vigorously. To retain such talent the firms need to do a better job of creating challenging opportunities within the firm.

My work for Philadelphia Gas Works soon brought me into the international arena. One of the company's top executives, Charles Frazier, recognized that meeting energy peak demand would require the importation of natural gas, which could be accomplished only if gas were condensed into a liquid that could be loaded onto tankers for travel across the ocean. We traveled to Caracas, Venezuela, and Algiers, Algeria, on many occasions to negotiate supply contracts. Storing the liquefied gas presented a major challenge. We worked with various government agencies to meet the safety challenges involved in building a storage facility and negotiated a contract to build a facility for the Port of Philadelphia. There had been several terrible explosions in other areas, and although our engineers thought they had solved the safety problem, I insisted that the building contract we negotiated be insured by Lloyd's of London, in case the project was canceled. After the construction started there was another terrible explosion in Tipton, Massachusetts, and the PGW project was abandoned. Lloyd's of London paid every penny of PGW's outlay. Nonetheless, given the importance of natural gas today as an alternative to coal-burning utilities in meeting targets for greenhouse-gas reduction, it is disappointing that we were not able to complete the project.

As the Dilworth firm gained stature and as I took on the leadership of a respected litigation department, that I had initially broken the color barrier became increasingly irrelevant. I was accepted for membership in the Midday Club, the Union League of Philadelphia, and the Philadelphia Club, the first person, or among the first persons, of color to be admitted to these venerable institutions. I also joined the board of trustees of the Philadelphia Art Museum and became its vice chair.

Other doors began to open. I joined the boards of the Western Savings Fund Society of Philadelphia and the Penn Mutual Life Insurance Company. In 1964 our firm was retained to establish a national bank called the Lincoln Bank, and I was invited to join its board, where I served for about three years. Then the first Pennsylvania Bank and Trust Company, the largest bank in Philadelphia, asked me to join its board. I was also on the Philadelphia Electric board.

Lovida's close friends Tom and Betty Harvey had a bucolic vacation farm in South Pomfret, Vermont, about ten miles from Woodstock.[3] We started to spend about six weeks each summer there and continue to do so to this day.[4] I confess I never actually spent six weeks in South Pomfret, but I would often fly up to West Lebanon, where Lovida met me at the airport for a long weekend together at the farm. In Vermont we got to know Dr. Stanley J. Sarnoff and his talented wife, Lolo, who lived in Bethesda, Maryland, and also had a rustic home in Barnard, Vermont, which they had purchased from Dorothy Thompson and Sinclair Lewis.[5] An artist, Lolo has been very active in numerous philanthropic organizations. Twenty-three years ago she founded her own very special charity, Arts for the Aging (AFTA), combining her two interests in art and health care.[6]

A number of years later in the mid-1960s, when our three children were enrolled in Germantown Friends School, I asked Lovida if there was anything she particularly wanted. She asked for help in managing the house two days a week, as she had just been accepted as an art history student at the Barnes Foundation. Albert C. Barnes established the foundation in 1922 to promote fine arts education and appreciation.[7]

The Barnes Foundation set aside one day each year when a student could bring his or her spouse to visit the private collection. It was a special all-day event. Lovida had reserved October 15, 1965, on my calendar many months in advance. As luck would have it, the Supreme Court scheduled an oral argument on one of my cases for the very same day. Under the Court's well-established tradition it would have been fruitless to petition for a change of date.

By that time I had gotten to know Chief Justice Warren through my work on the Warren Commission, the federal Civil Rules Advisory Committee, and the Legal Defense Fund's Earl Warren Legal Training Program. Given the importance of this Barnes Foundation occasion to Lovida, I decided to call on the chief justice. With some trepidation, I asked for a meeting, which he granted. After some small talk about the Warren Commission and the Warren scholarship program I said, "There is something else, Mr. Chief Justice, that I have to ask you. I am scheduled for an argument on October 15th, and I simply cannot be present on that day. I can come the day before or the day after or any other day but that is the one day that I simply cannot come."

"Okay, Bill. Let's set a different date." The chief was too much of a gentleman to ask me why, but he had this quizzical look on his face that made me feel very guilty about withholding the reason.

"To be honest, Mr. Chief Justice," I blurted out with my eyes lowered, "for more than six months, Lovida has scheduled a special event at the Barnes Foundation where she is an art history student. She would be deeply hurt if I did not attend."

"Why, Bill, that's the best reason I've heard all week—and I've heard more than a dozen oral arguments."

Balancing family and work was always a challenge. There were times when I would take the first flight back from a business meeting in Europe to make a track meet in which one of my children was participating. They were all better-than-average athletes, and while I missed many games, the ones I made a special effort to attend are among my fondest memories.

In 1969 I received a call from Cyrus Vance, who was then a partner in the New York law firm of Simpson, Thatcher, and Bartlett. Cy was forming a group to go to London to engage in a discussion with representatives from the Middle East on how to resolve the Israeli-Palestinian controversy. At his request, I joined them. One of the Americans at the meeting in London was Najeeb Halaby, who was then the chief executive of Pan American World Airways.[8] Halaby and I hit it off really well during the discussions. The day after I got back to Philadelphia, he asked me to join Pan Am's board of directors.

Membership on the Pan Am board was a real plus for the Coleman family. My wife and I and our three children all had free first-class passes, enabling us to travel almost anywhere in the world on international routes. One day when I was rushing through Heathrow Airport in London, I bumped into my son, Bill, who was studying at Yale Law School. His embarrassment was fully justified.

"What the hell are you doing here, Bill? You should be in New Haven studying for your exams," I said.

"Well, Dad, to be honest, I had a date in Los Angeles on Saturday night. Since Pan Am has no domestic flights, I decided to return to New York via London. I'll take the train back to New Haven late tonight. Look, Dad," as he raised three law casebooks to my line of vision, "I get more studying done on these long flights than I ever could in my house in New Haven."

Somewhat relieved I said, "I can see your point, what with that roommate of yours always asking to borrow your class notes to make up for all the classes he's skipped."

"That's true, Dad, when my roommate is not on a date with Hillary Rodham, he's out campaigning for some local official. What bugs me is that he'll ace every exam. The guy is a real quick study."

"Sounds like Bill Clinton's more interested in politics than practicing law," I said before Bill III rushed off to catch his Pan Am flight to New York.

The experience of practicing law is a continuous education, constantly presenting new situations. Given our hourly rates, we are rarely asked to perform routine or repetitive duties. Each new case or transaction presents novel and untested issues that challenge the intellect and force us to dig deeper into the many layers of the law. While I relished the intellectual challenge and the joy of successful results, I also learned from my senior and junior colleagues certain fundamental principles. Let me share ten points that reflect lessons learned during my sixty years of law practice.

First, read completely and master the underlying documents, whether they be the Constitution, a federal or state statute, a corporate charter, regulations, by-laws, a contract, or pleadings already on file with the court.

Second, if you want to climb to the top of the ladder, start at the bottom and accept menial tasks cheerfully and responsibly as part of a team effort.

Third, if you are given a small part of a major transaction or litigation, understand the full context to which your responsibilities will contribute—imagine yourself as the senior partner in charge in achieving your client's objectives.

Fourth, keep your colleagues and clients fully informed about what you are doing and the status of the matters you are working on.

Fifth, understand the common-law roots that breathe life into the language of the Constitution, federal and state statutes, judicial precedents, and legal documents.

Sixth, keep up-to-date on developments in all of the principal areas of law to ensure that you understand the full context of representations that you undertake.

Seventh, because the best business development is usually success for an existing client, make sure that providing timely, high-quality, and responsive advice to your clients is your highest professional priority.

Eighth, as your career progresses, stay in touch with your colleagues, former law school classmates, clients, and other professional relationships. Throughout your career your paths will cross, providing mutually beneficial opportunities.

Ninth, diversity pays. Working with a diverse group of people is not only stimulating and enjoyable, it also creates new opportunities for challenging and interesting work.[9]

Tenth, devote time and effort to public interest law and public service, which not only is personally rewarding but also is good business development.

TWENTY-SIX

The *Girard College* Case

*The Lord so constituted everybody that no matter what color
you are you require the same amount of nourishment.*

—WILL ROGERS

STEPHEN GIRARD, A PHILADELPHIA MERCHANT and banker, was in 1813 the
richest man in America. He had made his fortune in developing trade with
China. When in 1811 Congress refused to renew the charter of the Bank of
the United States, Girard purchased the bank's nonfinancial assets. During
the War of 1812 with Great Britain, he lent the U.S. Treasury more than
$8 million, enabling the young nation to defend itself and end the war on
respectable terms in the 1814 Treaty of Ghent. Girard was a great patriot and
philanthropist. When he died in December 1831 in Philadelphia, his slave,
Hannah, was at his bedside. He freed his slave but left no heirs.

In his will, probated in 1831, he left a trust for the construction, maintenance, and operation of a "college" for "as many poor white male orphans,
[to begin school] between the ages of 6 and 10 as the said income shall be
adequate to maintain." The sole trustee named in the will was the city of Philadelphia. The school was located in North Philadelphia and opened in 1848.
At that time there were fewer than ninety thousand people living in Philadelphia, including a significant number of white and colored people living in
poverty. In 1776, when Girard arrived in the Philadelphia area, there were as
many as fifteen hundred African slaves living there, and under the phased-
in Pennsylvania Emancipation Act of 1780, there were still a few slaves at
the time the college opened. Even free blacks were treated more restrictively
under commonwealth law. In later years, inspired by the Quakers, Philadelphia would become a hotbed of abolitionist fervor.

In 1869 the Pennsylvania legislature enacted the first of several laws providing for the administration of the Girard College by a board of directors of
Philadelphia's City Trust. Board members included leading citizens, some of
whom had attended the college. Although the college never received public
money, as a charity it qualified for federal and state tax exemptions.

As the years passed the beautiful walled campus of Girard College became a fortress. Shabbily constructed public housing in the neighborhood deteriorated into a dilapidated urban Negro ghetto. The people of color who surrounded the campus enviously observed the well-dressed white orphans, who received an excellent education and often went on to successful careers. Some became chief executive officers of major Philadelphia companies.

In 1955, shortly after the Supreme Court's decision in *Brown* v. *Board of Education*, Raymond and Sadie Alexander filed a lawsuit in the Orphans' Court of Philadelphia County against the Philadelphia City Trust. Their clients were two orphan boys of color, William Ashe Foust and Robert Felder, who sought and were denied admission to the Girard elementary school.

The Alexanders argued that the racial restrictions of the will were against public policy, urging the court to eliminate the word *white* from the City Trust. The Alexanders also relied on an English case involving the will of Cecil Rhodes. The Rhodes will had excluded people of color from India and other British colonies from the Rhodes Scholarship Program at Oxford College. The House of Lords had struck the exclusionary provision as disruptive to the Commonwealth of Nations with racially diverse populations. The Philadelphia Orphans' Court, which handled estate and trust matters, rejected the Alexanders' argument. It held that the city's role in administering the trust was not state action and therefore not a violation of the Fourteenth Amendment. The Supreme Court of Pennsylvania affirmed.

Still basking in the afterglow of *Brown* v. *Board of Education*, I read about the Girard College decision in the local press with shock and amazement. A couple of weeks later as I was leaving the courthouse, I bumped into Raymond Alexander on the street. I told him I thought the Pennsylvania Supreme Court's decision that the city's involvement was not state action was outrageous. I asked him if I could work with him on a voluntary basis to seek a review by the U.S. Supreme Court. He was delighted to get the extra help.

I called Lou Pollak, who was then a professor at Yale Law School. The two of us joined the Alexanders in filing a petition for a writ of certiorari on January 2, 1957. We were opposed by Owen B. Rhodes of Dechert, Price, and Rhodes, who was assisted by a bright young partner and a friend of mine, Hasting Griffiths. The cocky Hasting bet me a hat that the Supreme Court would deny our petition—not bad odds given that the Supreme Court only grants about 1 percent of the certiorari petitions filed. If the petition had been denied, it would have been the third straight victory for the defenders of the City Trust—a "hat trick" in British cricket, rewarded by the gift of a hat to the winner.

Hasting lost his bet. On April 29, 1957, the Supreme Court took the case and summarily reversed the Pennsylvania court without oral argument. The Supreme Court held that the Board which operated Girard College is an agency of the State of Pennsylvania. Therefore, even though the Board was acting as a Trustee, its refusal to admit Foust and Felder to the college because they were Negroes was discrimination by the State. Such discrimination is forbidden by the Fourteenth Amendment. *Brown* v. *Board of Education,* 347 U.S. 483. Accordingly, the judgment of the Supreme Court of Pennsylvania is reversed and the case is remanded for further proceedings not inconsistent with this opinion.

As in its decision in *Cooper* v. *Aaron,* the Supreme Court showed zero tolerance for state resistance to the *Brown* policy—and this was Philadelphia, not Little Rock. As a true Philadelphia gentleman, a chastened Hasting promptly arrived at my door with an elegant black fedora hat in hand. Our victory unfortunately was short lived. What followed was truly incredible.

The Orphans' Court on its own motion, without any notice, briefing, or hearing, removed the city as trustee. Instead, it set up a board of twelve so-called independent trustees, requiring each of them to swear they would uphold the racial restrictions. The ten who had been members of the board of directors of the City Trust resigned from the board to accept the new appointment. We objected. The Orphans' Court overruled our objections. The Pennsylvania Supreme Court affirmed. We filed a second petition for certiorari in the U.S. Supreme Court, which was denied. We had hit a dead end.

As if the speedy action by the Pennsylvania courts were not enough, the proceedings took a nasty personal turn. Charles Klein, chief judge of the Orphans' Court, telephoned me demanding that I be in his chambers in City Hall the next day at 4:00 p.m. I arrived ten minutes early. Lawyers who practice in the Orphans' Court often come in to see the judges to get informal advice about how to handle a particular estate or trust matter. There must have been about twenty lawyers in the judge's waiting area when I arrived. About twenty after four, Judge Klein strolled out of his private office into the reception area and said to me in a booming voice, clearly intended for everyone's ears, "Coleman, you aren't fit to be in my office, get the hell out!"

I was shocked. He had summoned me to his chambers and I had dutifully arrived early. Now he was throwing me out of the office before some twenty witnesses, who must have assumed that I had mishandled a client's will or estate. Apparently he so resented our challenge to the Girard Trust that he could not control his anger. I left greatly upset but neither intimidated nor deterred. The next day Judge Klein called the senior partners in the Dilworth firm and urged them to kick me out of the firm. He strongly implied that my partners would not fare so well in the Orphans' Court if I remained in the firm. This was particularly troubling in a court where the judges have broad discretion and the power to appoint lawyers in disputes involving wealthy estates, a source of significant income for estate lawyers.

My partners at the Dilworth firm rejected his demand. It was, however, the only year in which I did not receive a bonus. The Orphans' Court also removed my estate-planning partner Douglas Paxson from its advisory committee, a prestigious position for estate lawyers. My admiration for Doug only increased when he called me in and told me to keep on doing what I was doing. "That," he said, "is what the Constitution is all about."

With our legal remedies exhausted, we seemed at an impasse; but a couple of years later agitation over Girard College started again. This time Cecil B. Moore Jr., a firebrand trial lawyer of color, mobilized a street protest against Girard College's racially restrictive admissions policy. He generated a lot of publicity and disrupted a lot of traffic in downtown Philadelphia. The picketing became so intense that the new governor of Pennsylvania, Bill Scranton, announced that he had hired two attorneys, Charles Biddle of Drinker, Biddle, and Reath, and me, to advise him on whether the racial restrictions at Girard College could be removed. Governor Scranton hoped that his announcement would stop the citywide picketing, but it did not. In fact, Cecil decided to organize a picket at my house in Mount Airy. I called him and said, "Okay, Cecil, you can picket my house as long as you personally lead the picketing. But remember, there is a steep hill in front of my house, and you had better get in better shape if you expect your pickets to last very long."

Cecil laughed. "Okay, Coleman, just file the damn suit. Then I'll stop the protest." We filed the suit, and Cecil stopped the picketing—after one last fling that disrupted the entire city for most of the day.

Charles Biddle was the epitome of a Philadelphia Main Liner. He once told me his wife couldn't understand why he would represent colored kids seeking admission to Girard College. "Bill," he said sheepishly, "my wife is from Louisiana." I replied, "Mr. Biddle, I don't find that a valid excuse. My wife also is from Louisiana, and she completely understands."

With the full support of our respective law firms, Biddle and I worked long hours, evenings and weekends, to prepare a new lawsuit. This time we filed in the federal district court. Not surprisingly, we concluded that we would not get a fair hearing in the Orphans' Court. Representing the trustees of Girard College were Arthur Littleton and his partners from Morgan, Lewis, and Bockius, which more than matched us with the number of lawyers they threw on the case.

We prevailed in the federal court, citing a state statute that required all schools in Pennsylvania to admit student applicants without regard to race. The U.S. Court of Appeals for the Third Circuit, Judge William H. Hastie presiding, reversed, holding that the Pennsylvania statute on which we had relied was not applicable to Girard College. That Hastie would rule against us is a tribute to the legal preciseness and impartiality he assumed when donning judicial robes. We knew where his heart was. His reversal, however, forced us to improve our case and withstand further appellate review.

We retried the case in the federal court. This time we demonstrated that even though the college had been funded privately there was sufficient state involvement to constitute "state action" under the Fourteenth Amendment. Joseph S. Lord, chief judge of the U.S. District Court for the Eastern District of Pennsylvania, decided the case for the plaintiffs of color. This time the Third Circuit Court of Appeals affirmed. The trustees of Girard College petitioned for certiorari to the U.S. Supreme Court, but it was denied.

As a result, the plaintiffs of color were admitted to Girard College. In later years, relying on the precedent we set, girls also were admitted to Girard College. Today almost all the students are persons of color and other minorities—male and female. That there are few white children at Girard College these days truly saddens me; this is not the integration we fought for.

In the struggle to open Girard College to persons of color, the emotions among the notoriously competitive Philadelphia law firms ran particularly hot. The litigation generated huge media attention. We were challenging the very roots of the Philadelphia establishment. Stephen Girard may not have been Ben Franklin, but he was a greatly admired historic figure. Many Main Line lawyers thought the courts had no right to interfere with his decision on how to bequeath his substantial legacy.[1] My emotions were also overheated. I could not understand why the Philadelphia establishment, whose revered ancestors embraced the very concepts of liberty that gave birth to the nation, would fight so passionately against providing to poor orphans of color the same opportunities accorded to poor white orphans. That the extraordinary beneficence of Stephan Girard should be available to all poor orphans, regardless of color, seemed to me in the late 1950s self-evident. Like Alexander Hamilton, writing about a constitutional provision, I found it "astonishing that so simple a truth should ever have had an adversary." Yet to realize this simple, self-evident truth took fifteen court opinions from five courts over fourteen years.[2]

While the lawyer's task consists of many hours of research, drafting, typing, editing, revising, and filing of briefs and arguing abstractions in a sterile, decorous environment, every so often a more tangible experience brings home the purpose of it all. In 1975 when I was serving in President Ford's cabinet, Georgetown University conferred on me an honorary degree at its June graduation ceremony. After the ceremony I descended the platform to rejoin Lovida. A young man of color, dressed in whites and carrying a tennis racket, asked me, "Excuse me sir, but are you the Mr. Coleman who at one time lived in Philadelphia?"

I said, "Yes."

"I am Theodore Louis Hicks. My brother and I graduated from Girard College. My brother Charles is now a lawyer in Texas. I am a junior at Georgetown, and when I graduate I intend to go to law school and join him in the practice of law."

What a thrill it was to hear his story. Several days later I shared this information in an emotional moment with Judge Lord.

The ever-unfolding story does not end there. In February 2009, during Black History month, Senator Casey of Pennsylvania, joined by Senator Specter, introduced a resolution on the Senate floor honoring my career.[3] At the reception that followed I was taken completely by surprise when a young person of color stepped up to the podium and presented me with a plaque on behalf of dozens of Girard College graduates of color, expressing appreciation for the work we did in revoking the exclusionary language in the Stephen Girard will and trust. As I mingled with some of the successful alumni of this fabled institution, I again experienced the very tangible blessings that often come from the tenacious pursuit of abstract principles.

TWENTY-SEVEN

The Legacy of
Houston-Hastie-Marshall

*The pioneering work in civil rights must go on. Not only
because discrimination is morally wrong but also because its
impact is more than national—it is worldwide.*

—PRESIDENT DWIGHT D. EISENHOWER

AFTER I HAD ACCEPTED THURGOOD Marshall's request in 1958 to become
chairman of the board of directors of the LDF, I began to broaden my involvement in its multifaceted legal assault on racial discrimination, while remaining a full-time partner in the Dilworth firm. As the leading civil rights group
dedicated to securing equal opportunity for people of color through law, the
LDF has focused on school integration, education equity, voter rights and
protection, economic justice, fair housing, employment discrimination, capital punishment, reform of the criminal justice and prison system, the right to
marry interracially, and the selection of judicial nominees who will uphold
constitutional protections for Americans of color and vulnerable minorities.
The LDF model has been so successful that other minority constituencies
have replicated it, such as the Children's Defense Fund, the Mexican American Legal Defense and Educational Fund, the Puerto Rican Legal Defense
and Educational Fund, the NOW Legal Defense and Educational Fund, the
Asian American Legal Defense and Educational Fund, and human rights
groups in South Africa, Canada, and Brazil.

Since the 1930s LDF lawyers have forged much of the transformative legal
precedent on civil rights through litigation in the federal and state courts and
appeals to the Supreme Court. The Inc Fund has attracted some of the finest
lawyers, regardless of color, who have gone on to extraordinary careers as federal judges, law school professors, leading law firm partners, and elected officials. Some eighty LDF alumni serve as judges of federal, state, or municipal
courts. At the risk of omission, some notable alumni include Derek A. Bell Jr.,
professor at Harvard and New York University law schools; Robert L. Carter
and Constance Baker Motley, federal district court judges; Drew S. Days III,
assistant attorney general for civil rights and U.S. solicitor general; Bill Lann
Lee, assistant attorney general for civil rights; Marian Wright Edelman, the

founder of the Children's Defense Fund; Jack Greenberg, dean of Columbia College; Eric Holder, attorney general of the United States; Deval Patrick, governor of Massachusetts; and, of course, Thurgood Marshall. And I omit from this short list such eminent and successful civil rights advocates as Elaine Jones, the first female director counsel for the LDF; Julius L. Chambers, former president of the LDF; Constance L. Rice, Ted Shaw, John Payton, and Lani Guinier. There are many others.

After President Kennedy appointed Thurgood Marshall to the U.S. Court of Appeals for the Second Circuit in 1961, I appointed Jack Greenberg to take his place as director counsel of the Legal Defense Fund. My decision was controversial, since both Jack and Constance Baker Motley had extraordinary abilities of leadership and successful Supreme Court practices, as did Bob Carter, who had left the LDF to serve as general counsel to the NAACP. Although my critics argued that I should have selected a person of color, I knew we were fighting for the principle that color should not determine qualifications for the job. Jack did a superb job at the Legal Defense Fund for many years, and Connie continued her great legal career, rising to chief judge for the Southern District of New York. I served as chair of the LDF from 1958 through 1975, when I was appointed secretary of transportation, and returned as co-chair, along with Robert Preiskel, in 1977 until I was kicked upstairs to co-chair emeritus. As chairman of the LDF, I argued three Supreme Court cases involving race, *McLaughlin* v. *Florida* (1964), *Bradley* v. *School Board of Richmond* (1974), and *School Board of Richmond* v. *State Board of Education* (1973). My record was 2-1.

I was in Washington in 1964, working on a natural gas case, when Jack Greenberg called. He explained that the state of Florida prohibited mere cohabitation in a room during the night by a white person and a colored person of different sexes. Dewey McLaughlin and his female companion were about to go to jail because the Florida Supreme Court had affirmed their conviction under the state statute. Initially, Greenberg had placed the call simply to inform me about the litigation. The LDF had a firm policy not to engage in litigation involving allegations of sexual relations between whites and blacks. Why? Because in every school case our lawyers were constantly confronted with the accusation that they were trying to promote sexual relationships among the races. Thurgood Marshall would often laugh, saying he was not aware that colored kids were so promiscuous in kindergarten. Jack Greenberg asked, "Bill, McLaughlin has asked us to represent him in this case. Given our policy, what do you think we should do?"

I replied, "How can we let two fellow American citizens go to jail merely because of their race?" Jack agreed. He then added, "Bill, you must brief and argue the case if the writ of certiorari is granted." Louis Pollak, then at Yale

Law School, once again joined me in the effort. We argued that Florida presented no overriding statutory purpose to justify prohibiting cohabitation (that is, merely occupying the same room during the night) by a racially mixed couple. If there was a justification for such a prohibition, why didn't it include couples of the same race? In the absence of such a showing, the racial classification was an invidious discrimination forbidden by the equal protection clause.

During the oral argument Justice Potter Stewart asked what was wrong with a statute that makes sexual intercourse between two unmarried persons illegal. The justice wanted to know whether I was asking the Court to overrule the fornication statutes of every state. He said that these laws were mostly codifications of common law.

I replied to Justice Stewart that this was not the case at bar, that the Florida statute prohibited two persons of different races and different sexes from occupying the same room during the night time. They would have been guilty under the Florida statute if all they were doing was reading Dylan Thomas.

Chief Justice Warren asked if McLaughlin and the white female defendant were married. I hesitated and then indicated that there was evidence in the record that they were married, and there was evidence in the record that they were not married. The Florida trial judge had removed the issue, noting that another Florida statute prohibited interracial marriages.

The chief justice then asked why the defendants were not put on the stand to testify whether or not they were married. I confessed to the Court that I did not know because I had not tried the case below. On the train ride back to Philadelphia after the argument I was mulling over how I could have better answered the question (a common affliction that all appellate litigators will understand), and it suddenly hit me that the antimiscegenation statute prohibiting interracial marriage carried a ten-year prison sentence, whereas occupation of the same room carried only a two-year sentence. No lawyer would have exposed his client to the risk of a ten-year sentence by putting him on the stand in defense of a statute that carried a maximum penalty of only two years.

The Supreme Court reversed the convictions 9-0, holding that Florida had provided no rational reason in support of the statute. Justice Stewart and Justice Douglas went even further. They rejected any possible implication in the majority opinion that the statute could be found constitutional if the state could demonstrate an overriding rational purpose or reason.[1] The Court's reasoning was so forceful that in retrospect I wondered whether if I had admitted that the couple were married and argued that the Florida statute prohibiting interracial marriage violated the Fourteenth Amendment, I would have accelerated by three years the Court's decision in *Loving* v. *Commonwealth of Virginia*. There the Court held unconstitutional a state ban on interracial marriage, citing the *McLaughlin* case in support of its ruling at least seven times. While we savored the Supreme Court victory in *McLaughlin,* I was surprised, and frankly offended, that neither of the defendants ever called or wrote to thank us for the hundreds of hours of time we put into the case. We never heard from them again.

Another success was *Bradley* v. *School Board of Richmond* (1974), in which we persuaded the Court that a provision in a new civil rights statute providing for counsel fees for the winning plaintiffs' attorneys in civil rights cases applied even to those parts of the court proceeding occurring before the new statutory provision was enacted. This victory became a significant source of revenue for the LDF.[2]

My other Supreme Court argument in *School Board of Richmond* v. *State Board of Education* (1973) did not fare so well. The federal district judge Robert R. Merhige Jr. had held that owing to state and city racial policies the city of Richmond was so racially segregated that it was impossible to desegregate the Richmond public schools unless the surrounding, predominantly white counties of Chesterfield and Henrico were included in the desegregation plan. Judge Merhige wrote a brilliant opinion, ordering busing across county lines. It was a tremendous victory for those of us seeking to desegregate public schools in urban communities whose inner city was overwhelmingly black and the surrounding counties overwhelmingly white.

On appeal, the Fourth Circuit reversed the decision by a 2-1 vote. The LDF asked me to represent the plaintiffs in the Supreme Court. Justice Powell, who had just been appointed to the Supreme Court, disqualified himself because he had been president of the Richmond school board. Only four days after the argument, the Court entered an order with no opinion, stating the "the Judgment below is affirmed by an equally divided court."[3] Without Powell's participation, there was no tiebreaker.

In many jurisdictions, local authorities had bused students across county lines to maintain segregation. I have always thought that if the record in the lower court had included evidence of cross-county busing in the Richmond school system, we might have been able to get the fifth vote necessary to reverse.

In *Millicent* v. *Bradley,* the Court again rejected interdistrict relief in a Detroit school desegregation case. Justice Marshall dissented in language I wish I had used in my argument in the *Richmond School Board* case:

Desegregation is not and was never expected to be an easy task. Racial attitudes ingrained in our Nation's childhood and adolescence are not quickly thrown aside in its middle years. But just as the inconvenience of some cannot be allowed to stand in the way of the rights of others, so public opposition, no matter how strident, cannot be permitted to divert this Court from the enforcement of the constitutional principles at issue in this case. Today's holding, I fear, is more a reflection of a perceived public mood that we have gone far enough in enforcing the Constitution's guarantee of equal justice than it is the product of neutral principles of law. In the short run, it may seem to be the easier course to allow our great metropolitan areas to be divided up each into two cities—one white, the other black—but it is a course, I predict, our people will ultimately regret. I dissent.[4]

In the 1960s, when I was back in Washington working on yet another natural gas matter, Jack Greenberg called me at the Madison Hotel one evening. He asked me to represent several LDF lawyers in an appeal before the Fifth Circuit Court. Harold Cox, chief judge of the federal district court in Mississippi, had held several LDF lawyers in contempt for not appearing in his courtroom when only minor uncontested motions of a strictly procedural nature were presented, even though our local counsel was present.

After the LDF's success in several cases in Mississippi, Judge Cox had issued an order that required every lawyer who had signed the original complaint or any other pleading or motion to appear in the court for every proceeding. The evident targets of the order were Jack Greenberg, James Nabrit, and Constance Baker Motley, members of the New York bar who had prepared, in cooperation with local counsel, the original pleadings. Cox usually waived the order for out-of-state lawyers. The order was just meant for "Jews and niggers from New York," he once stated—on the record.[5]

It seems that Judge Cox was angry at these Yankee lawyers' meddling in the long-standing traditions of Old Dixie. The Cox order was a direct threat to LDF's ability to implement a nationwide legal strategy ultimately aimed at Supreme Court review. I agreed to argue the appeal in the Fifth Circuit, but I asked the court to move up the date of my oral argument by two days, explaining by letter that I had to be in Caracas, Venezuela, on a natural gas matter on the date originally set for the argument. I emphasized at the oral argument that in the 1960s it was common for lawyers all over the country to work with local counsel in bringing actions in the federal courts. To drive the point home, I cited the experience of the presiding chief judge, John R. Brown, who, in private practice as an admiralty lawyer and member of the Texas bar, had tried admiralty cases in federal courts on the East and West coasts as well as the Great Lakes region. As I referred to Judge Brown's earlier peripatetic practice, he smiled and leaned forward from the bench, displaying in a southern drawl the trademark irony for which he was known: "Why,

Mr. Coleman, good lawyers not only have to be in federal court throughout the United States, but sometimes they even have to go to Caracas, Venezuela, on important legal matters."

The Fifth Circuit Court of Appeals reversed Judge Cox's order and established a valuable precedent for the LDF to invoke on future occasions when southern judges expressed annoyance at our meddling in their courts.[6]

TWENTY-EIGHT

The Nixon Years

*There are few things wholly evil or wholly good. Almost
everything, especially of governmental policy, is an insepa-
rable compound of the two; so that our best judgment of the
preponderance between them is continually demanded.*

—Abraham Lincoln

Shortly after the election of Richard Nixon in 1968, I received a call
from William Rogers, his secretary of state designee. President-elect Nixon
had asked him to contact me and request that I come to Washington for
a meeting. When I arrived at his office at the State Department, Rogers
came right to the point. Nixon had recommended me for appointment as
legal adviser to the Department of State. It was an intriguing offer. The legal
adviser, comparable to the general counsel of Defense or Treasury, had at his
service an elite cadre of lawyers that rivaled the best law firms in the country.
I used to kibitz with Adrian "Butch" Fisher, former Frankfurter law clerk and
legal adviser to Secretary of State Acheson, about some of the fascinating
international legal challenges he had confronted. There was a catch, however.
Rogers wanted me to say yes on the spot because Nixon had planned to make
the announcement on television the next morning at the Pierre Hotel in New
York, where his transition team was ensconced.

If I had been given the opportunity for further reflection, I might well have
accepted this position. But I felt pressured and uneasy about the motivation
underlying the president-elect's offer. I was wary of the Nixon campaign's so-
called Southern Strategy, and I feared I was being used as the token person
of color in a senior position in his administration. Unlike President Johnson, Nixon had not appointed an American of color to his cabinet. The legal
adviser certainly was high among the second-tier positions in the federal government, but I politely declined the offer.

In the ensuing months I was to realize that I may have badly misjudged
Richard Nixon on this issue. As president he took significant aggressive steps
to improve the conditions of minorities by adopting strong affirmative action
programs, hiring and recruiting blacks for key government jobs, and ensuring
that minorities had a fair shot at government contracts. He appointed cabinet

officers like Elliot Richardson as secretary of health, education, and welfare and George Shultz as secretary of labor, men who were firmly committed to continuing the progress initiated under the Eisenhower and Johnson administrations. He appointed distinguished civil rights leaders to key subcabinet posts, such as Arthur Fletcher at Labor, James Farmer at Health, Education, and Welfare, Samuel Jackson at Housing and Urban Development, and General B. O. Davis at Transportation. Later in his administration he offered me the position of undersecretary of commerce with an implied commitment to promote me to the top job in six months, when Pete Peterson planned to leave. I even learned from listening to his notorious tapes that he considered me for appointment to the Supreme Court. Nixon never held it against me that I had turned down his offer of legal adviser. With three children in private schools, two of them in college, I had practical financial reasons to turn down a full-time government job.

The Nixon administration nonetheless reached out to me for advice on several other occasions. In 1969 the president appointed me as alternative delegate to the Twenty-Fourth General Assembly of the United Nations. This exposed me to foreign policy issues and enabled me to work with the national security adviser, Henry Kissinger, and Shirley Temple Black on United Nations resolutions to free Namibia from South Africa.

Faced with spiraling inflation, the president later appointed me to a productivity commission. Our job was to recommend ways to reduce inflation by making American business and labor more efficient and competitive internationally. Invoking the theories of the University of Chicago economist Milton Friedman, I worked with both George Shultz and Don Rumsfeld, then on the White House staff, in helping to fashion government policies that would promote technologies to hold down costs and prices.

About a year later President Nixon established the Price Commission and the Pay Board. I was one of seven members on the Price Commission, which included J. Wilson Newman, the chief executive of Dunn and Bradstreet Company, and former governor Bill Scranton. The much-maligned commission, a futile exercise in inefficient price controls by a purportedly conservative Republican president, lasted only a year. At least we learned how ineffectual this type of government intervention into the economy can be.

One of the great ironies of history is that the Nixon administration had a record of solid achievement in both domestic and foreign policy, and yet it will always be remembered for the resignation of a flawed and prideful president who could not bring himself to admit the errors of judgment that engulfed him in the Watergate scandal.

The Watergate tragedy has been retold on many occasions. After serving only six months as secretary of defense, Elliot Richardson was asked to move to the Department of Justice as attorney general, replacing his predecessor, John Mitchell, who had been forced to resign. Aware of the conflicts that were to confront him, Elliot did not want the job. At one point he suggested my name as an independent outsider who could bring integrity and order to the Justice Department. President Nixon insisted, however, that Elliot take the job. Elliot handled masterfully the resignation of Vice President Agnew, who appallingly had continued to receive envelopes of cash in the vice-presidential office. This unconscionable act of disrespect for the second-highest office in the land, as the horrified Elliot once confided in me, offended him more deeply than any other transgression he had confronted during his long public career.

With the vice-presidency vacant at a time of national crisis, President Nixon wisely nominated the experienced, easy-going, and self-assured Republican minority leader of the House, Gerald R. Ford, who was confirmed by the Senate in accordance with the Twenty-Fifth Amendment to the Constitution. Perhaps Nixon thought that the selection of Ford—the very antithesis of the mercurial Nixon—would discourage the majority Democrats in Congress from demanding his ouster. As it turned out it was an astute choice. Ford was able to restore a sense of calm and confidence to the nation as the Watergate storms subsided.

With the Agnew crisis behind him Elliot turned his attention to the demands of the special prosecutor appointed to investigate the Watergate break-in and alleged cover-up. Earlier, Elliot had asked me if I would be interested in the independent prosecutor job. "Are you kidding?" I said. "Absolutely not!" He then appointed Archibald Cox, our mutual friend and former Harvard Law School professor, to this onerous task. When Nixon ordered Elliot to fire the special prosecutor, who had demanded unrestricted access to the White House tape recordings, Richardson refused and resigned in the infamous Saturday Night Massacre. The deputy attorney general, William Ruckleshaus, also resigned, and the third-ranking official at Justice, the solicitor general Robert Bork, became the acting attorney general. He followed the president's order, as he was obligated to do if he would keep his job, and fired Archibald Cox. The credibility and authority of President Nixon spiraled downward, cascading toward its inevitable conclusion.

As a private citizen who had served as an adviser in several capacities in the Nixon administration, as a confidant of Elliot Richardson, as an admirer of the new vice president, Gerald Ford, with whom I had worked on the Warren Commission, and as a lawyer who had fought hard to help make this "a more perfect Union," I was deeply troubled by the turn of events. On August 7, 1974, I published an op-ed piece in the *New York Times*. In the article I acknowledged that President Nixon had lost the confidence of the American people and could no longer be an effective leader in a democratic society. Given the challenges we faced internationally and domestically, I argued, it was essential that there be an effective transition, and I proposed the following:

> Resignation is the only solution and we must, therefore, offer the President inducements to take that step. The Republican and Democratic leadership in Congress should propose and enact into law the following measures: "First, the President should be guaranteed whatever retirement benefits he would otherwise have received at the end of his term. Second, he should be granted absolute immunity from all prosecution, Federal or state, for all acts before resignation, and also absolute immunity from subpoenas to testify or produce documents at the trials of others or before Congressional committees. Third, he should be permitted, if he desires, before resignation to destroy tapes, memoranda and other material connected in any way with Watergate and related matters.[1]

My op-ed piece was strongly criticized even by some of my closest friends, but I continue to believe that my advice was sound. The Nixon impeachment process in the House was sapping the energy and diverting the focus of the nation's leadership. Critical foreign and domestic policy matters were being neglected. The always volatile Middle East was on the verge of war. As the midterm elections approached, it was likely that a new House and Senate would have to start the process all over again. If the president were impeached and convicted in the Senate, and if he later were tried and convicted in a criminal court, there would be an uproar in the country. Critical national security matters would continue to be neglected. Only the long view of history will determine whether any of my proposals made sense.

My op-ed piece was overtaken by events. Two days later President Nixon resigned. In *United States* v. *Nixon*, the Supreme Court had required him to turn over the Watergate tapes in response to the special prosecutor's subpoena. Leading members of his own party had convinced him to leave office. Gerald Ford was sworn in as president. Shortly thereafter, President Ford granted Nixon a full pardon. This may well have cost Ford the election in 1976, when he was defeated by Georgia governor Jimmy Carter. In retrospect, however, history appears to have vindicated President Ford's decision to pardon Nixon. Even the Kennedy family came to support his decision: they awarded President Ford its Profiles in Courage Award. President Ford would have been spared a lot of grief if Congress had expressly provided for the pardon as belatedly proposed in my op-ed piece.

With the ascendancy of Gerald Ford to the presidency, the long national nightmare was over. The dawn of a new morning brought a surprising opportunity for me, which would change the course of my life.

For twenty-three years, from April 1952 until March 1975, I had lived the dream of my life as a Philadelphia lawyer. I had an exciting and profitable career at the Dilworth firm. When I started, the firm had about 25 lawyers; when I left, it had grown to 125 lawyers. My name had been added to the firm's title. The firm had established a national reputation. While the job was demanding and required many late evenings, the Dilworth firm, like Paul, Weiss before it, fully supported my public service ventures and voluntary work on civil rights litigation. I had acted as counsel for a wide variety of situations. My legal skills had been stretched and contorted in every possible way. Now, I was about to take a break from my career ambitions, adapt to an entirely new "situation," and apply the tools of law to the challenge of public policy.

PART V

Serving in the Ford Cabinet

Our long national nightmare is over. Our Constitution works; our great Republic is a government of laws and not of men. Here the people rule.

—President Gerald R. Ford

TWENTY-NINE

Change in Course

In a political sense, there is one problem that currently under-lies all others. That problem is making government sufficiently responsive to the people. If we don't make government respon-sive to the people, we don't make it believable. And we must make it believable if we are to have a functioning democracy.

—GERALD R. FORD

MY GREATEST AMBITION—THE UNRELENTING CAREER focus of my life since my sophomore year in college—was to be a successful practicing lawyer in an outstanding private law firm. I love the law, the courtroom clashes, the demands of anxious clients, the challenge of complex transactions, the reso-lution of conflicts through reason, and the income that a law practice can generate. But that world was about to change. In his genial, disarming way, President Ford had drafted me onto his team. The former star center at the University of Michigan was facing the greatest challenge of his career, and I was to join him on the front line.[1] The goal: restoring the confidence of the American people in the integrity of their governmental institutions. As the president had said at his swearing in, "Truth is the glue that holds government together, not only our government but civilization itself. That bond, though strained, is unbroken at home and abroad. In all my public and private acts as your president, I expect to follow my instincts of openness and candor with full confidence that honesty is always the best policy in the end."[2]

After the president sent my nomination to Capitol Hill, I met with the White House congressional relations staff to arrange courtesy calls on key senators. Armed with heavy briefing books, I endured the senate confirmation hearing without any unexpected surprises and was confirmed unanimously by the full senate. There was no turning back now.

A couple of days before I was sworn in, I was at a dinner party at the Brit-ish embassy. A member of the British cabinet asked me about the budget and workforce of the Department of Transportation. From my confirmation brief-ings, I knew that the department had a budget of more than $80 billion and about 118,000 employees, making it at that time the fourth largest in the fed-eral government—facts I rattled off with cocky confidence. But his next ques-tion stunned me. He asked, "How many people have you ever managed?" On the way home that night I began to feel like Robert Redford in the movie *The Candidate*: I've got the job, what do I do now? In a near state of panic I called Elliot Richardson, who by that time had served in four federal departments. He had just been nominated by President Ford to be the U.S. ambassador to the Court of St. James. The Richardsons had offered us the use of their house on the bluffs overlooking the Potomac River in McLean, Virginia.

In my call to Elliot I accepted the Richardsons' kind offer of a riparian home and told him I had a pressing problem that I needed to discuss with him. Although it was quite late he invited me over to his house, where we discussed what it takes to be an effective cabinet officer. In the wee hours of the morning I took copious mental notes from my Professor of Secretary for Everything 101. I came away from that conversation with twelve aphorisms that I recall to this day.[3]

First, my loyalty first and foremost should be to the American people and to the president who appointed me. On important matters I should ask to see the president and argue vigorously for the department's position, but once the president makes a decision, I had an obligation to carry out his policies, unless I was convinced that they were either unethical or so abhorrent to my principles that I had no option but to resign. (Obviously, Elliot knew whereof he spoke on this issue.) The president and White House staff quickly detect those cabinet officers who are charting their own course, dealing surreptitiously with the media to advance their own agenda, and making deals with members of Congress that undercut the president's policy. Ultimately, they are ineffectual and replaced, often under a cloud.

Second, most federal departments are conglomerates of older, long-standing, autonomous fiefdoms that have their own direct contacts with members of Congress and constituent groups to which they give their primary loyalty. In my case the Federal Highway Administration, the Federal Aviation Administration, and the Coast Guard, for example, were established decades before the Department of Transportation. The secretary's responsibility is to fashion a coherent, integrated policy that demonstrates that the whole is greater than its component parts. For a department like Transportation, this means demonstrating the interconnectedness of the nation's transportation system and fashioning policies that promote seamless efficiency and evenhandedness among transportation modes. Convening staff meetings of the various administrators and assistant secretaries on a weekly or biweekly basis to promote common goals and objectives is one way to foster a cohesive departmental mission.

Third, politics is the lifeblood of the nation's capital, indeed of any constitutional democracy, but it was important to make clear to all the principals in the department that politics should be used only as a tool by which we advance the public interest. The power we exercise over funding, regulation, and media access should be used to achieve what's best for the American people, not to advance personal or party political agendas.

Fourth, since I was entering office during the middle of an administration, with most of the key positions in the department filled, I should assess the quality of the executives there, decide whom I wanted to retain, and look for opportunities to select my own people for key positions such as deputy secretary and general counsel. I should then schedule a meeting, preferably on a Friday, with each of the principals and ask them what their responsibilities, objectives, and priorities had been and how they had worked with my predecessor. The following Monday I should invite them back, explain my priorities, and establish lines of communication between us. Even if I reassigned them the same responsibilities, I would be sending a message that they were now working with me and that my style of operation would differ from that of my predecessor.

Fifth, I should spend at least a quarter of my time on Capitol Hill talking with senators, members of the House, and senior staff, especially on committees with authorization, appropriations, and oversight jurisdiction over the department and its component parts. I should also regularly invite the chair and ranking members of the key committees to the department to a breakfast or lunch meeting for open-ended discussions, even when we did not have a pressing issue to resolve.

Sixth, I should get to know and spend time with the White House chief of staff, the director of the Domestic Policy and Economic Policy councils and their staffs, the director and deputy director of the Office of Management and Budget, and the analyst responsible for my department's budget.

Seventh, I should identify the outside organizations that are most affected by, and interested in, the department's work—trade associations, unions, consumer and environmental groups, state and local government associations, and transportation companies—and open up lines of communication with them. I especially should consult with governors and mayors who have major or controversial transportation projects before the department. They should know that I am interested in and will listen to their advice. Even if I decide against their position, they will appreciate being consulted. The most hostile criticism of government policy usually comes from those who have been denied a voice in the process.

Eighth, I should read the morning newspapers before I arrive at work. It is embarrassing to appear before a congressional committee to testify on a subject without being informed about a scandal that has just broken and is reported on the front page of the *Washington Post*. I should anticipate spending some time most days looking into an issue raised in the *Post* or the *New York Times* or responding to questions from the White House staff or members of Congress about a breaking story. The media truly are the fourth branch of government.

Ninth, I should be selective about speaking opportunities, choosing from among the hundreds of invitations I would receive the appropriate forum for important policy announcements and opportunities to jawbone the public on issues like buckling seatbelts.

Tenth, I should carefully read letters prepared for my signature and guard the use of my signature machine, giving authority to only my most trusted assistants to use it on my behalf. I must constantly press my staff to ensure that responses to letters from elected leaders at the federal, state, and local levels and to heads of key constituent groups are promptly prepared. Cabinet officers pay a huge penalty for failing to respond in a timely manner to inquiries from key congressional leaders.

Eleventh, I should select a top-notch lawyer as my general counsel. Specific expertise is less important than a lawyer who is innovative, commands respect, and is able to ensure that the department's decisionmaking responsibilities are carried out with integrity and in an open and fair process. Elliot and I shared an appreciation for the importance of a general counsel, on whom we would rely not only for sound legal and policy advice but also to ensure that we complied with the many laws and regulations that governed our conduct as federal officers.

Twelfth, I should hire an immediate staff that is bright, loyal, and knowledgeable about how government works. I should not hire a team of special assistants vested with subject matter expertise that duplicates that of my career departmental advisers. My staff should not create a barrier between me and the principal officers of the department but rather should facilitate the gathering of information and policy options in a fair and evenhanded way and ensure that I am presented with all reasonable alternatives and the recommendations of my principal subordinates, members of Congress, and key constituency groups before I make a decision. In this regard Elliot recommended Donald T. Bliss, whom Elliot had selected as the first executive secretary to the Department of Health, Education, and Welfare to manage the decisionmaking process at the sprawling HEW bureaucracy. Don became my principal special assistant. Elliot and I recalled simultaneously the pertinent couplet from Alexander Pope, "For forms of government, let fools contest; whate'er is best administered is best."[4]

When I got back to the Madison Hotel early in the morning I was exhausted, but I felt prepared, ready to go. Armed with good advice from Elliot, I began to assemble the rest of my immediate office team. I brought along a young partner from the Dilworth firm, Michael Browne, who agreed to trek down to Washington and continue our close working relationship.

My next objective was to hire a superb general counsel. From my work on the Warren Commission I had grown to admire John Hart Ely, then a professor at the Harvard Law School and a former law clerk to Chief Justice Warren. John's book *Democracy and Distrust* was to become one of the most cited scholarly works in judicial opinions.[5] John had turned down my previous attempts to hire him, and so I decided to approach this task with a more calculated plan. I called John and asked to see him in Cambridge, Massachusetts. He and his wife Nancy invited me to dinner. I invited John to become general counsel of the Department of Transportation. John's reaction was predictable: "Come on, Bill, be serious. I don't know anything about transportation. The only thing I know how to do is start my car by turning the key to the right in the ignition. Besides, I really like teaching and writing. Why would I want to spend two to three years supervising a lot of lawyers dealing with issues I know nothing about and, frankly, have no interest in?"

"John," I replied, "I don't expect you to be a transportation lawyer. I want to use you the same way Dean Acheson used Butch Fisher as legal adviser to the State Department."

This appealed to John. He knew Butch Fisher, who was the dean of Georgetown Law School, and he was intrigued by my proposition. He accepted, and we closed the deal. Back in Washington, I bumped into Butch Fisher and asked him how Secretary Acheson had used him. I told him I had made a commitment to John Ely that I would use him the same way. Butch rolled with laughter, telling me that he had attended all the policy briefings of the secretary of state, read all the memos that Acheson read, and was briefed on all conversations between the secretary and the president.

John Ely came to work in the department and brought with him two young *Harvard Law Review* editors, Phil Ward and Ladd Levin, as his special assistants. John and his team brought an extraordinary quality of legal analysis and writing to the general counsel's office, upholding a long tradition in the department. His two predecessors, after graduating from Yale Law School, where they served as editors of the *Yale Law Journal*, had been partners in the prestigious New York law firm of Cravath, Swain, and Moore. One of them, John Barnum, had been promoted to deputy secretary of transportation by my predecessor, Claude Brinegar. I gave Barnum the Elliot Richardson workout, and I decided to keep him. Barnum was a superb deputy. We worked well together, and I benefited greatly from his knowledge of the department and the key issues we were facing. I have continued to benefit from his counsel and friendship in subsequent years. My deputy undersecretary was John Snow, a lawyer and Ph.D. economist, who was a rare breed—a charismatic policy wonk who knew how to work the bureaucracy to get results. Later in his career, John became the successful chief executive officer of CSX Transportation and thereafter secretary of the treasury under George W. Bush.

John Ely's skill at assembling a strong team in the general counsel's office presented me early on with a difficult and unanticipated choice. After about three months on the job, Ely had become frustrated at his inability to find a deputy general counsel who would help him manage the large office of lawyers and free up his time to spend on key decisions facing the department. Impressed with my special assistant's work on several key decisions, John came to me and asked if he could appoint Don Bliss as deputy general counsel. I said, "No, John, go find your own deputy general counsel."

John replied, "I did come up with a candidate, but the White House vetoed him, and quite frankly, Bill, I'm getting pretty frustrated. If I can't have Don Bliss as my deputy, I'm inclined to go back to Harvard next semester and resume teaching."

I must have had a look of panic on my face. Like Acheson in his relationship with Butch Fisher, I relied on John's participation in all the key decisions facing the department. I caved. "Okay, John, I'll make you a deal. You can have Don Bliss as deputy general counsel as long as you allow him to continue to work on special projects for me from time to time."

I bumped Mike Browne up to principal special assistant and hired Elaine Jones, an LDF staff attorney, as my second special assistant.

In my final year, and on my recommendation, President Ford appointed John Snow as administrator of the National Highway Traffic Safety Administration, and I moved Mike Browne over to deputy undersecretary and Elaine Jones up to principal special assistant. In June 1976 John Ely returned to Harvard Law School to retain his teaching tenure, and Don Bliss became acting general counsel for the remainder of the Ford administration.

On March 7, 1975, I was sworn in at the White House at a ceremony hosted by President Ford with some three hundred guests. Justice Marshall administered the oath. Among my guests were Joe Rauh, who had testified in the Senate against Gerald Ford's nomination for vice president, several of my Quaker friends, who left their pickets just outside the White House protesting against the Vietnam War, and Mattie Guinan, head of the Transit Workers Union. President Ford showed great magnanimity in reaching out to all people, a fact that was noted in a *New York Times* editorial the following morning.

At 7:00 a.m. on March 8, 1975, I showed up for work. From my spacious office in the Volpe building, I could look out over the Potomac River and watch the cars, buses, and trains crossing the 14th Street bridge. My eyes traveled from the boats on the river to the planes taking off from Washington National Airport. It was truly an intermodal transportation perspective.

My first meeting of the day was a one-on-one in the Oval Office with President Ford. As a representative from Grand Rapids, Michigan, Ford had had a strong appreciation for the importance of transportation to local communities. We discussed the challenges of completing the interstate highway system envisioned by President Eisenhower, the inefficiencies and high costs of the overly regulated transportation sector, and the need to create jobs to address the high rate of unemployment.

As busy as he was, the president always had time to meet with me on important transportation issues, particularly those on which there were differences among the cabinet that needed to be resolved. He was also a delegator. He expected me to make the decisions, and he would back me up and hold me accountable for the results. Unlike so many White House occupants during my lifetime, he had no interest in micromanaging transportation decision-making. I left the Oval Office supremely confident that I had made the right decision in coming to Washington.

THIRTY

Cabinet-Style Government

Some are born great, some achieve greatness, and some have greatness thrust upon them.

    —WILLIAM SHAKESPEARE, *Twelfth Night*

HAVING HAD THE PRESIDENCY SUDDENLY thrust upon him, Ford spent the first six months assembling his own team, combining new faces with trusted veterans from the Nixon administration. Attending my first cabinet meeting in April 1975 was a thrill for me. In the historic cabinet room, I felt humbled by the examples of such awe-inspiring predecessors as Alexander Hamilton, Thomas Jefferson, James Madison, William H. Seward, George C. Marshall, and Frances Perkins.

Assembled around the table were the newly confirmed vice president, Nelson Rockefeller; Henry Kissinger, the secretary of state; Edward Levi, the new attorney general; Carla Hills, secretary of housing and urban development; William Simon, secretary of the treasury; George H. W. Bush, director of the CIA; Daniel Patrick Moynihan, ambassador to the United Nations; Brent Scowcroft, director of the National Security Council; and Alan Greenspan, chairman of the Council of Economic Advisers, among others. It was an eclectic group of independent thinkers and achievers from many walks of American life—academia, banking, law, and public service. It was not top-heavy with elected officials—senators, representatives, or governors stolen from their constituents—as the cabinets of more recent administrations have been. Diversity of experience and perspective and depth of knowledge and expertise were virtues of the Ford cabinet.

The cabinet meeting lasted about three hours. Kissinger led a discussion about issues relating to the Soviet Union, our European allies, and China. The president described his plans to control inflation and create new jobs. No decisions were made. The purpose of a cabinet meeting as I saw it was twofold.

First, it was an opportunity for cabinet officers to get to know one another on a personal level so they could better work together in coordinating policy and resolving interdepartmental conflicts. Many of the controversies I faced as secretary were with my cabinet peers or with agencies like the Environmental Protection Agency or the Office of Management and Budget. Personal collegiality facilitated the resolution of strong disagreements. Disputes were grounded in differences in our respective missions, often defined by conflicting statutory mandates. The Environmental Protection Agency wanted cars that created less air pollution, and the Department of Transportation wanted cars that were safer and more fuel efficient.[1] Where one stood on an issue depended on where one sat. Usually there was no single right answer. We had to reconcile various public interest objectives in coming to an optimal result. When we could not reach agreement, we would ask for a meeting with the president, who often invited us to the White House on a Saturday afternoon to discuss conflicting policy recommendations. Ford would listen to each point of view and then render a decision. The meetings would start in the early afternoon, as President Ford often played golf in the morning with his close friend, Democratic House Speaker Tip O'Neill.

The other principal purpose of a cabinet meeting was to keep us informed on the administration's key foreign and domestic policy issues. We raised questions and provided insights from our perspective that helped articulate a coherent, consistent message of the administration's priorities. As cabinet officers, we were frequently called on to discuss the president's policies in various forums, and it was important that this choir all sing from a single sheet of music.

During the Ford administration the president's cabinet usually met about once every ten days. The meetings usually started at nine in the morning and continued until noon or early afternoon. On occasion some or all of the cabinet members would be called to the White House at the end of the day for a discussion of issues of concern to the president. I recall one cabinet meeting in particular, which illustrates the way in which President Ford effectively used his cabinet.

The night before a regularly scheduled cabinet meeting word had flashed across the television screens that Syria had invaded Lebanon, which at the time was partially occupied by Israel. The president and Secretary Kissinger had been on the phone most of the night and had met earlier in the Oval Office that morning. When the cabinet convened, Kissinger gave the briefing. Contrary to the fears of those of us less schooled in foreign policy, Kissinger did not see the Syrian invasion as a threat to Israel but rather as an attempt to check the dissident, anti-Israeli Lebanese, who wanted to take aggressive action to push the Israelis out of southern Lebanon. Perhaps because he had worked in the House for so long President Ford quickly grasped the political maneuvering of the contentious Lebanese factions. He was also skeptical of Israel's claim to certain territories as a rationale for its occupation of southern Lebanon.

We then turned to a presentation by the new secretary of defense, Donald Rumsfeld, who had been replaced as White House chief of staff by his deputy, Dick Cheney. Rumsfeld described his plans to rebuild and retool the U.S. armed forces, which were under strain from the costly war in Vietnam. The next issue on the agenda was the crisis facing the Social Security fund, which would soon run into a deficit, followed by an update on the administration's program to fight inflation. Two nights earlier, the president had made a nationally televised address on the economy, using a visual aid to illustrate how high he would let the deficit go. Being left-handed, like myself, President Ford drew the last third of the line a bit higher than he had intended.*

The next item on the agenda was the financial crisis facing New York City. Treasury Secretary Simon advised that the city needed the federal government to guarantee loans to meet its financial obligations. A bill was pending in Congress to authorize the guarantee the city had requested. Unfortunately, the legislation was festooned with extraneous provisions to protect existing labor contracts, prevent the layoff of city employees, and provide for wage escalators, all of which would have hamstrung the city's efforts to make the financial reforms necessary to come out of the crisis with a viable plan. There was strong sentiment in the cabinet for the president to veto the legislation.

Attorney General Levi suggested that New York City should consider filing for bankruptcy and let a federal judge make the tough decisions necessary to come up with a financial plan. There was no consensus on an approach. President Ford asked for further review of the various options and said, "Let's turn to the next issue."

That issue was the busing of school children to desegregate the public schools in Boston, Massachusetts. Although legally imposed racial segregation had ended in Massachusetts more than a hundred years earlier, there still existed de facto (and de jure) school segregation because the neighborhoods in Boston, as in many U.S. cities north and south, were highly segregated, attributable in part to federal public housing policies dating back to the Franklin Roosevelt administration. In a lawsuit brought by parents of color, federal district court judge W. Arthur Garrity, who had been my classmate at Harvard Law School, issued a courageous order requiring the busing of black and white kids out of their residential neighborhoods to attend desegregated schools.

There was a huge public outcry. The Irish American white parents from South Boston were in revolt. Unruly crowds hung Judge Garrity in effigy. They yelled racial epithets and threw stones at the buses carrying black

---

*I hoped the American public realized that this is a common characteristic of left-handed people when we attempt to draw a line from left to right.

students to schools across town. President Ford sent federal marshals and FBI agents to assist Governor Sergeant and Mayor White in keeping order. This was not Montgomery, Alabama, or Jackson, Mississippi. This was Boston, the home of the abolitionists.

Boston politicians remained mum as the U.S. Court of Appeals for the First Circuit affirmed Judge Garrity's order. The white parents then petitioned for a writ of certiorari to the Supreme Court. The issue for discussion at the cabinet meeting was whether to authorize then solicitor general Robert Bork to file a brief *amicus curiae* asking the Supreme Court to grant the writ of certiorari supporting the white parents who opposed the busing. The attorney general recommended that the government file the brief. He argued that Judge Garrity's order involved far too much busing over long distances and that federal judges should not interfere with the operations of public schools, which were a local matter. In almost any other administration I would not have had the opportunity to weigh in on this issue, even though as secretary of transportation I could argue that school buses were a form of transportation, which gave me at least a jurisdictional toehold. In the Ford administration, the cabinet was invited to comment.

President Ford's views on busing were well known. He took pride in the fact that he had walked to school, even when suffering from football injuries, and he thought that neighborhood schools were important to ensure parental involvement and participation in extracurricular activities. He had spoken out against busing on the House floor and signed legislation restricting the forced busing of school children shortly after he took office.

"Mr. President," I said, "the last two issues we have discussed present an interesting contrast. The attorney general has suggested that all fiscal, budget, and operational problems of New York City be turned over to an unelected public official, a federal district judge. We would ask a bankruptcy judge to make decisions that normally locally elected officials should make. On the other hand, when we are discussing the Boston school case, where the local public officials have remained silent for decades on ending racial segregation in the public schools, we are criticizing the federal courts for meddling in local affairs. In my judgment, the courts are simply acting, with great restraint, to enforce the Fourteenth Amendment to the Constitution."[2] A hushed silence fell on the cabinet room. I thought I noticed a suppressed smile on the faces of the vice president, Secretary Hills, and the secretary of health, education, and welfare, David Mathews, who had been president of the University of Alabama. But no one spoke up in support of my position.

So I continued: "Mr. President, when the politicians at the federal, state, and local levels have failed to take action to address the continuing practice of school segregation, lest they offend their white majority constituents, it has been the federal courts that have courageously stepped up and acted. Many communities, Pasadena, California, for one, have embraced school busing without violence and without diminishing the quality of education. Starting with Herbert Brownell and Lee Rankin in the Eisenhower administration, the Justice Department has consistently supported federal judges as they have fashioned remedies to enforce the Supreme Court's mandate. If you wish to reverse course at this point and withdraw the support of the executive branch for these brave federal judges, I only ask that you explain to the American people your reasons for this shift in position—that as a strong proponent of neighborhood schools, you are opposed to the excessive use of busing as a judicial remedy. Then, I will fully support you."

Disguising any annoyance, the president concluded the discussion with the comment, "Both the New York City and Boston issues are really tough. Let me think about them some more."

On the Boston school case the administration decided not to file a brief *amicus curiae* in support of the white parents. Judge Garrity's school busing plan went into full force and effect. On New York City finances, with strong lobbying from the White House, Congress eliminated the overly restrictive and costly provisions in the bill, and President Ford signed it into law. With federal loan guarantees, New York was able to emerge from its financial crisis, which would not have been possible had the original legislation been enacted.

Another illustration of the special relationship between President Ford and his cabinet involved my efforts to secure the financing necessary to complete a ninety-eight-mile subway system plan. The Washington Metropolitan Area Transit Authority, or Metro, plan had been carefully designed to serve the District of Columbia and the Maryland and Virginia suburbs in a way that would ensure community and financial support from each jurisdiction. Two federal dollars would be provided for every local dollar contributed. Construction of the first lines was under way. In 1969 the initial projected cost was grossly underestimated at about $3 billion. By the time I took office, the projection was up to almost $5 billion, still less than half the final $10 billion completion cost in January 2001. The Nixon administration had guaranteed about a billion dollars in bond financing to build the subway, but as the cost projections escalated, this proved to be woefully inadequate.

With the skillful assistance of my budget director Ted Lutz, my deputy John Barnum, and my general counsel's office, and with the wise advice and cooperation of Walter Washington, mayor of the District of Columbia (a friend of my father's, Washington had also operated a boys' club, his in New York), we proposed to use newly authorized congressional authority to transfer interstate highway funding to the transit authority for subway construction. This meant that portions of the interstate system planned for the District of Columbia would never be built and that the Metro would be an essential method of commuting from the suburbs to government jobs in the city.

We planned to raise almost a billion dollars from such transfers, but additional financing would still be required. We had made a proposal to the Office of Management and Budget for an additional $1.26 billion, which Jim Lynn, director of the agency, thought was overly extravagant. In fact, he viewed the transit authority's ninety-eight-mile subway plan as far too expansive and expensive. It would be the largest public works project since the interstate highway system. Conservatives had criticized Metro as an exorbitant display of big government in Washington using the taxpayers' money to build a monument to itself. They referred to the proposal as the biggest boondoggle in the history of mankind. Instead, Lynn proposed a truncated forty-one- or sixty-eight-mile system.

I had worked hard with all the jurisdictions to support a plan that would serve the entire metropolitan area fairly, facilitate the commute for the many government employees who lived in distant suburbs, and provide a first-class transportation system for tourists and visitors to the nation's capital from all over the world, comparable to the grand systems in London, Paris, or Moscow. I was not about to give up on the ninety-eight-mile plan. I asked for a meeting with President Ford.

The atmosphere was tense as Ted Lutz, Don Bliss, and I entered the Oval Office on a Monday morning. Director Lynn argued eloquently for the scaled-back plan, making a number of points that resonated with the fiscally conservative president. I explained the importance of sticking with the original plan to which all the local jurisdictions had committed. I didn't appear to be making much headway with the president, so I ratcheted up the argument.

As we had discussed in the New York and Boston situations, at that time American cities were near a state of crisis—facing financial distress, racial unrest, high unemployment, rising crime rates, and the scourge of drug addiction. Our cities should be the citadels of our civilization, as they are in other parts of the world, but they are becoming increasingly isolated, segregated urban ghettos, as the middle class flees to the suburbs. Having worked in the Washington area for many years, the president perked up a bit. He was all too familiar with the deterioration of many parts of Washington, the urban dead spots between the Capitol and the White House. I argued that the Metro system would knit together the entire metropolitan area as the interstate highway system had knit together the entire country. With hubs and spokes reaching out to distant suburbs, the city center would once more flourish as a magnet for entertainment, sports, and culture.

The president asked some direct questions of each of us. He then paused, puffed on his pipe, and said, "Bill is correct. We should build the ninety-eight-mile system. Let's find the money, Jim."

It was not an easy decision. Shortly before this meeting, the president had directed Lynn to find ways to cut the federal budget deficit. But it was the right decision. We continued to place stringent conditions on federal funding and imposed a $4.7 billion cap because we were concerned about questionable design features and cost overruns that had plagued construction. Studies to consider more efficient alternatives continued. Today Metro runs 118 miles of track with a couple of additional stations and intermodal access to Reagan Washington National Airport. George W. Bush's transportation secretary, Mary Peters, also approved an extension by light rail to Dulles International Airport. By some studies, automobile congestion in the metropolitan area ranks second only to that in Los Angeles. Since coming to the Washington area, I have been blessed with a car and driver, enabling me to read the newspapers, use the phone, and get a lot of work done during my commute; but for the life of me I cannot understand how so many single-occupant auto commuters tolerate the long delays and lost productivity of driving to work. And there is the cost to energy security and the environment. Without the Metro system, there would be absolute gridlock.

Most important, however, in the past twenty-five years downtown Washington has flourished. The Verizon Center and dozens of new theater groups have sprung up around town. Visitor access to the Smithsonian museums and the many monuments spawning on the National Mall has greatly improved. Young people flock to the capital as one of the most livable and exciting urban areas in the country, and even in such a hardworking town, the lights are on into the wee hours as the young singles dance the night away.

We probably made two major mistakes in the financing and design of the Metro subway system. First, we did not put into place an effective areawide system of funding the operation, maintenance, and modernization of the system. Other jurisdictions have enacted a penny sales tax for this purpose. Thus as the system ages, securing adequate financing to maintain it continues to be a challenge.[3] A series of safety problems that occurred in 2009, including a tragic collision of rail cars, ought to provide the impetus for regional cooperation in resolving this matter. When the Metro system was launched a half century ago, it made sense to assemble a governing board of public officials from the three participating jurisdictions, Virginia, Maryland, and the District of Colombia, with the chair rotating each year. Recently a federal representative wisely was appointed to the governing board. In a mature system, it may be useful to select a full-time chairman and board of professionals who would put safety and financial stability of the regional system ahead of the parochial interests of their jurisdictions.

Second, in approving the original plan, we did not provide for direct service between the suburban counties in Maryland and Virginia—a circle line, sometimes called the "missing Purple Line" to complement the Red, Blue, Green, Orange, and Yellow Lines that serve as spokes into the District of Columbia. There is a discussion today of constructing segments of such a line, partially as a light-rail system, to serve the substantial populations that move between job and home in the suburbs, often working for the so-called beltway bandits.* On the other hand, the hub-and-spoke system has worked beyond my wildest imagination to recreate the District of Columbia as the focus of the metropolitan area as it should be.

Shortly before the 1976 New Hampshire primary, when Governor Reagan challenged President Ford for the Republican Party nomination, the governor of New Hampshire called the president to complain that the U.S. Coast Guard had just determined that Lake Winnipesauke, a major resort and tourist attraction for the state of New Hampshire, was a navigable waterway subject to federal jurisdiction and regulation. Tourist and recreational boats would have to obtain federal licenses, and New Hampshire could no longer collect a tax on boats, a major source of state revenue. What really set the governor off, though, was the bold headline on the first page of the arch-conservative, statewide New Hampshire newspaper, the *Manchester Union Leader:* "FEDS INVADE NEW HAMPSHIRE."

Given the high stakes involved, President Ford reacted with his usual calm and said, "Secretary of Transportation Bill Coleman was an excellent lawyer before I convinced him to enter public life. I suggest you have your attorney general call him and arrange for an appointment."

The attorney general called that afternoon and we set an appointment for three days later. I asked my then acting general counsel Don Bliss to put together a team to analyze the law. The issue was whether there was navigable water flowing between Lake Winnipesauke and Massachusetts, which would make the lake part of an interstate waterway. At one time water from Lake Winnipesauke flowed through rivers joining the Merrimack River and on through Massachusetts to the ocean. By 1976, the rivers had mostly dried up or been filled in with development. New Hampshire attorney general David H. Souter arrived in my office well prepared. He made a factual

---

*Corporations sited around the beltway that profit principally from government contracts.

showing that you could not float a straw from the lake into Massachusetts. His presentation was consistent with the findings of my legal team.

On matters of law the general counsel of the Transportation Department was empowered to overrule the chief counsel of the Coast Guard, who reported to the commandant. It was an authority rarely exercised. In this case we felt the law was strongly on our side, and my acting general counsel wrote a legal opinion that overruled the Coast Guard and restored Lake Winnipesauke to New Hampshire state jurisdiction. Whenever I ran into Justice David Souter (who recently retired from the U.S. Supreme Court), he thanked me for my decision on Lake Winnipesauke. He once told me that during his Supreme Court confirmation hearing he wore the same necktie that he had worn the day he visited me on Lake Winnipesauke. He considered it his lucky tie and wore it on occasions when he hoped for a good result. I told him I would ask to borrow that tie the next time I made an argument before the Supreme Court.

The Coast Guard did not give up easily on its attempt at territorial acquisition. A few weeks after I left office on January 20, 1977, a memorandum showed up on the desk of my successor, Brock Adams. It was an opinion by the Coast Guard declaring Lake Winnipesauke to be navigable waters of the United States. Only the date had been changed. Wisely, Secretary Adams called the general counsel's office and got Don Bliss on the phone. Bliss filled him in on the interesting history behind the Coast Guard's attempt to invade New Hampshire.

When I accepted my appointment to President Ford's cabinet, I could not have realized the extent to which the president intended to rely on his cabinet for key decisionmaking. He delegated broadly but insisted on accountability. He listened to advice from individuals who were far more expert than he in their fields, but where there were conflicts, he made the decisions and insisted that his cabinet implement them faithfully. Compare his attorney general, Edward Levi, a renowned legal scholar and president of the University of Chicago, to John Mitchell, Richard Nixon's former law partner, or Bobby Kennedy, the president's younger brother. Don't get me wrong; I greatly admired Bobby, especially his tenacity on civil rights. But he was hardly an independent attorney general. Consider Ford's choice of a vice president, Nelson A. Rockefeller, a man of enormous experience and an independent political base, or the retention of Henry Kissinger as secretary of state. As the opportunity arose he brought back Elliot Richardson from London to head Commerce, moved Rumsfeld to Defense, and brought in experienced labor negotiators like John Dunlop and W. J. Usery as secretaries of labor, who were respected by labor and management alike. He selected a rival, George H. W. Bush, as director of central intelligence.

An unassuming but effective leader, President Ford inspired collegiality and teamwork, in ways reminiscent of what Doris Kearns Goodwin has called Abraham Lincoln's "team of rivals."[4] I admired him very much. I am greatly indebted to him for the confidence and support he gave me as I tackled some controversial issues in what Henry Kissinger described, in the context of my Concorde decision, as my own "inimitable style."

THIRTY-ONE

Getting to Know the
Department of Transportation

Prepare the way for the people, build up, build up the
highway.

—Isaiah 62:10

CONGRESS CREATED THE DEPARTMENT OF Transportation on October 15,
1966, to bring together under one roof the disparate federal transportation programs and to develop a comprehensive, coordinated transportation policy. The
department began operations on April 1, 1967, in President Johnson's administration under the leadership of its first secretary, Alan S. Boyd. At the time
of my arrival in June 1975, it consisted of seven agencies, most of which had
direct access to Congress at least equal to that of the secretary of transportation.

Superimposed on the seven modal administrations was the Office of the
Secretary, whose job was to address cross-cutting issues, such as safety, transportation policy, international negotiations and agreements, the environment,
transportation of hazardous materials, pipelines, research and development,
public-private financing of transportation, and congressional, intergovern-
mental, and media relationships. These functions were managed by a number
of assistant secretaries, deputy assistant secretaries, and office directors.

HIGHWAYS

The administrator of the Federal Highway Administration, Norbert T. Tiemann, had been governor of Nebraska. His effervescent personality and ability
to dole out federal highway funds to states made him popular among members
of Congress. I learned from Nobby Tiemann how to exercise executive power
to achieve policy objectives in the political environment.

Most of my work with the highway administration involved the interstate
system. A little history is in order. On July 7, 1919 (exactly one year before my
birth), a young U.S. Army captain, bored with peacetime duties, volunteered
for a mission that would take him throughout the United States. The purpose
of the trip was to evaluate the status of America's roadways and determine

the feasibility of federal support for a highway system that would serve both commerce and defense requirements. His evaluation confirmed the wretched conditions of U.S. roadways. The young captain prepared a task force report that recommended "a comprehensive system of national highways."[1]

He went on to perform heroically for his country and was promoted to the rank of five-star general and chief of the Allied Forces in World War II. In 1952 he was elected president of the United States and served two terms. But the disturbing picture of the nation's transportation infrastructure remained firmly etched in Dwight D. Eisenhower's mind. As president, he was in a position to do something about it. He proposed, pushed through Congress, and signed into law the National Interstate and Defense Highways Act of 1956.[2]

Based on an extensive survey, with substantial state participation, a plan was developed to build an interstate highway system of exactly 39,425 miles. The federal government would provide 90 percent of the funding and the states a 10 percent match. The U.S. Highway Trust Fund was established, funded by a federal four-cent-a-gallon tax on gasoline and additional motor carrier charges. Planned, funded, and constructed as a single nationwide integrated highway system, it remains today, at a cost of $129 billion, the largest public works project in the history of the world.[3]

By the time I took office, about 80 percent of the system was complete; however, we ran into roadblocks. The 1970 National Environmental Policy Act required a thorough analysis of the environmental impact of each new federally funded project. Most of the incomplete highway segments were in urban areas and caught up in lawsuits by environmental and community groups. This created glaring gaps in an integrated system. A prime example was the Overton Park segment of I-40 in Memphis, Tennessee, which became the subject of a seminal Supreme Court decision written by Justice Thurgood Marshall, ensuring that environmental impacts and alternatives would be carefully assessed before any highway project could proceed.[4] In some cases, partially built highways stopped in the middle of an overpass, creating a bridge to nowhere.

I made the completion of the interstate system a high priority. We would work through the environmental issues and decide on alternatives that would meet environmental objections and withstand judicial scrutiny. I personally conducted several public hearings and studied the environmental impact statements to impress on the Federal Highway Administration the importance of resolving these controversies expeditiously and in an environmentally sensitive way. We also issued and applied new department regulations requiring a review by metropolitan planning organizations to provide the most efficient transportation systems for metropolitan areas. We broke the logjam and began the construction on I-40 in Memphis, I-70 in Colorado, and I-66 in Virginia. Designs were modified to accommodate environmental concerns. Carpool, bus-only, and other restricted access lanes were built, and right-of-ways were reserved for public transit. In other cases, such as in the District of Columbia, interstate highway funds were transferred to public transit agencies for light-rail or subway construction. By the time I left office, President Eisenhower's bold vision was just about completed.

In some cases where it was decided not to complete a particular segment, the mileage would be returned to the 39,425-mile pot to be reallocated.[5] The power to allocate interstate miles proved to be a useful chit.

President Ford and budget director Lynn called me one day and said they had decided to limit yearly expenditures from the Highway Trust Fund in order to reduce the federal deficit, for which they needed the consent of the Senate and House appropriations committees. They asked me to visit each of the committee chairs and seek their approval. I first went to see Birch Bayh, senator from Indiana. He withheld his approval but added, to his later regret, that if I could convince the chair of the House Appropriations Committee, George Mahon of Texas, he would report President Ford's proposed appropriations amendment out of his committee without objection. The next day I visited Mahon. He started the conversation, "Mr. Secretary, I have a highway problem in my district. I need eight miles of interstate."

"Mr. Chairman," I interrupted, "you have it, assuming it meets all the legal requirements." I then explained my request. Having gotten what he wanted, Mahon assured me that he would support President Ford on reducing Highway Trust Fund expenditures.

The next day I told Senator Bayh that the chair of the House committee had agreed to the president's proposal. The senator's response is unprintable; however, as a man of honor he kept his word. The Senate committee passed through the Ford amendment. When I called Jim Lynn and told him that I had successfully accomplished the president's assignment, he laughed and said he had thought he was sending me on a fool's errand. Apparently Ford had told Lynn, "If anybody can do it, Coleman can. Give him a try." Lynn asked how I had succeeded. I disclosed my special pool of returned interstate highway mileage.

A few weeks later President Ford called and told me he was having trouble getting the defense appropriations bill through Congress. "Bill," he asked, "do you suppose you can get me forty-eight miles of interstate highway?"

"Of course, Mr. President, assuming that all the legal requirements are met."

Years later, in 2006, I attended a Transportation Development Foundation dinner celebrating the fiftieth anniversary of the interstate highway system. The keynote speaker was my neighbor, Colin Powell. That evening I came to appreciate that not only did the interstate highway system greatly facilitate the logistics of troop and supply movements for the U.S. military, but, according to General Powell, it also facilitated the demise of the hateful practices of segregation in the South. Colin, a child of Jamaican immigrants who grew up in the Bronx and found his footing in the City College of New York's reserve officer training program, had married Alma, a child of Alabama. During his military years in the early 1960s, when she and Colin traveled between New York and Alabama, they would plan their trip carefully. There were only a few places along the route where they could stop and use the bathroom facilities, have a meal, or spend the night—such as the Ghana Motel in South Carolina. With the construction of the north-south interstates, they could make the trip more quickly, and he also noticed that racial segregation had begun to fade. The nationwide restaurant chains, like Howard Johnson, Stuckey's, and Cracker Barrel, that had sprouted up along the interstates understood the commercial benefit in serving all travelers. Those that did not change soon found their northern franchises subjected to a picket or boycott. I was thrilled to hear that my sometimes obstinate efforts to strong-arm the Federal Highway Administration into finishing the interstate highway system complemented in purpose and effect my life-long commitment to equality of treatment for all of America's citizens.

AVIATION

One of my first (and most unpleasant) duties as secretary of transportation was to replace the administrator of the Federal Aviation Administration (FAA). President Nixon had appointed Alex Porter Butterfield as administrator shortly after Butterfield disclosed to Congress the existence of the clandestine recording apparatus in President Nixon's White House office, the source of the so-called Watergate tapes. Soon after I took office, the Ford White House decided to replace Butterfield with Secretary of the Air Force John McLucas, and I was assigned the task of requesting Butterfield's resignation.[6] McLucas had a strong technical aviation background and proved to be an effective leader in resolving new and challenging issues, such as the increasing impact of aircraft noise on local communities.

Some FAA administrators have suggested that the FAA has a dual mission of safety and promoting civil aviation and that decisionmaking requires balancing or reconciling these two objectives. I made it clear to McLucas that, in my judgment, the FAA's overriding mission was safety. I told him that the FAA had the delegated authority to make final decisions on aviation safety. I would not question his safety judgments. Some transportation secretaries have been accused of second-guessing safety calls at the behest of airlines or aircraft manufacturers, but I wanted to make sure that the technical experts made such calls with the full backing of the political appointees. On other issues like aircraft noise, FAA authorization and appropriation legislation, international trade disputes, and major airport development, I retained concurrent authority and worked closely with the FAA.

On my arrival at the transportation department, I was pleasantly surprised to find that my former commander at Fort Godwin, Benjamin O. Davis Jr., a genuine American hero, had been appointed as assistant secretary of transportation for safety and consumer affairs. It felt somewhat awkward to have the leader of the fabled Tuskegee Airmen now working for me. But I was extraordinarily lucky to have as an adviser a person of General Davis's experience, judgment, and character.[7]

After Davis's retirement from the air force in September 1970, transportation secretary John Volpe had appointed him to the newly created post of director of civil aviation security in the Office of the Secretary. Alarmed by a proliferation of hijackings in the late 1960s and early 1970s, Volpe asked Davis to develop a comprehensive aviation security program for the department. Davis organized and trained the first crew of air marshals and developed within the FAA a cadre of security professionals who instituted the first airport screening operations to keep passengers with guns and other weapons from boarding aircraft.[8] In recognition of his exceptional work, President Nixon appointed him assistant secretary.

By the time I arrived at the department, Davis's security program had been very effective in reducing the number of successful hijackings. I did face one incident in which a hijacked plane landed in Paris. With the able assistance of the Coast Guard in the U.S. embassy in Paris and Pan Am's worldwide communications network, we were able to arrange for the release of all the hostages without any loss of life. When Davis and I conducted a review, we agreed on a commonsense approach to preventing future hijackings. We issued an order that before leaving the gate commercial airline pilots must lock the cockpit door and not open it until the aircraft had landed and begun disembarking passengers at the arrival airport.

I understand that my successor, Brock Adams, revoked this order when the pilots complained that during long flights they needed to have access to the bathroom facilities. Based on my experience with army air corps pilots during World War II, I did not find this excuse persuasive. I won't go into details.

What if my explicit order to lock the cockpit door had still been in effect on the morning of September 11, 2001?

COAST GUARD

The U.S. Coast Guard was then part of the Department of Transportation, although it was subject to transfer to the command of the Defense Department during time of war. I had great respect for the Coast Guard and its leadership. My relationship was greatly facilitated by the assignment of a young commander, Ted Leland, as my military aide. Ted was an invaluable adviser on many issues and a good friend through the years. As secretary I also had the benefit of flying in Coast Guard One, a Gulf Stream jet that would take me to the West Coast for a luncheon speech and back to my own bed in McLean, Virginia, by the end of the evening.[9]

My special assistant Elaine Jones and my civil rights director Carmen Turner kept bugging me to convince the Coast Guard commandant to admit women to the Coast Guard Academy in New London, Connecticut. One day, I asked Ted Leland to set up a meeting with the commandant, Owen W. Siler. When I broached the issue, Admiral Siler said, "Mr. Secretary, none of the other academies admits women. We are the smallest. Remodeling facilities to accommodate women would be very expensive within our tight budget. We do accept women in our Officers Candidate School."

"Look, Si," I interrupted, "this would be a great move for the Coast Guard. You would be the first, leading the way for the other academies. This is going to come. It's inevitable. Why not be the first?"

Si graciously implemented what he interpreted as a military command. Despite the grumblings of some of his headquarters staff, women were admitted to the academy the following fall. The other military services followed the Coast Guard's example. The Coast Guard and Admiral Siler received a lot of favorable publicity for their groundbreaking decision. The admission of women into the service academies opened up many new opportunities for women—as they had for men of color in previous decades—and changed the culture of military service for the better. I was pleased to read in 2009 that a woman had been appointed regimental commander of the Corps of Cadets.

Elaine and Carmen were elated by this development and soon pressed me on another issue. They urged me to ask the commandant why Coast Guard women were not permitted to go to sea, particularly since the navy had adopted a policy whereby women were eligible for sea duty. I set up a meeting with the commandant to discuss a number of issues, and at the end invited Elaine and Carmen to join us. I asked the commandant point blank, "Why is it women in the navy are permitted to go to sea but women in the Coast Guard are not?"

The commandant replied, "Mr. Secretary, Congress has enacted a statute that requires the navy to permit women to go to sea, but it has not made any such requirement of the Coast Guard."

"Why don't we just do it ourselves and not wait until we are ordered by Congress?" I responded.

"Quite frankly, Bill," the commandant replied with a chuckle, "my wife would strongly object. She claims that because the Coast Guard women wear skirts, the male sailors would look up their dresses when they climb the ropes on the mast."

At which point Carmen interrupted, "Commandant, why don't you just require the women to wear pants when they have sea duty?"

The next day (having apparently won over his wife), the commandant personally brought to my office an order for my concurrence, declaring that thereafter women sailors would be assigned to sea duty in the Coast Guard on the same basis as men.

Shortly after President Ford lost the November 1976 election, we were confronted with an environmental crisis. In December 1976 there were four oil spills involving Liberian tanker vessels, resulting in the discharge of about 7.5 million gallons of oil in or near U.S. waters. There was a massive explosion of one ship in Los Angeles, the grounding of ships off the coast of Massachusetts and in the Delaware River, and a spill of five thousand gallons of oil in the Thames River in Connecticut. A fifth vessel was grounded in San Juan harbor in Puerto Rico, but oil discharge was prevented. When the *Argo Merchant* ran aground off the coast of Nantucket island, I flew to the site with the Coast Guard commandant to observe the impact of the oil spill and begin a cleanup plan. Then near the end of December the SS *Olympic Games* spilled 133,000 gallons of crude oil in the Delaware River. Having flown to Massachusetts, I could not neglect my hometown of Philadelphia. The commandant, Don Bliss, and I spent New Year's Day traveling to Philadelphia and viewing the spill from a helicopter. Much of the damage was covered by freshly fallen snow. On the way back I instructed the commandant and my acting general counsel to put together a task force to undertake a comprehensive review of marine safety regulations and their effectiveness in preventing and containing oil spills.

The task force issued a report on January 11, 1977, which included twenty-five specific recommendations to prevent oil spills and provide for more expeditious and effective cleanup when they did occur.[10] I left office before I was able to implement them. My successor, Brock Adams, was confronted with an oil spill in the Gulf of Mexico off the coast of Texas in late January. He was able to put many of these recommendations into effect in response to that crisis. In two weeks of intensive work we were able to lay the foundation for a tougher oil tanker regulatory regime and a more effective, coordinated Coast Guard–led response to ocean oil spills—steps that would be strengthened in future decades as the Coast Guard faced unprecedented catastrophes such the *Exxon Valdez* oil spill in March 1989 and the explosion of BP's deep water offshore rig in April 2010.

RAILROADS

The railroad system in the United States was in crisis when I moved into the secretary's office. It was crumbling both physically and financially. In the months before I took office, several bridges had failed, and repair, strengthening, or replacement was required for many of the 860 bridges in the Northeast corridor. Service was rapidly deteriorating owing to deferred maintenance. Financially, six railroads of the Northeast and Midwest, including the fabled Penn Central and Reading railroads, had declared bankruptcy. Competition from trucks on the interstate highways, archaic regulations that prevented the railroads from responding to changes in market demand, and high labor costs were contributing causes. As freight revenues declined, service levels deteriorated.

The agency charged with the overwhelming infrastructure challenges was the Federal Railroad Administration. Ace Hall, former chief of staff to my predecessor, Claude Brinengar, was the administrator. The agency set safety standards for the railroads, not an easy task given the economic and physical deterioration of the nation's railroads at that time. It was also charged with performing engineering studies to improve the Northeast rail corridor. The improvements were intended to repair the worst track conditions and improve current service, but they also laid the foundation for high-speed rail passenger service in the corridor.[11] The challenge was compounded by the many jurisdictions involved. In preparing a plan to upgrade the Northeast corridor, we consulted with ninety-three federal, state, regional, and municipal organizations that had significant planning responsibilities in the corridor.

To prevent the complete shutdown of rail service in the Northeast the federal government had stepped in, taking bold action as it has on many occasions when the marketplace has failed. Since the days of the founding fathers, Americans understandably have retained a healthy skepticism of government, but when the marketplace fails, they look to Washington to save the companies that are too big to fail, restore lost jobs, ensure the continuation of necessary services, and stimulate economic growth. In 1971 the government established and funded Amtrak to take over inter-city passenger service. In 1973 Congress passed the Regional Rail Reorganization Act, which provided interim funding for the bankrupt freight railroads and established the U.S. Railway Association (USRA) to solve the problem of the bankrupt railroads. USRA was directed to develop a final system plan. It created a new entity called the Consolidated Rail Corporation (Conrail) and designated the rail lines to be included in the new entity. Other lines would be sold to Amtrak, state governments, regional transportation authorities, or solvent private railroads.

The final system plan was almost complete when I arrived on the scene and started to ask some hard questions.[12] With fresh eyes, and informed by my decade of experience in holding down costs at the regional transportation authority in southeastern Pennsylvania, I had several concerns. First, it seemed that everybody would benefit from the plan except the taxpayers. The plan included an open-ended commitment to fund billions of dollars of Conrail's deficits for the foreseeable future. Second, while the plan rationalized the route system, it did not adequately address the underlying inefficiencies and high cost structure of the Northeast freight railroads. Third, it did not address the government-imposed regulatory barriers that would prevent Conrail from responding efficiently to changes in consumer demand. Fourth, it would give Conrail monopoly power in the Northeast. I felt it would be preferable to have more rail competition from the major eastern railroads, the Southern Railway and the Norfolk and Western Railway (which merged to form the Norfolk Southern) and the Chessie System (now CSX Transportation).[13]

Although I got lots of resistance, I decided to explore other options including one that had been rejected earlier.[14] After consulting with John Barnum, John Ely, and Mike Browne, I decided that the best solution would be to scrap Conrail and sell the Penn Central to the Southern, the Norfolk and Western, and the Chessie. I proposed that the federal government make one lump-sum payment to each of the railroads to assume the financial obligations and capital investments required to upgrade the deteriorating infrastructure. Then it would be up to the privately run railroads to make a go of it. There would be no open-ended federal subsidy, as had been proposed, for Conrail.

The opposition was fierce. Many USRA staff were planning on taking top executive positions in Conrail. The unions were opposed because the government would not be obligated to put up money each year to keep the railroads running, and the Democratic Congress supported the more favorable labor conditions that the USRA had proposed to give the unions.

Despite the opposition, I was not ready to give up on my idea. I called in the chief executives of the railroads and described to them my counter plan. They agreed that it made sense. We decided that I would first negotiate with the Southern for its part of the system. Chief executive Graham Claytor and I met for about three days and worked out tentative terms, including the labor terms under which the present employees of the Penn Central would become employees of the Southern. The stumbling block was that the Penn Central unions not only wanted the Southern to guarantee the jobs of all their existing workers, but they also insisted that the terms of the Penn Central labor agreements should apply to all new employees hired by Southern. Graham Claytor could not go along with this demand. He would accept the Penn Central labor agreements only for the existing employees. I called an all-day meeting with Claytor and the presidents of the six railway labor unions in my conference room at the Department of Transportation. We were quite close to an agreement. We simply wanted the unions to recognize that although we would protect all current Penn Central employees and those of the other bankrupt railroads under their existing labor agreements, we would not guarantee these benefits to new hires after Southern and the other private railroads acquired the assets of the bankrupt railroads. Many of the union leaders seemed to agree that this was a reasonable compromise, but one union leader was particularly unyielding. He had a prior commitment to give a speech in Philadelphia. To keep the discussions going, I offered to supply a Federal Aviation Administration plane to take him to Philadelphia and bring him back after the speech to continue with the negotiations. After his departure, negotiations started to go really well. By ten in the evening we were close to reaching an agreement when we were informed that the plane was on the way back with the missing union leader and approaching Washington National Airport. My special assistant radioed the pilot with the following instructions: "Secretary Coleman is close to an agreement. He wants you to keep that turkey in the air for an extra fifteen minutes so he can close the deal before your passenger comes back and messes things up." Unfortunately, the voice speaker in the plane was open, and the union leader overheard the remark. He insisted, quite rightly, on an immediate landing and showed up at the meeting in time to bust the negotiations wide open. The next morning, Fred Rooney, a Democratic representative from Allentown, Pennsylvania, may have saved my job by arranging an off-the-record meeting with the six union presidents. I apologized for the unfortunate language of my aide. But we could never get the negotiations back on track again.

As a result, the USRA plan went into effect. Conrail began operations on April 1, 1976. It continued to post losses of as much as a million dollars a day and received billions of dollars in federal subsidies for the first seven years. We were able to give Conrail a little more flexibility when President Ford signed the Railroad Revitalization and Regulatory Reform Act, which included some deregulatory provisions enabling management to respond more efficiently to the marketplace. Real progress was made, however, when Congress enacted the Staggers Rail Act of 1980, which significantly deregulated the rail industry, and the Northeast Rail Service Act of 1981, which required the secretary of transportation to sell the government's interest in Conrail. Thereafter Conrail began to show a small profit. Given Conrail's increasing success, attributable to billions of dollars of federal investment in upgrading the infrastructure and deregulating economic controls over the industry, the two eastern private rail competitors engaged in a takeover battle to acquire Conrail. In 1997 the two railroads, CSX Transportation and the Norfolk Southern Railway, struck a compromise agreement to acquire Conrail jointly and split most of the assets between them. The buyout was approved by the

Surface Transportation Board (the successor agency to the Interstate Commerce Commission) on August 22, 1998. As a result the Norfolk Southern acquired 58 percent of Conrail's assets and CSX received 42 percent. Today the two eastern railroads compete vigorously throughout the eastern United States. The private, efficiently managed railroads have done quite well. Former secretary of transportation Elizabeth Dole, a Reagan appointee, deserves a lot of credit for encouraging the split and privatization of Conrail. In the end, the proposal I made back in 1976 essentially came into effect in 1998. It's too bad that we were not able to complete our negotiation in 1976. We might have been able to save the government a few of the billions of dollars it expended in the twenty-two-year life of Conrail.

MASS TRANSIT

The Urban Mass Transportation Administration was primarily a grant-making agency. Just before I took office President Ford had signed into law the National Mass Transportation Assistance Act of 1974, authorizing $11.8 billion in funding over six years for mass transit projects—a large amount of money even by today's standards. This landmark legislation presented an extraordinary opportunity to assist urban and rural communities in developing transportation alternatives in an era of increasing environmental consciousness and high energy costs. We funded major projects in Detroit, Atlanta, New York City, Chicago, Los Angeles, Baltimore, Philadelphia, Cleveland, Miami, Salt Lake City, Boston, and the New Jersey statewide system. At a time of high unemployment these projects created many new jobs for minority contractors and workers.

I worked closely with the urban mass transit administration to decide which new light-rail and subway starts made economic sense, how to address the needs of physically challenged passengers, and how to ensure that transit alternatives were fully considered and appropriately funded as part of the metropolitan regional planning process. The agency has since been renamed the Federal Transit Administration, which better reflects its increasing attention to public transit in rural as well as urban areas.

AUTOMOBILE SAFETY

The federal role in automobile safety regulation essentially began in the late 1960s, so in 1975 we were still in the early stages. The challenges were great. In 1972 alone, 54,589 motorists had died on U.S. highways. That was unacceptable—an American tragedy. Our primary mission was to bring down this rate. John Snow, administrator of the National Highway Transportation Safety

Administration (NHTSA), joined me in taking aggressive action. We identified seven priorities: Half of all traffic fatalities involved the abuse of alcohol, so we initiated a tough program to curtail drunken driving. There was a strong correlation between high speed and fatalities (and an urgent need to combat fuel shortages), so we enforced an unpopular nationwide 55-mile-an-hour speed limit. We promulgated new standards to improve crash survivability. We ran campaigns to encourage the use of seat belts. We developed and publicized uniform standards to grade passenger car tires, refined and issued an antilock air-brake standard, and promoted the use of motorcycle helmets. We launched a passive-restraint (air bag) demonstration program. And we initiated special programs to address the safety challenges posed by younger and older drivers.[15]

At the end of my last full year (1976) the total number of annual fatalities was 45,523—down 16 percent from 1972 but still far too high. As the NHTSA continued to upgrade automobile safety standards, Congress pulled the plug on the 55-mile-an-hour speed limit, and fatalities spiked again. Over time cars became much safer but unfortunately not as fuel efficient as I thought necessary. By 2007, despite the increase in traffic and average speed, the number of fatalities declined to 41,059.

As safer cars meeting tough new standards gradually came into operation, entirely new challenges have arisen. Most troubling are the distractions of cell phones and text messaging, driver and mechanic interaction with complex computer technologies, and the mix of fuel-efficient small cars, sport utility vehicles (SUVs), and large trucks on increasingly congested interstates. Ray LaHood, the current secretary of transportation, has effectively raised public awareness of the epidemic of driver distraction. The Transportation Department has also published a model state law to encourage states to address the issue. Cell phone use and text messaging while driving simply cannot be tolerated. It is as serious as the drunken-driving challenge I faced in the 1970s. There are other forms of driver distraction as well, including grooming, eating, and fiddling with the radio, a CD, or a GPS. Department statistics indicate that distracted drivers are four times as likely to cause injury-creating accidents. All told, driver distraction is a factor in 80 percent of automobile accidents. Using the carrot and the stick, the federal government must ensure tough state laws against cell phone use and text messaging while driving and their strict enforcement.

New technologies offer many safety advances, but the interaction between the driver and sophisticated computer technologies often presents unforeseen problems. An example would be sudden, uncontrolled acceleration. As I learned from my work on the antilock braking standard, it is difficult for government regulators to keep up with fast-changing technologies. Perhaps the department should appoint a council on safety and technology, consisting of the best experts around the country from the National Academies of Sciences and Engineering, universities, and industry to monitor safety issues that arise from operator interaction with sophisticated technologies. We face a similar challenge in aviation, where pilots who learn to fly in glass cockpits in simulators may be less prepared to fly today's complex aircraft when computer systems fail.

Government also has to address the conflicting demands for safer, more fuel efficient, and greener automobiles. According to the Insurance Institute for Highway Safety, passengers in minicar crashes suffered three times as many deaths as those in large cars. The tensions between safety, environmental consciousness, and energy security (and their respective advocates in government) have grown increasingly taut. The National Research Council reported that the increase in the number of smaller cars on the road as a result of the 27.5-mile-a-gallon fuel economy standard contributed to about two thousand additional highway deaths. What will be the effect on safety of the new 35-mile-a-gallon combined average for cars and trucks? Government has not effectively reconciled these conflicting objectives. Given the safety threat posed by mixed vehicular traffic congestion on the highways, we should invest in new freight rail corridors and new highways for interstate trucking in addition to high-speed passenger rail service between major metropolitan areas.

During my tenure I was concerned about the fragmentation of the federal government's involvement with the U.S. automobile industry. Over the years, as U.S. manufacturers have faced multiple challenges, the federal government has failed to address automobile issues comprehensively. Safety, fuel efficiency, emissions, job creation and retention, labor, international trade issues, health insurance, pensions, tax and financing issues, all affect the viability of the automobile industry, and yet the government's policy—in both the executive branch and Congress—has been fragmented, often inconsistent, and frequently changing, making it difficult for automobile manufacturers to make long-term investments and respond to consumer demand for their products. Well before the current crisis facing U.S. manufacturers, the federal government was heavily involved in the automobile industry. While U.S. manufacturers are not blameless, I believe the government's failure to develop a long-term consistent and comprehensive policy was a major contributing factor to the industry's current condition.

In recent years, the federal government has invested billions of dollars in two U.S. auto manufacturers, created an automobile czar at the Department of the Treasury, and hired financial consultants from Wall Street to manage the investment. While this may have been a necessary expedient during a time of economic crisis, it does not address the root causes of the car manufacturers' financial health. A high-level interagency council, aided

On August 28, 1958, Wiley Branton, Thurgood Marshall, and Bill Coleman emerge from the U.S. Supreme Court after Marshall's successful argument in the Little Rock school case. With the strong support of President Eisenhower, the Court's unanimous decision in *Cooper* v. *Aaron* transformed the idea of *Brown* into the reality of public school desegregation

Raymond Pace Alexander, Bill Coleman, and Martin Luther King Jr. meet at Bill's Philadelphia office in October 1960. King dropped by to thank Bill for his help in obtaining his release from prison, and Bill took the opportunity to introduce him to one of Philadelphia's preeminent attorneys and trial judges.

In June 1966, Attorney General Nicholas Katzenbach, Morris Abrams, and Bill Coleman discuss with President Johnson the recommendations of the White House Conference on Civil Rights, titled "To Fulfill These Rights." Coleman and Abrams co-chaired the conference planning session. Standing in the back are Johnson advisers Cliff Alexander and Lee White.

In a 1967 meeting, Bill explains to President Johnson why he cannot accept appointment to the Third Circuit. The press release announcing the appointment was destroyed.

Bill Coleman and Thurgood Marshall share a light moment after Marshall swore in Coleman as the fourth U.S. secretary of transportation in March 1975

Secretary Coleman and President Ford discuss the Boston school busing crisis in September, 1975.

Republican Bill Coleman and Democrat Ted Kennedy worked closely together on many issues, including transportation deregulation, the Voting Rights Act, and the failed nomination of Judge Bork to the Supreme Court. Senator Kennedy's adviser Stephen Breyer and Coleman collaborated in shaping the first airline deregulation legislation.

Bill Coleman discusses transportation deregulation with President Ford's chief of staff, Dick Cheney, in 1976.

In 1975, Coleman fights for funding for the Washington, D.C., Metro subway system as James Cannon, domestic policy director, listens.

President Ford approves the Metro funding plan with Secretary Coleman and James Cannon looking on.

Bill Coleman visits the Concorde assembly plant in Toulouse, France, several months after making the Concorde decision in 1976.

"YOUR KEEPING IT OUT WOULD BE A SERIOUS BLOW TO OUR RELATIONS —— WITH OUR ALLIES, OF COURSE"

©1975 HERBLOCK

Washington Post cartoonist Herblock expressed the public cynicism about government decisionmaking in his 1975 cartoon. Coleman sought to address the public's concerns in his public hearing and reasoned February 1976 decision to allow the SST Concorde to fly to the United States under stringent conditions.

Bill and Lovida Coleman with President George H. W. Bush and First Lady Barbara Bush at the White House in February 1990.

Bill Coleman is recognized by President George W. Bush on February 12, 2008, at a White House program for Black History Month. First Lady Laura Bush beams to his left. Secretary of State Condoleezza Rice is partially hidden in the first row.

Honorary pallbearers at the funeral services for President Gerald Ford, Washington National Cathedral, January 2, 2007. From the left are Henry Kissinger, Donald Rumsfeld, Alan Greenspan, James Baker, Brent Scowcroft, Carla Hills, and Bill Coleman.

Associate Justices Antonin Scalia and Stephen Breyer toast their friend Bill Coleman at his 90th birthday party on June 2, 2010.

Photo by Carl Cox Photography

by consumer, academic, labor, and industry advisers, should be created to develop a comprehensive federal policy based on a rigorous cost-benefit analysis that recommends consistent, coordinated federal objectives, mandates, tax incentives, and targeted investment to optimize safety, U.S. job retention, green and "smart car" technologies, fair competition, trade and export promotion, and fuel economy. The emphasis should be on consistent and predictable federal policy that would enable the private sector to plan and implement effectively. We should learn from the experience of World War II, when the federal government worked with the car industry to mobilize for the war effort. We need a similar coordinated approach today to mobilize our nation's response to the challenges of job creation, climate change, energy security, and transportation safety.

MARINE TRANSPORTATION

When Congress created a cabinet-level department in 1966 to oversee the nation's transportation by land, sea, and air, it left out pieces of the puzzle. The Maritime Administration remained in the Department of Commerce, probably because it was subject to the jurisdiction of a different congressional committee, which did not want to relinquish its power over shipping and inland waterways. Years after my departure, the Maritime Administration was transferred to the Department of Transportation. In my time, however, Transportation did have two functional responsibilities in marine transportation: the St. Lawrence Seaway Development Corporation and the Office of Deepwater Ports.

The St. Lawrence Seaway corporation was a self-sustaining government-owned business, funded by fees and charges assessed for the use of the Eisenhower and Snell locks. Other than a few courtesy visits from the administrator, I spent little time worrying about this efficiently run operation.

With the nation's increasing dependence on foreign oil, a large amount of imported crude petroleum was carried by the new supertankers, very large crude carriers whose size and draft precluded the use of most ports and harbors in the United States. Congress sought to encourage the development of offshore port facilities that would accommodate these vessels. Recognizing that many federal and state government agencies would have a say in regulating such facilities, Congress wisely enacted the Deepwater Ports Act of 1974. It directed the secretary of transportation to receive applications from proposed deepwater ports, hold hearings, consult with other government agencies, reconcile any conflicting recommendations, and issue a port license incorporating conditions that reflected the concerns of the relevant government agencies and the public.

I received two applications from consortiums of oil and pipeline companies to construct deepwater ports in the Gulf of Mexico off the coast of Louisiana and Texas.[16] We met all the statutory deadlines, and I issued both licenses, jam-packed with tough conditions.[17] No party was completely satisfied, but I think we did a good job in reconciling many conflicting points of view in a fast-track procedure that enabled one of the ports—the Louisiana offshore oil port (Loop)—to be constructed, meeting an important national need at the time. The other applicant—Seadock—off the coast of Texas received a license but did not build the facility. It may have found the conditions recommended by the Department of Justice and the Environmental Protection Agency too onerous.[18] Government certainly hasn't gotten any less complicated since the mid-1970s. The Deepwater Port Act is an interesting model that can be adapted to other circumstances, offering a single-window approach to the private sector in dealing with increasingly complex and fragmented government agencies.

There really is no adequate education or professional skill set that prepares one to be a cabinet officer. While I got some useful advice from Elliot Richardson, I basically brought to the job my own set of experiences as a practicing lawyer. I approached problems differently from the way a former member of Congress or a corporate executive might. I believed strongly in a fair and open process of decisionmaking, in which the issues are clearly defined, the interested parties can present their case in a transparent process, and my decisions are explained and supported by a record.

A lot of my time was spent testifying before Congress, explaining the administration's priorities, defending our decisions before oversight committees, and seeking funding for our programs—far too much time, I believe, given the many congressional committees and subcommittees that claimed jurisdiction over some of the department programs. I also made many speeches before constituent groups with an interest in transportation, seeking public support for our priorities and listening to the concerns and advice of the professionals—public and private—who managed and operated transportation services and the environmentalists and safety advocates who kept a vigilant eye on departmental decisionmaking.

THIRTY-TWO

Making Transportation Policy

*In a scheme of policy which is devised for a nation, we should
not limit our views to its operation for a single year, or even
for a short term of years. We should look at its operation for a
considerable time.*

—HENRY CLAY

DURING THE CONFIRMATION PROCESS SEVERAL senators had pressed me on
a particular issue: What was the Department of Transportation's purpose? It
had been in existence since 1966. Its enabling statute had expressly directed
the secretary to develop a national transportation policy. Why? Congress created the department to coordinate the federal funding and regulation of transportation systems to promote safe, efficient, and seamless interstate and local
transportation of people and goods.[1] Yet almost a decade later, no transportation policy statement had been issued.

In 1791 Alexander Hamilton had prepared what essentially was the nation's
first national transportation policy. It was called the "Report on Manufactures." It stressed the importance of a comprehensive approach to the development of commerce and trade among the states in the young nation.[2] In 1808
Albert Gallatin, secretary of the treasury under President Jefferson, presented
the first federal transportation plan to Congress. It proposed the construction of a series of canals to connect interstate commerce efficiently, knitting
together the diverse regions of a dynamic, growing economy. Implementing the federal plan, the Erie Canal was completed in 1835, followed by the
construction of a network of canals in the East. Five years later a competitor
emerged, the railroad, culminating in the laying of the first transcontinental
tracks in 1869. What was the policy, if any? Through land grants, the federal
government provided the railroads generous rights of way but did not provide
a continued funding source for the railways.

In 1895 the first American automobile was issued a patent. The federal
government helped fund highway construction (but not maintenance) at
different levels with a maximum of 90 percent federal and 10 percent state
matching for the interstate highway system launched in 1956. Federal funding

was recouped through gasoline and motor carrier taxes. Funding for public transit came later and was less generous, but both capital and operating costs at times were subsidized by federal and local governments.

In 1903 a new form of transportation was born in Kitty Hawk, North Carolina. In the succeeding decades, the United States would lead the world in the development of global aviation. The fledgling airline industry was supported by federal mail contracts. Airports were funded primarily through a ticket tax on passengers and local airport user fees paid by the airlines.

Since 1808 federal transportation policy has evolved willy-nilly. How did all these federal programs fit together? Did they encourage a rational, efficient transportation system?

NATIONAL TRANSPORTATION POLICY

On September 17, 1975, my department issued the first statement of national transportation policy. It consisted of general principles that would guide federal transportation decisionmaking, emphasizing the federal responsibility to promote safe, environmentally sensitive, and consumer-responsive transportation through a competitive private sector. We stressed the importance of efficient connections between different forms of transportation, facilitating the transfer of passengers and freight. This meant, among other things, rail and truck connections to ships at ports, public transit access to airports, and park-and-ride facilities to encourage commuters to use public transit in the cities. It also meant better coordination between federal, state, and local governments, including stronger regional planning authorities to ensure efficient trade-offs between highways and public transit in accordance with a regional master plan.[3] We sought to minimize distortions in federal funding and regulation that might favor one mode of transportation over another.

My first attempt at issuing a national transportation policy met with mixed reviews. Several members of Congress expressed displeasure with our policy. They apparently were looking for a plan that would essentially map out the country's transportation infrastructure requirements for the next twenty-five years. I did not believe that, in an economy that relies primarily on the private sector to make capital investments and operate transportation services, the federal government should be in the business of creating such a plan. Nevertheless, I asked my assistant secretary for policy, plans, and international affairs to develop a transportation plan that would be consistent with the policy guidelines we had just issued. After much discussion, we concluded that it was not feasible for the federal government to issue a static twenty-five year plan in a dynamic, changing economy and in a system of federalism in which states and local governments have transportation-planning authority.

Instead, on January 5, 1977, we issued a four-hundred-plus-page document packed with charts, graphs, and maps entitled *National Transportation: Trends and Choices (to the year 2000)*.[4] The document provided a useful springboard for the incoming Carter administration on the transportation policy choices confronting it. *Trends and Choices* provided the most comprehensive basis for transportation decisionmaking since Albert Gallatin's 1808 plan and served the department well until September 5, 2000, when Rodney E. Slater, Clinton's appointee as secretary of transportation, issued two reports: *The Changing Face of Transportation* and *Transportation Decision Making: A Policy Architecture for the 21st Century*. The opening sentence of chapter 1 of Slater's first report states:

> A quarter century ago, William T. Coleman, Jr., the fourth Secretary of Transportation, opened a window into the lives of Americans that was extraordinary. In a report that most people in America never saw, he painted a picture of American society, the ways in which they traveled and interacted, their economic lives, their safety and health, their environment, and their use of natural resources. But he also went further than that. He used the knowledge of the past to look into the future, and then he set about to create a planning and decision making framework to guide that future. Over the next two and a half decades, the document itself would fade from view. But planning and decision making did change. And, remarkably, the future unfolded in many ways just as Secretary Coleman had envisioned in the 1977 report, *National Transportation: Trends and Choices*.[5]

It was the articulate visionary Rodney Slater, the second secretary of transportation of color, who picked up the baton and carried the department's statutory mandate—transportation policy—into the twenty-first century.

FEDERAL AVIATION NOISE ABATEMENT POLICY

Another area in which clear federal policy was long overdue involved increasing community aggravation about aircraft noise. With the advent of jets, some 6 million to 7 million Americans, mostly in major metropolitan areas, were subjected to the significant annoyance (and health-related effects) of aircraft noise. Lawsuits against airports sprang up around the country. Local noise restrictions and curfews proliferated, creating a patchwork of inconsistent regulatory requirements that greatly disrupted interstate commerce and caused havoc in the nation's air transportation system.

In 1968 Congress had directed the Federal Aviation Administration to regulate aircraft noise at its source. The agency issued noise standards for new jet aircraft.[6] When I became secretary, the outstanding issue was how to quiet the noise of older jet aircraft still operating in the commercial fleet, which still had a substantial life cycle ahead.

My staff and I met with T. A. Wilson, the impressive chief executive officer of Boeing, to explore potential technologies to quiet existing aircraft and increase energy efficiency. Wilson provided a thorough briefing, which convinced me that retrofitting the old B-707s with noise suppression technology would not be cost effective. Instead, I thought, we should provide incentives to encourage U.S. air carriers to purchase the next generation of quieter, fuel-efficient aircraft then on the drawing board. After the briefing Wilson and I had lunch at the Sans Souci restaurant, then one of the popular hangouts of Washington power brokers. As we ate lunch, I noticed White House reporter Helen Thomas at a corner table. On the way out, Helen asked me with her usual no-nonsense directness, "Secretary Coleman, I would like to know who is paying for the lunch you just had with Mr. Wilson." I replied, "Helen, why don't you ask the head waiter?" She did. The head waiter informed her that in making the reservation my assistant had asked for two separate checks. I could see the look of disappointment on Thomas's face when the maitre d' informed her that according to his waiter, "Mr. Coleman was a slightly more generous tipper than Mr. Wilson."

As I delved deeper into the aircraft noise issue, it became clear that even if we reduced aircraft noise from the operating fleet, we would not substantially mitigate the adverse effect on local communities unless appropriate action were taken at other levels of government. As airplanes became quieter, we would need effective zoning and land-use planning in areas surrounding airports to ensure that builders did not simply move their developments in closer. Moreover, if the airlines were to invest millions of dollars to quiet their aircraft fleets, then at least the Department of Transportation should take action to eliminate inconsistent local noise restrictions that severely disrupted air commerce.

We needed a comprehensive approach to the issue. I asked my acting general counsel, Don Bliss, to work closely with FAA administrator John McLucas, the FAA chief counsel's office, and noise experts to develop a comprehensive aircraft noise policy.[7] On November 18, 1976, John McLucas and I released a statement on our noise abatement policy, which called for a balanced, cooperative approach.[8] The federal government would reduce aircraft noise at its source by requiring all commercial aircraft that did not meet stringent new noise standards to be retired from the fleet or retrofitted with noise suppression equipment in accordance with a phased-in compliance schedule for each aircraft type. The deadlines were based on what was technologically practicable and economically reasonable. To ensure compliance by foreign air carriers serving U.S. cities, the United States committed to work through the

International Civil Aviation Organization to reach an international agreement applying the same noise standards to all aircraft globally. The organization amended Annex 16 to the Chicago Convention very much along the lines of U.S. noise policy.

The FAA also agreed to propose tougher noise standards for new aircraft designs by March 1, 1977, to develop and implement flight operational procedures for noise abatement, and to manage air traffic control and navigable airspace to minimize noise impact on residential areas. Takeoff and landing patterns were redesigned to reduce the noise impact on neighborhoods. Finally, the Department of Transportation agreed to provide financial and technical assistance to airports for noise reduction planning and abatement activities.

Our preparation of the comprehensive noise policy was greatly aided by a Supreme Court victory by Warren Christopher, a future secretary of state and my future law partner at O'Melveny & Myers. In a 1973 decision, *City of Burbank* v. *Lockheed Air Terminal,* the Supreme Court had held that the control of aircraft noise at its source was a federal responsibility that preempted all state and local regulation of aircraft noise. There was, however, a significant loophole. In footnote fourteen in the decision, the Supreme Court recognized the responsibility of local airport proprietors to take appropriate action to minimize their liability for the adverse effects of aircraft noise.[9] We thought the Supreme Court had established a useful foundation on which we constructed our policy statement. We therefore recognized that airport proprietors could adopt reasonable local restrictions on airport use that did not unjustly discriminate against any airport user, impede the federal interest in the safety and management of the air navigation system, unreasonably interfere with interstate or foreign commerce, or conflict with federal noise regulations. My noise policy, however, made crystal clear that state and local governments had no authority to regulate aircraft noise. Their responsibility was to limit the use of land near airports to purposes compatible with aircraft operations.

It must have been a slow news day because the *Washington Post* announced the aircraft noise abatement policy as the lead story on the first page of its Saturday edition.[10] The policy established the framework that continues to this day, parts of it endorsed by Congress in legislation,[11] its principles adopted by the International Civil Aviation Organization in its "balanced approach,"[12] and its legal underpinnings enforced by the courts as they have protected the efficient flow of interstate air commerce from local curfews and a hodgepodge of inconsistent airport noise restrictions.[13] The policy also has enabled the FAA to spur the manufacturers and airlines to bring into operation new generations of aircraft that are 70 percent quieter and more fuel efficient than the early jets,[14] far surpassing that which has been accomplished in most other industries.[15]

TRANSPORTATION DEREGULATION

In the Ford administration we devoted an enormous amount of energy to another important area of policy development, which came to full fruition in the subsequent Carter administration—economic deregulation. In this area President Ford was the antithesis of Richard Nixon, who had experimented with such intrusive regulation as wage and price controls (as I knew all too well from my service on the Price Commission). Nixon had appointed committed regulators to the independent agencies, such as the Civil Aeronautics Board and the Interstate Commerce Commission, but President Ford was impressed with multiple studies demonstrating the enormous inefficiencies of economic regulation. Ralph Nader, in his seminal 1970 *Report on the Interstate Commerce Commission*, had shown how economic regulatory agencies had often become the captives of the industries they were supposed to regulate.[16] The agencies' policies protected the economic welfare of the status quo players. Thoughtful analysis by academic writers such as Paul MacAvoy, who was a member of President Ford's Council of Economic Advisers, Jim Miller, later director of the Office of Management and Budget, and Cornell economist Alfred E. Kahn, who spearheaded airline deregulation in the Carter administration, demonstrated the substantial efficiencies that could be achieved if transportation companies were released from the regulatory strictures that prevented vigorous competition and responsiveness to consumer demand.

Despite little media interest, President Ford set up the Domestic Council Review Group on Regulatory Reform under the leadership of White House staffers Rod Hills, Ed Schmults, and Paul MacAvoy.[17] Much of the initial focus was on transportation, since the airlines, the motor carriers, and the railroads were among the most regulated—and least profitable—industries. In those days government agencies regulated just about everything—routes, rates, and services. Entry by new companies was greatly restricted or denied altogether. For example, the Interstate Commerce Commission had to approve every minor change in the types of products that could be transported and the routes over which the truckers traveled. All too often a truck would be required to take a circuitous route to reach its destination and then return empty to its point of origination. Federal regulation drove up costs, wasted fuel, and polluted the environment. Escalating labor costs and inefficient work rules were simply passed through to consumers in rate or fare increases. Both the regulated companies and the unions strongly supported the status quo, from which they greatly benefited, as they were protected from new upstart low-cost (nonunion) competitors.

With strong support from the president, the Department of Transportation assembled a team led by John Snow.[18] We cranked out deregulation bills for the railroads, the trucking companies, and the airlines and sent them up to Congress. Support for transportation deregulation brought together an odd coalition of smart, innovative, and philosophically diverse people. Senator Kennedy, with the able assistance of his counsel Stephen Breyer, then a Harvard Law School professor and now associate justice of the Supreme Court, pushed hard in Congress for airline deregulation. We worked closely together and I accepted a number of Breyer's suggestions. One of the earliest advocates was Ralph Nader who, in a televised debate with Ronald Reagan of California said, much to the audience's surprise, "Governor, if you will campaign for president on the platform of economic deregulation even I could support you." (When the topic turned to motorcycle helmets, however, their newfound affinity quickly dissipated.)

The impetus for transportation deregulation was motivated in part by the distressed state of legendary transportation companies, like Pan Am, which continued to bleed losses, and the Penn Central railroad, which had filed for bankruptcy. In May 1975 we submitted to Congress the proposed Railroad Revitalization and Regulatory Reform Act, which coupled funding for the creation of Conrail with pricing flexibility for the railroads. President Ford told me to spread the word on Capitol Hill that there would be no funding for Conrail without the deregulatory provisions. If the iron triangle—a coalition of industry, unions, and veteran lawmakers who supported the status quo— succeeded in stripping the deregulatory provisions, the president would veto the bill. Our first partial deregulatory effort was enacted in 1976.

We had proposed comprehensive trucking deregulation legislation in November 1975. It was my task to brief the president of the teamsters union. He almost threw me out of his office. I did not fare any better with the major trucking companies. When President Ford was informed of my failures of persuasion, he remarked, "Well, if the teamsters and truckers are against it, it must be a pretty good bill." Enactment would have to wait until the Carter administration.

Meanwhile President Ford started to appoint deregulators to the independent regulatory agencies. John Robson was appointed chairman of the Civil Aeronautics Board. He began to phase in competition as best he could within the statutory straitjacket he inherited. He allowed airlines to raise or lower prices within zones of reasonableness and to enter and exit certain routes without board approval. The board awarded routes to new carriers, ending the freeze that had protected the lethargic incumbents for so many years. Robson also allowed the air carriers to charge discount fares, despite the solid opposition of their competitors. My general counsel's office flooded the agency with briefs advocating less regulation and more competition.

With the able assistance of his brilliant aide, Stephen Breyer, Senator Kennedy held a series of hearings that uncovered tremendous inefficiencies in the regulated system as well as efforts by the pre-Robson Civil Aeronautics Board to cover up illegal political contributions by airline executives. The scandal attracted media attention, and the hearings started to warm up enthusiasm for deregulation.

On October 8, 1975, President Ford submitted an airline deregulation bill to Congress. It encouraged new entrant air carriers, liberalized charter service, phased out restrictions on entering and leaving routes, and phased in pricing flexibility. Both Robson and I testified in favor of the legislation, explaining how the present system of regulation did not serve the interest of the traveling public.

One noon I invited the chief executive officers of the major U.S. airlines to lunch in the secretary's dining room, a Coast Guard mess adjacent to my office. I told them that deregulation might not happen during the Ford administration but it was coming. I told them they had a choice: They could continue to oppose deregulation and sit on the sidelines, or they could become players and help shape the contours in a way that would enable the carriers to make a smooth transition to a deregulated environment. It was up to them. Pan Am was the first major airline to support deregulation. The Civil Aeronautics Board had restricted Pan Am to international routes, and it was losing the competitive battle to other major U.S. carriers with strong domestic feeder operations that were expanding into international markets. Pan Am badly wanted to build a domestic system and thought deregulation would enable it to do so.[19] Shortly thereafter, United Airlines endorsed airline deregulation. Gradually, others came on board.

With the exception of the first phase of railroad deregulation, none of the Ford administration's transportation deregulation proposals was enacted by Congress. But because these proposals reflected a uniquely bipartisan effort, President Carter and Alfred Kahn, his Civil Aeronautics Board chairman, enthusiastically accepted the baton and carried on the work to a successful conclusion.[20] As a result, both the Civil Aeronautics Board and the Interstate Commerce Commission were phased out and no longer exist. There are few examples in American history of the termination of substantial federal programs and agencies. It is a precedent well worth considering during times of significant budget deficits and growing federal bureaucracies.

Transportation deregulation was not achieved easily. Since deregulation, the airlines have taken a roller-coaster ride, traveling through periods of new entry by low-cost carriers, bankruptcy by the established "legacy carriers," mergers and consolidations, terrorist attacks, and the demise of some of the great names of American aviation like Pan Am, Eastern, TWA, Braniff, and Northwest. Today air travel is no longer the preserve of the elite; the number of passengers has tripled. On an inflation-adjusted basis, average fares are lower today than they were in 1978.[21]

In retrospect, I believe we could have done a better job in managing the transition, and so could some of the airline chief executives. But I remain convinced we did the right thing. It is a lot less fun to fly today, but that is because we have created an equal opportunity for all Americans to enjoy the benefits of fast travel for business, recreation, or family purposes. As we face congressional gridlock today on many major initiatives, even when one party controls both the White House and Congress, we can learn from the success of transportation deregulation. Good legislation must be based on solid, independent analysis by academics and think tanks and wide consultation with industry, labor, and public interest groups. The legislation should be modified on a bipartisan basis to reflect legitimate concerns raised during congressional hearings and to build in a reasonable transition period. Over two administrations and several Congresses, the deregulation bills took shape and gradually gained public support.[22]

The Ford administration's airline deregulation initiative was primarily focused on domestic aviation. At the same time, the Department of Transportation had prepared an international aviation policy statement.[23] We advocated greater competition on international routes, the elimination of government subsides, and more reliance on the marketplace in pricing and entry. In retrospect, we were not as bold as we should have been. Subsequent administrations have pushed hard for "open skies" bilateral air service agreements with other countries. By negotiating more than fifty such agreements, including the extraordinary aviation liberalization agreement with the European Union, the United States has led the world in promoting price competition, free entry into markets, and fully competitive international air service.

In one area, however, the United States has fallen behind most of the rest of the world. That is restrictions on cross-border investment in the airline industry. By statute the U.S. limits to 25 percent the amount of voting stock that a foreign investor can hold in a U.S. air carrier. Granted, there are legitimate national security and labor concerns that need to be taken into account; however, there is no justification, in my judgment, for treating the airlines in such a protective, restrictive fashion, unlike other major industries, where cross-border investment facilitates the flow of capital. If U.S. airlines are to compete globally with the best available technology, they need to have access to foreign capital, as other industries do. It's time to rethink these arcane restrictions and regain our leadership in promoting global free markets in aviation.[24]

Finding the right balance between regulation and competitive free markets is never an easy task. In transportation, we retained federal oversight in safety, antitrust, and consumer protection. We also designed a transition period that was intended to minimize market disruption. Too much regulation creates enormous inefficiencies and higher prices, but too little regulation creates its own set of dangers, as recent experience in the financial markets has shown. While there is no magic formula, I believe that we are more likely to find the right balance if we rely on thoughtful, independent studies, work on a bipartisan basis, and plan transitions carefully. We also need to monitor vigilantly the effects of deregulation and be prepared to do some fine-tuning if unanticipated market disruptions or abuses occur.

TRANSPORTATION REORGANIZATION POLICY

Deputy Secretary Barnum and I issued a fifty-four-page proposed Transportation Reorganization Policy Plan on January 19, 1977, the day before we left office.[25] It has yet to see the light of day. It was based on the principles set forth in our statement of national transportation policy to provide cost-effective, evenhanded government support for a comprehensive, integrated, seamless nationwide transportation system. Because this initiative would have reduced federal funding distortions and replaced the various transportation fiefdoms with functional programs, it would have faced fierce opposition from the powerful lobbies of stakeholder organizations.

Here is how we would have reorganized the department. The various administrations (highways, mass transit, railroads, and automobile safety) would have been reorganized into three new agencies dealing with safety, interstate transportation, and regional and local transportation. The FAA would have retained its aviation safety responsibilities. Its air traffic management operations would have been spun off into a quasi-government corporation, subject to strict FAA safety oversight. Environmental policy would have been coordinated by an assistant secretary for the environment, although each administration would have had an environmental office.[26]

Perhaps the most controversial aspect of our proposal was the creation of a unified trust fund that would have funded the three new transportation administrations. At the time there were only two significant user charges in place: gas and other taxes for highway users and an aviation ticket tax. We proposed a substantial increase in the federal gasoline tax, the introduction of waterway user charges (ports, locks, and fuel fees), and a possible tax on rail services.

In light of the shortfall in recent years of highway trust fund revenues and the extraordinary cost to the nation of our increasing dependence on imported oil, my biggest regret today is not having proposed to replace the cents-based gas tax with a percentage tax that would have increased revenues as the cost of a gallon rose. If I had proposed a 15 percent federal gas tax in 1976, it would not have seemed threatening, but it would have generated eight to ten times the revenues today. And it would have reduced consumption.

In the ensuing thirty-five years, the challenges have increased. Our dependence on imported oil from unstable foreign regimes, our neglected transportation infrastructure (failing bridges, congested roadways, deteriorating passenger rail service), and the trust fund revenue shortfall all call for bold action. In its February 2009 report the congressionally established National Surface Transportation Infrastructure Financing Commission found that the gap between projected trust fund revenues and required federal highway and transit infrastructure investments would reach $400 billion during the period 2010–15 and grow to $2.3 trillion by 2035. This translates to billions of dollars in lost productivity, for example, as workers stall in snarled traffic. The commission recommended replacing the gas tax with a mileage-based fee.[27] If we have grown numb in recent years talking about billion- and trillion-dollar deficits, then consider the scarier prognosis of highway and transit deaths from collapsing bridges, deteriorating infrastructure, and failing equipment.

The simplest approach to funding the shortfall would be the institution of a carbon tax or petroleum tax. This would create a dedicated revenue source to fund the nation's transportation infrastructure, including safety, highways, bridges, public transit, Amtrak or alternative passenger rail options, airport capacity development (including new runways and satellite-based navigation technologies), high-speed rail corridors for passengers and freight,[28] and maintenance of inland waterways by the Army Corps of Engineers.[29]

Bold action will be required to modernize the nation's aging transportation infrastructure, reduce our dependence on foreign oil, protect the environment for future generations, and create domestic jobs. Economic stimulus funding is at best a temporary fix. I hope some future Congress will seize the opportunity. Congress seems far more willing to spend money on specific home-state transportation projects (sometimes bearing the name of a member of Congress) than to raise revenues to pay for an efficient nationwide system. Perhaps as a starting point it would be helpful to dust off some old files from my days at the Department of Transportation, when we began to think about these issues but ran out of time before we could begin to implement them. We might even consider taking the transportation trust fund out of the federal budget and have it administered by a quasi-governmental authority that could approve multiyear obligations, raise funds in the capital markets, and enter into public-private partnerships.

DIVERSITY POLICY

We made tangible progress in creating a level playing field for Americans of color. The Department of Transportation was a major job creator. By conditioning federal funding, the department could promote opportunities for minority contractors and employment. In this area the Nixon administration had taken aggressive action. I fully intended to build on that foundation.[30]

Through regulations and grant conditions we opened up opportunities for previously excluded minority contractors and encouraged the training and hiring of minority construction workers and transportation operators. In those days the unions did not always welcome minority workers. Their excuse was a lack of skills training and on-the-job discipline. We conditioned federal funding on providing on-the-job training and apprenticeships. We tailored our conditions to the particular funding mechanism and project. In funding major transit systems in Detroit and Atlanta, for example, we included specific minority contracting, recruiting, training, and hiring goals. In a multibillion-dollar upgrade of the Northeast rail corridor, we built in the strongest conditions ever for the use of minority contractors and the hiring and training of minority construction workers.

In approving the West Side Highway project for Manhattan, we negotiated with government, business, and union leaders to leverage more than $7 billion in new private, state, and city investment to revitalize New York City, including the construction of new educational, health care, cultural, and park facilities as well as retail, residential, and office space. The project would have provided fifteen thousand person years of new on-site construction jobs, with strong union commitments to recruit and train minorities and youth at a time when the unemployment rate in the construction industry exceeded 30 percent. Environmentalists, however, killed the project. They persuaded the courts instead to save the Hudson River striped bass.[31]

We also made progress with the airports. By chance I ran across a federal statutory provision requiring that the accounts of every airport be audited by a public accounting firm each year. After some inquiries, I discovered that none of the work had been given to minority accounting firms. I directed that notice be given to qualified minority firms in addition to the larger accounting firms. Every so often when walking through an airport, an accountant of color will come up to me and say thanks for giving him or her the first opportunity to take on a client of such size.

Shortly after I took office, Andrew Young, one of the representatives from Atlanta, Georgia, invited me to lunch on Capitol Hill. When I showed up at his office he said he was going to order sandwiches for us to eat rather than go to the congressional dining room. Knowing Andy quite well, I asked why. He replied, "Bill, you're a Republican and I'm a Democrat." I responded, "Andy, how many times did the Legal Defense Fund keep you out of jail when you were leading those protest marches down South? Don't tell me, seriously, that you are ashamed to be seen with me in public." We went to the congressional dining room.

Working with Andy and Atlanta's mayor, Maynard Jackson, the department provided substantial funding for the Atlanta airport and the construction of its new subway system. We provided for strong diversity programs, including work for experienced minority contractors and subcontractors. For the Atlanta subway I included a special provision requiring that half of the stations be designed by respected minority architects. As I believe visitors during the Olympics will attest, those architects designed some of the best subway stations in the world. The attractiveness of these stations was further enhanced by local artwork created through a department-sponsored arts program—following a suggestion made by Charles Ansbacher, the White House Fellow assigned to my department (and an orchestra conductor).

With millions of dollars of federal funding going out the door, I was surprised and disturbed by the low level of minority participation I observed when I arrived. We pursued an aggressive diversification policy, and as a result we increased significantly the number of minority contractors and minority workers in construction and in the management and operation of transportation services. When given the opportunity, they performed for the most part with great skill and success. We had to break down some long-standing traditions, open up some good-old-boy networks, and reach out to some new faces to bring about this change. I strongly believe it was the right policy at the time. And it worked. However, diversity policies must be constantly updated to reflect changing circumstances.

THIRTY-THREE

The Decisionmaking Process

The history of liberty has largely been the history of the observance of procedural safeguards.

—Justice Felix Frankfurter

In the Ford administration, we were fully committed to restoring confidence and trust in the federal government as the nation healed from the Watergate trauma. Since my training and experience had been exclusively as a lawyer, the tools I brought to this task were a commitment to a process that is fair, rational, transparent, and understandable to the public. Too often decisions in Washington were made behind closed doors, influenced by powerful interests with deep pockets and special access, and explained with a distorted spin that only increased public distrust and cynicism.

When I assumed office I faced a number of highly controversial issues. Should I approve the construction of a proposed eight-lane interstate highway through northern Virginia—I-66—that would feed traffic into the District of Columbia? Should I allow the European-made supersonic transport, the Concorde, to fly into the United States? Should I mandate air bags for passenger cars? Should I build a grand new airport for the St. Louis area across the Mississippi River in southern Illinois? In the past some of these decisions might have been made over a private lunch between a senator and a cabinet officer, perhaps as a quid pro quo for an increased appropriation for a pet project or some other earmarked piece of pork.

There were times, of course, when I played my political cards. We used a profusion of political tools to negotiate a good policy result, especially when dealing with powerful congressional chairs. My use of the pool of unused interstate highway mileage is a case in point, although no interstate would ever actually be built without going through a rigorous review process. On major, controversial issues, however, in which there were strongly voiced conflicting views and for which public acceptance was critical, my lawyerly instincts for a fair and open process prevailed.

One management tool that is second nature to a practicing lawyer but too often ignored in government is the setting of deadlines. Even statutory deadlines are often ignored. I was constantly setting tight deadlines that kept the civil servants scrambling. There was always the temptation to postpone controversial decisions, but by establishing due dates, I was able to bring a number of long-standing issues to resolution.

To bring some sunshine into the decisionmaking process I decided as a first step to publish in the *Federal Register* the issues and alternatives under consideration. The issues often involved reconciling various public interest objectives, such as safety, environmental protection, job creation, promotion of new technologies, cost efficiency, quality of transportation services, and benefits to the economy. The second step would be to invite written comments from interested parties. Third, I would hold a public hearing, extending as long as six hours. Based on my reading of the written submissions, I would have some tough questions for the hearing participants. Finally, as the decisionmaker, I would write out the reasons for my decisions, explaining how I had analyzed and reconciled conflicting public interest considerations.

1-66

The first controversial case I faced was the proposal by Virginia governor Mills Godwin to build an eight-lane freeway through northern Virginia to the Potomac River that would feed commuter traffic from the western suburbs over the Theodore Roosevelt Bridge into Washington. There was a lot of opposition to the highway from within the District of Columbia and close-in Arlington County, Virginia, and a lot of strong support from the further-out suburban communities whose residents faced increasing congestion in their commute to jobs in the capital.

There were many conflicting considerations, some of which were set forth in a comprehensive environmental impact statement. The metropolitan area had committed to building a ninety-eight-mile fixed-rail rapid transit system and had transferred funds originally planned for District of Columbia freeways to the construction of the new subway. At that time the Organization of the Petroleum Exporting Countries' oil embargo had quadrupled the price of imported petroleum, precipitating an energy crisis. Air pollution was becoming a serious regional problem. The District of Columbia originally had planned to build the Three Sisters Bridge to accommodate the increased traffic flow across the Potomac to Virginia but had recently decided to withdraw the bridge from its transportation plan. Clearly there were disconnects in the planning of the two neighbors.

On June 21, 1975, I held all-day public hearings and heard arguments by elected officials and organizations both for and against the proposal. After the hearing, I reviewed the extensive record and wrestled with the decision. I asked Don Bliss to prepare two written decisions, one approving the project and one disapproving it. I outlined the issues for each and scheduled a press conference to explain my decision. The preceding evening, still at the office near midnight, I called in Don and told him I was going to disapprove the proposal. Although it was a well-designed proposal, this was simply the wrong place and the wrong time to build it. I was concerned that constructing a major new highway to serve peak-hour commuter traffic to an urban center was inconsistent with emerging policies on energy conservation, air quality, noise, conservation of public parks, and the quality of urban living. I was also concerned that an eight-lane highway would generate additional traffic congestion in Washington and promote land-use patterns that would increase reliance on the automobile at a time when we were promoting the use of public transit.

I told Don to add several qualifications to my decision of disapproval. The first was to direct the department to recommend ways to improve access to Dulles International Airport from downtown Washington and to improve public transit alternatives in the corridor that would alleviate congestion. The second was that my decision would be without prejudice to any further modified design proposal by the commonwealth of Virginia to build a highway in that corridor that would meet the environmental and other concerns raised in my decision.

Don pointed out that if I invited Virginia to submit another proposal, I probably would have no choice but to approve it. It simply was not fair to ask the Virginia Department of Transportation to expend millions of dollars in designing a new highway proposal and to disapprove it a second time. I told him that the condition was essential. I would not reject the eight-lane highway proposal without it.[1]

Public reaction to my decision ranged from extremely favorable to extremely hostile. A *Washington Post* editorial strongly praised the decision as a wise and forward-thinking view of national transportation policy, recognizing the need for alternatives to the automobile and highway construction.[2]

Less than a year later, Virginia proposed a new, redesigned highway. My staff worked closely with the commonwealth, the Federal Highway Administration, and the Metropolitan Planning Organization (under new regulations requiring its review of urban highway projects) to come up with a design that was compatible with regional transportation planning, a proposal that I approved. It consisted of four lanes with a median strip that would be reserved for an above-ground metro line to Vienna, Virginia, preserving the option of eventually continuing rail service to Dulles airport.[3] In recent years there have been proposals to widen certain parts of I-66 to facilitate the ever-increasing congestion of commuter traffic. Members of Congress have asked me whether my initial decision would preclude any changes to the highway design, and I have told them of course not. Congress or the secretary of transportation can always adjust the decisions of their predecessors to accommodate changing circumstances. Nevertheless, I believe the approach I took to the I-66 decision remains valid today. We cannot simply build highways willy-nilly. We need coordinated regional transportation plans that preserve the quality of urban life, conserve energy, and reduce air pollution, including that from the new threat of greenhouse gas emissions.

SUPERSONIC TRANSPORT

An even more controversial issue than I-66 was whether to grant the Concorde supersonic transport landing rights in the United States. The United States abandoned its government-subsidized supersonic transport program in 1972 because of rising fuel costs; however, the French and British proceeded with the development of a commercial supersonic aircraft, the Concorde. When British Airways and Air France purchased the first Concordes, they sought permission from the Federal Aviation Administration to amend their operations specifications to allow the new aircraft to operate between London and Paris and various cities in the United States.

Under most circumstances, an amendment of an airline's operations specifications would be approved routinely by an FAA regional director. Given the controversy of this case, I reserved for the secretary the authority to make the decision. As was my practice I published a statement of the issues. They included safety, the supersonic boom, the effect of subsonic aircraft noise on communities, the impact of stratospheric supersonic flying on the ozone layer, the value of developing and testing new technologies through commercial application, the importance of free trade and fairness to our oldest allies, who had developed this technology and depended on service to the United States to recoup their investment, and U.S. obligations under international aviation treaties to recognize technologies developed in other nations.

After the submission of written comments, I scheduled a six-hour public hearing. The State Department had warned me that the governments of France and the United Kingdom would never agree to testify at my hearing. But they did, along with representatives from the Environmental Protection Agency and several environmental groups that strongly opposed admitting the Concorde.

After the public hearing, I caucused with a small group of advisers from the general counsel's office, including John Ely and Don Bliss. We agreed that

I would rely completely on the FAA administrator, John McLucas, to determine whether the Concorde was safe. After a technical review, McLucas ruled that the aircraft met the FAA safety requirements.

I then decided that the best way to reconcile the conflicting positions was to allow a sixteen-month demonstration project. I wrote out the terms of the demonstration in long hand and asked my lawyer colleagues to prepare a draft decision explaining how we weighed and balanced the various public interest considerations.[4]

When the written decision was finished, I called a press conference. We had put a lot of hard work into the decision, considering all the relevant issues and explaining my reasons in detail. I did not want the press running off with a one-line announcement without fully understanding the process and rationale. Accordingly, I invited the press to come to the Department of Transportation at nine in the morning, at which point they would be locked in a conference room and given the 120-page decision to read. I planned to show up an hour later, issue the press release, and answer any questions.[5] By that time I hoped the press would have some pretty tough questions. There were widely reported rumors that President Nixon had made a secret deal with President Pompidou of France to approve the Concorde's application. To ensure the integrity of the decisionmaking process, I did not inform either the secretary of state or the president in advance of my decision. The National Security Council sent over two annoyed staffers to sit in the locked room and read the opinion. That morning I had to give a short statement to a congressional committee on Capitol Hill. When I left the hearing, I was trailed by a friendly *Washington Post* reporter trying to get a scoop on the decision. I stopped at a pay phone and dialed the White House to inform President Ford of my decision. I misdialed and had to borrow a quarter from the reporter to redial. I told the president that if I had made the wrong decision, I would offer to resign and he should accept my resignation.

I then returned to the department and began the press conference. I confessed that this was a very close and tough decision and I had gone to extraordinary lengths to assure the public that their views were heard. I recognized the seriousness of the environmental objections, especially the impact of aircraft noise on local communities, but I also recognized my responsibility to treat our oldest allies—France and the United Kingdom—fairly and to adhere to our treaty obligations. By testing new technologies in the marketplace, we would ascertain their economic viability and determine whether they could be improved. For these reasons, I decided that a controlled demonstration project that would minimize and monitor the environmental effects was the best way to reconcile the conflicting concerns. Apparently one reporter from Norway was able to sneak out and release the news to the European wire services before the conference was concluded. (This was well before the days of cell phones and text messaging.)

Although not everybody was pleased with the decision allowing the Concorde to fly to two U.S. airports for a sixteen-month trial period, there were quite a few compliments on the way it was explained. The next day's *New York Times* (February 5, 1976) carried my public statement in its entirety.[6]

The department was immediately sued by environmental groups. My decision was subject to review by the U.S. Court of Appeals for the District of Columbia Circuit. The clerk of the court put the issue on a fast track for briefing and oral argument, probably because there were press accounts that the president of France was planning to fly the Concorde to the United States for a state visit in the near future. I called Attorney General Levi and said I wanted my general counsel, John Ely, to argue the case for the government. Levi's initial reaction was negative: it was the Justice Department's responsibility to defend federal agencies in court, but he acquiesced, and John did a superb job in defending the decision.[7] A few hours after the argument, the court affirmed my order in a *per curiam* decision. Some months later I ran into the presiding chief judge, James Skelly Wright, at a cocktail party. He told me that as a staunch environmentalist he wanted to reverse my decision but could find no basis to do so. He said our reasoning was airtight, and so he agreed to a *per curiam* approval without a precedent-setting opinion.

The environmental groups also sued the Port Authority of New York and New Jersey (which operates Kennedy Airport), seeking to bar the Concorde from landing there. The district and appellate courts upheld my decision and allowed the Concorde to participate in the sixteen-month demonstration project, which was extended by my successor. Writing for the court, Irving R. Kaufman, chief judge of the U.S. Court of Appeals for the Second Circuit, relied heavily on my decision, concluding that "Secretary William T. Coleman's decision is the very paragon of a clear and considered administrative action."[8]

Many months later on a trip to Toulouse, France, where the Concorde was manufactured, I was asked to make a few remarks at the beginning of dinner. To show respect for the local language I tried to recall some of my schoolboy French. In an attempt to tell the group how very happy I was to be there, I said, "Je suis très jolie." The room burst out into laughter. My American dinner companion explained to me that what I had actually said was "I am very pretty."

AIR BAGS

Whether to require automobile manufacturers to install passive restraint systems in new cars presented another controversial issue. Seat belts and shoulder harnesses had proved effective in most accidents, but they required an affirmative act by the consumer. Rates of usage were dismally low—less than 25 percent. I confess I was less than vigilant myself in buckling up. In 1972–74 the National Highway Traffic Safety Administration had experimented with an interlock system under which the ignition would not start until the driver was buckled up. The public revolted, and it became clear that public acceptance had to be an important part of implementation. Ralph Nader and certain members of Congress, Senator Magnuson and Representative John Moss in particular, strongly supported mandating the new air bag technology. The auto companies resisted for reasons of costs, concerns about public acceptance, and potential liability from technical problems such as inadvertent deployments. I reviewed one safety study estimating that the installation of air bags would prevent 11,600 fatalities each year.

I established a task force under my special assistant, Mike Browne, who worked closely with the new NHTSA administrator, John Snow, and the general counsel's office to define the issues for publication in the *Federal Register*. Four issues were of special concern to me: What was the usage rate of seat and shoulder belts, and would it be substantially increased through mandatory seat belt laws? What were the safety benefits of seat belts compared with air bags, which deploy automatically on impact? Would the public be willing to pay the additional cost of installing air bags? What was the risk of inadvertent deployment, causing injury to passengers, especially elderly persons and small children?

We then scheduled a public hearing. One well-intentioned participant got off on the wrong foot. Testifying for a regulation mandating air bags, Ralph Nader began with a comment: "Mr. Secretary, some of us feel as strongly about automobile safety as you do about civil rights." My response: "Mr. Nader, I resent your comment. I am not sitting up here for six straight hours listening to testimony because I have less concern for the safety of the American traveling public than you." Why the outburst? I had enormous respect for Nader and his dedicated band of consumer advocates, who have done so much to shape a more consumer-responsive government. But I was offended that he would view me as a single-issue secretary. All my life I had worked to contribute constructively to the enrichment of the American mainstream. The purpose of my voluntary civil rights advocacy was to facilitate this ambition. On that morning, my mandate was automobile safety, and the color of my skin and views on racial equality were irrelevant.

At the conclusion of the hearing, I was troubled by several unresolved technical questions, especially the safety implications of unscheduled deployments for small children. I was also concerned about public acceptance of this new technology. The evidence showed that seat and shoulder harnesses were more effective than air bags against side collisions and other types of accidents. I worried that the installation of air bags would cause people to neglect buckling their seat belts. I concluded that air bags were an additional but not alternative safety measure. It was important that the department continue through public relations campaigns and our work with state motor vehicle agencies to urge consumers to use both seat and shoulder belts.

Ralph Nader had become increasingly impatient about the lengthy process of analysis I had undertaken, calling me "an absolute coward in refusing to stand up to the automobile industry's pressures." I wrote him a personal letter: "I hope I can demonstrate to you that I was not and am not a coward." He later intimated that I was doing to automobile safety what the Ku Klux Klan did to civil rights, which was more than mildly annoying. But I admired Nader's passion and persistence and that of his colleague Joan Claybrook, who later became the NHTSA administrator in the Carter administration. Their tireless efforts have saved thousands of lives on America's roads. They made a strong case for air bags at my public hearing. The automobile manufacturers had made some excellent technical points as well.

As I thought through these issues, I was convinced that it was important to phase in the installation of air bags and to monitor how they worked technically, what effect they had on seat belt use, and how the public accepted them. I was personally convinced that air bags would prove to be an important safety initiative and that the public would gladly pay the extra cost when it recognized the additional safety protection provided. I decided to establish an experimental program and reach out to the automobile manufacturers.

The sixty-six-page decision explaining my reasons for the trial period was released to the public in a press conference on December 6, 1976.[9] By now the approach I was taking to many of these decisions should not have been a surprise to close observers. Resistance and fear often accompany a substantial change in public policy. As I had proposed unsuccessfully after the *Brown* decision during the Legal Defense Fund's internal debate on school segregation remedies, I had come to believe in the benefit of a reasonable transition to bold new initiatives. If we carefully plan a transition period, often that fear dissipates as the benefits of the new initiative are demonstrated. Public acceptance then increases.

How could we design and finance a demonstration program for airbags? Usually the federal government issues a final command-and-control regulation after a notice of proposed rulemaking and public comment. In the case of air bags, there wasn't time to complete the administrative process before the end of the Ford administration. I also thought it was important to get the automobile companies, each of which had a different set of issues and technical concerns, to buy into the concept since they would have to invest in the technology and market air bags to the consumer. So I decided to take a novel approach and negotiate a demonstration program directly with each of the car manufacturers.

On advice of my general counsel to avoid any antitrust concerns, Mike Browne and I negotiated with each car manufacturer separately. At first General Motors and Ford were reluctant to enter into negotiations. Mike warned them that if we failed to reach agreement, I would issue an industry-wide air bags mandate before I left office. Mike was a tough negotiator. When he reached an impasse, I would step in and offer a carrot to the companies. With time running short, we ran our "good cop, bad cop" routine. We signed separate agreements with General Motors, Ford, Chrysler, and Mercedes Benz pursuant to which they would develop the production capacity to install air bags in at least a half million cars for model years 1980 and 1981. They agreed to cap the cost to purchasers at a specified amount. They also agreed to invest a specific amount in marketing air bags to consumers.[10] In return for the signed agreement, I terminated the passive restraint rulemaking three days before I left office.

Unfortunately, President Ford lost the election. The next secretary of transportation, Brock Adams, canceled the agreements with the car companies. He rushed through a regulation mandating the installation of air bags. The department was immediately sued, and after years of litigation, the U.S. Supreme Court invalidated the regulation. As a result, the installation of air bags as a safety measure was delayed another five years.

In 1989 John D. Graham, an expert on auto safety, assessed my handling of the air bag issue:

> Coleman's administrative strategy was innovative. Rather than use regulation to compel technological progress, he used regulatory authority as a threat to induce voluntary action by auto companies. It was an especially appropriate strategy for an air bag advocate in a pro-business administration. Claybrook, for instance, believes that Coleman did as much as he could for air bags as part of the Ford administration and was "sincere in his support for the air bag."[11]

I remain convinced that the approach I took would have resulted in faster implementation and acceptance of an important safety initiative as well as technical improvements that would have minimized some of the adverse effects of unscheduled deployments. I am told that many of the NHTSA scientists and engineers agreed with me. As one engineer put it, "There was a consensus in the technical community that Coleman's plan was a brilliant idea. It would resolve any lingering technical questions while building confidence in the technology. Once on the road in large numbers, the air bag would sell itself."[12]

THE AIRPORT THAT NEVER WAS

Another controversial decision I made was relegated to the dustbin of history: whether to approve the construction of a new airport to serve the St. Louis area. The existing airport, Lambert Field, was in St. Louis County, Missouri, west of the city. It was greatly constricted by surrounding development, which prevented expansion to alleviate congestion and accommodate increasing air service demand. The proposal before me was to build a spacious new airport in Waterloo, Illinois, across the Mississippi River, east of St. Louis. What made this decision particularly tough was that many Missouri residents and their elected representatives, including the vast majority of air travelers who lived in the suburbs to the west of St. Louis, greatly enjoyed the convenience of Lambert Field and strongly opposed moving their airport across the river. Local opposition and convenience to the traveling public were certainly important considerations. I spent a full day in St. Louis listening to residents and their elected representatives at a public hearing.

But there were other public interests to consider: long-term aviation growth, reducing the adverse impact of aircraft noise on the surrounding community, and ensuring a continuing vital role for the St. Louis area in interstate commerce. I was particularly troubled by the demographics east of St. Louis, a perpetually depressed area with one of the highest unemployment rates in the nation. A new airport would be a huge economic boost for the entire area, pulling commerce and industry east from St. Louis. Interestingly, the mayor of St. Louis supported the Illinois airport, as did elected Illinois politicians. However, Kit Bond, for whom I had great respect, was in a tight reelection race for governor of Missouri. He and other Missouri elected officials strongly opposed the Illinois airport proposal.

I pondered my decision far too long. As the fall election approached, local politics intensified the controversy. As I lay awake one night mulling over the pros and cons, I thought to myself what if, in 1959, the FAA administrator Elwood "Pete" Quesada had decided not to build that white elephant called Dulles International Airport way out in the Virginia sticks, so far from Washington? After all Washington already had the convenient close-in National Airport. I headed down to the office early the next morning and started to work with my staff to prepare an eighty-eight-page decision that would thoroughly analyze traffic projections, capacity, safety, noise, and other relevant considerations. I decided to approve the grant for a new airport in southern Illinois. I hoped that by explaining in detail the reasons for my decision, I would at least convince those people who disagreed with me that the democratic process had not failed. Their views had been heard. Judging by the editorials in the two leading St. Louis newspapers the next day, I was only halfway successful in achieving this modest objective. The *St. Louis Post-Dispatch* called the decision "a thorough and impartial study," "a fair proposition for both sides of the St. Louis area," and "a thoughtful blueprint for balanced airport progress as far as can be seen from the vantage of 1976." The *St. Louis Globe-Democrat* described it as "an act of unparalleled arrogance by a Washington bureaucrat" and "the biggest sky jacking ever attempted."

Governor Bond lost his reelection bid, possibly because of ads run in the St. Louis area about my decision to highjack his airport and move it to Illinois. St. Louis County and the state of Missouri hired my former law school dean Erwin Griswold to bring a lawsuit challenging my decision. But my decision prevailed and was upheld at every level in the federal courts.

History will not determine whether or not I made the right decision. One of the first acts of the incoming secretary of transportation in the Carter administration was to meet privately with Senator Eagleton of Missouri to discuss the "airport problem." Shortly after the meeting, Secretary Adams instructed the staff to overturn my decision, but to do it in a way that met the due process standards of the Coleman decision and would be upheld in the courts. Since the decision had already been made in a private meeting with the Missouri senator, it was an impossible task to replicate the Coleman process, but at least Secretary Adams did not have to endure any sleepless nights while he ruminated over what was the right course of action.[13]

After American Airlines acquired TWA, which had been the major carrier in St. Louis for decades, scheduled service plummeted. With significant improvements made to Lambert Field, it may well be that the current airport will adequately serve the traveling public for the foreseeable future.[14] As far as I can tell, there has been little economic progress to the east of the city in southern Illinois. So perhaps we will never know who was right, Secretary Coleman or Secretary Adams. For me it was a close decision in the first place. Reasonable public officials can and should disagree on the substance of policy. That is why it is so important that we use a process that is open and fair. It will not always lead to the best decision, but it should assure the people that their government is acting responsibly and fairly to address their concerns. As Justice Frankfurter said, "The history of liberty has largely been the observance of procedural safeguards."[15] So the responsiveness of government to the people must largely be a result of the fair and open process by which government decisionmaking is conducted.

THIRTY-FOUR

A Time of Transition

*I am a Ford, not a Lincoln. My addresses will never be as
eloquent as Mr. Lincoln's. But I will do my best to equal his
brevity and plain speaking.*

—President Gerald R. Ford

During my twenty-three months as secretary of transportation, my
respect and admiration for President Ford grew immensely. His guileless style
was the polar opposite of that of his two immediate predecessors. His calm,
warm, engaging, self-assured personality was exactly what the nation needed.
As a congressional leader, he was well versed in domestic and international
affairs, an excellent judge of character, a good listener who sought many
diverse points of view, decisive, and willing to delegate to persons in whom he
had confidence. He was not particularly interested in, or good at, public relations. The media's projection and public perception of President Ford ("can't
walk and chew gum at the same time") were in stark contrast to the person we
knew and worked with in the Oval Office.

It is ironic that the most centered president of that era had not clawed his
way to the White House. He had never run for public office outside his safe
congressional district. This was about to change. President Ford announced
his decision to run for election for a full term of the presidency in the Rose
Garden in July 1975. I was fully committed to work hard for his election for
the good of the nation and because I felt a personal stake in the outcome.

In less than three years, President Ford had brought the nation out of the
nightmare of Watergate as he worked to restore trust and confidence in government. His pardon of Richard Nixon had cost him dearly, but he knew it
was essential to refocus the nation on the future and address the smoldering
international and domestic crises that confronted us. When Vietnam and
Cambodia fell, in part because the public would not support further U.S.
intervention, he was able to put these divisive episodes behind us and begin
the national healing process. He laid the groundwork for a new arms control
agreement with the Soviets and a major peace agreement in the Middle East.
He engineered the Helsinki Accords, reducing tensions in Eastern Europe

and beginning a thaw in the cold war that eventually led to the disintegration of the Soviet bloc. He ended the recession he had inherited and cut the inflation rate in half. Unlike some other presidents, he had no enemies list and did not obsess about single issues, as did Johnson (Vietnam), Nixon (Watergate), or Bush 43 (Iraq). He used the cabinet more effectively than any modern president, and his scandal-free administration mirrored his own standards of integrity and accomplishment. Precisely because he was the only president in our history who'd never been elected to nationwide office, I fervently hoped that the American people would ratify his successful leadership.[1]

On a more personal level, I had gotten to know President Ford well over many years. I really liked him. I thought the administration was beginning to hit its stride and hoped that our policy initiatives would be implemented in a full term. I had reason to anticipate that Ford's election would bring some exciting new opportunities for me. Ed Levi had told the president he planned to retire as attorney general at the end of the term. President Ford told me that I would be his choice for attorney general if he were elected president. This would have brought me back to my first love—the practice of law—at a most exalted level.

For all of these reasons, I campaigned with the president in Michigan and for him in my home state of Pennsylvania and in Ohio, New York, and New Jersey. By March 1976 the pollsters told us that President Ford faced a tough election fight. Through the good offices of my special assistant, Michael Browne, I was named a member of the Pennsylvania delegation to the Republican National Convention. The Republican Party had planned a late convention in Kansas City from August 16 to 19 on the assumption that there would be no primary contest and the publicity surrounding the convention would launch the general election campaign after Labor Day.

California governor Ronald Reagan, however, had different ideas. He mounted a formidable challenge for the nomination. In one artful move, he announced that Richard Schweiker, senator from Pennsylvania, would be his vice-presidential running mate. One of the first issues the convention delegates faced was a proposal to the rules committee by the Reagan camp that each presidential nominee should name his vice president before the presidential nomination. Obviously, Reagan wanted to force President Ford's hand. If Ford retained the liberal northeasterner Nelson Rockefeller on the ticket, Reagan thought he could shore up his conservative support in the South and West. If Ford replaced Rockefeller with a more conservative candidate, the northeastern moderates might be offended and impressed by Reagan's choice of a moderate Pennsylvania senator as his running mate. The Reagan motion was put to a vote. The head of the Pennsylvania delegation, Drew Lewis, had committed to support President Ford before Reagan entered the race. Lewis faced an unwelcome dilemma. Senator Schweiker was one of Lewis's best friends; they each had served as the other's best man. Moreover, having a Pennsylvanian on the national ticket would be a great boost for the state. However, in politics keeping one's word is a matter of honor. Drew Lewis worked for four straight days and nights in a second-rate hotel far from the convention center to convince the Pennsylvania delegation to vote against Reagan's motion to compel a presidential nominee to state his choice for vice president in advance. The crucial motion was defeated by only seventeen votes. President Ford won the nomination and thereafter announced that Kansas senator Robert Dole of Kansas was his choice for vice president. Ronald Reagan obviously respected Drew for keeping his commitment because later as president he appointed Lewis secretary of transportation. Drew's many accomplishments in that position (including amending the highway trust fund to dedicate a penny of the gas tax for mass transit) would rank him among the best ever to occupy that office.

Having survived a bruising primary campaign and convention, President Ford was off to a rough start in the general election, trailing the Democratic nominee, Governor Carter of Georgia, by some twenty points in the polls.[2] While both candidates endured their share of bad publicity, Ford was especially hurt by false allegations that he had accepted illegal campaign cash payments from the Marine Engineers Beneficial Association. Attorney General Levi referred the issue to the special prosecutor, Charles Ruff, who took his time in finding that the allegations were completely baseless. But the damage had been done as Carter concluded each stump speech with "President Ford should tell the American people the truth, the whole truth, and nothing but the truth."

President Ford outperformed Jimmy Carter in the first debates, looking far more presidential than the nervous governor, who sounded as if he had a mouth full of grits. Then agriculture secretary Earl Butz served up Carter a slow pitch. In an interview with John Dean for *Rolling Stone* magazine, Butz made the indelicate, false, and frankly stupid comment that the Republican Party couldn't attract more black votes "because coloreds only want three things: . . . first, a tight pussy; second, loose shoes; and third, a warm place to shit."[3] Ford issued a strong statement condemning the remarks, but in a few days, at the insistence of his wife, Betty, he asked for Butz's resignation. Out on the campaign trail, I took a deep breath and tried to fend off questions about Butz's stupidity as best I could: "In a lousy attempt at humor, Butz was simply quoting an old ward politician from the Midwest to illustrate why Republicans failed to attract black voters."

In the second debate Ford made his famous gaffe, denying that the Soviet Union dominated Eastern Europe. Although he did not express himself artfully, the president clearly intended to say that the Soviet Union could never dominate the spirit, aspiration for freedom, and cultural self-determination of the peoples of Poland and other Eastern European countries. Ford's sentiment was absolutely right, as subsequent history has shown.

In the final debate, Ford emphasized his success in reducing inflation and creating 4 million jobs. I believe Ford was helped by his overall performance in the three debates. The polls indicated that he was fast closing in on Carter's lead.

It turned out to be a very close race. I stayed up watching the returns until four in the morning, when it became clear that Carter was victorious. Carter won by 2 percent of the popular vote, with 297 Electoral College votes to Ford's 241. Among the tough battleground states, President Ford won Michigan and New Jersey. Sadly, he lost Pennsylvania, which, had he won, would have taken him over the top. I believe to this very day that if we had had one more week, President Ford would have won the election.

The day after the election I showed up at the Department of Transportation tired and disappointed. Nonetheless, the people's business must continue. In our democratic tradition, we would provide for a smooth transition. President Ford and I would remain in office for another two and a half months. I gathered my staff and told them that in my life the most exciting event I had ever witnessed was the birth of a child. From conception to birth, it takes nine months. If such a miracle can be accomplished in such a short time, the department could complete the work we had begun in the time remaining to the Ford administration. I intended to work until 11:59 a.m. on January 20, 1977, to resolve all the issues pending before me that were ripe for decision. Having undertaken the analysis, reviewed the options, and considered the views of Congress and the constituent organizations, I thought the only responsible course of action was to make a decision, which my successor could then implement or reverse. He did plenty of both. For those on my staff who had worked exceedingly hard in the months preceding the election, and perhaps had intended to take some time off to regenerate and search for a job, this could have been unwelcome news. But my staff felt as I did; we had invested time and effort into working through important issues. We owed it to the new administration and the American people not to leave them with unfinished business.

We worked long hours over the next two and a half months. We completed a comprehensive report on the prevention and cleanup of oil spills. We promulgated new departmental regulations on ethics—the toughest in government at the time, as we intended to hold the incoming administration to its lofty campaign rhetoric on morality. We signed off on highway, Northeast rail corridor, and mass transit projects that were ready for approval.

One such project was the Massachusetts proposal to build a tunnel under Boston Harbor to connect Logan Airport to downtown Boston. The project acquired the name the Big Dig. I had spent a fair amount of time on this project, listening to Senators Kennedy and Brooke, who strongly supported it, and visiting on several occasions with Tip O'Neill, the Speaker of the House. Although we had just about completed our review, I thought that I should defer to the incoming Democratic administration the fanfare that would accompany approval of the project. To my surprise, when I arrived at work in the morning of January 20, I received a call from the Speaker a little after nine, urging me to sign the letter of approval. I told him I had to make one call and promised to call him back later that morning. I then called President Ford and explained the situation to him. I told him the project would cost $2.6 billion but I thought it made sense because it would facilitate transportation within Boston, reduce congestion and pollution, and increase safety. President Ford responded: "Of course, Bill, if you have all the information and have concluded the project is cost effective, there is no reason why you shouldn't sign the letter and make the Speaker happy." Given the long-standing friendship between Ford and O'Neill, who had served many years together in the House and spent many Saturday mornings together on the links, the president's response was not unexpected. I believe O'Neill really appreciated President Ford's granting him this request. He never developed the same affection for Jimmy Carter, even though they shared the same political party.

I signed the letter of approval and delivered it to the Speaker's office for arrival thirty minutes before President Carter was sworn in.

Unfortunately, the Big Dig experienced a number of scandals and huge cost overruns. When the project was finally completed in 2007, the cost had reached almost $22 billion. In June 2006 I visited former president Ford in his Palm Springs home. I apologized for telling him that the Big Dig project would only cost $2.6 billion and for failing to anticipate the construction deficiencies that delayed its completion by so many years. As he did so often, President Ford looked at the brighter side: "Well, Bill, at least when the ribbon is finally cut on the project, it will be by a Republican governor, Mitt Romney."[4]

About eight o'clock on the night of January 19, I invited Chuck Percy, senator from Illinois, to the secretary's conference room, where we announced before the assembled Chicago press a major federal grant to the Chicago Transit Authority. It was my last press conference in the Ford administration.

One of my practices at the department was to open up my office on Saturday mornings to any employee who wished to drop by and discuss any matter of interest. Before my departure I invited all the employees to come by so I could shake their hands and thank them for the work they'd done during my tenure. A long line spiraled down the hallway through the reception area and out into the main corridors of the department. As I made eye contact I could feel the dedication and commitment of so many fine federal civil servants who worked on behalf of the public interest for far less compensation than they could have received in the private sector. We had accomplished a lot in twenty-three months, and it was possible only because so many talented and expert people had worked long hours to improve the nation's transportation system. In recent years so many of our presidents—both Republican and Democrat—have campaigned against the federal government, denigrating the term *bureaucrat* and asserting that government is the problem, not the solution. While there are huge institutional problems in the structure of the federal government and we all suffer from imperfectly drafted statutory and regulatory mandates, I believe that the individuals who have chosen to work for the federal government, with few exceptions, uphold the highest standards of integrity, competence, and self-lessness of any Americans in the workforce. My last Monday in office, Lovida and I also hosted a luncheon at the Cincinnati Club for the reporters who had covered the department. They were a delight to associate with.

As time was running out, it finally dawned on me that after January 20 I would have the very practical problem of no job, no office, and no place to go during the day. Lovida had married me for better or worse, in sickness and in health, but not every day for lunch. As luck would have it, Vice President Rockefeller had graciously called me to thank me for my hard work as secretary and offer his vacation home in Venezuela for up to a month immediately after January 20 so that Lovida and I could decompress—an offer we were pleased to accept.

Fortunately, I had a place to come back to because a couple of days before the inauguration, Elliot Richardson had given me another valuable tip. He suggested that I call George Packard, who was then the deputy director of the Woodrow Wilson International Center for Scholars, and ask if he would take me on as a Woodrow Wilson Scholar to write a paper about cabinet government in the Ford administration. Packard liked the idea and offered me an office, secretarial assistance, and a stipend comparable to my compensation in the Ford cabinet. I stayed there for about three months and completed my paper on cabinet government, which was well received.

As I observed the transition from the Ford to the Carter administration, I thought there was a major flaw in our governmental system, which continues to this day. So many of the senior positions in the executive branch turn over when an administration changes. Of the dozens of senior political appointments at the Department of Transportation, only Don Bliss was asked to stay on in the Carter administration. (He left six months later to join me in the practice of law.) It took many months to fill all the vacancies, and much was lost in continuity, institutional memory, and momentum. There would be great value in adopting the British tradition of having a principal career deputy in each department remain to ease the transition.

It is unconscionable that a year into President Obama's administration, only 55 percent of the positions subject to Senate confirmation had been filled. I attribute this poor record to three factors: there are too many political appointees at senior levels; the White House employed an unrealistically burdensome "vetting" process; and under its arcane rules, the Senate can ignore its constitutional responsibility to render "advice and consent." For example, a single senator can indefinitely hold up a nomination for reasons unrelated to the nominee's qualifications. In 2010 one Republican senator incredibly attempted to put a hold on all seventy of the president's nominees then pending confirmation unless Congress and the president agreed to fund some local facilities in this state. In my view the president has a constitutional right to an expeditious up or down vote on his nominations.

My scholarly pursuits at the Wilson Center were constantly interrupted by some pleasant phone calls, inviting me to join various boards of directors. Among the phone calls I received were invitations from Tom Watson of IBM, Don Kendall of PepsiCo., Bill Sewall of Pan Am, David Rockefeller of Chase Manhattan Bank, and the chief executives of American Can, Philadelphia Electric, INA, J.P. Morgan Bank, American Airlines, and the Chessie Railroad. Philadelphia Electric and INA, the oldest insurance company in North America, were former clients and were headquartered in my hometown of Philadelphia. I readily accepted their offers and others from PepsiCo, IBM, and American Can. I knew I could choose only one of the three transportation companies that offered me a directorship. I accepted the invitation from Pan Am because I had previously served on its board, enjoyed my associations with fellow directors, and looked forward to using again that wonderful perk, a free family first-class pass on international service. There was no way I could turn down David Rockefeller, the chief executive officer of Chase Manhattan Bank, with whom I had worked so closely in the founding of the Trilateral Commission.

While I had postponed any discussions with law firms, I assumed that Lovida and I would return to Philadelphia and I would rejoin the Dilworth firm. To my surprise I started to get calls from other law firms asking if I would be interested in joining them. A couple of weeks after returning from Venezuela, I received a call from my old classmate at Penn and Harvard, Leonard Joseph, who was then the head of Dewey, Ballantine in New York. Joseph said he wanted me to head up the firm's new Washington office and would add my name to the firm's title in Washington.

About the same time, Warren Christopher, who was chair of the law firm O'Melveny & Myers, called me from Los Angeles. He said that he was leaving the firm to become deputy secretary of state in the Carter administration but that the firm had recently opened a seven-lawyer Washington office, its first

U.S. venture outside of Los Angeles. He told me to expect a call from Richard C. Warmer, the head of the new office. I was familiar with O'Melveny, one of the the oldest law firms in Los Angeles. I had also known and admired Warren Christopher from his days as deputy attorney general in the Johnson administration, where he was a strong supporter of school desegregation.

I received several other inquiries from law firms in Washington, Philadelphia, and New York. I actually entered into some serious discussions with a couple of white-shoe Philadelphia law firms (which had denied me an interview in the 1950s). I also had discussions with the Dilworth firm. I narrowed my options to the Washington offices of Dewey, Ballantine and O'Melveny & Myers. Why not an established Washington-based firm rather than the Washington office of an out-of-town firm? My concern was that Washington-based firms were focused primarily on the federal government—legislation, regulation, contracting, and lobbying. In a New York or Los Angeles firm, I expected to find a more diversified practice as I had found at Paul, Weiss and the Dilworth firm. A broad-based practice would better withstand business cycles and the phasing out of regulatory practices in areas such as natural gas, trucking, and aviation. Another consideration was the challenge of building a new Washington practice in support of the Fortune 500 client base of a first-class, out-of-town firm.

Dick Warmer from O'Melveny's Washington office called me and arranged for discussions with the O'Melveny partners from Los Angeles and the local lawyers who had come east, in a reverse of manifest destiny, to pioneer the Washington office. In taking what was considered to be a controversial step at the time, Warren Christopher and the management committee had selected Warmer, one of the most impressive young litigators, to head up the new office and had armed him with a team of associates who were among the best in the firm. They came with a strong sense of O'Melveny's tradition and values and ensured that the development of the Washington office would be fully integrated with its Los Angeles base.

The discussions with O'Melveny went very well. I had a real feeling of empathy for one of the Los Angeles partners, Richard Sherwood, because he had clerked for Justice Frankfurter and also because he had broken a barrier as the first Jewish partner of a major non-Jewish law firm in Los Angeles. A truly renaissance man who chaired the Los Angeles County Art Museum and took sabbaticals to teach art and law at Yale and antitrust law at the University of Tokyo, Dick Sherwood also was the only father of whom I am aware whose two children were both Rhodes Scholars. I also was most impressed by the outstanding young partners from the West Coast whom I had gotten to know as I interviewed and later joined the firm. O'Melveny had an extraordinary client base of blue-ribbon corporations, which it shared with Cravath,

Swaine, and Moore, in New York, and Covington and Burling, and Wilmer, Cutler, and Pickering, in Washington, as they bounced matters back and forth from coast to coast. In my discussions with the two firms, I learned that Dewey, Ballantine represented AT&T, a major competitor of IBM, whose board I had just joined. O'Melveny, on the other hand, had represented IBM in several major antitrust law suits that had been brought on the West Coast. This seemed a better match.

After a certain amount of ruminating, I accepted the offer from O'Melveny & Myers to become a full-share partner and member of its management committee. I was the first lateral partner to join the firm since Justice Louis Myers resigned from the California Supreme Court to join Henry O'Melveny in 1929.

From the start, O'Melveny's Washington lawyers considered themselves an integral part of the firm and not employees of a branch office. I remember a few months later at a Chase Manhattan Bank board meeting, the general counsel was briefing the directors on a troubling lawsuit against the bank in California. A fellow board member suggested to the chairman, "Why don't you retain Bill's firm, O'Melveny & Myers, to represent the bank in the lawsuit?" David Rockefeller looked surprised as he turned to me and said, "Why, Bill, you never told me your firm had a Los Angeles branch."

PART VI

A Washington Lawyer

*First say to yourself what you would be; and then do what
you have to do.*

—Epictetus

THIRTY-FIVE

The Sun Also Rises in the East

The wilderness and dry land shall be glad, the desert shall rejoice and blossom.

—ISAIAH 35:1

SINCE ITS FOUNDING IN 1885, O'Melveny & Myers had been an integral part of the growth of Los Angeles from a sleepy Mexican town to the second-largest city in the United States. Over the decades O'Melveny had established an extraordinary reputation on the West Coast, representing the major California banks, IBM, Occidental Petroleum, General Motors, major motion picture studios, Lockheed Aircraft, the department store Carter Hawley Hale, and, more glamorously, Bing Crosby, Shirley Temple, William Holden, Gregory Peck, James Stewart, Gene Autry, and Ingrid Bergman. In 1976 its fewer than two hundred lawyers were housed in downtown Los Angeles and a satellite office in Century City, where its entertainment department was located. There was a small outpost in Paris, France, established shortly after World War II to service movie studio executives and stars, as many films were then being made in Europe.

O'Melveny recruited the top students at the best law schools, many of whom grew into outstanding lawyers and community leaders. Because it was one of the go-to firms in Los Angeles, there was little interest in, or emphasis on, business development. Some of the finest East Coast firms referred their major clients to O'Melveny for work on the West Coast. Understandably, they greeted O'Melveny's opening of a Washington office with little enthusiasm, and some of my Los Angeles partners were concerned that the East Coast referral business would dry up. Some were also hesitant to refer their West Coast clients to the embryonic Washington office, which had yet to prove itself, instead of established Washington firms like Covington and Burling or Wilmer, Cutler. We had to persuade our own partners that we would serve their clients well and add a new dimension to O'Melveny as a full-service law firm.

When O'Melveny set up stakes in Washington in 1976, there were only a few out of-town firms with Washington offices, often staffed by local lobbyists or former federal agency heads. In making this move, O'Melveny changed the rules of the game. The next decade would see a cascade of Washington offices opening up from all the major U.S. cities, and not surprisingly a number of East Coast firms decided to open up offices in Los Angeles.

O'Melveny also was being challenged by other first-rate law firms in Los Angeles: Gibson, Dunn; Latham and Watkins; Paul, Hastings; and others. O'Melveny could not rest on its laurels as the best in the West. In my judgment, it had to move to a higher platform and compete effectively on the national and international stage. The Washington office would show the way. Although controversial in its inception, the success of the new office paved the way for a proliferation of O'Melveny offices around the world. There are now fourteen, including five in Asia.*

In 1977 the challenge was to convince my partners that O'Melveny had the quality and talent to compete nationally and internationally, to persuade our existing clients that we could meet their legal requirements anywhere in the country (or the world), and to attract new clients by building a reputation as a full-service law firm with strong litigation, transactional, and other practice specialties that even the best Washington-based firms, with their emphasis on federal regulatory issues, could not hope to replicate. Washington itself was changing. With the trend toward deregulation there was demand for innovative multidisciplinary teams of lawyers who could help formerly regulated industries thrive in a more competitive environment.

Over the next several years we were able to demonstrate with a string of successes how the Washington office could substantially raise the profile of the firm internationally. We assembled teams of expert lawyers in diverse specialties from our various offices to meet the challenges of, or seize opportunities for, major global corporations. Few clients ever hired O'Melveny to perform routine legal services. But when a "bet-the-company" crisis occurred, we became one of the few go-to major law firms on the general counsel's short list.

Of course, O'Melveny did not open the Washington office with such a grandiose view. The firm had several existing clients in need of legal services on the East Coast. A former O'Melveny associate, Frank Loy, the president of the Pennsylvania Company (the successor to the old Penn Central, no longer in the railroad business) moved the company's headquarters to the Washington area. Its principal outside counsel, John Roney, a senior corporate partner in Los Angeles, spent so much time in Washington that he became an enthusiastic supporter of opening an office there.

---

*Los Angeles, Century City, San Francisco, Newport Beach, Silicon Valley, New York, Washington, London, Brussels, Tokyo, Beijing, Shanghai, Hong Kong, and Singapore.

The Pennsylvania Company was a source of significant corporate and tax work in the opening months of the Washington office. In addition, O'Melveny had been the principal outside counsel for the Alyeska Pipeline Service Company, the consortium of oil companies that constructed the eight-hundred-mile Trans Alaska pipeline from Prudhoe Bay to Valdez. About this time tariff proceedings were initiated before the Federal Energy Regulatory Commission, and several O'Melveny attorneys moved to the Washington office to participate in this proceeding.

IMPERIAL VALLEY

The Washington office added a new dimension to the firm's representation of existing clients, such as the farmers of the Imperial Valley in California. About the turn of the twentieth century, family farmers in the Imperial Valley began, in the words of Isaiah, to make the desert bloom, creating acres of fertile farmland. They brought in water from Mexico by canal and constructed tens of thousands of miles of drainage systems to leach the salt out of the desert soil. To finance this investment over several generations, the farmers incorporated into larger tracts of six hundred to twelve hundred acres owned by extended family members.

When the Boulder Dam was constructed in the late 1930s, the United States decided for foreign policy reasons to discontinue the importation of water from Mexico and instead divert water from the Colorado River through the All-American Canal to irrigate the Imperial Valley farmland. Several lawsuits were brought against the family farmers seeking to invoke a 1902 National Reclamation Act provision and a similar requirement in the 1929 Boulder Canyon Project Act that prohibited the delivery of Colorado River water to farms of more than 160 acres or which were owned by persons living more than fifty miles away. After the plaintiffs' success at the federal district court level, the Carter administration's secretary of the interior, Cecil Andrus, began a rulemaking proceeding to implement the requirements nationwide.

While there were some large corporate farms in central California using federal water, the Imperial Valley was unique. The development of Imperial Valley had preceded by many decades the construction of the Boulder Dam (now the Hoover Dam), and the farmers had received assurances from the federal government that they were a grandfathered exception to the regulatory restrictions. Our expert economists predicted that if the reclamation restrictions were applied and the farms were broken up into 160-acre plots, most of the farmland would revert to desert.

Chuck Bender, a Los Angeles litigation partner who later became chair of the firm, led the appellate litigation team in the Ninth Circuit Court and eventually in the Supreme Court, challenging the trial court's decision to apply the 1902 Reclamation Act to the Imperial Valley.

By now there was a Washington dimension. First, I tried unsuccessfully to convince my law school classmate, U.S. solicitor general Wade McCree, to recognize the farmers' grandfather rights in the government's Supreme Court brief. Second, the farmers sought relief in Congress, relying in part on assurances from previous administrations. Third, the farmers participated in the Department of the Interior's rulemaking proceeding. O'Melveny also filed a lawsuit in California and succeeded in persuading a federal court to enjoin Interior from implementing the restrictive regulations without first preparing an environmental impact statement.[1]

The Interior Committee of the House of Representatives decided to schedule a hearing in Palm Springs, California. Rarely have farmers come so well prepared to testify before a congressional committee. Although the committee chair was anxious to wrap up the hearings by late morning so the members could make their tee times, Representative Burgener, whose district included the Imperial Valley and who sat by invitation on the committee, persuaded the members to stay and listen to the entire testimony of the farmers. It was quite compelling. We had hired an expert economist to demonstrate that the Imperial Valley would revert to desert if the restrictions were implemented, but his written statement read like a doctoral thesis, intelligible only to his faculty adviser at MIT. My partner John Daum, a brilliant and scholarly litigator, stayed up all night and completely rewrote the statement in simple, clear language. He presented it to the economist in the morning, an hour before he was to testify. At first the economist balked, saying that this simply was not his statement. John explained to him, "All I have done is translate your economic analysis into language that lawyers can understand. Most of the members on the committee are lawyers, and none is an economist. It is important that the lawyers fully understand your very thoughtful analysis." Our economic expert acquiesced and read the statement that John had prepared, as the committee members nervously eyed their watches.

In the end, Chuck Bender made a brilliant argument to the Supreme Court, which held that the Imperial Valley land developed before the Boulder Dam was exempt from the reclamation restrictions.[2] Interior then terminated its rulemaking, and Congress followed up by enacting legislation to exempt the remaining land. Don Bliss and I decided to sit in the Senate gallery and watch the debate on the legislative amendment we had recommended. Senator Mathias looked up and saw me there. He signaled for me to meet him in the lobby outside the Senate chamber.

"Bill, I saw you up there and figured you must be interested in this Imperial Valley legislation. What is this all about?"

Understandably, the senator from Maryland was not up to date on a western water issue unique to one county in Southern California. I explained the situation, and the senator went back into the chamber to cast his vote aye and inform some of his puzzled colleagues from northeastern states, who also voted aye.

A team effort brought complete success for the Imperial Valley farmers. Most important, we had demonstrated that the Washington office could contribute an additional dimension to the firm's practice. And we had shown how effectively lawyers from the various O'Melveny offices could work together to achieve a common objective.[3]

PAN AM

Within a few months our business development efforts (like the Imperial Valley desert) began to bear fruit, and the Washington office began attracting clients on its own.[4] The first major opportunity came from Pan Am, which sought to acquire another airline, the first merger since enactment of airline deregulation under the Carter administration. During the phase-in period of the new law, traditional antitrust principles were to be applied by the Civil Aeronautics Board in analyzing proposed mergers, a significant departure from the previous regulatory regime, under which only the acquisition of a failing carrier would be entertained. The board would now apply the antitrust standard of section 7 of the Clayton Act, barring a significant lessening of competition in any relevant market. Although Pan Am had excellent regulatory counsel in the law firm established by Berl Bernhard and Harry McPherson, my friends from the Johnson administration, their Washington-based firm did not then have a traditional antitrust practice. At the request of Pan Am's general counsel, we were added to the team.

My experience with Pan Am dated back to the days of Juan Trippe, the brilliant and innovative visionary who launched Pan Am as the first international airline carrying mail from Key West, Florida, to Havana, Cuba, and built the company into the world's largest international carrier, serving the Asia-Pacific, Europe, Africa, and South America, launching the clipper ships, and eventually introducing the first jet aircraft (the Boeing 707) and later the widebody Boeing 747. With its extensive worldwide network, Pan Am's principal competitors were foreign air carriers. The Civil Aeronautics Board prohibited Pan Am from serving any U.S. domestic routes. However, as deregulation evolved, the major U.S. airlines, like United and American, began serving international routes, where they had a substantial competitive advantage over Pan Am because they could feed their U.S. gateways with extensive domestic connecting service. Pan Am determined that to remain competitive there was an urgent need to develop a significant domestic network. Pan Am decided that the fastest way to develop a domestic system was to acquire National Airlines, a midsized domestic airline based in Miami, Florida, which could bring passengers to Pan Am's international gateways at Miami for service on to Latin America and to Kennedy airport in New York for service to Europe.

I asked my partner Dick Sherwood, an antitrust litigator in our Los Angeles office, to head up the O'Melveney team. Dick spent many weeks in the Washington office working with Don Bliss, who understood the airline industry and the Airline Deregulation Act well from his Department of Transportation experience. We put together a strong case, and an administrative law judge, after an extensive hearing, approved the acquisition. I was in Beijing with the Pan Am board when I received a phone call at my hotel at three o'clock in the morning from Don Bliss informing me of Judge Dapper's decision. The Civil Aeronautics Board affirmed the judge's decision, and the merger went through, sparking off a round of mergers and consolidation in the airline industry.

From a business standpoint, integrating the two workforces proved enormously challenging. The cultures of the two airlines were very different. A small domestic airline, National had the easygoing southern style of its Miami base in contrast to the cosmopolitan, New York–based, global Pan Am. In retrospect, Pan Am probably should have gradually developed its own domestic route system during the phase-in period under the Airline Deregulation Act.[5] A similar lesson could be learned from many of the copycat airline mergers that followed. Integrating the diverse unionized workforces of two culturally different airlines presented significant and costly challenges. Some of the mergers that followed could not be called an unmitigated success.

From the Washington office standpoint, however, the Pan Am acquisition demonstrated how our antitrust expertise in Los Angeles could be combined with our aviation experience in Washington to provide full-service representation. With airline deregulation, the airlines were in need of full-service legal representation in Washington, and O'Melveney's Washington office soon developed a premier antitrust practice.

ASBESTOS

Some of my business development activities inured to the benefit of Los Angeles. At the Dilworth firm I had represented the Insurance Company of North America, founded in Independence Hall in Philadelphia in 1792. The company retained our Los Angeles office in May 1979 in the California coordinated asbestos insurance coverage litigation. In the 1970s thousands of personal injury lawsuits had been filed against asbestos producers by workers who had been exposed to asbestos. The Insurance Company of North America had insured all five asbestos manufacturers at one time or another. Because of the long latency of asbestos-related diseases, there were many questions about the liability of insurers to defend and pay such claims. Potential asbestos liability placed the entire company at risk. As my litigation partner John Niles undertook this representation, he quickly realized the scope of the litigation and assembled a team of dozens of lawyers who tried cases and engaged in a complex settlement process under the auspices of the nonprofit Center for Public Resources, moderated by Henry Wellington, the dean of Yale Law School.[6]

In 1982 the Insurance Company of North America merged with Connecticut General of Hartford, Connecticut, a leading life insurance and employee benefits company founded in 1865. We continued to represent the combined company, CIGNA, in both Los Angeles and Washington and later in New York. In 1999 CIGNA sold its property and casualty business to ACE, a Bermuda-based international insurance and reinsurance business. O'Melveny continued to represent both CIGNA and ACE, which CIGNA's general counsel had made part of the deal.

By January 2000 more than two hundred thousand asbestos suits had been filed. O'Melveny became a principal counselor to CIGNA on a broad range of insurance coverage issues, including environmental remediation (superfund sites), exposure to toxic substances, and construction defects. The firm's CIGNA representation expanded into additional areas, including antitrust, bad-faith litigation, disputes with agents and brokers, and managed care.[7]

GENERAL MOTORS

The opportunity to resume my Supreme Court practice came early on. The general counsel of General Motors, Otis Smith, whom I had known through my former classmate Wade McCree, asked me to represent General Motors in an antitrust matter pending before the Supreme Court. Otis explained that our client, the named plaintiff Orrin W. Fox, was a GM car dealer.[8] The defendant was the New Motor Vehicle Board, a California state agency. The case, Otis said, was really about a constitutional challenge by General Motors of a California statute that protected automobile dealers from competition. He told me that O'Melveny had won the case before a three-judge district court in Los Angeles. The Supreme Court had noted probable jurisdiction of the appeal. He thought the O'Melveny lawyers were superb trial lawyers but wanted someone with Supreme Court experience to handle the appeal.

After consulting with the management committee, I accepted Otis Smith's request. Regretfully, I failed to contact personally Gerry Boudreau and John Niles, who had handled the trial. This was insensitive on my part, and it caused some discontent in the Los Angeles office. The O'Melveny tradition was that lawyers who had handled the trial also handle the appeals. Unlike many other law firms, O'Melveny had not established a separate appellate practice. Gerry and John put their resentment behind them and worked closely with my Washington associate and later partner, Carl Schenker, a former law clerk to Supreme Court Justice Powell and president of the *Standford Law Review*, on the appellate briefs, although the bad feeling generated by this clash in cultures took a while to overcome. Indeed, a short time later Gerry Boudreau decided to leave O'Melveny and join an Atlanta firm. To make matters worse, I lost the case in the Supreme Court, 8-1.

While O'Melveny continued to represent General Motors, primarily in Los Angeles, our focus in the Washington office was about to shift to a competitor—a competitor that I had represented at the Dilworth firm.

THIRTY-SIX

Building the Washington Practice

*Mere access to the courthouse doors does not by itself assure a
proper functioning of the adversary process.*

—Justice Thurgood Marshall

Early in 1978 I got a call from Hank Nolte, general counsel for the Ford
Motor Company. Nolte had been general counsel of Philco when I arranged
a meeting with Attorney General Kennedy to discuss Ford's acquisition of
Philco. We also had worked together closely to negotiate an agreement as part
of my air bags experiment when I was transportation secretary. Hank's boss,
Phil Caldwell, the chief executive officer of Ford, was on the Chase Manhattan board with me. Nolte wanted to speak with me about representing Ford
on a very serious automobile safety matter. I flew out to Detroit, accompanied
by Dick Warmer and Don Bliss, to discuss this new matter.

AUTO SAFETY

The National Highway Traffic Safety Administration (NHTSA) had recently
begun investigating the safety of the transmissions in 23 million Ford automobiles. The allegation, which was based on complaints and statistical reporting, was that Ford transmissions had a tendency inadvertently to shift from
park into reverse when the motor was left running. A driver, for example,
would pull into a driveway, shift into park, and run out behind the car to check
the mailbox. The car would slip into reverse and run over the driver walking
behind it. There were several heartbreaking incidents in which young children
were run over by a car that had shifted into reverse.

In their presentation, the Ford executives recommended that we develop
a statistical comparison showing that Ford transmissions were no more likely
than those of its competitors to shift into reverse. They contended that these
rare incidents were caused by the driver's failure to place the vehicle properly
in park. I looked over at Dick Warmer, who shared my apprehension. I called
an immediate halt to the presentation and asked for a few minutes to caucus

with my O'Melveny colleagues. Because we had represented General Motors, we did not think it would be appropriate for us to take on a representation that might depend in part on making a comparison of the safety performance of Ford vehicles with those of General Motors. I came back to the room and reluctantly told Ford that owing to a conflict of interest we could not undertake the representation. Ford hired another law firm to represent it on this matter.

Although Ford was disappointed, it soon called on us for another project. The NHTSA had made an initial determination that certain Ford Pinto fuel tanks were defective. Under the procedures, after an initial defect determination is made, the manufacturer has the opportunity to respond. This issue did not present a conflict, and we undertook the representation. By that time the office was really busy, and we reached out for assistance from Los Angeles. John Beisner, a young associate, came out to work in Washington for about six months. We sent Beisner over to the NHTSA to analyze its safety defect files. He prepared a historical study showing that, compared with past defect proceedings, the statistical incidents of alleged fuel tank failures were insufficient to support a final defect determination. Based on this analysis the NHTSA closed the proceeding without further action.

As he was on the way out of the Department of Transportation building, the NHTSA's chief counsel handed Beisner a letter to deliver to Ford. John had no idea what was in the letter, but he called Ford on his return to our office. Ford's safety counsel John MacNee asked Beisner to open and read the letter to him. To everyone's surprise, the letter was an initial defect finding on the Ford transmission park-to-reverse matter. Having heard nothing from his outside counsel, MacNee hit the roof. Shortly thereafter I got another call from Hank Nolte.

Nolte told me that if the NHTSA proceeded on this course and Ford was required to replace the transmissions on 23 million vehicles, it would bankrupt the company. He said that Ford had decided not to pursue the statistical comparison to its competitors. After further consideration we told Ford that we could undertake the representation.

The Center for Auto Safety, a Ralph Nader organization, took on the Ford transmissions in the media and urged the NHTSA to require a recall. The NHTSA alleged that the design of the Ford transmissions made it possible for a driver inadvertently to fail to put the gear shift lever properly into the parked position. If this happened, and the engine were left running, vibration could move the lever back into the reverse position, causing the car to move backward.

Ford contended that this would not happen if drivers properly placed the shift lever in park. If drivers were careless it is possible that in rare cases there could be unintended reverse movement in vehicles of all manufacturers. The NHTSA had collected a number of consumer complaints about the Ford transmissions, but Ford contended that these complaints were largely a result of the widespread publicity generated by the Center for Auto Safety and the NHTSA investigation itself.

Most initial-defect proceedings are settled by negotiations between the NHTSA and the automobile manufacturer, resulting in an agreed voluntary corrective action plan. In this case the NHTSA staff wanted to require a recall and retrofit of almost all Ford cars made over an eight-year period. This could have been the end of the company. Accordingly, Ford insisted on a public hearing. Over four days each side presented its case. Joan Claybrook, the NHTSA administrator who previously had been head of the Ralph Nader organization, presided over the hearing. Dick Warmer and I presented Ford's case.

Despite the adverse media publicity and strong pressure from the Nader group, our factual presentation convinced the NHTSA to return to the negotiating table with Ford and work out a reasonable remedy. Ford agreed to provide its automobile owners a dashboard sticker explaining how to park properly and avoid unintended vehicle movement. The Center for Auto Safety challenged the settlement in federal court. We joined the government to defend the settlement, and the district court upheld it. In *Center for Auto Safety* v. *Lewis*, the appeals court affirmed the agreement, calling this "the largest and most difficult and complex investigation ever conducted [by the NHTSA]."[1] The courts agreed with Ford that no specific defect had actually been shown and that park-to-reverse incidents could be prevented if drivers adhered to the warning labels and placed the gear shift in park correctly.[2]

CLASS ACTIONS

Not surprisingly, the NHTSA investigations precipitated class action lawsuits seeking a recall or damages. The granddaddy of these lawsuits was *Walsh* v. *Ford Motor Co.*, which was filed in August 1981 in the U.S. District Court for the District of Columbia.[3] The purported class constituted all purchasers of Ford vehicles for model years 1976-80, some 12 million to 15 million automobiles. The complaint alleged that under the Magnuson-Moss Warranty Act plaintiffs were entitled to damages for the difference between the value of their cars as warranted and their actual value as diminished by the alleged defect. The damage claim was in the range of $1.2 billion to more than $7 billion, with the potential for punitive damages on top of that. While the attempt to invoke the class action rule for this type of case was deeply flawed, Ford obviously had to take the enormous liability risk seriously and mount a comprehensive defense.

Unfortunately, frivolous class action claims alleging huge damages are still a common phenomenon. Plaintiffs' attorneys in class action lawsuits all too often seek to coerce major companies to settle by offering token consumer benefits and demanding large counsel fees. Companies often agree to such terms to avoid the litigation costs of discovery and the risk of an unconscionable damage award from a maverick judge or jury.

Ultimately, each of these class action lawsuits against Ford failed. O'Melveny's work in these cases seasoned an experienced and knowledgeable class action defense team in the Washington office.[4] The *Walsh* plaintiffs persisted for some ten years, generating thirteen published opinions, 550 court docket entries, and more than 700 entries in the docket of a court-appointed special master, Frank Flegal, of the Georgetown University Law Center.

When Chief Justice Earl Warren appointed me to the Civil Rules Advisory Committee in 1959, the most contentious issue at the time was a new Rule 23, providing for class action lawsuits. I was greatly concerned that the rule would open a Pandora's box of abuse, but I never envisioned that it would be invoked to rationalize a class of 15 million automobile purchasers who bought different car models in different years with different types of transmissions and control systems and had had entirely different driving experiences. The overwhelming majority of the plaintiff class had never experienced the rare park-to-reverse phenomenon.

In my argument in the *Walsh* case before the U.S. Court of Appeals for the District of Columbia Circuit in 1981, I could speak with some authority, having participated personally in the creation of Rule 23. We envisioned a situation, for example, in which a group of people suffered similar damages in responding to a fraudulent advertisement, and the amount of damages was so small as to make the pursuit of an individual law suit infeasible. Class action lawsuits had worked quite well in addressing widespread employment discrimination. There was a legitimate need and purpose for the class action procedures envisioned in Rule 23(b)(2), which was proposed in 1966. But the *Walsh* case had taken the rule to an illogical extreme.

Despite many ingenious arguments made by the *Walsh* plaintiffs' counsel, who made the Ford transmission case his life's work, the district court belatedly came to the inevitable conclusion that there were too many variables to allow a class action to proceed. The District of Columbia Circuit Court affirmed the district court's decision dismissing the class action in an opinion by appellate court judge Ruth Bader Ginsburg, who later became an associate justice of the Supreme Court.

After the dismissal of the Walsh appeal, the plaintiffs' class counsel filed copycat class actions in Philadelphia, the Superior Court of the District of Columbia, and Chicago. All of these cases were eventually dismissed. Over the years we developed a strong cadre of class action defense specialists, including dozens of partners on both coasts. We have branched out into health care, prescription drugs, financial services, securities law, product liability and mass torts, wage and hour, environmental, and insurance class actions. More recently, the general counsel and executive vice president of Merck Corporation came to me, and we began working on class action litigation involving the drug Vioxx.

In 1996 I testified before the Civil Rules Advisory Committee, proposing modifications to Rule 23(b)(2) from the perspective of one who was "present at the creation"—to quote Dean Acheson, who chaired the committee at the time Rule 23 was created. Heeding Plato's admonition that the one person who does not know the meaning of the words of a poem is the author thereof, I did not claim to be the drafter. I acknowledged that in some respects Rule 23(b)(2) had served the legal community well through the years. As a civil rights litigator, I found it an effective tool in the fight against employment discrimination. In other respects, Rule 23(b)(3) was becoming an unmitigated disaster because of the way some plaintiffs' counsel and courts had abused it. Some attorneys have used the device responsibly; but Max Boot of the *Wall Street Journal* and other observers of our judicial process amassed considerable evidence that too many practitioners were filing too many ill-conceived class actions for one purpose: to make a quick buck. Their anecdotal research indicated that the following scenario was all too common:

An attorney brings a complaint claiming that the defendant has caused loss to thousands of people by some action. The complaint is bare bones—it is a formbook job, reflecting no thoughtful case preparation at all. Often, before the complaint is even served, the attorney seeks publicity about his or her lawsuit. The morning headline screams that Corporation X has done some supposedly horrible deed. Other attorneys copy the complaint and file the same action before another court. Then, one of the attorneys calls up Corporation X. "Even though I just sued you," he says, "I'm a nice guy. I'm very reasonable. I can make this whole problem disappear very cheaply. Just provide some very, very modest benefit to the proposed class members, pay me a basket load of attorney's fees, and this painful chapter will be history."

Now, why doesn't defendant's counsel just hang up the receiver? Because when a class action is filed—even one that is downright frivolous, as many are—a defendant corporation with substantial assets cannot ignore it. Typically, the purported claims are brought on behalf of so many people that the exposure is enormous. Hypothetically, if a class action was brought on behalf of the 8 million car owners and the claim is for $1,000 in damages to each class member, the exposure would be $8 billion. If the likelihood of success were assessed at a minuscule 2 percent, the exposure still would be $160 million. If there is the customary claim for punitive damages, the stakes are even greater.

No right-minded general counsel can turn a blind eye to that kind of financial risk. Thus even where the claims involved are utterly without merit, Rule 23 hands plaintiffs' counsel a fully loaded gun to press to the heads of corporate defendants and individuals with deep pockets. In too many cases, defendants have been forced into settlements driven not by the best interests of the putative class members but rather by the financial interests of class counsel.

Let me give an example. I picked up the *Wall Street Journal* one morning and read the lead article about a Department of Justice investigation of alleged price signaling by the airlines through the use of secret codes in computer reservation systems. Were the airlines fixing prices in violation of the antitrust laws? Within a few hours, complaints were filed in several federal courts around the country, with numbered counts that matched almost word for word paragraphs in the *Wall Street Journal* article. There was a mad rush to a friendly court, and a lot of jockeying among plaintiffs' lawyers to get a hometown judge, which would give them a financial premium as lead counsel. After a flurry of conferences, motions, hearings, and discovery over many months, we reached a settlement in which dozens of plaintiffs' lawyers received generous payments and air travelers got a coupon, good for a discount on their next flight—a promotion that the airlines readily agreed to.

O'Melveny worked hard to reform class action abuses. We advised the U.S. Chamber of Commerce on class action reform and worked with Congress to enact the Class Action Fairness Act of 2005 curbing the most excessive abuses. We have made progress, but some abuses continue.

AVIATION

We continued to do a lot of work for the airlines. For many years O'Melveny represented the Air Transport Association, the trade association of the major U.S. airlines, in various airport noise disputes. We brought actions challenging local noise regulations, curfews, and restrictions on airport access throughout the United States.[5]

We also continued to represent Pan Am, as it struggled to make the transition to a deregulated market. The airline was forced to sell assets to offset its mounting losses. Among its most valuable assets were its routes to Tokyo and other Asia-Pacific points. Pan Am and Northwest Airlines had grandfathered air rights to Japan, dating back to the post–World War II period. Only these two U.S. air carriers were allowed unlimited service between the United States and Japan and permission to pick up passengers in Japan and take them to various points beyond. No carrier had ever sold an international route before, and we were concerned that the Department of Transportation might balk at our putting a government license up for sale. We knew from the sale of National to Pan Am, however, that we could sell an airline. If we could sell an airline, then why not a subsidiary or a division?

Accordingly, we created the Pan Am Pacific Division and put all the valuable Japan and beyond routes into the package. We also transferred into the Pacific Division some thirty Boeing 747s and our old Lockheed L-1011s as well as flight crews and ground employees who served the routes and maintained the aircraft and ground facilities. We negotiated the sale of the Pacific Division to United Airlines for $750 million. United was represented by Covington and Burling. There were a few tough issues the lawyers could not resolve. I suggested that the two airline chief executive officers meet in a conference room at Covington and Burling. I had arranged an appointment with Secretary of Transportation Dole at nine o'clock the following morning to brief her on the sale, but at nine the night before we still had not reached agreement on which Pan Am pilots would be transferred to United. Given the morning deadline, we finally reached an accommodation and signed the letter of intent. There is nothing like a deadline to force the resolution of those last few sticky issues.

The transfer required the approval of the Department of Transportation, which assigned the case to an administrative law judge for a three-week hearing. The Department of Justice Antitrust Division opposed the transaction and argued that United should be required to spin off several of Pan Am's routes to Tokyo. Most of the other major U.S. airlines also appeared in opposition to the transfer, as did all the unions. After the multiparty hearing, the administrative law judge wrote an opinion approving the transaction. All the opposing parties appealed to the department, which affirmed the judge's decision. Thereafter, the unions representing Pan Am employees filed a petition to review Transportation's decision in the U.S. Court of Appeals for the Ninth Circuit, arguing that the department should have required United to take on the Pan Am employees at their existing seniority, applying what was known as labor protection provisions. Don Bliss argued the case for Pan Am in the Ninth Circuit Court, which upheld the department's decision, ruling that such labor-protective provisions were no longer required under the Airline Deregulation Act.[6]

We then had to convince Japan to accept United in place of Pan Am. This should have been a ministerial act, but Japan had been complaining for years that its aviation agreement with the United States was imbalanced in favor of U.S. carriers. Now Japan was concerned that United Airlines, with its substantial U.S. domestic feeder system, would have a substantial competitive advantage over the Japanese airlines. Several years before, when United applied for a single route from Seattle to Tokyo, Japan stalled for six years before granting United permission to begin service. We wanted to ensure that Japan would act quickly to grant United its landing rights and the landing and takeoff slots at the Tokyo airport, which were in short supply.

At our request the assistant secretary of transportation for aviation and international policy, Jeffrey Shane, traveled to Tokyo over the holidays to meet with high-level Japanese officials. We arranged for my partner Warren Christopher to meet with the U.S. ambassador to Japan, Mike Mansfield, and senior officials in the Japanese foreign affairs and transportation departments in Tokyo. Don Bliss and I urged U.S. State Department officials to communicate with the Japanese Ministry of Foreign Affairs. We understood that the Japanese Ministry of Transportation strongly opposed the transfer, but Secretary of State James Baker raised the issue with the foreign minister on a trip to Tokyo. He was successful in getting the Japanese government to agree to permit United to start service immediately in exchange for an unrelated concession that was important to Japan.

Our next challenge was to arrange for the transfer of the aircraft and engine titles from Pan Am to United. This proved to be more complicated than I had anticipated. Most of the aircraft were financed, and we needed the approval of the lenders. There was the added problem of locating airplanes that were flying under a full schedule around the globe. Long-haul international flights are often subject to substantial delays, and consequently the schedules were continually changing. Even if we could identify a specific airport where a plane was scheduled to be at a certain time, we had to take into account the potential tax consequences of that particular jurisdiction. Finally, we had to make sure that the Federal Aviation Administration's office in Oklahoma City was open to record the transactions at the time of the transfer. The transfer of the engines was even more complicated since they were often rotated among various aircraft as the planes were being overhauled. We developed a complicated schedule that emphasized locations that would minimize the transfer tax, including the transfer of title over the Pacific Ocean, where no transfer tax was applicable.[7]

As was the case in Pan Am's acquisition of National Airlines, the transfer of its Pacific Division provoked a series of copycat mergers and acquisitions throughout the airline industry—a second round of industry consolidation. After the department approved the Pacific Division transfer, it became fairly common practice for the airlines to sell international routes.

Delighted with the success of the Pacific Division transfer, Pan Am's chair, Edward Acker, called me to set up a meeting at Kennedy Airport when Acker would be returning from Caracas, Venezuela. Don Bliss and I flew to New York and met Acker in the Pan Am lounge at Kennedy. After some initial pleasantries, Acker said, "I would like to create a Pan Am subsidiary to run a shuttle service between Boston and New York and New York and Washington. I think we could compete very effectively for some premier business traffic in this corridor. My problem is that LaGuardia and Washington National are very restricted. Airlines have to obtain landing and takeoff slots, and there are not any available to run an hourly shuttle service. It's also very difficult to get gates at these airports. Do you have any thoughts about how I might go about getting the slots and facilities to initiate a competitive shuttle service?"

"Why," I asked, "would you want Pan Am to operate a shuttle centered at New York's LaGuardia airport when your international operations are all at Kennedy, and there are no good connections between the two airports?"

"Well, you know, Bill," Acker responded, "the shuttle is used mainly by business travelers, many of whom are Pan Am's customers. We can develop loyalty through our frequent-flyer programs and encourage shuttle users to fly internationally with Pan Am rather than United, American, or a foreign air carrier. It's all about building customer loyalty with the premium business traveler."

"I guess that makes sense, Ed," I answered. "Let us give this some thought and get back to you on it."

On the way back to Washington, Don Bliss and I came up with a plan. At that time Frank Lorenzo, who had founded Texas Air Corporation, was seeking to become the chief executive officer of the world's largest airline. With his holding company he had acquired New York Air, which operated a shuttle service in the corridor in competition with the Eastern shuttle. He also owned People's Express, which operated out of Newark, New Jersey. Lorenzo now sought to acquire Eastern Airlines. This was the opening we needed.

Don Bliss and I made an appointment with the Justice Department's Antitrust Division. We urged the Department of Justice to oppose Lorenzo's acquisition of Eastern Airlines on the ground that it would eliminate competition in the highly restricted Boston, New York, and Washington shuttle marketplace. The Justice Department did not need much convincing on this point. However, we offered a solution. We said that Pan Am would be willing to negotiate with New York Air to purchase its slots and gates at the three airports in order to operate a competitive shuttle service. The department's aviation antitrust expert thought that the spin-off of New York Air's shuttle operations might well eliminate the anticompetitive problem. We then advised Ed Acker to negotiate with Frank Lorenzo for the purchase of New York Air's shuttle facilities. After some tough negotiations and many government approvals, the Pan Am shuttle was up and running profitably out of LaGuardia's Marine Air Terminal.[8] Pan Am's financial situation, however, continued to deteriorate. Pan Am later sold the shuttle to Delta Airlines, and it now operates as the Delta Shuttle.[9]

ENERGY

The Synthetic Fuels Corporation, otherwise known as Synfuels, was a corporation established and funded by the federal government to finance private industry research into alternative fuels. The OPEC embargo during the Carter administration caused substantial fuel shortages, and oil prices sky rocketed. The nation was committed to developing alternatives to imported petroleum. As counsel to Synfuels, we worked on a project to finance private industry research into the production of oil from shale. Unfortunately, as the energy crisis faded and the price of oil declined, the nation lost interest in many of these projects, and Synfuels went out of business. Given the spike in fuel prices in 2008 and the tremendous cost we have paid for our increasing dependence on imported oil, it is indeed tragic that the country did not have the resolve to follow through on the Synfuels project. The Reagan administration criticized such government-funded efforts because when the price of fuel declined, there would be no marketplace demand for the product. I again regretted that we had failed to address this situation by imposing a significant tax on petroleum.

An important alternative to oil, greatly underused in this country, is nuclear power. As a board member of Philadelphia Electric, I had become a strong advocate of nuclear energy as an environmentally clean alternative to carbon fuels. I admired the way France had developed this power source based on a proven model facility. Philadelphia Electric operated the Peach Bottom Atomic Power Station at Delta, Pennsylvania, on behalf of itself and three other utilities. On March 31, 1987, the Nuclear Regulatory Commission ordered the plant closed because of alleged mismanagement and misconduct by control room employees. Three of the owners of the facility sued Philadelphia Electric, the fourth owner, in the federal district court in Camden, New Jersey, seeking more than $1 billion in actual and punitive damages based on breach of contract. I asked Dick Warmer to work with me on the litigation, assisted by a number of partners and associates. Through this kind of case, the office became adept at managing complex litigation in cases involving numerous issues and massive discovery. O'Melveny's litigation department has always ranked among the top firms, having been selected in 2003 as the number-one litigation firm in the country by the *American Lawyer*.

The Peach Bottom fact development was particularly challenging because the closure of the facility had resulted in the termination of top management. When the district court denied our motion to dismiss, we agreed to an alternative dispute resolution process before a former federal district judge, Harold Tyler, who conducted a mini-trial involving the executive officers of all the parties. The matter was settled on terms that were favorable to Philadelphia

Electric, as indicated by a three-dollar increase in its stock price the day the settlement was announced.

Because of our success in the Peach Bottom case, I was engaged to represent Pacific Gas and Electric in the U.S. Court of Appeals for the District of Columbia Circuit. An environmental group had appealed the Nuclear Regulatory Commission's decision granting a license to the utility for the Diablo Canyon nuclear facility in San Francisco. Among other things, the petitioners alleged that the facility had been constructed in mirror reverse from the approved architectural plan. We were able to convince the court that the commission had done a thorough investigation and that its safety findings were based on substantial evidence in the record.

Practicing law in Washington with O'Melveny also gave me the chance to continue my Supreme Court practice. One early opportunity came with a phone call from the chief justice of the United States.

THIRTY-SEVEN

The *Bob Jones* Case

*I have a dream that my four little children will one day live
in a nation where they will not be judged by the color of their
skin but by the content of their character.*

—MARTIN LUTHER KING JR.

ON A LATE FRIDAY AFTERNOON in April 1982, my office telephone rang.
When I picked up the phone the voice on the line said, "The chief justice of
the United States, the Honorable Warren Burger, wishes to speak with you."
Was this a belated April fool's joke? I decided to play along. "Go ahead and
put him through," I said.

"Mr. Coleman, this is Chief Justice Burger." The melodious, deep bass
voice was unmistakable. With his flowing white hair and modulating intona-
tions, Warren Burger fit the public image of a chief justice. Hollywood could
not have improved on the typecasting.

"Mr. Coleman, the Supreme Court has a case before it, entitled *Goldsboro
Christian Schools, Inc.* v. *United States*. The U.S. government was successful in
the Fourth Circuit below, but the Justice Department has informed me it has
changed its position on the law and is no longer willing to defend the appellate court's opinion."

"I am frankly not familiar with the case, Mr. Chief Justice," I replied.

"Well, actually, there are two consolidated cases. One involves the Goldsboro Christian School, which does not admit Negroes, and the other involves
Bob Jones University, which did not formerly admit Negroes but has now
changed its policy and admits Negroes subject to certain racial restrictions on
campus," the chief justice elaborated.

"Of course, I know the *Bob Jones* case," I said, my blood pressure slightly rising. "I've followed the press accounts. The Reagan administration has reversed
the government's position. It would now give tax breaks to racially discriminatory private schools."

"That's the case, Mr. Coleman," the chief justice continued. "Bob Jones
has appealed the Fourth Circuit's decision revoking its tax exemption, and the
U.S. government now refuses to defend its victory below. I need a counsel who

will argue in support of the Fourth Circuit's decision. The purpose of my call is to invite you to serve as *amicus curiae* appointed by the Court, to defend the position of the court below. Would you be willing to take this on?"

"Absolutely, I would love to do it, Mr. Chief Justice," I said without hesitation.

"Bill, don't you first have to check and see if there is a conflict of interest in your law firm?" Burger continued. "Your firm may have clients who support the new IRS position."

Unable to restrain my unbridled enthusiasm, I blurted out, "I can assure you, Mr. Chief Justice, that if my firm has a conflict, we will no longer represent the other client."

"Well, you know, Bill, the Court cannot pay your law firm for its legal services," he continued, hoping to brake my perhaps precipitous response. "The most we can pay for is printing your brief and your transportation expenses from your offices to the Court on the date of the argument."

"That won't be a problem. My firm has a long tradition of undertaking voluntary legal services. I'm sure the firm will gladly take on this opportunity. As far as travel expenses go, I work here in Washington, so that shouldn't be a burden."

"Well, that's good news, Bill. I'll prepare the order," the Chief said, and then added with a chuckle, "and by the way, Bill, when I last saw you it looked like you've put on some weight. You might consider walking up to the Court for the argument. You could use the exercise."

I feigned a laugh and hung up the phone, elated at the opportunity to tackle yet another threat to the *Brown* legacy. In the Little Rock case, the Inc Fund had fought to fortify the federal government's resolve to end public school segregation expeditiously. In a fourteen-year struggle, we had finally busted the Girard College trust that excluded children of color. But like a giant sponge, when we pressed down in one spot, another trouble spot popped up. President Reagan had reversed Richard Nixon's decision to deny substantial indirect federal subsidies to private schools that discriminated against Americans of color. If whites-only private schools offered a backdoor exit from desegregated public schools, then we faced a threat not only to *Brown* but to the public school system itself. I also greatly feared that if the Reagan position prevailed in the Supreme Court, tax-exempt private schools, colleges, and universities in the South (and perhaps elsewhere) would be encouraged to discriminate against persons of color in admissions and to adopt discriminatory rules and practices on campus. We must close the loophole: the federal government should not do indirectly what the Supreme Court forbade the states to do directly.

O'Melveny & Myers undertook this new assignment with great enthusiasm. We assembled a strong legal team, which included my partners Dick

Warmer, Don Bliss, John Stamper, and Ira Feinberg along with David Beddow, Randy Hardock, and many others.

Before 1970 the IRS had granted tax-exempt status under section 501(c)
(3) of the Internal Revenue Code to private schools without regard to their
policies on race. Contributions to such schools also qualified for charitable
deductions under section 170 of the code. Charities, schools, churches, and
other nonprofit institutions received a substantial financial benefit from these
indirect federal subsidies based on the presumption that they served a useful
social or public policy purpose.

After the *Brown* decision, several southern school districts had closed the
public schools to avoid judicial desegregation orders. Mississippi, Georgia,
South Carolina, and Virginia had encouraged the establishment of whites-
only private tax-exempt schools. It appeared that the federal tax exemption
was being used to raise funds to thwart the Supreme Court's mandate.[1] In
July 1970 the IRS issued a general ruling that it could not legally justify tax-
exempt status to private schools that discriminated based on race. President
Nixon expressly approved this decision.[2]

In April 1975 the IRS revoked the tax-exempt status of Bob Jones University and the Goldsboro Christian School. The schools protested the IRS ruling, claiming their racial policies were based on sincerely held religious beliefs.
Although Bob Jones had begun to accept students of color, it prohibited interracial dating and fraternization. A student who violated this rule would be
expelled. Bob Jones University paid the taxes but challenged the ruling in
the U.S. District Court for the District of South Carolina. The district court
ruled for the university, holding that the revocation of the tax exemption violated the religious freedom clause of the First Amendment. The government
appealed to the U.S. Court of Appeals for the Fourth Circuit.[3]

Meanwhile, Goldsboro Christian School filed a suit in the U.S. District
Court for the Eastern District of North Carolina claiming that it had been
improperly denied section 501(c)(3) tax-exempt status and seeking a refund
of taxes paid. The district court entered summary judgment for the IRS, and
Goldsboro appealed to the Fourth Circuit.[4]

In both appeals, the Fourth Circuit upheld the IRS's denial of tax exemptions to racially discriminatory schools. The appellate court reasoned that
eligibility for a tax exemption must be considered in light of the common-law
history of charitable trusts, which "must not be contrary to public policy." The
circuit court held that a charitable institution cannot obtain tax-exempt status
if it practices racial discrimination, as it is against public policy. The Supreme
Court agreed to hear the appeals of Bob Jones and Goldsboro.

The incoming Reagan administration, in a dramatic reversal, determined
that nothing in the Internal Revenue Code barred the two schools from

tax-exempt status, despite their practice of racial discrimination. Only Congress could deny tax-exempt status to racially discriminatory private schools, the Reagan administration concluded, and Congress had not done so explicitly. The solicitor general announced to the Court that the U.S. government would not defend its victories in the circuit court. In an act of great courage, the career deputy solicitor general, Lawrence Wallace, signed the statement with a footnote indicating that he did not agree with the U.S. government's altered position.

Given the intellectual challenge presented by the *Bob Jones* case and the public policy principles implicated, I had tremendous volunteer support, from senior partners to summer associates, in researching the law, writing the briefs, and preparing for oral argument. We left no stone unturned. Indeed, I must confess that few firm clients would have been willing to pay the hourly billable rates of O'Melveny & Myers to undertake the comprehensive research we undertook pro bono in support of our brief. In private moments I felt badly for the Reverend Bob Jones, who I expect would not have been in a position to finance such comprehensive research.

Work on this case reconfirmed my long-standing view, dating back to my legal training at Harvard, that knowledge of the English common law is often essential to understand the meaning of language used in many acts of Congress. Based on our research of legislative history, principles of statutory interpretation, and the English common law, we argued in our brief that section 501(c)(3) was intended to provide tax-exempt status only to charitable organizations that contribute to the general welfare. Since the early days of common law, tax exemptions were not granted to educational or other nonprofit charitable institutions if their purposes were inconsistent with law or fundamental public policy. Since *Brown* v. *Board of Education,* the decisions of the Supreme Court and the actions of Congress had expressed a fundamental public policy—firmly rooted in the Fifth, Thirteenth, and Fourteenth Amendments to the Constitution—condemning state-supported racial discrimination in education, both public and private. The Court had consistently and unequivocally ruled that government support of segregated schools "through any arrangement, management, funds or property" was unconstitutional. Congress had consistently ratified and approved this policy.

The day of the argument arrived on October 12, 1982. The Supreme Court was packed with lawyers, reporters, and spectators. On the way in I overheard the petitioner, university president Bob Jones Jr., arguing with a guard who stopped him outside the Court because the spectator section was full. I intervened with the guard and explained why the Reverend Jones should be admitted. Jones recognized me and said he had prayed that God would resolve the case properly. I told him I shared that hope, although perhaps with a different outcome—that the Court would hold that racial discrimination in private educational institutions was contrary to public policy.

This was no run-of-the-mill Supreme Court argument, if there ever is any such thing as a run-of-the-mill Supreme Court argument. The United States rose to argue in support of the discriminatory schools, in direct opposition to the position the government had taken successfully in the court below. The government and the taxpayer schools divided their argument, and each made a persuasive and skillful case for their position. The United States was represented by Bradford Reynolds, the assistant attorney general for the Civil Rights Division. He and the counsel for the schools argued that the Internal Revenue Code specifically permitted nonprofit educational institutions to receive a tax exemption. There was no statutory requirement that an educational institution be a common-law trust charity and act consistently with any particular view of public policy. Their argument was fairly straightforward and simple, relying on the statutory language and pointing out that Congress was perfectly capable of writing in provisions prohibiting racial discrimination but had chosen not to do so. The schools also argued that denial of their tax exemptions would violate their free exercise of religion. The government did not support the schools' First Amendment claim.

As the appellants sat down, I rose to approach the lectern. My knees wobbled weakly under the weighty responsibility to help the Supreme Court affirm a decision of one of its more conservative appellate courts, despite the opposition of all the original parties to the decision of the lower court. To accomplish this, I would have to ask the Court to look beyond the simple language in the statute and understand the context in which these provisions were drafted. I would ask the Court, once again, to affirm the public policy against racial discrimination for which we had fought so long and hard in *Brown* v. *Board of Education* and its progeny.

I pointed out that under section 501(c)(3), a tax-exempt institution not only had to be a legitimate charity or educational institution but also must demonstrably serve, and be in harmony with, the public interest. This Court had taken the position in *Brown* v. *Board of Education* that racial discrimination in education not only violated the Fourteenth Amendment but was against the public interest. In our brief and at the oral argument, we pointed out that over the past twenty-five years the executive, judicial, and legislative branches of our government had repeatedly affirmed a national prohibition against racial segregation and discrimination in our public schools. We had enumerated these actions in our brief, which the Court incorporated into its opinion. Private schools seeking tax-exempt status as charitable institutions, like public schools, were obligated to serve the public interest.

We opposed the schools' argument that their practice of racial discrimination was protected from government interference by the First Amendment's free exercise clause. We pointed out that under Supreme Court precedent the free exercise clause did not mean that all actions by government affecting religion were unconstitutional. In *United States* v. *Lee,* the Court held that a "state may justify a limitation on religious liberty by showing that it is essential to accomplish an overriding governmental interest." In 1980 eliminating government-supported racial discrimination was an overriding interest. We argued that federal and state tax exemptions were indirect government subsidies. The government could not subsidize racial discrimination in the guise of religious freedom because discrimination was a clear violation of overriding public policy.[5]

Finally, we pointed out that since 1970, Congress had received various notices of the IRS position that charities discriminating on race were not entitled to tax-exempt status. Congress took no action to reverse this position. It had even amended section 501(c)(3) to add subparagraph L, extending this prohibition to social groups that discriminate. Congress made clear that discriminatory social groups, like country clubs, were no longer entitled to tax exemption.

As I neared the end of my oral argument, Justice Powell leaned forward on the bench and asked, "Mr. Coleman, if you are correct that these two appellants are not entitled to a tax exemption because of their discriminatory policies, what about Smith College, which accepts only women as students?"

I knew that Justice Powell's wife was on the board of Smith College, which accepts only females. Preparing for the argument, I had been concerned that some of the justices, perhaps Justice O'Connor, might hesitate to affirm the court below for fear that it might set a precedent that would deny tax-exempt status to women's colleges and private girls' schools. My reply to Justice Powell was simple and direct, if not entirely responsive: "Mr. Justice, this nation fought a war over racial discrimination. It did not fight a civil war over sex discrimination."

One question I had anticipated, but fortunately never got, was why the Court should decide this issue at all since arguably at that time there was no "case or controversy" between Bob Jones University and the federal government. They both agreed that the charitable exemption should not be affected by racial discrimination. Article III of the Constitution requires an actual controversy between the parties for a federal court to decide a case. Because the government tax collector now said no tax was due, and the appellant taxpayers agreed, it was not clear what controversy requiring adjudication remained. If I had been asked the question, I would have simply responded by citing the cases holding that once the Supreme Court grants a petition for a writ of certiorari, neither party can withdraw without the permission of the Court.

For me the *Bob Jones* case was a natural culmination of many years of hard work persuading the Supreme Court that school segregation based on race—at any level and in most any form—violated the fundamental principles of our nation's governing documents. Through the tax code, Congress has consistently advanced various social and economic policies, sometimes doing indirectly what it dared not do more directly through regulation or subsidy. The Reagan reversal opened an escape hatch through which die-hard segregationists could retreat. They could simply boycott the integrated public schools and establish tax-exempt all-white academies. I also was concerned that private colleges and universities would engage with impunity in more subtle forms of racial discrimination in admissions policies and campus rules and practices. The Fourth Circuit had properly extended the national policy against government-sanctioned racial discrimination in the schools—whether public or tax-exempt private. As a nation we had come far in a few short years. Despite the toll of all-nighters and long weekends and the sacrifices of my family, it had all been worthwhile. That's why I responded so quickly and enthusiastically to Chief Justice Burger's call and why I was so gratified by the enthusiastic support of my law firm. There is no question I had an emotional commitment to this case. I had felt personally the pain of the loss in the *Richmond School Board* case, believing that it set back our efforts for decades toward meaningful public school desegregation in metropolitan areas. I thought the Reagan administration's reversal of the IRS's position in the *Bob Jones* case was a similar setback. For this reason, my argument in the Supreme Court may have displayed an excess of impatience, passion, and impertinence, causing me to depart from the traditional decorum. I will let others be the judge of this, but I quote below at length a story in the *New York Times* that commented somewhat favorably on my argument.

Ask a friend for advice and you sometimes get more than you bargained for. That may have happened to the Supreme Court when the Justices heard William Coleman, Jr., their invited "friend of the Court," argue against tax breaks for schools with racist policies. Here was a friend and professional peer who spoke straight from the shoulder.

It was quite a scene. Mr. Coleman, a patrician lawyer from Philadelphia who became Secretary of Transportation and later head of an influential Washington law office, was there to make a legal argument.

Yet this black lawyer, whose own brilliant career has helped pave the way for other black professionals, was also there to express outrage over the antics of the Reagan Justice Department that made his appearance necessary. He did it all, with drama and class.

He used his technical skill to shred the argument of William Bradford Reynolds, Assistant Attorney General for Civil Rights. Mr. Reynolds contended that the Internal Revenue Service lacked the authority to deny tax breaks to entities that violate public policy. Why, he said, Congress proved that every time it amended the charitable exemption section of the law, not leaving it up to the I.R.S.

Nothing doing, Mr. Coleman explained in response; in nearly all those cases, Congress was merely ratifying previous I.R.S. rulings. Mr. Coleman's bluntest talk was aimed at Justice William Rehnquist, who challenged the assertion that the two schools involved, Bob Jones University and the Goldsboro Christian Schools, had violated the law.

Rehnquist: What law does it violate?

Coleman: It violates Section 1 of the Act of 1866. It violates the 13th Amendment, for starters.

Q: Has that been held?

A: What?

Q: Has that been held by this Court?

A: Well, I—yes, even you, in your opinion which you—in the Operating Engineers (case last June), you finally held, you finally recognized even though you dissented before, that Section 1 of the Act of 1866 made illegal racial discrimination even among two private persons.

That "even you" had a tone of familiarity—and authority—the Court doesn't often hear. Mr. Coleman also returned fire from Justice Byron White. Over and over, the lawyer told the skeptical Justice that the law has always given the Revenue Service the right to decide whether a school forfeited its tax benefits by violating public policy.

Coleman: The statute has always said—

White: There has been a change in the I.R.S.'s construction of it.

Coleman: No, no.

Q: What about the application of it?

A: Well, no sir. (Then, working hard to be patient) I will try once again, Your Honor . . .

Pressed by Justice Lewis Powell about how far his argument went, he asked the Justice, "Hear me out." He proceeded to explain that racial discrimination was in a class by itself historically. Mr. Coleman well knew that Justice Powell himself has written that sex discrimination claims don't rate the same scrutiny the Court has given to charges of racial bias. Sex discrimination is indeed serious, but, he said, "We didn't fight a Civil War over sex discrimination."

Not long ago, it was the Justice Department to which the Court often turned for expert advice and straight talk. One day, the department may yet again lead the way on civil rights with broad and worthy arguments. Meanwhile, the Court can add the argument of William T. Coleman, Jr. to its treasury of proud moments.[6]

On May 24, 1983, while I was in New York attending a meeting of the IBM directors, I was informed that the Supreme Court had decided the cases. I immediately slipped out of the board room and rushed to a telephone, where I learned that the Court, by a vote of 8 to 1, had held that private educational institutions practicing racial discrimination are not entitled to tax exemptions.[7] In an opinion written by the chief justice, the Court stated emphatically that "there can no longer be any doubt that racial discrimination in education violates deeply and widely accepted views of elementary justice." Driving a final stake in *Plessy,* the Court continued: "Over the past quarter of a century, every pronouncement of this Court and myriad acts of Congress and Executive Orders attest a firm national policy to prohibit racial segregation and discrimination in public education." Not just segregation but "racial discrimination in education violates a most fundamental public national policy, as well as rights of individuals."[8] The lone dissenter was then associate justice William H. Rehnquist, who simply was not persuaded that section 501(c)(3), as written, required that a charity operate consistently with public policy. He thought it was Congress's responsibility to legislate expressly.

Emotions ran high after the Supreme Court's decision. President Bob Jones Jr. ordered the American flags on campus flown at half mast. In 1998 a public relations spokesman for the university explained the university's rationale: "God has separated people for his own purposes. . . . God has made people different from one another and intends those differences to remain."[9]

The times they are a-changin'. In 2000 the university ended its official prohibition against interracial dating. In 2009 tears welled up in my eyes as I read a statement by Stephen Jones, the great grandson of the founder and the fourth president of Bob Jones University. Jones apologized for the institution's racist past: "For almost two centuries American Christianity, including BJU in its early stages, was characterized by the segregationist ethos of American culture. Consequently, for far too long, we allowed institutional policies regarding race to be shaped more directly by that ethos than by principles and precepts of the Scriptures. . . . In so doing, we failed to accurately represent the Lord and to fulfill the commandment to love others as ourselves. For these failures we are profoundly sorry."[10]

I have always thought that the Supreme Court's decisions in *Little Rock* and *Bob Jones* were critical in changing American attitudes on race. Education from kindergarten through college—public and private—has led the way, demonstrating the benefits of bringing all American citizens into the cultural and economic mainstream.

THIRTY-EIGHT

Supreme Court Practice

The Constitution, on this hypothesis, is a mere thing of wax in the hands of the judiciary, which may twist and shape it into any form they please.

—Thomas Jefferson

HAVING SERVED IN THE EXECUTIVE branch and testified on many occasions before Congress, I would have to say that for a practicing lawyer, there is no experience more exhilarating than advocacy before the Supreme Court of the United States. I am far from an expert in antitrust law, natural gas regulation, public transit, constitutional law, the Internal Revenue Code, or even interracial cohabitation, but then neither are the nine justices. When called on to represent clients in these and other areas, I would totally immerse myself in the record, the judicial precedents, and the prior positions of the justices. In the Supreme Court, I am dealing with a concrete case or controversy in a specific factual setting, but I appear before the highest court because an issue of fundamental national significance, perhaps a conflict among the appellate courts, must be resolved. And we are confident that the Court's resolution will be based on reason and reason alone. Though brilliant men and women of different views may reason to different conclusions, they must explain their reasons in writing. That is not always true of the other branches.

Whereas Congress properly reflects the popular emotions and the executive branch must respond to fast unfolding current events, fighting fires and coping with crises, the Supreme Court remains committed to reflective reasoning, to a rational search for sometimes elusive constitutional values, and to the peaceful resolution of conflict that transforms the tensions of a pluralistic society into creative progress toward a more workable civilization. Anchored in history, the Court can resist the shifting tides of public emotion and, at the same time, keep the nation on course as it strives to realize the Constitution's promise. In addressing specific factual situations, the Court brings broad policies and principles into the daily lives of Americans.

The creation of this third branch to balance the more democratic branches of government was a brilliant compromise between a government that reflects the will of the people and a government that is reflective, consistent, and principled. The Supreme Court does not have a standing army or the periodic affirmation of a popular election. The efficacy of its decisions depends on their acceptance by the other branches and the general public, especially its decisions protecting the rights of minorities and the most vulnerable in our society, which may be politically unpopular. To maintain its legitimacy and relevance, the Court must strive for a delicate balance, applying the changeless values of the Constitution to changing contemporary circumstances while respecting and not intruding on the constitutional responsibilities of the other branches to legislate and to execute.

In fulfilling its unique role, the Court has benefited from great leaders like Chief Justices John Marshall and Earl Warren and great thinkers and pragmatists like former associate justices Holmes, Brandeis, Frankfurter, Marshall, O'Connor, Stevens, and both Harlans. By adhering to the constraints of the judicial craft, grounded in the English common law, the justices have applied fundamental constitutional powers and rights to circumstances beyond the imagination of the framers, demonstrating through powerful analysis and reason how established precedent has been applied, distinguished, or, in rare cases, overruled. Preserving the Court's credibility and its leavening influence in a maturing constitutional democracy requires continuing diligence and calibration.

We should not hesitate to ask certain fundamental questions: Does the proliferation of dissenting and concurring opinions undermine the Court's moral force? Are we appointing justices who bring the intellect and life experiences to the Court that will enrich its understanding and articulation of fundamental constitutional values? Are we appointing justices simply to reflect diverse elements of our population rather than for the wisdom they bring to reasoned decisionmaking? Is the Court taking on too many cases, resolving conflicts prematurely, relying too heavily on law clerks, and completing the unfinished work of legislators? Can we still agree with Justice Brandeis's statement "The reason the public thinks so much of the Justices of the Supreme Court is that they are almost the only people in Washington who do their own work"?[1]

I will leave it to future generations to answer these questions. It is their responsibility to monitor the work of the Court and educate the American public to understand and appreciate the intricate role the Court has played and will continue to play in our republic. In my legal practice, my nineteen appearances before that venerable institution were always—win or lose—an exhilarating experience.

BANKING LAW

In 1982 my Los Angeles partners Ted McAniff and Fred McLane counseled the firm's client, Security Pacific National Bank, then the largest bank in Los Angeles, on a strategy for entering the discount brokerage business. In those days interstate banking was prohibited by the McFadden Act. On Ted's advice, the bank asked the comptroller of the currency for approval to establish a new subsidiary to engage in a discount brokerage business throughout the country. When the comptroller general approved the bank's application—the first of its kind for a national bank—the Security Industry Association, fearing competition from the banks, filed suit in the U.S. District Court for the District of Columbia to overturn the comptroller's ruling. The association argued that the Glass-Steagall Act permitted banks to purchase securities only for the accounts of established banking customers. While the court rejected this contention, it did accept the association's argument that a bank's discount brokerage business was restricted to established bank branches.[2] This ruling was affirmed by the U.S. Court of Appeals for the District of Columbia Circuit.[3] Under this ruling, Security Pacific could not operate discount brokerage offices outside of California. At this point, Ted McAniff and my Los Angeles litigation partner Boyd Hight petitioned the Supreme Court for a writ of certiorari. McAniff called and asked whether, assuming the Supreme Court agreed to hear the case, I would serve as counsel of record. I readily agreed.

One sunny spring day in 1987 my new partner John Beisner burst into my office with the news: "This morning the Supreme Court has granted two of our petitions for certiorari—*Clarke* v. *Security Industry Association* and *Alaska Airlines* v. *Brock*. That must be a first, two Bill Coleman petitions granted on the same day. What are the odds on that, especially since the Court only grants about 1 percent of the petitions filed?" Noticing the scowl on my face, John continued, "Don't you find that incredible?"

"That means we're going to have to file two briefs on the merits on the same day, John. You better start preparing a petition to extend the due date for the *Alaska* case." John readily understood, as he was the junior partner on both cases. McAniff, Beisner, associate Jake Lewis, and I got to work immediately on the Security Pacific brief.

Ted and I developed the argument that the McFadden Act's prohibition on interstate banking was limited to "core banking functions," which did not include discount brokerage services. Our research of the legislative history supported this argument, which had not been made in the lower court. Fortunately the Supreme Court agreed with my argument.[4] In *Clarke* v. *Security Industry Association* (1988), the Court held that discount brokerage is not a core function of a national bank and therefore Security Pacific's subsidiary was free to operate the discount brokerage business throughout the United States.

The Supreme Court's definition of *core banking functions* became an important principle in banking law. Security Pacific's innovative entry into the discount brokerage business reflected a trend that would continue during the next two decades. The historical lines of demarcation between traditional banking and brokerage and investment banking established by the 1939 Glass-Steagall Act, initially intended to protect depositors from risky investment and speculation, were repealed in 1999 during the Clinton administration. This enabled major banking enterprises to underwrite mortgage-backed securities and launch other risky structured investment vehicles. The consolidation of financial institutions was a parallel trend; for example, Security Pacific merged into the Bank of America. Our Supreme Court victory in the Security Pacific case was an early indication that the pendulum was swinging toward deregulation and market flexibility for large financial institutions. Has the pendulum swung too far?[5]

SEPARATION OF POWERS

Through my work with the Legal Defense Fund I had become deeply immersed in the jurisprudence of the post–Civil War amendments. In private practice I had ample opportunity to delve deeply into other areas of constitutional law, including the evolving doctrine of separation of powers and the enigmatic Tenth Amendment.

My partner Don Bliss had been representing the Air Transport Association on a number of regulatory and litigation issues. One issue involved a troubling provision in the Airline Deregulation Act that was added at the insistence of the unions after I left the Department of Transportation. The theory was that under deregulation some carriers would do well and others would not. Section 43(f) directed the Department of Labor to issue regulations, subject to a legislative veto by either house of Congress, requiring the airlines that did well to hire the employees laid off by their competitors as a result of deregulation.

The airlines strongly objected to this duty-to-hire requirement, in part on safety grounds. As a frequent air traveler, I agreed it was essential that airlines have complete discretion to hire the very best pilots and not be compelled to hire a pilot who had been laid off by a failing competitor. Each airline should be able to select the applicants best suited for its training and promotion protocols and cockpit culture to minimize human factors as a cause of most accidents. The Department of Labor ignored the airlines' extensive comments, and fourteen airlines brought a lawsuit in federal district court challenging the regulations.[6]

Congress obviously had reservations about entrusting the Department of Labor (which had no aviation safety expertise) with the regulatory responsibility because it reserved the power for either house of Congress to veto the labor department's regulations. We thus argued that section 43(f) was invalid because of the one-house legislative veto provision. In *Immigration and*

Naturalization Service v. *Chadha* (1983), the Supreme Court had held that legislative veto provisions are unconstitutional because they violate the separation of powers provisions of the Constitution. By establishing three equal branches of government—legislative, executive, and judicial—the framers intended that one federal branch should not interfere impermissibly with the performance of the constitutionally assigned functions of another branch. The separation of powers doctrine is violated when one federal branch assumes a function that the Constitution has more properly entrusted to another federal branch or when one branch acts in ways beyond its constitutional authority. Laws are enacted by the legislative branch only when they pass both houses of Congress and are signed by the president or when a presidential veto is overridden by a two-thirds vote of each house. Here, under section 43(f), one house of Congress could interfere with the responsibilities of the executive branch to implement the laws through regulations.

We had a bit of a problem, though, because Congress had not actually exercised the legislative veto. Nonetheless, we argued that by incorporating a one-house veto in the statute, Congress had exceeded its constitutional authority. Federal district judge Gerhard Gesell agreed and found section 43(f) unconstitutional. Congress could not reserve to either house a second bite of the apple. If Congress wanted to enact employee protection provisions it should do so in a constitutionally proper way.

The Department of Labor appealed our victory to the District of Columbia Circuit Court, which reversed the district court. The Supreme Court granted our petition for certiorari but affirmed the circuit court and remanded the case back to the federal district court to consider our other objections to the Department of Labor regulations.[7]

A few years later we found ourselves on the opposite side of a legislative veto controversy. Some background will help put this case in context. When I left the Department of Transportation at the end of the Ford administration, there were at least three major issues that I was not able to resolve successfully. Indeed, these issues had haunted every secretary of transportation before and after me until Elizabeth Dole was appointed by President Reagan, as the first woman to hold that post and, thereby, the first to head a branch of the U.S. military—the Coast Guard.

First, as previously discussed, as transportation secretary I was unable to arrange for the sale of the bankrupt northeastern railroad assets to the two competitive East Coast–based railroads, the Norfolk Southern and the Chessie. Second, the historic Union Station in Washington, designed by the architect Daniel Burnham as the railroad gateway to the capital, had become a debilitating eye sore. Despite my efforts to generate the financing to rehabilitate it, when I left office it constituted one huge hole in the ground. Third, for decades the Federal Aviation Administration had owned and operated the two commercial airports serving the city—Washington National and Dulles International. National was badly in need of modernization, and Dulles of substantial expansion to serve the increasing demand for transcontinental and international service. Management by the federal government, subject to the whims of the annual congressional appropriations process, was no way to run an airport. Various proposals to establish a regional authority, which could sell bonds to finance airport improvements, met with strong resistance from Congress, which jealously guarded the close-in National Airport and its free congressional parking spaces as essential to quick egress from Washington back to their home districts for long weekends to reestablish contact with their constituents and raise money for reelection.

When Elizabeth Dole assumed office in 1983, her predecessors advised her to avoid these three sand traps. Secretary Dole, however, ignored our advice. She was up to the challenge. Among her major successes were the sale of Conrail to the Norfolk Southern and CSX, the rehabilitation of Union Station into a grand citadel of welcome to people traveling to Washington by rail, and the transfer of the two airports to a new regional authority, the Metropolitan Washington Airports Authority, whose board of directors was appointed by the governors of Virginia and Maryland and the mayor of Washington. The authority was able to raise funds in the bond market to finance the modernization of National and the expansion of Dulles into a thriving international gateway.[8]

In agreeing to the transfer of the airports to local control, however, Congress sought to ensure that the interests of nationwide users of the airports would be protected. It therefore conditioned the transfer on the creation of a board of review consisting of nine members of Congress serving in their individual—not legislative—capacities. The review board was authorized to disapprove certain major actions by the airports authority that in its view could diminish the airports' special role as gateways to the nation's capital. The congressional concern was not without justification. National Airport, though only a ten- or fifteen-minute ride from the Capitol, was surrounded by fairly dense development. There was strong organized local opposition to aircraft noise and calls for closing the airport. Congress feared that local control could result in reduced flight schedules if not closure of National in response to local demands. Like the *Alaska Airlines* case, the disapproval power was never exercised.

After the airports authority was up and running, a preeminent local businessman and philanthropist, John Hechinger, and a group of anti-noise activists, who called themselves the Citizens for the Abatement of Aircraft Noise, brought a lawsuit challenging the constitutionality of the new authority. The anti-noise advocates wisely hired as their counsel an experienced Supreme Court advocate, Alan Morrison, who, besides being the head of Public Citizen, a Ralph Nader organization, was, fortuitously, the attorney who successfully argued the Supreme Court case in *Chadha*. Morrison saw the opportunity to apply the *Chadha* decision, which invalidated legislative vetoes, to a nonfederal agency, a regional airport authority.

The first chair of the board of review was Norman Mineta, who also had been the chair of the House of Representatives Public Works and Infrastructure Committee, which drafted the airport transfer legislation. After the lawsuit was filed, the chief executive officer of the airports authority and Chair Mineta asked me to represent the authority and the board of review jointly in the litigation.[9] We defended them successfully before the federal district court but lost on appeal to the District of Columbia Circuit Court. The Supreme Court granted our petition for certiorari. After oral argument, the Court affirmed the circuit court, holding that the board of review was acting as an agent of Congress and its veto power (though never exercised) exceeded Congress's authority under the Constitution.[10]

Over the next several years, the O'Melveny team traipsed up to Capitol Hill to work with the House committee on remedial amendments to the federal legislation and then defended the authority against additional challenges.[11] Over a five-year period the O'Melveny team was batted back and forth between Congress and the courts like a badminton shuttlecock. Congress finally adopted a new structure that survived all judicial challenges.

Meanwhile, the airports authority proceeded uninterrupted with the modernization of National (now Ronald Reagan Washington National Airport), designed by architect Cesar Peli, and with the expansion of Dulles in harmony with the stunning original design of Eero Saarinen. We were able to keep the litigation from interfering with the authority's mandate to upgrade the airports, which was skillfully accomplished under the leadership of its chief executive officer James A. Wilding and his successor, James E. Bennett, demonstrating Congress's wisdom in transferring the airports to a regional authority.

THE TENTH AMENDMENT

Our third constitutional excursion during this period involved a bit of an enigma, even to constitutional scholars. The Tenth Amendment provides that "the powers not delegated to the United States by the Constitution, nor prohibited by it to the States, are reserved to the States respectively, or to the people." Until the Supreme Court's 5-4 decision in *National League of Cities* v. *Usery*, the Tenth Amendment was thought of as something of a truism: whatever powers the federal government did not exercise belonged to the states or the people. In *National League of Cities,* the Supreme Court held that the Tenth Amendment did create boundaries on the constitutional powers of the federal government. Under the commerce clause, Congress could not regulate the wages and hours of employees of state and local governments who were operating in "traditional governmental functions." This decision breathed new life into the Tenth Amendment in defining a system of federalism under which core state functions were protected from federal regulation.

Despite the decision in *National League of Cities,* the Department of Labor, at the behest of the public transit unions, sought to apply the wage and overtime compensation policies of the federal Fair Labor Standards Act to bus drivers and other local public transit workers. My partner, Don Bliss, and I were approached by the American Public Transit Association.[12] The association's members were greatly concerned that attempting to apply the straitjacket of the Fair Labor Standards Act (requiring forty-hour weeks plus overtime) to bus drivers would force a complete restructuring of scheduling practices and substantially increase the cost of highly subsidized transit services. Ninety-four percent of transit operations at that time were owned by state, regional, or local governmental authorities. In the transit association's view, public transit operations were as much a traditional governmental function as police and fire protection, both of which were explicitly protected under the *National League of Cities* decision.

This was a great case to work on because it went to the heart of the nation's system of federalism: What are the limits on federal power? What are the constitutional rights of states? It also tugged at my heart. As a civil rights litigator I was not enamored with certain claims of states rights. On the other hand, as a Republican, I thought there should be legitimate constitutional limits on the powers of the federal government, especially in areas where the federal bureaucracy interfered directly with the fiscal and operational functions of states. Without any constraints, federal mandates could bankrupt state governments. Before the ratification of the Seventeenth Amendment in 1913, senators were chosen by the state legislatures, a practice that provided a check on federal power. With the popular election of senators, that political check was diminished and the constitutional protections of the Tenth Amendment gained importance.

Working with the San Antonio Metropolitan Transit Authority, we filed suit against the secretary of labor in the U.S. District Court for the Western District of Texas, seeking a declaratory judgment that under *National League of Cities,* the Fair Labor Standards Act could not be applied to public transit employees. We selected San Antonio in part because the unions were seeking damages there for past wages under the act and partly because we thought it would be a sympathetic venue. My team consisted of Don Bliss and Zoe

Baird, who later was nominated by President Clinton to be the first woman attorney general of the United States (but unfortunately withdrew when allegations surfaced that she had not paid social security taxes for her children's nanny). We worked closely with George Parker, counsel to the San Antonio authority, and after briefing we trekked down to San Antonio for oral argument before district court judge Clyde Frederick Shannon Jr. The unions' lawsuit was consolidated with ours, and after listening to arguments by the federal government, the unions, the transit authority, and the public transit association, the self-confident thirty-eight-year-old judge, ruling from the bench (a practice more common in Great Britain) announced his decision holding that the San Antonio Metropolitan Transit Authority's bus drivers were state or local governmental employees operating in a traditional state or local governmental function. As such, under *National League of Cities*, the Fair Labor Standards Act could not be applied to the transit authority.

The U.S. government appealed the decision directly to the Supreme Court, which remanded the case back to the federal district court for reconsideration in light of a Supreme Court decision the previous year, *Transportation Union* v. *Long Island Railroad* (1982), holding that the Railway Labor Act applied to employees of a state-owned railroad because they were not performing traditional governmental functions.[13]

In our reargument before Judge Shannon in San Antonio, we presented a strong statistical case that distinguished bus operations, which were overwhelmingly governmental and heavily subsidized, from rail operations, which were overwhelmingly private. Shannon agreed: "I was right the first time and I am still right. But this time I will take a few days and write up my decision so that the Supreme Court will have more to review than simply a transcript." True to his word, Judge Shannon wrote a crisp and straightforward twelve-page decision holding again that the operations of the San Antonio Metropolitan Transit Authority served a traditional government function, protected by the Tenth Amendment in a system of federalism articulated in *National League of Cities*. The federal government promptly returned to the Supreme Court, using the same mandatory right of appeal that we had so deftly invoked in the *Brown* v. *Board of Education* cases.[14]

On March 14, 1984, I argued the case in the Supreme Court on behalf of both the American Public Transit Association and the San Antonio Metropolitan Transit Authority, showing how local transit operations were similar in nature to local police and fire protection and how in recent decades they had become traditional governmental functions rather than proprietary activities operated in competition with the private sector. Theodore B. Olson, the assistant attorney general in charge of the Office of Legal Counsel, argued for the federal government.[15]

On June 16, 1984, the last day of the Supreme Court term, no decision had been issued. Instead, the clerk of the Court issued an order setting down the case for reargument in the next term, asking the parties to address the following question: "Whether or not the principles of the Tenth Amendment as set forth in *National League of Cities v. Usery* . . . should be reconsidered."[16] From Justice Harry Blackmun's papers at the Library of Congress I later discovered that we had actually won the case 5-4 in the conference following the oral argument. But the chief justice—to his later regret—assigned the opinion to Justice Blackmun, who was the swing vote in *National League of Cities*.

Blackmun said that he "decided to come down on the side of reversal because I have been able to find no principled way in which to affirm." The justice substituted an opinion drafted by a persuasive law clerk reversing the decision below without explicitly overruling *National League of Cities*. He recognized that in light of his change of position, the justices might want to set down the cases for reargument. Justice O'Connor and Justice Powell responded to Blackmun's memo, expressing surprise and urging reargument.[17] An annoyed Blackmun suggested that if the case were reargued, *National League* might well be overruled.[18]

Blissfully unaware that the swing vote in *National League* was about to swing the other way, we spent the summer researching the history of the Tenth Amendment and the expectations of the states when they ratified the Bill of Rights. In my second argument I had a heavier burden. I had to convince the Supreme Court that Justice Rehnquist's 5-4 majority opinion in *National League*, interpreting the Tenth Amendment, was correct and should be affirmed. I then had to convince the Court that public transit was a traditional local governmental function within *National League's* umbrella of protection. My opponents this time were the solicitor general, Rex Lee, and Laurence Gold, an eminent appellate litigator for the AFL-CIO, who argued the case for the unions.

After reargument, the Court dramatically overruled *National League of Cities*, in another 5-4 decision.[19] Switching sides and making good on his veiled threat, Justice Blackmun wrote a sweeping opinion for the majority, consigning the Tenth Amendment to the ash heap of constitutional doctrine. For the Supreme Court to overrule its own precedent in fewer than two years on a constitutional issue that goes to the very heart of the nation's system of federalism sent shock waves through the legal community. Justice Rehnquist wrote a bitter separate dissent, predicting that the Tenth Amendment would one day again "command the support of the majority of this Court." He proved prophetic. In subsequent years, the Court has chipped away at the Blackmun majority opinion in *Garcia* v. *San Antonio Metropolitan Transit Authority* without actually overruling it to establish the boundaries of state sovereignty in a system of federalism.

Having served as a Frankfurter clerk during a fractious Court term, I should not have been so surprised by the turn of events in the *Garcia* case. It certainly made me appreciate the leadership of Chief Justice Warren in forging a unanimous decision in *Brown* v. *Board of Education*. When the Court can swing back and forth in 5-4 decisions reversing and then overruling its own decisions on a major constitutional issue in the space of a few years, it is not likely to engender great public confidence. Especially on matters of constitutional impact, there is great value in unanimity and consistency.

While I was disappointed in the results of these constitutional cases, I fared better in other Supreme Court matters. Early in 1985 the chief judge of the U.S. District Court for the Southern District of New York, my former colleague from the Legal Defense Fund Constance Baker Motley, asked me to represent a federal judge in her district. Lawrence Tribe of the Harvard Law School, representing Cable News Network (CNN), had filed a petition for a writ of certiorari seeking to force the federal district court judge to permit TV cameras in the courtroom during the libel trial brought by General Westmoreland. On behalf of the judge, we opposed the petition, which was denied by the Supreme Court.

With the advent of C-Span and the Freedom of Information Act and its progeny, the proceedings of Congress and, to a lesser extent, the executive branch are immersed in the warmth of sunshine. There has been a swelling of similar demands to bring more transparency into the secretive deliberations of the Supreme Court. Some have advocated having C-Span cameras cover oral arguments. I do not see the value in this recommendation. I have no problem with the release of transcripts or radio broadcasts of significant arguments after the fact. But I would hate to see Supreme Court advocates grandstanding before the cameras like some members of Congress to generate media attention for their position. Of the three branches of government, the Court should be the least responsive to prevailing public opinion and popular politics. It resolves specific controversies with adherence to reason and precedent, explains its reasoning, and publishes its decisions for all to read and critique. The Supreme Court provides a check on the exuberance of a political system battered by competition for sound bites and shrill commentary. Its deliberations should be insulated so that at least one branch of government may transcend the moment and ground its decisions in history and reason that will stand the test of time.

Over several decades, I was honored to work on dozens of cases before the Supreme Court and to argue nineteen, winning more than I lost. If I had been a pitcher, this would not have gotten me into the Hall of Fame, but for a private practitioner it was a pretty good record. Arguing before the Court requires peripheral vision because there are nine justices who can throw questions at you at any time, and many of them do so with Gatling-gun rapidity, except for Justice Clarence Thomas, who rarely asks a question during oral argument, expressing his views in written opinions. A Supreme Court advocate will not have much of an opportunity to read a prepared statement. It is therefore a good idea to make the two or three key points that are critical to your case in the first couple of sentences and to have in mind a summation that reemphasizes those points at the end of your argument, after the white light goes on and you know you have five minutes to sum up. You will have to sit down promptly when the red light goes on, unless you wish to risk the ire of the chief justice. For the casual observer the best Supreme Court argument is rarely a Clarence Darrow–like performance of eloquence and rhetorical flourish. Rather, the argument may sound jittery and helter-skelter as the attorney seeks to emphasize points that are important to specific justices who may be on the fence, reinforcing, wherever possible, the client's position by referring to a previous opinion written by a justice that supports that view.

Mastering the record is essential. First-time advocates often forget that the Court is resolving a specific dispute, a case or controversy, and not engaging in scholarly, lofty, abstract speculation. The ability to cite to a specific page in an appendix where the record demonstrates a fact that is critical to the case can make all the difference in a closely contested argument.

Most Supreme Court advocates prepare by staging one or more moot courts (practice sessions) in which colleagues throw out tough questions enabling the counsel to formulate succinct, accurate, and persuasive replies. It is important that counsel listen carefully to the justice's questions and answer them directly. Evasive answers that fall back on previously prepared platitudes or scripted sound bites should be reserved for political campaigns or perhaps White House press conferences, as they are a disaster in the Supreme Court. By listening carefully, sometimes you can detect whether a justice is trying to help you in building support for his or her position among his or her colleagues or is seeking to create a record that will support an opinion against your client's position. Sometimes it is difficult to tell which. That's why I seldom predict what the Supreme Court will decide.[20]

THIRTY-NINE

The Robert Bork Hearings

Justice in the extreme is often unjust.

—RACINE

ON MY RETURN TO THE private sector, I was honored to be asked to resume a leadership role in the NAACP Legal Defense and Educational Fund as the co-chair of its board. The fund had had many successes in resuscitating the Thirteenth, Fourteenth, and Fifteenth Amendments from decades of somnolence. It had fought hard to ensure the enforcement of a great deal of recently enacted civil rights legislation. To preserve and protect these successes, it was essential that federal judges be appointed who would not turn back the pages of history.

Of the many judicial nominees the Legal Defense Fund reviewed and discussed, the most vexing for me was the Honorable Robert W. Bork, who was nominated by President Reagan in July 1987 to replace retiring Justice Powell on the Supreme Court. Judge Bork had had a brilliant legal career as a popular professor of law at the Yale Law School (he taught my older son), solicitor general of the United States, and at the time of his nomination, a respected judge on the U.S. Court of Appeals for the District of Columbia Circuit. I knew Judge Bork quite well and had—and still do have—great respect for him. At the time of his nomination to the U.S. Court of Appeals for the District of Columbia Circuit in 1981, I was the member of the American Bar Association's Standing Committee on the Federal Judiciary assigned to investigate Judge Bork's fitness to be a judge on the circuit court. After the investigation, I recommended him without any reservation as being "exceptionally well qualified," the highest rating possible. The full committee upheld my recommendation. His service on the circuit court was fully consistent with that finding.

I won the one case I had argued before him. In that case, the NAACP had sued the NAACP Legal Defense and Educational Fund seeking to have *NAACP* dropped from its name. Judge Bork joined the three-judge appellate panel in unanimously upholding my position on behalf of the Inc Fund. In 1957 Thurgood Marshall had severed the formal ties between the two organizations to protect the independence of the tax-exempt Inc Fund, allowing it to pursue an aggressive litigation strategy free from the NAACP's internal politics, but he kept *NAACP* in the name of the independent entity. After all, as counsel to the NAACP, Marshall had won many landmark civil rights cases, including *Brown* v. *Board of Education,* and it was important to the Legal Defense Fund to retain continuity as we continued to pursue our mission. Concerned about public confusion, the NAACP objected. This unfortunate and embarrassing internecine dispute among fellow warriors in the civil rights struggles could only be resolved by resort to the District of Columbia Circuit Court, pitching former senator Edward Brooke as counsel for the NAACP against yours truly on behalf of the Legal Defense Fund. With Judge Bork's vote, we prevailed.[1]

Since all my experiences with Judge Bork had been highly positive, what was so vexing about his nomination to the high court? There was no question about his intellect, integrity, character, and experience. While attempting to cast Supreme Court justices into stereotyped ideological corners is in my judgment a fruitless exercise, there was a general perception at that time that the Supreme Court was divided into two camps of four justices in each camp. President Reagan had already made two appointments to the Court. Many liberals feared that Bork's appointment would secure a conservative majority. Attorney General Edwin Meese added fuel to the fire when he inartfully said, "We now have our fifth vote."[2] Would a Bork appointment undo the progress on racial issues made under the Warren Court? Jack Greenberg and most of the Legal Defense Fund staff were among those who expressed this concern.

About a week after the Bork nomination, Joe Rauh invited me to lunch at the Metropolitan Club, a downtown dining facility a few blocks from the White House where many issues of historic import have been discussed over a glass of sherry. Joe described the many opinions and articles Bork had written expressing views that threatened to unravel some of our hard-fought victories. He cited, for example, Bork's frequent criticism of judicial remedies to redress racial discrimination in both public and private facilities. He reminded me that as solicitor general during the Ford administration Bork urged the government to intervene on behalf of the white parents in Boston opposing the busing of school children.

Joe Rauh urged me as chair of the Legal Defense Fund to testify against Bork's nomination before the Senate Judiciary Committee. At the end of the lunch, I told Joe that I was torn by his recommendation because I had always thought that Judge Bork was an intellectually brilliant lawyer. With his broad experience in the private sector, the Justice Department, as an appellate judge, and in academia, he seemed exactly the type of nominee that I had always thought would be the ideal Court appointment.

Jack Greenberg called the next day. He said the Legal Defense Fund staff recommended that we thoroughly investigate Judge Bork's entire record and consider whether his positions were so detrimental that we should publicly oppose his confirmation. I assured the director-counsel that I would not over-rule the staff if, after a diligent, complete, and balanced inquiry, they con-cluded that opposing Judge Bork's nomination was important to preserve and continue the progress to end racial discrimination for which the Legal Defense Fund had labored so long. I also told Jack that I would submit his recommendation to the Legal Defense Fund board of directors, and if the board voted to oppose the nomination, I would not stand in the way. I did express concern about the repercussions of the Legal Defense Fund's actively opposing a nominee who might be sitting on the Supreme Court for the next twenty or thirty years, and I suggested to Jack that my vote as a member of the board would probably be against opposing the confirmation. That was before I began to delve into the extensive public record of Bork's speeches and articles.

As the public debate intensified, it became apparent that I could not side-step the controversy. On many occasions I had gone to members of Congress asking them to take unpopular positions publicly. My own career as a public servant and practitioner of law and my participation in public policy and cor-porate decisionmaking would never have been possible if the Supreme Court had not acted to eradicate the discriminatory laws and practices existing at the time of my birth and after graduation from law school.

The Inc Fund had invoked the aid of the courts because ultimately we had faith that the Supreme Court eventually would act to realize the Constitution's unfulfilled promise of equality of opportunity regardless of race and gender. As the final guardian of the constitutional legal principles that resolve our nation's most controversial disputes, the Supreme Court, in more recent decades, had for the most part kept the protest against racial injustice from exploding into violent confrontation in the streets. That has not always been the case.

When I sat next to Thurgood Marshall during his oral arguments in *Brown* and *Aaron* v. *Cooper,* we could only hope that the dark decades of the *Dred Scott* decision and *Plessy* v. *Ferguson* were behind us, never to return. We had fought a great Civil War and endured decades of Jim Crow laws, lynch-ings, and Black Codes until a courageous Supreme Court had taken a highly unpopular stand—a stand that our elected officials had opposed or deferred for almost a century; and with that decision, the battle had only begun. We had inched our way forward case by case, suffering setbacks along the way, such as my loss in the *Richmond School* case. The battlefields were now squarely in the courts, the boardrooms, the churches, and the legislative halls. Robert

Bork was an extraordinary lawyer and judge. From personal experience, I knew there was not a racist bone in his body. He was eminently fair and unbiased in his personal relationships. That did not resolve the fundamental issue. Would Judge Bork use his brilliant and persuasive intellect on the Court to continue to move us forward on the long march to eradicate racial discrimination and preserve the rights of minorities and the less advantaged in our society? Given his well reasoned but, in my judgment, incorrect judicial philosophy as expressed in scholarly writing, I thought it unlikely. I felt we should not take a chance. Too much was at stake. As one who had benefited so greatly from this nation's difficult but steady march toward a free, fair, and open society, the handwriting on the wall—"mene mene tekel upharsin"—would condemn my failure to testify against the confirmation of Judge Bork. ("Thou art weighed in the balance, and art found wanting" (Dan. 5:25–27 AV).

With some trepidation, I decided to oppose Judge Bork's nomination and agreed to testify at the hearing of the Senate Judiciary Committee on September 22, 1987. As co-chair of the Legal Defense Fund board, I had a responsibility to respect its concerns. It had undertaken a comprehensive review of Bork's writings and speeches and concluded that his elevation to the Supreme Court at that time would place in jeopardy a decade of hard-fought victories.

Facing the klieg lights, TV cameras, and the full array of the Senate Judiciary Committee (a rare event), I nervously approached the witness table, settled into my chair alone, and began to read slowly and with a heavy heart my prepared statement opposing the nomination, giving the following reasons:

First, as a legal scholar Judge Bork had rejected many of the leading Supreme Court decisions on the fundamental constitutional rights to liberty and privacy. In articles and speeches, Judge Bork had on occasion rejected the well-established line of Supreme Court decisions holding that the word *liberty*, which appears in the Fifth and Fourteenth Amendments and the preamble to the Constitution, protects Americans against governmental invasion of our substantive personal liberty and privacy. Judge Bork, for example, criticized as "wrongly decided" the first decision in this important line of cases, *Meyer* v. *Nebraska* (1923) (holding that the word *liberty* in the Constitution means more than "merely freedom from imposed, bodily restraint").[3] The *Meyer* decision had been followed by the Supreme Court in numerous cases. By rejecting this line of cases, Judge Bork apparently would have excluded from constitutional protection "the right of the individual . . . to acquire useful knowledge, to marry, establish a home and bring up children . . . and generally to enjoy those privileges long recognized at common law as essential to the orderly pursuit of happiness by free men."[4]

Judge Bork's narrow view also would have excluded the constitutionally protected liberty of mobility. He rejected Justice Stewart's position in *Shapiro* v.

Thompson (1969) that the concept of liberty embraces the fundamental right to travel. This rejection hit a raw nerve. The constitutional right to travel is especially important for minorities and the poor, who seek out communities that will provide them a meaningful opportunity for jobs and individual fulfillment. A sensitive reading of history would show how important mobility has been for persons of color—from the Underground Railroad (which my great uncle operated in St. Louis), to the Black Codes in the South, which restricted the mobility of former slaves, to the great migration to northern urban cities.[5]

Judge Bork's philosophy of almost complete deference to the majoritarian will of local legislative bodies, reflecting prevailing community mores and biases, was similar to that of Justice Holmes, one of our greatest jurists. Holmes's record on matters of race and protection of minorities, however, was completely out of step with the mainstream of constitutional interpretation by the time of the Bork nomination.

Judge Bork, in scholarly writing both before and after joining the bench, rejected the long-established view that the meaning of *liberty* in the Constitution encompasses a fundamental right to privacy, including personal decisions relating to marriage: *Loving* v. *Virginia* (1967) (interracial marriage); *Turner* v. *Safley* (1987) (procreation, right to marry even though in prison); *Griswold* v. *Connecticut* (1965) (contraception); *Prince* v. *Massachusetts* (family relationships); *Roe* v. *Wade* (1973) (abortion); *Pierce* (1925) (child rearing and education); and *McLaughlin* v. *Florida* (1964) (right of two persons of different races and different sexes to occupy the same room during the nighttime).

The respect for individual privacy is deeply embedded in our nation of diverse peoples and beliefs. We harbor an inherent distrust of a powerful government's capacity to infringe on basic individual substantive liberties. No concept is likely to be more important to the preservation of a free democratic society over the next fifty years because of advances in computer technology, science, telecommunications, medicine, and the mapping of the human genome, all of which substantially increase the government's capacity to invade individual privacy.

In *Griswold*, the seminal privacy decision, the Court struck down a Connecticut ban on the use of contraceptives by a married couple as a violation of the fundamental right to privacy protected by the due process clause. Judge Bork, before going on the bench, wrote as follows:

> *Griswold*, then, is an unprincipled decision, both in the way in which it derives a new constitutional right and in the way it defines that right, or rather fails to define it. We are left with no idea of the sweep of the right to privacy and hence no notion of the cases to which it may or

may not be applied in the future. The truth is that the Court could not reach its result in Griswold through principle. . . . All law discriminates and thereby creates inequalities. The Supreme Court has no principled way of saying which non-racial inequalities are impermissible. What it has done, therefore, is to appeal to simplistic notions of "fairness" or to what it regards as "fundamental" interests in order to demand equality in some cases but not in others, thus choosing values and producing a line of cases as improper and as intellectually empty as *Griswold* v. *Connecticut*.[6]

In scholarly writing and speeches after becoming a federal judge, Bork continued to criticize *Griswold*. He wrote disdainfully that the result in that case could not "have been reached by interpretation of the Constitution"[7] and that *Griswold*, along with "all the sexual freedom cases," reflected the Court's "imposition of upper middle class, college educated, east-west coast morality."[8] In his view, "since there is no constitutional test or history to define the right[,] privacy becomes an unstructured source of judicial power."[9] His views did not moderate. In an interview in 1985 he restated the criticism he first expressed fifteen years earlier, saying, "I don't think there is a supportable method of constitutional reasoning underlying the *Griswold* decision."[10]

Bork, like many other respected scholars, also criticized the decision in *Roe* v. *Wade,* the abortion rights case. In 1981 he testified that *Roe* v. *Wade* "is an unconstitutional decision, a serious and wholly unjustifiable judicial usurpation of State legislative authority" and, as he later reiterated in a speech, has "no constitutional foundation."[11] After becoming a judge in 1982, Bork, in his nonjudicial writings and speeches, continued his attacks on *Roe* and described the result of that case as the outgrowth of the "gentrification of the Constitution"[12] and the Court's attempt at the "nationalization of morality through the creation of new constitutional rights."[13] In an interview in 1984 Judge Bork repeated his view that the Constitution has nothing to say about the right to have an abortion.

Some acknowledged scholars supported Bork's nomination on the grounds that his expressions of "judicial restraint" place him in the tradition of Justices Frankfurter and Harlan. I refuted this argument by attaching as appendixes A and B to my written testimony before the Senate Judiciary Committee a discussion of opinions written by Justices Frankfurter and Harlan that showed their views to be wholly at odds with the positions taken by Judge Bork, as a scholar, on substantive liberty and privacy.[14]

The Supreme Court, by recognizing the constitutional basis for the protection of such fundamental liberties, has been able to respond in a principled fashion to unforeseen problems and abuses that the framers could not have possibly anticipated. In another important branch of constitutional law, the commerce clause, Judge Bork correctly recognized the necessity of a pragmatic and sensitive constitutional interpretation that reflects the changing "needs of the nation."[15] Yet where the privacy of individuals and families is involved, Judge Bork exhibited none of this pragmatism.

Unlike freedom of the press and freedom of religion, the right to privacy was not explicitly spelled out in the Bill of Rights. But the concept of privacy in a free society is so central to the founding premise of respect for individual dignity and liberty that any attempt to define all its dimensions would only have served to constrain its essential function in preserving the rights of individuals to be free from overly intrusive government seeking to impose the beliefs of the majority. External manifestations of an individual's private views in speaking, writing, praying, or assembling are explicitly protected, as are the right to be free from illegal search and seizure, the right to due process, and the right against self-incrimination. Privacy is central to and inherent in most of the constitutional amendments. If we are to continue on the long march toward a more perfect union, and if the Supreme Court is to discharge its constitutional responsibilities to protect the rights of individuals, the Court must have the flexibility to apply unchanging constitutional values to changing contemporary circumstances. The discipline of the time-tested judicial process, rooted in the English common law and anchored to established precedent, enables the Court to take a principled path toward progress that is not frozen in eighteenth-century language, custom, and tradition.

While sitting as a judge on the intermediate court, Judge Bork might have felt bound by the Supreme Court decisions with which he disagreed, although he wasn't shy about criticizing them in speeches and interviews. If Bork were to be confirmed as associate justice, he most likely would feel much less bound by earlier decisions of the Supreme Court (and correctly so, on occasion).

My second concern was Judge Bork's criticisms of landmark civil rights cases under the equal protection clause and his skepticism about the effective use of the equal protection clause to protect women, aliens, the poor, or illegitimate children. In his writings and speeches, but not in his opinions, he had concluded that several leading constitutional decisions protecting the rights of people of color were wrongly decided and had no basis in the Constitution, including its amendments. Bork criticized *Shelley* v. *Kraemer* (1948), decided by a unanimous Court (with three justices not participating), in which the majority opinion was written by Chief Justice Vinson, never thought to be a flaming liberal. The Court in *Shelley* addressed the issue whether a state court can enforce a racially restrictive covenant prohibiting the sale of real estate to a black person. The Fourteenth Amendment prohibits state action denying due process or equal protection of the law. But a racially restrictive covenant is only a private contract. The Court in *Shelley* held that the judicial enforcement of a racially restrictive covenant by a state court constitutes state action prohibited by the Fourteenth Amendment. Today, the decision simply reflects the reality that when a state judge acts to interpret and enforce a repugnant racial restriction in a written contract, it is as much state action as when a state legislature enacts a statute.

Judge Bork's failure to appreciate the scourge of restrictive covenants was particularly disturbing to people of color and to many Jews. Racial segregation (and often religious discrimination) in residential housing, apartments, and hotels was the way of life in this country at least through 1945. The historic struggle to eradicate these pervasive practices is a long and dramatic one. As early as 1917, the Supreme Court in *Buchanan* v. *Warley* (1917) correctly held that a city could not create racial ghettoes by ordinance. Even as the legal barriers were eliminated, the perverse result was achieved through private racial or religious restrictive covenants (often enforced by state and federal courts) and by the refusal of private hotels and apartment houses to rent to people of color or Jews. In most cities, North and South, the dominant residential pattern was—and, unfortunately, too often remains—racially segregated. If state courts enforce these private racial restrictions, then the state is perpetuating segregation, which obviously has an effect on the composition of public schools and the ability of people to get to know one another and work together, even where state-mandated segregation has been abolished.

Chief Justice Vinson's opinion in *Shelley* v. *Kraemer* was based in part on section 1 of the Civil Rights Act of 1866, which provides that "all citizens of the United States shall have the same right, in every State and Territory, as is enjoyed by white citizens thereof to inherit, purchase, lease, sell, hold, and convey real and personal property."[16] Five years later, in *Barrows* v. *Jackson* (1953), the Court, clearly relying on *Shelley*, held that under the Fourteenth Amendment, a state court cannot award damages against a white seller who sold property to a black buyer in breach of a restrictive covenant.[17]

In 1971, twenty-three years after the *Shelley* decision, eighteen years after *Barrows*, and despite numerous decisions supporting the principle in *Shelley*, Bork took the position that the restrictive covenant cases were wrongly decided. Lest there be any doubt, this is what Judge Bork wrote: *"Shelley v. Kraemer* . . . converts an amendment whose text and history clearly show it to be aimed at governmental discrimination into a sweeping prohibition of private discrimination. *There is no warrant anywhere for that conversion.*"[18]

Bork believed that judicial enforcement of private agreements to exclude people of color by a state or federal court, clearly organs of government, does not involve discriminatory state action based on race. Most Americans believe that a court is as much an arm of the state as the legislature, a mayor, or a governor. Only three years before the Bork hearings, in *Palmore* v. *Sidoti* (1984), Chief Justice Burger, writing for a unanimous Court, cited *Shelley* for the proposition that "the actions of state courts and judicial officers in their official capacity have long been held to be state action governed by the Fourteenth Amendment."[19]

Having reviewed Bork's scholarly work in this area before and after he became a judge, I came to the painful realization that if his views had prevailed in the Supreme Court, my fourteen years of litigation in the Girard College case would have gone for naught.

Bork's views were especially puzzling given that three years before his 1971 law review article criticizing *Shelley*, the Supreme Court had held (by a 7-2 majority) in *Jones* v. *Alfred H. Mayer Co.* (1968) that the 1866 Civil Rights Act relied on in *Shelley* did not require any state action at all.[20] The *Jones* decision held that the Thirteenth Amendment bars racial discrimination in public places, like restaurants and hotels, because such discrimination is a badge of dishonor and reflective of past slavery. The decision was reaffirmed and extended in the 1986 term when the Court held 9 to 0 that private discrimination violates the 1866 act even when the victims are Arabs or Jews.[21]

Other significant civil rights precedents criticized by Bork include the decision in *Regents of University of California* v. *Bakke* (1978) (affirmative action) and the state poll tax cases. In 1973, before going on the bench, he had targeted the decision in *Harper* v. *Virginia Board of Elections* (1966), which struck down a Virginia poll tax as impermissibly discriminating on the basis of wealth. He said the case was wrongly decided and could not be defended on equal protection grounds.

As a scholar, Bork often argued that it was the responsibility of Congress and not the courts to outlaw discriminatory practices. Yet even when Congress acted to address civil rights violations, Bork sometimes questioned the constitutionality of the federal legislative action. Bork took the position, for example, that section 5 of the Fourteenth Amendment granted the power to Congress "to enforce, by appropriate legislation" only actions that would be *per se* illegal under the amendment.[22] The Supreme Court unanimously rejected this view in *Oregon* v. *Mitchell* (1970), which held that section 5 authorized Congress to prohibit literacy tests that were designed and used to disqualify people of color from voting in state elections even though the Court previously had held that such tests were not *per se* unconstitutional.[23] Contrary to Judge Bork's view, section 5 also has been invoked to support legislation applying a "discriminatory effects" test under the Voting Rights Act of 1965, as amended (*Rome* v. *United States* [1980]), to enact Title VII to the Civil Rights Act prohibiting employment discrimination on the basis of race, religion, sex, or national origin (*Fitzpatrick* v. *Bitzer* [1976]), and to punish private conspiracies that violate constitutional rights (*United States* v. *Guest* [1966]).[24]

In applying the Fourteenth Amendment, the Supreme Court had devised a "strict or heightened scrutiny" test to sustain a racial classification. Over time the Court applied the test to its review of the constitutionality of governmental actions that discriminate on the basis of gender, illegitimacy, poverty, or alienage. Bork's scholarly writings suggest that he had rejected or would have greatly limited the use of this test in determining the constitutionality of state action.[25]

That the protections accorded by the equal protection clause are broader than the prohibition of state action discriminating on race or ethnicity is manifest from the text and history of the Fourteenth Amendment. The Court rightfully has applied the clause to prohibit other forms of invidious discrimination. Unlike the Thirteenth and Fifteenth Amendments, the Fourteenth Amendment does not expressly limit equal protection to matters of race or prior servitude, although that clearly was its fundamental purpose. Bork's view is based on a selective interpretation of the legislative history, a practice he might otherwise eschew. In recent decades the Supreme Court, usually in a sensitive and perceptive manner, had recognized that the bigotry long directed at people of color has been also directed at other groups as well, including women, aliens, poor people, Jewish people, and illegitimate children. The salutary application of this grand principle of antidiscrimination to the complex realities of American life was too often dismissed by Bork as merely the result of "fads in sentimentality."[26]

From an intellectual standpoint, Bork's scholarship was well reasoned and provocative. From my point of view, it was regressive in refusing to accept the validity of Supreme Court decisions that had affirmed fundamental human rights.

I conceded to the Senate Judiciary Committee that I was unaware of any judicial opinion of Judge Bork incorporating his more extreme views. Nevertheless, many of his writings and speeches postdated his appointment to the bench.[27] I thought it appropriate for the Senate to give weight to the views reflected in those statements. Judge Bork and his supporters in the Reagan administration had implied that the power of appointment is an effective way of overturning wrongly decided cases.[28] I thus urged the Senate committee to bear in mind what Judge Bork had said before the hearings about overruling constitutional precedents with which a justice disagreed. Robert Bork had written: "Since the legislature can do nothing about the interpretation of the Constitution given by a court, the Court ought to be always open to rethink Constitutional problems. . . . At bottom, a judge's basic obligation or basic duty is to the Constitution, not simply to precedent."[29] "If a court became convinced that it had made a terrible mistake about a constitutional ruling in the past, I think ultimately the real meaning of the Constitution ought to prevail over a prior mistake by the court."[30] "Certainly at the least, I would think an *originalist* judge would have no problem whatever in overturning a nonoriginalist precedent, because that precedent by the very basis of his judicial philosophy, has no legitimacy. It comes from nothing that the framers intended."[31]

At the outset of my oral testimony, I informed the Senate Judiciary Committee that I was a member of the American Bar Association's Standing Committee on the Federal Judiciary in 1981, which rated Judge Bork as exceptionally well qualified for appointment to the U.S. Court of Appeals for the District of Columbia Circuit, that I had led the committee's investigation of him, and that I fully agreed with that rating. I testified that nothing Judge Bork had done or written as a judge on the court of appeals would have changed in any way my opinion and recommendation on that appointment. Other witnesses had argued that this 1981 rating should have been conclusive. Senator Hatch persistently pressed me on this issue. I gave the committee three reasons why my earlier finding should not determine Judge Bork's qualifications to sit on the Supreme Court.

First, the American Bar Association's criteria for nomination to the Court of Appeals address "professional qualifications, competence, integrity and judicial temperament." The committee recognizes that "the Senate may consider other aspects of the prospective nominee's qualifications."[32]

Second, the bar association's procedure and rating system for Supreme Court nominees are different from those applicable to the court of appeals. The instructions provide that "the significance, range and complexity of the issues considered by the Supreme Court, the importance of the underlying societal problems, the need to mediate between tradition and change and the Supreme Court's extraordinarily heavy docket are among the factors which require a person of exceptional ability. To fulfill the responsibilities of a Supreme Court Justice, it is not enough that one be a fine person or a good lawyer."[33]

Third, few cases in the U.S. Court of Appeals for the District of Columbia Circuit involved constitutional, civil rights, and liberty issues. In Judge Bork's five years on the circuit court, he had written only one opinion in this category, *Dronenburg v. Zech* (1984) (the Navy's policy of mandatory discharge for homosexual conduct does not violate constitutional rights to privacy or equal protection).[34] Moreover, lower court judges are obligated to follow the precedents of the higher court.[35] An associate justice is not under the same stricture.[36] Judge Bork had criticized many of the Supreme Court decisions discussed above as wrongly decided. His writings suggested that he would not have felt bound to follow those prior Supreme Court decisions with which he had expressed strong intellectual disagreement.

At the end of my lengthy testimony before the Senate Judiciary Committee, Senator Kennedy said that he wanted

> to acknowledge the remarkable career of Secretary Coleman; not only his academic career at college, at the University of Pennsylvania, at Harvard Law School and the Law Review and then coming down and serving as law secretary for Felix Frankfurter, then serving in President Ford's Cabinet with great distinction. In practice, he appeared before the Supreme Court on 18 different occasions over three decades, and he has really reached the pinnacle of success both in the public and private sectors. I think all of us who have listened to him this morning [have enlarged] our knowledge of the Constitution and [been impressed] by his review of the many cases that have made this a better society and a better country.[37]

Senator Biden, then chair of the Judiciary Committee, made the following remarks:

> Mr. Secretary, I must tell you, I have not been here as long as my colleagues on my left and my right, but I have sat here for 15 years. I thought I knew you before you came up because I was here when you were Secretary of Transportation. On mass transit issues, I was often petitioning you with regard to Amtrak and other things. I thought I knew you, and I was impressed then. . . .
>
> I have been more impressed by you as a witness today than any witness I have ever sat and listened to in any hearing. I knew you were a man of great integrity and passion and feeling, but I am amazed and impressed by the depth of your knowledge of the law, your reverence for the Constitution, and your facility to discuss it.
>
> Whether or not Judge Bork should or should not be on the Court will be decided by the whole body, but I want to tell you, there is not a President now or in the future who would have made a mistake by putting you on the Supreme Court of the United States of America.[38]

After twelve days of testimony—five by Bork—the Senate Judiciary Committee on October 6, 1987, failed to approve the nomination by a vote of 5 in favor and 9 against. The committee nevertheless voted to send the nomination to the Senate floor. The Senate on October 23, 1987, rejected the nomination by a vote of 42 for and 58 against.

Although it was difficult testimony to give, I believe I made the right decision. Unlike some of the shrill commentary that accompanied Bork's nomination, my testimony was not personal. It was grounded in comprehensive research into Bork's extensive written record. That doesn't mean I haven't had regrets, particularly when I have observed how the nomination and confirmation process has evolved since then. My testimony was not intended to deter presidents from nominating brilliant minds like Robert Bork who have spoken and written provocatively. I suspect sadly that it has. I have never believed that the life experience or the political and philosophical views of a nominee can predict how he or she will rule from the bench.

Since the Bork hearings, presidential nominees to the Supreme Court have undergone exhaustive scrutiny. A nominee's philosophy, opinions, and utterances caught on tape or in an e-mail are fully examined and often elevated to shrill sound bites for talk shows on radio and TV. The confirmation process has been greatly elongated. This is a historic sea change. Despite rumors about his prior membership in the Ku Klux Klan, Hugo Black was confirmed only five days after President Roosevelt nominated him. Harold Burton was confirmed the day he was nominated. When President Kennedy nominated Byron "Whizzer" White, it took only eight days to confirm him. Abe Fortas's confirmation took only fourteen days (although the nation may have paid a penalty for rushing through that nomination, since he later was forced to resign). In contrast, Thurgood Marshall's nomination took seventy-eight days.[39]

There is today an awkwardness and ambiguity in the confirmation process. Nominees should not be asked their views on issues likely to come before the Court lest they be forced to prejudge the outcome before the specific factual context is presented. Yet almost every issue of national importance eventually will come before the Court. Does this mean that the Senate should address only the integrity, the experience, and the qualifications of the nominee, deferring to the elected president on philosophy? As a senator, President Obama voted against the nominations of Chief Justice John Roberts and Justice Samuel Alito. There certainly was no argument that they were not qualified and experienced. The issue was pure philosophy. The defeat of Bork's nomination raised a lot of issues that are still unresolved.

Recent Senate confirmation hearings have been like a kabuki dance as senators posture for the media and nominees equivocate and evade the questions following the script of their White House lawyer advisers. The hearings have become a huge waste of time. This was not the lesson of the Bork hearings, but it may well have been the effect.

In the end, I opposed Judge Bork's nomination because he had repeatedly, consistently, and passionately expressed views with clarity of reason that threatened to reverse the hard-won victories the Legal Defense Fund had achieved in the Supreme Court. For Americans of color and other minorities, the post–Civil War amendments to the Constitution were the realization of the founding fathers' unfulfilled promise of equality of opportunity for all Americans. In *Brown* v. *Board of Education* and other decisions that followed, the Court had finally turned the page and extended these living mandates to other disadvantaged individuals. We had come too far to risk a retreat.

Of all the tasks I undertook as chair of the Legal Defense Fund, testifying at the Bork confirmation hearings was the most challenging and unsettling.

FORTY

Is Race Still Relevant?

There are no "white" or "colored" signs on the fox holes or graveyards of battle.

—JOHN F. KENNEDY

PRESIDENT KENNEDY'S OBSERVATION IS A self-evident truth, but a truth whose significance unfortunately has eluded many Americans for too many years. Even after the adoption of the Thirteenth and Fourteenth Amendments, the Supreme Court in 1896 essentially endorsed a system of American-style apartheid.[1]

I was born only twenty-four years after the *Plessy* decision. I became conscious of differences in skin color at a very young age, and experienced various forms of Yankee-style racism. My parents emphasized the value and contributions of people of color throughout world history and to the American experience. What they taught me was important to the development of my self-confidence.

Over my life of fourscore and ten years, we have made enormous progress in this country in breaking down the barriers of discrimination. Most Americans no longer accept in law the racial views of Thomas Jefferson, Chief Justice Taney, Justice Brown, or even the beloved Abraham Lincoln or the respected Justice Holmes. We have created a legal framework that enables successful people of all races to rise to the top of their calling on merit. But we have not reached utopia. We are not yet a color-blind society. Americans of color and white Americans remain conscious of race, and we all still struggle to adapt our views to changing circumstances.

In a pluralistic society, race and ethnicity perhaps remain relevant, but must be considered in the context of the American experiment in which the whole is greater than its parts. As John Dewey said in 1916, ethnicity is but "one note in a vast symphony." We must extract from "each people its special good, so that it shall surrender into a common fund of wisdom and experience." The dangerous thing," Dewey continued, "is for each factor to isolate itself, to try to live off its past and then to attempt to impose itself upon other elements,

335

or, at least to keep itself intact and thus refuse to accept what other cultures have to offer, so as thereby to be transmuted into authentic Americanism."[2]

Authentic Americanism is not a self-evident concept easily within grasp. I admire what Louis D. Brandeis said to the New Century Club on November 28, 1905: "There is no place for what President [Theodore] Roosevelt has called hyphenated Americans. There is room here for men of any race, of any creed, of any condition of life, but not for Protestant-Americans, or Catholic-Americans, or Jewish-Americans, not for German-Americans, Irish-Americans, or Russian-Americans."[3] Why should it be any different for Americans of African ancestry? On the other hand, authentic Americanism is not frozen in time. It is ever changing and expanding and embraces the contributions of all races and ethnicities to a diversified cultural mainstream.

Appreciating one's heritage is a healthy intellectual exercise that can provide emotional reward. I have always admired Alex Haley, the author of *Roots* (after all, he spent a career in the Coast Guard). Haley showed us how to explore our African heritage, and Harvard professor Louis Henry Gates brought a scholarly dimension to the practice.

The idea of America as a melting pot is not inconsistent with having pride in one's ancestry and in the customs and traditions that may have contributed in some fashion to the American experience. Immigrant Americans in varying degrees have passed along certain customs and traditions to their children and celebrated their cultural affinity. Preserving cultural traditions and special skills passed down through generations has greatly enriched the mainstream culture. Gospel music, rhythm and blues, jazz, storytelling, agricultural and medical innovation, equitable justice, and athleticism are but a few examples of the contributions that Americans of color have made to enrich the quality of life for *all* Americans. The success of President Barack Obama, Hank Aaron, Jackie Robinson, Roy Campanella, W. E. B. DuBois, Charles Houston, William Hastie, Thurgood Marshall, James Earl Jones, Dick Parsons, Colin Powell, Ursula M. Burns, Lorraine Hansberry, Ralph Bunche, George Washington Carver, Daniel Drew, and countless others is not attributable to their race but to their contributions in government, diplomacy, national security, law, sports, music, business, literature, science, and medicine to the quality of American life.

The first time I walked into College Hall at the University of Pennsylvania, Langdell Hall at Harvard Law School, Justice Frankfurter's chambers at the Supreme Court, a board meeting at IBM, the Cabinet Room at the White House, or my office at each of my three law firms, I felt enormous pride, not so much as an American of color but as an American who had been given the opportunity to stretch my God-given talents to the fullest and to realize my potential. Meeting the challenges presented in these forums has informed my views about how best to work for unity and progress in our beloved country.

There is a risk that overemphasis on race and ethnicity will divide us and diminish the growing strength of a diverse mainstream. In the 1970s and 1980s, years after we had overturned the separatist doctrine of *Plessy*, there was a revolt among the Young Turks in the civil rights movement. They called themselves "Black" and later "Afro-" or "African American." "Black is beautiful" was their mantra. Some advocated racial separation as a vehicle for expressing racial pride. I fully appreciate that their objective was to rebut centuries of white-perpetuated libel that Negroes were inferior. Employing an extraordinary range of fictional arguments falsely rooted in theology, biology, paleontology, anthropology, sociology, philosophy, and law, this mendacious message of Negro inferiority was conveyed by preachers, teachers, politicians, and merchants as though mere repetition made it true—like the earth is flat or the sun revolves around the earth.[4] So why not rise up and rally in support of the beauty of blackness? Even if for some it meant creating a fortress of separateness to keep out the false idols of racism.

My oldest son was at Yale Law School during the heyday of African American studies and black separatism. He tells me that his classmate Bill Clinton and Bill's girlfriend, Hillary Rodham, were two of the few people who insisted on the right to sit at the all-black table during meals. Bill Clinton and my son even shared the same house in their first year in law school. Good for the Clintons.

Having fought to expunge all vestiges of racial segregation my entire life, I find the concept of black separatism unacceptable. I prefer not to use (but cannot always avoid) the appellations "Black" and "African American," which I consider inconsistent with my personal heritage.

At different periods of history Negro (capitalized or not, which means black in Spanish and Portuguese), colored, Black (capitalized or not), or African American has been the preferred (some would say politically correct) appellation. The preference has differed among generations, races, and regions. My mother and father preferred "colored" but would not be upset if called Negro. Justice Thurgood Marshall and many of his contemporaries agreed.[5]

At the start of the Nixon administration the census included only two categories: white and nonwhite. President Nixon's counselor, Patrick Moynihan, was offended by this limited categorization. He established a task force under James Farmer, then assistant secretary of health, education, and welfare, to recommend new designations. The task force came back with a divided opinion. The older advisers recommended "Negro," the younger advisers recommended "black."[6] In 1977 the U.S. census adopted the terms *black, white,*

American Indian or Alaska native, and *Asian or Pacific Islander.* Twenty years later the U.S. government changed the census categories to American Indian or Alaska Native, Asian, Black or African American, Native Hawaiian or other Pacific Islander, and White. In 2000 the census added a sixth category: Some other race. There also were two categories for ethnicity: Hispanic or Latino and Not Hispanic or Latino. Hispanics and Latinos could be of any race.[7] Since 2000, Americans are allowed to check more than one box. About 6.83 million people, 2.11 percent of the population, have done so.

It seems that the government also has trouble making up its mind. We keep changing what we call ourselves because none of the appellations is completely satisfactory. As we lawyers like to say, the term *colored* is over-inclusive and the term *black* is under-inclusive. All races could qualify under the term *colored.* The so-called whites come in varying shades ranging from albino to fleshy pink to various shades of tan or Mediterranean brown. I was taught in grammar school that Asians are the "yellow" race, although this seems a bit of a stretch. On the other hand, "black" is misleading. Black people come in varying shades of brown. If anything I am a shade of brown—a darker shade in the summer after a hour by the pool.

Sometimes we are called a minority, but that is the most over-inclusive term of all. These days just about everybody is a minority of one kind or another. Elliot Richardson used to say that the only unprotected class of minorities is the male WASP (white Anglo-Saxon Protestant). I told him to stop complaining. It is worthy of reflection, however, that soon this nation will simply be a collage of minorities. How will this change the way we view racial issues? Let's hope we will not choose our leaders solely to reflect the colors of the rainbow. Let's hope we will finally realize that the greatness of our nation lies in our being the world's first pluralistic meritocracy. The strength of our diversity comes from the freedom of each of our citizens to maximize her or his potential, without artificial constraints of prejudice, past practice, or tradition. It does not come from setting quotas based on race, gender, or ethnicity.

We are one nation. From our cultural and ethnic diversity, we grow into a more advanced and modern civilization, rising above the restrictive cultural practices that constrain so many of the societies from which we or our ancestors have come. We fought to end state-sanctioned public school segregation because we believed that Americans of color should be fully integrated into a more enriched and tolerant mainstream of American life and culture, fully enabled to contribute to the progress of a secular society. Americans of color have made enormous contributions in every sector of our society, but integrated schools need to do a better job of recognizing their accomplishments.

While I wish we could eliminate race completely as a relevant criterion today, we cannot do so until we have eliminated all vestiges of slavery, including the lingering effects of the post–Civil War Black Codes and Jim Crow laws, government policies of racial discrimination in housing and employment during the last century, de facto segregation in neighborhoods and schools today, and continuing manifestations of racial discrimination. The ideal may be color blindness, but the reality is that some degree of color consciousness is still necessary to fulfill the promise of equal opportunity for Americans of color. The elimination of state-sanctioned discrimination, the recognition of the constitutional right to equality of opportunity, and the rise of elected officials of color have changed the rules of the game, but they have not eradicated social, economic, and cultural discrimination. Too many Americans of color continue to live in segregated urban or rural ghettos. Americans of color suffer disproportionately from high unemployment, high rates of incarceration, recidivism, poor health care, absent fathers, inferior segregated education, and unremitting crime. It is premature to divorce these problems entirely from the issue of race, not when Americans of color make up only 13 percent of the population but 40 percent of America's prisoners. Not when the median income of black families in 2010 is only 62 percent that of white families. Not when the unemployment rate for Americans of color is double that for whites and exceeds 25 percent in some urban areas.[8]

As long as significant segments of the nonwhite population are identified in the popular mind with crime, drugs, joblessness, parental neglect, and educational underachievement, all Americans of color will face subtle prejudice, stereotyping, and racial profiling. These are the issues that civil rights and political leaders must face square on. At the top of the list is the retention and creation of good jobs and the education, skills training, and character building that is necessary for successful employment in a competitive economy.

We need to fine-tune legal tools such as affirmative action or diversification used successfully in the past to remedy the effects of state-sponsored discrimination. Today, race in and of itself usually is not an impediment to success at the highest levels of our society or at any level for that matter. We need therefore to modify our diversification policies to focus more on creating opportunities for people entrapped in a cycle of poverty and those with special needs and challenges or who have not had the benefit of strong family and community support systems. We need to keep in mind the original purpose of diversification—eliminating the badge of slavery—but we must also take into account generations of poor whites in rural and urban areas, some of whom have been disadvantaged by government policies that focus only on providing racial preferences, regardless of circumstances.[9]

Attorney General Holder has challenged Americans to engage in a candid discussion about race, calling us "a nation of cowards."[10] While I agree that there are forums in which it is helpful to discuss issues of race candidly and openly, I believe we should also spend more time talking about poverty, national security, the quality of healthcare, the responsibility of parents in their children's education, and the responsibility of individuals to accept the challenge of living productively in a free society. These are the underlying issues that are the root cause of racial discrimination and unrest.[11]

We need a healthy dialogue about how to bring all Americans, regardless of race or ethnicity, into the expanding mainstream of our economy and culture. We take pride in a society that, unlike Europe, is purportedly free of tradition-bound class stratification, a society that supposedly offers unlimited potential for upward mobility. But we also are a society that has been largely unleashed from traditional bonds of community, extended family, and intergenerational rites of passage. Instead, we venerate competition, reward individual achievement, and create transitory and not always exemplary role models. Succeeding—indeed, coping—with the pressures of such a culture requires qualities of self-confidence, self-discipline, acceptance of personal responsibility, and knowledge of the rules of the game. Too often good-faith government interventions increase dependency instead of instilling the virtues needed to survive and thrive. Unless we are prepared to write off another generation, we need to delve deeply into the still-segregated, poverty- and crime-infested neighborhoods and isolated rural areas and teach the values of successful living in a free society and competitive economy. We will need to draw on the great American reservoir of philanthropy and volunteerism as we work through our religious institutions, nonprofits, and other local charitable organizations to reach the hearts and minds of our youngsters.

In this book I have often used racial appellations that were appropriate during the relevant period. While terms such as *Negro* and *colored* may sound off-key today, they were the references commonly used in discussions at the time and enable me to describe accurately how the issue of race has affected my career in different ways during different periods of time.

More generally, today, I prefer the term *Americans of color* because it is less divisive and because the word *Americans* comes first. I long for the day when my family and I will be simply Americans, not hyphenated Americans. When a journalist and friend I really admire, Al Hunt, then a reporter for the *Wall Street Journal*, interviewed me after I became secretary of transportation, his first question was, How does it feel, Mr. Coleman, to be the first Afro-American secretary of transportation? I said I wasn't sure. I would have to ask Henry Kissinger how it felt to be a Jewish secretary of state, or Carla Hills how it felt to be the first woman secretary of housing and urban development. But I said I thought it was challenging and rewarding to be the fourth U.S. secretary of transportation. Dan Rather, anchor for the CBS Evening News, announced one evening that "the first black Secretary of Transportation, Bill Coleman, has ordered the installation of air bags in a half million automobiles." I wrote him a letter and asked him of what possible relevance was my race in the announcement of that decision? I had not ordered air bags installed only in black automobiles. I never got an answer to my letter.[12]

In 1949 when I was denied interviews at many Wall Street, Boston, Washington, and Philadelphia law firms, I considered myself only a Negro lawyer. Today, sixty years later, I consider myself an American lawyer, proud of my special heritage and the contributions of all races and ethnicities to enriching the American mainstream.[13]

With the election of President Barack Obama, this would be an appropriate time for all of us simply to consider ourselves "Americans."[14] According to demographic projections, by 2050 whites will be just another minority.[15] Increasingly the American melting pot embraces mixed races and mixed ethnicities, making racial and ethnic attribution a thankless task.[16] In his memoir, True Compass, Edward M. Kennedy writes of his father's frustration that he "would always be an 'Irish Catholic' first. When a newspaper referred to him as an Irishman, he blurted out, 'I was born here. My parents were born here. What the hell do I have to do to be called an American?'"[17] The challenge of this century is to fully recognize the contributions and talents of all Americans.

An important part of that challenge is moving into the American mainstream the 12.7 million Americans who have emigrated from or whose parents have come from Mexico. Mexico will continue to grow as an important economic and cultural power on the world stage. We need to be a better neighbor and a better host to the Americans who have legally emigrated from Mexico, helping them bring their talents and traditions into the American mainstream as they become an integral part of our culture and way of life.

In a multiracial society, we will need to broaden our education system to recognize the diverse contributions of people of many backgrounds and races, especially non-European, which have enriched our culture and strengthened our economy. School integration was an important—and still incomplete—beginning. The schools themselves must offer a diverse student population an appreciation for the multiple roots of American society, the historical contributions of people of all colors, and the responsibility of each citizen to be an active, informed, and constructive participant in democratic self-government and an increasingly competitive global economy.

FORTY-ONE

Opportunities for Public Service

There is a debt of service due from every man to his country, proportioned to the bounties which nature and fortune have measured to him.

—Thomas Jefferson

ONE BLUSTERY DAY IN EARLY 1977 I got a call from Cy Vance, then secretary of state in President Carter's administration. Cy told me that President Carter was very concerned about deteriorating relations with Latin America. While President Kennedy had made a noble effort to improve relations through the Alliance for Progress initiative, in recent years elected officials had blithely ignored our neighbors to the south. This was fast reaching a boiling point, with virulent attacks on the United States and angry protest mobs, no doubt provoked by young Latino revolutionaries. The central rallying point at the time was U.S. ownership of the Panama Canal. The president appointed two experienced ambassadors, Ellsworth Bunker and Sol Linowitz, to negotiate transfer of the canal to Panama. This reversed a Carter campaign promise. It drew fire from conservatives, especially Senators Helms and Thurmond and Governor Reagan: the canal was ours, we built it, we paid for it, and we should keep it, they argued.

Secretary Vance was forming a committee bringing together diverse points of view that would review the treaty being negotiated with Panama. He wanted to ensure long-term U.S. interests and help gain the broad domestic support necessary to ensure ratification, which required a two-thirds vote of the Senate. I accepted Vance's invitation to serve on the committee. We worked with the State Department in reviewing provisions for the canal's transfer over a transitional period.

Resolution of this issue was essential if the United States were to reverse disintegrating relations with Latin America. When we were satisfied that the U.S. delegation had negotiated a responsible treaty, balancing the protection of U.S. national security interests with improved hemispheric relationships, we recommended that President Carter sign it.[1] With our support, the Senate ratified the treaty on April 18, 1978, by one vote more than the required two-thirds (68 to 32). Governor Reagan invoked the Panama Canal "give-away" as a wedge issue in the next presidential election. It may well have contributed to President Carter's defeat after one term. President Carter's courageous stance was one of his finer moments. Transfer of the canal proved to be in the best interest of the United Staes. In reversing his campaign position, the president was well advised by Secretary Vance, his deputy Warren Christopher, and former ambassador to the Organization of American States, Sol Linowitz.

JUSTICE O'CONNOR

In 1981 I was appointed a member of the Standing Committee on the Federal Judiciary of the American Bar Association by its then president, Bernard G. Segal, a great "Philadelphia lawyer."[2] I have already described the exceptionally well qualified rating that we gave Robert Bork on his nomination to the District of Columbia Circuit Court. A special opportunity came to us in 1981 when, owing to the retirement of Justice Stewart, President Reagan sent up to the Senate Sandra Day O'Connor as the first woman to be nominated as a justice of the Supreme Court. At that time she was a state circuit judge in Arizona. I could empathize with O'Connor's legal career. In 1952 she and Chief Justice Rehnquist had finished as the top two in their class at Stanford Law School and served together as members of the *Stanford Law Journal*. Rehnquist immediately became an associate at a premier law firm in Phoenix, but when O'Connor was interviewed at several West Coast law firms, she was offered only the position of secretary to an attorney. She decided instead to become active in state politics and ended up serving as Speaker of the Arizona House of Representatives. She also served briefly as a state circuit court judge.

The O'Connor nomination presented a dilemma for the American Bar Association's judiciary committee. To achieve the highest ranking of exceptionally well qualified, a nominee should have had substantial experience as a practicing lawyer. Given O'Connor's diversion into state politics, this was a difficult hurdle. The committee was torn. I suggested that the committee adopt the statement that it was expected that she would prove herself exceptionally well qualified. Judge O'Connor was easily confirmed by the Senate and exceeded the committee's expectations. She became one of the nation's most respected and admired jurists.[3] Given the equally divided Court during the Clinton and Bush years, some advocates can perhaps be forgiven for focusing their arguments almost exclusively on Justice O'Connor, who in close cases would often be the decisive vote. During her twenty-four-year tenure, I was always impressed by her probing, practical parsing of the issues and factual predicates of the case during oral argument. She applied commonsense, calm, and balanced judgment to the whirligig of ideological abstractions. Her career outside the judiciary brought depth and realism to her analysis. We would do well to bear in mind the value of such experience in selecting future justices. Justice O'Connor and her husband, John, a leading tax lawyer, became good friends of Lovida and me and not infrequent dinner guests at our home in McLean. In 2007 the retired justice, as chancellor of the College of William and Mary in Williamsburg, Virginia, conferred on me an honorary Doctor of Laws degree.

As Lovida and I had remained in the Washington area for four years after I left the Department of Transportation, we regretfully were not likely to return to Philadelphia. Lovida found an excellent location in McLean and we purchased a one-acre plot and built a beautiful house.

As we settled into our new home, we enjoyed giving parties for a cross-section of the Washington community. These intergenerational get-togethers were our way of trying to recreate the spirit of the House of Truth from my clerkship days, where Supreme Court justices, cabinet officers, and senators of all philosophies and persuasions would mix with the younger generation in a spirit of collegiality.

SOUTH AFRICA

In 1986 I got another call from a secretary of state. This time it was during the Reagan administration. George Shultz invited me to serve on an advisory committee on South Africa. The United States had been pursuing a policy of constructive engagement with the government of South Africa, led by P. W. Botha of the Afrikaner National Party. Through government channels, the United States sought to induce reforms in the abominable system of apartheid—enforced racial separation. Under the apartheid laws, adopted in 1948, the 74 percent black African majority was forced to live in segregated townships confined to 13 percent of the least desirable land, required to obtain work permits to travel to cities, overwhelmingly disenfranchised, and subjected to segregated facilities, brutal harassment, and racial discrimination. The law categorized the population into four groups with varied rights and restrictions and created a massive bureaucracy to enforce the classifications: Whites, Indians, Coloureds (mixed race), and Blacks.

"Constructive engagement" was not working. The situation was deteriorating. Sparked by the Soweto protests in 1976, black resistance began to build. Government repression intensified. Nelson Mandela and other leaders of the African National Congress were imprisoned. As the Shultz advisory committee was formed and began its deliberations, the Botha government adopted a hard-line siege mentality. Botha cracked down on the political opposition, ignored the legislature in asserting executive authority, forced the relocation of blacks to designated "homelands," drastically censored the media, and restricted intellectual activity in black schools. Between September 1984 and the date we issued our report, more than two thousand people were killed. In June 1986 a nationwide state of emergency was declared.

The Reagan administration recognized that its policies were not effective. Mineral-rich South Africa was the dominant military and economic power in sub-Saharan Africa. Two hundred and forty-one U.S. companies did business there, and they could play a constructive role in creating jobs and encouraging reforms. The Soviets were actively promoting communism among the black majority in South Africa and the neighboring countries. If the situation were to implode into a race war, the consequences for U.S. domestic pluralism and politics were significant. President Reagan issued Executive Order 12,532 calling for the creation of this advisory committee to provide recommendations on measures to encourage peaceful change in South Africa.

Frank Cary, the former chair of IBM, and I agreed to serve as co-chairs. The committee members represented the perspectives of American business, the civil rights community, unions, religious organizations, foreign policy experts, and Congress.[4] To its credit, the Reagan administration wanted a diversity of views and out-of-the-box thinking. Otherwise, how could it have appointed Vernon Jordan, Franklin Thomas, and the Reverend Leon H. Sullivan to the committee? I enlisted the help of a senior associate of my law firm, Debra A. Valentine, who accompanied the committee on an investigative trip to South Africa.

To come face to face with the regime of apartheid was a brutal experience. We interviewed black Africans who had been subjected to the most degrading physical and mental abuse, denied basic human rights, and shunted into shanty township ghettos. Having not grown up in the Jim Crow South, I had only read about the inhumane treatment that scarred our own nation's history. Here I was confronted with the reality. It was as though the words of the *Dred Scott* decision had flown off the pages of the Supreme Court reporter, like an evil genie emerging from a bottle—blacks are "so far inferior that they [have] no rights which the white man [is] bound to respect."

A purported democracy that had benefited from technology, trade, and investment from Western nations, South Africa denied any meaningful participation in government to the overwhelming majority of its inhabitants. This vividly reinforced the value of our work back home to enact and enforce the Voting Rights Act. It was a chilling reminder of how only very recently in our own history were Americans of color and women able to participate fully in our democracy and serve as elected representatives. On our trip, we could not meet with Nelson Mandela, who was still in prison on Robben Island. We did get to know and appreciate the struggles of Bishop Tutu, who in subsequent years would visit me on trips to the United States. In August 2009 President Obama awarded him the Presidential Medal of Freedom.

The committee delivered its report, "A U.S. Policy toward South Africa," to Secretary Shultz in January 1987. The report included a detailed history and accounting of the practice of apartheid in South Africa, the evolution of U.S. policy, and the status of various so-called reforms. We made many recommendations to the U.S. and South African governments and the private sector. We urged the South African government immediately to release Nelson Mandela and other political leaders of the resistance movement who had been imprisoned for their political beliefs without trial. We urged South Africa to remove the ban on political organizations and establish the right of all South Africans to form political parties, express political opinions, and participate freely in the political process. We urged the government to terminate the state of emergency and release the detainees held thereunder.

Because we were concerned about the potential for a racial war, we recommended that the foremost priority of U.S. policy should be to facilitate good-faith negotiations between the South African government and representatives of the black majority. We recommended that the United States work with our major allies to help South Africa shape a nonracial democratic political system. Negotiations must be based on recognizing the black majority's rights for political justice and economic opportunity and the legitimate concerns of the white minority about their future. We concluded that piecemeal reforms had not been successful and that pressure should be applied on the South African government to take comprehensive steps to restore full citizenship to all Africans born or naturalized in South Africa, to repeal the legal structures of apartheid, and to create a legal system that ensured due process and fair trials for all citizens.

We urged the U.S. government to build working relationships with the black majority and expand contacts with opposition organizations. We called on President Reagan to initiate negotiations to implement the Comprehensive Anti-Apartheid Act of 1986, recently enacted by Congress, working with our allies to develop a multilateral program of tough sanctions that would pressure the South African government to negotiate immediately and seriously. We made a host of recommendations to U.S. educational, religious, and legal organizations to initiate programs with the black population to prepare them for the postapartheid period, which, in my view, could not come too soon. We proposed U.S. assistance in developing small black-owned businesses. We urged U.S. companies in South Africa to adhere to the fair labor practice standards commonly referred to as the Sullivan Principles that were developed by my fellow committee member Leon Sullivan and adopted by Congress in the Anti-Apartheid Act. We urged U.S. companies that were divesting to make every effort to enable black employees and investors to participate in the purchase of their businesses. I thought that U.S. companies in South Africa were—and continue to be—a highly constructive force in improving the lives of the black majority by providing training, housing, and good jobs.

I believe that the committee's report contributed to important changes in the attitude and policy of Western nations toward South Africa and ultimately led in some small way to Nelson Mandela's release from prison on February 11, 1990. Having served twenty-seven years on Robben Island, in 1994 he became the first president of South Africa to be elected in a fully representative multiracial democracy. He showed no bitterness as he sought to heal the wounds of apartheid, respect and encourage the continued contributions of the white minority to South Africa's economic development, and create a society in which people of all races would bring their skills and talent to advance the greater good. Mandela has to rank alongside Gandhi, Lincoln, and Simon Bolivar as one of the greatest political leaders the world has ever known.

While I was pleased with the report's recommendations and commonsense judgment, I felt it did not adequately portray the unconscionable treatment of black Africans by the dominant white minority. I expressed my true indignation at the inhumanity and cruelty that I had learned about on my South African trip in additional comments at the end of the committee report.[5]

One benefit of being a partner in a major law firm is that I was able to draw on the support of younger, conscientious, hardworking associates and partners whose handling of client matters made it easier for me to devote time to public service opportunities and whose support, research, and advice on public service opportunities enabled me to contribute substantively in areas where I had no particular expertise or experience. For example, I served on a commission to improve science education in the nation's public secondary schools, a presidential advisory committee on federalism, and the NASA advisory council task force on the effective use of the shuttle.

Working on these various advisory projects over the years, I encountered many familiar faces, superb human beings. Griffin Bell, Lloyd Cutler, Vernon Jordan, Cy Vance, Bill Webster, Carla Hills, Franklin Thomas, and others were frequently recycled for public service duty on myriad issues. As our resumes lengthened, we appeared all the more qualified. Undoubtedly, because we had worked together so much and had experience in the potential and pitfalls of government advisory work, we could hit the ground running. In a way, it is unfortunate that elected and appointed leaders too often resort to the same small talent pool for advice. So many of the faces I repeatedly encountered were products of the same schools, churches, and political associations. At least the talent pool was more diverse than it had been in the earlier days of my career. There is an enormous reservoir of untapped talent in our universities, corporations, and nonprofit institutions that is overlooked by political leaders, who too often overvalue familiarity, personal loyalty, and ideological compatibility.

THE GORE COMMISSION

At 8:31 p.m. on July 17, 1996, TWA flight 800, a Boeing 747-131 with 230 people on board on a scheduled flight from JFK to Rome through Paris, exploded in midair and crashed into the Atlantic Ocean near East Moriches, New York. There were no survivors. Some eyewitnesses thought they saw an external missile strike the aircraft, possibly, some said, from a U.S. Navy vessel or a terrorist. Others speculated that there might have been a bomb on board, which caused the huge fiery explosion. Because of the fear of possible terrorism, parallel investigations were initiated by the FBI and the National Transportation Safety Board. There was some tension between the two. Amid the swirling speculation, President Clinton announced the creation of the White House Commission on Aviation Safety and Security under the chairmanship of Vice President Gore, often referred to as the Gore Commission. I was asked to join the commission along with CIA chief John M. Deutch, FBI director Louis J. Freeh, National Transportation Safety Board chair Jim Hall, transportation secretary Federico Pena, Air Force retired general John M. Loh, and safety advocate Victoria Cummock, whose husband had been killed in the Lockerbie crash of Pan Am flight 103 eight years earlier.

As a Pan Am board member at the time of Lockerbie, I was fully aware of the devastating effect of a terrorist attack on an airline. All major aviation accidents are tragedies that generate huge media attention. The fear of terrorism has extraordinary negative consequences for U.S. flag carriers, which are presumed to be targets. While those of us on the Pan Am board struggled for many years to adjust to the deregulated, competitive aviation environment, I personally believe that it was Lockerbie that sealed Pan Am's eventual demise. In the case of TWA flight 800, there was the additional speculation about a cover-up of a U.S. missile gone awry, speculation irresponsibly promoted by former Kennedy press secretary Pierre Salinger.

The Gore Commission got off to a shaky start. The members were extremely busy with challenging full-time government and private sector responsibilities. Most of the work was undertaken by staff before Vice President Gore actually called a meeting. We were all geared up to deal with a major terrorist event. As the accident investigation unfolded, the National Transportation Safety Board concluded that the crash was caused by an explosion of the center wing fuel tank. The flammable fuel and air mixture in the tank was ignited by a short circuit in the electrical wiring of the fuel quantity indication system.

The commission's final report, released on February 12, 1997, contained more than twenty recommendations. Most of the recommendations dealt with enhanced aviation security procedures, many of which had been identified after the Lockerbie disaster but never implemented.[6] Because the federal agencies had concluded that the crash of TWA flight 800 was not caused by a terrorist act, the momentum for implementing the commission's recommendations was stalled. Although President Clinton could be faulted for establishing the commission precipitously before there was a better understanding of the cause of the accident, the recommendations were helpful in raising public awareness of the security threat to our nation and preparing the public for the inconvenience that eventually would come as we recognized the necessity of a comprehensive aviation security program.

CLOSING PENNSYLVANIA AVENUE

Two advisory projects I undertook during the Clinton administration are worthy of some additional comment. At 1:49 a.m. on September 12, 1994, a Cessna 150L airplane crashed onto the south lawn of the White House, killing the pilot and coming to a halt against the south wall of the executive mansion. President Clinton and his family were away at that time and were never in any danger. The next month a lone individual, Francisco Martin Duran, fired twenty-nine rounds from a semiautomatic assault rifle into the north side of the White House. Three nearby citizens subdued him, and the Secret Service took him into custody.

Because of these and other incidents, I received a call from the undersecretary of the treasury for enforcement, Ronald K. Noble, asking me to participate in a White House security review of these incidents.[7] We were asked to critique the response of the Secret Service and to make recommendations on the adequacy of procedures used to protect the president and First Family within the White House complex. We retained a number of expert consultants to advise us and issued a classified report of more than five hundred pages.[8]

Many of our recommendations were never released to the public, and others were not controversial, but there was one recommendation that caused a stir. We recommended that Pennsylvania Avenue in front of the White House be closed to traffic. We consulted with several architects and historians who endorsed the idea of converting the roadway into a pedestrian plaza.

I was one of the last members of the committee to be convinced of the need to close the avenue. I was concerned about the substantial inconvenience to vehicular movement that this would create in an already congested city. The public enjoyed driving along Pennsylvania Avenue to view the White House grounds lit up at night. I was concerned about creating what might be perceived as a barrier between the president and the people. Having reviewed all the classified information and been briefed thoroughly by the experts, I came to the chilling conclusion that there was no alternative that would amply protect the presidential family during an age of terrorist attacks. Had the passengers on United Airlines flight 93 on September 11 not frustrated the hijackers' ability to carry out their operations according to plan, it is possible that even the recommendations of our committee would not have been sufficient. Having witnessed what has happened in places like Lebanon, Iraq, Kenya, and Tanzania, when heavy vehicles filled with explosives are rammed into buildings, I believe we made the right decision. Although progress has been made in beautifying the closed Pennsylvania Avenue segment, I believe more can be done to create the type of pedestrian plaza that the committee members envisioned.

ADVISING THE DEPARTMENT OF DEFENSE

My work on the TWA flight 800 crash and the White House security review preceded September 11, 2001, but deeply involved me in issues of enhanced security against the threat of terrorism. After September 11, Secretary Rumsfeld asked me to participate on a part-time basis in three separate matters: advising the secretary on establishing military commissions to try the "enemy combatants" at Guantanamo Bay who were alleged to have been involved in terrorist acts against the United States; ensuring that advanced information-gathering technologies to identify terrorists before they act were applied consistent with U.S. law and American privacy values; and serving on a military commissions appellate review panel.

The Defense Department had developed the Terrorism Information Awareness Program to mine data on the activities of potential terrorists from multiple sources of information. The U.S. government and other entities, including foreign and U.S. airlines, banks, and other companies, receive a wealth of personal information and data from individuals. To develop appropriate safeguards, the secretary of defense appointed the Technology and Privacy Advisory Committee, of which I was a member.[9] Our report to the secretary was delivered and relased on March 1, 2004.[10]

While I agreed with the report in general, including its description of potential cyber-security threats to the nation, I dissented on one point. The committee recommended that data submitted to public and private entities that could be mined through the Terrorism Information Awareness Program should not be turned over to the U.S. intelligence agencies unless authorized by the Foreign Intelligence Surveillance Court.[11] Most of these data were voluntarily provided without any restriction on their transfer. I was not aware of any Supreme Court decision holding that such information cannot be transferred to a federal agency without the court's permission.[12] I frankly found quite impractical the committee's recommendation that the government be forced to go to a court for approval to transfer information from one agency to another when that information had been willingly given without restriction. Although I undoubtedly irritated my more liberal colleagues on the eight-person task force, I did not see the merit in jumping ahead of the Supreme Court and Congress by creating additional road blocks on the gathering of intelligence information to protect the American people.

Finding the right balance between protecting individual liberty and protecting national security is a constant challenge. It is critical that we not tip the scales too far in either direction if we are to preserve a nation in which liberty is possible. I thought Justice Jackson got it right in *Terminiello* v. *Chicago* when he said, "The choice is not between order and liberty, it is between liberty with order and anarchy without either. There is a danger that if [this] Court does not temper its doctrinaire logic with a little practical wisdom, it will convert the constitutional Bill of Rights into a suicide pact."[13]

When in 1945 I turned down a promotion to major and an invitation to join the U.S. Army Air Corps Reserve, I thought my military career was over. Secretary Rumsfeld, however, drafted me back into military service. He asked me to serve as one of four attorneys on the Court of Military Commission Review to hear appeals from the convictions of so-called enemy combatants at Guantanamo. The U.S. Court of Appeals for the District of Columbia Circuit had exclusive jurisdiction over final decisions by military commissions, and that court's decisions could be appealed by certiorari to the Supreme Court. On September 21, 2006, in advance of my appointment, I was sworn in as a major general of the U.S. Army under a statute that permits the president to grant commissions of general rank for up to three years without congressional confirmation.[14] Because the entire military commission procedure was tied up in the federal courts for much of my tenure, the only meeting of the military review commission I attended was called to adopt rules and procedures to handle appeals from convictions by the military commissions. I found these delays enormously frustrating, especially because there was so much criticism about the retention of enemy combatants at Guantanamo without trial. But the wheels of justice grind slowly. It would have been foolish to proceed with military trials without a green light from Congress and the Supreme Court. Shortly after I received my two stars as a major general, retired four-star general Colin Powell wrote me: "Dear Bill: Congratulations on your appointment as Major General. If you lose some weight, you can wear my uniform."

During my days as a legal counsel to the Warren Commission, I had witnessed firsthand the complexities involved in balancing the work of intelligence operatives in protecting national security and the values of individual privacy and due process of law. In the post-9/11 period, emotions have run high as some have argued we have tipped the scale too far in one direction or another. Often these opinions are rendered with twenty-twenty hindsight after a quiet period of relative safety and security. The greatest criticism often comes from those unburdened with the responsibility for the consequences of inaction. While this is not the time or place to engage in this debate, I do believe, as a participant and witness to some of the decisionmaking process, that people in good faith struggled long and hard to get the balance right as circumstances unfolded. Those in positions of responsibility with access to intelligence information acted with respect for the law and the judicial process. They sought the advice of outside experts, and they patiently waited as litigation wound its way up to the Supreme Court. There were strong disagreements as lawyers struggled to fine-tune the balance by applying detached analysis and reverence for the Constitution's commands to protect both the nation and the rights of its citizens. Of course, the balance must constantly be recalibrated as circumstances change.

The officeholders were patriotic Americans seeking to apply the law to new and unprecedented threats to the national security. While I can understand the strong disagreements some have had with the decisions made, I am frankly appalled by the vitriolic (and hypocritical) criticism of some legislators and academics who seemed to forget that we are all Americans committed to securing our freedoms and seeking to plot the right course through turbulent seas.

History will judge whether the right decisions were made at the time they were made. Sometimes the long view of history brings a surprising perspective. Lest we all be prematurely judgmental, I am reminded of the opposition to Governor Warren's nomination as chief justice because of his actions in support the relocation of Japanese Americans during World War II. Had Warren been denied the nomination, I shudder to think how much worse off we would be as a nation. And as Justice Frankfurter used to tease me, it was Chief Justice Taney who stood up for constitutional rights when Abraham Lincoln suspended habeas corpus. Judged by their overall record, who now is most revered by history—the history that casts such a long shadow?

Sometimes we need to just turn off the TV chatter, set down the *New York Times,* and take a very deep breath.

After reading the intelligence reports, I had to take a deep breath and retreat to my comfortable home in Virginia, take off my shoes, and settle deeply into my leather chair with a gin and tonic and the latest book by David McCullough or David Stewart. Lovida and I greatly enjoyed our new home in McLean and especially frequent visits from our three grown children (and now five grandchildren). If parents can take credit for the success of their children, the credit goes to Lovida. That does not prevent me from joining her in the pride we feel about the careers of each of our children.

William T. III (Billy) graduated from Williams College in 1970 and Yale Law School in 1973, where he roomed his first year with Bill Clinton (the stories he can tell!). Following a clerkship with Judge Gignoux, of the U.S. District Court for Maine, he practiced law in Savannah, Georgia, and a few years later at Pepper, Hamilton, and Sheetz in Philadelphia and Detroit. In 1983 he became a partner in the same Pepper firm that had refused me an interview in 1949. President Clinton appointed him general counsel of the Army in 1994. He has one step-child by his first wife and two adorable sons with his present wife. His wife and children keep him young, and he is busy practicing law at Berger and Montague in Philadelphia.

Our daughter, Lovida, started college at Smith, took a year off in Europe, and finished her degree at Radcliffe College (which has since been absorbed into Harvard University) in 1972. She also studied at the Sorbonne in Paris. Apparently more intent on following her older brother than her father, she graduated from Yale Law School in 1975. She clerked for Wilfred Feinberg, judge of the U.S. Court of Appeals for the Second Circuit. She has worked for several great law firms, Williams and Connolly, White and Case, and Sutherland, Asbill, and Brennan, where she became a partner, specializing in white-collar criminal defense work. Like her father, she has served in government as a special assistant to U.S. attorney general Benjamin Civiletti and as a special assistant U.S. attorney.

Our youngest, Hardin, following in his mother's footsteps, is pursuing a career in education. In youth the most rebellious of our children, he has charted a steady path toward great success in adulthood. He and his wife, Gail, were married in a Quaker ceremony near Philadelphia. They have two college-age sons. Hardin graduated from Williams College and earned a master's degree in counseling at the University of Vermont and a doctorate from Stanford University. He taught counseling at Shanghai Teachers University in China for a year and religion for two years at Westtown, a Quaker school near Philadelphia. He later became a professor of counseling psychology and associate dean of the School of Education at the University of Wisconsin in Madison. In 2008 he was appointed dean and professor at Boston University's School of Education, his mother's alma mater. Hardin has co-written three books on school counseling and many articles in professional journals.

In almost sixty-five years of marriage, Lovida has been the one person who has always told me exactly what I needed to hear. She has been—and remains—my staunchest critic and defender. Wooing her away from her many suitors was by far my largest success and accomplishment.

FORTY-TWO

Reflecting on Republicans and Race

I recognize the Republican Party as the sheet anchor of the colored man's political hopes and the ark of his safety.

—FREDERICK DOUGLASS

I HAVE BEEN A REGISTERED Republican for sixty-five years, and my father and his father before him were Republicans. Lovida's father was a Republican in the best southern tradition. The Coleman and Hardin roots are firmly planted in the party of Lincoln. Indeed, I was born less than sixty years after Lincoln was elected president. So I tend to take a long view of the Republican Party.

Being a registered Republican doesn't mean I have to vote the straight party line. As a moderate on many issues, I am free to vote for the candidate who has the most integrity, intellect, and innovative skill to represent me effectively. Indeed, I campaigned and voted for Lyndon Johnson and Richardson Dilworth.

Through the years, I have had many mentors, advisers, colleagues, and friends in both political parties who have opened doors and taught me wisely. Some of the Democrats included President Johnson, Justice Frankfurter, Judge Goodrich, Mayor Dilworth, Louis Weiss, Louis Pollak, and Vernon Jordan. A few of the Republicans were President Eisenhower, Chief Justice Warren, President Ford, Nelson Rockefeller, David Rockefeller, Senator Hugh Scott, Elliot Richardson and his uncle Henry Shattuck, Governor Scranton, and Senator Baker—and one who has switched back and forth, Senator Specter.

In my work with elected leaders through the years, I have enjoyed constructive professional and personal relationships with presidents, senators, members of Congress, governors, and party leaders from both sides of the aisle. The vast majority of my civil rights compatriots have been Democrats. Thurgood Marshall, a registered independent, knew I was a Republican and encouraged me to remain a Republican. He recognized that it was important to have people of color in both political parties. If all people of color registered as Democrats, they soon would be taken for granted by the Democratic Party. This has too often been the case. According to recent exit polls, the overwhelming majority of Americans of color feel more at home in the Democratic Party. This has not always been the case. I believe the Republican Party would greatly benefit by going back to our roots and building on a record of historical achievement. On the issue of race, for example, we can learn a lot from history. To bring more balance and perspective to the political debate, I would like to paint a different historical picture than most Americans of color are accustomed to viewing. Consider this more a brief than a balanced judicial opinion; there are plenty of briefs on the other side of this issue.

The roots of the Democratic Party lie with Thomas Jefferson, whose decentralized, agrarian view of the nation's destiny was all too compatible with the perpetuation of slavery.[1] Some years later the first real Democratic president, Andrew Jackson, appointed Roger Taney, also a Democrat, as chief justice. He gave us the erroneous *Dred Scott* decision. The two dissenters in the *Dred Scott* decision were Justices Benjamin Curtis and John McLean, one a Republican before he was appointed and the other a Republican after his appointment.

It was Abraham Lincoln, the first Republican president, however imperfect his views on race, who preserved the Union and issued the Emancipation Proclamation in November 1862. His Republican attorney general issued an opinion rejecting the language of *Dred Scott* and declaring Negroes to be American citizens. In the Gettysburg Address, Lincoln invoked the phrase "All men are created equal" from the Declaration of Independence, to proclaim the cause for which the Union was fighting in the Civil War.[2]

With the death of Chief Justice Taney in 1864, Lincoln appointed his secretary of the treasury and former rival, Salmon P. Chase, a Republican, as chief justice. Chase was a strong advocate of civil rights and a staunch defender of voting rights for Negroes. He appointed the first attorney of color, John Rock, to argue cases before the Supreme Court.

After Lincoln's assassination, the Republicans in Congress pursued with great vigor the Thirteenth, Fourteenth, and Fifteenth Amendments to the Constitution, the Civil Rights Acts, and the Reconstruction Acts, which brought about radical, albeit short-term, changes in the South. With the ascendancy to the presidency of Vice President Andrew Johnson, a Democrat from Tennessee, the momentum toward racial equality slowed and then reversed.[3]

As southern Democrats gained seniority in the congressional committee structure, a long legislative drought began. As I recount in chapter 15, the Supreme Court, consisting of appointees by both Republican and Democratic presidents, significantly undermined the Thirteenth, Fourteenth, and Fifteenth Amendments, ignoring their underlying purpose and nullifying important post–Civil War civil rights legislation. The one eloquent dissenter (a true advocate of racial equality) was John Marshall Harlan, a Republican appointed by a Republican president.

In 1938 Charles Houston had his first Supreme Court victory, recounted in chapter 20, chipping away at the pernicious separate-but-equal doctrine of *Plessy* v. *Ferguson*. The opinion in *Missouri ex rel. Gaines* v. *Canada* was written by Chief Justice Charles Evans Hughes, a Republican appointed initially by President Theodore Roosevelt, a Republican, and reappointed as chief justice by President Hoover, a Republican.

In the executive branch, most U.S. presidents of both parties from Andrew Johnson to Franklin Roosevelt condoned benign neglect, at best, and at worst moved the clock back substantially.[4] Woodrow Wilson, a Democrat, resegregated Washington, D.C.

With the election of President Franklin Roosevelt, the issue of race became more complicated. In acting boldly to address the Great Depression, Roosevelt initiated programs that may have marginally improved the lives of people of color and attracted Negroes to the Democratic Party. While his housing policies improved the living conditions for the poor and racial minorities, they also created segregated vertical urban ghettos that have persisted to this day. When Thurgood Marshall and William H. Hastie sought the help of Roosevelt's Justice Department in support of *Smith* v. *Alwright*, which challenged the exclusion of blacks from voting in southern Democratic primaries, they were turned down on the ground that the Roosevelt administration could not afford to irritate southern Democratic Party chairs whose support was needed to pass important New Deal legislation.[5] Moreover, despite Eleanor Roosevelt's constant nagging (she was a true champion of racial equality), Franklin Roosevelt failed to integrate the armed forces during World War II.

Eleanor Roosevelt created opportunities for soldiers of color to demonstrate their patriotism and courage, and President Truman ordered the armed forces to integrate. It was President Eisenhower, however, who fully implemented the order. On civil rights, Truman was more in sync with Eleanor than Franklin. He appointed a prestigious White House Civil Rights Committee and on the strength of the recommendations of its report, *To Secure These Rights*, called on Congress to make lynching a federal offense, prohibit the poll tax, end segregation in interstate transportation, permanently enact the Fair Employment Practices Commission, and establish a civil rights commission. By executive order, Truman also prohibited racial discrimination in federal employment. Truman's attorney general, Tom Clark, came in on the side of the Legal Defense Fund in *Shelley* v. *Kraemer,* urging the Supreme Court to bar judicial enforcement of racially restrictive covenants. The Court did so in an opinion by Truman appointee Chief Justice Vinson. Ironically, the Truman administration continued segregation policies in federal housing and the administering of the G.I. Bill of Rights, which accelerated the trend toward racially isolated urban neighborhoods.

All of Truman's appointments to the Supreme Court joined the unanimous opinion in *Brown*.[6] And Truman appointed a brilliant federal judge of color—the first such appointment in history, William H. Hastie—to the Third Circuit Court of Appeals. Truman's courage on race issues caused the Dixiecrats to leave the Democratic Party and nominate South Carolina governor Strom Thurmond. Miraculously in the 1948 election, Truman beat Republican Tom Dewey and Dixiecrat Thurmond anyway.

In my life experience, the tipping point in terms of government policy on race relations came in a Republican administration with the election of President Eisenhower and his appointment of former California Republican governor Earl Warren as chief justice. Some historians have questioned President Eisenhower's support for school desegregation. Even Chief Justice Warren, in his autobiography written eight years after President Eisenhower's death and published two years after his own death, stated that "I have always believed that President Eisenhower resented our decision in *Brown* v. *Board of Education* and its progeny." I believe that Eisenhower's disappointment in the Warren Court related to its civil liberties decisions, which he thought undermined national security. In the heat of the times, I know Thurgood Marshall also was skeptical of Eisenhower's commitment to the *Brown* decision.

I believe, however, that Eisenhower's record speaks for itself. President Eisenhower personally read, edited, and approved Solicitor General Lee Rankin's legal briefs in *Brown* v. *Board of Education* urging that public school segregation be held unconstitutional and that *Plessy* v. *Ferguson* be overruled. After the first decision in *Brown* v. *Board of Education,* without waiting for the reargument on remedy, he ordered the immediate desegregation of the public schools in Washington, D.C. In the Little Rock school case, President Eisenhower acted forcefully to ensure that the Little Rock Nine could attend Central High School. He ordered the 101st Airborne Division to move from Memphis to Little Rock to enforce the Supreme Court's order, and he federalized the Arkansas National Guard, removing it from the control of Governor Faubus, who had used the Guard to prevent desegregation of the high school.

As supreme Allied commander, Eisenhower developed great respect for the heroism of troops of color in holding back the Germans at the Battle of the Bulge and in the success of the Tuskegee Airmen. He was a strong advocate of enabling soldiers of color to volunteer for combat. As president, he appointed the first presidential assistant of color on the White House staff, Frederick Morrow. He also appointed Ernest J. Wilkins, as the first under secretary of labor. Wilkens attended many cabinet meetings as the first known cabinet participant of color in the nation's history. President Eisenhower ordered the desegregation of all federal facilities. He approved the U.S. government's position in the *Thompson* case, which outlawed racial segregation in Washington's private restaurants, hotels, and theaters, and he pressured the city's theater owners to end racial segregation in movie houses.

When the sit-in movement began in 1958, President Eisenhower persuaded many national chains to desegregate lunch counters and other facilities in the South. He also actively supported two civil rights bills: the Civil Rights Act of 1957, the first such act since Reconstruction eighty-one years earlier, eliminating racial segregation in most state facilities; and the Civil Rights Act of 1960, protecting the voting rights of Americans of color, which passed with the able support of Lyndon Johnson, majority leader of the Senate. There were many more Republican than Democratic votes in support of these two civil rights bills, which were strongly opposed by the conservative southern Democrats.

In my experience with President Eisenhower on the Branch Rickey Committee and in visits to his Gettysburg farm after his presidency, I found him to be a forceful advocate for opening up opportunities for people of color in the military and civil service. In summarizing Eisenhower's record, Adam Clayton Powell, the charismatic Harlem member of Congress, said succinctly, "The Honorable Dwight D. Eisenhower has done more to eliminate discrimination and to restore the Negro to the status of first-class citizenship than any President since Abraham Lincoln."[7]

On race issues, President Kennedy's speeches were lofty and inspirational, but his term of office was tragically cut short. He supported civil rights legislation but agreed to compromises that diluted federal enforcement power, arguing that weakening the legislation was necessary to get it through Congress. Even then he failed to get the legislation passed while in office. His attorney general, Robert Kennedy, was a strong supporter of civil rights, although as a political adviser, he also was cautious about confronting southern Democrats. He initially criticized Eisenhower for sending troops to Little Rock, but ultimately realized that enforcing the law would require federalizing the National Guard on certain occasions.[8] Senator Edward Kennedy was an unwavering advocate for civil rights, working hard to pass civil rights legislation and for the appointment of progressive federal judges. As chair of the Legal Defense Fund board, I knew we could always count on his leadership and legislative prowess, persistence, and mastery of detail. Although a leading Senate liberal, Kennedy was a master at reaching across the aisle to get results, with Senator Hatch on children's health, with President George W. Bush on education, and with Senator Dole on voting rights. He fought hard to renew and strengthen the 1965 Voting Rights Act. He was especially proud of his success in enacting the Americans with Disabilities Act because of his respect for his older sister Eunice and her Special Olympics.

I have only praise for the courage and leadership of President Johnson on matters of race. Despite his southern roots, Johnson rose to the occasion.

With his masterful legislative skill he seized the momentum of the nation's post-assassination soulful unity to propel the pending civil rights legislation into law. I sat in meetings with Johnson and listened to his advisers warn him that his stance on civil rights would shift voting patterns in the South from Democrat to Republican, which in fact has come to pass. I heard him reply that "when you're a president you have to do what's right even if it has a temporary adverse effect on your own party." During the Johnson presidency, the Justice Department vigorously enforced the civil rights laws, intervened in the courts on the side of racial justice, and nominated progressive judges. President Johnson appointed Thurgood Marshall as solicitor general and then associate justice of the Supreme Court. He also appointed my LDF colleagues Spottswood Robinson (to the D.C. Circuit), Constance Baker Motley (to the U.S. District Court for the Southern District of New York), and Jack Weinstein (to the U.S. District Court for the Eastern District of New York).

I do have one criticism of the Johnson administration. The well-intended War on Poverty, which undoubtedly improved conditions for many Americans and solidified the support of voters of color for the Democratic Party, created a huge government-dependent constituency. Too often the beneficiaries of some of the Great Society's programs have claimed racial entitlements that in my judgment are neither warranted nor helpful in eliminating the vestiges of discrimination. While some of Johnson's initiatives, such as the Head Start Act of 1981 and the Legal Services program created by the Economic Opportunity Act of 1964, did enormous good, other programs tended to increase dependence on the federal largess, deterring minorities from competing in the economic mainstream.

While I did not have great expectations for the Nixon administration, I was encouraged by President Nixon's strong commitment to creating affirmative opportunities for Americans of color to get a good education and good jobs. Maybe I am unduly influenced by the title of the first progressive federal affirmative action program, the Philadelphia Plan. The Nixon administration worked to increase funding for elementary and secondary schools that served disadvantaged children, seeking to upgrade the quality of education in de facto segregated inner-city school districts. Nixon's judicial appointments were mixed, but he did appoint Legal Defense Fund and NAACP counsel Robert Carter to the District Court for the Southern District of New York. And I am personally grateful that his administration extended the national policy against racial discrimination to tax-exempt private schools and that his appointee, Chief Justice Burger, affirmed that decision in the *Bob Jones* case. The Nixon administration was a paradox. Although I did not think much of Nixon's "Southern Strategy" and appeal to the "Silent Majority," I believe that people of color, like all Americans, breathe cleaner air, drink purer water, work in safer conditions, and have a stronger safety net due to laws passed during his administration.

The Ford administration continued the diversity policies of its predecessor. As a member of the administration, I will let others judge its effectiveness. My efforts to continue to condition federal grants on strong diversity programs are detailed in chapter 32.

President Carter was a strong advocate of human rights, but for a candidate who won office with 98 percent of the black vote in the South, he was surprisingly silent on issues of race. Although never presented with a Supreme Court vacancy, Carter did make a number of diversified appointments to the federal bench. Indeed, President Carter appointed more persons of color and women to the federal bench than all of his predecessors combined. I was also especially delighted with his appointment of Louis Pollak to the federal district court in Philadelphia. He appointed my Harvard Law School classmate Wade McCree as solicitor general with the prospect of elevation to the Supreme Court if a vacancy had occurred.

I never thought President Reagan condoned racial discrimination, and I respected the emphasis he placed on eliminating federal programs that deterred Americans of color from accepting and acting on the basis of personal responsibility. I believe Reagan was color blind—prematurely so in his failure to recognize, as had his predecessors Nixon and Ford, that government action was still necessary to eradicate the vestiges of slavery. In his administration, civil rights enforcement was uneven at best. I have detailed in chapter 37 my views on his switching sides in the *Bob Jones* case and in chapter 39 my views on his nomination of Robert Bork to the Supreme Court.

President George H. W. Bush appointed more judges of color in one term than President Reagan had in two terms—not all of them cheered by the civil rights community. He appointed Clarence Thomas to the Supreme Court after the retirement of Justice Marshall. Because of Thomas's conservative philosophy and his record on the Equal Employment Opportunity Commission, his nomination drew the ire of some liberals. I was approached by both sides to testify for or against the nomination but decided not to testify. Justice Thomas demonstrates that people of color do not adhere to a monolithic ideology, and that is a good thing.

The Clinton administration professed a strong commitment to civil rights, earning Bill Clinton the moniker "the first Black president." During his tenure, civil rights laws were reasonably well enforced, and most judicial appointments were progressive. If President Clinton had come out of the closet and admitted he was a Republican, I would rank him among the best since Teddy Roosevelt. He shrunk the size of the federal government, balanced the budget, promoted free trade, reformed the welfare system, and deregulated the financial markets. (On this last achievement, it appears he went too far. Some of his economic advisers have been drafted into the Obama administration to fix the effects of their deregulatory exuberance.) Some argue that the Clinton administration placed an inordinate emphasis on the rainbow coloration of appointments, both in the executive branch and the judiciary—that quality took a back seat to obtaining the right ethnic composition. This is a trend that worries me. By working to create a legal foundation for all Americans, regardless of race or ethnicity, to enter the expanding mainstream, we did not seek to dilute the importance of meritocracy. To the contrary, we sought to improve the quality of leadership by opening up opportunities for all Americans to succeed based entirely on merit.

President George W. Bush appointed the first secretary of state of color and the first woman of color as secretary of state, the preeminent executive appointment in our constitutional form of government. These were not token appointments for a rainbow composition of the cabinet seating chart. These two appointees were the representatives of the United States to the world at large, and they were superbly qualified. No president has done more to raise the profile of Africa. Humanitarian assistance to the continent tripled during his administration. His first successful initiative, No Child Left Behind, demonstrated a strong commitment to realize the human potential of all children, regardless of race. He was convinced that with good education and proper incentives, the achievement gap would narrow, if not disappear. I always felt that President Bush dealt with all Americans, regardless of color, with equal attention and respect.

For the Obama presidency, the issue of race relations presents a distinct challenge. He is plainly aware that his first duty is to serve all the American people. On the other hand, he cannot neglect issues of importance to the Americans of color who helped elect him. In addressing the nation's economic crisis, he understands that promoting economic growth and job creation will benefit all Americans and proportionately those minorities who have suffered disproportionately from the economic downturn. Progress in the minority communities will depend on creating good paying jobs and improving the nation's education and health-care systems.

Taking the longer view, which at my age is one of the few things I can do more easily than most others, I believe that both political parties have contributed to racial progress in this country and both political parties have taken steps that have periodically set us back. From a historical perspective, the Republican Party has accomplished more on the race issue. As Jack Kemp once said, "The Republican Party has had a great history with African Americans and they turned away from it. The Democratic Party has had a terrible history, but they overcame it."[9]

The Republican Party can learn a lot from its own history. It is important that both political parties reach out to people with different ideas and perspectives. Efforts by the Club for Growth and other ideological conservatives to drive moderates—sometimes called RINOS (Republicans in name only)—out of the party by challenging them in primaries is a kamikaze mission. If Republicans take their party down the road of ideological purity, it will most likely become a small, predominately regional minority party without real influence at the national level. If the party gains the reputation of saying "no" to all initiatives without offering viable alternatives, it could suffer the fate of the Know Nothing Party, which opposed German and Irish Catholic immigration in the 1850s. Polls indicate that an increasing number of Americans consider themselves politically independent, and an even larger majority consider themselves in the mainstream of political philosophy. A party that no longer attracts mainstream voters in any democratic society is destined to extinction.

As to race, this should not be a wedge issue that divides the parties. An honest debate about how to improve race relationships and create opportunities for minorities to succeed in a democratic free market society should be the subject of continuing thoughtful discussion.

Elected leaders and the civil rights community face new challenges today. Many legal barriers inhibiting the progress of minorities have been removed. Americans of color and women have entered the mainstream, rising to positions of leadership. Of this there can be no doubt. Yet there remain enormous inequalities. Large segments of our population remain mired in poverty because access to the skills required for upward mobility remain beyond their reach. This is as much an issue of poverty and culture as race, but race remains a factor as the vestiges of slavery and two hundred years of apartheid cannot be eradicated by the sweep of a pen. Integrating immigrant populations, many of them undocumented, presents a new set of challenges.

Well-intentioned programs by government and private institutions have failed to solve this problem. The voice of these communities appears to have less influence in legislative halls today even as more minorities and women are elected. It will require a sustained and targeted partnership of government and the private sector to focus on education, skills training, housing, jobs, and the administration of justice that are the root causes of racial inequality. To be blunt, civil rights leaders should focus less on historical grievances and more on restoring the family and community support systems that are needed to facilitate social mobility into the mainstream of American culture. The government's responsibility is to establish a legal framework that ensures all Americans have access to education and good jobs; but success comes from hard work and accepting personal responsibility and accountability and is not dependent on government largess.

A healthy democracy works best when honest public debate between different philosophical points of view flushes out the alternatives and informs the electorate. Legislative success, however, depends on a group of practical centrists who put the public interest above party interest and who come together and form a majority to fashion a reasonable compromise that serves all the people whether they know it or not. This is called leadership, and it is not subject to the transitory whims of opinion polls or the exigencies of reelection. The landmark Civil Rights Act of 1965 was enacted only because midwestern conservative pragmatic Republicans such as Bill McCulloch, the ranking member on the Judiciary Committee from Piqua, Ohio, Tom Curtis, of St. Louis County, Missouri, and Everett Dirksen, a senator from Illinois, worked with Hubert Humphrey and a few personally committed northern liberals to secure a majority despite the opposition of the southern Democrats.[10] This formula has worked time and again to pass progressive but practical legislation.[11]

So taking the long view, I believe we need committed, innovative leadership from both parties. Real progress is made by centrists who use politics as a means to solve real problems. All Americans, but especially minorities, benefit when government works effectively in partnership with a responsible private economy to advance the public good. On national security issues, we need a realistic, hard-headed approach to protect the interests and rights of U.S. citizens. We need constantly to fine-tune the balance between national security and civil liberties in response to a realistic appraisal of potential threats to the nation. Liberty thrives in an ordered society.

On economic issues, a properly regulated, free market economy makes better choices about allocating resources than government does. I believe that the federal government should be involved only in those essential activities that it can perform efficiently and that cannot be performed in the private sector or by the states. I believe that the closer the government is to the people the more responsive it can be to their needs and concerns. I believe that government should not unduly interfere with the liberty and privacy of individuals. I believe in federal and state fiscal responsibility, which means a balanced budget. I would like to see both an operating budget and a capital budget to encourage more investment in the nation's infrastructure.

I would like to see a line-item veto to enable the president to exercise fiscal responsibility by cutting out earmarks and "pork" from the flatulent appropriations bills he receives. Congressional abuse of earmarks is a national disgrace. How can we have confidence in the legislative process when we witness the profligate waste of taxpayer money at a time of rising deficits? Finally, I also believe that incremental progress is usually the best course. Our nation is too large, diverse, and complex to adjust to radical, comprehensive change efficiently. We need to be taking small steps in the right direction, constantly evaluating the results, making midcourse corrections, and gaining public confidence and acceptance. This was the way the LDF progressed in civil rights, patiently, persistently, and ably pursuing a step-by-step strategy to achieve the equal opportunity promised—but so long denied—by the Constitution.

As the parties have become increasingly polarized, we have lost many centrist members of Congress. I worry who will replace them. We must cultivate a new generation of leaders who are firmly rooted in strong principles that underlie the greatness of the American experiment but who are also pragmatic and focused on problem solving. Strong centrist bipartisan leadership will be critical in bringing *unsustainable* federal entitlements, state mandates, budget deficits, and the mushrooming national debt under control. I do not underestimate the challenge, but if we are to have any chance of success, we must work within both political parties to demonstrate that in a democratic, free enterprise system, politics is the means by which we make good policy choices and not an end in and of itself.

FORTY-THREE

Counsel for the Situation

*Give a wise man an honest brief to plead and his eloquence is
no remarkable achievement.*

—EURIPIDES, *The Bacchae*

JUSTICE BRANDEIS DESCRIBED HIS LEGAL practice before ascending to the
Supreme Court as "counsel to the situation." In his view, the lawyer was more
than an adversarial advocate. The lawyer was a counselor, a negotiator, a problem solver who sought to advance the client's objectives while maintaining the
highest standards of ethics and serving the public interest.[1]

At the Senate confirmation hearing on his Supreme Court nomination,
Brandeis was berated for serving as a "counsel to the situation" instead of
counsel to his client. Did he not have a duty, he was asked, to represent vigorously his client's interest, even if the interests of other parties and the public
suffered? In some specific situations Brandeis may have taken the concept
too far (compromising his obligation first and foremost to serve the client),[2]
but I fully agreed with his broader conception: first, in representing clients, a
member of the bar has an obligation to uphold the highest standards of integrity and inform the client of the public interest considerations at stake, and
second, a truly outstanding lawyer is able to represent a client on a broad range
of issues, calling in specialists as needed, but also capable of mastering a set of
complex interrelated issues and moving nimbly among legal disciplines. The
kind of legal practice defined by Brandeis has been my aspiration as a lawyer.
My informal advice to Bill Levitt while I was at the Dilworth firm, that his
early policy of racial exclusion from the Levittown projects was unwise and in
conflict with emerging national policy against racial discrimination in housing, illustrates the point. To distinguish my nuanced interpretation of the
Brandeis philosophy, I have coined the term *counsel for the situation.* I would be
counsel to the client but willing and able to deal with any situation.

In the Washington context, the counsel for the situation acts as a mediator
between the private sector and government, a bridge between law and public
policy. Effective counsel is able to explain to government officials how the

government's statutory obligations can be met in the most efficient way and how sometimes conflicting public interest considerations can be reconciled. To function effectively, government requires substantial information from the private sector and a full understanding of the consequences (intended and unintended) of the exercise of its regulatory and fiscal powers. Counsel can marshal and present complex information in a credible, skillful way that facilitates good policymaking.

Counsel can explain to a private sector client how Washington works (or doesn't work) and how to achieve the client's objectives within the statutory framework that drives government policy. Many clients complain about the heavy hand of bureaucracy (sometimes for good reason). Astute counsel knows how to bridge the communications gap and negotiate a positive outcome. The counsel's greatest creative challenges often come in helping clients adapt their business models to emerging legislative policies. Many government objectives—safe transportation, quality health care, energy security, and environmental protection among them—can only be met through efficient private sector initiatives. Counsel also can help shape and pass legislation or regulations that open up new private sector business opportunities.

As counsel for the situation, I would assemble a team of legal experts to undertake strategic or corporate crisis counseling, working with clients in developing new business horizons or handling bet-the-company situations. A major corporate takeover, enforcement action, scandal, or product liability exposure can subject a company to the glare of media, congressional oversight, an agency investigation, and multiple lawsuits. In such circumstances, full-service client representation may involve interaction with all three branches of government and the media in preparing clients to testify before congressional committees, participating in regulatory proceedings, negotiating with federal officials, and defending clients against enforcement actions and private lawsuits arising out of federal actions.

Some say that the counsel for the situation—the Tommy Corcorans, Clark Cliffords, Edward Bennett Williams, Lloyd Cutlers—are dinosaurs. They argue that only specialists can effectively address increasingly complex legal systems. I beg to differ. There has always been, and will always be, a demand for specialists. There will also continue to be a demand for generalists who can view the forest and fight the fires from the perspective of twenty-five thousand feet, especially in Washington, where the failure to understand the interconnectedness of public policy so often results in unintended consequences.

This concept of counsel for the situation certainly applied to our representation of the insurance giant CIGNA. In Washington, we undertook many different kinds of projects. When CIGNA was interested in getting into the health insurance and managed-care business, it requested a comprehensive analysis of the statutory and regulatory environment at the federal and state level in which such a business would operate, including trends and potential new regulatory obstacles. Don Bliss, Tom Donilon, David Beddow, and I prepared a compendium of federal and state statutes and regulations and pending legislative initiatives and proposals that could present opportunities or hurdles for profit-making institutions providing managed care. Relying on that analysis, the general counsel briefed the board of directors, which then approved CIGNA's acquisition of a managed-care company and a strategic plan to enter into the health insurance business.

After entering the health care business, CIGNA continued to call on us to review proposed legislation, draft amendments, analyze significant regulatory proposals, and, as a last resort, seek judicial relief.[3] We collaborated on ways to expand CIGNA's employee benefit business. Working with an eminent Harvard professor, we developed a privatized-option proposal for Social Security beneficiaries and a state Medicaid voucher proposal that would allow low-income beneficiaries to purchase a managed-care policy in lieu of the regular government fee-for-service reimbursement. We worked with CIGNA on alternatives to costly fee-for-service (indemnity) health-care financing that would encourage prevention and wellness. We advised CIGNA on proposed legislation addressing toxic waste and asbestos liability and analyzed its methods and techniques for managing and litigating insurance claims, recommending alternatives to the traditional law firm hourly-rate billing arrangements. While some may have regarded this as putting the fox in charge of the chicken coop, we came up with some useful ideas that helped CIGNA manage its litigation costs more efficiently. This assignment put us ahead of the curve, as law firm billing practices have become a major issue over the past few years.

In recent years, especially during economic downturns and intense global competition, law firms have experienced increasing cost pressures. In 2009, for the first time, the largest 250 law firms laid off 5,259 (4 percent) of their lawyers. Many firms deferred the arrival of incoming associates. Clients urged law firms to change the way they charge for services. Some argued that a variety of factors had converged, like perfect storms, to batter the dot.com, financial, and real estate markets. Were law firms next?

Since the advent of the *American Lawyer* and other legal trade publications, there has been a healthy disclosure of law firm revenues and profitability. Easy comparisons have intensified competition among law firms, transforming them from professional partnerships to sometimes brutally competitive business enterprises, many of them obsessed, like so many U.S. corporations, with the short-term bottom line. The changes have been dramatic. Historically, corporate clients relied on deep and long-standing relationships with trusted law firms; today, clients often shop around for the cheapest services. Historically, law partners planned to spend their careers in professional relationships with respected colleagues; today, productive partners jump from firm to firm in search of greater compensation. Rainmaking (bringing in legal business) too often has superseded scholarship, judgment, and community outreach as the most valued quality of partnership. Historically, the law firm model was based on collegial relationships in service to a community. Today, great law firms span the globe; through mergers and acquisitions and lateral hires, some firms have grown to more than a thousand partners, most of whom do not even know one another.

Historically, high-achieving law students joined the great law firms, often after judicial clerkships, with the prospect of disciplined training and promotion to partnership in seven or eight years. Today, many law firms neglect the cultivation and promotion of their associates, preferring to attract lateral partners with business portfolios. Today, in many firms, fewer than 10 percent of the incoming recruits actually advance to partnership. The competition for young lawyers has become fierce. After all, law firms do not sell widgets; they sell the best and brightest minds to tackle complex problems and resolve unprecedented challenges. Top law firms compete intensely for the few students at the top of their class in the best law schools or coming off prestigious clerkships. When I finally got a job after my Supreme Court clerkship, my starting salary was $6,700. By 2007 the starting salary at a major law firm could be $160,000 or more, and a former Supreme Court clerk could attract an additional signing bonus of $250,000 or more. We were approaching the stratospheric realm where the top professional athletes dwell, although the athlete's career span is a bit shorter than the lawyer's—in my case, more than sixty years!

To finance this competitive model, major law firms have raised hourly billing rates, and clients are increasingly unwilling to pay $300 to $400 an hour for a clever but completely untrained novice. Like fee-for-service reimbursement in health care, charges based on billable hours do not necessarily reflect outcomes nor encourage efficiency. That is why many clients are searching for alternative models like flat-fee contracts.

According to a recent *American Lawyer* survey of the two hundred largest U.S. law firms, 93 percent are willing to discuss alternative fee arrangements. In lieu of the billable hours model, firms are agreeing to flat fees for specific tasks; a lower base rate combined with a substantial bonus or "success fee" for a positive result; blended rates that offer more predictability by averaging the rates of individual attorneys of varying experience working on a case; and fees contingent on the completion of a transaction or litigation. Firms also are working with clients as partners, in-house attorneys performing specific tasks in close coordination with outside counsel. Law firms are often asked to propose a detailed budget for a case or transaction. If the time expended exceeds the projected budget, law firms must seek advance approval and negotiate additional fees. O'Melveny & Myers has been a leader in developing alternative fee arrangements that reward law firm efficiency, increase predictability for clients, and ensure that the cost of outside legal services is commensurate with the value received by the client.

In both medicine and the law, responsible billing practices must return to basics. As professionals, we have an obligation to adhere to high standards in providing quality services at a reasonable cost that reflects the value received. If our primary motivation is to make as much money as possible, we are in the wrong business. Law firms and medical providers have a responsibility to calibrate billing practices to provide the right incentives and rewards for cost-effective, outcome-focused services. I would encourage the professional associations (the American Bar Association and the American Medical Association) to promote billing practices that appropriately compensate professional services.

The law firm model has significantly changed. Every quality law firm today is struggling with these issues in searching for the most efficient way to serve its clients and retain top-notch lawyers. We must adapt to changing conditions, but in doing so I hope we will preserve certain basic values that have characterized the legal profession historically and are essential to good government and an efficient economy. These values include the law firm's obligation to train and advance its young lawyers, to encourage voluntary legal work and public service, and to emphasize that the practice of law is a profession that requires high ethical standards and a commitment to serve the client efficiently and consistent with the public interest.

A law firm's reputation for objectivity and professionalism is critical. For example, in 1998 I got a call from Dr. Thomas Frist, a founder and principal shareholder of the Hospital Corporation of America and brother of then majority leader of the U.S. Senate, Tennessee senator Dr. Bill Frist. I got to know Tom when we served together as IBM directors. Tom had retired from active leadership of the corporation, but recent events involving allegations of Medicare fraud and mismanagement of the company greatly disturbed him. He decided to return to the company as chief executive officer and wanted to bring in two new respected outside directors to help him restore the financial strength and the reputation of the company he founded. The two prospective directors were the dean of the Harvard Business School and a former member of the president's Council of Economic Advisers. I knew both gentlemen quite well. They told Tom that they could not agree to join the board unless he provided them with an independent outside review of the corporation's liability. They suggested me as someone who could advise them on any liability they might be assuming as directors.

I went to Nashville to visit with Tom and wisely brought with me A. B. Culvahouse, an experienced troubleshooter who could help me assess the merits and potential liabilities of the lawsuits filed against the Hospital Corporation of America. A.B. had served as White House counsel to President Reagan and successfully shepherded that administration through the thicket of Irangate. We assembled a team and conducted a top-to-bottom review of the company. Tom was pleased with our report, which persuaded the two new directors to come on board. We have continued to do significant legal work for the corporation.

A bachelor friend once told me that attracting a new client was more fun than seducing a pretty woman. New clients come in strange and random ways. While I was in Lisbon, Portugal, for a meeting of the Trilateral Commission, I shared a cab with Steve Friedman, then the chief executive officer of Goldman Sachs, on the way to a restaurant one evening. The driver got terribly lost. He spoke no English, and we spoke no Portuguese. Steve and I passed the time discussing how a range of issues being debated in Washington might impact Goldman Sachs. Finally, after driving around for an hour and a half, we left the cab and found another taxi to take us to the restaurant, where our colleagues had been waiting impatiently for dinner. The following Tuesday, after he returned to the United States, Steve called and said he had found our conversation stimulating. He wanted to involve me in some of Goldman Sachs's legal work and asked me what my specialty was. I suggested that having spent several hours with me cruising aimlessly around the streets of Lisbon, he should realize that I was a person without a specialty. However, I did think of myself as counsel for the situation. I suggested that I bring up to New York three or four of my bright young partners who were quite expert in many of the areas in which Goldman Sachs did business and introduce them to his team. I told him that by the end of the day, we would understand fully Goldman Sachs's business and objectives. The meeting went well, and our firm began doing (and continues to do) a lot of legal work for Goldman Sachs in Washington, New York, Japan, China, the United Kingdom, Europe, and elsewhere.

My membership on corporate boards was also a valuable source of new business. Although highly remunerative, my board duties were demanding in terms of travel and time. I often found myself addressing difficult and complex problems for which my legal skills offered an important perspective. While many of my associations were enjoyable and some of the challenges intellectually exhilarating, I also faced unwelcome personnel situations and financial and ethical crises that were not conducive to a good night's sleep. As an IBM director, I considered the bold recommendation of outside counsel to challenge Judge Edelstein's handling of the U.S. antitrust case against IBM. Having reviewed the allegations of bias, I advised the board of my agreement with this high-stakes strategy. IBM was successful in convincing the judge to recuse himself. Eventually, the government dropped the lawsuit.

As a director of Philadelphia Electric, I confronted serious challenges with the regulatory closure of the Peach Bottom nuclear plant and the need to replace senior managers. Serving on the board of American Can and then AMAX, I confronted contentious issues of chief executive officer succession and acquisitions as well as problematic dealings with developing countries in international mining ventures.

As a board member of INA Corporation, I helped to engineer a merger with Connecticut General, which became CIGNA. We negotiated an agreement that would keep the corporate headquarters in Philadelphia rather than move it to Hartford, the hometown of Connecticut General, and a plan of executive succession that would integrate two very different cultures on fair terms. As a director of PepsiCo, I learned a lot from the politically savvy chief executive, Don Kendall, and worked to diversify the business, expand its global reach, and retain its dominant position in Russia.

As a director of the Chase Manhattan Bank, I participated in several acquisitions but retired before Chase merged with J.P. Morgan to create the banking giant J.P. Morgan Chase. At the request of Bob Bass, I also served on the board of directors of New American Holdings, which became Washington Mutual before it was acquired by J.P. Morgan Chase. I have already recounted many of the challenges I faced as a Pan Am director as we watched this venerable institution slowly disintegrate in the deregulatory climate I had helped bring about.

The advice of attorneys on corporate boards is valuable as companies struggle to comply with post-Enron statutory and regulatory requirements, epitomized by the Sarbanes-Oxley legislation. Directors today accept more responsibility (and liability) for the ethics of their companies and the welfare of their shareholders. Having served on multiple boards, I could bring a perspective to board deliberations, drawing from lessons learned on one board to avoid a pitfall on another.

The business that my board participation brought to O'Melveny could have incurred criticism. Former Securities and Exchange Commission chair Harold Williams, for example, advised lawyers to resign from boards for which their law firms do legal work, positing a conflict of interest between board membership and serving as outside counsel. Can a director act independently if she or he is concerned about retaining the company as a client? It is a fair question. On balance, from my experience, I believe there is a net benefit from attorney participation on corporate boards even when serving as outside counsel. The potential for conflict can be minimized by taking the following steps: the relationship should be fully disclosed; the director should be recused in certain circumstances from board deliberations on matters where he or she serves as outside counsel; the law firm should screen the director from involvement in certain cases in which his or her firm serves as counsel; the director's law firm should not be the general outside counsel on all corporate matters; and the legal fees received from the corporation should not constitute a significant and disproportionate share of the law firm's revenues.[4] By adhering to these conditions, I believe my service on corporate boards was a net benefit.

Good law firms are highly professional in addressing conflicts and other ethical considerations. They usually are more adept at handling them than university presidents, investment bankers, or corporate executive officers who sit on boards of companies with which they do business, all of which present a potential for conflicts. My work as an outside counsel increased my understanding of the company's business, the quality of its management, and the challenges it faced. On a few occasions, as outside counsel, I was able to ensure that the board was informed about a company's potential liability where management was reluctant to be forthcoming. At least I was able to offer another perspective where management understandably was not eager to disclose its own shortcomings. With due respect for the conventional wisdom, I thought this made me a better director.[5]

When I joined O'Melveny in 1977, I expected that the diversified skills and values of this Los Angeles–based firm would have much to contribute on the world stage. Over the past thirty-two years we have succeeded beyond my expectations. Without the talent, energy, and commitment of my partners and associates, it would not have been possible for me to attract new global clients and business to the law firm. Through the many networks I developed through my career in the practice of law, public service, and on boards of directors, I have had the opportunity to match O'Melveny's talent with the legal needs of many clients—Ford Motor Company, CIGNA, PepsiCo, Merck, Goldman Sachs, Hospital Corporation of America, Aetna, AMAX, Pan Am, Washington Mutual, Philadelphia Electric, Republic Properties, the West Group, Greenbrier, the American Public Transit Association, the Southeastern Pennsylvania Transportation Authority, the JER Companies, the Philadelphia Gas Works, Ocwen Co., Ace Ltd., TPG-Axon Capital, and other institutions and individuals. My partners and associates performed brilliantly for these new clients, expanding the scope of work we undertook for them, developing strong professional relationships with general counsels and management, and generating billions of dollars of revenue for the firm.

In addition to the major transactional and litigation work I have described above for major corporations, as counsel for the situation I have enjoyed the challenge and constant variety of a diverse practice for dozens of other clients. To cite but a few examples over the past thirty years at O'Melveny, I advised a Chinese importer to repackage his suits as coats and trousers as they traveled across the Pacific Ocean so that they would be accepted in the United States under the yet unfulfilled quotas for jackets and pants. I arranged for the signature of a half dozen tribal chiefs in North Dakota and Montana during a blinding blizzard on New Year's Eve to meet the year-end statutory deadline for a swap of valuable coal-mining land on the reservations for valuable tracts in the Powder River Basin in Wyoming.

Expanding my knowledge of public transit, I demonstrated to a federal district judge in Washington how she could get from the Los Angeles airport to the federal court house in Los Angeles by public transit as I sought to demonstrate the adequacy of the environmental assessment in support of rerouting of the proposed Los Angeles subway system around methane gas deposits. I proposed to federal and regional transit authorities that they encourage the use of a safety device that would reduce insurance costs by preventing fatalities and serious injuries to persons who slip and fall under the rear wheels of a bus. When SEPTA had a series of rail accidents, I led a team that reviewed the safety practices and procedures of the regional transit authority from top to bottom and reported my recommendations to the board of directors.

Moving on to sea transportation, I tried unsuccessfully to persuade the Department of Defense and the Maritime Administration in the Department of Transportation to provide loan guarantees to build a new FastShip to transport roll-on-roll-off containers. Powered by Rolls Royce jet engines, FastShip would cut in half the time it takes to cross the North Atlantic and would connect to special intermodal ports at Philadelphia and Cherbourg, France, transporting valuable cargo to any city in Western Europe within seven days. The ship could be adapted for military use, to move heavy tanks and aircraft quickly to respond to hot spots around the globe. On the air side, I worked with tech companies seeking to transform the antiquated radar-based air traffic control system into a modern satellite-based system.

On the rail front, I am currently working with Washington, Virginia, Maryland, and CSX on a proposal to relocate railroad tracks and develop a grand new corridor to the nation's capital along Maryland Avenue. I also represented the largest manufacturer of railcars on some tricky competition issues.

My farmer friends from the Imperial Valley asked for help in amending the 2008 farm bill to allow the development of an innovative facility that would process sugar beets in the winter and sugar cane in the summer, providing full-time jobs to replace migrant labor, generating excess energy from bio fuels to sell to the California grid, and eliminating pollution by fully using all the by-products.

As an arbitrator, I have been asked to resolve a dispute between a Swedish company and the country of Kazakhstan and to set the rates of New Hampshire public utilities after recent deregulation by the state legislature.

On behalf of AMAX, my tax partner Ben Benjamin and I restructured a pension fund that freed up $60 million for investment in new mines and established a model that was approved by the Internal Revenue Service and the Pension Benefit Guaranty Corporation. I then explained the model in testimony before Congress.

In my Supreme Court practice, I have worked with such diverse clients as the estate of Howard Hughes, Mobil Oil, a wrongfully convicted Philadelphia socialite, and Cowles Media in seeking or opposing Supreme Court review on a range of novel issues.

It has been a great ride. With each new week, new surprises, challenges, and opportunities would present themselves. I would immerse myself in the banking or insurance industry, the operation of a bus system, or sugar growing and processing in the Imperial Valley. And yet I did not have to spend my entire life farming, driving a bus, approving loans, or writing insurance policies. I could pack all of these careers and many more into a lifetime of adventure and fun.

In my initial decision to come to O'Melveny, one of the values I found most attractive was the long tradition of public service. This was best exemplified by the former chair of the firm, Warren Christopher, who served not only as deputy attorney general and deputy secretary of state in the Johnson and Carter administrations but also as President Clinton's secretary of state during his first term. Christopher also has undertaken numerous part-time public service assignments during his long career. President Carter awarded him the Presidential Medal of Freedom, the highest honor that can be bestowed on a civilian in the United States.

When we moved into our new spacious offices two blocks north of the White House in 2002, my partners surprised me by including my picture and biography in a large display in the reception area alongside Warren Christopher's, highlighting perhaps the only law firm ever to boast two practicing attorneys who were recipients of the Presidential Medal of Freedom.[6]

For yes, I was privileged to receive this honor from William Jefferson Clinton in 1995. In a way this was a validation of my lifelong choice to be a counsel for the situation and a creative part of the American mainstream—to chart a course that would add value to the flow of history. President Clinton summed up succinctly and all too graciously what I have been attempting to do over my long legal career. "For four decades in the courtroom, the boardroom, and the halls of power, Bill Coleman has put his brilliant legal intellect in service to our country. . . . I can honestly say if you are looking for an example of constancy, consistency, disciplined devotion to the things that make this country a great place, you have no further to look than William T. Coleman Jr."[7]

EPILOGUE

Having represented Frank Sinatra at the request of my law school class-mate Mickey Rudin, I became a big fan of his music. Before Elvis and the Beatles, this skinny boy from New Jersey rose to the top of his profession. And he did it through sheer talent, persistence, and tenacity. He did it his own way. As his career was coming to a close, his still rich voice filled the concert hall with an anthem to a life well lived—in his own inimitable style. In my ninetieth year, the song resonates well with me. While I could never sing it, I set it forth below with a few personal modifications.

My Way
And now, the end is here
And so I face the final curtain
My friend, I'll say it clear
I'll state my case, of which I'm certain
I've lived a life that's full
I've traveled each and ev'ry highway
And more, much more than this, I did it my way

Regrets, I've had a few
But then again, too few to mention
I did what I had to do and saw it through without exemption
I planned [almost] each charted course, each careful step along the byway
And more, much more than this, I did it my way

Yes, there were times, I'm sure you kn[o]w
When I bit off more than I could chew
But through it all, when there was doubt
I ate it up and spit it out
I faced it all and I stood [firm] and did it my way

I've loved [Lovida], I've laughed and cried
I've had my fill, my share of losing
And now, as tears subside, I find it all so amusing
To think I did all [what's herein]
And may I say, not in a [too] shy way,
"Oh, no, oh, no, not me, I did it my way"

For what is a man, what has he got?
If not himself [and his family, his friends, his law partners, his clients, and
his nation], then he has naught
To say the things he truly feels and not the words of one who kneels
The record shows I took the blows and did it my way!

Yes, it was my way.

I have been blessed with great work and challenging opportunities. I urge each
generation to reach out to help the younger generation, regardless of color, gender, or religious beliefs. This is essential if our nation is to remain a world leader,
for diversity is our greatest strength. It is essential in the interconnected world
in which we now live. We are no longer an isolated oasis protected by two great
oceans. We must remain vigilant and ready to rise to the occasion if another
Dred Scott or *Plessy* v. *Ferguson* comes along to challenge the rights of a substantial group of Americans. I continually challenge my children, Bill III, Lovida Jr.,
and Hardin, as well as my grandchildren, Jesse, Aaron, Bill IV, and Amadeus, to
swim boldly in the mainstream and to strive for that more perfect union.

*(I would like to thank Paul Anka, who wrote the original English lyrics of "My Way." Mr. Anka
personally authored the English lyrics to "My Way" for his dear friend Frank Sinatra, who recorded
the original English version.)*

English Lyrics by Paul Anka
Original French Lyric by Gilles Thibault
Music by Jacques Revaux & Claude Francois
©1967 Chrysalis Standards, Inc. (BMI)/Warner Chappell Music France (SACEM)/Editions
  Jeune Musique (SACEM)/Jingoro Music Co. (BMI)/Architechtural Music Co. (BMI)
All Rights In the USA Administered by Chrysalis Standards, Inc. (BMI), Jingoro Music Co.
  (BMI) and Architechtural Music Co. (BMI)
Copyright Renewed. International Copyright Secured
All Rights Reserved. Used By Permission

ACKNOWLEDGMENTS

IT IS IMPOSSIBLE TO MENTION all the people who have contributed to a book that reflects my life experience. I am grateful to my mother and father and extended family who taught me to have pride in my heritage as an American citizen and be resolute in my commitment to the equality of all human beings. Without the courage of national leaders who have opened doors for me and shown me the path of a responsible citizenship, I would not have had the opportunities and blessings of working on challenging issues and contributing to solutions. To mention but a few: Presidents Dwight Eisenhower, Lyndon Johnson, and Gerald Ford, Presidents George W. Bush and William J. Clinton and their families; Vice Presidents Nelson Rockefeller, Dick Cheney, and Joseph Biden; Boston Brahmins Elliot Richardson, Henry Shattuck, and William Putnam Bundy; Brahmins of color Charles Houston, Chief Judge William H. Hastie, Justice Thurgood Marshall and Cecilia Marshall, Julius Chambers, Raymond Pace Alexander and Sadie T. Alexander, General Colin Powell, Vernon Jordan, Robert Tresville, Dr. Melvin Chisum and Dr. Gloria Chisum; Supreme Court justices Felix Frankfurter, Earl Warren, Hugo Black, Steven Breyer, Ruth Ginsburg, Sandra Day O'Connor, Anthony Scalia, John Paul Stevens, David Souter, and Clarence Thomas; law school deans and professors Erwin Griswold, Paul Freund, Henry Hart, Thomas Reid Powell, Lon Fuller, Jack Greenberg, Charles Ogletree Jr., and John Hart Ely (who was also my general counsel at the Department of Transportation); law firm leaders Louis Weiss, Richardson Dilworth, Warren Christopher, Lloyd K. Garrison, James Wilson, John Hannum, and Cy Vance; Judges Louis Pollak (also a dean of both Yale and Pennsylvania Law Schools, law professor, fellow law clerk, and lifelong friend), Herbert F. Goodrich, Learned Hand, Edward Becker, Robert Carter, and Constance Baker Motley; Philadelphia colleagues Harold Kohn, Sam Evans, and Jean Palmer Greer Zeiter; cabinet officers Dean

Acheson, Henry Stimson, Carla Hills, Henry Kissinger, Edward Levi, Jim Lynn, Condoleezza Rice, Don Rumsfeld, and Hank Paulson; business leaders David Rockefeller, Steve Friedman, Don Kendall, Tom Watson, Joe Robert, and Walter Wriston; 100 senators but especially Hugh Scott, Ted Kennedy, Howard Baker, Orrin Hatch, and Arlen Specter; Transportation Department colleagues John Barnum, John Snow, Carmen Turner, Judith Connor, Mike Browne, Ted Leland, Don Bliss, Heather Adams, and Elaine Jones (who was also my fellow warrior at the LDF). Each of these individuals—and many more—have touched me with fire. To any I have omitted, forgive me, please.

In the preparation of this book, I am grateful to my coauthor, Don Bliss, former ambassador, top lawyer at the Department of Transportation, and law partner; Patricia Hass, senior editor and adviser; Ellen Sandel, my administrative assistant; Andrew Eveleth, senior paralegal; Doris Beckett, assistant to Don Bliss; Judge Louis Pollak; Elaine Jones; Debbie Fisher; Martha Cocker; and my daughter Lovida Jr. Many scholars, from Richard Kluger in *Simple Justice* to David Nichols in *A Matter of Justice,* have thoroughly plowed the ground, to which I add only some personal recollections. I hope I have given them all proper credit. I have tried to capture the spirit of some conversations that took place a long time ago, but I accept any flaws in memory as my responsibility only.

I am blessed with a wonderful family of independent thinkers and fierce advocates who chart their own course: my children, William T. III, Lovida Jr., and Hardin, and their children, Flavia, Jesse, Aaron, Bill IV, and Amadeus. I am indebted most of all to my wife of sixty-six years, Lovida, who has endured beyond all measure my reliving the past, gently attempted (not always successfully) to keep my ego contained, and served as my most cherished adviser, critic, and loving companion.

WILLIAM T. COLEMAN JR.

McLean, Virginia
August 2010

CHRONOLOGY OF THE LIFE
OF WILLIAM T. COLEMAN JR.

1915   William T. Coleman Sr. and Laura Beatrice Mason married, June 29, Baltimore, Maryland.

1920   William T. Coleman Jr. born, 12:15 a.m., July 7, North Philadelphia.

1938   Graduated Germantown High School, January 29.

1941   Graduated University of Pennsylvania summa cum laude, June.

1941   Entered Harvard Law School, September.

1942   Invited to join the *Harvard Law Review.*

1943   Volunteered for the U.S. Army Air Corps, reported for basic training March 4, Biloxi, Mississippi.
Attended Harvard Business School.
Commissioned as second lieutenant and assigned to the 477th Composite Fighter-Bomber Group, Godman Field, Kentucky, as a statistical control officer.

1945   Married Lovida Hardin, February 10, New Orleans.
Defended Tuskegee Airmen in court martial proceedings after they entered a whites-only officers' club at Freeman Field, Indiana.
Honorably discharged from the Army Air Corps.
Worked for the law firm of Raymond Pace and Sadie Alexander in Philadelphia, among the top law firms of color in the nation.
Reentered Harvard Law School in the fall, where he served as an editor of the *Harvard Law Review.*

1946   Graduated Harvard Law School, first in the class of 1946/1943.
Employed as Langdell Teaching Fellow at the Law School.
Passed Pennsylvania Bar exam.

1947   William T. Coleman III born on April 20.
Began clerkship for Judge Herbert F. Goodrich on the U.S. Court of Appeals for the Third Circuit in May, the first American of color to clerk for a federal appellate judge.

1948   Began clerkship for U.S. Supreme Court Justice Felix Frankfurter
        on September 1, the first American of color to clerk for a Supreme
        Court justice, co-clerking with Elliot Lee Richardson.

1949   Daughter Lovida Jr. born, May 21.
        Pounded the pavement in Philadelphia, Boston, Washington, and
        on Wall Street in an unsuccessful search for a law firm job.
        Completed Supreme Court clerkship, August 31.
        Finally was offered, and accepted, an associate position at the New
        York firm of Paul, Weiss, Wharton, and Garrison, to which he com-
        muted from Philadelphia by train for two years, the first American
        of color to join a major law firm.

1950   Joined the civil rights litigation team led by Thurgood Marshall
        and the NAACP Legal Defense and Educational Fund (LDF) on a
        voluntary basis while continuing to practice law.

1952   Third child, Hardin, born on January 30th.
        Accepted a position as an associate at the Philadelphia law firm of
        Dilworth, Paxson, Kalish, and Green, the first attorney of color to
        join a major Philadelphia firm.

1953   Sat next to Thurgood Marshall at the counsel table during re-
        argument of *Brown* v. *Board of Education* after having worked on the
        brief and argument preparation with the LDF team.

1954   State-sanctioned school segregation declared illegal by the U.S.
        Supreme Court under the Fourteenth Amendment to the U.S.
        Constitution, May 17.
        Worked with the LDF Team on briefing the Supreme Court on the
        appropriate remedy.

1956   Elected a partner of the Dilworth law firm.
        Represented the Southeastern Pennsylvania Transportation Author-
        ity, Triangle Publications, Levitt and Sons, and American Homes in
        litigation, labor, corporate, and real estate matters.

1957   Undertook representation of students of color seeking to enter
        Girard College in Philadelphia, which was open only to white male
        orphans under the trust of Stephen Girard. After fourteen years
        and fifteen court opinions, Girard College finally open to persons of
        color and, eventually, to women.

1958   Sat at counsel table with Thurgood Marshall during Marshall's
        argument in *Cooper* v. *Aaron*, the Little Rock school desegregation
        case, in August; in September, Supreme Court unanimously ordered
        that the students of color be admitted to Central High School and
        issued an opinion personally signed by all nine justices—the only
        unanimous decision personally signed by the entire Court.

1958   Represented Frank Sinatra at the Dilworth firm.
Thurgood Marshall asked Coleman to chair the LDF board of directors. Coleman accepted and served for many years as chair, president,
or co-chair before and after his appointment to the president's cabinet.

1959   Appointed by President Eisenhower to the Committee on Employ-
ment Policy (the Branch Rickey Committee).
Appointed by Chief Justice Earl Warren to the Civil Rules Advisory
Committee under the chair of Dean Acheson.

1963   Appointed a senior counsel to the Warren Commission Investigating the Assassination of President Kennedy and tasked with
determining whether the Soviet Union or Cuba was involved in a
conspiracy to assassinate the president.
Became head of the Litigation Department of the Dilworth firm,
and his name added to title of the firm. Represented Philadelphia
Gas Works, United Gas Improvement Company, Triangle Publications, and Ford Motor Company.
Appointed as consultant to the U.S. Arms Control and Disarmament Agency.

1964   After Coleman's successful argument in *McLaughlin* v. *Florida,* the
U.S. Supreme Court invalidated a Florida statute that prohibited
persons of different races from spending the night together.

1965   Argued successfully in the Supreme Court several cases for the
Philadelphia Gas Works involving natural gas regulatory issues.
Appointed by President Johnson as co-chair of the Planning Session
of the White House Conference on Civil Rights, entitled To Fulfill
These Rights, June 1966.

1969   Member of the U.S. Delegation to the United Nations General
Assembly.

1971   Appointed by President Nixon to the National Commission on
Productivity and the Price Commission.

1974   Won one case in Supreme Court awarding attorney fees to winning
counsel and lost another involving intercounty busing in the Richmond school desegregation case.

1975   Sworn in as the U.S. secretary of transportation in the Ford administration in March, the second known person of color ever to
serve in the cabinet. As secretary, issued the nation's first national
transportation policy, initiated transportation deregulation legislation, established the Federal Aircraft Noise Abatement Policy, and
decided such controversial issues as the introduction of air bags,
granting the supersonic Concorde conditional U.S. landing rights,
and opening the Coast Guard Academy to women.

1977   Appointed a Distinguished Fellow of the Woodrow Wilson International Center for Scholars, February.

Joined the law firm of O'Melveny & Myers, Washington, D.C., as full partner and member of its Management Committee in June.

Joined the board of directors of IBM, Pan Am, Chase Manhattan Bank, INA, PepsiCo, American Can, and Philadelphia Electric, among others.

Appointed by Secretary of State Cyrus Vance to the Panama Canal Advisory Committee in President Carter's administration.

1978   Represented General Motors before the Supreme Court in an antitrust case, the first of several Supreme Court arguments as an O'Melveny & Myers partner, which included representing Security Pacific National Bank in affirming the decision of the comptroller of the currency to allow national banks to enter the discount brokerage business nationwide and representing the Washington Metropolitan Airports Authority, the American Public Transit Association, and fourteen major airlines on various constitutional issues involving separation of powers and federalism.

1979   Nominated by the president of France as an officer of the National Order of the Legion of Honor.

1982   Appointed by Chief Justice Burger of the Supreme Court as *amicus curiae* to defend the decision of the Fourth Circuit Court denying tax-exempt status to private schools that practice racial discrimination after the Reagan administration reversed the position of the federal government and refused to defend the appellate court's decision in the Supreme Court. Coleman won in an 8-1 decision.

1986   Appointed by Secretary George Shultz as co-chair of the State Department's Advisory Committee on South Africa in President Reagan's administration.

1987   Testified before the Senate Judiciary Committee against President Reagan's nomination of Judge Robert Bork to the Supreme Court.

1994   Appointed to serve on the White House Security Review, which recommended the closing of Pennsylvania Avenue.

1995   Awarded the Presidential Medal of Freedom, the highest honor accorded a civilian in the United States, by President Bill Clinton, in a White House ceremony.

1996   Appointed to the White House Commission on Aviation Safety and Security, chaired by Vice President Albert Gore, after the crash of TWA 800.

1997   Presented with the Thurgood Marshall Lifetime Achievement Award by the LDF.

2000 Awarded the Judge Henry J. Friendly Medal by the American Law
      Institute.
2004 Awarded the Chief Justice John Marshall Award, recognizing
      extraordinary achievements in the administration of justice, by the
      American Bar Association.
      Served on the Technology and Privacy Advisory Committee of the
      Department of Defense.
2006 Sworn in as a major general in the U.S. Army to serve on the Court
      of Military Commission Review to review appeals from military
      commission convictions of Guantanamo detainees.
2007 Awarded Spirit of Excellence Award by the American Bar
      Association.
2010 Awarded, belatedly, the Harvard Law School's Fay Diploma for
      having attained the highest ranking in his class of 1946.
      Continues to serve as the senior partner and senior counselor of
      O'Melveny & Myers LLP.

ADDITIONAL FACTS IN THE LIFE
OF WILLIAM T. COLEMAN JR.

Mr. Coleman has served on the Board of Directors of Chase Manhattan Bank, N.A.; Chase Manhattan Corporation (now J.P. Morgan Chase); CIGNA Corporation; IBM Corporation; Pan American World Airways; PepsiCo; American Can; AMAX; New American Holdings (later Washington Mutual); and the Philadelphia Electric Company. Before joining the Ford cabinet, he served on the Boards of the Penn Mutual Insurance Company, the Western Saving Fund Society, the Lincoln Bank, the First Pennsylvania Bank, and the American Stock Exchange. He has been a trustee of the Business Enterprise Trust, the Urban Institute, and the Carnegie Institution of Washington and is currently a trustee of the Philadelphia Museum of Art, of which he is also vice president. He is an honorary trustee of the Brookings Institution and serves on the board of the New York City Ballet, the Advisory Board of the Metropolitan Opera Association, the Trustees Council of the National Gallery of Art (until March 2004), and the Council of the Woodrow Wilson Center. From 1975 to 1978, he served on the Board of Overseers of Harvard University. He is a member of the Council on Foreign Relations and a lifetime member of the Executive Committee of the Trilateral Commission.

In addition to the public service assignments listed above, Coleman was a member of the NASA Task Force on the Effective Utilization of the Shuttle, the Presidential Advisory Committee on Federalism, the Private Sector Survey on Cost Control (the Grace Commission), the American Bar Association's

Standing Committee on the Federal Judiciary, and the Lawyers' Committee for Civil Rights under Law; the chair of the Philadelphia Citizen's Police Review Board; and representative of the Greater Philadelphia Movement on the Philadelphia Citizen Advisory Poverty Committee.

Among the professional organizations in which Mr. Coleman holds membership are the American College of Trial Lawyers, the American Law Institute (he is also a member of its Council), the American Bar Association, the American Society of International Law, the American Academy of Appellate Lawyers, and the American Academy of Arts and Sciences. He was recently elected a Fellow of the American Bar Association.

Mr. Coleman is a member of the Pennsylvania and District of Columbia Bars, the Bar of the Supreme Court of the United States, and many of the appellate and district courts of the federal court system.

He holds honorary degrees from Harvard University, Amherst College, Williams College, Yale University, Central Michigan University, the University of Pennsylvania, Bates College, Drexel University, Swarthmore College, Saint Michael's College, Lincoln University, Syracuse University, Howard University, St. Joseph's College, Tulane University, Georgetown University, Columbia University, Bard College, Marymount University, University of the District of Columbia, College of William and Mary, Roanoke College, and Boston University.

In March 2000 the Public Interest Law Center of Philadelphia conferred on him the Thaddeus Stevens Award, and in April 2000 the Black Leadership Forum conferred on him the Lamplighter Award for leadership. In October 2000 Mr. Coleman received the Fordham-Stein Prize from the Fordham University School of Law, a prize presented annually to a member of the legal profession whose work exemplifies outstanding standards of professional conduct, promotes the advancement of justice, and brings credit to the profession by emphasizing in the public mind the contributions of lawyers to our society and to our democratic system of government. In March 2004 he was awarded the Marshall-Wythe Medallion from the Marshall-Wythe Law School of the College of William and Mary. *American Lawyer* magazine in May 2004 named him one of the twelve outstanding lawyers of the past twenty-five years. In September 2004 Mr. Coleman received the We the People award from the National Constitution Center for his lifetime achievements in civil engagement. In June of 2006 he received the Academy of Achievement's Golden Plate Award. Later that month, he received the District of Columbia Bar Association's Legends of the Bar Award. In May 2007 he received the University of the District of Columbia Law School's David A. Clarke School of Equal Justice Award; and the following week he received the Historical Society of Pennsylvania's Founder's Award. On June 7, 2010, he received the Rex

E. Lee Advocacy and Public Service Award of the J. Reuben Clark Society, which was presented by the dean of Brigham Young University Law School.

Mr. Coleman is a member of Phi Beta Kappa, Pi Gamma Mu, the American Academy of Arts and Sciences, the American Philosophical Society (founded in 1745 by Benjamin Franklin and Thomas Jefferson), the Order of the Coif, and the Alpha Phi Alpha fraternity.

He is the author of "The Supreme Court of the United States: Managing Its Caseload to Achieve Its Constitutional Purposes" (1983); "Mr. Justice Felix Frankfurter: Civil Libertarian as a Lawyer and as Justice: Extent to Which Judicial Responsibilities Affected His Pre-Court Convictions" (1978); "The Foreign Corrupt Practices Act of 1977 Regulation of Foreign Business Practices: A Reassessment" (1980); "Corporate Dividends and Conflict of Law" (1950); "Effect of the Presence of a State Law Question on the Exercise of Federal Jurisdiction" (1947); "Pennsylvania Marital Communities and Common Law Neighbors" (1947) (written with Judge Herbert F. Goodrich, U.S. Court of Appeals for the Third Circuit); "A Tribute to Mr. Justice Thurgood Marshall" (1991); "Mr. Justice Thurgood Marshall: A Substantial Architect of the United States Constitution for Our Times" (1991); "In Tribute: Charles Hamilton Houston" (1998); "A Friend's Portrait of Henry W. Sawyer III" (1999); and "Tribute to Mr. Justice Thurgood Marshall" (1999).

Mr. Coleman is a member of the Philadelphia Club, the Union League, the Cosmos Club, the Metropolitan Club, and the Alfalfa Club.

Mr. Coleman is married to the former Lovida Mae Hardin of New Orleans, Louisiana, a graduate of Boston University. The Colemans have three adult children. William III and Lovida Jr. are practicing lawyers. Hardin is dean of the School of Education of Boston University. The Colemans have four grandchildren.

PRINCIPAL CASES CITED

Alaska Airlines v. *Brock*, 480 U.S. 678 (1987)

Bailey v. *Alabama*, 219 U.S. 219 (1911)

Baker v. *Carr*, 369 U.S. 186 (1962)

Belton v. *Gebhardt*, 87 A.2d. 862 (Del. Ch. 1952), *aff'd*, 91 A.2d 137 (Del. 1952).

Berea College v. *Kentucky*, 211 U.S. 45 (1908)

Bob Jones Univ. v. *United States*, 461 U.S. 574 (1983)

Bolling v. *Sharpe*, 347 U.S. 497 (1954)

Boynton v. *Virginia*, 364 U.S. 454 (1960)

Bradley v. *Sch. Bd.*, 416 U.S. 698 (1974)

Briggs v. *Elliott*, 98 F. Supp. 529 (1951)

British Airways v. *Port Auth.*, 558 F.2d 75 (2d Cir 1977)

British Airways Bd. v. *Port Auth.*, 564 F.2d 1002 (2d Cir 1977)

Brown v. *Bd. of Educ.*, 347 U.S. 483 (1954)

Brown v. *Bd. of Educ. II*, 349 U.S. 294 (1955)

Brown v. *Bd. of Educ.*, 98 F. Supp. 797 (D. Kan. 1951)

Bryant v. *Yellen*, 447 U.S. 352 (1980)

Buchanan v. *Warley*, 245 US 60 (1917)

Center for Auto Safety v. *Lewis*, 685 F.2d 656 (D.C. Cir. 1982)

Citizens to Preserve Overton Park v. *Volpe*, 401 U.S. 402 (1971)

City & County of San Francisco v. *FAA*, 942 F.2d 1391 (9th Cir. 1991)

City of Burbank v. *Lockheed Air Terminal*, 411 U.S. 624 (1973)

Clarke v. *Sec. Indus. Ass'n,* 479 U.S. 388 (1988)

Clearfield Trust Co. v. *United States,* 318 U.S. 363 (1943)

Coit v. *Green,* 404 U.S. 997 (1971)

Colegrove v. *Green,* 328 U.S. 549 (1946)

Cooper v. *Aaron,* 358 U.S. 1 (1958)

District of Columbia v. *John R. Thompson Co.* 346 U.S. 100 (1953)

Envtl. Def. Fund v. *Dep't of Transp.,* 1976 U.S. App. LEXIS 11275 (May 25, 1976)

Evans v. *Jeff D.,* 475 U.S. 717 (1986)

Fed. Power Comm'n v. *Sunray DX Oil Co.,* 391 U.S. 9 (1968)

Garcia v. *San Antonio Metro. Transit Auth.,* 469 U.S. 528 (1985)

Green v. *Kennedy,* 309 F. Supp. 1127 (D.D.C. 1970), *appeal dismissed sub nom.* *Cannon* v. *Green,* 398 U.S. 956 (1970)

Hall v. *DeCuir,* 95 U.S. 485 (1878)

Indep. Union of Flight Attendants v. *United States Dep't of Transp.,* 803 F.2d 1029 (9th Cir. 1986)

MacDougall v. *Green,* 335 U.S. 281 (1948)

McLaughlin v. *Florida,* 379 U.S. 184 (1964)

Meyer v. *Nebraska,* 262 U.S. 390 (1923)

Missouri ex rel. Gaines v. *Canada,* 305 U.S. 337 (1938)

Mitchell v. *United States,* 313 U.S. 80 (1941)

Morgan v. *Virginia* (1946)

NAACP Legal Def. & Educ. Fund v. *NAACP,* 753 F.2d 131 (D.C. Cir. 1985)

Permian Basin Area Rate Case, 390 U.S. 747 (1968)

Pierson v. *Post,* 3 Cai. 177, 2 Am. Dec. 264 (N.Y. 1805)

Plessy v. *Ferguson,* 163 U.S. 537 (1896)

Sanders v. *Russell,* 401 F.2d. 241 (5th Cir. 1968)

School Board of Richmond v. *State Bd. of Educ.,* 412 U.S. 92 (1973)

Scott v. *Sanford,* 60 U.S. 393 (1857)

United Gas Improvement Co. v. *Callery Props.,* 382 U.S. 223 (1965)

United Gas Improvement Co. v. *Cont'l Oil,* 381 U.S. 392 (1965)

United States v. *Morton Salt,* 338 U.S. 632 (1950)

Virginia v. *West Virginia,* 222 U.S. 17 (1911)

Wolf v. *Colorado,* 338 U.S. 25 (1949)

BIBLIOGRAPHY

Acheson, David C. *Acheson Country: A Memoir*. New York: W. W. Norton, 1993.

Bates, Edward. "Citizenship." In *Opinions of the Attorney General* 10 (1862).

Bickel, Alexander M. "The Original Understanding and the Segregation Decision." *Harvard Law Review* 69 (1955).

Bird, Kai. *The Color of Truth*. New York: Simon and Schuster, 1998.

Bliss, Donald T. "A Challenge to U.S. Aviation Leadership: Launching the New Era of Global Aviation." *Ripon Forum* (July 1991).

"Bob Jones Apologizes for its Racist Past." *Journal of Blacks in Higher Education* (Winter 2008–09).

Bork, Robert H. Address to Catholic University, March 31, 1982.

———. Address to the Federalist Society, Yale University, April 24, 1982.

———. Address to the University of San Diego Law School, December 1983.

———. "Civil Rights: A Challenge." *New Republic*, August 31, 1983.

———. *Constitutionality of the President's Busing Proposals*. American Enterprise Institute, 1972.

———. "Judicial Review and Democracy." In *Encyclopedia of the American Constitution*, vol. 3. Edited by Leonard Levy and others. New York: Macmillan, 1986.

———. "Neutral Principles and Some First Amendment Problems." *Indiana Law Journal* 47 (1971).

———. *The Tempting of America: The Political Seduction of the Law*. New York: Simon and Schuster, 1990.

Boys and Girls Club of America. *Changing Lives, Changing America: 100 Years of Boys and Girls Clubs*. 2006.

Brandt, Nat. *Harlem at War: The Black Experience in WWII*. Syracuse University Press, 1996.

Bucholtz, Chris. *332nd Fighter Group: Tuskegee Airmen*. Oxford, U.K.: Osprey Publishing, 2007.

Bureau of National Affairs. *BNA General Policy*. November 22, 1976.

Cannon, James. *Time and Chance: Gerald Ford's Appointment with History*. New York: Harper Collins, 1994.

Chaffee, Zachariah. "Freedom of Speech in War Time." *Harvard Law Review* 32 (1919).

Clary, Everett B. *History of the Law Firm of O'Melveny & Myers LLP*. 4 vols. Los Angeles: O'Melveny and Myers, 2001.

Coleman, William T., Jr. "In Honor of John Hart Ely: John Hart Ely, Counsel for the Situation." *Stanford Law Review* 40 (1988).

———. "In Memoriam: A Friend's Portrait of Henry W. Sawyer III." *University of Pennsylvania Law Review* 148 (1999).

———. "In Tribute: Charles Hamilton Houston." *Harvard Law Review* 111 (1998).

———. "Mr. Justice Thurgood Marshall: A Substantial Architect of the United States for Our Times." *Yale Law Journal* 101 (1991).

———. *National Transportation: Trends and Choices (to the year 2000)*. PB[H]282[H]30. U.S. Department of Transportation, 1977.

———. "A Tribute to Justice Thurgood Marshall." *Harvard Law Review* 105 (1991).

Colonial Williamsburg Foundation. *Jamestown, Williamsburg, Yorktown: The Official Guide to America's Historic Triangle*. Williamsburg, Va., 2007.

Crain, Andrew Downer. *The Ford Presidency: A History*. Jefferson, N.C.: MacFarland Publishing, 2009.

Davis, Benjamin O., Jr. *Benjamin O. Davis, Jr., American: An Autobiography*. Smithsonian Institution Press, 1991.

DeFrank, Thomas. *Write It When I'm Gone: Remarks and Other Off-the-Record Conversations with Gerald R. Ford*. New York: Putnam's Sons, 2007.

Dempsey, Paul Stephen. *Public International Air Law*. McGill University Press, 2008.

Denniston, Lyle. "Justice Robert H. Bork: Judicial Restraint Personified." *California Lawyer* (May 1985).

Douglas, William O. *The Court Years, 1939–1975: The Autobiography of William O. Douglas*. New York: Random House, 1980.

Dryden, Charles W. *A-Train: Memoirs of a Tuskegee Airman*. University of Alabama Press, 2002.

DuBois, W. E. B. *The Souls of Black Folks*. Chicago: A. C. McClurg, 1903.

Dunham, Allison, and Phillip B. Kurland. *Mr. Justice*. University of Chicago Press, 1964.

Ellis, Joseph. *Founding Brothers: The Revolutionary Generation*. New York: Vintage Books, 2002.

———. *His Excellency: George Washington*. New York: Alfred A. Knopf, 2004.

Ely, John Hart. *Democracy and Distrust: A Theory of Judicial Review*. Harvard University Press, 1980.

Fairman, Charles. "Does the Fourteenth Amendment Incorporate the Bill of Rights? The Original Understanding." *Stanford Law Review* 2 (1949).

Farmer, Lawrence. "When Cotton Mather Fought the Smallpox." *American Heritage Magazine*, August 1957.

Federal Bar Association. *A Report on Transportation Restructuring: The Legal Challenges*. Arlington, Va., 1995.

Fellmeth, Robert. *The Interstate Commerce Commission: The Public Interest and the ICC; Ralph Nader's Study Group Report on the Interstate Commerce Commission and Transportation*. New York: Grossman Publishers, 1970.

Ferren, John M. *Salt of the Earth, Conscience of the Court: The Story of Justice Wiley Rutledge*. University of North Carolina Press, 2004.

Ford, Gerald R. *A Time to Heal: The Autobiography*. New York: Harper and Row, 1979.

Francis, Charles E. *The Tuskegee Airmen*. 4th ed. Boston: Branden Publishing, 1997.

Franklin, Benjamin. *The Complete Works of Benjamin Franklin*. 10 vols. London: Longman, Hurst, 1806.

———. *The Writings of Benjamin Franklin*, ed. Jared Sparks. 10 vols. London, 1882.

Franklin, John Hope. *From Slavery to Freedom: A History of Negro Americans*. New York: Alfred A. Knopf, 1947.

Friedman, George. *The Next Hundred Years: A Forecast for the Twenty-First Century*. New York: Doubleday, 2009.

Garrow, David J. *Liberty and Sexuality: The Right to Privacy and the Making of Roe v. Wade*. University of California Press, 1994.

Goodrich, Herbert F., and William T. Coleman. "Pennsylvania Marital Communities and Common Law Neighbors." *University of Pennsylvania Law Review* 96 (1947).

Goodwin, Doris Kearns. *Team of Rivals: The Political Genius of Abraham Lincoln*. New York: Simon and Schuster, 2005.

Goodwin, Richard N. *Remembering America: A Voice from the Sixties*. Boston: Little, Brown, 1989.

Gordon, John Steele. *Hamilton's Blessing: The Extraordinary Life and Times of Our National Debt*. Darby, Pa.: Diane Publishing, 1997.

Graham, John D. *Auto Safety: Assessing America's Performance*. Dover, Mass.: Auburn House, 1989.

Greenberg, Jack. *Crusaders in the Courts*. New York: Basic Books, 1994.

Greenfield, Meg. *Washington*. New York: PublicAffairs Books, 2001.

Greenspan, Alan. *The Age of Turbulence: Adventures in a New World*. New York: Penguin Books, 2007.

Hager, Barry M. "Lawyers on Corporate Boards: Resisting SEC Pressure." *Legal Times of Washington* 2, no. 18 (October 15, 1979).

Hamilton, Alexander. "The Report on Manufactures" (1791).

Hartmann, Robert Trowbridge. *Palace Politics: An Inside Account of the Ford Years*. New York: McGraw-Hill, 1980.

Hill, Oliver. *The Big Bang: Brown v. Board of Education and Beyond; The Autobiography of Oliver Hill, Sr.* Jonesboro, Ark.: Grant House, 2007.

Holder, Eric. Remarks prepared for African-American History Month Program, Department of Justice, February 18, 2009.

Holmes, Oliver Wendell. "The Path of Law." *Harvard Law Review* 10 (1897).

Homan, Lynn M., and Thomas M. Reilly. *The Tuskegee Airmen Story*. Illustrated by Rosalie M. Shepherd. Gretna, La.: Pelican Publishing, 2002.

Irons, Peter, and Stephanie Guitton, eds. *May It Please the Court: The Most Significant Oral Arguments Made before the Supreme Court since 1955*. New York: New Press, 1993.

Isaacson, Walter. *Benjamin Franklin: An American Life*. New York: Simon and Schuster, 2003.

Jackson, Robert H. "Full Faith and Credit: The Lawyer's Clause of the Constitution." *Columbia Law Review* 45 (1945).

James, Rawn, Jr. *Root and Branch: Charles Hamilton Houston, Thurgood Marshall, and the Struggle to End Segregation*. New York: Bloomsbury Press, 2010.

Jefferson, Alexander, with Lewis H. Carlson. *Red Tail Captured, Red Tail Free: Memoirs of a Tuskegee Airman and POW*. Bronx: Fordham University Press, 2005.

Katzenbach, Nicholas. *Some of It Was Fun: Working with RFK and LBJ*. New York: W. W. Norton, 2008.

Keynes, John Maynard. *The General Theory of Employment, Money, and Interest*. London: Palgrave Macmillan, 1936.

Kluger, Richard. *Simple Justice: The History of Brown v. Board of Education and Black America's Struggle for Equality*. New York: Alfred A. Knopf, 1975.

Kurland, Philip B., and Gerhard Casper, eds. *Landmark Briefs and Arguments of the Supreme Court of the United States: Constitutional Law; Brown v. Board of Education (1954 & 1955)*. Bethesda, Md.: University Publications of America, 1975.

Kushner, David. *Levittown: Two Families, One Tycoon, and the Fight for Civil Rights in America's Legendary Suburbs*. New York: Walker and Company, 2009.

Lacovara, Philip. "A Talk with Robert H. Bork." *District Lawyer* 9 (May–June 1985).

Liu, Meizhu, Barbara Robles, and Betsey Leondar-Wright. *The Color of Wealth: The Story behind the U.S. Racial Wealth Divide*. New York: New Press, 2006.

Locke, Alain. *The New Negro*. New York: Albert and Charles Boni, 1925.

Marshall, John. *An Autobiographical Sketch*. University of Michigan Press, 1937.

McConnell, Michael W. "Originalism and the Desegregation Decisions." *Virginia Law Review* 81 (1995).

McCullough, David. *1776*. Simon and Schuster, 2005.

McNeil, Genna Rae. *Groundwork: Charles Hamilton Houston and the Struggle for Civil Rights*. University of Pennsylvania Press, 1983.

Menand, Louis. *The Metaphysical Club: A Story of Ideas of America*. New York: Farrar, Strauss, and Giroux, 2001.

Morrison, Steven, and Clifford Winston. *The Economic Effects of Airline Deregulation*. Brookings, 1986.

Motley, Constance Baker. *Equal Justice Under Law: An Autobiography*. New York: Farrar, Strauss, and Giroux, 1998.

National Research Council. *Effectiveness and Impact of Corporate Average Fuel Economy (CAFE) Standards*. Washington: National Academy Press, 2002.

National Urban League. *State of Black America*. New York: National Urban League, 2009.

———. *State of Black America*. New York: National Urban League, 2010.

National Surface Transportation Infrastructure Financing Commission. *Paying Our Way to the Future: A New Framework for Transportation Finance*. February 2009.

Newmyer, John. *John Marshall and the Heroic Age of the Supreme Court*. Louisiana State University Press, 2007.

Newton, James S. *Justice for All: Earl Warren and the Nation He Made*. New York: Riverhead Books, 2006.

Neyland, James. *Crispus Attucks*. Los Angeles: Holloway House, 1995.

Nichols, David A. *A Matter of Justice: Eisenhower and the Beginning of the Civil Rights Revolution*. New York: Simon and Schuster, 2007.

Patterson, James T. *Brown v. Board of Education: A Civil Rights Milestone and Its Troubled Legacy*. Oxford, U.K.: Oxford University Press, 2001.

Peppers, Todd. *Courtiers of the Marble Palace: The Rise and Influence of the Supreme Court Law Clerk*. Stanford University Press, 2006.

———. "William Thaddeus Coleman, Jr. Breaking the Color Barrier at the Supreme Court." *Journal of Supreme Court History* 33, no. 3 (2008).

Pipes, Kasey. *Ike's Final Battle: The Road to Little Rock and the Challenge of Equality*. New York: World Ahead Media, 2007.

Powell, Colin L., with Joseph E. Persico. *My American Journey*. New York: Random House, 1995.

Report of the President's Commission on the Assassination of President Kennedy. Government Printing Office, 1964.

Roberts, John. Commencement address. Georgetown University Law Center, May 2006.

Rosen, Jeffrey. *The Supreme Court: The Personalities and Rivalries That Defined America.* New York: Times Books, 2007.

Rossiter, Clinton. *1787: The Grand Convention.* Macmillan, 1966.

Savage, Carter. "In the Interest of Colored Boys: The History of Boys' Clubs in Black Communities." Paper prepared for the annual meeting of the Association for the Study of African American Life and History, Atlanta, Ga., September 26, 2006.

Schwartz, Bernard. *A History of the Supreme Court.* New York: Oxford University Press, 1993.

Silber, Norman I. *With All Deliberate Speed: The Life of Philip Elman; An Oral History Memoir.* University of Michigan Press, 2004.

Simon, James F. *Lincoln and Chief Justice Taney: Slavery, Secession, and the President's War Powers.* New York. Simon and Schuster, 2006.

Slater, Rodney. *The Changing Face of Transportation.* Department of Transportation, September 5, 2000.

Specter, Arlen, with Charles Robbins. *Passion for Truth: From Finding JFK's Single Bullet to Questioning Anita Hill to Impeaching Clinton.* New York: William Morrow and Company, 2000.

Stewart, David O. *Impeached: The Trial of President Andrew Johnson and the Fight for Lincoln's Legacy.* New York: Simon and Schuster, 2009.

———. *The Men Who Invented the Constitution: The Summer of 1787.* New York: Simon and Schuster, 2007.

Tocqueville, Alexis de. *Democracy in America.* 2 vols. London: Saunders and Otley, 1835–40.

Transportation Research Bureau. *Winds of Change: Domestic Air Transport since Deregulation.* Washington: National Research Council, 1991.

Twyman, Wink. "Heritage Profile: Against All Odds; The Story of Sadie Tanner Mossell Alexander." *Pennsylvania Lawyer* 28 (2006).

Tyler, Samuel. *Memoir of Roger Brooke Taney LL.D.: Chief Justice of the Supreme Court of the United States.* Baltimore: John Murphy and Company, 1872.

Urofsky, Melvin I. *Louis D. Brandeis: A Life.* New York: Pantheon Books, 2009.

U.S. Congress. Senate. Committee on the Judiciary. *Confirmation of Federal Judges: Hearings before the Senate Committee on the Judiciary.* 97th Cong., 2nd sess., 1982.

———. *Hearings on the Bork Nomination.* Senate Hearing 100[H]1011, serial J[H]100[H]64. September 1987.

————. *Human Life Bill: Hearings on S. 158 before the Subcommittee on Separation of Powers.* 97th Cong., 1st sess., 1982.

————. *Nomination of Joseph T. Sneed to Be Deputy Attorney General and Robert H. Bork to Be Solicitor General: Hearings before the Senate Committee on the Judiciary.* 93rd Cong., 1st sess., 1973.

U.S. Congress. Senate. Committee on Labor and Public Welfare. *Equal Educational Opportunities Act: Hearings on S. 3395 before the Subcommittee on Education.* 92nd Cong., 2d sess., 1972.

U.S. Department of State. *A U.S. Policy toward South Africa: Report of Secretary of State's Advisory Committee on South Africa.* February 10, 1987.

U.S. Department of Transportation. *Aviation Noise Abatement Policy.* November 18, 1976.

————. *A Progress Report: Implementation of the 1975 Statement of National Transportation Policy.* September 17, 1976.

————. *Reorganization of the Department of Transportation and Its Programs.* January 19, 1977.

————. *Report of the Task Force on Oil Spills and Clean-up.* January 16, 1977.

————. *Secretary's Decision in Interstate Highway 478 New York City.* January 4, 1977.

————. *Secretary's Decision Concerning Vehicle Occupant Crash Protection.* December 6, 1976.

————. *A Statement of National Transportation Policy by the Secretary of Transportation.* September 17, 1975.

————. *Transportation Decisionmaking: A Policy Architecture for the 21st Century.* September 5, 2000.

U.S. Department of War. *Annual Report of the Chief of the Motor Transport Corps to the Secretary of War.* Government Printing Office, 1920.

Ward, Artemus, and David L. Weiden. *Sorcerers' Apprentices: 100 Years of Law Clerks at the United States Supreme Court.* New York University Press, 2006.

Warren, James C. *The Tuskegee Airmen Mutiny at Freeman Field.* Vacaville, Ca.: Conyers Publishing, 2001.

Washington, Booker T. *Up from Slavery.* New York: Doubleday, 1901.

Wilentz, Sean. *The Age of Reagan: A History, 1974–2008.* New York: Harper Perennial, 2008.

————. *The Rise of American Democracy: Jefferson to Lincoln.* New York: W. W. Norton, 2005.

Williams, Juan. *Thurgood Marshall: American Revolutionary.* New York: Times Books, 1998.

Wood, Gordon S. *Revolutionary Characters: What Made the Founders Different.* New York: Penguin Press, 2006.

NOTES

PROLOGUE

1. For a discussion of the founders' dilemma in reconciling the early republic's ideals with its treatment of persons of color, see, for example, Ellis, *Founding Brothers,* pp. 81–119. "The largest unmentioned and presumably excluded constituency was the black population, about 90 percent of which was enslaved. [From the beginning of our nation, 10 percent of blacks were free individuals.] [President] Washington said nothing whatsoever about slavery in his Farewell Address, sustaining the silence that the Congress had adopted as the official posture early in his presidency." Ibid., p. 157. The final draft of the U.S. Constitution avoids explicit mention of slavery. "It would, James Madison said, be wrong to admit in the Constitution the idea that there could be property in men." Wilentz, *The Rise of American Democracy,* p. 34. "Silence, of course, can speak volumes, and in Washington's case, the unspoken message was that a moratorium had been declared on this most controversial topic, which more than any other issue possessed the potential to destroy the fragile union that [the President] saw as his life's work and chief political legacy. Since the primary purpose of the Farewell Address was to affirm that legacy and further the promotion of his national vision, the last thing Washington wanted to mention was the one subject that presented the most palpable threat to the entire enterprise. Like Madison in 1790, he wanted slavery off the American political agenda. Unlike Madison, however, and unlike most of his fellow Virginians, including Jefferson, there is reason to believe that President George Washington thought this extension on slavery as a political problem should lapse in 1808, when the Constitution permitted the slave trade to end." Ellis, *Founding Brothers,* pp. 157–58.

2. At our breakfast table, the Coleman family talked about "The Autocrat at the Breakfast Table" and other writings of Dr. Oliver Wendell Holmes Sr., the father of Oliver Wendell Holmes Jr. (who spent three years after graduating from Harvard College fighting in the Civil War and was then an associate justice of the U.S. Supreme

397

Court). I had assumed that the Holmeses, father and son, not only were antislavery but were in favor of the integration of people of color into American life. Thus it was a great shock when I learned that Dr. Holmes, while dean of Harvard Medical School, had expelled three colored medical students because the white-student majority in 1850 had signed a petition stating that "we cannot consent to be identified as fellow students with blacks, whose company we would not keep in the streets, and whose society as associates we would not tolerate in our houses" and that "we feel our grievances to be but the beginning of an evil, which, if not checked will increase, and that this number of respectable white students will, in future, be in inverse ratio to that of blacks." Quoted in Menand, *The Metaphysical Club,* p. 8. When I started college at the University of Pennsylvania (in January 1938), I knew that a number of distinguished white Boston intellectuals, such as William James and Theodore Parker, believed "in the natural inferiority of Black people" and that Louis Agassiz, the "man for whom the Lawrence Scientific School [at Harvard] was created," taught the inferiority of people of color. Quoted ibid., pp. 87, 97. Also see Josiah C. Nott, *Two Lectures on the Natural History of the Caucasian and Negro Races* (Mobile: Dade and Thompson, 1844), pp. 23–24. More troubling is the case of Samuel Gridley Howe, physician, philanthropist, and abolitionist, who was married to the author of "The Battle Hymn of the Republic" and had been appointed by President Lincoln in 1863 to head the American Freedmen's Inquiry Commission, which was charged with formulating policies for dealing with a large freed black population. Howe accepted "as scientific" the erroneous racial myths (the inherent biological inferiority of blacks) set forth by Nott, William James, Theodore Parker, and Agassiz, which "helped sustain a hundred years of segregation." Quoted in Menand, *The Metaphysical Club,* p. 116.

3. Marshall, *An Autobiographical Sketch,* p. 3.

4. See chronology in this volume. Also see Kluger, *Simple Justice,* pp. 292–93, 321, 399, 553, 555, 601, 624, 638–39, 643, 722–23, 726, 776; and DeFrank, *Write It When I'm Gone,* pp. 49, 92, 207.

CHAPTER TWO

1. John Marshall, the fourth chief justice of the United States, was also born in a place called Germantown, but his Germantown was in Virginia. However, as a young man he fought in the battle of Germantown, Philadelphia, on October 3 and 4, 1777. He was wounded slightly. In each of my junior and senior high school years there would be a reenactment of the Battle of Germantown. We would mark the high point of the advance of the American revolutionary forces toward downtown Philadelphia and look at the battle marks still on buildings on Germantown Avenue just below Chestnut Hill. The revolutionary forces were not able to advance into the heart of Philadelphia, and they were forced to retreat to Valley Forge, Pennsylvania, where they endured the horrors of a cold and snowy winter. Elite Philadelphians, on the other hand, spent a very social winter with the British officers. Chief Justice Marshall never forgot "that Americans did not rally en masse to the war effort or queue up to

bolster Washington's depleted ranks when things got desperate in 1777 and 1778. Ninety thousand on paper, two thousand in the field, said a lot about human nature to those inclined to listen." See Newmyer, *John Marshall and the Heroic Age of the Supreme Court*, pp. 24–25.

2. "Letter to Miss Stephenson," June 11, 1760, in *The Complete Works of Benjamin Franklin*, 2:95.

3. *Seventh Lincoln-Douglas Debate, Alton, Illinois*, October 15, 1858.

4. "It is long past time to reclaim Thaddeus Stevens as a great American figure." Stewart, *Impeached*, p. 319. As a final act of defiance, Stevens sold two family plots in a whites-only cemetery, and he was buried at Shreiner's Cemetery in Lancaster, Pennsylvania, which accepted all races, noting that fact on his tombstone. Ibid., p. 306.

CHAPTER THREE

1. Much to my surprise, the noted journalist Juan Williams brought to my attention a full-page federation advertisement in *USA Today* that highlighted the work of my father: "Both mentor and inspiration, . . . Coleman provided both hope and opportunity, establishing dozens of Clubs that made a profound, positive impact on thousands of young lives." *USA Today*, February 26, 2006, p. 15A. My father's contributions were also recognized in 2005, when the William T. Coleman Fellows program was founded to support the career development of black professionals.

2. Boys and Girls Club of America, *Changing Lives, Changing America*, pp. 36–37.

3. Savage, "In the Interest of Colored Boys."

4. Father received much recognition for his work. At the 1926 National Boys Clubs Convention, he received the Distinguished Service Award, and at the 1953 convention, the Bronze Keystone Award. In 1931 he chaired the National Boys' Clubs Conference in New York, and in 1942 he received the Stubbs Plaque for his outstanding contributions to the Germantown community. The achievement of which he was most proud, however, was the first prize won by the woodworking class of the Wissahickon Boys' Club at the Chicago Exhibition in 1919. My father had taught the class himself.

5. Franklin, "Letter to Thomas Brand Hollis," October 5, 1783, in *Writings of Benjamin Franklin*, 9:104.

CHAPTER FOUR

1. Compare DuBois, *The Souls of Black Folks* with Washington, *Up from Slavery*.

2. *Missouri ex rel. Gaines v. Canada*, 305 U.S. 337 (1938). For a brief description of Houston's legal strategy in *Gaines*, see Coleman, "In Tribute: Charles Hamilton Houston," pp. 2159–60.

3. Katzenbach, *Some of It Was Fun*, pp. 58–59.

4. See Locke, *The New Negro*.

5. See Brent Staples, "Editorial Observer: Back When Skin Color Was Destiny—Unless You Passed for White," *New York Times*, September 7, 2003.

CHAPTER FIVE

1. See Bucholtz, *332nd Fighter Group: Tuskegee Airmen*, pp. 44–45. Bob's widow later married the journalist Carl Rowan.

CHAPTER SEVEN

1. Tocqueville, *Democracy in America*.
2. Holmes, "The Path of Law," p. 469.
3. Keynes, *General Theory of Employment, Money, and Interest*.
4. See Twyman, "Heritage Profile: Against All Odds," pp. 40–41.

CHAPTER EIGHT

1. *Pierson* v. *Post*, 3 Cai. 177, 2 Am. Dec. 264 (N.Y. 1805).
2. Jackson, "Full Faith and Credit," p. 16.
3. Peppers, *Courtiers of the Marble Palace*, p. 103.
4. *Urgency Deficiencies Act of 1913*, Public Law 63[H]32, chap. 32, *U.S. Statutes at Large* 38 (1913): 208, 220–21, *amended by* Public Law 77[H]515, chap. 210, sec. 3, *U.S. Statutes at Large* 56 (1943): 198, 199.
5. In 2005 I was reading the biographical sketch of a new law firm associate, Derek Douglas, a Yale Law School graduate, who joined us after spending three years with the NAACP Legal Defense and Educational Fund. As an undergraduate at the University of Michigan, he had won the Harold D. Osterweil Prize in Economics (awarded to the most outstanding graduating economics student.) Harold's family had established this prize after Harold's death. Derek now serves in the Obama White House.
6. Bird, *The Color of Truth*, pp. 74–79.

CHAPTER NINE

1. Coleman, "In Tribute: Charles Hamilton Houston," p. 2155.
2. Kluger, *Simple Justice*, p. 110. According to family legend, Houston's grandfather was an aide-de-camp to General Grant and one of the pallbearers who brought Lincoln's body back to Springfield. Ibid., p. 106.
3. Brandt, *Harlem at War: The Black Experience in WWII*, p. 119.
4. See *Mitchell* v. *United States*, 313 U.S. 80 (1941). A unanimous Supreme Court held that the black member of Congress Arthur Mitchell of Illinois could not be removed from the whites-only car when the segregated car was inferior.
5. On the morning I was to leave the cadet officers group at San Antonio Air Base for Harvard Business School, the commanding officer asked me to take command of all of the troops in my cadet officer class and lead the proceedings, which took place before breakfast, including marching into the breakfast building and thereafter back to the barracks. Being the only soldier of color in the class, I was in command of about

a thousand white soldiers. But in those years, even when the United States Army did the right thing, it never gave 100 percent. The published order transferring the selected cadets to the Harvard Business School contained two groups: group A included all the white cadets; I was the only cadet in group B. Nevertheless, I did get a first-class Pullman ride from San Antonio to Boston as a troop train was moving thousands of soldiers, black and white, up to Boston Harbor for embarkation to Europe. I also know that before the end of World War II the navy had commissioned several officers of color; they later served on combat ships, to my knowledge without racial discrimination.

6. Dryden, *A-Train;* Jefferson, *Red Tail Captured, Red Tail Free.* The story of the Tuskegee airmen has also made its way to film and children's literature. See, for example, *The Tuskegee Airmen,* directed by Robert Markowitz (HBO, 1995), and Homan and Reilly, *The Tuskegee Airmen Story.*

7. The story is well told in Warren, *The Tuskegee Airmen Mutiny at Freeman Field,* pp. 103–04, and Francis, *The Tuskegee Airmen,* pp. 243–45.

8. Warren, *The Tuskegee Airmen Mutiny at Freeman Field,* pp. 103–04.

9. Ibid., pp. 63–64.

10. Ibid., pp. 92–94.

11. Ibid., p. 154.

12. Nichols, *A Matter of Justice,* pp. 42–50, 275.

13. Thanks to Joseph Ellis and David M. McCullough, we now know, very late in American history, the story of Billy Lee, Washington's "mulatto slave, who came on the scene in 1768" and "accompanied him on foot and horseback, at all times." Ellis, *His Excellency,* pp. 44, 46, 79. See also McCullough, *1776,* p. 42. Of Billy Lee, McCullough writes: "Billy Lee, the body servant, rode with him, rode like the wind by all accounts and no less fearlessly than his master." Ibid., p. 48. "Riding with Washington . . . , Billy Lee became as familiar a figure, a large spy glass in a leather case slung over one shoulder." Ibid., p. 42. Washington's last will and testament freed Lee "outright upon Washington's death." It also "provided [Lee] with a small annuity along with room and board, 'as a testimony to my sense of the attachment to me, and for *his faithful service during the Revolutionary War*'"(emphasis added). Ellis, *His Excellency,* p. 263. See also Stewart, *The Men Who Invented the Constitution,* p. 257.

14. At least five thousand soldiers of color fought in the Continental army and colonial militias in the Revolutionary War. According to historian Joseph Ellis, that was a matter of necessity: " In this first year of the war, when the revolutionary fires burned their brightest, Washington presumed that he would enjoy a surplus of recruits. In October 1775 a council of war voted unanimously "to reject all slaves & by a great Majority to reject Negroes altogether." The following month Washington ordered that "neither Negroes, Boys unable to bear arms, nor old men unfit to endure the fatigues of the campaign, are to be enlisted." But within a few months, as it became clear that there would not be enough new recruits to fill the ranks as the militia units disbanded, he was forced to change his mind: "It has been represented to me," he wrote Hancock, "that the free negroes who have Served in this Army, are very much dissatisfied at being discarded—and it is to be apprehended that they may Seek employ in the ministerial Army—I have presumed to depart from the Resolution respecting them, &

have given license for them being enlisted; if this is disapproved of by Congress, I will put a stop to it." In that backhanded fashion Washington established the precedent for a racially integrated Continental army. Except for a few isolated incidents, it was the only occasion in American military history, until the Korean War, when blacks and whites served alongside one another in integrated units. Ellis, *His Excellency*, p. 84.

15. See "The Fourth of July; How a Battle in New Orleans Confirmed its Meaning," *Washington Post*, July 4, 2008.

16. Stewart, *Impeached*, p. 48; see also Goodwin, *Team of Rivals*, p. 548. Many were fighting soldiers. The historical record contains some glorious fighting by colored people, such as those who stormed Fort Wagner; those, including some of my relatives, who stormed up Lookout Mountain in Tennessee; and those who fought at Port Hudson and Milliken's Bend. By the last year of the Civil War "black soldiers had become so integral to the War effort that some of the commanders of our armies in the field who have given us our most important successes, believe the emancipation policy, and the use of colored troops, constitute the heaviest blow yet dealt to the rebellion." Goodwin, *Team of Rivals*, p. 554.

17. Warren, *The Tuskegee Airmen Mutiny at Freeman Field*, p. 19.

18. Nichols, *A Matter of Justice*, pp. 9–10.

19. See Davis, *An Autobiography*.

CHAPTER TEN

1. In my senior year on the *Review*, I wrote a note entitled "The Doctrine of Preclusion against Inconsistent Positions in Judicial Proceedings" (*Harvard Law Review* 59 [1946]). Shortly after my graduation in October 1946, while I was a Langdell teaching fellow at Harvard, I published an article entitled "Corporate Dividends and the Conflict of Laws" (*Harvard Law Review* 63 [1950]).

2. The word *Brahmin* was adopted by Dr. Oliver Wendell Holmes of Boston. It meant for him, as well as for me, a person of good family but in addition a scholar, or what today many would call an intellectual.

CHAPTER ELEVEN

1. This story is recounted in Peppers, "William Thaddeus Coleman, Jr., Breaking the Color Barrier," and Ward and Weiden, *Sorcerers' Apprentices*, p. 93.

2. About the same time I got a job offer from Judge Wyzanski of the U.S. District Court for Massachusetts. Barbara Scott, daughter of a leading colored family in Washington, was finishing Yale Law School. I told her about Judge Wysanki's inquiry and she applied for and got the job. Several years later, I told her about Donovan, Leisure's attempt to hire me after I had started at Paul, Weiss; she applied for and got that job. Barbara later became a lawyer for the Motion Pictures Association of America, ending her career as its general counsel. She married her law school classmate, Robert Preiskel, who became an outstanding tax lawyer at Fried, Frank, and Shriver. Bob and I served for many years as co-chairs of the board of directors of the NAACP Legal Defense and Educational Fund.

3. Goodrich and Coleman, "Pennsylvania Marital Communities and Common Law Neighbors."

4. The American Law Institute was founded in 1923. Its membership consists of judges, practicing lawyers, and legal scholars from all areas of the United States as well as some foreign countries, selected on the basis of professional achievement and demonstrated interest in the improvement of the law. The institute's incorporators included the chief justice of the United States, former president William Howard Taft, future chief justice Charles Evans Hughes, and former secretary of state Elihu Root. Judges Benjamin N. Cardozo and Learned Hand also were among its early leaders. The Institute's restatements, model codes, and legal studies are used as references by the entire legal profession.

5. On May 15, 2000, the American Law Institute awarded me its Henry J. Friendly award. It was a special thrill because two of the previous recipients were Paul A. Freund and Edward J. Levi, former law dean and president of the University of Chicago who, as attorney general, became my colleague in the Ford cabinet.

CHAPTER TWELVE

1. Isaacson, *Benjamin Franklin*, p. 453.

2. Quoted in "Life of Franklin," in *The Complete Works of Benjamin Franklin*, 1:523.

3. Quoted in Peppers, *Courtiers of the Marble Palace*, p. 104.

4. Ibid., 107.

5. *Wolf* v. *Colorado*, 388 U.S. 25 (1949), was overruled in 1961 by *Mapp* v. *Ohio*, 367 U.S. 643 (1961).

6. Three years after my clerkship, Justice Frankfurter, in his concurring opinion in *Youngstown Steel and Tube Co.* v. *Sawyer*, 543 U.S. 579, 594–95 (1952), set forth clearly his views on a justice's task: "The Framers . . . did not make the judiciary the overseer of our government. They were familiar with the revisory functions entrusted to judges in a few of the States and refused to lodge such powers in this Court. Judicial power can be exercised only as to matters that were the traditional concern of the courts at Westminster, and only if they arise in ways that to the expert feel of lawyers constitute 'Cases' or 'Controversies.' Even as to questions that were the staple of judicial business, it is not for the courts to pass upon them unless they are indispensably involved in a conventional litigation—and then, only to the extent that they are so involved. Rigorous adherence to the narrow scope of the judicial function is especially demanded in controversies that arouse appeals to the Constitution. . . . Due regard for the implications of the distribution of powers in our Constitution and for the nature of the judicial process as the ultimate authority in interpreting the Constitution has not only confined the Court within the narrow domain of appropriate adjudication. It has also led to 'a series of rules under which it has avoided passing upon a large part of all the constitutional questions pressed upon it for decision.' Justice Brandeis, in *Ashwander* v. *Tennessee Valley Authority*, 297 U.S. 288, 341, 346 (1936). A basic rule is the duty of the Court not to pass on a constitutional issue at all, however narrowly it may be confined, if the case may, as a matter of intellectual honesty, be decided without even considering delicate problems of power under the Constitution. It ought to be,

but apparently is not, a matter of common understanding that clashes between different branches of the government should be avoided if a legal ground of less explosive potentialities is properly available."

7. *Youngstown Steel and Tube Co. v. Sawyer,* p. 596.

8. Roberts, Commencement address at Georgetown University Law Center.

9. See Rosen, *The Supreme Court,* 120–21; Chaffee, "Freedom of Speech in War Time."

10. One scholar has observed that in most cases involving race, Justice Holmes thought that "if the white South as the 'de facto dominant power in the community' wanted to subordinate the black citizens under the thinnest cover of formal-legal equal treatment, the federal courts could or should do nothing about it." Rosen, *The Supreme Court,* p. 88.

11. There were two justices named John Marshall Harlan, a father and son. The father often is referred to as the first Justice Harlan.

12. See Simon, *Lincoln and Chief Justice Taney,* pp. 5–13. Perhaps Frankfurter was correct in his overall evaluation of Chief Justice Taney. "Indeed, two [well-respected] Chief Justices of the present [20th] century, Hughes and Warren, have delivered public addresses according him praise." See Carl Brent Swisher, "Mr. Justice Taney," in *Mr. Justice,* ed. Dunhan and Kurland, p. 203, also pp. 222–23.

13. During much of the Supreme Court's history, there was usually one seat tacitly reserved for a Catholic. To remedy a brief gap, Eisenhower appointed Justice Brennan to restart the tradition. Today, six of the nine justices are Roman Catholic.

CHAPTER THIRTEEN

1. There was ample precedent for the exchange of ideas that accompanied inter-branch walking. Chief Justice Marshall "was the chief walking companion and confidant of President John Quincy Adams." See Newmyer, *John Marshall and the Heroic Age of the Supreme Court,* p. 31.

2. *Doubleday & Co. v. New York,* 335 U.S. 848 (1948).

3. One tidbit we might have enjoyed but only surfaced recently: During much of the October 1948 term Justice Frank Murphy was often not present for oral arguments nor in his office. But he still voted, apparently by telephone or memo, on whether particular cases should be heard. In late 2005 I learned that he had given his proxy to Justice Rutledge, who often voted the proxy without prior consultation with Justice Murphy. See Ferren, *Salt of the Earth,* p. 406.

4. For a slightly different version, see Newton, *Justice for All,* p. 271.

5. Frankfurter to Coleman, letter, August 21, 1949, in possession of author.

6. Frankfurter to Coleman, letter, February 9, 1950, in possession of author.

7. Frankfurter to Coleman, October 6, 1948, in possession of author.

8. "Attorney General Eric Holder at the Department of Justice African American History Month Program," February 18, 2009 (www.justice.gov/ag/speeches/2009/ag-speech-090218.html).

9. Kluger, *Simple Justice;* Reed quotation from p. 598.

CHAPTER FOURTEEN

1. When a young associate complains about assignment of a menial task, I also cite the experience I had later at the Dilworth firm in Philadelphia. My senior partner, Harold E. Kohn, had asked me to serve a subpoena on Father Divine. It took a lot of finesse to work through the various layers of angels around him. I said I had to touch him with the subpoena, which he agreed. When I offered him the witness fee, which I assumed he might refuse, he said, pointing to one of the ladies, "Give it to my angel." I did, thanked him, and left. The case settled favorably to our client the very next day.

2. Adlai Stevenson really did not want to go to law school. After leaving Harvard Law School, he joined the family newspaper in Illinois. After a few years, he went to Northwestern Law School, graduated, and had a successful legal career. He served two terms as governor of Illinois and twice ran for president against Eisenhower (in 1952 and 1956), losing both times. Probably no other mortal could have won. He then joined Paul, Weiss and continued there until President Kennedy appointed him ambassador to the United Nations, where he delivered an elegant performance debating the Russian ambassador during the Cuban missile crisis.

CHAPTER FIFTEEN

1. Kluger, *Simple Justice,* pp. 136, 149, 156, 173–84, 220–24, 252. See also Williams, *Thurgood Marshall,* p. 107.

2. Williams, *Thurgood Marshall.* Williams writes, "Oddly, of the three leading black liberators of twentieth-century America—Thurgood Marshall, Martin Luther King Jr., and Malcolm X—Marshall was the least well known. . . . It was Marshall who ended legal segregation in the United States. He won Supreme Court victories breaking the color line in housing, transportation, and voting, all of which overturned the "separate-but-equal" apartheid of American life in the first half of the century. . . . It was Marshall who won the most important legal case of the century, *Brown* v. *Board of Education,* ending the legal separation of black and white children in public schools. The success of *Brown* sparked the 1960s civil rights movement, led to the increased number of black high school and college graduates and the incredible rise of the black middle class in both numbers and political power in the second half of the century." Pp. xv–xvi.

3. In 1957 the Legal Defense Fund was spun off as an independent entity, with Thurgood Marshall as its first director-counsel.

4. On January 7, 2003, at the dedication of the U.S. postage stamp depicting Justice Marshall in Washington, I attempted to describe certain essentials of his vital contribution to American history: "Only one other great American jurist, Chief Justice John Marshall, compares to Justice Thurgood Marshall in formatting our constitutional structure to breathe life into a document that has so well served this nation. They shared a mission; they shared a devotion to the nation and the law; they shared a name. It is striking that the two justices who did the most to bring to life a constitutional structure that makes possible one nation with equal justice for all, were both named Marshall." See Coleman, "Mr. Justice Thurgood Marshall"; Coleman, "A Tribute to Justice Thurgood Marshall."

5. Franklin, *From Slavery to Freedom*. Marshall called on Franklin in 1953 to document the way the South had ignored and undermined the Fourteenth Amendment. Franklin's stinging monogram was used in the NAACP's trial brief. See Kluger, *Simple Justice*, p. 627. Also see Walter Dellinger's op-ed piece on the death of John Hope Franklin, on March 25, 2009, at the age of ninety-four: "[Franklin knew that] we are still always crossing that bridge from Selma to Montgomery. But John Hope always looked at the State trooper blocking the bridge, the figure standing in the way of freedom and saw another child of God." Dellinger, "The Historian Who Lived What He Taught," *Washington Post*, March 26, 2009, p. A21.

6. Pedro Alonso Niño (also Peralonso Niño) (1468–1505) was a Spanish explorer who was known as el Negro (the Black). He accompanied Christopher Columbus on his third voyage to the New World and explored the West Indies independently thereafter. He became quite wealthy but was accused of cheating the King of Spain out of his 20 percent of the profits. He died before his trial. Thus the first black man to arrive in the New World came not only as a free man but as a leader of men.

7. Records from 1623 and 1624 list the Africans as servants, and later records show an increasing number of free blacks, some of whom were land owners. See Colonial Williamsburg Foundation, *Jamestown, Williamsburg, Yorktown*, pp. 34–36.

8. In 1706 the black slave Onesimus told the preacher Cotton Mather how Africans used the fluid from a mild smallpox infection to inoculate the healthy against the disease. Mather inoculated his son, who almost died, but in 1721 introduced smallpox inoculation to combat an epidemic. Mather conducted one of the first clinical trials on the Negro slaves. The mortality rate of those inoculated was only about 2.5 percent compared with 14 percent of those infected naturally. See Farmer, "When Cotton Mather Fought the Smallpox."

9. Crispus Attucks, who was shot and killed by the British on the Boston Commons, was the first casualty of the American Revolution. A runaway slave and free sailor, Attucks was the leader and instigator of the protest. As the son of an African man and an Indian mother, he was considered a mulatto. The British soldiers were defended by John Adams and acquitted of murder, as Adams argued that the six foot two, twenty-seven-year-old Attucks, "whose very looks was enough to terrify any person," had struck the first blow. After some controversy, the abolitionists erected a monument to Attucks on the Boston Commons in 1888 as "the first to defy, the first to die, the first to pour his blood as precious libation on the altar of a people's rights." Neyland, *Crispus Attucks*, pp. 180–82.

10. *Scott v. Sanford*, 60 U.S. 393, 576 (1857) (Curtis, J., dissenting).

11. See Goodwin, *Team of Rivals*, p. 190.

12. See U.S. Const. art. I, sec. 2. See also Rossiter, *1787: The Grand Convention*, pp. 266–67; Stewart, *The Men Who Invented the Constitution*, pp. 59–100, 119–26, 196–99, 204–06, 262. The 3:5 ratio gave slave states fourteen extra seats in the House in 1793, twenty-seven additional seats in 1812, and twenty-five added seats in 1833. Ibid., p. 262. Thus "when Southern guns fired on Fort Sumter in April 1861, a grandson of former President John Adams wrote in his diary, 'We the children of the third and

fourth generation are doomed to pay the penalties of the compromises, made by the first.'" Ibid., p. 206. David Stewart's wonderful book fully explains how the three-fifths compromise was reached. The larger Southern states wanted to encourage ratification by the smaller southern states, and the North wanted to limit the number of southern representatives in the House. The three-fifths clause also limited the tax contributions by the southern states. According to Stewart, John Rutledge of South Carolina and his Committee of Detail "reconceived the powers of the national government, redefined the powers of the states, and adopted fresh concessions on that most explosive issue, slavery. It is not too much to say that Rutledge and his Committee hijacked the Constitution. Then they remade it." Stewart, *The Men Who Invented the Constitution*, p. 165. As a result of the 3:5 ratio provided in Article I of the U.S. Constitution, the commonwealth of Virginia in the 1790s had six more representatives than did Pennsylvania, even though both states had roughly the same number of free inhabitants.

13. See Menand, *The Metaphysical Club*.

14. See Ellis, *Founding Brothers*.

15. For example: "The hero of State Street was Daniel Webster, whose 'Seventh of March Speech' in the United States Senate, invoking the principle of union above section, had cleared the way for the Compromise of 1850. That act—really a series of acts—dealt with the status of slavery in the new territories and in California in a manner satisfactory to the South. It also responded to southern demands for reinforcement of the fugitive slave laws. Laws affirming the property rights of slaveholders in former slaves who had escaped across state lines had been on the books since 1793; under the terms of the Compromise, their enforcement became for the first time a federal responsibility, which meant that southern slaveholders could enlist federal marshals and magistrates in their efforts to hunt down and retrieve refugees in the North—thereby trumping the authority of local officials and state 'liberty laws.' The new Fugitive Slave Law was the least-debated item in the Compromise of 1850, but it radicalized the North. It pushed many previously passive unionists into active animosity toward the South—not because they considered the law an encroachment on the liberties of black Americans, but because they considered it an encroachment on the liberties of Northern whites. It was a 'degradation which the North would not permit,' wrote Ulysses S. Grant near the end of his life, and he regarded it as the prime instigator of the war. 'The great majority of the people of the North had no particular quarrel with slavery, so long as they were not forced to have it themselves. But they were not willing to play the role of police for the South in the protection of this particular institution.'" Menand, *The Metaphysical Club*, pp. 10–11.

16. See *Scott* v. *Sanford*, p. 410.

17. Ibid., p. 407.

18. Taney quoted in Tyler, *Memoir of Roger Brooke Taney LL.D.*, pp. 599–600; Simon, *Lincoln and Chief Justice Taney*, pp. 156–57.

19. See Goodwin, *Team of Rivals*, p. 190.

20. "Citizenship," 10 Op. Att'y Gen., pp. 382–413.

21. *1866 Civil Rights Act*, chap. 31, sec. 1, 14 Stat. 27.

22. Kluger, *Simple Justice,* pp. 630–37.

23. Quoted ibid., pp. 58–59, 655.

24. One of Lincoln's most unfortunate decisions was to allow the replacement of his first-term vice president Hannibal Hamlin of Maine with a Democrat, Andrew Johnson of Tennessee. Lincoln claimed he was neutral on the issue of the vice president, and Johnson won the nomination on the second roll call at the Baltimore convention. See Stewart, *Impeached,* p. 347 n. 8. Presumably Lincoln thought that Johnson would improve his reelection prospects and help reunify the nation and heal its wounds. In 1844 Johnson had not been bashful about stating his views on blacks, who were "inferior to the white man in point of intellect—better calculated in physical structure to undergo drudgery and hardship," and "many degrees lower in the scale of graduation . . . between God and all that he had created in the white man." Ibid., p. 16. Johnson had opposed one bill because it "would place every splay-footed, Bandy-Shanked, humpbacked, thick-lipped, flat-nosed, wooly headed ebon-colored negro in the country upon an equality with the poor white man." Ibid. Johnson opposed the Fourteenth Amendment and vetoed much of the Radical Republicans' reconstruction legislation. When his vetoes were overridden, he undermined their implementation. Johnson ignored the rise of violence against freed slaves in the South and opposed giving blacks the vote, which would force white Southerners "to degrade themselves by subjection to the negro race." Ibid., p. 108.

25. For the full context of the horror that underlay the Jim Crow laws, see Kluger, *Simple Justice,* pp. 3–113 passim; 160; 202–54 passim; 312; 455–530, passim; 616; 624.

26. A 1936 NAACP flyer claimed that 5,105 people were lynched in the United States between 1882 and 1936. Williams, *Thurgood Marshall,* p. 81.

27. Kluger, *Simple Justice,* p. 89.

28. Ibid.

29. *Roberts* v. *City of Boston,* 163 U.S. 537, 550 (1896).

30. Ultimately, Harlan's prophetic vision would prevail in *Brown* v. *Board of Education.*

CHAPTER SIXTEEN

1. See Coleman, "In Tribute: Charles Hamilton Houston."

2. See James, *Root and Branch,* pp. 119–20, for the frustrating tale of Gaines's disappearance. See also Williams, *Thurgood Marshall,* pp. 97–99.

3. While the Supreme Court victory in *Sweatt* laid the foundation for the *Brown* strategy, the reality, as in *Gaines,* was not so pleasant. Williams, *Thurgood Marshall,* p. 185.

4. While the judicial outcome in *Sipuel* was less helpful than that in *Gaines,* the reality was more encouraging. See Williams, *Thurgood Marshall,* p. 179; James, *Root and Branch,* pp. 203–04.

CHAPTER SEVENTEEN

1. Hill, *The Big Bang.*

2. Motley, *Equal Justice under Law.*

3. See Greenberg, *Crusaders in the Courts.*

4. The Ming argument, in part, was based on his reading of Article VI of the U.S. Constitution: "This *Constitution,* and the laws of the United States which shall be made in Pursuance thereof; and all Treaties made, or which shall be made, under the Authority of the United States, shall be the supreme Law of the Land; and the Judges in every State shall be bound thereby, any Thing in the Constitution or Laws of any State to the Contrary notwithstanding." In other words, he read Article VI as saying that a treaty signed by the United States outranks even the U.S. Constitution itself. Thus the Migratory Bird Treaty case, *Missouri* v. *Holland* (1920), would become relevant as the U.N. Charter treaty provisions would then override the Fourteenth Amendment even if the Fourteenth Amendment as held in 1898 in *Plessy* v. *Ferguson* authorized racial segregation.

5. Juan Williams, in his biography of Marshall, recounts one participant pounding the wooden table in the conference room in reaction to Carter's doll proposal: "We'll absolutely lose. It's weak, it's a weak legal decision, the justices won't buy it, they won't go for it." Quoted in Williams, *Thurgood Marshall,* p. 209.

6. Patterson, *Brown* v. *Board of Education,* p. 44.

7. Marshall undoubtedly was influenced by his late mentor, Charles Houston, who was known for his philosophy of social engineering. Houston once said "a lawyer is either a social engineer or he's a parasite on society." By social engineer, he meant a highly skilled, perceptive, sensitive lawyer who understood the Constitution and knew how to explore its uses in solving the "problems of . . . local communities" and "bettering conditions of underprivileged citizens." Quoted in McNeil, *Groundwork,* p. 84.

8. Not only did we submit substantial sociological and psychological evidence at the trial level, but we also incorporated such evidence in our briefs to the Supreme Court. And the Court relied upon the evidence in the unanimous *Brown* decision. Could it have been a determinative factor? The information appealed to the politician in Chief Justice Warren and may have helped him persuade some of his colleagues. I remain personally convinced that we would have been better off if we had relied on a purely legal argument. The chief summarized the nonlegal evidence in footnote 11 to the *Brown* decision, which listed six psychological and sociological studies showing the detrimental effects of segregation on colored children. Footnote 11 became a source of great controversy. Southern critics argued that the Court had strayed too far from the Constitution and legal precedent by relying on the opinions of antisegregation sociologists for whom the traditions of the South were not in vogue. Footnote 11 became another arrow in the quiver of southern resistance.

9. *Mitchell* v. *United States,* 313 U.S. 80 (1941).

10. Kluger, *Simple Justice,* pp. 302–03. For example, Judge Waring of the federal district court in South Carolina was a renegade who supported school desegregation. He was the sole dissenter on the three-judge panel in the *Briggs* case that ruled against the NAACP. Ibid., pp. 366–67.

11. *Brown* v. *Bd. of Educ.,* 98 F. Supp. 797 (D. Kan. 1951).

12. *Briggs* v. *Elliott,* 98 F. Supp. 529, 548 (D.S.C. 1951) (Waring, J. dissenting).

13. *Belton* v. *Gebhardt,* 87 A.2d. 862 (Del. Ch. 1952), *aff'd,* 91 A.2d 137 (Del. 1952).

14. *Bolling* v. *Sharpe,* 347 U.S. 497 (1954).

CHAPTER EIGHTEEN

1. See Coleman, "In Memoriam: A Friend's Portrait of Henry W. Sawyer III," p. 7. In those days gentlemen like Henry Sawyer usually refrained from telling a friend what he had done for him to advance his career.

CHAPTER NINETEEN

1. The leading firms were Morgan, Lewis, and Bockius; Dechert, Price, Rhodes, and Clarke; Ballard, Spahr, and Ingersoll; Drinker, Biddle, and Reath; Pepper, Hamilton, and Sheatz; and Schnader, Harrison, Seagal, and Lewis. Wolf, Block, Shorr, and Solis-Cohen and Blank, Rhome, and Comisky were the leading Jewish firms.

2. The reputation for cross-examination of another young litigator, Aaron Fine, was so great that often a witness, seeing him move to pull a deposition out of his files, would simply say to the judge, "Let Mr. Fine remind me what I said a year ago in the deposition," preferring not to be exposed in a contradiction through a skillful cross-examination. The Republican contingent at the Dilworth firm included Doug Paxson, whose family owned part of the Pennsylvania Railroad, and Howard Dilks and Leo Sutton, who together led the estate and trust practice. Harry A. Kalish and Richard L. Levy were expert at getting business and along with James Sutton led a thriving transactional practice. Dolores Korman Slovitor joined the litigation practice a bit later. Note editor of the *University of Pennsylvania Law Review,* she taught at Temple University and then pursued a successful career as a trial lawyer until she was appointed by President Carter to the U.S. Court of Appeals for the Third Circuit, where she served as chief judge for seven years. Another young litigator, Louis Hill, was a stepson of Dilworth. He had married into the *Wall Street Journal* family. He tried a number of libel cases, accumulating the best won-and-lost record on the team. Hill lived a block away from my family, and our children got to know one another well, swimming in the Hills' beautiful backyard pool. Louis and I became partners at the Dilworth firm on the same night.

3. A year later I got what every lawyer craves, an extraordinary assistant, in Jean Palmer Greer. Born in Scotland, she had attended Germantown High and graduated from Beaver College with a major in English. She worked long hours, weekends, and holidays to make this ambitious young attorney look good, applying her extraordinary writing skills to leavening the language of my briefs. She worked on my many pro bono matters, including my work for the Warren Commission, the *Girard* case, my work for the LDF on *Brown* v. *Board of Education,* and other matters. Eleven years after joining our firm she married William Zeiter, an associate at Morgan, Lewis, and Bockius. She left my office two years later only because his law firm had hinted that if he became a partner there might be a conflict of interest. Zeiter became a leading partner at his firm, and the Zeiters became close friends of the Colemans.

4. See *Clearfield Trust Co.* v. *United States,* 318 U.S. 363 (1943).

5. According to one report, upon hearing the bad news on the way to a board meeting, a furious McShain ordered his chauffeur to stop his limousine as he instructed his discharged lawyer to exit the vehicle.

6. We also had an excellent relationship with Robert Turner, the city manager, and Seth Taft, who was on the city council.

CHAPTER TWENTY

1. Kluger, *Simple Justice*, p. 584; Newton, *Justice for All*, p. 305.

2. Newton, *Justice for All*, pp. 307–08; see also Kluger, *Simple Justice*, p. 619.

3. Douglas, *The Court Years*, p. 113.

4. *Brown v. Bd. of Educ.*, 345 U.S. 972 (1953), pp. 972–73.

5. At the time, the *Brown* team was fully aware of the uphill battle we were waging to apply the Fourteenth Amendment to state-sanctioned public school segregation. There was ample scholarship by respected academics that the Fourteenth Amendment, "as originally understood, was meant to apply neither to jury service nor suffrage, nor anti-miscegenation statutes, nor segregation." See Bickel, "The Original Understanding and the Segregation Decision," p. 58; but see McConnell, "Originalism and the Desegregation Decisions," pp. 950–54 (noting the scholarly consensus that the framers of the Fourteenth Amendment did not intend to prohibit segregation but ultimately finding the historical record to be less conclusive).

6. Greenberg, *Crusaders in the Courts*, p. 181.

7. Tennessee was readmitted before passage of the Reconstruction Act of 1867; it was therefore the only Confederate state to be readmitted under its antebellum constitution, amended only to abolish slavery. S. Con. 73, 39th Cong., 1st sess., 14 *U.S. Statutes at Large* 364 (1866). Half of Tennessee had remained loyal to the Union. Michael W. McConnell concluded in 1995, as I did in 1950–53, that such actions by the southern states is compelling evidence that the language used in the Fourteenth Amendment was meant to forbid legally imposed racial segregation in public schools. McConnell, "Originalism and the Desegregation Decisions," pp. 962–67.

8. Quoted in Kluger, *Simple Justice*, p. 658.

9. See Bickel, "The Original Understanding and the Segregation Decision."

10. On rare occasions, Marshall did perform. Juan Williams recounts a story told by Lou Pollak. During an intense mock argument a faculty member asked if the court had the power to end school segregation unilaterally. "Thurgood fell on one knee, Al Jolson–like, and said supplicant-like: 'Power? Power? White boss, you got the power to do anything you want!'" Williams, *Thurgood Marshall*, p. 223.

CHAPTER TWENTY-ONE

1. Kluger, *Simple Justice*, pp. 672–73.

2. Davis quoted in Kurland and Casper, *Landmark Briefs and Arguments of the Supreme Court*, pp. 33–43.

3. Ibid.

4. John Barrett to author, October 3, 2007, e-mail, "Jackson List: Thurgood Marshall in the Supreme Court."

5. See Nichols, *A Matter of Justice*, pp. 50–63.

6. See, generally, Silber, *With All Deliberate Speed*.

7. Quoted in Newton, *Justice for All*, pp. 324–25.

8. Ibid., p. 325.

CHAPTER TWENTY-TWO

1. Kluger, *Simple Justice*, pp. 701–02.

2. Meizhu Lui, "The Wealth Gap Gets Wider," *Washington Post*, March 23, 2009.

3. See Pipes, *Ike's Final Battle*, p. 175.

4. Brief of the United States, quoted in Nichols, *A Matter of Justice*, p. 71.

5. *Brown v. Bd. of Educ. of Topeka*, 349 U.S. 294 (1955), pp. 300–01.

6. *Griffin v. Sch. Bd.*, 377 U.S. 218, p. 229.

7. Nichols, *A Matter of Justice*.

CHAPTER TWENTY-THREE

1. Nichols, *A Matter of Justice*, p. 173.

2. As Kasey S. Pipes writes in the prologue to his book *Ike's Final Battle: The Road to Little Rock and the Challenge of Equality*, "The greatest American leader of his time was forced to confront the greatest American dilemma of all time. . . . On matters of race, he had always preferred the velvet cords of persuasion to iron bonds of federal law. He had always been more interested in leveling the playing field than in dictating scores. As long as people had a fair shot at the starting line he wasn't too worried about different outcomes at the finish line. . . . But civil rights may well have been an issue where conservatism simply didn't have enough to offer. The promise of incremental change over time was little solace to a poor black family in Selma or a young child of color in Albany. If ever an issue cried out for dramatic, federal action it was racial [in]justice. If ever policymakers should have sought to 'begin the world over again,' it was on civil rights." Ibid., p. xxxiii. "And so Eisenhower now genuinely believed in and embraced the cause of racial justice. He had been outraged by Goldwater. He had quietly worked with Kennedy to support civil rights. He even campaigned for black candidates for office and served as honorary chair for a fundraising drive to benefit the Tuskegee Institute. When Harvard's first black professor willed that his life's savings go to the establishment of a Dwight D. Eisenhower Scholarship Fund, Ike said he 'could not recall a personal distinction that had touched me more deeply.'" Ibid., p. 297.

3. Irons and Guitton, *May It Please the Court*, p. 254.

4. *Cooper v. Aaron*, 358 U.S. 1, 4 (1958). Excising racial discrimination from American public schools has often taken an incredibly long time. On Monday, June 26, 2006, "a federal appeals court . . . upheld a decision keeping the Little Rock School District under federal desegregation monitoring, which had been in effect since 1965. A three-member panel of the Eighth Circuit Court of Appeals in St. Louis agreed with a 2004 ruling by district court judge William R. Wilson in the long-running desegregation case involving the Little Rock district, the North Little Rock District,

and the Pulaski County Special School District. Wilson had ruled that the Little Rock district had not successfully evaluated its academic programs for how well they helped black students. Otherwise, the district would have been released from the remaining desegregation monitoring it had faced since 1965. The district had been released in 2002 from all aspects of its monitoring except those relating to program evaluations. In his opinion, Wilson held that the district would remain under court order through the 2005–06 school year. He ordered the district to hire outside experts and design a program assessment process." Noah Trister, "Federal Appeals Court Upholds Order in Little Rock Desegregation Case," Associated Press, June 27, 2006.

CHAPTER TWENTY-FOUR

1. The President's Committee on Government Employment Policy was created on January 18, 1955, by Executive Order 10,590 (20 *Federal Register* 409), which prohibited discrimination in government service. In addition to making policy, the committee reviewed 1,053 discrimination complaints and took corrective action in 96 percent of them. Nichols, *A Matter of Justice*, pp. 39–40.

2. The executive director of the committee was Berl Bernhard, who later became staff director of the U.S. Commission on Civil Rights, an adviser to secretaries of state Dean Rusk and Edmund Muskie, and a founding partner of one of the leading law firms in Washington. Elizabeth Drew, who later became a leading journalist and author, was communications director.

3. At the second of these meetings, Eisenhower recalled that he had met me in 1952 in Chicago and again in 1956 in Philadelphia, when Lovida's father was a delegate from Louisiana to the Republican conventions. It was also at these meetings that I first met Richard Nixon, Eisenhower's vice president. We had meetings with senators, including Hugh Scott, and members of the House of Representatives. It was there that I met Gerald R. Ford, member of Congress and the future minority leader of the House and president. Around this time I also met Lyndon B. Johnson, then a freshman senator from Texas, who had recently had a heart attack and was recuperating at Walter Reed Hospital. Justice Frankfurter had also had a heart attack at about the same time and was also resting up at Walter Reed, where one or more of his law clerks visited him each week. Often the tall gangling freshman Texas senator would come to the Frankfurter suite to join the gossip. We shared quite a few stories.

4. See Goodwin, *Remembering America*, pp. 121–22.

5. Another version of the story and the election statistics is recounted in Newton, *Justice for All*, pp. 376–78.

6. See Specter, *Passion for Truth*, p. 303.

7. William T. Coleman Jr. and W. David Slawson to J. Lee Rankin, memorandum, 1964.

8. Specter, *Passion for Truth*, pp. 44–125.

9. *Report of the President's Commission on the Assassination of President Kennedy* ("Warren Commission Report") (1964).

10. Ibid., p. 17.

11. Ibid., p. 21.

12. Coleman and Slawson to Rankin, memorandum, p. 89.

13. President Johnson's concerns with the nomination of Thurgood Marshall were recounted in Juan Williams's biography, where he refers to a meeting between the president and his attorney general, Nicholas Katzenbach. According to Williams, "Johnson, standing toe-to-toe with the equally tall balding Katzenbach, told him, 'Marshall's not the best—he's not the most outstanding black lawyer in the country.' Katzenbach grimaced as the imposing Johnson listed prominent, supposedly better qualified black lawyers such as William Coleman and Bill Hastie. Finally, Katzenbach, who had come to be friends with Marshall, faced up to Johnson's charge. He replied, 'Mr. President, if you appoint anybody, any black to that Court but Thurgood Marshall, you are insulting every black in the country. Thurgood is *the* black lawyer as far as blacks are concerned—I mean there can't be any doubt about that." Williams, *Thurgood Marshall,* p. 8.

CHAPTER TWENTY-FIVE

1. Among the issues discussed were the beginning of a proceeding, called AR 61-21, to fix the price of distributing newly produced natural gas in southern Louisiana through the interstate pipelines, and the *Permian Basin* case, to determine how the refunds from a Federal Power Commission rate reduction would be allocated to the distribution companies.

2. See Kushner, *Levittown.*

3. Betty was a member of the Strawbridge family, who founded the department store Strawbridge and Clothier, and her mother, as previously noted, served on the board of directors of the Wissahickon Boys' Club.

4. One Vermont neighbor, John Jones, a graduate of Harvard Law School, was a leading tax lawyer in the prominent Washington law firm of Covington and Burling. He also served in the Kennedy administration in the department of the treasury. His brother-in-law, Frank Coffin, is a former Frankfurter law clerk and now a professor of law at Harvard Law School.

5. Lolo Sarnoff has a studio adjacent to her Bethesda home, where she has created extraordinary sculpture using fiber optics, Plexiglas, chrome, and other metals. She has had many shows, and her favorite piece—The Flame, in memory of President Kennedy—is exhibited in the Kennedy Center Opera House in Washington.

6. Recognizing the aging demographics and growing scourge of Alzheimer's and other forms of dementia, and appreciating the value of struggling artists and their contribution to the nation's quality of life, Lolo came up with a wonderful idea. Drawing on her connections in the diplomatic community and the Washington arts establishment, she raises funds for an organization that recruits talented young artists, musicians, dancers, sculptors, painters, and storytellers and gives them special instruction on how to work with elderly citizens in low-income daycare centers, many of whom are struggling with dementia. The artists are paid to conduct interactive workshops. The results are quite extraordinary. A young Harvard-educated guitarist and songwriter

would visit a senior center in Northeast Washington and lead poor elderly persons in singing songs from the 1920s and 1930s. Some of them could remember every word, even though they could not remember the name of their spouse. Lolo is a pioneer in showing how the arts can contribute to healthy aging and slow the deterioration that so often accompanies the aging process.

7. Barnes became very wealthy after developing an antiseptic silver compound, Argyrol. He had accumulated one of the world's largest collections of impressionist, postimpressionist, and early modern paintings, including extensive holdings by Picasso, Matisse, Cezanne, Renoir, and Modigliani as well as African art and sculpture. Something of an eccentric, he did not like the trustees of the Philadelphia Art Museum and decided to start his own foundation to house his diverse collection and provide an art school for about fifty people. As a child, Barnes had attended African American revival meetings with his mother, who was a devout Methodist. During those religious retreats Barnes developed an appreciation for African American culture, especially its music and art. Barnes was also very supportive of African American artists.

8. Halaby was a leading star in the early days of aviation, having served as an adviser to President Kennedy, the chief negotiator of international aviation agreements for the U.S. Department of State, and the first head of both the Civil Aeronautics Board and the Federal Aviation Administration. Of Lebanese descent, he was actively involved with the Middle East. His beautiful daughter, after marrying King Hussein of Jordan, became Queen Noor. Halaby was a lawyer who had started his career with O'Melveny & Myers, the Los Angeles–based law firm that I would join after my tenure as secretary of transportation. His other daughter, Alexa, became an associate in O'Melveny's Washington office after I joined it in 1977.

9. In recent years, the number of Americans of color serving in top executive positions and as general counsel of major companies has exploded. Law firms wishing to do business with these companies had better be able to show a diversified group of attorneys. In 2005 I saw a survey of minority general counsel in Fortune 500 companies. They included Vernon Baker, senior vice president and general counsel, Arvin Meritor; Paula Boggs, executive vice president and general counsel, Starbucks Coffee; James Breedlove, vice president and general counsel, Praxair; C. Michael Carter, vice president, general counsel, and secretary, Dole Foods; M. Javade Chaudri, executive vice president and general counsel, Sempra Energy; Michele Coleman Mayes, senior vice president and general counsel, Pitney Bowes; James C. Diggs, senior vice president and general counsel, PPG Industries; Frank Fernandez, general counsel, Home Depot; Kenneth C. Frazier, senior vice president and general counsel, Merck; Alberto Gonzales-Pita, executive vice president and general counsel, Tyson Foods; Carlos M. Hernandez, general counsel and secretary, International Steel Group; Charles James, vice president and general counsel, Chevron Texaco; James Jenkins, vice president and general counsel, John Deere; Leonard J. Kennedy, senior vice president and general counsel, Nextel Communications; James Lipscomb, senior vice president and general counsel, MetLife; Don H. Liu, general counsel, Toll Brothers; George W. Madison, executive vice president, general counsel, and secretary, TIAA-CREF; Ronald

McCray, senior vice president for law and government affairs, Kimberly-Clark; Stacey J. Mobley, senior vice president, chief administrative officer, and general counsel, DuPont; Alberto Moreno, senior vice president and general counsel, Levi Straus; Roderick Palmore, executive vice president, general counsel, and secretary, Sara Lee; Gloria Santona, executive vice president, secretary, and general counsel, McDonald's; Charles Tanabe, senior vice president and general counsel, Liberty Mutual; Larry Thompson, senior vice president and general counsel, PepsiCo; Lawrence P. Tu, senior vice president and general counsel, Dell; Kellye Walker, vice president and general counsel, BJ's Wholesale Club; Paul S. Williams, executive vice president, chief legal officer, and secretary general counsel, Cardinal Health; Andrea Zopp, executive vice president and general counsel, Sears, Roebuck.

CHAPTER TWENTY-SIX

1. The leading Philadelphia lawyers and the law firms who vigorously opposed us were Owen B. Rhoads and Hastings Griffin of Decker, Price, and Rhoads; Thomas J. Gaffney of Gaffney and Gaffney; and Arthur Littleton, John Russell Jr., Ernest R. von Starck, and Richard P. Brown of Morgan, Lewis, and Bockius. On the other hand, two major Philadelphia law firms, Drinker, Biddle, and Reath led by Charles Biddle, Lewis H. Van Dusen Jr., and Henry L. Sawyer, and Dilworth, Paxson, Kalish, Levy, and Coleman, led by Richardson Dilworth and Douglas Paxson, extended their legal talents, voluntary time, and courage on behalf of poor orphans of color.

2. The judicial opinions are *Girard Estate*, 4 Pa. D. & C.2d 671 (Phila. Orphans' Ct. 1955), *aff'd*, 127 A.2d 287 (Pa. 1956), *rev'd sub nom; Pennsylvania* v. *Bd. of Dirs. of City Trusts*, 353 U.S. 230 (1957), *reh'g denied*, 353 U.S. 989 (1957); *Girard Estate*, 7 Pa. Fiduciary Rptr. 555 (Phila. Orphans' Ct. 1957), *reh'g den.*, 7 Pa. Fiduciary Rptr. 608 (Phila. Orphans' Ct. 1957), *aff'd sub nom; Girard College Trusteeship*, 138 A.2d 844 (Pa. 1958), *appeal dismissed and cert. denied sub nom; Pennsylvania* v. *Bd. of Dirs. of City Trusts*, 357 U.S. 570 (1958), *reh'g denied*, 358 U.S. 858 (1958); *Pennsylvania*, 260 F. Supp. 323 (1966); *Pennsylvania* v. *Brown*, 260 F. Supp. 358 (E.D. Pa. 1966); *Pennsylvania* v. *Brown*, 373 F.2d 771 (C.A. 3d Cir. 1967); *Pennsylvania* v. *Brown*, 270 F. Supp. 782 (E.D. Pa. 1967), *aff'd*, 392 F.2d 120 (3d Cir.), *cert. denied*, 391 U.S. 921 (1968).

3. Tribute to William T. Coleman, 154th Cong., 1st sess., *Congressional Record* 154 (February 23, 2009): S2357–59.

CHAPTER TWENTY-SEVEN

1. *McLaughlin* v. *Florida*, 379 U.S. 184 (1964).

2. *Bradley* v. *Sch. Bd. of Richmond*, 416 U.S. 698 (1974). Once again we relied on Supreme Court precedent that had nothing to do with race and were able to persuade the Court to extend the principle underlying its prior holdings to the civil rights cases at hand. The basic principle was that a change in the law must be given effect in a pending case unless there is a clear intention in the new statute that it was not to be applied retroactively.

3. *Sch. Bd. of Richmond* v. *State Bd. of Educ.*, 412 U.S. 92 (1973).

4. *Millicent* v. *Bradley*, 418 U.S. 717, 814–15 (1974) (Marshall, J., dissenting).

5. Quoted in Greenberg, *Crusaders in the Courts*, p. 348.

6. *Sanders* v. *Russell*, 401 F.2d. 241 (5th Cir. 1968).

CHAPTER TWENTY-EIGHT

1. William T. Coleman Jr., "Inducing Mr. Nixon to End His Seventh Crisis," *New York Times,* August 7, 1974.

CHAPTER TWENTY-NINE

1. In 1980 Robert Hartmann wrote, "He [President Ford] is, actually, color blind and (if there is such a word) creed-oblivious. He chose Bill Coleman for his Secretary of Transportation not because he wanted a token black face at the Cabinet table, but because he had been impressed with Bill as a young lawyer on the Warren Commission Staff. And Coleman richly returned Ford's confidence as one of his finest Cabinet choices." Hartmann, *Palace Politics*, p. 216; see also Ford, *A Time to Heal*, p. 238; and DeFrank, *Write It When I'm Gone*, pp. 49, 92, 207.

2. Quoted in Crain, *The Ford Presidency*, p. 36.

3. Additional insight into Elliot Richardson's style and approach to governance may be found in his books, *The Creative Balance: Government, Politics, and the Individual in America's Third Century* (New York: Holt, Rinehart, and Winston, 1976) and *Reflections of a Radical Moderate* (New York: Pantheon Books, 1996).

4. Alexander Pope, "Of the Nature and State of Man, With Respect to Society," in *Essays on Man*, epistle 3.

5. John Hart Ely's first love was writing. He was an original thinker and graceful writer who stressed quality over quantity. His book *Democracy and Distrust: A Theory of Judicial Review* (Harvard University Press, 1980) established his reputation as one of the nation's leading constitutional scholars. His later books, *War and Responsibility* (1993) and *On Constitutional Ground* (1996), reinforced his position as one of the sages of our time. His untimely death from cancer at the age of sixty-four deprived the nation of clear and thoughtful analysis at a time when it was most needed. I wrote a tribute to John in the *Stanford Law Review:* "John could transform the driest of investigatory prose into an exposition of lyrical clarity and insight." Coleman, "In Honor of John Hart Ely," pp. 357–58.

CHAPTER THIRTY

1. Even within the Department of Transportation, there was a tension between fuel economy and safety. Larger vehicles tended to be safer but less fuel efficient. See Sam Kazman, "Small Cars Are Dangerous Cars: Fuel Economy Zealots Can Kill You," *Wall Street Journal,* April 17, 2009; see also Robert E. Grady, "Light Cars Are Dangerous Cars: And Other Unintended Consequences of Strict Fuel-Economy Standards,"

Wall Street Journal, May 22, 2009; National Research Council, *Effectiveness and Impact of Fuel Economy Standards.* In fairness, Ray LaHood, secretary of transportation, has argued that meeting the tough new fuel economy standards would not necessarily require downsizing all vehicles because there also would be improved technologies in larger vehicles.

2. Discussion of cabinet meeting from Crain, *The Ford Presidency,* p. 189; my comments to the president are my own recollection. See also Wilentz, *The Age of Reagan,* p. 44.

3. See Lena Sun, "D.C. Out of Sync on Metro Funding," *Washington Post,* April 19, 2005.

4. Goodwin, *Team of Rivals.*

CHAPTER THIRTY-ONE

1. "The necessity for a comprehensive system of national highways," the report notes, "including transcontinental or through routes east and west, north and south, is real and urgent as a commercial asset to further colonize and develop the sparsely settled sections of the country, and finally as a defensive military necessity." Department of War, *Annual Report of the Chief of the Motor Transport Corps,* p. 11.

2. George F. Will eloquently describes the significance of this act in "Interstate Ribbons of Progress," *Washington Post,* July 9, 2006.

3. Federal Highway Administration, Department of Transportation, Frequently Asked Questions, "What Did It Cost?" (www.fhwa.dot.gov/interstate/faq. htm#question6 [April 8, 2010]).

4. *Citizens to Preserve Overton Park* v. *Volpe* (1971).

5. My predecessor had delegated the authority to reallocate the mileage, but I revoked the delegation and consequently the FHWA administrator would recommend an alternative project for my approval. I found it somewhat amusing that if I disapproved a particular recommendation, I would receive shortly thereafter a letter from a powerful senator or House committee chair, urging me to approve the project. The letter read an awful lot like the administrator's memorandum, sometimes containing the same typos and misspelled words.

6. Butterfield submitted a draft resignation letter that was highly critical of President Nixon and President Ford. I called him into the office and asked him candidly why he wanted to write such a critical letter. I thought his letter would be a one- or two-day sensation in the press and that would be the end of it. Butterfield felt betrayed because in accepting the administrator position, which President Nixon had urged him to take a few months earlier, he had had to resign his military commission in accordance with a congressional statute requiring that civil aviation be kept separate from the military. He therefore would have no job or source of income. Under the circumstances, I thought it only fair that we enter into a six-month consulting agreement. Butterfield provided some valuable advice to me and the FAA through the transition. He destroyed his vitriolic resignation draft and submitted a short and gracious letter of resignation.

7. My high regard for General Davis apparently was reciprocated. He wrote in his autobiography, "William Coleman had become an outstanding Secretary, brilliant in

his analysis of problems. Agatha and I hoped to see him appointed to the Supreme Court." Davis, *Autobiography*, p. 386.

8. From the peak year in 1969, when forty airliners were hijacked to Cuba alone, there were only twenty-two hijackings worldwide in 1973 and 1974. Although the Cuban hijacking threat had been mostly eliminated, we were facing the emerging threat of terrorism, much of it arising from conflicts in the Middle East. This called for continuing vigilance. In the last full year before my arrival, General Davis's successful screening program had denied boarding to 2,663 passengers and detected and confiscated 2,450 guns, 14,928 explosive and ammunition rounds, including fireworks, 21,468 knives, and 26,864 other dangerous articles. Davis, *Autobiography*, p. 386.

9. With such amenities I can perhaps overlook the fact that the Coast Guard had its own very strong relationships on Capitol Hill. One day the powerful chairman of the House Appropriations Committee asked me to see him about the inadequate funding of an important Coast Guard procurement. As I arrived for the meeting, I was told that the chairman was tied up and would be with me shortly. As I cooled my heels in the outer office, who should burst out of the chairman's door but the Coast Guard commandant and his legislative aide. When I walked in, the chairman had been fully briefed. Reading from his talking points, he made a most persuasive argument that I should find more money to meet the Coast Guard's demand. When I got back to the department, the commandant and I worked out a compromise by shifting around procurement funding within the budget mark.

10. Department of Transportation, *Report of the Task Force*.

11. Comprehensive engineering studies were carried out, involving track and structure design, upgrading, electrification, passenger and freight operations, terminals and shops, rolling stock, grade crossings, fencing, signaling, and operations. An assessment of the bridges in the corridor found that many of the pre-1895 bridges were inadequate for anticipated loadings in the 1990s and had not been properly maintained.

12. The final system plan was three years in the making, and a lot of vested interests were involved in getting the plan approved, including Edward G. Jordan, president of the USRA, his staff, its board, and its chairman, Arthur D. Lewis; the railroad unions who thought that government funding would protect their high wages and labor agreements; and even the bondholders and shareholders of the bankrupt railroads who would receive some compensation from the transfer of railroad assets to Conrail.

13. I was also concerned that because the freight railroads were shareholders in Amtrak and users of the Northeast corridor in which the federal government was investing billions of dollars to upgrade track, improve the train stations, and fix the bridges, they would be receiving a windfall. Recalling my class with Professor Leach at the Harvard Law School, I wanted to make sure that when the government made all these improvements, benefits didn't accrue solely to the private owners and that the government would retain ownership of its investments.

14. My friend Walt Wriston, chief executive of Citicorp and a former fellow Pan Am board member, called a meeting of the railroad chief executive officers, trustees, and commercial and investment bankers in New York. Wriston asked me to attend. The USRA presented its plan, and the bankers and lawyers discussed it. In the course

of the meeting, I said that I thought huge mistakes had been made by the management of the railroads and by the commercial banks that had made foolish loans to the Penn Central and other bankrupt railroads. I thought that the USRA proposal was too generous and that the banks ought to make some sacrifices to get the freight railroad operations off their hands. It would be a great understatement to say that my comments were not appreciated. I was fortunate not to have been thrown out of a high floor window of the Citicorp building.

15. The responsibility for regulating the safety of trucks was bifurcated between the Federal Highway Administration and the NHTSA, and in later years motor carrier safety was spun off into a separate administration (the Federal Motor Carrier Safety Administration), which doesn't make a lot of sense to me.

16. The Deepwater Ports Act required public hearings and set tight deadlines. A decision was required within ninety days after the last public hearing. In deciding whether to issue licenses to the two applicants, I was compelled to evaluate and consider a broad range of expert advice and information from federal agencies, adjacent states, and the general public. I was further directed to make specific findings that would protect, promote, and in some cases reconcile national priorities in energy, the environment, the economy, safety, and navigation on the high seas. In issuing licenses to the two applicants, I incorporated tough conditions that had been recommended by the Environmental Protection Agency, the National Oceanic and Atmospheric Administration, state environmental agencies, the Department of the Interior, the Federal Energy Agency, the Departments of State, Justice, and Defense, the U.S. Army Corps of Engineers, the attorney general, the Federal Trade Commission, the governors of Florida and Texas, and the Coast Guard. With the ninety-day statutory deadline and the end of the Ford administration looming, my general counsel's office negotiated day and night with the applicants and other federal agencies to develop workable licensing conditions. Essentially, I was acting as an honest broker between the various government agencies and the applicants.

17. Licenses were issued for Loop, Inc., and Seadock, Inc. Located in 110 feet of water in the Gulf of Mexico eighteen miles south of Grand Isle, Louisiana, Loop is the only U.S. port where deep-draft tankers can be offloaded.

18. Both deepwater port applicants were represented by Washington counsel. Given the tight deadlines, the complexity of the issues, and disagreement among the federal and state regulatory authorities, the Washington lawyers played an important role in the licensing process. The style and approach of the two attorneys could not have been more different. The lawyer for one of the applicants forcefully fought every proposed condition and restriction, displaying a disdain for federal bureaucrats who simply did not understand the oil-shipping business. The other attorney worked closely with my general counsel's office to draft language that would meet the federal objective in the most efficient way possible. He understood the statutory mandate but suggested ways in which government objectives could be achieved more efficiently. It was not a coincidence that the license negotiated with the more accommodating attorney was actually implemented. The experience was instructive for me in later years when I decided to practice law in Washington.

CHAPTER THIRTY-TWO

1. See 49 U.S.C., sec. 101(b): "A Department of Transportation is necessary in the public interest and to . . . develop and recommend to the President and Congress transportation policies and programs to achieve transportation objectives considering the needs of the public, users, carriers, industry, labor, and national defense." During the George W. Bush administration, Congress created a new position, under secretary for transportation policy, and the president appointed an experienced transportation policymaker, Jeffrey Shane, to the position to provide leadership in the development of policy. 49 U.S.C., sec. 102(d).

2. Hamilton, "Report on Manufactures."

3. Department of Transportation, *Statement of National Transportation Policy;* Department of Transportation, *A Progress Report.*

4. Coleman, *National Transportation.* The report provided a framework for long-range resource allocations, indicating the potential consequences of policy options, relating transportation to broader national goals, and encouraging forecasting and planning, performance measurement, program evaluation, and informed public debate. At the time it was issued, heavily regulated transportation industries were facing significant financial challenges and energy shock from the OPEC oil embargo. Energy conservation and independence were great concerns that unfortunately faded from the public consciousness all too quickly when gas prices declined.

5. Slater, *The Changing Face of Transportation;* Department of Transportation, *Transportation Decisionmaking.*

6. Section 611 of the Federal Aviation Act of 1958, *as amended* (1968), *codified at* 49 U.S.C., sec. 44715.

7. Chief counsel for the FAA Bert Goodwin, environmental counsel Len Ceruzzi, Department of Transportation environmental director Marty Convisser, Department of Transportation environmental counsel Greg Wolfe, and FAA noise expert John Wesler, among others, worked under the leadership of my acting general counsel to prepare the noise policy.

8. Department of Transportation, *Aviation Noise Abatement Policy.*

9. *City of Burbank* v. *Lockheed Air Terminal,* 411 U.S. 624, 635 n. 14 (1973).

10. Doug Feavor, "U.S. Moves to Cut Noise at Airports," *Washington Post,* November 19, 1976.

11. *Aircraft Noise and Capacity Act of 1990,* 49 U.S.C., sec. 47521 *et seq.*

12. Annex 16 to the *Convention on International Civil Aviation,* 61 Stat. 1180, T.I.A.S. no. 1591, August 9, 1946. See Dempsey, *Public International Air Law,* pp. 426–42, 426.

13. See, for example, *City and County of San Francisco* v. *FAA* (9th Cir. 1991) (prohibition of aircraft type held to be unjustly discriminatory).

14. See Bureau of National Affairs, *BNA General Policy,* pp. A[H]17–19. Today there is another compelling reason to encourage the use of newer, more fuel efficient technologies—reducing the impact of aircraft emissions on the climate. New engine and aircraft designs, alternative fuels, and satellite-based navigation technologies offer

the prospect of substantial reductions in carbon-based fuel. Incentives to accelerate the development and application of these technologies would be a triple winner, reducing airline costs, reducing carbon dioxide and other greenhouse gas emissions, and enhancing U.S. energy security and independence.

15. There was one issue in our aviation noise policy with which I was not completely satisfied. By adopting a phased-in compliance schedule, we encouraged operators to replace rather than retrofit some of the older aircraft for which hush kits were expensive and highly fuel inefficient, but I thought we should do more to assist the airlines to acquire new fuel-efficient aircraft. This would be good policy because it would support new aircraft development (greatly benefiting the U.S. balance of trade) and would reduce the nation's dependence on foreign oil. But because the airlines earned a very poor rate of return, they could not attract the capital to stimulate the design and production of the next generation of aircraft. To address these concerns I circulated a proposal for a special financing program to assist U.S. air carriers in purchasing replacement aircraft. To raise the funding, I proposed several alternative mechanisms, including a surcharge on the airline ticket tax, an aircraft noise pollution charge that would be returned to the airlines for the purchase of new aircraft, the extension of government loan guarantees for the purchase of replacement aircraft, or the use of airport development grants for this purpose. Not surprisingly in a conservative Republican administration, there was much opposition to my proposal. I took it to the president in a Saturday afternoon debate with Jim Lynn, director of the Office of Management and Budget, but President Ford agreed with the budget office that the proposal intervened too much into marketplace decisionmaking.

16. See Fellmeth, *The Interstate Commerce Commission*.

17. Crain, *The Ford Presidency*, pp. 202–09.

18. Key players in the department included Bill Kutzke, assistant general counsel for litigation, Peyton Wynn and Ray Young, policy analysts, and, of course, my deputy, John Barnum, and my lawyers, John Ely, Don Bliss, and Mark Aaron.

19. I was concerned about the sudden impact of complete deregulation on an industry that had grown up in the sheltered environment of federal protection. It was essential, I thought, to phase in deregulation in an ordered and predictable way, enabling airlines and their employees to adjust to a fully competitive environment.

20. During the Carter administration, airfreight was deregulated by the Air Cargo Deregulation Act of 1977, and passenger traffic was deregulated by the Airline Deregulation Act of 1978. The trucking industry was substantially deregulated by the Motor Carrier Act of 1980, and the deregulation of the railroads was completed by the Staggers Rail Act of 1980.

21. See Morrison and Winston, *The Economic Effects of Airline Deregulation;* Transportation Research Bureau, *Winds of Change*. Forty years ago, the average price to fly one mile was 34 cents and there were 172 million passengers. In 2009, the average price had dropped to 14 cents and the number of passengers had increased to 770 million. Scott McCartney, "The Golden Age of Flight," *Wall Street Journal*, July 22, 2010.

22. See Greenspan, *The Age of Turbulence*, p. 71 (describing deregulation as the Ford administration's "great unsung achievement").

23. The first draft I presented to President Ford's Economic Policy Board was roundly criticized, even by Elliot Richardson, secretary of commerce. I spent some time visiting the critics, such as deregulation advocate Paul MacAvoy, and we inched toward a common deregulatory approach to international air service, which was reflected in the final version issued by the department.

24. When President Roosevelt convened the Convention on International Civil Aviation in Chicago in 1944, seeking to establish a global framework for international aviation, the United States strongly promoted free markets, but the British and other Europeans were fearful of U.S. dominance. We were unable to address these concerns on a global basis at that time. Some sixty-five years later, it may now be the time to replace the fragmented structure of thousands of bilateral and multilateral air service agreements with an international agreement providing for a truly competitive global aviation market. See Bliss, "A Challenge to U.S. Aviation Leadership."

25. Department of Transportation, *Reorganization of the Department.* See William A. Jones, "Coleman Legacy: A Plan for DOT Reorganization," *Washington Post,* January 31, 1977. See also Federal Bar Association, *Report on Transportation Restructuring.* The Clinton administration Department of Transportation restructuring proposal would have consolidated ten modal administrations into three. The largest— the Intermodal Transportation Administration—would oversee highway, transit, rail, and maritime interests. The second component, the Aviation Administration, would have consolidated FAA safety and Transportation Department commercial space promotion but removed air traffic control management to a governmental corporation. The third component would have been the Coast Guard. I frankly preferred the Ford administration's approach, which created a separate safety administration. I was concerned about consolidating the safety oversight of the National Highway Traffic Safety Administration with the Federal Highway Administration and Federal Transit Administration grant-making authorities. Ibid., p. 2.

26. The Transportation Safety Administration would have been responsible for setting safety standards for all modes of transportation except aviation—automobiles, trucks, railroads, mass transit, and pipelines. To this day there is no effective federal safety oversight of local mass transit despite the fact that more people commute by public transit than by air. The new agency also would have sponsored research and shared best practices with state and local governments. Because safety is a top priority of the department, the administrator would have a dual appointment as under secretary for safety and would be responsible for coordinating with the FAA on aviation safety issues and with other nations and international organizations on cross-border safety issues, such as Mexican trucking. The Interstate Transportation Administration would have worked with the states in developing and implementing a national transportation plan. The Regional Administration would have provided urban and rural block grants to regional planning organizations and local governments.

27. National Surface Transportation Infrastructure Financing Commission, *Paying Our Way to the Future.*

28. One of my regrets, as I look back from a vantage of thirty-five years, is that I did not push hard enough as secretary for the development of high-speed passenger rail

service between major urban areas where it is economically feasible, especially funding research for the new technology of levitation. France, Germany, Japan, and China have all surpassed the United States in using the highly efficient mode of high-speed rail because some of us were asleep at the switch when we should have promoted this energy-efficient form of transportation.

29. In the reorganization plan, Deputy Secretary Barnum and I also proposed moving the Maritime Administration, which deals with water-borne transportation, including shipping, ports, vessel operations, the environment, safety, and the U.S. Merchant Marine, from the Department of Commerce to the Department of Transportation. We proposed folding these maritime programs into the Interstate Transportation Administration. Although our plan was never implemented, the Maritime Administration eventually was transferred to the Transportation Department, which was the right thing to do, since inland waterways and shipping are an important part of a seamless national transportation system.

30. My first step was to find a new director of the office of civil rights. Elaine Jones recommended Carmen Turner, a GS-4 clerk-typist, who displayed a certain toughness, charm, innovative spirit, and leadership potential that we recognized immediately. After she became the director, we made a lot of progress in the recruiting, hiring, and retention of minorities and in motivating our state and local counterparts and constituent organizations to do the same. Carmen went on to become the highly successful general manager of the Washington Metropolitan Area Transit Authority as it completed its 118-mile subway system. The media widely promoted her as a candidate for mayor of the District of Columbia when sadly breast cancer struck her down at the young age of fifty-seven.

31. Department of Transportation, *Secretary's Decision in Interstate Highway 478.*

CHAPTER THIRTY-THREE

1. Department of Transportation, Secretary of Transportation's Decision on Whether the Department of Transportation Should Approve the Construction of Interstate Route 66 in Arlington and Fairfax Counties, Virginia, August 1, 1975.

2. Editorial, *Washington Post,* August 2, 1975.

3. Department of Transportation, Secretary's Decision on Interstate Highway 66, Fairfax and Arlington Counties, Virginia, January 5, 1977.

4. At one point during the preparation, while reading the three-volume environmental impact statement, I came across some technical language that was hard to decipher. I asked Don Bliss to bring up the FAA noise expert John Wesler, who patiently explained the meanings of various noise measurement protocols. At one point a somewhat frustrated Don Bliss said to me, "Bill, you don't have to read every word of the environmental impact statement. That's what you have staff for." I replied, "But I read in the National Environmental Policy Act that the decisionmaker has to review the environmental impact and alternatives. If I am the decisionmaker then I have to read the environmental impact statement in order to understand the environmental implications and the alternatives."

5. Department of Transportation, The Secretary's Decision on the Concorde Supersonic Transport, February 4, 1976.

6. Excerpts from my public statement, which was published in full by the *New York Times*:

Few decisions I have made as Secretary of Transportation have caused me greater concern than this one. How could anyone, no matter what the objective statistics show, not be concerned about any increase in the noise levels around John F. Kennedy and Dulles? But at the same time, who—placed in a position of decision rather than advocacy—could confidently take it upon himself to treat the aircraft of our allies worse than other nations have historically treated ours, and single handedly to close the door on what is at least potentially an extremely significant technological advance? Perhaps my greatest worry, however, is that those who are disappointed by this decision will conclude that because their will did not prevail, the democratic process had somehow failed. That is why I have struggled so long to make the opinion I have distributed reflect what is in fact the case, that everyone's concerns were taken seriously in an honest attempt to reach a decision that is as fair as possible to all concerned, but that also expresses what is in the public interest that we all struggle to define.

One cannot hide from decision because decision is difficult, however, and after careful deliberation, I have decided for the reasons set forth in detail in the opinion to permit British Airways and Air France to conduct limited scheduled commercial flights into the United States for a trial period not to exceed 16 months under certain limitations and restrictions.

I am therefore directing the F.A.A. administrator, subject to any additional requirements he would impose for safety reasons or other concerns within his jurisdiction, to order provisional amendment of the operations specifications of British Airways and Air France to permit those carriers, for a period of no longer than 16 months from the commencement of limited commercial service, to conduct up to two Concorde flights a day into JFK by each carrier, and one Concorde flight a day into Dulles by each carrier.

These amendments may be revoked at any time upon four months' notice, or immediately in the event of an emergency deemed harmful to the health, welfare or safety of the American people.

1. No flight may be scheduled for landing or take-off in the United States before 7 a.m. local time or after 10 p.m. local time.

2. Except where weather of other temporary emergency conditions dictate otherwise, the flights of British Airways must originate from Heathrow Airport and those of Air France must originate from Charles de Gaulle Airport.

3. Authorization of any commercial flights in addition to those specifically permitted by this action shall constitute a new major Federal action within the terms of the National Environmental Policy Act and therefore require a new environmental impact statement.

4. In accordance with F.A.A. regulations, the Concorde may not fly at supersonic speed over the United States or any of its territories.

5. The F.A.A. is authorized to impose such additional noise abatement procedures as are safe, technologically feasible, and necessary to minimize the noise impact, including, but not limited to the thrust cut-back on departure.

I am also directing the F.A.A. to proceed with a proposed high altitude pollution program, to produce the database necessary for the development of national and international regulation of aircraft operations in the stratosphere.

I herewith also direct the F.A.A. to set up monitoring systems at JFK and Dulles to measure noise and emissions levels and to report the results thereof to the Secretary of Transportation on a monthly basis. These reports will be made public within 10 days of receipt.

I shall also request President Ford to instruct the Secretary of State to enter into immediate negotiations with France and Great Britain so that an agreement that will establish a monitoring system for measuring ozone levels in the stratosphere can be concluded among the three countries within three months. The data obtained from such monitoring shall be made public at least every six months.

I shall also request the Secretary of State to initiate discussions through the International Civil Aviation Organization and the World Meteorological Organization on the development of international stratosphere standards for the SST.

It is an understatement to say this has not been an easy decision. I am aware it will be unpopular in some quarters; indeed, I doubt it will meet with unalloyed acclaim in any quarter. But it has been made openly and in accordance with our democratic traditions.

"Concorde Flights to U.S. Approved for 16 Months,"
New York Times, February 5, 1976.

The *Washington Post* editorialized: "Secretary Coleman's decision to permit the Concorde to land in the United States on a trial basis strike us as a sensible answer to a close and difficult question. He has weighed the right issues—international fair play and technological progress on the one side and environmental consequences on the other—and concluded that only a test under operating circumstances will provide the right answer." *Washington Post*, editorial, February 5, 1976. Aside from some complaints from the press about the unusual procedure (locking the reporters in a room to read the entire decision), the coverage generally was quite thoughtful and reflected the time and investment the reporters made in reading the decision.

7. *Envtl. Def. Fund* v. *Dep't of Transp.* 1976 U.S. App. LEXIS 11275 (May 25, 1976).

8. *British Airways* v. *Port Auth.*, 558 F.2d 75, 80 (2d Cir. 1977).

9. Department of Transportation, *The Secretary's Decision Concerning Vehicle Occupant Crash Protection*.

10. See Department of Transportation, Results of the Secretary's Negotiations Concerning Motor Vehicle Occupant Crash Protection Demonstration Program, January 18, 1977.

11. See Graham, *Auto Safety,* p. 104.

12. Ibid., p. 103. My demonstration program called for the negotiation of agreements with Ford, General Motors, Chrysler, and Mercedes Benz to make available to customers at least five hundred thousand air bag–equipped vehicles at a modest additional cost, starting as early as September 1, 1978. Over the following five years, we would have had the opportunity to evaluate the technology and public acceptance of air bags, addressing potential concerns about unintended deployments and harm to children and the elderly. It is probable that improved technology would have been in general use by 1983. Regretfully, my successor, Brock Adams, scuttled my demonstration program and rushed through a rulemaking mandating installation of air bags or automatic seat belts starting by September 1981. The four-month rulemaking ignored substantial concerns raised by the manufacturers and other groups. In the words of John Graham, "In medical terms it was like introducing a new vaccine into the marketplace with no clinical trial experience with humans. That meant the air bag became an all or nothing experiment with the American driver as a guinea pig." Quoted in David B. Ottaway and Warren Brown, "From Life Saver to Fatal Threat: How the U.S., Automakers, and a Safety Device Failed," *Washington Post,* June 1, 1997. The Pacific Legal Foundation challenged the flawed administrative process, ultimately prevailing in the Supreme Court, which invalidated the mandatory requirement. The Reagan administration repealed all passive-restraint requirements. Secretary Dole reinstated the program as of September 1986 under a plan that required states to pass mandatory seat belt laws. In December 1991 President George H. W. Bush signed legislation mandating installation of driver-side air bags in new cars by September 1997. Meanwhile data continued to emerge concerning unintended consequences. In November 1996 the NHTSA issued a rule requiring warning labels, allowing the depowering of air bags, and introducing smart air bags.

13. Ernest Holsendolph, "Adams Cancels Plan to Put a New Airport in the St. Louis Area," *New York Times,* March 31, 1977.

14. An attempt to develop commercial aviation at Scott Air Force Base in southern Illinois (also known as MidAmerica St. Louis Airport) failed when Allegiant Air discontinued service in January 2009. So in today's economic environment, at least, the Illinois airport may not be viable.

15. *McNabb* v. *United States,* 318 U. S. 332, 347 (1943).

CHAPTER THIRTY-FOUR

1. See Crain, *The Ford Presidency;* Cannon, *Time and Chance;* Ford, *A Time To Heal.*

2. See Crain, *The Ford Presidency,* pp. 270–82.

3. Quoted in "Exit Earl, Not Laughing," *Time,* October 18, 1976.

4. As of this writing the governor of Massachusetts is Deval Patrick, the first governor of color of a northeastern state, who started his career on the staff of the Legal Defense Fund.

CHAPTER THIRTY-FIVE

1. I took some satisfaction in the trial judge's order enjoining the Interior Department from proceeding with the regulations until an environmental impact statement had been prepared. The solicitor of the department at the time was the former general counsel to the Environmental Defense Fund, which had often sued the Department of Transportation during my tenure for what he then argued was an inadequate environmental analysis. As solicitor of Interior he now had to defend his finding of "no significant impact" without doing any environmental assessment at all. I guess this demonstrated, once again, that where you stand on an issue depends on where you sit.

2. *Bryant v. Yellen* (1980). See also Clary, *History of the Law Firm of O'Melveny & Myers*, 3:693–94 and 4:965–90.

3. There was another dimension to the Imperial Valley representation. For Don Bliss and me, it was a special pleasure to work with the farmers who rose in the dark of early morning to till the hard desert soil. The farmers simply could not understand why federal bureaucrats, who had never been to the valley, wanted to destroy the fruits of three generations of hard labor. As we were transitioning out of government, it was a helpful reminder that all the answers are not found in Washington. The private sector deserves quality representation in making its case to the government.

4. As a director of several major corporations, I would subtly look for opportunities to inform my fellow directors of O'Melveny's many talents. Sometimes the company on whose board I sat retained the firm to represent it in a new matter. We were always careful in those cases to disclose fully the firm's representation, as required in the company's reports, and to maintain the integrity of my distinct roles as a director and as outside counsel. We also made sure that my participation and that of Don Bliss was fully consistent with all post–federal employment ethical requirements.

5. At the time, Pan Am had the world's most powerful international reservation system. With hindsight, I ask myself whether future events would have unfolded differently had Pan Am instead used the investment it made in National to develop the first global computer reservation system. As it turned out, American and United successfully developed this new technology.

6. See Clary, *History of the Law Firm of O'Melveny & Myers*, 4:947–61.

7. In 1994, with the dissolution of the Mudge Rose law firm in New York, Paul Koepff joined O'Melveny's New York office, bringing with him a team of lawyers who had handled CIGNA's East Coast coverage litigation. Every year since 1980, CIGNA has been one of the firm's top clients.

8. At Wade McCree's request I had presided over a law school moot court in which Otis Smith made a stellar argument. I wonder whether, if Otis had lost his first argument, he still would have called me to represent GM.

CHAPTER THIRTY-SIX

1. *Center for Auto Safety, Inc. v. Lewis*, 685 F.2d 656, 663 (D.C. Cir. 1982) (quotation to district court opinion omitted).

2. As complaints continued to come in, the Nader's group brought another unsuccessful action a couple of years later. The House of Representatives Committee on

Energy and Commerce, at the instigation of the Center for Auto Safety, held public hearings and summoned Ford executives to testify. The General Accounting Office, an arm of Congress, also conducted an investigation of the NHTSA proceedings and settlement. Our Washington office team worked intensively on all of these matters, preparing testimony for Ford executives and defending both the company and the agreement reached with the NHTSA. All these investigations ended without adverse impact on either Ford or the NHTSA.

3. *Walsh* v. *Ford Motor Co.*, 106 F.R.D. 378 (D.D.C. 1985), *rev'd*, 807 F.2d 1000 (D.C. Cir. 1986), *cert. denied*, 482 U.S. 918 (1987), *on remand at* 130 F.R.D. 260 (D.D.C. 1990), 945 F.2d 1188 (D.C. Cir. 1991).

4. In addition to Dick Warmer, the Ford team included Carl Schenker, John Beisner, and Brian Anderson.

5. On behalf of the Air Transport Association, Don Bliss filed a lawsuit against my old department, challenging noise regulations proposed for Washington National Airport. We were able to settle that lawsuit in a way that eased the restrictions on airport access for the new generation of quieter aircraft.

6. *Indep. Union of Flight Attendants* v. *U.S. Dep't of Transp.* (9th Cir. 1986).

7. When as secretary of transportation I worked on the first airline deregulation bill, I did not fully anticipate the extent to which deregulation would create such a dynamic, changing marketplace, opening up opportunities for law firms such as mine to exercise their creative talents in responding to changing market conditions. A Washington-based Civil Aeronautics Board regulatory law firm could not handle a transaction like the Pacific Division transfer because it called for expertise in so many diverse areas. Jeff Rosen, a former law clerk to Justice Brennan, and Michael Masin helped me negotiate the complicated transaction under which we created the Pacific Division and then sold it to United. Ben Benjamin dealt with all the complex tax implications of the various components of this transaction. Bob Siegel of our Los Angeles office, one of the top airline labor lawyers in the country, dealt with all the challenging problems of the transfer of Pan Am employees to United and the unraveling and reconstitution of various labor agreements. Warren Christopher and Ko Yung Tung (later general counsel to the World Bank) helped with the delicate diplomatic negotiations with Japan. Don Bliss and I helped shape the transaction in a way that would increase its prospects for regulatory approval and shepherded it through the administrative proceedings at the Department of Transportation and the appellate court. It was an extraordinary team effort, again demonstrating the value of close cooperation between our offices in California, New York, and Washington. O'Melveny handled the entire unprecedented transaction in record time, without the assistance of an investment bank adviser, and we were well compensated for our work.

8. Acker and Frank Lorenzo negotiated the purchase agreement, although for some reason, Acker did not get quite enough slots to operate the hourly shuttle service. Mike Masin and Don Bliss went up to New York and spent the night negotiating all night a purchase agreement, which unfortunately contained a few holes where we had not been able to get the slots we needed. We then filed a petition with DOT seeking to have additional slots made available to us to fill in the gap so that we could operate the hourly service as a full competitor. The Department of Transportation sat

on the petition but fully understood the point we were making. It disapproved Tex Lorenzo's application to acquire Eastern Airlines on the grounds that the spin-off of New York Air facilities was insufficient to ensure competition. After the disapproval, Lorenzo got the message and provided Pan Am with the missing slots. Now able to operate a competitive hourly service, we arranged to purchase the old marine terminal at LaGuardia Airport to house the new Pan Am Shuttle as well as provide marine transport from LaGuardia to Manhattan.

9. We handled a number of other interesting projects for Pan Am. After World War II, Pan Am had received the rights to operate a German service connecting Berlin to other key German cities. After the fall of the Berlin Wall, with the unification of Germany imminent, Pan Am wisely decided to sell its intra-German service to Lufthansa. I asked A. B. Culvahouse, who had recently returned to the firm after having served as White House counsel in the Reagan administration, to handle this transaction, which presented some unique questions of international law. We were able to complete the transaction and generate some badly needed cash for Pan Am before its rights would inevitably have been terminated with German unification. Unfortunately, Pan Am continued to bleed losses. In its continuing struggle to survive, Pan Am's chairman decided to sell its transatlantic air service from various U.S. cities to London Heathrow airport. Having established the precedent in the Pacific Division transfer case that international routes could be bought and sold, we negotiated the sale of Pan Am's Heathrow routes to United Airlines for $350 million.

CHAPTER THIRTY-SEVEN

1. On January 12, 1970, the three-judge U.S. District Court for the District of Columbia issued a preliminary injunction in a case called *Green* v. *Kennedy*, prohibiting the IRS from awarding tax-exempt status to a private school in Mississippi that refused to admit Negroes.

2. The district court upheld the IRS's denial of tax-exempt status for the Mississippi school, a decision that was affirmed by the Supreme Court in *Coit* v. *Green* (1971).

3. Bob Jones University filed returns under the Federal Unemployment Tax Act for the period from December 1, 1971, to December 31, 1975, and paid a tax. It sued the government for a refund. The federal government filed a counterclaim for unpaid federal employment taxes for the taxable years 1971–75 in the amount of $489,675.59 plus interest. The U.S. District Court for the District of South Carolina decided that no tax was due. It held that the revocation of the university's tax exemption was improper under the IRS rules and procedures and violated the university's rights under the religious clause of the First Amendment. See *Bob Jones Univ.* v. *United States*, 468 F. Supp. 890, 901–08 (D.S.C. 1978). In a divided opinion the U.S. Court of Appeals for the Fourth Circuit reversed and held that section 501(c)(3) must be read against a background of charitable trust law. A charitable institution is eligible for an exemption under that section only if the "institution [is] 'charitable' in the broad common law sense, and therefore must not be contrary to public policy." *Bob Jones Univ.* v. *United States*, 639 F.2d 147, 151 (4th Cir. 1980) (footnote omitted).

4. Goldsboro never received a determination by the IRS that it was an organization entitled to tax exemption under section 501(c)(3). Upon audit of Goldsboro's records for the years 1969 through 1972, the IRS determined that Goldsboro was not an organization described in section 501(c)(3) and therefore was required to pay taxes under the Federal Insurance Contribution Act and the Federal Unemployment Tax Act. Goldsboro paid the IRS $3,459.93 in withholding, Social Security, and unemployment taxes with respect to one employee for the years 1969 through 1972. Thereafter, Goldsboro filed a suit seeking refund of that payment, claiming that the school had been improperly denied section 501(c)(3) exempt status. The IRS counterclaimed for $160,073.96 in unpaid Social Security and unemployment taxes for the years 1969 through 1972, including interest and penalties. *Goldsboro Christian Schs., Inc. v. United States*, 436 F. Supp. 1314, 1315–16 (E.D.N.C. 1977). The U.S. District Court for the Eastern District of North Carolina decided the action on cross-motions for summary judgment. In addressing the motions for summary judgment, the court assumed that Goldsboro's racially discriminatory admissions policy was based on a sincerely held religious belief. The court nevertheless rejected Goldsboro's claim to tax-exempt status under section 501(c)(3). Ibid., p. 1318. The Court of Appeals for the Fourth Circuit affirmed. That court found an "identity for present purposes" between the *Goldsboro* case and the *Bob Jones University* case, which had been decided shortly before by another panel of that court and affirmed for the reasons set forth in *Bob Jones University. Bob Jones Univ. v. United States*, 461 U.S. 574, 584–85 (1983).

5. The religious belief argument always troubled me. What about Americans of color who clung to the belief that God created all her children equally? Why should the government trample on the free exercise of that belief?

6. John MacKenzie, "The Editorial Notebook: Friend of the Court," *New York Times*, October 15, 1982.

7. *Bob Jones Univ. v. United States*, 461 U.S. 574 (1983).

8. Ibid., pp. 592–93.

9. Quoted in "Bob Jones Apologizes for Its Racist Past," *Journal of Blacks in Higher Education* (Winter 2008–09).

10. Ibid.

CHAPTER THIRTY-EIGHT

1. Schwartz, *A History of the Supreme Court*, p. 22.

2. *Sec. Indus. Ass'n v. Comptroller* (D.D.C. 1983).

3. *Sec. Indus. Ass'n v. Comptroller* (D.C. Cir. 1985).

4. *Clarke v. Sec. Indus. Ass'n*, 479 U.S. 388 (1988).

5. I did not fare so well in my next argument. *Evans v. Jeff D* involved the right to attorneys' fees under the Civil Rights Attorney Fees Awards Act of 1976. Our client had brought a lawsuit against the state of California seeking injunctive relief on behalf of a class of emotionally and mentally handicapped children. As part of the settlement the state demanded and obtained a waiver of attorney fees, which was approved by the district court. This seemed grossly unfair to me and a terrible deterrent to

hard-working civil rights lawyers to settle cases. The Ninth Circuit Court reversed striking down the fee waiver as contrary to the federal statute. The Supreme Court nevertheless granted certiorari and, despite my passionate argument, reversed the circuit court and upheld the fee waiver provision in the settlement agreement.

6. Although we had represented the Air Transport Association in the rulemaking proceeding at the Department of Labor, the lawsuit was brought on behalf of fourteen individual airlines, which were expanding and hiring under deregulation. The case was captioned *Alaska Airlines, Inc.* v. *William E. Brock, Secretary or Labor*. Brock was the former senator from Tennessee and later chair of the Republican National Committee.

7. *Alaska Airlines* v. *Brock,* 480 U.S. 678 (1987).

8. In achieving this success Secretary Dole enlisted the support of the respected former governor of Virginia, Linwood Holton, who worked closely with the key congressional committees to design the plan that was enacted into law. The secretary and the governor got wonderful support from airports director Jim Wilding and attorneys Ed Faggen, in the FAA, and Greg Wolfe, in the Department of Transportation's general counsel's office.

9. The representation was fraught with irony. It is conceivable that the airport authority would not have been completely disappointed if a court had ruled that the review board was without constitutional authority to veto its decisions. But the Metropolitan Washington Airports Authority's board and management were fully committed to respect the compromise that had made possible the transfer of the airports and insisted on a unified front.

10. *Metro. Wash. Airports Auth.* v. *Citizens for Abatement Aircraft Noise, Inc.,* 501 U.S. 252 (1991).

11. Under an amended statute, a list of nominees for the board of review would be prepared by the Speaker of the House and the president pro tem of the Senate, but the actual appointments would be made by the authority's board of directors. In addition, the board could no longer veto a decision by the authority. It could make recommendations, but if the authority did not follow the recommendations, it was required to submit its decision and the reasons for it to both houses of Congress and wait sixty days before implementing the decision. This would give the full Congress an opportunity to enact curative legislation. That approach was rejected in *Hechinger* v. *Metro. Washington Airports Auth.* (D.D.C. 1994), in part because almost all the original congressional members of the board of review were reappointed. Finally Congress passed an amendment abolishing the board of review and providing for the appointment of an additional director to the airports authority board of directors to represent the federal interests.

12. The chairman of the American Public Transit Association at that time was David Girard-diCarlo, who was chairman of the Southeastern Pennsylvania Transit Authority. David was a lawyer who got his start at the Dilworth firm, working with me on Southeastern Pennsylvania Transit Authority matters. He recently served as U.S. ambassador to Austria.

13. The unions were elated. They sought to compare bus and subway operators to railroad operators. Both types of employees had unusual schedules that did not fit

neatly into the structure of a forty-hour workweek plus overtime as mandated by the Fair Labor Standards Act. On the other hand, most railroads in the United States were privately owned and operated. There were fewer than a handful of state-owned railroads. Railroads clearly were not a "traditional governmental function."

14. By this time there was a proliferation of lawsuits around the country, many brought by the unions seeking to enforce the Fair Labor Standards Act against local transit agencies. We often intervened or filed *amicus curiae* briefs at the appellate level. We also participated in oral arguments before several federal circuit courts with successful results.

15. Olson later became solicitor general and as a private lawyer argued the famous *Bush* v. *Gore* case that resulted in the presidency of George W. Bush.

16. Order of Supreme Court, June 16, 1984.

17. Chambers of Justice Sandra Day O'Connor to the Conference, memorandum, June 11, 1984.

18. Chambers of Justice Blackmun to Justice Powell, memorandum, July 3, 1984.

19. *Garcia* v. *San Antonio Metropolitan Transit Authority* (1985).

20. Historically, O'Melveny had eschewed the idea of establishing a separate appellate practice group. Instead, our litigators had the opportunity to take a case up from the trial through the appellate process, and sometimes ultimately to the Supreme Court, over a period of many years. For example, former firm chairman Chuck Bender successfully brought closure to the Imperial Valley cases by making an excellent argument before the Supreme Court. In 1998 the Washington office decided to establish a first-class appellate practice group and persuaded Walter Dellinger, former assistant attorney general, head of the Office of Legal Counsel at the Justice Department, and acting solicitor general during the Clinton administration, to join the firm. Walter had argued nine cases for the U.S. government before the Supreme Court. He was a respected professor of constitutional law at Duke Law School. Walter attracted a number of Supreme Court clerks to O'Melveny's appellate practice, and he has argued some of the most interesting and challenging cases in recent years on behalf of clients as diverse as Exxon Mobil and the District of Columbia. A brilliant but deeply humane and humorous colleague, Walter has been a tremendous asset to O'Melveny & Myers over the past decade. More recently, Walter was joined by Sri Srinivasan and Jon Hacker, two experienced appellate advocates who are racking up some significant victories in the Supreme Court.

CHAPTER THIRTY-NINE

1. *NAACP Legal Defense and Education Fund, Inc.* v. *NAACP* (D.C. Cir. 1985).

2. "Liberals were alarmed. President Ronald Reagan, a staunch conservative, had already appointed two justices—Sandra Day O'Connor in 1981 and Antonin Scalia in 1986, the latter at the same time that William Rehnquist was named to replace the retiring chief justice, Warren Burger. A moderate, Powell had voted with liberal justices on issues such as affirmative action and abortion. But Powell's departure now meant that liberals could count on only four justices—Harry A. Blackmun, William J.

Brennan, Thurgood Marshall, and John Paul Stevens. The conservative wing of the court consisted of Rehnquist, O'Connor, Scalia, and Byron White. With his selection of Powell's replacement, President Reagan could swing the balance in favor of the conservatives—and no one doubted that he fervently desired to do just that." Jason Manning, "The Bork Nomination," The Eighties Club, 2000 (http://eightiesclub. tripod.com/id320.htm [July 3, 2010]).

3. Bork, "Neutral Principles," p. 11. In fact, the *Meyer* line of case may be traced back to a Supreme Court decision of more than a century ago: "In a line of decisions . . . going back perhaps as far as *Union Pacific R. Co. v. Botsford*, 141 U.S. 250, 251 (1891), the Court had recognized that a right of personal privacy, or a guarantee of certain areas or zones of privacy, does exist under the Constitution." *Roe* v. *Wade*, 410 U.S. 147, 152 (1973); see also ibid., pp. 214–15 (Douglas, J., concurring), and pp. 167–71 (Stewart, J., concurring).

4. *Meyer* v. *Nebraska*, 262 U.S. 390, 399 (1923).

5. Justice Stewart's view in *Shapiro* v. *Thompson* was that the concept of liberty embraces the fundamental right to travel: "The constitutional right to travel from one State to another . . . has been firmly established and repeatedly." *United States* v. *Guest*, 383 U.S. 745, 757 (1966). This constitutional right, which, of course, includes the right of "entering and abiding in any State of the Union" (*Truax* v. *Raich*, 239 U.S. 33, 39 [(1915)]), is not a mere conditional liberty subject to regulation and control under conventional due process or equal protection standards. "The right to travel freely from State to State finds constitutional protection that is quite independent of the Fourteenth Amendment." *United States* v. *Guest*, p. 760, n.17. As we made clear in *Guest*, it is a right that can be broadly asserted against private interference as well as governmental action. Like the right of association, as in *NAACP* v. *Alabama*, 357 U.S. 449 (1958), it is a virtually unconditional personal right, guaranteed by the Constitution to us all. *Shapiro* v. *Thompson*, 394 U.S. 618, 642–43 (1969) (Stewart, J., concurring).

6. Bork, "Neutral Principles," pp. 8–9, 11–12.

7. Bork, address to Catholic University, p. 4.

8. Bork, address to Federalist Society, Yale University, pt. 2, pp. 8–9.

9. Bork, address University of San Diego Law School, p. 10.

10. Quoted in Garrow, *Liberty and Sexuality*, p. 256; see also Bork, "Neutral Principles." Research had revealed no judicial opinion in which Judge Bork has rejected, revised, or modified these views; Robert Bork, "Robert Bork: In His Own Words," *Washington Post*, July 5, 1987.

11. Senate Judiciary Committee, *Human Life Bill: Hearings*, p. 315; Robert Bork, address to the Seventh Circuit Court of Appeals (c. 1981), pt. 2, p. 7.

12. Quoted in Bork, *The Tempting of America*, p. 242.

13. Bork, address to Federalist Society, p. 8.

14. It has become an established part of our legal tradition to view the Constitution as forbidding government abuses that, in the words of Justice Frankfurter, "offend those canons of decency and fairness which express the notions of justice of English-speaking peoples." *Adamson* v. *California*, 332 U.S. 46, 59, 66–67 (1947) (Frankfurter,

J., concurring opinion); see also *Poe* v. *Ullman,* 367 U.S. 497, 522, 543 (1961) (Harlan, J., dissenting opinion). The conclusion that *liberty* as expressed in the Fifth and Fourteenth Amendments and the preamble to the Constitution each has substantive content in the realm of personal rights, indeed had been accepted by every justice then on the Court with the possible exception of Justice Black, whose somewhat distinctive jurisprudence results from his personal premise that the first eight amendments in their entirety are incorporated in, but represent both the floor and the ceiling of, the Fourteenth Amendment. See also Fairman, "Does the Fourteenth Amendment Incorporate the Bill of Rights?"

15. Senate Judiciary Committee, *Hearings on the Bork Nomination,* p. 180.

16. 42 U.S.C. 1982.

17. Chief Justice Vinson dissented. He fully accepted *Shelley,* which he had written, but argued that since the lawsuit in *Barrows* was between two whites who had signed the restrictive covenant, and the house had already been conveyed to the black buyer, and no claims for damages or other relief were being brought against the black buyer, there was, in Chief Justice Vinson's view, no one before the Court whose constitutional rights would be violated by an award of damages by the state court against the white seller who clearly had broken the contract.

18. Bork, "Neutral Principles," p. 16 (emphasis added).

19. 466 U.S. 429, 432n2 (1984). Thus Judge Bork's scholarly conclusion failed to come to grips with the fact that, much before *Shelley* and in the decades since then, the Supreme Court has recognized in a wide variety of contexts that "the action of state courts and judicial officers in their official capacities" is state action subject to the commands of the Constitution. *Shelley* v. *Kraemer,* 334 U.S. 1, 14 (1948). Chief Justice Vinson's list of those cases in *Shelley* included *Ex parte Virginia,* 100 U.S. 313 (1880), holding unconstitutional the actions of a [state] judge restricting jury service to whites; *American Federation of Labor* v. *Swing,* 312 U.S. 321 (1941), holding enforcement by state courts of common law to restrain peaceful picketing constituted state action prohibited by the Constitution; *Cantwell* v. *Connecticut,* 310 U.S. 296 (1940), holding state conviction for common-law crime of breach of peace to violate due process guarantee of freedom of religion; *Bridges* v. *California,* 314 U.S. 252 (1941), holding enforcement of common-law rule relating to contempt by publications constituted unconstitutional state action.

20. *Runyon* v. *McCrary,* 427 U.S. 160 (1976) applied this principle to private schools. The U.S. government filed a brief in the Supreme Court as *amicus curiae* urging affirmance. Solicitor general Bork, along with the deputy solicitor general, Lawrence Wallace, and the assistant attorney general for civil rights signed the brief. The official report of the Supreme Court shows no indication that Bork made an oral argument.

21. *St. Francis College* v. *Al-Karzaraji,* 481 U.S. 604 (1987); *Shaare Tefila Congregation* v. *Cobb,* 481 U.S. 615 (1987).

22. Judge Bork's published constitutional beliefs, again written as a scholar, if sustained by the Supreme Court, would have imposed severe, unfair, and unwarranted restrictions on the power of Congress under section 5 of the Fourteenth Amendment,

restrictions that the Court had already rejected. Section 5 provides that "the Congress shall have the power to enforce, by appropriate legislation, the provisions of this article." U.S. Const. amend. XIV, sec. 5. There are two possible positions regarding the scope of section 5. The narrow view adhered to by Judge Bork in his public speeches and writings is that Congress cannot enact any statute that would make illegal an action that would not violate the amendment *per se* in the absence of such statute. Under this cramped view Congress can only add penalties or remedies to what is already a constitutional violation. Bork, "Civil Rights," p. 22. See also Bork, *Constitutionality of the President's Busing Proposals*, p. 10 ("The [*Katzenbach* v.] *Morgan* (1966) decision embodies revolutionary constitutional doctrine"); Senate Judiciary Committee, *Confirmation of Federal Judges: Hearings*, p. 16 (Bork calls *Katzenbach* "incorrect"); Senate Judiciary Committee, *Human Life Bill: Hearings*, p. 310 ("I agree entirely with the dissent . . . in *Katzenbach v. Morgan*"); Bork, address to Seventh Circuit Court of Appeals, p. 5 ("*Katzenbach v. Morgan* is terrible law").

23. See *Lassiter* v. *Northhampton County Board of Elections*, 360 U.S. 45 (1959).

24. Not only did Judge Bork believe that under section 5 Congress could not establish rights not already found in section 1 of the Fourteenth Amendment, he also believed that Congress, believe it or not, can cut down on the remedy that courts could otherwise impose under the Fourteenth Amendment. For example, in *Swann* v. *Charlotte Mecklenburg*, 402 U.S. 1 (1971), the Court, in an opinion written by Chief Justice Burger, held 9 to 0 that once a district court had found that the school board had discriminated on the basis of race, the district court could order school busing to desegregate the school system in the same area in which the school board had exercised its power to segregate. The Court said: "As with any equity case, the nature of the violation determines the scope of the remedy." Ibid., p. 16. Professor Bork, however, in 1972, maintained that Congress, by statute, could reduce the Court's power to desegregate. Senate Committee on Labor and Public Welfare, *Equal Educational Opportunities Act: Hearings* (statement of Professor Robert Bork, Yale University Law School).

25. See Bork, address to Catholic University, pp. 16, 18, 19; Bork, "Neutral Principles," pp. 5, 17; Robert Bork, comments at the Justice and Society Seminar, Aspen Institute for Humanistic Studies, August 1985, transcript of tape recording.

26. Bork, address to Catholic University, pp. 18–19.

27. Nothing in Judge Bork's actions as U.S. solicitor general dispelled the honestly held fears of the civil rights communities generated by his erroneous views of the meaning and the effect of the Fourteenth Amendment. The reasons are crystal clear. First, he expressed many of these same views even after he left the office of the solicitor general. Second, briefs that he filed in his capacity as solicitor general seldom if ever had any direct bearing on the equal protection clause, since the cases generally involved statutory rather than constitutional issues. Third, it would be inappropriate to attempt to draw from Judge Bork's work as solicitor general any conclusions about his personal views on the constitutional issues discussed above. The solicitor general is the government's lawyer in Supreme Court cases, charged with presenting in that Court policies and legal views that other officials of the federal government, usually policy officials, are primarily responsible for formulating. At his confirmation hearings

for solicitor general in 1973, Judge Bork acknowledged that he would be prepared to "put aside [his] personal philosophy" and represent the government "on the basis of the policy as enunciated by the agencies and the Attorney General and on the basis of the law as it presently stands." Senate Judiciary Committee, *Nomination of Joseph T. Sneed to Be Deputy Attorney General and Robert H. Bork to Be Solicitor General: Hearings*, p. 5.

28. Robert Bork, "Judicial Review and Democracy," 3:1062; see also Senate Judiciary Committee, *Confirmation of Federal Judges: Hearings*, pp. 1, 13.

29. Lacovara, "A Talk with Robert H. Bork" (emphasis added).

30. Senate Judiciary Committee, *Confirmation of Federal Judges: Hearings*, p. 13.

31. Bork, address to Federalist Society, p. 126.

32. American Bar Association, "ABA Standing Committee on the Federal Judiciary: What It Is and How It Works" (1983), pp. 3–4.

33. Ibid., pp. 1, 4, 7–8.

34. *Dronenburg* v. *Zech*, 741 F.2d 1388 (D.C. Cir. 1984) (rehearing *en banc* denied, November 15, 1984).

35. In addition, an erroneous constitutional decision by a circuit judge is effective only for that circuit, not for the nation as a whole.

36. I referred the committee to appendix C attached to my written testimony submitted to the Senate Judiciary Committee for a discussion of Judge Bork's public statements about when a justice is obligated to follow the Court's precedents and when he is free to overrule them. One of the cases listed I knew all too well; I was the unfortunate lawyer who argued and lost it, 5-4. In *Garcia* v. *San Antonio Metropolitan Transit Authority*, 469 U.S. 528 (1985), Justice Blackmun had rejected his own previous concurring opinion and instead wrote the opinion that overruled *National League of Cities* v. *Usery*, 426 U.S. 833 (1976).

37. Senate Judiciary Committee, *Confirmation of Federal Judges: Hearings*, p. 999.

38. Ibid., pp. 1001–02.

39. Williams, *Thurgood Marshall*, p. 14.

CHAPTER FORTY

1. *Plessy* v. *Ferguson*, 163 U.S. 537, 543 (1896).

2. Quoted in Menand, *The Metaphysical Club*, pp. 400–01. In his chapters on pluralism and pragmatism (pp. 337–408), Menand discusses authors of the historical span including Charles Pierce, Thorstein Veblen, William James, August Weismann, Herbert Spencer, Franz Boas, and W. E. B. DuBois, who struggled with the issue. But the real challenge is how to determine what traditions and qualities from the cultures of diverse groups, races, and religions ought to be kept and encouraged into America's mainstream, in hope that they will be passed on to surviving generations.

3. Quoted in Urofsky, *Louis D. Brandeis*, p. 400.

4. Menand, *The Metaphysical Club*, p. 116.

5. At one time it was not uncommon for the media to refer to blacks as "darkies" and "shines." One of Marshall's early efforts for the NAACP was to convince major companies to stop using crude racial stereotypes on their products, such as Nigger

Head Shrimp, Pickaninny Peppermints, and Nigger Hair Pipe Tobacco. Williams, *Thurgood Marshall,* pp. 105–06.

6. Stephen Hess, letter to the editor, *Washington Post,* February 17, 2009.

7. American residents with a Spanish-speaking heritage still argue about whether the correct appellation is Hispanic or Latino. Daniel Fears, "The Roots of 'Hispanic': 1975 Committee of Bureaucrats Produced Designation," *Washington Post,* October 15, 2003.

8. National Urban League, *State of Black America.*

9. Senator James Webb of Virginia has criticized expanding government diversity policies giving preferences solely on the basis of race as treating "whites as a fungible monolith." He points out that in 1860, at the height of slavery, only 5 percent of whites in the South owned slaves. Many southern whites have lagged far behind the national average in education, income, and employment opportunities. Webb recommends abolishing all distinctions based on race and ethnicity except targeted programs to assist African Americans still in need in order to remedy the vestiges of slavery and government-sanctioned policies of racial discrimination in education, employment, and housing. Webb's recommendation, in my judgment, would reduce the white backlash against diversity programs and restore them to their original purpose—"eliminating the badge of slavery." James Webb, "Diversity and the Myth of White Privilege," *Wall Street Journal,* July 23, 2010.

10. Holder, remarks for African-American History Month.

11. See Liu, Robles, and Leondar-Wright, *The Color of Wealth.*

12. See also Rawn James Jr., letter to the editor, *Washington Post,* May 30, 2009. (The *Post* refers to Colin Powell "as one of the country's leading black political figures." James notes, "Nowhere in the 19-paragraph article was Powell's race even remotely relevant, and, pointedly he was the only person in the article described by his race.")

13. Apparently, the *American Lawyer* agrees, naming me as one of America's twelve outstanding lawyers of the past twenty-five years (*American Lawyer Lifetime Achievers,* May 2004). And apparently the *Washingtonian* concurs, having named me as one of ten preeminent lawyers in Washington over the years. "Legendary Lawyers," *Washingtonian,* December 2009, and "Local Lawyer Legend Bill Coleman," *Washingtonian,* February 2010.

14. Michael A. Fletcher, "Obama Talks of Significance of His Race," *Washington Post,* January 19, 2009.

15. Sam Roberts, "Projections Put Whites in Minority in U.S. by 2050," *New York Times,* December 18, 2009; see also Friedman, *The Next Hundred Years.*

16. Mixed race is hardly a new phenomenon. By the end of the Civil War "mulattoes actually outnumbered Negroes in the United States, a statistic not exactly comparable with the notion that racial interbreeding is instinctively repugnant and leads to extinction." See Menand, *The Metaphysical Club,* p. 115. Depending on the time and place, mixed-race persons might be called "octoroons," "quadroons," "creoles," "creamies," "half-caste," "half breeds," "coulored," or "President of the United States."

17. See also Edward M. Kennedy, *True Compass: A Memoir* (New York, Grand Central Publishing, 2009), p. 47.

CHAPTER FORTY-ONE

1. On September 7, 1977, President Carter signed the Panama Canal Treaty and the Neutrality Treaty promising to turn over control of the canal to Panama by 2000.

2. I applaud President Obama's decision to restore the American Bar Association's traditional role in vetting judicial nominees. There is value in the peer review of lawyers in assessing qualifications and judicial temperament.

3. President Reagan nominated O'Connor on July 7, 1981. She was confirmed by the Senate on September 22 and took the oath of office on September 25, 1981. She retired from the Court in January 31, 2006, and was replaced by Justice Alito.

4. The other members of the advisory committee were Griffin Bell, attorney general in the Carter administration; Father Timothy S. Healy, S.J., president of Georgetown University; Vernon E. Jordan Jr., a partner in Lazard Frères and former head of the National Urban League; Franklin A. Thomas, president of the Ford Foundation; Lawrence S. Eagleburger, who became secretary of state during the first Bush administration; Owen F. Bieber, head of the United Auto Workers; John R. Dellenback, president of the Christian College Coalition; Helene Kaplan, president of Barnard College; Roger B. Smith, chairman of General Motors; and Reverend Leon Sullivan, of the Zion Baptist Church in Philadelphia.

5. "Participation in this report has been a searing and shattering experience. For it revealed the stark reality that most whites in South Africa, even though they claim to have Western civilized values and have gained so many advantages from Western capital and technology, treat the overwhelming number of their black citizens and residents in inhumane ways, denying them even the basic human rights. Also upsetting is the utter lack of indignation and the acceptance of the status quo among a small number of people in the United States." Coleman, A U.S. Policy toward South Africa: The Report of the Secretary of State's Advisory Committee on South Africa (Department of State, 1987), p. 42. After becoming a partner at O'Melveny, Debra Valentine, the associate who worked with our committee, later became general counsel of the Federal Trade Commission. She is currently general counsel to Rio Tinto, the international mining conglomerate, based in London.

6. White House Commission on Aviation Safety and Security, report, February 12, 1997.

7. The other members of the six-person review team were David C. Jones, who had served as chairman of the Joint Chiefs of Staff; Robert Carswell, former deputy secretary of the treasury; Charles Duncan, former deputy secretary of defense; Judith Rodin, president of the University of Pennsylvania; and William H. Webster, former director of both the FBI and the CIA.

8. Department of the Treasury, *Public Report of the White House Security Review* (May 1995).

9. I was privileged to work with Newton Minow as chair of the committee and fellow committee members Floyd Abrams, Zoe Baird (a former law partner), Griffin B. Bell, Gerhard Casper, Lloyd N. Cutler, and John O'Marsh Jr. Fred H. Cate, the director of the Center for Applied Cybersecurity Research at Indiana University, was the committee reporter.

10. U.S. Department of Defense, Technology and Privacy Advisory Committee, *Report of the Technology and Privacy Advisory Committee, Safe Guarding Privacy in the Fight against Terrorism* (March 2004).

11. Ibid. "For all other government data mining that involves personally identifiable information about U.S. Persons, we recommend below that the government be required to first establish a predicate demonstrating the need for the data mining to prevent or respond to terrorism, and second, unless exigent circumstances are present, obtain authorization from the Foreign Intelligence Surveillance Court for its data mining activities. As we stress, that authorization may be sought either for programs that include data mining known or likely to include information on U.S. persons, or for specific applications of data mining where the use of personally identifiable information concerning U.S. persons is clearly anticipated. Legislation will be required for the Foreign Intelligence Surveillance Court to fulfill the role we recommend." Ibid., p. 40.

12. I wrote in dissent, in part: "My basic difficulty [with the report] is that the report talks mainly about 'data mining' in the broader sense, thus putting databases where the U.S. person willingly has supplied the data to the Government or a third person (and that person has willingly given it to the Government) in the same category as when the Government obtains the data by another method. . . . The Supreme Court of the United States has rejected the notion that there is a constitutional privacy right when the person has willingly given the information to the Government or to a third person who then willingly gives it to the Government. The depositor takes the risk, in revealing his affairs to another, that the information will be conveyed by that person to the Government. This Court has held repeatedly that the Fourth Amendment does not prohibit the obtaining of information revealed to a third party and conveyed by him to government authorities, even if the information is revealed on the assumption that it will be used only for a limited purpose and the confidence placed in the third party will not be betrayed." Ibid., pp. 82–84.

13. *Terminiello v. Chicago*, 377 U.S. 1, 37 (1949).

14. The other members of the military review court were former attorney general Griffin B. Bell; the chief justice of the Supreme Court of Rhode Island, Frank J. Williams; and Edward G. Beister, senior judge of the Court of Common Pleas in Doylestown, Pennsylvania.

CHAPTER FORTY-TWO

1. "This agrarian vision of America's future was fundamental to the separation between the Jeffersonian Republicans and the Federalists." Wood, *Revolutionary Characters*, pp. 108–09. See Wilentz, *The Rise of American Democracy*, p. 307.

2. As Lincoln was aware, by the end of the Civil War nearly 20 percent of the North's fighting forces were black, a significant number of whom were free negroes. Powell, *My American Journey*, p. 61.

3. President Andrew Johnson replaced several generals from southern commands whom he thought too aggressive and instructed that military force could be applied

only on his order. As a consequence in 1868, more than a thousand blacks and white unionists were killed in Louisiana, more than six hundred in Kentucky, and a black Republican congressman in Arkansas was assassinated. The Ku Klux Klan claimed credit for murdering leading Republicans in Alabama, Georgia, Texas, and South Carolina. Stewart, *Impeached*, pp. 302–03.

4. A Republican, Ulysses S. Grant, won the election in 1868 and served two terms. For a time the army restored some protection for freed slaves and unionists in the South, and the Fifteenth Amendment was ratified. Some six hundred Klansmen were convicted, and additional civil rights legislation was enacted. Ibid., p. 314. The election of 1876, however, brought the Hayes-Tilden Compromise in which Republican Rutherford Hayes agreed to withdraw federal troops in return for the Electoral College votes of Florida, Louisiana, and South Carolina, which put him over the top despite his loss of the popular vote. Thus the work of the Radical Republicans went into a long Rip Van Winkle dormancy, to be awakened during the Eisenhower administration by the Warren Court.

5. Williams, *Thurgood Marshall*, p. 82.

6. Some say Truman's appointments to the Supreme Court were mediocre. In 1970 Senator Hruska, in an unfortunate attempt to defend President Nixon's Supreme Court nominee G. Harold Carswell against accusations of mediocrity, proclaimed, "Even if [Carswell] were mediocre, there are a lot of mediocre judges and people and lawyers. They are entitled to a little representation, aren't they, and a little chance? We can't have all Brandeises, Frankfurters and Cardozos." Quoted in William H. Honan, "Roman L. Hruska Dies at 94; Leading Senate Conservative," *New York Times*, April 27, 1999.

7. Nichols, *A Matter of Justice*, p. 292, n.37.

8. Senator John Kennedy had criticized President Eisenhower for sending troops into Little Rock, Arkansas, saying that no American president should ever use military troops against U.S. civilian citizens. President Eisenhower clearly recognized the difficulty: He often said "sending in the troops was the hardest decision I have made since D-Day . . . but it was the only thing I could do." Jean Edward Smith, "We Should Still Like Ike," *New York Times*, July 7, 2008. At the University of Mississippi in the Meredith case in 1962, President Kennedy used only U.S. marshals at first, but the mobs soon overran them and President Kennedy, contrary to his criticism of Ike, sent in U.S. troops.

9. Quoted in Kathleen Parker, "Can the GOP Speak to Blacks?" *Washington Post*, September 3, 2000.

10. See Greenfield, *Washington*, pp. 187–90.

11. Historically, there were many more moderates or middle-of-the-roaders in Congress, who would cross party lines to forge a compromise and eschew partisan advantage to act independently in the public interest. We can learn a lot from the likes of Hugh Scott, Jacob Javits, Jack Kemp, Tom Davis, Connie Morella, Chris Shays, Tom Kuchel, Clifford Case, Mac Mathias, Gilbert Gude, Robert Stafford, Jim Jeffords, Bill Cohen, Mark Hatfield, John Heinz, Sherry Boehlert, Chuck Percy, Bill Green, Howard Baker, and Jim Leach, among many others.

CHAPTER FORTY-THREE

1. Urofsky, *Louis D. Brandeis,* p. 67.

2. For example, in a bankruptcy proceeding, Brandeis had been criticized for compromising a client's position by making sure that all the parties were treated fairly.

3. For example, we developed a litigation strategy to seek Supreme Court review of state "any willing provider" laws.

4. See Hager, "Lawyers on Corporate Boards."

5. My board memberships were not limited to global corporations. I also served as a trustee of the Brookings Institution, the Business Enterprise Trust, the Carnegie Institution of Washington, the Philadelphia Museum of Art (where I served as vice president), the Urban Institute, the New York City Ballet, the National Gallery of Art, the advisory board of the Metropolitan Opera Association, the advisory council of the Woodrow Wilson Center, and on the Harvard Board of Overseers.

6. When I arrived at the firm, the most junior associate in the Washington office was A. B. Culvahouse. He now serves as chair of the firm, based in Washington. He has also served as White House counsel in the Reagan administration and legislative assistant to senate majority leader Howard Baker. The firm's Washington office is now led by Brian Brooks, a leading financial services litigation and regulatory specialist who is active in the Washington think-tank community and in Republican presidential politics. The current generation of practice leaders also includes Tom Jerman, labor and employment law; Rich Parker, Dave Beddow, Mike Antalics, Ian Simmons, Christine Wilson, and Ben Bradshaw, antitrust; Brian Anderson, Brian Boyle, Matt Shors, and Steve Brody class-action defense; Walter Dellinger, Sri Srinivasan and Jon Hacker, appellate; Bob Eccles, Karen Wahle, and Gary Tell, Employee Retirement Income Security Act (ERISA) practice; Ted Kassinger and Greta Lichtenbaum, international trade; Bill Satchell, Martin Dunn, Barbara Stettner, Rob Plesnarski, Richard Grime, and Chris Salter, financial services; Andrew Varner, Todd Triller, Ken Yellen, and Marita Okata, corporate law; Robert Rizzi, tax law; Jeff Kilduff, Robert Stern, and Kim Newman, securities litigation; Steve Smith, international litigation; and Ken Wainstein, Lee Blalack, Steve Bunnell, and Jeremy Maltby, national security, legislative, and white-collar defense.

7. President Clinton, statement at Presidential Medal of Freedom ceremony, September 29, 1995, at the White House.

INDEX

The letter "n" following a page number refers to a note, followed by note number or both chapter and note number when it is unclear which chapter the note number pertains to.